Mediation
in an Evolving World

Mediation
in an Evolving World

Theory and Practice

James Alfini
PROFESSOR OF LAW EMERITUS AND DEAN EMERITUS
SOUTH TEXAS COLLEGE OF LAW HOUSTON

Donna Erez-Navot
LEGAL SKILLS PROFESSOR AND ASSOCIATE DIRECTOR OF THE INSTITUTE
FOR DISPUTE RESOLUTION
UNIVERSITY OF FLORIDA LEVIN COLLEGE OF LAW

William Froehlich
LANGDON FELLOW IN DISPUTE RESOLUTION AND DIRECTOR OF THE DIVIDED
COMMUNITY PROJECT
THE OHIO STATE UNIVERSITY MORITZ COLLEGE OF LAW

Sharon Press
PROFESSOR OF LAW AND DIRECTOR OF THE DISPUTE RESOLUTION INSTITUTE
MITCHELL HAMLINE SCHOOL OF LAW

Joseph B. Stulberg
PROFESSOR EMERITUS
THE OHIO STATE UNIVERSITY MORITZ COLLEGE OF LAW

Oladeji M. Tiamiyu
ASSISTANT PROFESSOR OF LAW
UNIVERSITY OF DENVER, STURM COLLEGE OF LAW

CAROLINA ACADEMIC PRESS
Durham, North Carolina

ISBN   978-1-5310-2936-4
eISBN   978-1-5310-2937-1
LCCN   2024931824

Carolina Academic Press
700 Kent Street
Durham, NC 27701
(919) 489-7486
www.cap-press.com

Printed in the United States of America

To Barry, Carol, Edo, Jessie, Midge, and Muibi

Table of Contents

Preface and Acknowledgments

A distinguishing feature of twenty-first century jurisprudence and legal practice has been the global embrace of mediation to resolve disputes. Many law schools worldwide include mediation courses as a staple in their curricular offerings. *Mediation in an Evolving World: Theory and Practice* offers a comprehensive text for the study of this increasingly important field.

This book is an outgrowth of *Mediation Theory and Practice*, a law school textbook authored by three of the contributors to this textbook. It has been their good fortune to be joined by three superb colleagues whose perspectives, abilities, and interests prompted the creation of this new work that captures the richness and complexities of this dynamic field. The theory and practice of mediation has been transformed by significant social and historical developments — the technology revolution of the internet and its use in conducting mediation sessions; a global Covid-19 pandemic; and intensified political and social polarization in many communities — and by the writings of a new generation of legal academics, social scientists and communication theorists that deepen our understanding and analysis of such topics as mediator roles, styles and orientations, confidentiality in mediation, mediator ethics, challenges in institutionalizing mediation, and diversity, power and justice. This text examines these and other matters by combining excerpts from seminal writings in the field with these contemporary contributions, offers notes and questions to enrich reflective practice, and discusses professional and career paths.

We are indebted to many who offered kind support and encouragement. The generosity of our home institutions cannot be overstated. We shamelessly took advantage of our colleague, Sharon Press, who appeared to us to have access to important resources, considering her position as Director of the Dispute Resolution Institute at Mitchell Hamline School of Law. Lindsay Hanson, Staff Attorney at the University of Florida Levin College of Law, was exceptionally generous in organizing and implementing a plan for obtaining permissions to publish excerpts from the writings of numerous scholars and commentators. We thank these authors for kindly granting us permission to share their knowledge and wisdom in this book. Our students also deserve our gratitude for giving us the opportunity to see if the book's materials met our pedagogical goals. Some of our students also rendered excellent research assistance. Thanks especially to Josh Fojtik, a 3L at South Texas College of Law Houston and Nina Hylton, a 3L at the University of Florida Levin College of Law. Finally, we thank Krystal Norton at Carolina Academic Press for her steady assistance in guiding us through the publication process.

Online Materials

Additional content for *Mediation in an Evolving World: Theory and Practice* is available on Carolina Academic Press's *Core Knowledge for Lawyers* (CKL) website.

Core Knowledge for Lawyers is an online teaching and testing platform that hosts practice questions and additional content for both instructors and students.

To learn more, please visit:
coreknowledgeforlawyers.com

Instructors may request complimentary access through the "Faculty & Instructors" link.

Mediation
in an Evolving World

Chapter 1

Conceptual Framework and Historical Context

A. Introduction

Why Study Mediation?

Lawyers are problem-solvers. They are professionally trained to help persons deal with differences in a constructive, principled way. They participate in multiple settings, and their skillset includes practitioner talents for both effective advocacy and expertise in designing an appropriate dispute resolution process to match a client's goals.

There are many ways to solve a problem: submit it to a judge; negotiate a deal; seek expert advice; flip a coin; go to war. Mediation is one more process option for addressing disputes. Courts have supported its use to resolve civil cases involving personal injury claims, contract disputes, insurance claims, intellectual property conflicts, family separations, and employment challenges. Businesses, schools, health care institutions, and other organizations regularly use it to resolve conflicts arising from in person and on-line transactions.

Mediation is a facilitated negotiation. It is a procedure in which an independent, neutral intervener assists two or more negotiating parties identify matters of concern, develop a better understanding of their situation, and, based on that improved understanding, develop mutually acceptable settlement proposals. It has four distinguishing features: first, the parties identify, as broadly as they choose, each issue they want to address; second, the mediator acts as a neutral, not an advocate; third, the mediator has no authority to impose a binding decision on the parties, should they not succeed in developing mutually acceptable settlement terms; and fourth, the parties reach agreement — settle the matter — only if every party accepts the proposed settlement terms for each issue. Why might an advocate suggest that a client consider using mediation to address their concerns? Participating in mediation enables persons to talk directly with one another to shape settlement possibilities; the mediator's presence provides a valued structure to those settlement efforts. More fundamentally, mediation enables stakeholders enmeshed in a conflict — *i.e.*, those who live that conflict's tensions and, simultaneously, are best positioned to know its settlement possibilities — to engage in and accept responsibility for resolving it.

While the mediation process is private and confidential, its use — and success — has regularly garnered prominent public attention about high profile matters, such as the $787.5 million resolution of the Dominion Voting Systems complaint against Fox News Corporation; the $500 million settlement of sexual harassment claims by female athletes against Michigan State University and its sports doctor, Larry Nassar; the $765 million resolution of the litigation by retired professional football players against the National Football League over concussion-related brain injuries; and the land-claim settlement between New York State and the Six Nation Iroquois Confederacy governing the use of lands in the Adirondack Park.

B. Mediation's Development

1. Historical Perspective

Mediation has a distinguished history. In international affairs, political leaders and institutions have long undertaken a mediating role to promote negotiations to stop hostilities among warring parties or to create economic development packages among national partners. Family elders in indigenous tribal groups in Central America and Africa have assumed a mediating role to promote problem solving among disputing community members; in China, community leaders in rural areas assume a similar role. In the more structured global commercial sector, the European Union has mandated member nations to develop implementing legislation to support using mediation to resolve cross-border civil and commercial disputes, and the ICC International Court of Arbitration, a distinguished organization that has administered arbitration cases involving international parties throughout the world since 1923, more recently developed and adopted Rules for administering mediation services.

In the United States, religious, immigrant and trade groups in colonial New England sustained their ethical and religious traditions in part by using mediation to resolve conflicts among group members. Mediation's more systemic use took hold in the early 20th century with the passage of the Railway Labor Act to govern union-management relations in the railroad industry. Following World War II, the United States Congress created the Federal Mediation and Conciliation Service (FMCS) to provide mediation services to private sector union and management personnel engaged in collective bargaining over wages, hours, and terms and conditions of employment; beginning in the 1960s, various state governments enacted laws that authorized state and local government employees to create and join public sector unions to negotiate employment terms with management personnel, and those laws created state-agency mediation services to facilitate those talks.

Mediation's prominence and expanded use, however, emerged in the late 1960s as part of the contemporary "Alternative Dispute Resolution" (ADR) movement. ADR proponents advocated using such dispute resolution procedures as negotiation, mediation, arbitration, elections, summary jury trials — that is, "alternatives" to traditional trials — to resolve conflicts ranging from interpersonal conflicts that were swamping local court dockets to polarizing community disputes stemming from social protests seeking enhanced civil rights. Mediation emerged as ADR's "darling-child process." Its development in the United States can be viewed as consisting of three historical periods: its Foundational years (1969–1989), ripe with experimentation; its years of institutionalization (1990–2011) within court systems, businesses, and civic organizations; and its transformative years of intersectional values (2012–present) in which sophisticated technology and social justice demands shape and propel its deployment in the life of each community.

2. Foundational Years: (1969–1989)

Particular dispute settings gained urgent salience during this period: group protests demanding social change; citizen and judicial calls for court reform to address interpersonal disputes laced by socio-economic disparities; changing social mores impacting family practices and divorce procedures; and public education efforts designed to support the learning development of all students.

a. Group Conflicts

Group conflicts erupted over multiple matters: community protests regarding police practices and demands for citizen oversight; parent resistance to federal court-ordered school desegregation plans; indigenous nation demands for tribal lands; university student sit-ins seeking expanded curricular offerings; and environmentalists picketing companies that were constructing nuclear power plants. The conventional — and understandable — law enforcement response to these developments was to arrest, then prosecute, the protestors for failing to obey orders to disperse; that response stimulated satellite litigation, further depriving the disputing stakeholders from meeting together to negotiate about their concerns.

Mediation efforts launched to address these conflicts by not-for-profit organizations, such as the American Arbitration Association (AAA) and the Institute for Mediation and Conflict Resolution (IMCR), received significant program and financial support from private sector sources, including the Ford Foundation and the William and Flora Hewlett Foundation. Their success varied. In the public sector, the U.S. Congress stabilized the delivery of such services when creating the Community Relations Service (CRS) as part of the Civil Rights Act of 1964. The CRS mandate is to recruit, train, and deploy persons skilled at developing and implementing conciliation and mediation processes to resolve controversies in local communities laced with racial and ethnic tensions. In its early history, CRS personnel, operating administratively within the U.S. Department of Justice, intervened as mediators in such matters as citizens protesting the implementation of the Boston School desegregation orders, and citizen opposition to the march of the Ku Klux Klan in the predominantly Jewish suburb of Skokie, Illinois; more recently, CRS has provided mediating services in such polarizing situations as the shooting of Sikh worshippers in Oak Creek, Wisconsin (2012), police-community confrontations at the Unite the Right rally in Charlottesville, Virginia (2017) and the citizen protests of the police shootings of Michael Brown in Ferguson, MO, Breanna Taylor in Louisville, KY, and George Floyd in Minneapolis, MN. Various states, including Minnesota, California, and New Jersey, have created state dispute resolution offices to provide comparable services.

b. Court Cases

To assist municipal court systems address and resolve interpersonal disputes among neighbors, local bar association leaders, court personnel, and community activists created court-annexed programs using trained citizen volunteers to mediate such cases. Beginning with the Night Prosecutor's Program in Columbus, Ohio, the Arbitration as an Alternative ("4-A") program of the American Arbitration Association (AAA), and the Citizen Dispute Settlement (CDS) programs in selected Florida counties, mediation proponents and sympathetic judicial personnel offered a new approach and philosophy to service such matters. Their programs' design and values were importantly crystallized by Harvard Law Professor Frank Sander's presentation at the 1976 Pound Conference entitled *Varieties of Dispute Processing* and endorsed by Chief Justice Warren Burger. The idea was straightforward: bring the disputing neighbors into a room. Have them meet with one another in the presence of a volunteer community resident trained in conducting problem-solving dialogues. Try, through that discussion, to have the parties discuss their concerns, communicate their aspirations, and develop mutually acceptable settlement arrangements. If the matter was resolved, the case would be removed from the court docket. Such programs, enhanced in 1977 by the U.S. Department of Justice launching three experimental Neighborhood Justice Centers (NJC) in Kansas City, Missouri, Atlanta, Georgia, and Los Angeles, California, quickly established dramatic results: settlement rates often exceeded 75% of the cases, and evaluation studies confirmed sustained party compliance with negotiated outcomes and strong party satisfaction with both the process and its results. These mediation programs received wide-spread judicial endorsement; some state legislatures passed statutes providing program funding to judicial budgets or not-for-profit organizations to sustain them, with New York, Florida, Texas, and Colorado among the jurisdictions to lead this movement. Variously referred to as Neighborhood Justice Centers, Citizen Dispute Settlement programs, or Community Dispute Resolution Centers, these programs now number more than 400 throughout the country, many of which are connected through the National Association for Community Mediation; all retain the feature of using trained, volunteer citizens as mediators to service these disputes.

c. Family Mediation

Divorce mediation is now a profession; it did not exist in 1980. To obtain a civil divorce in the United States, parties must meet the statutory requirements of a particular state's jurisdiction. Even though "no-fault" divorce statutes make securing a divorce less onerous, the divorcing couple must still resolve matters relating to the division of real and personal property, payment of debts, and, where appropriate, such matters as pension benefits, health care coverage, spousal and child financial support, and parenting arrangements. As the divorce rate in the United States increased during the 1970s and 1980s, the experience of securing a legal divorce remained not only financially and psychologically costly but also intensely polarizing: as lawyers communicated offers and counteroffers, the estranged spouses often developed an increasingly bitter picture of their spouse's being selfish, manipulative, or mean, thereby exacerbating their willingness to interact constructively. And the impact of this entire process on the psychological health of the affected children remained troublesome.

Mediation proponents cautiously urged the experimental use of mediation to resolve these matters. The practice grew in both the public and private sphere. The Association of Family and Conciliation Courts (AFCC) was originally organized by a group of California court employees who were trained as mental health professionals and had statutory responsibility for protecting the welfare of children whose parents were seeking a divorce; with the increasing divorce rate, their focus shifted from exploring possible reconciliation by the divorcing couple to assisting them resolve financial and parenting issues in a manner that enabled each affected party to retain maximum dignity, strength, and respect as they moved on to their separate lives. That new dimension quickly led AFCC members to embrace a mediation model for assisting families; AFCC expanded into a national organization of practitioners, court personnel, and scholars and assumed a leadership role in advancing this emerging practice field. From a private-provider perspective, O.J. Coogler, based in Atlanta, Georgia, was the first person to design and use a "structured mediation process" for handling divorces. Leaders of the AAA soon developed its Family Mediation programs. Dr. John Haynes, a psychologist, helped launch and sustain the Academy of Family Mediators to feature and support the training of practicing mental health professionals to incorporate mediation into their professional services.

More recently, some matrimonial lawyers have adopted the Collaborative Law approach. In this framework, each advocate and their client seeking a divorce contractually stipulate that the lawyer will represent their clients in all efforts to negotiate a resolution of all matters, including using mediation, but that if such settlement efforts are not successful, the lawyer will not represent their client in subsequent litigation efforts. While this approach has generated significant professional discussion and debate, it reflects an important effort to design and use a dispute resolution process that assists parties to effectively resolve practical issues in what is understandably an emotionally-complex situation.

The private practice of divorce mediation is now widespread, and it remains the one substantive area of court-annexed mediation in which non-lawyers serve as mediators. But court-sponsored mediation programs were also developed and are currently used to address two other dimensions of legal matters involving family members. The first targets the situation in which a parent seeks court assistance to supervise their child. A parent, for example, might disapprove her teenage child's boyfriend or girlfriend, so the parent imposes curfew hours or attempts to prohibit their socializing; the child, protesting the rule, leaves the house and moves in with a friend — or simply lives on the street. A parent seeks court assistance to structure a parent-child relationship that attempts to stabilize their relationship; many courts have created mediation programs to address these petitions (often referenced as PINS [Persons in Need of Supervision] or CHINS [Children in Need of Supervision] petitions).

But parents themselves might behave in ways that endanger their child's wellbeing. A parent's abuse of drugs or alcohol or their experiencing depression can trigger conduct that jeopardizes their child's safety. For such matters, a public agency charged with protecting children's welfare must secure court assistance to protect the child, including, where warranted, the child's removal from the parent's home; multiple participants, including lawyers, guardian *ad litem*, and others meet in a "family conference" setting to attempt to work out sustainable living arrangements.

d. Mediation in Education

In 1973, Congress passed the Rehabilitation Act. The law requires school districts to develop individualized educational plans (IEPs) for each student certified to be in need of special services, with the overall goal of integrating that student into the normal tempo of school life to the maximum feasible extent. The statutory framework requires that the district's proposed plan be acceptable to the student's parents. If the parties cannot agree to a plan, the statute encourages them to use mediation to resolve their differences. While some school districts hired lawyers to serve as mediators, others trained school-based staff to mediate these situations. Taking a different tack, states such as Massachusetts hired full-time staff mediators into their education department to service these controversies.

In addition to using mediation for special education case conflicts, mediation programs also entered the school system via a different route.

A routine day in a middle school or high school often involves a student being disruptive in class or students getting into fights in the hallway. A typical school-district disciplinary policy response is to suspend the offending students for a minimum five-day period. But if the parents or guardians of those suspended students are working or otherwise occupied during that time-period so that the student is not supported or supervised, then those students often fall further behind in their classwork and the disruptive behavior remains uncorrected. That environment led mediation advocates to propose using mediation as an integral component of a school's constructive disciplinary response.

Community Boards (San Francisco) and The New York Peace Institute (New York City) developed programs in which they trained high school students to become mediators for such disciplinary matters; with staff supervision, these students, who themselves had been subjects of disciplinary penalties, mediated cases involving students — their "peers" — involved in disruptive behavior. The mediation process became a safety valve for the school: it was an affirmative response for dealing with student conflicts, a viable alternative to suspension, and a life-skills learning process for all participants. Peer mediation programs are currently ubiquitous in middle schools and high schools in the United States.

e. Public Disputes

Some federal government agencies augmented their administrative "publish and comment" statutory procedures for developing regulations with a mediation process entitled Regulatory Negotiation ("reg-neg"). In the "reg-neg" process, the agency and its private sector stakeholders hire a mediator to facilitate their collective negotiations of acceptable rules; the sponsoring agency pre-commits itself to adopting and publishing the rules developed through that process. The Environmental Protection Agency (EPA) and the Department of Labor's Occupational Safety and Health Agency, in particular, regularly use the "reg-neg" process.

f. Organizational Initiatives

The shifting economic climate continually triggers private sector initiatives targeted at helping companies compete effectively in a rapidly developing global economy; many businesses welcome any effort to improve total quality management, including those targeted at securing efficient, satisfactory resolution of disputes involving customers, suppliers, or employees. Organizations such as insurance companies and health-care providers have developed and implemented mediation programs to handle a variety of customer or patient complaints. General counsel of large corporations have publicly subscribed to the "Pledge" of the CPR International Institute for Conflict Prevention and Resolution to explore using alternative dispute resolution procedures, including mediation, to resolve their business and legal controversies. Trade organizations within the construction industry, a prominent user of arbitration processes, have developed rules for using mediation as a "pre-arbitration" step to resolve disputes arising from the construction of residential and commercial projects. The Better Business Bureau provides mediation services to assist its member businesses resolve customer conflicts regarding service delivery. And colleges and universities use mediation to resolve disciplinary matters involving students or conflicts involving a student and a faculty member. Such initiatives, episodic during the 1980s, are now widespread.

3. Institutionalizing Mediation's Use (1989–2012)

Beginning in the 1980s, mediation's use accelerated onto a flight path that would make its presence pervasive in the judicial system and, in more limited fashion, among federal government agencies. By the decade's end, mediation would be regularly used to resolve a broad range of conflicts, including not only such civil litigation claims as those involving personal injury, contract disputes, trust and estate conflicts, and the broad range of family law cases but also disputes over disaster relief claims, intellectual property, bankruptcy matters, tax challenges, and mortgage foreclosure controversies. Today's lawyer must be skilled both at counseling clients about mediation and in representing them in these structured, collaborative dispute resolution processes. As the practice of mediation has become more professionalized, the prospect of developing a career as a mediator is now viable.

a. State Courts

Given the expanded, though targeted use of mediation in court-related settings during the foundational years, it was only a matter of time until parties involved in virtually any civil action filed in a court would be encouraged or required to use mediation. And that dam broke in Florida in 1988.

By 1988, multiple mediation initiatives dotted the Florida landscape: citizen dispute settlement programs; family and divorce mediation; peer mediation; consumer mediation; and public policy mediation. In 1988, the legislature promulgated legislation authorizing civil trial court judges to promote pre-trial settlement by referring almost any civil court filing to mediation. The message was clarion: any case, large or small, "simple" or "complex," "important" or "unimportant," might be resolved through mediated negotiations. Disputes involving breach of contract, business dissolutions, catastrophic personal injuries, medical malpractice, construction projects, or trust and estates — not only neighborhood disputes or family matters — became eligible for mediation referral. The Florida Supreme Court was responsible for implementing the statute. It created a committee comprised of practicing lawyers, judges, mediators, and court administrators and charged it with creating proposed rules and standards for realizing the statute's promise. Professor James Alfini, then of Florida State University School of Law, together with Sharon Press and Michael Bridenback, then Director and Associate Director of the Dispute Resolution Center of the Florida Supreme Court, served as the Court and Committee's technical faculty and staff to help design and implement this unprecedented initiative. The committee worked rapidly, and, in consultation with a broad range of professionals from across the nation, developed its governing framework for implementation. The design questions they addressed included: what constitutes an eligible case for referral to mediation? Should the referral to mediation be decided by a judge on a case-by-case basis or apply to all cases of particular categories? Should the parties have the option of participating in mediation or should their engagement be mandatory? What constitutes qualification for service as a mediator? Should mediators be compensated for their services and, if so, by the parties or the court? What organization, public or private, should administer the mediation case? As the use of mediation emerged nationwide, different state courts, in their mediation rules, answered such questions differently.

Within 10 years of operation, Florida reported that more than 125,000 cases annually were being mediated, affirming that its legal culture had embraced its use. The Florida experience, with suitable adjustments, was soon replicated in multiple state court systems, and currently the availability of or mandate to use mediation to resolve a civil court filing is common in all state courts. And such innovation extends further: with strong support and guidance by judges, court administrators, Bar Association personnel and appropriate external stakeholders, some jurisdictions have designed and implemented a broad range of additional mediation initiatives connected to court services: Victim Offender Reconciliation Programs, for example, bring together the crime victim and perpetrator to discuss ways of engaging in reconciliation initiatives; students who are inexcusably absent from school now meet in mediation sessions with parents, school counselors, social workers and teachers to develop positive, realistic steps to correct the problem; family conferencing, previously referenced, is yet another development.

b. Federal Courts

The U.S. federal government legitimized and endorsed the use of mediation when it created federal processes for using mediation to resolve bargaining impasses in the transportation and private business sectors. It reaffirmed and expanded its public policy commitment by creating and funding the Community Relations Service of the U.S. Department of Justice.

But federal government support for using mediation within the federal court system or throughout its executive agencies was, until the 1990s, subdued. That has now changed. In 1990, Congress passed two laws affecting the use of alternative dispute resolution processes in federal agencies. The Negotiated Rulemaking Act made permanent the experimental uses of the "reg-neg" process referenced above. The Act establishes a framework whereby a federal government agency responsible for issuing various rules (e.g., the Environmental Protection Agency or the Federal Communications Commission) could engage a neutral third-party intervener (mediator) to facilitate rule development. Though the use of the "reg-neg" process has been uneven, it continues.

Congress also passed the Administrative Dispute Resolution Act in 1990. It authorizes and encourages each federal agency to consider using various dispute resolution processes, including mediation, to resolve any of the multiple conflicts that arise in the course of its work, from intra-agency controversies to agency/public interactions. This initiative received additional support from Executive Orders by Presidents George H.W. Bush (1991) and Bill Clinton (1998), directing or encouraging agencies and their litigation counsel to explore various resolution procedures in addition to traditional litigation. Currently, multiple federal agencies require the agencies and their sub-contractors to use mediation as a first step in resolving alleged contractual breaches in service delivery.

With the passage of the Civil Justice Reform Act of 1990 and the Alternative Dispute Resolution Act in 1998, Congress aligned the federal district courts with the ADR movement. Unlike state court initiatives which encouraged or mandated the use of mediation, the federal statutory framework required federal district courts to establish a more general ADR program, with mediation, advisory arbitration, mini-trials, or summary jury trials being among possible processes that district courts could make available to litigants. The 1998 Act also mandated that litigants consider using ADR processes at an appropriate time. Several district courts adopted advisory arbitration programs; soon thereafter, selected district courts adopted experimental mediation programs using volunteer attorneys as mediators. One unusual twist that first developed in the federal sector was the use of mediation within the federal circuit courts of appeal; a designated court employee serves as a full-time mediator of cases that are on appeal from the trial court's initial case disposition, conducting some mediation conferences in person and others by zoom or telephone.

c. The Internet

The Internet, publicly launched in the 1990s, transformed our interactions. It enabled previously unconnected business actors throughout the world — individuals or organizations — to develop commercial relationships and execute business transactions; it enabled organizations and individuals to communicate in unimagined ways, secure valued efficiencies in program administration, and capitalize on opportunities to provide access to justice for affected stakeholders. These technology developments also generated the need to create and administer dispute resolution processes to address and resolve complaints arising from user interactions.

i. On-line Dispute Resolution (ODR): The Internet in the Cyberspace Commercial Setting

The development of the Internet created multiple opportunities for businesses and individuals to engage in economic activity. These transactions were distinctive: they were conducted entirely on-line, involved geographically separated participants, and, typically, involved modest financial expenses. The actors in this space — particularly its commercial platform designers — quickly recognized that making commercial actors confident in conducting economic transactions exclusively on an electronic platform required providing them a quick, effective complaint resolution process to resolve such predictable conflicts as demands for financial damages stemming from delayed deliveries, complaints regarding product quality, and refund requests. Notably, eBay hired Colin Rule, skilled in both technology and dispute resolution practices, to develop an on-line dispute resolution system (ODR) to support resolving what it estimated would be approximately 60 million complaints annually. These systems designers built into their sequenced complaint resolution structure such ADR conceptual elements as interest identification, developing multiple settlement options, and securing finality in a prompt, cost-efficient manner.

ii. Technology's Impact on Public Dispute Resolution Programs

In the early years of the Internet's development, persons used e-mail, chat rooms, mobile communication apparatus, and videoconferencing to secure multiple efficiencies, including calendaring acceptable meeting dates, facilitating document transmissions, and reducing travel costs. This technology also facilitated broad-based community participation in discussing policy matters.

Court and Agency-Based Mediation Programs

During this 1989-2012 period of ADR program institutionalization, program administrators and mediation participants used technology primarily to support increasing the efficiency of conducting in-person conversations. Program records could be stored electronically; mobile phones enabled a party who was unexpectedly detained from physically attending a scheduled mediation session — a car breakdown or a child's caregiver becoming ill — to participate via phone so that the conflict would not linger; and an agency's form agreement containing boilerplate introductory language enabled mediators in appropriate settings to conclude successful mediation sessions by using agency desktop computers to draft the parties' settlement terms and secure their signatures.

Public Policy Discussions

Technology enabled facilitators to secure broad-based community participation to discuss policy matters. In 2002, facilitators conducted small-group discussions with more than 5,000 invited New York City residents to discuss and recommend proposed redevelopment uses of the former site of the World Trade Center in lower Manhattan. In the aftermath of Hurricane Katrina, facilitators used videoconferencing to conduct "public meetings" involving school leaders, state public officials, and concerned parents who were participating from a diaspora of forced relocation residences (from more than a dozen cities) to discuss rebuilding initiatives, restoration of public services, and school re-openings.

4. Transformative Years of Intersectional Values (2012 – Present)

The combination of continuous technological advances and intensified social justice events, each exacerbated by a world-wide public health pandemic, expanded and transformed mediation procedures and practices.

The COVID-19 public health crisis notably altered mediation service delivery and practice. In an environment in which personal interaction became severely limited, court systems and other businesses incorporated broad-based technological programs, such as Zoom, to conduct operations. Prior to the pandemic, many mediators and advocates were reluctant to rely on technology to conduct mediation. The forced isolation of the pandemic demanded rapid evolution. Mediation parties and mediators quickly embraced technology, and its impact on practice was immediate: parties could participate from multiple geographical locations in real time and select their mediator of choice wherever that person was located; process costs associated with travel, lodging, and meeting rooms for all participants vanished; mediators undertook technology training in order to seamlessly use such resources as chat rooms, break-out rooms, shared screens, and e-sign features to execute their role.

With this development, recurring normative issues emerged: did all parties to a mediation have access to the required technology? Did each participant possess the skillset to participate capably in a mediation session conducted in a virtual environment? Could a mediator continue to assure participants about the confidentiality of their conversations if any party in a remote location could be using phone apps to record or communicate with others about the matters being discussed? While there has been a resumption of convening in-person mediation sessions as the health-pandemic dangers eased, conducting mediation sessions entirely online remains a significant practice feature, hence a vital component of a client's justice experience.

The social and political divisions that permeate civic life in the United States have accelerated citizen polarization. The citizen involved killing of Trayvon Martin in Sanford, Florida, the police-officer involved killing of Michael Brown in Ferguson, Missouri, and, explosively, the murder of George Floyd in Minneapolis, Minnesota, generated nationwide protests and demands for broad-based race and equity reforms. The Me-Too movement intensified public concern and policy discussions regarding private parties in mediation having the power to secure non-disclosure provisions as part of their settlement terms. And controversies pivoting around immigration policies and practices, increased hate incidents targeting ethnic, religious and sexual-identity groups, and intensified citizen responses to such matters as public school gun shootings and raucous city government meetings have challenged dispute resolution professionals to shape engagement protocols that effectively facilitate dialogue, preserve safety, and address short-term disruptions and systemic inequalities. The fact that citizens acting in this reality use social media technology to advance and amplify their goals exponentially increases the complexity of the problem-solver's undertaking.

These transformative developments have crystallized crucial focal points for mediation theory and practitioner engagement. Scholarship now recognizes and explores the complexities of the multi-disciplinary features of the mediation process: its philosophical values, legal norms, economic structures, psychological dynamics, cultural norms, environmental settings, and historical practices. Community and organizational leaders identify conflict settings significantly beyond legal causes of action—from controversies surrounding historical monuments to conflicts over conduct codes that govern university student interaction at social events—as topics for which mediated conversations could be helpful. Practitioners now reflect multiple backgrounds and skillsets, from lawyers, therapists, urban planners and computer scientists to clergy, business leaders, law enforcement personnel, streetwise neighborhood leaders, and conscientious citizens. Mediation's process participants—advocates, parties, neutrals, and students—as well as the participants in the legal system writ large, have a continuing responsibility to identify the architectural guardrails of the mediation process (including party self-determination, mediator neutrality, confidentiality, and "coming to the table") and portray how those elements, when woven together, support a justice experience for its stakeholders that warrants a community's endorsement.

C. Enduring Challenges and Opportunities

The rule of law structurally shapes citizen interaction and engagement for resolving conflicts. It is a bedrock component for sustaining a stable, fair civil society. Contemporary ADR concepts — crucially, negotiation and mediation — enrich its resiliency and acceptability. Specifically, this transformative period raises important, new challenges, requiring practitioners and scholars to engage with heightened insight and sensitivity regarding matters identified during the foundational years: when does strong advocacy become bullying? Should we preserve the confidentiality of the professional relationships of lawyer-client-mediator if doing so endangers the emotional, financial, or physical well-being of others? In what ways are an individual's lived experiences germane to an equitable resolution of conflict? How do individual biases and the systems in which mediators operate infringe on key principles of neutrality and impartiality? Throughout the text, these and similar questions demand continuing reflection and analysis.

Notes and Questions

In ADR's foundational years, people used mediation to resolve many different conflicts, and the two challenges described below illustrate their breadth.

(1) A Hot City Night

Police officers are conducting a routine patrol of a city street that teems with people in bars and entertainment centers. Young car owners cruise the streets strutting their wheels. Crowds mingle. It is a typical, hot Saturday evening in August in one of the nation's medium-sized urban areas. Suddenly, two white police officers are involved in a scuffle with three female Black teenagers. Amid screaming and shouting of "pigs" and "honkeys go home," police try to wrestle the three girls to the ground to handcuff and arrest them on charges of drug dealing. They fiercely resist. Police aggressively use billy clubs to subdue them. By the time police officers shove them into the car, the girls' faces are notably bruised and one girl is spitting up blood. Thirty onlookers, all shouting hate slogans at the police, begin to "rock" the police car before it can pull away. The police officers fire warning shots into the air, and then accelerate the car; regrettably, one protester did not jump back in time and is fatally injured.

Pictures of the three arrested women appear in the next day's newspaper and are beginning to spread quickly on social media platforms. Two have swollen jaws, later determined to be broken. The third has a swollen eye; it is reported that this third individual, a 15-year-old, was six months pregnant but suffered a spontaneous abortion during the prior night's activity.

On Sunday morning, through church sermons and local news programming, the leadership of the African American community action agency calls upon all "decent members of the community" to participate in a mass demonstration in front of police headquarters on the following day, Monday, at 12:00 noon. Their goal is to "protest acts of police brutality" and demand that "the Police Commissioner create an independent citizen review board to investigate the Saturday night incident and all future citizen complaints of police misconduct." The Police Commissioner, in a Sunday night television interview, states that "all citizens have a right to engage in free speech and assembly, but if they are disruptive, they will be arrested." He further noted that the internal affairs division of the police department was already investigating the Saturday night situation and that an independent citizen board was both unnecessary and contrary to guidelines contained in the collective bargaining agreement negotiated between the City and the police officers' union. He explained that the officer body cameras are being reviewed to ensure officers followed department operating procedures. In a different television interview that night, the family of the fatally injured individual announces it will sue the city and the individual police officers. The family stated they are in possession of cell phone footage recorded by an observer which reveals clear and inappropriate action of more than one law enforcement officer.

You are a lawyer and concerned citizen of the community. You receive a telephone call from the Mayor late Sunday evening. She describes the above scenario and then asks: Can you help us solve these matters? How would you respond?

(2) Neighborhood Citizenship

As the new academic year began, four seniors who were living in an off-campus apartment for the first time in their college career decided to host a "welcome-back-to-campus" party. The party started on Friday evening and concluded Sunday afternoon! As the hosts described it: "lots of fun — football in the backyard, and food, television, dancing, music, booze, and sex throughout the house."

The party did not endear the students to the Smiths, their neighbors and thirty-three-year residents of the neighborhood. Several times during the weekend, the Smiths visited the house and requested that the noise abate; that effort seemed only to generate the opposite response: enhanced volume. Complaints to the police, as far as the Smiths were concerned, were ineffective. Officers stopped by to talk with the students, but no arrests were made, and the noise seemed to increase as soon as the police left.

Similar incidents continued throughout the fall. Tensions were exacerbated by the fact that the Smiths and their college neighbors shared a common driveway. The Smiths often left their car in the middle of the driveway close to their side-entrance door; only when students complained to them that they could not get their cars out of the driveway would the Smiths move their car to their garage in the back.

One morning in mid-October, a student resident bolted from the house to his car, needing to get to the university to take a mid-term exam. The Smith's car was blocking the driveway. The student frantically rang the doorbell. Mr. Smith answered, said that he would move the car as requested, but then took five minutes "to find his car keys." That delay caused the student to arrive at the university close to the beginning of classes, making it difficult for him to find an available parking spot. As a result, he arrived at the mid-term exam 15 minutes after the test had started, and he felt rushed and upset when completing the exam. The following week, he learned that he had failed the exam. Since he was certain that Smith had been slow to find his keys just to harass him, the student hosted "a very loud party for Mr. and Mrs. Smith's benefit" on the following Saturday evening. That night was an uncomfortable, aggravating one for the Smiths.

On the Sunday afternoon following the party, three of the student residents were playing catch with a football on their front lawn. An errant pass landed on Mr. Smith's front lawn. As a student went to retrieve the football, Mr. Smith, standing by his porch with his metal-prong rake, threw the rake at the student, yelling: "get off our lawn." By all accounts, the rake's prongs narrowly missed hitting the student's face.

The next day, Mr. and Mrs. Smith filed a criminal complaint for harassment against their college-student neighbors. As their evidence, the Smiths included a "DVD" which includes six hours of videotape recorded from their "doorbell" security camera. The Smiths must prove beyond a reasonable doubt that the defendants, with the requisite mental culpability, committed the acts of which they are accused.

The trial court administrator contacts you, describes the situation, and asks for your advice on "how to handle this—and lots of cases like it that don't seem to belong in court." What is your response?

Chapter 2

Negotiation Concepts for the Mediator

A. Overview

Mediation is commonly defined in relation to negotiation: mediation is negotiation in the presence of a third-party neutral (the mediator). Many who are parties to a mediation have often attempted to negotiate a settlement prior to mediation; some negotiate settlement following the conclusion of a mediation.

This chapter introduces some concepts about the negotiation process, with a particular focus on commentaries that would be helpful to the mediator. An extensive negotiation literature has evolved to explore psychological barriers to settlement, cross-cultural issues, and negotiator styles. Beyond academia, online booksellers, neighborhood bookstores, airport kiosks, podcast platforms, and digital media channels carry popular negotiation texts or offer guidance applying negotiation concepts to race and equity, hostage negotiation, business strategy and a range of other professional skills and concepts. As you review this chapter, consider how these concepts and skills might inform the mediator's role, paying particular attention to the vocabulary that emerges.

This chapter offers a sampling from the literature on negotiation. Section B focuses on negotiation strategies and behavior. Section C explores psychological and technological considerations for negotiators.

Note on Negotiation Terminology

Negotiation theorists have developed a distinctive vocabulary. Although this terminology may initially seem somewhat confusing, each of the authors whose writings are excerpted in this chapter views the negotiation process somewhat differently and seeks to develop a conceptual framework for understanding how *negotiation* and *bargaining* work. Indeed, commentators generally use the terms negotiation and bargaining as if they are interchangeable. Below we include two sets of terms. In the first chart, we define different styles of negotiation discussed in the articles herein. In the second chart, we highlight key negotiation terms which are widely used in negotiation literature.

Style	Author(s)	Definition & Explanation
Principled Negotiation	Fisher & Ury	An approach to bargaining that permits the subject of the negotiation ("the pie") to be expanded, resulting in so-called win-win solutions. This approach is often referred to as integrative bargaining or mutual gains bargaining.
Problem-Solving Negotiation	Menkel-Meadow	Calls upon negotiators to adopt a collaborative, *problem solving negotiation* process in the planning and execution phases, as opposed to using an adversarial style of negotiation that emphasizes compromise.
Competitive Bargaining	Goodpaster	Competitive bargaining, sometimes called hard, distributive, positional, zero-sum or win-lose bargaining, has the purpose of maximizing the competitive bargainer's gain over the gain of those with whom they negotiate.
Cooperative Bargaining	Williams	Negotiators seek a fair resolution by communicating a sense of shared values and attitudes, using rational persuasion as a means of seeking cooperation, promoting a trusting atmosphere.
Distributive Bargaining	Korobkin	Parties are rigidly locked into positions as they attempt to split a fixed pie. Rather than assuming that the pie is expandable, this form of bargaining assumes *zero sum negotiations*, where plus one for one party equals minus one for another.
Integrative Bargaining	Korobkin	All parties involved are better off as a result of the negotiation than they otherwise would be.

The following chart identifies fundamental negotiation terms and concepts which are used throughout negotiation literature.

Term	Definition
Position	"What" a party wants.
Interests	"Why" a party expresses a position or what underlies a position; according to Eckblad, interests may include the fears, concerns, desires, and motivations that underlie a stated position.
BATNA	Best Alternative To a Negotiated Agreement — not the minimum a party thinks they should get, but what will be the "best" result if the negotiation ends without an agreement.
Bottom Line or Reservation Price	The minimum for which a party will settle.
Separate the People from the Problem	Focus on the problem at hand, not the individuals advocating for a particular perspective.

Negotiable Issues	A behavior of one party which frustrates the need of another party that they have the ability to address.
Options for Mutual Gain	Proposed solutions which meet the interests of multiple parties.
Objective Criteria	Standards informed by traditions, customs, scientific findings, and market valuations, which are used to evaluate proposals and positions.
Anchoring	A reference point (often a proposal) which shapes and informs a negotiation.
Framing	Characterization or definition of concepts, positions, interests, or objectives.
Reactive Devaluation	Viewing a proposal less favorably because it is offered by an adversary.

A clear understanding of these terms and styles is crucial to adopting a comprehensive, flexible approach to serving as a mediator and working with parties in mediation. Indeed, parties to mediation and their counsel may use multiple, seemingly inconsistent, approaches in a single negotiation or mediation session. For example, a negotiator might commence a mediation using an *adversarial* or *competitive* approach and then transition toward a *problem-solving* approach when it appears a deal is not quickly forthcoming. As you read through the materials in this chapter, consider whether and how such combination of approaches might be sensible, consider how a mediator might work with adversaries taking each of these respective approaches, and identify how negotiation concepts might play a role in a mediation session.

B. Negotiation Strategies and Behavior

The materials below introduce some of the more prominent descriptions of negotiation strategy and behavior. Readings that discuss, critique, and re-imagine "principled negotiation" and integrative negotiation are excerpted in Section 1. Section 2 presents foundational materials on cooperative versus competitive negotiation. Section 3 outlines the "problem solving" approach to negotiation, which calls upon lawyers to rethink certain basic assumptions about lawyering.

1. Principled & Integrative Negotiation

Perhaps the approach to negotiation most consistent with a lawyer's training is distributive bargaining. In our adversarial system, lawyers are trained to develop and advance "positions" on behalf of their clients with adversarial zeal. Proponents of principled negotiation discredit that approach. Principled bargainers urge negotiators to abandon strategies and behaviors that require rigid adherence to their positions and argue that they adopt the precepts of the "principled" approach to negotiation. Students of mediation will notice how the Fisher, Ury, and Patton framework — classically articulated in *Getting to Yes* — fits into their work as a mediator by helping parties focus on interests rather than positions, elicit and emphasize objective criteria, or separate the people from the problem.

The following commentaries both recognize the value and framework of principled negotiation and offer thoughtful criticism of the merits of each framework. In the first excerpt, Russell Korobkin criticizes what he labels "the integrative supremacy claim." He does not argue that negotiators should avoid integrative bargaining, but rather that legal negotiations are often distributive in nature and therefore "lawyers would be better served, on balance, to think of distributive bargaining as the cake and integrative bargaining as the frosting, rather than the reverse." In the second commentary, Ebner and Kamp focus on the relationship aspect of principled negotiation, analyzing and critiquing the "separate the people from the problem" and suggesting concrete strategies for building relationships at the negotiation table. In the third article, Eckblad asks negotiators to re-consider assumptions about objective criteria and identifies practical suggestions of re-imagining classic concepts of principled negotiation.

Against Integrative Bargaining

58 Case W. Res. L. Rev. 1323, 1323-1328 (2008)*
By Russell Korobkin

Integrative bargaining, also known as "problem-solving," "value-creating," or "win-win" negotiation, is the centerpiece of normative negotiation scholarship and negotiation teaching. It has held this position at least since the publication of "Getting to Yes" by Fisher and Ury in 1981. . . .

To begin, let me admit that the title of this essay is somewhat misleading, or at least lacks the subtlety that I hope to convey. I am not really against integrative bargaining, by which I mean structuring negotiated agreements in such a way as to increase the joint value of a deal to the participating parties. As a matter of fact, I am firmly in favor of it. Through integrative bargaining, negotiators can make everyone involved in a transaction better off than they would otherwise be.

But the value of integrative bargaining, although substantial, has been oversold. This is true, I believe, with regard to negotiation generally, and especially concerning legal negotiations, the term I use for the negotiation contexts in which lawyers most routinely find themselves. For the past quarter century, the primary normative message of negotiation theory literature has been that negotiators will achieve better outcomes by focusing their attention on the integrative aspect of bargaining rather than its distributive aspect, by which I mean the division of resources in a way that makes one party worse off to the same extent that the other party is made better off. I call this the "integrative bargaining supremacy" claim.

In some cases, the dedication to the value of integrative bargaining often takes on a kind of missionary zeal. Practitioners of integrative tactics are seen as modern, sophisticated negotiators. In their search for "win-win" outcomes, they display subtlety, creativity, intelligence, and sophistication. In contrast, negotiators who employ distributive tactics are surly Neanderthals who try to use brute force and other boorish, knuckle-dragging behavior to subjugate their opponents. Teaching negotiation is viewed by many as the task of civilizing the great unwashed horde of naïve, instinctive negotiators and convincing them to renounce their backward, distributive ways.

Integrative bargaining supremacy is often defended with the assertion that, while most everyone has an intuitive sense of how to use some distributive tactics, such as taking a firm position and grudgingly making concessions, individuals who lack formal negotiation training are less likely to intuitively grasp the fundamental concepts of integrative bargaining. This point is probably accurate, but it can obscure the fact that negotiations generally, and legal negotiations specifically, have more distributive potential than integrative potential. For this reason, lawyer-negotiators would be better served, on balance, to think of distributive bargaining as the cake and integrative bargaining as the frosting, rather than the reverse.

. . .

I. Integrative and Distributive Value

An agreement is integrative to the extent that it creates additional cooperative surplus compared to some alternative. Because integrative value is relative, identifying it requires the specification of a baseline case for purposes of comparison.

Suppose that Bonnie Buyer is negotiating to purchase a house from Sam Seller. Bonnie's reservation price, defined as the maximum that she would be willing to pay, is $100,000. Sam's reservation price, defined as the minimum amount he would be willing to accept, is $90,000. An agreement, if one is reached, will create $10,000 in social value, or what I will call "cooperative surplus," relative to no deal, because Bonnie subjectively values the house $10,000 more than does Sam. How that $10,000 is split between them — whether, for example, the price agreed to is $90,000, $95,000, or $100,000 — is a matter of distributive bargaining; any gain for Bonnie means a loss for Sam, and vice versa. We can thus say that the deal will produce $10,000 in distributive value, divided based on distributive bargaining ability.

Now let's also assume that Sam is an excellent handyman and enjoys tinkering with things around the house. Bonnie, in contrast, cannot fix anything, and she hates having to call service people to the house because she fears that they will take advantage of her. These facts suggest that more cooperative surplus might be created by the sale of the house if Sam will promise to repair any item that breaks for one year after the sale. Let us assume, for example, that this would cause Bonnie's reservation price to increase to $110,000, while Sam's reservation price would increase only to $92,000. Any deal that included the repair agreement would be integrative because it would create more cooperative surplus than the parties could obtain through the sale of the house alone — the baseline case. The extra $8,000 can be understood as the value that can be generated by the negotiators' integrative bargaining ability.

This example demonstrates what an integrative agreement might look like, but it does not provide an analytically precise description of what the baseline point of comparison should be for a judgment whether an agreement is integrative. Let me suggest the following definition: for an agreement to be appropriately labeled integrative, it must create more cooperative surplus than the terms of whatever type of agreement would be customary under the circumstances. If houses were customarily sold with a one-year repair agreement, agreeing to a sale with such a repair agreement would still create $18,000 in cooperative surplus — which would have to be divided between the parties — but it would not be an example of an integrative agreement. This definition underscores that integrative bargaining requires creativity on the part of the negotiators — the ability to think "outside the box" rather than simply agree to customary terms.

II. Achieving Integrative Bargains

With this definition in place, it becomes possible to describe a set of tactics, or techniques, that negotiators can employ to reach integrative agreements: adding issues, subtracting issues, substituting issues, and logrolling. All four are variations on the theme of searching for ways to reconfigure the terms of a deal to increase its joint value.

A. Adding Issues

The simplest way to make an agreement integrative is to add one or more issues that the buyer values more than the seller to the customary set of terms, or what I will call the "negotiation package." . . . Of course, adding issues to the negotiation package is only integrative if the buyer values them more than the seller. Adding issues that the seller values more than the buyer would reduce the cooperative surplus. . . .

B. Subtracting Issues

The opposite of adding an issue that the buyer values more than the seller is subtracting something from the negotiation package that the seller values more than the buyer. Opportunities to profit from this integrative tactic are often more difficult to spot than opportunities to add issues because the negotiators first have to identify ways to unbundle what often appears to be a unitary, indivisible item. If the negotiation package consists of a single house, as in the example I used involving Sam and Bonnie, what is there to subtract? As it turns out, ownership of a house can be sliced and diced in many different ways, as can the contents of almost any negotiation package. Two examples: First, ownership can be divided into physical parts: if Sam loves the original chandelier in the dining room and Bonnie is indifferent, the chandelier can be subtracted from the package. Second, ownership can be divided temporally: if Sam wants to keep the house until his relatives visit in the spring and

Bonnie is in no hurry to move, cooperative surplus can be created by subtracting ownership for the next six months from the negotiation package.

C. Substituting Issues

Sometimes, parties can determine in the course of negotiations that the cooperative surplus they could create by entering an agreement would be greater if they completely changed the subject of the negotiation from what they originally assumed it would be. Perhaps when Bonnie visits Sam's house, she learns that he has another, similar property nearby. The main difference is that the second house is located on a main street and has associated traffic noise, so Sam would be willing to sell it for $85,000. The location makes it far more convenient to public transportation, however, which Bonnie values highly because she doesn't own a car, so she is willing to pay up to $110,000 for it. In this case, substituting the noisy, convenient house for the quiet, inconvenient house — which could be understood alternatively as subtracting one issue and adding another — should be considered an integrative move.

D. Logrolling

Finally, in many bargaining contexts, the baseline, or customary deal includes multiple issues, but the terms that deal with those issues can be changed. In this case, it provides conceptual clarity to think in terms of logrolling — that is, trading one issue for another — rather than adding or subtracting issues. For example, either Bonnie's or Sam's real estate agent might produce a copy of a standard form contract drafted by the local association of realtors that specifies that the sale will close in thirty days and provides the buyer with ten days in which to conduct a home inspection and cancel the transaction if defects are discovered. If Bonnie is leaving on vacation and wants to conduct the inspection when she returns, and Sam wants at least two months before he has to move, the parties can logroll by agreeing to extend the inspection contingency to twenty days and the number of days until closing to sixty.

. . .

Relationship 2.0*

in Rethinking Negotiation Teaching: Venturing Beyond the Classroom at 372-377,
382 (Christopher Honeyman, James Coben & Giuseppe De Palo, Eds., 2010)
By Noam Ebner & Adam Kamp

Getting to Yes purports to address a core problem: negotiators often find themselves cornered into a trade-off. . . . By exerting pressure on two fronts at once, demanding a better deal while threatening to withhold or damage a good relationship, negotiators try to maneuver their opposites into a concession on the former in return for an easing of the pressure in the latter. However, making these concessions or being "nice," as the authors state correctly, is no answer. On the contrary — it may

---

make a negotiator vulnerable, perceived as weak, and open to manipulation (Fisher, Ury, and Patton 1991: 8-9).

In essence, this is a relationship problem, and in that perspective one might say *Getting to Yes* is a relationship-oriented book. In order to avoid the relationship/substance trade-off, the *Getting to Yes* model suggests that negotiators *separate the people from the problem.* By dealing with their opposite in a respectful and open manner, while not going any easier on the substance of the deal, negotiators can avoid paying a price for relationship.

Separating the people from the problem is, in essence, the core framing of relationship in negotiation in the *Getting to Yes* model. Relationship exists *alongside* the substance of the negotiation. It should be a *working* relationship, one whose costs might be measured in terms of time, patience and communication, but not in concessions on the substance of the deal. Taken in context of the complete model the book presents, the essence of a "good" negotiation relationship would then be one that supports open communication, sharing of interests, exploration of options, and presentation of and comparison of standards.

. . .

We suggest that in attempting to create a clear scheme . . . to follow ("Form a good working relationship with the other without paying a price for it") we are actually sweeping a very challenging tension under the carpet. This separation between relationship and substance is a very tricky precept to master, practically speaking. As the *Getting to Yes* authors themselves state, negotiators are humans, and human nature and the dynamics of negotiation challenge our ability to separate relationship and substance. Manipulative negotiators you face — be it your boss or your three year old daughter — will *always* attempt to tie the two elements of relationship and substance together. More challenging, manipulative negotiators will often be supported in their behavior by internal and external forces affecting you.

. . .

. . . [I]t would seem that no sooner have we been offered a way out by striving towards a separation between people and problem, than we are once again sucked back into people-issues. Instead of leaving this notion of separation as a stand-alone, overarching precept, the authors attempt to simplify things by becoming prescriptive, breaking down just how this separation might be accomplished. We suggest that in this breakdown of do's and don'ts, the authors lead negotiators along a relationship-tightrope walk, along which human nature beckons them to fall into relationship-traps (or to use Fisher, Ury, and Patton's own terminology, situations in which negotiators will be tempted to pay a substantive price for maintaining the relationship) at every turn.

The *Getting to Yes* authors recommend four things regarding relationship:

1) You need to listen well, allowing the other to express themselves as best as they can;

2) You need to give the other space and allow them to vent, without reacting to emotional outbursts;

3) You need to step into the other's shoes, enabling yourself to see things from their perspective, and then reconsider your position; and

4) You need to view the other as a partner, not a competitor or enemy.

Each of these recommendations (intended to be "universally applicable") is hazardous to some extent in itself; in the aggregate, they are almost certain to cause the negotiator to fall into the very relationship traps he or she is attempting to avoid. We will briefly discuss some of the reasons we consider each of these recommendations to be hazardous, and then focus on the list as a whole.

Listen

Can it really be that the prescription to listen is *always* suitable, context notwithstanding? For example, this approach assumes an honest, straightforward speaker, and one who lacks the self-awareness to doctor one's statements for the benefit of one's counterpart. This is hardly the case. Such uncritical listening to a manipulative negotiator frames the entire discussion in a context that may have little bearing to the counterpart's actual reality, and can build sympathy for a situation that is in fact mostly or entirely illusionary. While it may of course be possible to counter this, later on, through reframing, it is setting the negotiator up for the challenge of applying that complex skill successfully. In any event, few teachers of negotiation discuss any potential value in *not* listening to the other party, or consider other models of discussion.

Allow Venting, Avoid Reacting

Not only is the expectation that we try to forego emotionality in the face of a heated outburst a sheer impossibility, but here in particular the suggestion that negotiators should allow the other party emotions they deny themselves has the result of valuing the other's feelings over their own. If venting serves a purpose in negotiation, then it might be something we should consider allowing ourselves to do as well—passing the onus to be accepting, understanding, forgiving (and perhaps even conceding) over to the other party. While there may be an advantage to recognizing a counterpart's emotions and stake in the game, this should not come at the cost of one's own emotional interests—yet that might be just the result of such a one-sided process-concession.

Recognize Partisan Perceptions

. . . [D]espite the *Getting to Yes* authors' protestations that one can understand another's perception without adopting it—is that necessarily true? Remember, we are being advised to understand the other's perception in a reality in which the other might not be concerned about understanding our own. This creates an imbalance: two parties understand Party A's perceptions, but only one party understands Party B's perceptions. Might this not have the effect of shifting the balance towards Party A's perceptions—which both parties can appreciate? For example, consider that better outcomes are generally a product of setting high values for oneself. When the *Getting to Yes* authors suggest that understanding another's perceptions may cause one to re-evaluate the merits of one's own claim, doing so is counter to keeping one's own goals high, and may result in unnecessarily lowering one's expectations.

Of course, whether one has a competitive or a cooperative bargaining style, one might still find it useful to understand the other's perceptions in order to better cast one's own response in terms one's counterpart may understand. But without clarifying the dangers of understanding those partisan perceptions so profoundly that they become the dominant frame of the conflict, this advice might lead the unwary reader awry.

Partnerize the Other

This is potentially the most dangerous trap, because it assumes mutuality of purpose. If the other side is treating you as a partner, then in most cases the most productive solution is going to be to treat the other as a partner as well. The book treats the creation of trust necessary to create such a partnership as simple, taken in stride. However, especially when considering an experienced and manipulative negotiator, those same overtures can be used to create a false sense of partnership; the trappings of trust-building, such as gifts or friendly statements, can lead us to make concessions based on preserving the relationship that we have assumed to exist.

Aggregate Hazards

Taken all together, these recommendations lead students down an even more hazardous path regarding relationship, owing to the potential implication of one party adopting this general mode of behavior regardless of their opposite's actions. If these recommendations (and others offered in Chapter Two of *Getting to Yes*) were made by a mediator speaking to both parties at once, or if one could promise that all negotiators would read *Getting to Yes* and adopt it to the same degree, these would be wonderful recommendations. As the authors say in their introduction to the method:

> Dealing with a substantive problem and maintaining a good working relationship need not be conflicting goals if the parties are committed and psychologically prepared to treat each separately on its own legitimate merits.

However, these recommendations are made to *individual negotiators*, who (in the rest of the chapter following the above quote) are charged with taking responsibility to conduct an effective negotiation for *both* parties, to ensure effective and productive communication between *both* parties, and for understanding the other party and where they are coming from. As a cluster of recommendations, this package seems highly likely to send the average negotiator . . . right back down the path of being *more concerned about the relationship than the other* — and falling into the same old trap of paying a price for it.

The risk associated with these recommendations might well be worthwhile if following them could be guaranteed to deliver the desired combination of a working relationship with no associated substantive costs, and the best deal possible for the individual negotiator following them. Obviously, that cannot be guaranteed in any individual case. . . .

. . .

For all these reasons, then, the foundational text for many negotiation classes is very much incomplete in the picture it paints of relationship. It admonishes readers not to pay a price for a good relationship — yet, at the same time, it extols the value of a good relationship to such an extent that it seems it is worth paying almost *any* price in order to obtain one! In a real-life situation, this might easily translate into even the most wary "separate the people from the problem" novice making seemingly small concessions in the deal in order to obtain a good relationship.

In Pursuit of Fairness: Re-Negotiating Embedded Norms & Re-Imagining Interest-Based Negotiation
26 Harv. Negot. L. Rev. 1, 6, 13, 20–28 (2020)*
By Ariel Eckblad

. . .

Interest-based negotiation centers on fairness and proffers "seven elements" toward achieving a fair outcome: relationship, communication, interests, options, objective criteria, alternatives, and commitment. A cursory review of the seven elements reveals the centrality of fairness to all parties in an interest-based practice. This centrality is distinctive. Other theories of action frame negotiation as an inherently adversarial process in which outcomes are seen as zero-sum — one party can gain only what another loses. Under some theories, parties are implored to leverage power, assert their rights, or push their positions in order to win more than the other parties. By contrast, an interest-based approach assumes that the best processes are collaborative and the best agreements are mutually beneficial.

. . .

IV. Embedding Fairness: Re-Imagining Interest-Based Negotiation

Acknowledging that norms may embed in criteria begets a twofold conclusion: First, many of the criteria previously presumed to be objective and fair cannot be relied upon to guarantee a fair distributive outcome. Second, negotiators should question whether unfair norms similarly taint other elements of an interest-based negotiation. Might embedded norms also influence negotiators' relationships, communications, and efforts at option generation? One cannot assume that fairness — whether in distributional outcomes or in the processes used to reach these outcomes — can be passively achieved.

Given that fairness is a core remit of interest-based negotiation, the approach should also provide negotiators with the tools necessary to begin identifying and

---

potentially redressing unfair norms at play in a negotiation. The current framework provides no such tools. While recognizing this deficit in the current framework is not a wholesale repudiation of interest-based negotiation, addressing the deficit does require a re-imagining of the framework. In this re-imagining, fairness cannot be presumed. Instead, negotiators must assume the omnipresence of embedded norms, question the fairness of said norms, and be prepared to proffer fairer alternatives.

. . .

C. Re-Imagining Fairness in Interest-Based Negotiation

. . . Negotiators would employ justice-oriented queries to identify unfair norms present in the execution of a particular element. If such norms are found, negotiators would look to procedural and distributive justice principles to determine what a fairer process or distribution would entail. This process can, and should, be imagined as a negotiation in and of itself in which the traditional negotiation around process (how the negotiation will be conducted) and distribution (who will get how much of what) is preceded by an explicit (re-)negotiation of formerly implicit norms.

. . . A foundational assumption of the existing framework is that so-called objective criteria are indeed objective and can therefore be relied upon to fairly answer the question of distribution. This article squarely challenges that assumption and as such, much of its exploration will be dedicated to the element of criteria. . . . Therefore, the following also touches on how an interest-based negotiator might reorient the remaining six elements toward fairness.

i. Criteria and the Question of Distribution

. . . [T]he recognition that embedded norms muddy the objectivity of so-called objective criteria casts doubt on the guarantee that even the well-intentioned use of objective criteria will necessarily lead to distributive fairness. In order to keep interest-based negotiation's promise of fairness, negotiators must therefore identify embedded norms and, when necessary, re-negotiate them. In their efforts to unearth embedded norms, negotiators can begin with justice-oriented queries.

Instead of accepting that a given criterion will lead to a fair distribution, a negotiator might ask:

- When using a proposed criterion, what person, group, or community might receive/has historically received an unfair allocation of resources?
- What norms, implicit or explicit, are being used/have been used to answer the question of distribution? Are these norms fair?
- What distributive norms should be re-negotiated to facilitate a fair distribution?
- What alternative norms might ensure a more equitable outcome?

At the core of this inquiry is a presumption not of objectivity, but inequity. This presumption is key. Presupposing inequity, instead of even-handed objectivity, puts the interest-based negotiator on alert. An increased alertness subsequently increases the likelihood that a negotiator will identify unfair embedded norms that might otherwise go unquestioned.

Once unfair norms have been identified, they can be re-negotiated. A fairness-oriented negotiator should then consider alternative norms to create a more equitable outcome. The distributive justice principles — equality, proportionality, compensatory justice, and need — proffer potential alternatives. In a re-imagined framework, an interest-based negotiator would always endeavor to assess the context of a negotiation and determine the fairest distributive norm available. The quest is not for criteria that are "objective" but for distributive norms that are fair.

For instance, in certain salary negotiations a fairness-oriented negotiator might challenge the use of salary history as criteria. Salary history is often interpreted as an indication of the value of an individual's work product, efficacy, skill, or merit. However, this purportedly objective precedent often reflects a myriad of patriarchal and racist norms. In the context of patriarchy and white supremacy, the labor of women of color, white women, and men of color is often deemed less valuable than that of cis-gendered white men. The result? A massive gender, race, and ethnicity pay gap. Salary history does not come to be in a vacuum; it is not created objectively. Instead, it is a direct reflection of certain persons having their work undervalued. As an entry point, a negotiator might ask themselves, "if I use salary history as a criterion for pay, would a person, group, or community receive an unfair allocation of resources?" This inquiry — even if negotiators have not determined *ex ante* what distribution of resources would be fair — invites the negotiators to consider gender and racial wage disparities and note the subjective nature of salary history.

If reliance on certain precedents has been shown to exacerbate inequality, a fairer distributive norm might be equality. The equality principle calls for an equal distribution of the benefits and burdens of a negotiated agreement. In the context of a salary negotiation, a negotiator might ask, "all other factors being equal, what is the average pay for cis-gendered white men in this position?" Using this salary range to guide distributive decisions could lessen the effect of patriarchy and white supremacy. The resulting negotiated agreement would likely be fairer than one based on the precedent of an individual's specific salary history.

Similarly, in a negotiation over housework it might be imprudent to rely on tradition as criteria. In a two-parent household with a cisgendered man and a cisgendered woman, traditional divisions of labor are embedded with patriarchal norms. One such norm is that women are subservient to men. Another is that women are expected to do the lion's share of domestic work — a trend which has continued even as women's work outside of the home increases. Negotiators seeking a fair distribution might ask, "would using tradition as criteria lead to an unfair allocation of domestic tasks?" This query necessarily compels negotiators to explore the patriarchal norms that inform the traditional allocation of domestic work. Should a negotiator determine that tradition cannot dictate distribution, they might consider adopting a compensatory norm. Compensatory distribution indemnifies parties for bearing undue costs or burdens. Reliance on such a norm could lead to a distribution of domestic labor that accounts for the "triple shifts" — labor in the home, labor outside of the home, and emotional labor for the family unit — many women already work.

. . .

The particular fairness norms proposed to replace objective criteria in the examples above are not meant to be dispositive. The goal, instead, is to examine how an interest-based negotiator might shift from assessing the "legitimacy" of a criterion, defined as whether the criterion is widely accepted by a "great many people," to assessing its fairness. As Carrie Menkel-Meadow notes:

> Negotiators will seldom agree a priori on what their own standards of fairness are, but merely raising the issue of whether we owe fellow negotiators some consideration of distributional fairness or justice in a negotiation is to raise ethical consciousness . . .

This proposed re-imagining, at a minimum, compels negotiators to begin answering the question of distribution by first considering what fairness requires. Does fairness require distribution based on need because certain groups — often women of color, white women, men of color, LGBTQIA+ individuals, working people, and people with disabilities — have been historically denied resources? When the labor and lives of a group of people have been consistently under or un-valued, does fairness require proportional distribution? Does fairness necessitate a compensatory norm to ensure that those who have been asked to shoulder a greater emotional, physical, or monetary burden are rightly compensated? Or, perhaps, does fairness call for a re-examination of what equal distribution truly entails? In outlining these questions and considering possible answers, negotiators can begin to "raise [the] ethical consciousness" of the interest-based framework.

ii. Relationship and Communication

. . . .

In the case of relationships and communication, the justice-oriented queries push negotiators to assess how both elements are influenced by the surrounding economic, political, and social infrastructure. In a traditional interest-based frame, the analysis around what comprises a good relationship and effective communication is relatively simple. Traditionally defined, a good relationship is "good enough to produce an acceptable agreement," while effective communication balances active listening, intentional inquiry, and clear assertion. A re-imagining of these elements requires a recognition that the nature of negotiators' relationships and communication is influenced as much by broader sociopolitical forces as by interpersonal chemistry and communication. Again, the structural is intimately linked to the interpersonal.

Therefore, when considering relationships and communication in a negotiation, a fairness-oriented negotiator might ask, "what components of the existing economic, political, and social infrastructure are shaping this negotiation?" and "what norms, embedded or explicit, are present?" Such questions invite negotiators to assess their relative positions in the surrounding social, economic, and political structures. Asking these questions pushes negotiators to consider how the structural realities of racism, classism, heteronormativity, and/or sexism shape their relationships and communication with other parties. For those interested in procedural and distributive fairness, this realization is key to promoting behavioral modification.

For instance, after posing these questions, a negotiator may find that as a result of privilege derived from class, gender, sexual orientation, or race, they have had a disproportionate influence over procedural choices and distributive outcomes. Consider a cis-gendered man, who because of patriarchal norms has been socialized to believe that he should dominate interactions, negotiating with a cis-gendered woman who has been socialized to believe the exact opposite. Perhaps, upon reflection, this cis-gendered man finds he spoke the majority of the time in a recent negotiation. Perhaps he realizes that as a result, his proposed agenda items were more readily adopted. And perhaps as a result, the final agreement was ultimately more reflective of his interests than hers.

In this instance, a procedural principle of "fair treatment and fair play" might help address inequities. This principle is meant to ensure that all negotiators have meaningful influence over process — influence that extends "beyond being invited to the table." Adopting this principle might lead negotiators to agree on explicit procedural norms that fairly allocate speaking time, prohibit interruptions, and require unequivocal consent before distributive decisions are finalized. Again, the hope is that these queries serve as a fruitful entry point. In sum, negotiators must recognize how structural inequity colors their interpersonal relations in order to redress its effects.

iii. Interests and Options

. . .

Justice-oriented questions can be used to assess the fairness implications of meeting a particular interest via a particular option. A negotiator might consider: "if this interest is met, would a person or group receive an unfair share of the available resources?", "did a party have sufficient decision-making authority in light of how a particular option will impact them?", "what parties that have a significant interest in what is being negotiated are absent from the table?", or, "what community would be harmed if a particular interest were left unmet?" Such questions force negotiators to assess the interpersonal and structural implications of advancing (or not advancing) certain interests and pursuing (or not pursuing) certain options.

After identifying these implications, fairness-oriented negotiators can adopt procedural or distributive remedies. For instance, a negotiator may realize that a party's interest in being meaningfully heard can be fairly met by ensuring all impacted parties are rightly involved in the negotiating process (i.e., able to voice dissent, advocate for their own interests, and have decision-making power proportionate to how they will be impacted). Alternatively, a negotiator may realize that meeting a specific interest would, in fact, unavoidably create an unfair outcome. In this case, a fairness-oriented negotiator should forgo this interest. For instance, after recognizing another party has greater needs, a negotiator might supplant an interest in attaining a disproportionately large share of resources, ignore a very real desire to exclude "irksome" stakeholders, and ultimately agree to an unequal distribution in another party's favor.

Consider an ongoing land negotiation where, because of white supremacy, people indigenous to the land have historically been excluded from the bargaining table. These indigenous people invariably have an interest in how this land is distributed. It is, after all, their home. Realizing that their absence from the table is (and was) supremely unjust, negotiators must consider new procedural and distributive norms. In this case, fairness might require a process governed by fair representation and fair treatment with a distribution determined by the compensatory norm. Fair representation would guarantee the indigenous peoples were present, fair treatment would ensure that their preferences were centered, and a compensatory distribution would indemnify them for historical injustices.

Further, certain parties to the negotiation who recognize that without white supremacy they would not even be part of this negotiation, would likely *not* pursue certain of their interests. For instance, in hopes of maintaining their dominion, they may in fact want an overwhelming share of the territory. Or, for fear of losing the land, they may want to completely exclude indigenous people from the negotiation. A party being asked to forgo privilege or power likely possesses a myriad of fears, concerns, desires, and motivations that are antithetical to fairness. A re-imaging of interests and options encourages negotiators to acknowledge this reality and modify the process of their negotiations and the norms they rely on accordingly.

iv. Commitment and Alternatives

The final step in an interest-based negotiation is determining whether to commit to the agreement on the table or pursue an alternative. The current framework suggests that negotiators should only commit to negotiated agreements that are better than their best alternative. A re-imagining of these two elements morphs this final decision point into a type of after-action review. Specifically, fairness-oriented negotiators might use the questions provided by transformative justice to assess the procedural choices they made and the distributive outcomes they settled on. For instance, a negotiator might ask, "did the process ensure that all persons significantly impacted by the outcome were present in the negotiation?", "did the process also ensure that these parties were meaningfully heard?", or, "does the final agreement have a certain party taking on a disproportionate amount of benefit or burden?" This type of reflection might drive negotiators to re-negotiate based on principles of procedural and distributive justice. And, should a fairness-oriented negotiator find that their counterpart is unwilling to do so, they can pursue their best alternative.

Notes and Questions

(1) Is Korobkin correct when he argues that although one may wish to begin a negotiation with an integrative approach, ultimately one needs to reckon with the distributive aspects of the negotiation, and one should thus view the distributive as the cake and the integrative as the frosting, rather than vice versa? Even in those negotiations where the distributive aspects are clear, is it possible to take an integrative approach? That is, although integrative and distributive approaches to bargaining provide distinct communication frameworks, are they reconcilable? How? Which of these communication frameworks do you think would be most suitable for a mediation? Why?

(2) James White, in *The Pros and Cons of "Getting to Yes"*, 34 J. Legal Education 115 (1984), suggests *Getting to Yes* oversimplifies the negotiation process by suggesting a "negotiator can make any negotiation intro problem solving and thus completely avoiding" problems connected to positional, distributional, or hard bargaining. According to White, the concept of "objective criteria" is "a particularly naïve misperception or rejection of the guts of distributive negotiation." He explains:

[T]he authors draw a stark distinction between a negotiator who simply takes a position without explanation and sticks to it as a matter of "will," and the negotiator who is reasonable and insists upon "objective criteria." Of course the world is hardly as simple as the authors suggest. Every party who takes a position will have some rationale for that position; every able negotiator rationalizes every position that he takes.

. . .

In short, the authors' suggestion . . . that one can avoid "contests of will" and thereby eliminate the exercise of raw power is at best naïve and at worst misleading. Their suggestion that the parties look to objective criteria to strengthen their cases is a useful technique used by every able negotiator. Occasionally it may do what they suggest: give an obvious answer on which all can agree.

Is White's framing more consistent with what a lawyer might be trained to do? How does Eckblad's argument mesh with White's?

(3) Ebner and Kamp criticize Fisher and Ury for insisting on "separating the people from the problem," particularly because it requires concession-making to preserve relationships that "may make a negotiator vulnerable, perceived as weak, and open to manipulation." However, there is no doubt that people problems, such as a growing dislike for the personality or attitude of the lawyer for the other side, may get in the way of one's ability to stay focused on one's client's interests. One of the more difficult people problems to deal with during a negotiation may arise when the lawyer for the other side makes offensive or demeaning comments.

(4) Ebner and Kamp (through the lens of Fisher and Ury) urge negotiators to consider relationships in negotiation. How might negotiators (and mediators)

demonstrate listening, demonstrate empathy, and build relationships with parties and negotiation colleagues via phone, or video, or via asynchronous communication?

(5) As you read the material in the next section, consider how the integrative/distributive dichotomy meshes with the cooperative/competitive dichotomy.

2. Cooperative Versus Competitive Negotiation

The behaviors that people exhibit when they negotiate or bargain have been the subject of considerable interest to social scientists. One set of research has sought to identify styles or patterns of negotiating behavior that might be deemed most "effective." Although there has never been a clear consensus over what is meant by negotiation effectiveness, these foundational studies have been very helpful in identifying varying negotiation styles or types. In particular, the identification of cooperative versus competitive negotiating styles emerged from this research. In the selections that follow, Professor Gary Goodpaster argues for a clearer understanding of competitive behavior in negotiation; and Professor Gerald Williams discusses the distinguishing characteristics of competitive and cooperative negotiators and reports on what makes each effective.

A Primer on Competitive Bargaining
1996 J. Disp. Resol. 325, 325–26, 341–43, 370–77 (1996)*
By Gary Goodpaster

One cannot understand negotiation without understanding competitive behavior in negotiation. It is not that competing is a good way to negotiate; it may or may not be, depending on the circumstances. Understanding competition in negotiation is important simply because many people do compete when they negotiate, either by choice or happenstance.

Competitive bargaining, sometimes called hard, distributive, positional, zero-sum or win-lose bargaining, has the purpose of maximizing the competitive bargainer's gain over the gain of those with whom he negotiates. He is, in effect, trying to "come out ahead of," or "do better than," all other parties in the negotiation. For this reason, we sometimes refer to this competitive bargaining strategy as a *domination* strategy, meaning that the competitive bargainer tends to treat negotiations as a kind of contest to win.

The competitive negotiator tends to define success in negotiation rather narrowly. It is simply getting as much as possible for himself: the cheapest price, the most profit, the least cost, the best terms and so on. In its simplest form, this strategy focuses on immediate gain and is not much concerned with the relationship between the negotiating parties. A more complex version of this strategy focuses on long-term gain. This focus usually requires some effort to maintain or further a relationship and usually moderates the competitive, often aggressive, behavior that jeopardizes relationships and possibilities of long-term gain. . . .

People bargain competitively essentially for three reasons, which often overlap. First, by inclination or calculation, they view the negotiation as a kind of competition, in which they wish to win or gain as much as possible. Secondly, they do not trust the other party. Where parties are non-trusting, they are non-disclosing and withhold information, which leads to further distrust and defensive or self-protective moves. Parties may be non-trusting because they are unfamiliar with the other party or because they are generally or situationally non-trusting. Finally, a party may bargain competitively as a defense to, or retaliation for, competitive moves directed at it.

. . . The competitive negotiator adopts a risky strategy which involves the taking of firm, almost extreme positions, making few and small concessions, and withholding information that may be useful to the other party. The intention, and hoped-for effect, behind this basic strategy is to persuade the other party that it must make concessions if it is to get an agreement. In addition to this basic strategy, competitive negotiators may also use various ploys or tactics aimed at pressuring, unsettling, unbalancing or even misleading the other party to secure an agreement with its demands.

In an important sense, the competitive negotiator plays negotiation as an information game. In this game, the object is to get as much information from the other party as possible while disclosing as little information as possible. Alternatively, a competitive negotiator sometimes provides the other party with misleading clues, bluffs, and ambiguous assertions with multiple meanings, which are not actually false, but nevertheless mislead the other party into drawing incorrect conclusions that are beneficial to the competitor.

The information the competitive negotiator seeks is the other party's bottom line. How much he will maximally give or minimally accept to make a deal. On the other hand, the competitive negotiator wants to persuade the other side about the firmness of the negotiator's own *asserted* bottom line. The competitive negotiator works to convince the other party that it will settle only at some point that is higher (or lower, as the case may be) than its *actual* and unrevealed bottom line. . . . Taking a firm position and conceding little will incline the other party to think the competitor has little to give. Thus, if there is to be a deal, then the other party must give or concede more.

. . . Competitive and cooperative bargaining strategies conflict. A simple cooperative strategy leaves the cooperator vulnerable to exploitation by a competitor. There is also good evidence that competitive negotiators who use the high demand, firmness, small concession strategy get better negotiation results than cooperators, at least where "better" means getting the most immediate gain.

Cooperative bargainers vary greatly in their sophistication. Innocent cooperators who, consciously or unconsciously, uncritically adopt the premise that cooperation begets cooperation may unwittingly engage in behavior that exposes them to possible exploitation. Potentially detrimental information disclosures, unilateral concessions, or excessive concession making are all examples of this kind of behavior. Some cooperators may even exhibit invariant, non-adaptive or "pathological" cooperation. That is, they either consistently and detrimentally misinterpret the other party's exploitive moves, or otherwise always respond to persistent hard bargaining with increasing deference or reasonableness and with more, or greater, concessions.

If the hard bargainer overreaches too much, the cooperator may feel pushed beyond his own boundaries of reasonableness and cooperation and break off the negotiations out of frustration and anger at the other party's unreasonableness. A canny, hard bargainer, however, who is skilled in reading the other party and sensitive to the possibility of pushing too far, can always take advantage of a naïve and inexperienced cooperative negotiator. Innocent or naïve cooperators tend to assume that the other party is bargaining non-exploitively. They want to be trusted and tend to trust others. In their desire to be reasonable and friendly, they assume that the other party will act the same way, even in the face of contrary evidence.

Cooperators may worry more about having a good relationship and keeping things calm, reasonable, and agreeable than they do about getting exactly what they want. Indeed, going into the negotiation, they may not specifically know what they would deem a good disposition. Instead, rather than enter the negotiation with certain figures or positions in mind as desirable results, they may enter with vaguer, more malleable and manipulable notions that they only want "what's fair" or "what's reasonable" under the circumstances. The lack of a clear reference point makes them less able to discern their own interest and, therefore, more vulnerable to competitive claiming.

The cooperator's desire to be a certain kind of person — noncompetitive, nonaggressive, fair, decent, honorable — may also result in turning the other cheek to the other party's hard-bargaining tactics. In fact, naïve cooperators may undercut getting what they want by assuming that they must make unilateral concessions or compromises without a return just to get an agreement. They sometimes fail to distinguish between their behavior toward others and their behavior toward the problem they are trying to resolve. In other words, they are "soft on the people" and "soft on the problem."

The cooperator faces a dilemma: the reasonable, compromising conduct in which he wishes to engage in order to obtain a fair and just agreement also puts him at risk. If the other party is also cooperative, all is well and good. The other party, however, may not be cooperative. Instead, the other party may either be overtly competitive or cooperative in demeanor and competitive in substance. If, for example, to be reasonable and attempt to have the union understand its point of view, management volunteers important information, such as planning a plant expansion, the union may simply take the information and use it to its advantage without volunteering information in return or reciprocating in any other way. Similarly, if Susan, being cooperative, makes a concession hoping to trigger a concession from Jerry, Jerry may simply take the concession and either give nothing in return or give a non-commensurate concession. Indeed, the cooperator's concession may encourage the other side to seek more or greater concessions. In this situation, the truly naïve cooperator may respond by conceding more in the hope of inducing a concession and movement toward an agreeable settlement rather than by noting the lack of reciprocity and adjusting his own behavior to protect himself.

The cooperator faces the dilemma that the way he wants to negotiate may put him at risk of being taken or exploited. Obviously, cooperative negotiators should not naïvely *assume* that the other party will also act cooperatively. Indeed, they must recognize that they cannot successfully bargain cooperatively unless the other party cooperates. They also need to devise ways to protect themselves from the other party's possible competitive moves that are often masked or hidden by a genial, reasonable, or cooperative demeanor.

Aware of the potential risks involved in their cooperative behavior, a negotiator could adopt a hard bargaining strategy. This strategy would certainly not be necessary in all cases. In fact, many negotiators might object to hard bargaining in principle. How does a wise and careful cooperative negotiator protect herself from competitive bargainers?

Defensive cooperativeness. During the initial stages of a negotiation the parties feel each other out, not only to gain information respecting positions, wants, and desires, but also to get a sense of whether, and how far, they can trust one another. Since trust, or providing security that one can trust, is a key issue, cooperators should try to anticipate negotiations, develop information about the other party, and build a relationship with the other party prior to negotiation.

Because cooperative behavior promotes trust, it tends to induce reciprocal cooperative behavior. Once in a negotiation, the careful cooperator adopts a cooperative, yet wary, demeanor and indicates a general posture of flexibility on issues. This may signal or hint at a willingness to make concessions on certain issues. Nevertheless, the defensive or cautious cooperator does not make significant concessions before determining whether the other party is trustworthy.

Fractionating concessions. A careful negotiator can, in part, fashion a self-protective concession strategy by fractionating concessions. One fractionates concessions by dividing an issue into smaller issues and, therefore, into smaller concessions where one gives on an issue. Using this method, the negotiator can make a small concession and wait to see how the other party responds. If the other party makes an equivalent concession, the negotiator can proceed.

Ambiguous or disownable signals. A negotiator makes a "disownable" concession move by making an ambiguous statement that suggests a willingness to make a concession but which can also be plausibly interpreted as not expressing such willingness. If the other party interprets the statement as offering a concession and reciprocates, then the negotiator confirms the other side's interpretation in some way. If the other party seeks to grab the assumed concession without offer-ing a return, the negotiator denies making it. Suppose, for example, that one party has repeatedly argued that two conditions had to be met before he would consider changing his position. After a time, however, he begins to mention only one condi-tion, thereby, signaling a willingness to drop the unmentioned condition.

This sort of signaling is, in effect, a testing of the other party. This test, however, does not run the actual risk of making a concession or exposing weakness. At most, it is an unclear expression of a contingent willingness to concede. As another exam-ple, consider two parties negotiating over contract terms. The buyer wants the seller to give her the same discount on equipment that the seller gives some of its other, much larger customers. The seller says, "We can write something like a 'favored nations' clause into the contract." The buyer responds, "I'll take that, and I appreci-ate getting the same discount as your larger customers," but he makes no concession in return. The seller then responds, "Well, you can have the clause, but it doesn't apply to discounts." Alternatively, had the buyer shown a willingness to concede, the seller could let the buyer's first interpretation of the statement stand.

If there is little trust, this process of signaling can be quite subtle because the target of the signal may be uncertain whether to interpret a statement as expressing a willingness to concede. If the target is uncertain, he may fear responding in a way which clearly shows his willingness to reciprocate because that may put him at risk. Consequently, the parties sometimes engage in trading ambiguous statements until one party feels secure enough to make a clear proposal or until both parties simul-taneously make a clear move.

"Directional" information. Sometimes a negotiator may encourage cooperative bargaining simply by indicating on which issues the other party should improve its proposals. This tactic provides the other party with some information about the negotiator's priorities but without clearly committing to anything.

Demanding reasoned justifications. A negotiator should make a practice of asking the other party to justify its positions in terms of some objective criteria. If the other party simply behaves competitively and attempts to extract whatever gains it can, it may have difficulty in stating satisfactory justifications for its positions.

Contingent cooperativeness and the reformed sinner strategy. There is good evi-dence that even those who wish to bargain cooperatively can succeed with competi-tive negotiators by adopting a shifting "competitive to cooperative" or "reformed sinner" strategy. This strategy involves making a high, initial demand, remaining firm initially, and then moving to a "contingently cooperative" strategy. Contin-gent cooperativeness involves behaving cooperatively if the other party reciprocates cooperative behavior and increasing cooperative behavior as the other party does so. Interestingly, the cooperator's initial firmness may signal to the other party that competitive behavior will not work.

. . .

The contingently competitive strategy appears to work by giving the other party evidence that its own cooperative behavior, but not its competitive behavior, has a desirable effect. In carrying out this general strategy, the cooperator may expressly negotiate over the negotiation ground rules and seek the other party's commitment to negotiate cooperatively as well, but, in any case, asserting a norm and expectation of cooperative behavior. The cooperator may then attempt to structure the negotiation to handle small issues first, where the risk of loss is not great. When ready to take some risks, the cooperator makes contingent proposals. The proposal expressly offers a concession or adopts a position closer to the other party's demands yet contingent on some specific concession or change of position from the other party.

Strategy imitation or tit-for-tat. Response — in-kind or tit-for-tat — is a form of contingent cooperation a negotiator can use to handle a competitor. If the cooperator observes competitive tactics, she can call attention to them and state that she knows how to bargain that way too and will respond in kind unless the other party bargains cooperatively. Alternatively, the cooperator can just respond in kind by using tit-for-tat to discipline the other party.

Tit-for-tat is a negotiation strategy designed to shape the other party's bargaining behavior. One dilemma negotiators face is figuring out whether to bargain cooperatively or competitively. If one wishes to be reasonable and bargain cooperatively, there is a risk that the other party will bargain competitively and gain an advantage. Using tit-for-tat, a negotiator solves that problem by competing just as the other party does and, in effect, sends the message that "I will bargain the way you bargain and will use the same tactics you use." This teaches the other party that it cannot get away with anything, and may lead to cooperative behavior.

In general, using a tit-for-tat or matching strategy appears to be an effective way to induce cooperation. The strategy makes it clear to the other party that it risks retaliation and increasing conflict if it continues to bargain competitively.

Time-outs. Negotiating parties deadlock when no party is willing to make a further concession to bring the parties closer together. When the parties are nearing a deadline and are deadlocked, they may realize that the negotiation will fail completely unless they cooperate. Declaring a time-out when a dead-lock is apparent gives the parties time to assess the situation without continued conflict, reconsider their reading of the negotiation thus far, and determine more rationally whether to risk trusting the other party. Often enough, when the parties return to formal negotiation, each side signals a willingness to move towards an agreement or make concessions leading to an agreement.

Because people bargain competitively for various reasons, negotiators and mediators need to understand competition in negotiation in order to respond appropriately. Some people bargain competitively without giving much conscious attention to the matter. Others compete in response to the other party's competitive behavior. In this response, they follow the common pattern that a particular kind of behavior elicits a similar behavior in response. In other words, one party frames the negotiation as a contest, and the other party picks up the competitive cues and behaves accordingly. Further, people naturally incline to competitive bargaining when they are non-trusting. In such situations, in order to avoid putting themselves at risk, non-trusting people act guardedly and adopt elements of the competitive strategy, for example, withholding information or misrepresenting a position. Finally, one can readily imagine ambiguous bargaining situations, in which at least one party is non-trusting, quickly devolving into a competitive negotiation between both parties. The non-trusting party acts defensively, and the other party senses this as competitive behavior and, therefore, acts in a similar fashion.

Negotiators, however, can also consciously adopt a competitive strategy. Negotiators are most likely to compete purposefully when

- the parties have an adversarial relationship;
- a negotiator has a bargaining power advantage and can dominate the situation;
- a negotiator perceives an opportunity for gain at the expense of the other party;
- the other party appears susceptible to competitive tactics;
- the negotiator is defending against competitive moves; or
- there is no concern for the future relationship between the parties.

This list suggests that competitive bargaining most likely occurs in situations such as labor and lawsuit negotiations, insurance and similar claims type settlements, and in one-time transactions between a relatively experienced party and a relatively inexperienced party. One would, for example, expect to see it in sales transactions where the parties will probably not see each other again.

Representative bargaining or bargaining for a constituency may also prompt competitive bargaining even when there will be future negotiations between equally sophisticated parties. The negotiator's accountability may override relationship concerns and reasons for cooperation. The concerned audience, consisting of a client, constituency, coalition partner, or other phantom party at the table, is, in effect, looking over the negotiator's shoulder. The negotiator, therefore, takes positions and makes moves she believes her client either expects or would approve. International negotiations between countries, union-management, lawsuit negotiations, and negotiations between different parties in interest-group coalition negotiations sometimes evidence this pattern.

Aside from circumstantial or situational pressures, there are some parties who bargain competitively because they believe that is the way to conduct business. There are also parties who are simply predisposed to bargain competitively and will incline to do so opportunistically in any bargaining situation if possible.

Finally, it is important to note that one can bargain competitively in a negotiation on some issues and cooperatively on others. In other words, a negotiator can selectively use competitive strategy or tactics on particular issues, while using a cooperative or problem-solving strategy on other issues. In such a case, extracting gain competitively may not greatly endanger future relationships. At least, there is a judgment call concerning this. The negotiator attempts to calculate the net effect of the overall results and skews the benefits, insofar as possible, to his side. In this kind of calculation, it is clear that there is some kind of assessment or balancing of short-term versus long-term gain. Again, there is no formula to calculate these gains, and the parties probably follow rules of thumb prevalent in the industry and developed from prior experience, or they calculate these gains based on hopes or individualized assessments.

Similarly, it is possible for negotiators to use an integrative or problem solving bargaining strategy in order to increase the amount of gain possible to the parties. At some point, however, notwithstanding cooperation to produce greater gain, the parties will have to distribute or divide the gain. Therefore, they may also engage in competitive bargaining.

Obviously, competitive bargaining covers a continuum of behaviors from the simplest, unreflective adversarial actions to highly conscious and virtually scripted contests. As such, competitive bargaining moves are natural responses in some negotiation situations and advantageous or profitable actions in others. This being so, what are the downsides to competitive negotiation?

At least in its full-blown form, competitive negotiation is risky bargaining. The competitor takes risks in order to secure gains. Among these is the risk that there will be no gains at all. The competitive strategy of staking out a position and holding firm, particularly when joined with various devious tactics, runs the risk of alienating, frustrating, or angering the other party and, thus, precluding a possible agreement.

Even if there is an agreement, it may not be a sustainable one. On reflection, the other party may conclude that it does not really like the deal or feels that it was "taken" in some way. Furthermore, even if there is a deal and it survives, the bargaining that occurred may adversely affect future relations between the parties. This is certain to happen if one party discovers that the other party actively misled or manipulated it. It may also happen just because of residual hard feelings or mistrust arising from the tactics used.

Beyond these concerns, competitive bargaining is neither efficient nor productive bargaining. It is inefficient and nonproductive because parties who withhold and manipulate information miss possibilities of cooperating to find or create additional value to divide between them. As a result, they can be said "to leave gains on the table."

Along this line, genuine cooperation and positive relationships are two real gains that competitive negotiators are unlikely to ever realize and bring to bear in immediate or prospective negotiations between themselves and others. Put another way, although a competitive negotiator may realize a gain in a particular negotiation, he may forgo far greater possible gains in doing so.

Legal Negotiation and Settlement

25–30 (1983)*

By Gerald R. Williams

[Ed. Note: Gerald Williams' research studied the negotiating behaviors of practicing attorneys in Denver, Colorado and Phoenix, Arizona. While Williams found that these lawyers could generally be placed in either the cooperative or the competitive category in terms of their negotiating behaviors, he concluded that there were effective and ineffective negotiators in both categories. That is, use of a cooperative style could, in and of itself, no more guarantee negotiating effectiveness than the use of a competitive style.]

In contrast to the friendly, trustworthy approach of cooperative effectives, effective/competitives are seen as dominating, competitive, forceful, tough, arrogant, and uncooperative. They make high opening demands, they use threats, they are willing to stretch the facts in favor of their clients' positions, they stick to their positions, and they are parsimonious with information about the case. They are concerned not only with maximizing the outcome for their client but they appear to take a gamesmanship approach to negotiation, having a principal objective of outdoing or outmaneuvering their opponent. Thus, rather than seeking an outcome that is "fair" to both sides, they want to outdo the other side; to score a clear victory. . . .

While there are differences in approach between the two types of effective negotiators, both types are, in fact, rated as highly effective. Our interest is in what makes them effective, *i.e.*, what traits they have in common. Common traits have particular importance, since law students and attorneys can seek to understand and emulate them irrespective of which pattern they prefer to follow. . . .

Both types of effective negotiators are ranked as highly experienced. This comes as no surprise, since we normally assume that negotiating effectiveness improves with experience. Its meaning here is illuminated by the comment of a responding attorney, who wrote: "it is important to have enough experience in order that you have confidence in yourself and be able to convey that confidence."

More importantly, both types are seen as ethical, trustworthy and honest, thus dispelling any doubt about the ethical commitments of effective/competitives. However, the priority of these traits is ranked much higher for cooperatives (3rd, 6th and 1st in priority) than for competitives (15th, 20th and 11th in priority). Given the current interest and concern about professional responsibility in the Bar, the high ratings on ethical and trustworthy for both effective groups are worthy of notice. Although literature on professional responsibility generally argues that high ethical standards are a precondition to success in practice, many law students and some practicing attorneys continue to believe or suspect that they must compromise their ethical standards in order to effectively represent their clients and attain success in practice. The findings of this survey suggest such compromises may be not only unnecessary, but actually counterproductive to one's effectiveness in negotiation situations.

In the same vein, we see that both types are careful to observe the customs and courtesies of the bar. While some attorneys have argued that there are tactical advantages in deliberately departing from the etiquette of the profession, as a general rule effective negotiators observe it. . . .

Although effective/competitives were seen as taking unrealistic opening positions, in general they share with cooperatives the traits of being realistic, rational, and analytical. These three attributes become very important in interpreting negotiator behavior. They mean more than the idea of "thinking like a lawyer"; they impose limits on how far a negotiator may credibly go in such things as interpretation of facts, claims about damages and other economic demands, and levels of emotional involvement in the case.

Both effective types are seen as thoroughly prepared on the facts and the law of the case. They are also described as legally astute. This, again, is something to be expected. But it bears emphasis because, as we shall see, ineffective negotiators lack these qualities. One attorney had these traits in mind when he wrote, "In my experience, the most important part of negotiation is thorough preparation and a complete knowledge of the strengths and weaknesses of your position. . . . I feel individual personality traits (*e.g.*, loud, forceful, quiet, reserved) are unimportant."

Legal astuteness means they have not only done their homework by informing themselves about the legal and procedural ramifications of the case, but they also have acquired good judgment about how and when to act with respect to this information.

Both types of effective attorneys are rated as creative, versatile, and adaptable. This is true even though competitive effectives are also labeled rigid. Apparently there is a distinction between being tough (which competitive attorneys are) and being obstinate. An attorney should not be so rigid that he is unable to seek creative solutions to problems. The flavor of the terms is suggested in a comment by an attorney representing a party who was involved in a very acrimonious dispute with a neighbor over an irrigation ditch. He wrote, "Our problem was solved by a simple relocation agreement executed by the parties and recorded. The opposition attorney and myself, after great study and much effort, came up with the simple solution of simply relocating the ditch."

Both types are self-controlled. . . .

One of the more important marks of effective negotiators is skill in reading their opponent's cues. This refers not only to the ability to judge an opponent's reactions in negotiating situations, but to affirmatively learn from the opponent. The old saying is that experience is the best teacher. Experience is only a good teacher for those who are skillful at learning from it. In the course of interviews connected with Denver attorneys, they were routinely asked what they did when they were faced with an inexperienced opponent — an opponent fresh out of law school. Their responses were very informative. One group of attorneys would get a sly grin on their face, their eyes would light up, and they would say "I hammer them into the ground." By far the larger number of attorneys responded quite differently, however. They said that when they had a "green" opponent, they slowed the case way down, tried to spell everything out as they went, and tried generally to show the younger attorney the right way to go about handling a case.

Consider this problem from the perspective of law graduates recently admitted to the bar. During the first few months of practice, they encounter some attorneys who hammer them into the ground, exploiting and taking advantage of them at every turn, and others who are trying to teach them how to be good lawyers. The experience is not calculated to engender trust in fellow officers of the court. Rather, the tendency in young lawyers is to develop a mild paranoia and to distrust everyone. This is unfortunate, because *some* opponents are providing valuable information, albeit in subtle ways. The key, then, is to learn to observe and "read" the opposing attorney and know who can be trusted and who cannot and then learn from both types without being misled by either.

Competitive and cooperative effectives are rated as perceptive, a term that goes hand in hand with skill in reading cues. It relates in part to the ability to perceive an opponent's strategy and his subjective reaction to your strategy. It also has a larger connotation, referring to the accuracy of one's perception of the whole case. One attorney in our study gave a telling description of his perception of a recently completed case: "I lost the case. Though my opponent was ineffective in preparation and presentation — and was a drunk — the judge *disbelieved* my key witness, a fundamentalist Minister, and the plaintiff got every cent he had wrongly demanded from my client."

Finally, it must be stressed that both types of effective negotiators are also rated as effective trial attorneys. As mentioned earlier, the alternative to settlement is trial. If an attorney is known as a weak trial attorney, it will often be more profitable for his opponent to take him to trial than agree to a reasonable settlement. This creates an awkward and troublesome dynamic, because the weak trial attorney knows that his client would be poorly served by an inept trial of the case. The weak attorney discounts the case as an inducement to the other side to settle and avoid the costs (and benefits) of trial. The interplay between fear of trial and discounting of the case is not healthy. There appears to be only one solution: to be taken seriously, lawyers who negotiate legal disputes (as opposed to non-actionable matters) must either develop substantial expertise as trial attorneys, or must openly associate themselves (whether by partnership, a referral system, or some other way) with very effective trial counsel.

Notes and Questions

(1) Would you characterize your negotiation style as cooperative or competitive? Why?

(2) Do Professor Goodpaster's suggestions for dealing with a competitive negotiator ("defensive cooperativeness," etc.) make you feel more comfortable about adopting a cooperative bargaining posture? Why or why not?

(3) Do you think a mediator's strategies might shift if they are working with cooperative or competitive negotiators?

3. Problem-Solving Negotiation

Toward Another View of Legal Negotiation: The Structure of Problem-Solving

31 UCLA L. Rev. 754, 817–29 (1984)*
By Carrie Menkel-Meadow

C. The Process of Problem-Solving Negotiation

The process of problem-solving negotiation is likely to be very different from the linear, reciprocal concession patterns leading to compromise in adversarial negotiation. This section reviews how problem-solving negotiation processes are likely to differ from adversarial negotiation.

1. Planning

As the discussion thus far should indicate, the crux of the problem-solving approach is the conceptualization and planning which precede any execution of the negotiation. A problem-solving conception of negotiation should be distinguished from cooperative or collaborative negotiation. The latter refers to particular behaviors engaged in during the negotiation, such as "being flexible, disclosing information and establishing good relationships with the other negotiator." These behaviors may be useful in problem-solving negotiations, but they can also be used as tactics in adversarial negotiations where their purpose is to achieve greater individual gain. The conceptualization used in planning problem-solving negotiation is useful in all negotiation, regardless of the particular behaviors chosen in the executory stages. Planning may indicate that needs are truly incompatible and call for the use of adversarial strategies to maximize individual gain, or that resort to adjudication is necessary.

Although economic evaluation of the case and some prediction of how a court would rule in a dispute resolution will still be appropriate, potential solutions need not be limited to some prediction of the mid-point compromise between estimated

---

first offers. Instead, the planning stages of a problem-solving negotiation resemble the brainstorming process described by Fisher & Ury in *Getting To YES*. The process emphasizes exploring and considering both parties' underlying needs and objectives and the devices suggested earlier in this Article for expanding resources. The problem solver who has engaged in a brainstorming planning session is likely to approach a negotiation with a number of possible proposals which can be offered for two-sided brainstorming with the other party. While the planning stages of an adversarial negotiation may narrow and make the offers more precise, the problem-solving planning stages are more likely to result in a broadening of solutions. As Fisher & Ury point out, the key to creative problem-solving is to separate the creative stages of planning from the necessarily more rigid judgment stages.[257] The more potential solutions a negotiator is able to bring to the bargaining table, the more probable it is that agreement will be reached; stalemate and rejection are less likely to occur. In the legal context these brainstorming sessions should include the client, as she may have some solutions of her own, as well as important insights into what the other party desires.

The planning discussed above is primarily substantive planning focused on potential solutions rather than strategic planning focused on what positions to take in the negotiation. Strategic planning may depend on how willing the other party is to depart from the more familiar adversarial negotiation process. At the intersection of substantive and strategic planning are considerations of what information about the other party's needs is necessary to plan for solutions acceptable to the other party. An example best illustrates this point.

Suppose that in a lawsuit based on concealment of a leaky roof in the sale of a residence, the plaintiff has sued for $10,000, the cost of repairing the roof. However, a more extensive portion of the roof was repaired than that which seemed necessary to prevent leaks. The plaintiff has been forced to take out a bank loan in order to repair the roof. This is a further encumbrance on the property, and the plaintiff is having a great deal of difficulty making all of the payments on the house. In addition, the plaintiff is concerned that her parents will learn she bought the house without following their advice to have an inspection made. The defendant seller of the house needs to make payments on her own house and is worried about the possibility of rescission. A bona fide dispute about the facts is whether the defendant misrepresented the facts, and if so, whether he did so negligently or intentionally. The seller holds a second mortgage on the house and the plaintiff now threatens to withhold payment. The plaintiff has taken the deposition of the defendant's former housekeeper who does remember a leaky roof when the defendant was in possession.

Assuming that we represent the plaintiff in this case, there are a number of needs that can be identified. Economically, the plaintiff would like to recover the cost of the roof repair, probably with a minimum of transaction costs. Depending on her

---

257. R. Fisher & W. Ury at 62-66. [R. Fisher & W. Ury, *Getting to YES* (1981).]

dealings and relationship with the defendant, the plaintiff might wish to have the defendant's actions declared legally fraudulent. Recall, however, that in this example the defendant holds a second mortgage on the house so that the plaintiff and the defendant will have a continuing relationship if the plaintiff remains in the house. The plaintiff's social needs may include preventing her parents from discovering that she bought the house without an inspection. Psychologically, it is possible that the plaintiff feels both foolish for not discovering the leak and angry because it was hidden. Furthermore, the plaintiff may feel that the defendant's deception was morally wrong and she may want an apology, payment as punishment, and/or an assurance that this is the only undisclosed defect.

At this point all we know of the defendant's needs may be what we learned from our client, the plaintiff. We know, for example, that the defendant needs the money from the second mortgage to pay the mortgage on her own new home. We may know that the defendant would prefer not to have a legal judgment of fraud entered against her because it will damage her credit rating. Similarly, the defendant may not want a lawsuit for fraud to become public because it could damage her relationship with business associates or her reputation in the community. Finally, it is possible that because the house-keeper has already given testimony against her, the defendant fears losing a lawsuit and may feel regretful or guilty about what she has done. Note that many of the assumptions or speculations about the defendant's needs have to be more fully discovered, either in pretrial discovery or in informal investigation, or tested in the negotiation.

Having identified the parties' needs, we can now begin to consider a number of general solutions. These may include such things as settling the case privately because both parties fear publicity, an apology and new promise that nothing else is defective, and perhaps a delayed or installment payment from defendant to plaintiff, or a reduction on the plaintiff's obligation on the second mortgage. The one remaining issue which is likely to result in conflicting views, the amount of the settlement, can be made less difficult either by having an independent determination of the proper amount to repair the original damage or by expanding the resources through time payments and tax structures that may permit the plaintiff to realize more dollars than the defendant actually pays out.

The structure of this example may not work in all cases, but it illustrates how the analysis of both parties' needs may lead to a number of possible solutions.

2. Execution

To the extent that both parties engage in a problem-solving negotiation structure, the negotiation is likely to resemble a fluid brainstorming session. Even if only one party has engaged in a problem-solving planning process, the negotiation need not be reduced to an adversarial exercise. First, the parties may begin with a greater number of possible solutions simply because two heads are better than one. In addition, as empirical research has demonstrated, when both parties approach negotiation with the objective of working collaboratively, more of the information reflecting the parties' needs may be revealed, facilitating the search for solutions. Thus, in the case of the leaky roof, the amount of damages might be easier to determine if both parties approached the problem by looking for ways to reach agreement than if one approached the problem as simply maximizing or minimizing payment, using litigation as a threat. On the other hand, even a single problem solver can propose alternative ways of measuring liability that may eventually be successful, if she has accurately determined the other party's needs.

When the problem solver is able to present a number of different solutions which potentially satisfy at least some of the other party's needs, it is more likely that the adversarial concession and argumentation pattern can be avoided than if she presents a single demand. The parties can consider variations of each of the proposals using the techniques of game theorists who simply alter the coordinates slightly at each play to see if a more efficient solution can be achieved. Thus, the negotiation game may be played on a multi-dimensional field rather than on one that is linear, or two-dimensional. In the leaky roof case one party may suggest a number of different methods of payment, such as reduction of the second mortgage, lump-sum, or installment payments at different discount factors, rather than simply demanding $10,000.

In addition to the different offer structure, problem-solving negotiations are likely to have different information sharing processes. As discussed above, many conventional works on negotiation urge the negotiator not to reveal information. The problem solver recognizes that he is more likely to develop solutions which meet the parties' needs by revealing his own needs or objectives, while at the same time trying to learn about the other party's. In short, there is no incentive to dissemble. When this is the goal, the process consists of asking questions in search of clarification and information, rather than making statements or arguments designed to persuade the other party to accept one's own world view.

On the other hand, totally uninhibited information sharing may be as dysfunctional as withholding information. In experimental simulations Pruitt & Lewis found that there was not necessarily a correlation between free information exchange and joint profit.[268] Instead, joint profit was associated with information processing — that is, the ability to listen to, receive, and understand the information and how it related concretely to the problem. Furthermore, information sharing in a thoughtless and unrestricted fashion may lead to the sharpening of conflict as value differences are revealed in competing goals and needs. In problem-solving negotiation it is crucial to understand the usefulness and function of particular pieces of information — such as exploring how strongly one party desires something — because each piece is related to possible solutions. Problem solvers must determine what information is needed and why, and must be able to absorb information from the other side to test assumptions about needs, goals or objectives.

---

268. Pruitt & Lewis at 170–72. [Pruitt & Lewis, *The Psychology of Integrative Bargaining, in* Negotiations: Social-Psychological Perspectives (D. Druckman ed. 1977).]

An example taken from my negotiation course can illustrate. In negotiating a partnership agreement, students are given information about each of the prospective partners. One partner has an immediate need for a relatively high salary because he must provide for a disabled child. The other partner would also like a high salary, but is more concerned about creating the partnership because he is excited about entering a new business. Students, who in my experience are more likely to be adversarial negotiators, have tended to approach the salary negotiation as a conventional zero-sum negotiation. When, as happens occasionally, one side reveals why the salary is needed, a greater variety of solutions seem to come unlocked, such as sliding scales, deferred versus immediate compensation, special provisions for the child, and salary trade-offs for other items. In this situation the party who learns of the disabled child either may be moved by sympathy or by the more instrumental realization that if this is of concern to his future partner it should be dealt with now so it is not a future drain on the partnership. Whatever the motivation, the new information can serve as a source of new solutions ending an otherwise stalemated salary negotiation. Obviously, not all negotiation problems will contain such useful information, but the problem solver is willing to share information about needs that may facilitate such solutions. Thus, problem solving produces a more sophisticated calculus concerning what information should be revealed.

Related to the information flow is the process by which the proposals are evaluated during the negotiation. Fisher & Ury describe this process in a problem-solving environment as principled movements which are reasoned, justified statements about why a particular proposal is important. Fisher & Ury distinguish such movements from the arguments over position which occur in conventional adversarial negotiation. In conventional negotiation, each party takes a position such as the first offer or target position, argues for it, and then makes unprincipled concessions to reach a compromise.

Even conventional adversarial negotiation, however, may be justified by principled movements. One of the most valuable contributions of the growing clinical literature on legal negotiation has been the analysis of using reasons for concessions. Thus, in order to avoid the pitfalls of totally unjustified concessions, negotiators are told that "it is important that the pattern and content of ... justifications [for concessions] will be well thought out in advance" as "the justification offered for a particular concession invariably will be assessed by one's opponent. . . ."[276] These suggestions about principled movement in the adversarial context, however, have been used largely to justify movements up and down the limited linear plane. Thus, although useful even in adversarial negotiation, principled movements are of a different sort and used for different purposes in a problem-solving negotiation.

According to Fisher & Ury, in the problem-solving context the negotiator will use principled movements to justify proposals and suggestions in terms of their

276. G. Bellow & B. Moulton, *The Lawyering Process: Negotiation* (1981).

relationship to the parties' underlying interests or objectives. Reconciling interests will be more effective than arguing over positions, they say, because "for every interest there usually exist several possible positions that could satisfy it. . . . Reconciling interests rather than compromising between positions also works because behind opposed positions lie many more shared interests than conflicting ones."[278]

In the process of considering possibilities, the problem solver articulates reasons why a particular solution is acceptable or unacceptable, rather than simply rejecting an offer or making a concession. Articulating reasons during the negotiation facilitates agreement in a number of ways. First, it establishes standards for judging whether a particular solution is sensible and should be accepted. If the reason is focused on the parties' underlying needs, the negotiator can consider whether the proposal is satisfactory to the parties. She need not be concerned with such conventional evaluation as "Is this the most I can get?" or its counterpart, "Is this the least I can get away with?" Second, principled proposals focus attention on solving the problem by meeting the parties' needs, rather than winning an argument. Furthermore, continuously focusing justification on the parties' needs may cause negotiators to see still other solutions, rather than simply to respond with arguments about particular offers. The use of principled proposals can decrease the likelihood that unjustified and unnecessary concessions will be made simply to move toward agreement. Finally, the use of principled proposals causes the parties to share information about their preferences that they might otherwise be reluctant to reveal.

Principled negotiations in the legal context may be more complex, however. In addition to proposals based on the parties' underlying needs, negotiators can focus on the legal merits as a justification for a particular proposal. In-deed, negotiators are told to use "the law" or "the facts" to make arguments or justify positions in analyzing how concessions can be justified in adversarial negotiations. For example, in deciding whether to accept a particular settlement offer a negotiator might say: "We might not agree on the percentage of responsibility, but in this jurisdiction there is comparative negligence so it is unlikely that our contributory negligence will bar recovery. My client is entitled to something." In some sense, all legal negotiations are measured against the legal merits because, in deciding whether to accept a particular proposal, the negotiator must also decide whether the negotiated agreement is better than the one which would be achieved at trial or in a form contract. In Fisher & Ury's parlance this is termed one of the BATNAs (Best Alternative to a Negotiated Agreement). All proposals in litigation negotiations will be measured against predictions about what the court might order.

Proposals justified by the legal merits can be problematic. Given a dispute where the parties have widely divergent views of the merits and how they will be determined by a fact-finder, negotiators may find themselves involved in precisely the sort of unproductive argumentation inherent in adversarial negotiation. Indeed, as

---

278. R. Fisher & W. Ury at 11, 41-57. [R. Fisher & W. Ury, *Getting to YES* (1981).]

some have argued, one of the primary advantages of negotiation over adjudication is that no judgment need be made about whose argument is right or wrong. Parties can agree to settle on principles such as community norms or values that are broader than those the court can consider. On the other hand, focusing on the merits as a justification still may be more productive than adhering to arbitrary positions simply out of competitive stubbornness.

Ideally, of course, proposals should be justifiable on a basis which integrates the parties' needs and the legal merits. Returning to the leaky roof example, consider how a demand by the plaintiff for $10,000 "because your client defrauded mine" contrasts with the following proposal to the defendant:

> "One solution here might be for your client to pay my client $7,000 by reducing the monthly payment on the second mortgage over the term of the five-year mortgage. It seems to me that this is fair because if we go to trial I think the court will find the defendant liable for at least $7,000 of the damages to the roof. The housekeeper's testimony will make it clear the defendant knew of the leak and the court will believe the housekeeper because she has no reason to lie. A payment of $7,000 is fair because it cost $3,000 to repair the roof, $3,000 to re-plaster the room and $1,000 to replace the ruined rugs. The proposal seems fair because it fits the needs of both of the parties. My client needs a reduction in her total monthly payments to meet all of her obligations, including the second mortgage payment to your client, and your client won't be out of any immediate cash to settle this case. If you prefer some other method of payment or other formulation, I'd be happy to discuss it with you."

The defendant's lawyer is now able to respond to the assessment of the legal merits and his client's needs and may modify this proposal, perhaps by offering a small cash payment with less of a reduction on the second mortgage to insure some future income. In addition, by presenting proposals with such justifications, each party reveals its assumptions about the other party's needs and legal positions, and can be corrected where wrong. When proposals are not justified in this way, the problem-solving negotiator should ask on what basis the proposal is made to be sure the principles are articulated and not assumed. Notice that the proposal is sufficiently flexible and indeterminate in terms of how the $7,000 second mortgage reduction will be structured. Both parties, therefore, can modify the proposal and contribute to the final solution without having to accept or reject the general principle of the solution.

Thus, although the relationship of the legal merits to the parties' underlying needs may be more problematic and complex than a simpler justification on the basis of the parties' underlying interests, these articulated rationales for negotiation proposals may be more likely to produce acceptable solutions.

Finally, a word should be said about the process of problem-solving negotiation from the perspective of the behavior of the parties. Problem-solving conceptions of negotiation do not necessarily result in weak or conciliatory strategies or tactics. As Fisher & Ury have stated, "being 'nice'" is not the answer to unproductive adversarial negotiations. Negotiating styles and behaviors are the means or procedures by which negotiation results and solutions are achieved, but they are not synonymous concepts. An overly cooperative negotiator may be just as likely to produce an ineffective compromise by giving in without basis as would a competitive negotiator who stubbornly holds to an unreasonable position. Some game theory suggests that cooperative strategies positively affect joint outcomes. Empirical studies of the effectiveness of cooperative versus competitive behaviors, however, are more complex and as yet inconclusive, both in legal negotiation and in more general negotiations studied by social psychologists. It is beyond the scope of this Article to discuss particular behaviors, other than in the context of negotiation structure. Furthermore, the state of negotiation art and science is not sufficiently advanced to permit accurate generalizations about specific behavioral choices.

Because problem-solving negotiations are likely to result in a greater number of potential solutions not contemplated in advance, the client in such negotiations is more likely to become involved in evaluating proposals. This will be particularly true where a client's objectives or needs may change over time, or need to be reevaluated as new proposals are forthcoming. Thus, the increased fluidity and emphasis on the parties' underlying interests may result in greater client involvement in the legal negotiation process. One of the key differences between the conventional adversarial model and the problem-solving model is the extent to which the parties and their lawyers engage in a continually interactive negotiation process, using the opportunity to seek new solutions rather than simply moving along a predetermined linear scale of compromise.

Notes and Questions

(1) Professor Menkel-Meadow states that the planning stage of problem-solving negotiation resembles a "fluid brainstorming session" and that, in the execution stage, the problem-solving negotiator should offer reasons why a solution may be acceptable or unacceptable. How are these aspects of the two stages related?

(2) May a problem-solving approach be used in connection with both integrative and distributive bargaining? By both cooperative and competitive negotiators?

C. Psychological & Technological Considerations

The materials below introduce key psychological and technological considerations for negotiators. First, Laura Frase identifies more than a dozen cognitive biases and discusses how they emerge in negotiation. Then, Noam Ebner identifies challenges that emerge when negotiation takes place via online dispute resolution (ODR) including via phone, video platform, or an asynchronous platform and suggests strategies for overcoming them. Ebner focuses on building trust: a fundamental tenet of integrative, principled, and interest-based bargaining, and (as Goodpaster notes), when absent, a key reason why negotiators engage in competitive bargaining. Finally, Jean Sternlight and Jennifer Robbennolt suggest considerations for engaging in in-person or technology-assisted dispute resolution processes. While they focus on dispute resolution processes broadly, their advice is applicable to the negotiator, mediator, and attorney alike. As you review these excerpts, consider how these concepts are applied in negotiation *and* how they might be valuable tools for a mediator.

Refining Our Thinking About Thinking: Battling the Sway of Cognitive Biases in Negotiation

51 Cumb. L. Rev. 347, 351, 353–64, 367–74 (2020-21)*
By Laura A. Frase

A. What is Important to Me Must Be Important to You: Egocentric Bias

Many of life's most important decisions start with self. We have "considerable difficulty casting aside [our] own unique perspective when attempting to take the perspective of another."[16] The "egocentric bias" means we assume that what is important to us or to our clients logically must be important to the other side; equally, what we consider unimportant is also unimportant to our opponent."[17] Because we believe we are rational in our perceptions, our priorities are thus also rational and logical (as are all things we conceive), and other rational perceivers, sensibly, will share our vision and goals. Assuming our negotiation goals are the same as another's is a ripe opportunity for significant miscalculation.

. . .

B. I Am Always Right: Overconfidence Bias

. . .

The overconfidence bias has a peculiar twist. Studies show that people are the most confident about circumstances in which they possess the least amount of information. One commentator suggests that for lawyers in particular, when a case is "unusual or outside the lawyer's experience, her overconfidence actually increases."[30] Clients believe we know the law, and know all of it, and it is sometimes hard to admit that our knowledge may be limited or out of date. Overconfidence supplants those gaps in our knowledge.

. . .

---

16. *Id.* [John R Chambers & Carsten K.W. De Dreu, *Egocentrism Drives Misunderstanding in Conflict and Negotiation*, 51 J. Experimental Soc. Psych. 15, 23 (2014).]

17. *Id.* at 16.

30. Michael Palmer, *Which Is Better? The Deal or the Ordeal? An Examination of Some Challenges of Case Valuation*, 36-Fall Vt. B.J. 34, 35-36 (2010) . . . .

C. Grander than All Others: Above-Average Effect

Sometimes referred to as the "illusionary superiority bias" or the "Lake Wobegon effect," the "above-average effect" means we believe that our abilities and capacities are superior to those of others.[37] It is not just about confidence (or overconfidence, for that matter). This effect means that when we compare ourselves to others, we believe we are above average in talent, tasks, and thinking.

. . .

Our practices are replete with examples of this effect. Our clients may think that their case is superior to similar cases and thus demand greater recompense. We may formulate negotiation plans that are unrealistic based solely on our perceived extraordinary capabilities. We may hold out for a better offer because we think we are more talented, which may create the setting for negotiation impasse. We may erroneously believe that we are more flexible, fair, competent, honest, or cooperative and thus ignore the demonstrated skillfulness of our counterparts. Assuming we are always above average impacts objectivity and risks underestimating our opponent. In pride and unearned arrogance, we may miss opportunities for our clients to get the resolution they desire.

D. Bad Behavior Speaks Volumes: Fundamental Attribution Error

Our motivational belief in our superiority is not limited to our own proficiencies or confidence. We may also believe we are superior at judging the foundation of another's personality and character. In "fundamental attribution error" ("FAE"), when confronted with another's perceived undesirable behavior, we may immediately assume that character flaws motivate that behavior.[48] Contrarily, we underestimate how outside or situational factors explain that same negative behavior. For example, if a person does not complete a task, we may say the person is lazy or unmotivated. We may not consider that perhaps the other person was given incomplete instructions or had an intervening family crisis. If someone completes a task ahead of a deadline, we may assume that the person had help or the assignment was too easy. In FAE, we evaluate behavior using assumptions and incomplete information, often about individuals we do not even know. "[P]eople are willing to make quick and confident judgements of a subject's personality trait based on a very limited data sample."[50]

. . .

---

37. Stoyan V. Sgourev, *Lake Wobegon Upside Down: The Paradox of Status-Devaluation*, 84 Soc. Forces 1497 . . . .

48. Lee Ross, *The Intuitive Psychologist and His Shortcomings: Distortions in the Attribution Process*, in 10 Advances in Experimental Social Psychology 173, 184 (Leonard Berkowitz ed., 1977). . . .

50. Andrew E. Taslitz, *Police are People Too: Cognitive Obstacles to, and Opportunities for, Police Getting the Individualized Suspicion Judgment Right*, 8 Ohio St. J. Crim. L. 7, 17 (2010).

FAE can play a confounding role in negotiations. For example, if the opponent does not respond to our offer right away, we may believe she is playing games or trying to gain strategic advantage. Instead, she may simply be delayed in discussing the offer with her client. Similarly, we may "attribute the negative aspects of the conflict to the dispositions and evil motives of the other party" while minimizing our own role in the dispute.[58] Now the parties are not arguing about the terms of a potential contract but rather about their own superb character while in combat with the opposing "reprobate." Such assumptions can change the entire tenor of the negotiation.

. . .

E. The Messenger Matters: Reactive Devaluation

As Groucho Max once crooned, "Your proposition may be good but let's have one thing understood. Whatever it is, I'm against it!" In "reactive devaluation," we judge the value of a message or offer based on our perceptions, typically negative, of the conveyor of the message or offer. The more we dislike our opponent, the stronger the reaction. Our unfavorable opinion of the messenger becomes inextricably intertwined with the import of the message.

Social scientists suggest different stimuli cause reactive devaluation. The bias may be triggered by fear that the opponent has access to undisclosed information. We may devalue an offer because we believe it is a signal that additional concessions may be forthcoming. Some suggest the bias is caused by cynicism. Spite may also explain the reaction; we reject a proposal because we view the opponent with such loathing that declining even the most beneficial terms keeps our opponent from obtaining what she wants. Whatever the cause, we react because the person making the offer or conveying the information is so distrusted that the value of the message is lost.

In negotiations, if an offer comes from an unrespected adversary, that offer may be undervalued. We may "see enemies where none exist." Conversely, if the exact same proposal is offered by a neutral party or a friend, that proposal may be treated with more deference. And if the offer or information comes from someone we highly regard, we may overvalue the benefits of the offer or information, thus failing to weigh its credibility and adjust our counteroffer.

Reactive devaluation is amplified further when we believe an offer is against the best interests of our counterpart; what is good for our counterpart must be automatically bad for us. We fail to understand that our counterpart may value terms of a potential agreement differently than we do, in part because we are mired in our own egocentric bias. The "possibilities for trades that benefit both sides would simply not be recognized."[67]

. . .

---

58. Adler, *supra* note 8, and 723 [Robert Adler, *Flawed Thinking: Addressing Decision Biases in Negotiation*, 20 Ohio St. J. on Disp. Resol. 683 (2005)].

67. Baron, *supra* note 65, at 439 [Jonathan Baron, Thinking and Deciding 438 (4th ed. 2008)].

F. "Draggin' the Line ": Anchoring Effect

One of the most well researched cognitive biases is the "anchoring effect," or "the human tendency to adjust judgments or assessments higher or lower based on previously disclosed external information-the 'anchor.'"[69] In attempting to make a decision, this mental shortcut starts with our selecting an initial known number or information and adjusting from that initial point until we reach the realm of what we think is a plausible answer. For example, we want to purchase a quart of cream but do not know the price. We know the price of a quart of milk, so we adjust from that number to estimate the cost of cream. If we want to buy a particular car, we may recall prices for similar models and use those numbers to estimate the cost of the car we want to purchase. The numbers or information we start with and use as comparisons are anchors.

. . .

. . . Sentencing guidelines, policy limits, jurisdictional limits, and damage may all serve as anchors. This effect is so powerful (and insidious) that the anchor need not be logically connected to what we are trying to determine. Studies show that an anchor sways judgments and influences our final estimation even though it is arbitrary, outrageous, or "incomplete, inaccurate, irrelevant, implausible or random."[82]

The anchoring effect also impacts how we assess information. The first information collected is often afforded greater importance, merely because it is the first piece of data received. In any subsequent analysis, we continually harken back to the first information, comparing it to the new information and testing the latter's credibility when weighed against the anchor.

. . .

Anchoring is particularly prevalent during negotiations. The party that goes first has more impact and control over the final agreed upon number, because the anchor characterizes the conversation and defines the bargaining zone. The more precise the number (*e.g.*, $19.99 versus $20.00), the stronger the anchor's influence, as the number implies credibility. The effect also sways evaluations as we prepare our negotiation plans. Information received at the beginning of the transaction or dispute process may carry greater weight or importance merely because it was first. The anchor weighs down negotiations.

. . .

G. Words Matter: Loss Aversion and Framing Effect

Losing is one of the more distasteful consequences of participating in life, society, and the economy. Losing can challenge our feelings of power, self-worth, and

---

69. Mark W. Bennett, *Confronting Cognitive "Anchoring Effect" and "Blind Spot" Biases in Federal Sentencing: A Modest Solution for Reforming a Fundamental Flaw*, 104 J. Crim. Law & Criminology 489, 495 (2014).

82. Bennett, supra note 69, at 495. . . .

self-preservation. Losing can also be motivational. Yet, ingrained within our psyche is this automatic repugnance to losing. We are thus laser-focused on averting and avoiding the potential of suffering losses.

Known as "loss aversion," multiple psychological studies prove that when deciding a course of action, we make different decisions when faced with a chance we will achieve a gain or sustain a loss.[100] And most illogically, we will take more risks to avoid losses than we will to attain gains.

. . .

H. Looking Through Rose-Colored Glasses: Confirmation Bias

One of the most common illusions that lawyers face in the cognitive bias catalogue is "confirmation bias"—the "tendency of people to search for and believe facts that support their opinions and ignore facts that contradict their beliefs."[120] In confirmation bias, rather than test our theories or assumptions critically, we seek, subconsciously, to prove them. Beliefs are "transmute[d] into evidence."[121] Thus, in confirmation bias, we are less concerned with "finding the truth as much as [we] are hell bent upon justifying [our] own views and thoughts."[122]

This breakdown affects us in two ways: the manner in which we search for information, and the degree to which we rely on corroborating-only data. When researching any new theory, the volume of information can overwhelm. "A systematic search through the 'whole universe' for [data] that could falsify the hypothesis can, from a pragmatic point of view, scarcely be accomplished."[123] So, in the name of efficiency, we subconsciously gravitate toward confirming information that supports our preconceived beliefs. This short-circuiting approach hinders critical evaluation of facts and case value. . . .

Even if we succeed in gathering balanced information, confirmation bias may still trip us up when we afford greater weight and credibility to the confirming information gathered. Additionally, we may challenge the research results differently; confirmatory evidence is more often "taken at face value while potentially disconfirmatory evidence is subjected to highly critical and skeptical scrutiny."[126] This

---

100. Robert A. Prentice, *Behavioral Ethics: Can it Help Lawyers (and Others) Be Their Best Selves?*, 29 Notre Dame J. L., Ethics & Pub. Pol'y 35, 49 (2015).

120. Margit E. Oswald & Stefan Grosjean, *Confirmation Bias*, *in* [Cognitive Illusions: A Handbook on Fallacies and Biases in Thinking, Judgment and Memory 79, 93 (Rüdiger F. Pohl, ed. 2nd ed. 2012)], *supra* note 73, at 79, 93.

121. Daryl Lim, *Predictive Analytics*, 51 Loy. U. Chi. L.J. 161, 216 (2019).

122. Cory S. Clements, *Perception and Persuasion in Legal Argumentation: Using Informal Fallacies and Cognitive Biases to Win the War of Words*, 2013 B.Y.U. L. Rev. 319, 353 (2003) . . . .

123. Oswald & Grosjean, *supra* note 120, at 81.

126. Lee Ross & Craig A. Anderson, *Shortcomings in the Attribution Process: On the Origins and Maintenance of Erroneous Social Assessments*, *in* [Judgement Under Uncertainty: Heuristics and Biases (Daniel Kahneman, Paul Slovic & Amos Tversky, eds. 1982)], *supra* note 107, at 129, 149. *See also* Charles G. Lord et al., *Biased Assimilation and Attitude Polarization: The Effects of Prior Theories on Subsequently Considered Evidence*, 37 J. Personality & Soc. Psych. 2098, 2099 (1979).

skewed perspective may cause us or our client to dismiss a good proposal because we think our facts are stronger than others view them. . . .

. . .

I. Like Where I Am: Status Quo Bias

. . .

The bias regularly plays out in negotiations, particularly if the debate surrounds changing relationships or statuses of the parties, such as with labor union contracts, divorces, and global trade deals. For instance, in settlement discussions, "[t]he typical person losing from his pocket a thousand dollars of past earnings feels more aggrieved than a person losing . . . a thousand dollars meant to compensate lost future earnings. A person palpably possesses the former and palpably feels the loss."[143] Because concessions may be viewed as losses (and thus trigger loss aversion), unaware clients may express preferences for leaving things as they are to their detriment.

. . .

J. Mine is Worth More Because It's Mine: Endowment Effect

Rationally, the value of an item should not change whether we own it. But because of our unwillingness to sustain losses (and our love of inertia), our subconscious reactions suggest otherwise. As a consequence of loss aversion and the status quo bias, under the "endowment effect" we believe that property we own is more valuable than others do. We may also demand more to sell something we own than we would pay to buy that same item from others. Our emotional attachment artificially increases our opinion of the value of our property. Further, if the property is acquired because of the demonstration of a skill or talent (*e.g.*, awarded versus received by chance), the effect becomes even stronger. If the item at issue is rare or scarce on the market, the effect intensifies. This effect impacts decision-making even if the ownership of the item is hypothetical. Simply, owning stuff is less risky than giving up stuff.

. . .

K. Losing More to Recuperate Losses: Sunk-Cost Fallacy

Most understand that future investments must be justified by the probability of future returns and not as a means of recuperating past expenditures. The "sunk-cost fallacy" may cloud that logic. This fallacy causes us to incorporate a project's spent resources into future goals of recovery. The United States' continued involvement in the Vietnam and Afghanistan wars are classic examples of the sunk-cost fallacy.

---

143. Schwade v. Total Plastics, Inc., 837 F. Supp. 2d. 1255, 1279 (M.D. Fla. 2011); see also Korobkin & Ulen, [*Law and Behavioral Science: Removing the Rationality Assumption from Law and Economics*, 88 Cal. L. Rev. 1051 (July 2000),] *supra* note 101, at 1107-13.

We continue to invest in losing propositions for a variety of reasons. Maybe we are trying to delay cognitive realization of the loss. Perhaps we want to prove that our original plan was appropriate. Or we want to avoid appearing stupid or foolish or wasting resources. Alternatively, we may be willing to pay more for vindication rather than compromise. Economically, none of these reasons justify throwing good money after bad or doubling down on commitment to an inferior plan.

. . .

The Human Touch in ODR: Trust, Empathy, and Social Intuition in Online Negotiation and Mediation
in Online Dispute Resolution: Theory and Practice, 80, 101-119
(Rainey et al., eds, 2d edition 2021)*
By Noam Ebner

Trust plays a key role in promoting cooperation, problem solving, information exchange, negotiator effectiveness, and achieving integrative solutions. Trust is a vital precondition for information sharing, which arouses generosity and empathy and reciprocation. . . .

. . .

3.6 Eight Challenges to Trust in Online Mediation and Negotiation

. . .

3.6.1 *Low Expectations of Trust*

Communicating via e-mail, negotiators experience lower levels of trust in their opposites than those experienced by negotiators in similar face-to-face interactions—at all stages of the process. Before the process' inception, parties negotiating via email report lower levels of trust in their opposite than do participants in face-to-face negotiations. This prophesy self-fulfills: low trust-levels persists throughout the course of the negotiation, resulting in diminished process cooperation and information sharing, and heightened suspicion: email are more likely to suspect their opposite of lying, even when no actual deception has taken place. The cycle culminates in email negotiators showing lower post-negotiation trust levels and less desire to engage with their counterparts in future interactions with them than do face-to-face dyads—even when there is no objective difference in the negotiation outcome.

One recent experiment has indicated that these findings regarding trust expectations may not apply in negotiation via videoconferencing.

3.6.1.1 *Implications for Negotiators*

Begin early: Trustbuilding attempts need to begin before your opposite's initial expectations turn into a self-fulfilling prophesy through attribution. Begin these

---

efforts right at the negotiation's launch, and even before the 'official' kick-off by means of informal, off-task communication.

Be prepared for rejection: Your opposite may expect you to be untrustworthy. Do not be surprised, or discouraged, if your early trustbuilding moves are rejected, misconstrued, unnoticed or ignored. Keep trying.

Do not stop at success: Initial trust needs building, but that is not enough. Trust must then be maintained in order to see the process through to its conclusion, and in a manner that naturally extends beyond the negotiation to support you in a future interaction with the same counterparty.

. . .

3.6.2 Lack of Contextual Cues

Perhaps underlying our low trust expectations is our intuitive sense that, negotiating online, our trust sensors are operating in the dark. Communicating with one another, people rely on contextual cues to interpret others' messages: their facial expressions, body language, tone of voice and other non-verbal hints. . . . We infer most of a message's meaning through these cues, in fact, rather than its words. In the rich medium of face-to-face communication we are so overcome with cues that we allow ourselves to ignore some of them (such as by looking away from our counterpart).

Communicating through leaner media, however, we seek out such cues more actively. Unable to see our interlocutor's face over the phone, we strain to infer meaning from their tone of voice. Text-based online communication, including e-mail and other communication systems common to ODR providers, is a very lean media for conveying contextual cues. . . . Indeed, in experiments comparing interactions through face-to-face, audio, video and text-based communication, found the last to be the least supportive of trust-building. Videoconferencing provides participants with more contextual cues in audio and visual form, and is therefore more supportive of trust building. Still, given the limitations of the video box and other constraints, these are still not the full array of cues provided in face-to-face communication. . . .

3.6.2.1 Implications for Negotiators

Learn to read: Text communication is full of cues — just not those we are used to. Never skim through a message, assuming you will get the gist of it. You will get the wrong gist. Read messages carefully, paying attention to details such as specific wording and phraseology.

Use what you've got: You can enhance your communication by utilizing every option your medium offers. In email, consider writing a new subject line each time instead of leaving the initial subject written three exchanges ago. In video communication, if you tend to communicate with your hands, make sure they are visible in the video box for your counterpart to see.

. . .

3.6.3 Increased Attribution, Increased Misunderstanding

Any medium diminishing in contextual cues causes parties to focus on the actual content of their counterpart's messages. At the same time, it denies them the means to interpret them accurately. Meaning ambiguity increases the tendency toward the fundamental attribution error: parties perceive negative actions or statements of their counterpart, and attribute these to the other's negative intentions and character rather than to any unmalicious circumstance. . . . Email negotiators ask fewer clarifying questions than face-to-face negotiators, leaving more room for parties to make and reinforce assumptions. Attribution dynamics nudge assumptions toward negativity and distrust. . . .

3.6.3.1 Implications for Negotiators

Slow down: Asynchronous text communication enables negotiators to slow down the pace of message crafting and improve their quality, preempting lack of clarity and misunderstandings.

Increase your social presence: Remind the other, repeatedly, that there is a real person opposite them. . . .

Communicate clearly: Preempt negative interpretations by enhancing clarity. In emails, clarify much more than you would face-to-face. In video interactions, be on the lookout for opportunities to verify your understanding or the others, even when you would not do so in an in-person encounter. . . .

Don't read too much intent into their style: Even as you mind your own writing style and framing, try not to read too much into stylistic issues in your counterpart's email. They may not be mindful, or skilled with the medium. . . .

Avoid delays, but do not sweat them: Waiting and perceived delay cause anxiety, which is, in turn, conducive to formation of negative attribution. Manage both sides of this cycle. . . .

Clear bottom line: More so than anything else, your basic message, offer, or statement must be kept clear. End every email message with a very clear 'to summarize' paragraph.

Save by the Bell: Concerned that all the intentionality and caution in the world might not suffice? Do not entrust the situation to text communication, if this is possible. If misconstrued messages threaten to derail the process, simply pick up the phone, or arrange a videoconference or an in-person meeting with your counterpart.

. . .

3.6.4 I Am Anonymous, the Other Is Faceless

A major challenge to one party's desire . . . to generate trust in their opposite arises from the setting of the encounter itself. Parties sit behind their computers, far away from their counterparts. In email negotiation, remoteness and intervening technology is augmented by facelessness, which only heightens the sense of anonymity, distance, and remote detachment. This engenders assumptions that one can get away with trust-breaking behavior at the same time as it lowers moral inhibitions against doing so. This, even when the process takes place between identifiable and accountable parties! The degree of effect this has on negotiation depends on how much effort parties put into 'unmasking' each other — or, more pro-actively, unmasking themselves toward the other. . . .

3.6.4.1 Implications for Negotiators

Meet if you can: The challenge of online bonding has led to recommendations that you would do well to hold a preliminary face-to-face meeting with your opposite before beginning an online process, given the potential for trust formed in one venue to spill over into the other.

Schmooze, and schmooze ahead: If a face-to-face meeting is impossible or impractical, as will often be the case in online processes, try to reach out, before initiating a negotiation process, in a short e-mail or phone call, to introduce yourself and to conduct some very basic 'schmoozing'. . . .

Work at rapport (rapport before work): In-person negotiators have always been advised to pre-personalize processes, using pre-negotiation interaction for 'bonding' and 'building rapport'. Such light social interactions do not manifest as intuitively or play out as smoothly in online conversations. In both emails and in videoconferencing, people tend to jump straight to the point. Sans rituals of handshakes and small talk, even introductions are more utilitarian than relationship building. Remember that even one lighter, bond-oriented sentence embedded in a businesslike e-mail can have great effect. Similarly, including a bit of personal information or commenting on your surroundings as you introduce yourself by video might elicit reciprocation.

Unmask yourself: As counterparts perceived as distant and faceless are less trusted, act intentionally to make yourself appear human, present, and real to the other. In email negotiation, self-unmasking might involve sharing personal information, or reducing perceived distance through shared language, or shared geographical or cultural references. In videoconferencing, attention to camera quality, angle, and background can further assist you to in providing your counterpart a humanized and engaging perspective of you and your surroundings. Express interest about an item in your counterpart's environment, and arrange your own background to provide fodder for such conversations.

Unmask the other: Remember, there is a person behind the other screen, whether they have had the foresight [to] unmask themselves or not. They are not computers or inboxes; they will respond to your messages on emotional, cognitive, and behavioral levels which you will then have to deal with. Encourage them to engage in unmasking by normalizing such behavior, by asking questions, and by providing references or cues for them to latch on to.

. . .

3.6.5 Physical Distance and Interpersonal 'Otherness'

In the previous section we explained how online communication transforms online parties' distance into a sense of being faceless (via email) or fuzzy and disembodied (via video) with a dash of (oft-unsubstantiated) sense of anonymity. We now add to this a related yet distinct challenge: Distance, facelessness and anonymity causes a perception of difference, of 'otherness' between the two parties, exacerbating the regular potential for 'otherness' effects to confound negotiation and conflict resolution. The structure of negotiation typically casts our counterpart in the role of the 'other' or 'opponent' — different from us and at odds with us. This poses significant challenges to identity-based trust, which relies on perceived similarities. Given our unfamiliarity with many of our online counterparts, this deficit in identification-based trust cannot be counterbalanced by knowledge-based trust. Indeed, the only thing we may know about them is that we need something from them, and/or that they need something from us. This can spiral parties into identification-based distrust, as we subconsciously assume that our mutual demands are manifestations of more fundamental dissimilarities; our opposites are nothing like us, and their attitudes, personality, and interests conflict with ours.

3.6.5.1 Implications for Negotiators

Do not just unmask, team up! Through initiating an unmasking process, you can potentially begin to dispel the 'otherness' obstacle and close distances perceived between you and your counterpart by tapping a particularly powerful source of identification-based trust: shared group membership. When we perceive ourselves as belonging to the same group as another, our perceptions of the other become more positive and our level of trust in them increases. This counteracts the 'otherness' obstacle, which essentially boils down to you and your counterpart perceiving yourselves as belonging to different 'out-groups', whose members are prone to mutual distrust. Development of positive attitudes and identification-based trust toward ingroup members plays out online much as it does offline, resulting in a greater likelihood of agreement between in-group members.

A new way of reading: Tune in closely to the other's messages, in order to discover things to connect to as members of a joint in-group. This involves a different type of message reading beyond the usual content-assimilation process. Glean any information you can from your counterpart's introduction and note personal information conveyed in later messages.

Link yourselves together: Use verbal mimicry of your counterpart's words to connect between you, particularly in the early stages of a negotiation.

3.6.6 Increased Contentiousness: A Vicious Cycle

As media richness is diminished, social presence is reduced and perceived social distance between parties increases. Negotiators feel disinhibited, less bound by normatively appropriate behavior than face-to-face negotiators. . . .

In email negotiation, the path to contentiousness is further smoothed by the medium's low synchronicity, which encourages what Anne Marie Bülow has dubbed a 'double monologue' style of interaction: Cherry-picking elements of a message to respond to while ignoring others, and relating to them in long, argumentative statements. Parties work simultaneously to persuade each other that they are right, rather than jointly exploring ways to work together. . . .

In this state of affairs, parties have little incentive to work at trust building. Au contraire, they are led down a path of competition if not downright aggression. Not only do parties to lean-media negotiation behave more competitively, they feel justified for choosing this behavior. Iterated rounds of contentious moves are likely to be mirrored in a cycle of trust-diminishment, and repeatedly justified by 'Well, they started it! I knew they couldn't be trusted.'

3.6.6.1 Implications for Negotiators

Use cooperative language intentionally: In both video and email, an intentional shift from contentious to cooperative language, such as by using the terms 'cooperation', 'agreement', or 'relationship' might ward off escalation. They remind parties (yourself included) what they are here to do, and steer them back toward trust-building, rather than trust-breaking, dynamics.

Step out, step in: Use your distance from the other to take time to 'step out' of the discussion in order to respond thoughtfully, rather than instantly reacting to the other party's moves. Encourage your counterpart to do the same (*e.g.*, 'I realize my "No" wasn't what you had hoped for; why not take some time to think it over, and get back to me tomorrow?'). Email's asynchronicity accommodates this quite naturally. Video negotiations are more easily broken down into several sessions than co-located negotiations; there are no travel costs and scheduling is simpler. Consider asking to take a break and reconvene at your counterpart's convenience, if things seem to be spiraling in a negative direction.

. . .

3.6.7 Privacy

Maintaining a negotiation process' privacy is never an easy task. In face-to-face negotiation, absent a confidentiality agreement (and too often, in practice, even when one exists!) parties can and do share information about the negotiation with anyone they like. However, meetings can at least be held behind closed doors, and sensitive information can be related in a lowered voice. Anything shared with external parties will always be subjective, after-the-fact, secondhand (and in legal terms, hearsay). . . . This balance between in-the-room privacy, and out-of-the-room sharing, is a familiar structural aspect of these processes.

In online processes, however, parties never know who is 'in the room' with them. Will my counterpart forward my message to their boss or colleagues? It my counterpart alone in the room, or is someone listening in, off-camera? Beyond immediate privacy issues is that of privacy over time. Messages transmitted via email are recorded, forever archived on your counterpart's computer, beyond your control.

Similarly, there is no way for one party to prevent another from recording a video-conference session without their knowledge or consent. . . .

. . .

3.6.7.1 *Implications for Negotiators*

Before sending emails: Consider each address field carefully. To whom should a message be sent? Should anyone appear in the 'cc' field? Do you want anyone invisibly lurking on the conversation, from the 'bcc' field?

When receiving mails: Use these information fields in reverse, alert for breaches of privacy. Review the address fields and tracking information visible in messages you receive, and read through previous messages recorded in the e-mail. Has your opposite included any internal correspondence you might want to see? CC'd someone on this latest message to you?

Consult: Unless you have agreed not to, share messages with anybody you feel can help you strategize and plan your responses.

Watch it: Increasingly, individuals' online activities are becoming public, widespread, sought out by future opponents and admissible in court. Be cautious of what you write in an e-mail, particularly before trust is established. A good rule of thumb might be: Do not write anything in an e-mail that you would not want shown on the news.

3.6.8 *Diminished Party Commitment, Investment, and Focus*

Parties to online processes might be somewhat less motivated than those participating in face-to-face processes, given investment's role in human motivation. In-person meetings involve preliminary coordination, dressing, and travel time, cost, and effort. Videoconferencing requires only coordination and dressing (and reduces investment in these areas as well); email eliminates all these completely. With no sunk costs in the process, online communication provides an easy option for 'shot in the dark' approaches with little follow-through. This might provide partial explanation for reports of higher rates of impasse in e-mail negotiation and for the phenomena of parties to text-based and email mediation and negotiation processes simply disappearing. From a trust perspective, one party's agreeing to participate may not induce a trust effect in the other, and a lack of constant, active participation might easily be interpreted by a counterpart opposite as untrustworthiness.

. . .

In general, research suggests that in the digital age, human attention span is decreasing. Proud of our ability to multitask, we fail to realize that we are not as good at this as we like to think we are. Heavy multitaskers suffer a range of shortcomings as opposed to 'focusers', many of which are pertinent to negotiation and mediation. They tend not to filter out irrelevant information, and are easily distracted. They often have low detail-recall, and despite their ability to switch between tasks rapidly, their performance of each suffers as their brain is always somewhat focused on the task they are not doing. Multitasking negotiators or mediators, or those working in crowded places or noisy work environments, might be cognitively overwhelmed, confused, or unfocused, without being aware. So too, might be parties participating via smartphone in noisy or crowded environments, without considering the effects their surroundings may have on their capacity to focus. . . .

3.6.8.1 *Implications for Negotiators*

Stay on top of things: To keep your counterpart engaged, maintain regular email contact, without being too pushy. Offer breaks to replenish during videoconferencing, or ask for one yourself.

Bridge time gaps: In email communication, use literary style to create the sense of uninterrupted conversation. For example, write 'As I wrote you . . .', followed by a quote pasted from your previous email.

Stay focused: The greater the importance of the negotiation to you, the more it pays to concentrate on it. Read and write messages in an environment that allows you to concentrate. Close your browser, and leave other devices out of reach, while negotiating via videoconference.

In-Person or Via Technology?: Drawing on Psychology to Choose and Design Dispute Resolution Processes

71 DePaul L. Rev. 537, 542, 591-607 (2022)*
Jean R. Sternlight & Jennifer K. Robbennolt

Just as decisionmakers must choose which dispute resolution processes to use (*e.g.*, litigation, arbitration, mediation, negotiation), so must they choose communication modalities, such as whether to engage in any of these processes in person, in a videoconference, by telephone, through e-mail, by text messages, or using an ODR platform. Similarly, just as a given dispute can move between and among processes-such as when negotiations occur at various points in a litigation process, or a filed case is ordered to arbitration-it is also possible and indeed common for multiple modes of communication to be used within a given process . . . .

. . .

III. Drawing on Psychology to Select Among and Effectively Use Dispute Resolution Communications Processes

The psychology that relates to dispute resolution and technology is informative, nuanced, and sometimes counterintuitive. Because the interaction between technology and human beings is complex, there are no one-size-fits-all recommendations. As one mediator recognized: "For each negative difference there appears to be a positive one. . . . No positive body language is offset by no negative body language.

---

* Reprinted with permission, all rights reserved.

No immediacy is set off by time to think. No face-to-face impression is set off by no initial prejudices."[305] . . .

Practical wisdom calls for an assessment of the "proper aims of the activity," the ability to balance and contextualize conflicting aims, and the capacity to account for others' perspectives and emotions. We, therefore, offer a set of questions for decisionmakers to consider in deciding how best to approach their dispute resolution tasks. First, decisionmakers must identify their goals, as it is difficult to choose an appropriate path without having clear objectives in mind. Second, decisionmakers will want to consider the participants in the process — the characteristics of the disputants, neutrals, or attorneys. Third, decisionmakers will want to examine the differences among disputes and the array of tasks that must be accomplished within disputes. Finally, once a communication medium is chosen or imposed, an understanding of the relevant psychology can also help participants to use that medium most effectively. Throughout, it will be important for decisionmakers to consider that reactions to different forms of communication will change over time and may vary with how participants use technology in other aspects of their lives.

A. What Are the Goals for the Process?

Decisionmakers' varying goals have implications for both what communication medium should be selected and for how the process might best be conducted in a given medium. These goals will differ in part by role — courts, for example, may have different objectives than attorneys; attorneys and clients may have differing interests or priorities; and mediators may have different concerns than judges or attorneys. But even within roles, individual courts, neutrals, lawyers, or disputants will have diverse aims. Participants will frequently have multiple interrelated goals and goals may differ across contexts or cases and need to be balanced against one another.

One goal, for example, might be ensuring that participants have access to the system. . . . Technology-assisted communication can both increase access by bridging distances and limit access for those without the necessary technology or skills. Asynchronous technologies may enhance access by making it possible for disputants to participate in hearings, negotiate, or take part in mediation without taking time off from work. The extent to which technology enhances or limits access will also depend on how it is utilized. . . .

Another goal might be efficiency-minimizing the expenditure of time and money by disputants, lawyers, courts, or neutrals. . . . Remote processes do not require costly travel and may also save participants and attorneys from having to sit in court waiting for other matters to finish. Text-based communication systems may

---

305. Mediator quoted in Hammond, [*How Do You Write "Yes"?: A Study on the Effectiveness of Online Dispute Resolution*, 20 Conflict Resol. Q. 261, 268 (2003),] *supra* note 61, at 276. *See also* Miguel A. Dorado, *Computer-Mediated Negotiation of an Escalated Conflict*, 33 Small Group Res. 509, 510 (2002)

be somewhat costly to develop, but perhaps these costs are not as significant as some might fear.

. . .

Lawyers and disputants will often be focused on how to use dispute resolution processes to persuade others with goals centered on persuading an adjudicator to rule in their favor or a counterpart to agree to a satisfactory resolution. We have seen that persuasion can happen across modes of communication, but decisionmakers can think about the nature of the arguments that are available to them and their own persuasive skills and choose a communication medium that best suits them or perhaps disfavors an opponent. An advocate with high-quality substantive arguments might prefer a communication medium that focuses attention on those arguments. Intricate arguments may facilitate persuasion in a medium that allows more rapid back and forth. A person who knows that they are skilled at building rapport may prefer an in-person or at least a video-conference medium. By contrast, a particularly talented writer may prefer a text-based communication format. Participants who are worried about being too easily persuaded might opt for an asynchronous process to allow them to fully consider and respond to a counterpart's proposals. If one is worried about a counterpart's persuasiveness, it may also be wise to choose an environment where one can fully focus and not become unduly fatigued.

. . .

A related goal might be to elicit or disclose as much information as possible, as shared information can be important to either truth-seeking or creative negotiation. If the goal of generating disclosure is focal, decisionmakers might lean toward modes of communication that are perceived to be private and within which they are best able to build rapport. They might also prefer the quicker back-and-forth of a synchronous process. On the other hand, decisionmakers might sometimes strive to minimize disclosure, perhaps during a deposition or a distributive negotiation. Decisionmakers whose goal is to minimize disclosure might prefer a mode of communication that is more formal or an asynchronous medium that allows more opportunity to choose their words carefully.

. . .

B. Who Are the Participants?

It is also important to consider the characteristics of the prospective participants and their relationships with one another. Disputants, attorneys, mediators, judges, jurors, or arbitrators will all vary in ways that can inform the choice of communication medium.

Individual participants, for example, will face a range of access issues. Some people will find it difficult to attend in-person proceedings, whether due to geographic impediments, cost, or scheduling issues. Similarly, asynchronous communications can be useful for those with limited access to the internet and those who might have a hard time attending meetings or hearings during business hours.

On the other hand, some will lack access to a good internet signal or computer, in which case in-person meetings or telephonic communications might be more accessible. . . .

We have also seen that differences among participants will affect their comfort with particular communication media and that greater comfort allows participants to use these modalities in more advanced ways. Stereotypically, but often true, younger persons may feel more comfortable than older persons using more sophisticated technology such as videoconferencing or texting. Some people will feel more at ease in person or on the telephone, whereas others will prefer writing. Persons who hold a lower status in a particular context might be more comfortable participating via a medium with fewer social cues. This comfort and familiarity is significant because those who are more familiar with a modality may have less need for synchrony. By contrast, a lack of familiarity with a particular medium or discomfort with the level of formality posed may tax attention in ways that are counterproductive. Comfort with particular forms of technology may also change over time and vary depending on the content of the communication.

Other differences among participants may also push toward one modality or another. Some clients may feel more "heard" if they have the chance to speak to a judge, mediator, or opponent in person; others may feel more heard if they can express themselves clearly using well-designed text boxes. A lawyer who believes she can make a quick, good impression may prefer a synchronous process. Some disputants may want to settle and move on or have their dispute resolved as quickly or economically as possible, caring less about future relationships or addressing broader issues; others may want a process that is more facilitative or transformative or that provides more procedural justice.

The use of technology may also play out quite differently depending on the nature of the relationships among participants. Although, as we have seen, it can take more time and effort to build rapport when communication channels are limited, communicators who are familiar and comfortable with each other are better situated to overcome these limitations. Such participants may not need an in-person meeting or videoconference to feel the trust or rapport that might enhance a negotiation or mediation. Similarly, we have seen that participants who are inclined to approach their interaction cooperatively are well-situated to use a variety of communication media effectively. Hopes or expectations for a positive future relationship may also moderate the potential negatives of leaner forms of technology. Thus, parties with an established working relationship — such as two attorneys who have dealt with each other in the past — or a set of participants who are inclined to take a cooperative stance, might work better together over the phone or in a text-based modality than parties or attorneys who are relative strangers.

Parties with negative relationships or those who are predisposed to be uncooperative, on the other hand, might prefer or be better served by more distanced forms of communication. We have seen that more synchronous and multi-channel modes of communication can intensify conflict for those who take an uncooperative stance. Similarly, some mediators have suggested that using text-based or phone mediation can be preferable to in-person mediation when parties have an unequal power relationship or a history of domestic violence, not only to preserve physical safety, but also to ensure that a richer communication medium is not used to intimidate the weaker or more vulnerable party. Leaner or asynchronous forms of communication may also help to tamp down negative emotions. Indeed, parties with a prior negative relationship might be more willing to participate if they would not need to confront one another face-to-face. At the same time, to the extent that parties with a prior negative relationship are interested in working to improve or repair that relationship, incorporating some face-to-face discussion might be useful. As noted above, some mediators have found it harder to engage in more facilitative processes through written modes of communication.

C. What is the Dispute or Task?

Just as goals and participants differ, the underlying disputes or tasks also vary in ways that should impact decisionmakers' technological choices. Whether the underlying dispute resolution process is adjudicative or consensual, whether the case is civil or criminal, whether the relevant task is information exchange or brainstorming or reaching an agreement, whether any agreement needs to be fine-tuned or just broadly principled, or whether the dispute is a one-off or likely to recur, all have implications for the choice of communication modality. Thus, a decisionmaker might believe it desirable to hold a trial of a certain matter in person, should trial prove necessary, but first try to settle the matter through text-based negotiation. Or a court might decide that jury selection is best done with a mix of written questionnaires and online *voir dire* but ask the selected jurors to deliberate in person.

The complexity of the dispute is one factor for decisionmakers to consider. Complicated and detailed proposals, for example, might best be communicated asynchronously, in writing, so that specifics are clear and there is a record that can be revisited as necessary. And large disputes that involve many different stakeholders might fruitfully incorporate technology-mediated processes that will better enable many people to be at the table. At the other end of the spectrum, some courts are setting up processes to handle more straightforward cases with online text-based processes rather than with a more labor intensive in-person or video-conferencing process, reserving these more intensive processes for more complicated cases.

Decisionmakers will also want to consider whether the dispute stems from a lack of shared information, whether the disputants or their attorneys need an opportunity to better explain their perspective, or whether there is a need for legal argumentation. Some disputes primarily turn on the exchange and review of documents and other information and are settled or adjudicated easily once the parties have exchanged relevant information or once they have provided that information to the court. . . . For such disputes or tasks, technological media can allow disputants to exchange documents with one another or to provide them to a judge or arbitrator quickly and easily. Asynchronous processes can also be effective for conveying information because they can facilitate the efficient transfer of large amounts of information, give communicators more time to digest and analyze that information, and allow more time to generate meaning. Conducting these sorts of proceedings more efficiently can also free up time and attention for other cases or tasks.

By contrast, some disputes or tasks do not turn on a lack of shared information. They require, instead, that the parties reframe their perspectives, that participants develop a more nuanced understanding of each other, or that participants come to a meeting of the minds. . . . The need for at least some convergence in these kinds of disputes may mean that relying on written forms of communication alone may not allow sufficient opportunity for disputants or their attorneys to try to persuade one another or a neutral of the validity of their position, or for the participants to reach a mutual understanding. A videoconference or an in-person meeting may be more productive for tasks involving convergence, coordination, and generative interaction. Some tasks, like brainstorming, might ideally incorporate a mix of synchronous and asynchronous processes to foster broad generative thinking.

D. Effectively Using Communication Processes

Advocates, parties, or institutions who have decided (or had it decided for them) that they will use a particular dispute resolution communication process can also use psychological insights to tailor and participate in that medium in ways that will best serve their purposes. Low quality audio or video, spotty or absent internet access, or poorly designed text-based systems, for example, will make any technology-mediated communication less effective. Designers and participants will also need to consider the effects of asymmetries in how different participants participate in the process.

Beyond the basic technological requirements, participants should focus on (and practice) effectively using communication modes in ways that account for human psychology. If they are videoconferencing, for example, participants should adjust their cameras to eye level. Placing speaking notes near the camera can also help participants ensure that their eye gaze is directed toward others. Participants can also potentially increase empathy by setting camera angles to show participants' entire upper bodies, rather than merely their faces. Keeping in mind counterparts' limited views and being transparent when needing to look elsewhere or speak to someone who is off camera can minimize the risks that such behaviors will lead to distrust or damage rapport. Communicators who are not meeting in person can try to build rapport by engaging in preliminary small talk. It is possible to smile and nod to connect with another person on a video call. Participants in videoconferences and phone calls can make facilitative sounds ("umhum").

Communicators can use explicit statements of relation, affinity, or affection when communicating in media that lack more subtle means of communicating. Indeed, more relational work is done via written verbal cues in text-based forms of communication as compared to in-person communication where nonverbal signals are possible. While food cannot literally be shared when communicators are not meeting in person, it may be possible to create an atmosphere of rapport by eating or drinking together during a video call. This attention to relationship building can also help to discourage the negative behaviors that can result from feelings of anonymity and perceived distance between communicators.

To the extent that communication via text-based modalities or video is more prone to misunderstanding, participants can take care to minimize ambiguity, communicate emotion more explicitly, provide thorough explanations, use clear descriptions in subject lines, and remind counterparts of the content of a prior conversation. Participants should be alert for potential misunderstanding, reading messages carefully, using more frequent and direct questions to detect confusion or crossed signals, and correcting mistakes quickly. Participants should also plan for the potential downsides of asynchrony, establishing a practice of timely response (at least to let others know that their messages have been received and when to expect an answer) or setting expectations at the outset for the pace of exchanges.

. . .

When using any mode of technology-mediated communication, participants should take advantage of the helpful features provided by the tool. If transparency is important, participants should use the options provided by the medium to provide live access or to create a video, audio, or written record. Or, if privacy is important, parties should set ground rules such as requiring doors to be shut, requiring participants to use headphones, and prohibiting recording to minimize the risk that discussions will be overheard or recorded. Using the available formatting options, attachments, chat boxes to share links, or embedded whiteboards or screensharing can facilitate clear explanation, information exchange, or collaboration, support the use of other technological aids (*e.g.*, litigation analytics), or increase persuasive effect. Similarly, to provide privacy, mediators can use breakout rooms for caucusing, clients and their attorneys can use them for consultation, and judges could ask attorneys to go into a breakout room to attempt to settle a case. Backgrounds can be used thoughtfully to convey or obscure information, to make an impression, or to signal solemnity. When using asynchronous media, participants should use the opportunities inherent in that medium by taking time to reflect. Participants might also combine modes of communication to use the advantages of one to make up for the deficiencies of another. Research has found, for example, that it can be effective for negotiators using text-based systems to start with a brief phone call to schmooze and get to know each other in order to establish rapport more quickly.

Fatigue and distraction might be managed by scheduling shorter sessions and taking breaks. This can be helpful across modes of communication but might be particularly useful given the fatigue-inducing features of videoconferencing. Making deliberate choices about whether to view videoconferences in speaker view or gallery view, how large or small to set views of other participants, when to hide self-view, and when to use only audio can also reduce the demands on attention. Video-conference participants can decrease fatigue by using external cameras and keyboards to increase the distance between themselves and their screens. Given the risks of multitasking, lawyers or neutrals may want to insist that those viewing screens or on conference calls shut off potential distractions, leave their phones in another room, or even download software that will prevent them from multitasking.

Participants' effectiveness, their trust in the system and the neutrals, and their sense of procedural justice can also be enhanced by clear instructions. Making sure that all participants know how to use the relevant technology, that they understand what to expect from the process, and that they know what will be asked of them can improve their ability to express themselves and increase the likelihood that they will feel that they have been treated with dignity and respect. Participants can be instructed about how to set cameras, how to dress, and other best practices to enhance their persuasive capabilities. Conveners could start sessions by "orienting a remote participant to the courtroom space" or giving a "guided tour" of the platform. Procedures to usher participants into the dispute resolution setting may help focus attention and signal the appropriate level of solemnity. Text-based systems should similarly be equipped with clear and understandable instructions. Protocols should be established to help all participants understand each participant's role and to help them understand when proceedings have started or finished, how to handle documents, and when they can be seen on camera.

Process designers can also take other steps to help provide participants with procedural justice or to provide the community with a feeling that they have fully observed and participated in a dispute resolution process. Some important symbolic aspects of in-person proceedings might be replicated in video hearings, text-based platforms, or phone calls. . . .

Notes and Questions

(1) Some commentators have pointed to less tangible factors that may influence negotiation behavior but have not been considered by social science researchers. In *The Role of Hope in Negotiation*, 44 UCLA L. Rev. 1661, 1684–85 (1997),* Jennifer Gerarda Brown criticizes economic theories of negotiation for failing to recognize a role for hope:

> Hope is part emotion, part preference structure, part cognitive process. Hope affects people's behavior, as much in negotiation as in any other context. . . .
>
> Hope may not be easily subject to manipulation. Even if hope is not fixed, we may be unable to find and operate the mechanism that moves hope up or down. So if hope is not malleable — or if we are unable to change malleable

hopes — why focus on it? Why not just take hope as a psychological wild-card — like pride, anger, or love — that may affect the negotiation, but not in a manner that economists would study or care about?

Even if we cannot manipulate hope, we might want to include it in models of negotiation because more inclusive models will be better predictors of negotiation processes and outcomes. . . .

Similarly, hopeless models that fail to incorporate optimism will overestimate the probability of settlement, because they will wrongly assume that negotiators accurately calculate the probable distribution of the other side's reservation price. Realizing that an optimistic seller might inflate the range of the buyer's possible reservation prices will show that such parties are less likely to come to terms than we might at first predict.

Measuring hope — even if we cannot manipulate it — might also be useful. Negotiators should try to assess the other side's optimism or satiation point if these variables might affect behavior in negotiation. For example, if a buyer was able to discover that a seller might be sated easily, this could affect the buyer's first and subsequent offers. Or if the buyer knew that the seller had an unrealistically optimistic view of the buyer's reservation price, the buyer might plan to bring to the negotiation some "proof" that would educate the seller away from her optimism. In either case, measuring hope prior to a negotiation might help a negotiator prepare more thoroughly.

For interdisciplinary commentary on negotiation, see The Negotiator's Desk Reference (Andrea Schneider & Christopher Honeyman, eds., 2017); and *Rethinking Negotiation Teaching Series* published by DRI Press (2009–2012), at https://open.mitchellhamline.edu/dri_press/.

(2) A multidisciplinary team of scholars at Stanford created a body of research generally referred to as "barriers research" because it explores certain barriers to settlement. Professor Robert Mnookin discusses these barriers in his article *Why Negotiations Fail: An Exploration of Barriers to the Resolution of Conflict,* 8 Ohio St. J. on Disp. Resol. 235, 238–49 (1993). One such barrier is sometimes referred to as the "principal/agent" problem:

> The basic problem is that the incentives for an agent (whether it be a lawyer, employee, or officer) negotiating on behalf of a party to a dispute may induce behavior that fails to serve the interests of the principal itself. The relevant research suggests that it is no simple matter — whether by contract or custom — to align perfectly the incentives for an agent with the interests of the principal. This divergence may act as a barrier to efficient resolution of conflict.

One of the more common circumstances where a counsel's interests in settlement negotiations might diverge from those of their client is the case where the attorney is paid by the hour and thus has little or no incentive to work towards an early settlement. How might an attorney work to bring their interests in line with those of their client?

(3) Are lawyers held to a high standard of truthfulness in mediation? As indicated in the discussion of this topic in Chapter 10, the ABA Model Rules of Professional Conduct permit "puffery" in negotiations (and mediations). In her article, *Chipping Away at Lawyer Veracity: The ABA's Turn Toward Situation Ethics in Negotiations*, 1990 J. Disp. Resol. 103, Professor Ruth Fleet Thurman states: "If many lawyers shade the truth when they negotiate on behalf of clients, the practice will spread by imitation or retaliation and will spill over into more serious distortions. The ultimate outcome is loss of trust and goodwill toward lawyers and the law." In light of these concerns, should the ethics rules for lawyers be changed to require a higher standard of truthfulness for lawyers in negotiation and mediation settings?

Chapter 3

Mediation Process and Skills

A. Introduction

This chapter highlights the substantive skills and strategies which shape the distinctive role of the mediator. It identifies possible contributions and constraints of taking on the role of mediator, points out deliberate strategies which the mediator may adopt in attempting to build a settlement, and indicates the activities which the mediator must avoid. Beyond the skills required for effective mediation, additional characteristics are important, because mediation is mostly an art, not a science. While mediation, at its core, is based on a set of foundational values, each mediator has a distinctive mediation style that is shaped by one's individual personality traits.

As discussed in Chapter 4, *infra*, there are different orientations and styles to which mediators subscribe. The three most widely used approaches are facilitative, evaluative, and transformative. For purposes of understanding the skills of the mediator, this chapter focuses primarily on the facilitative style of mediation for several reasons. First, the facilitative style most underscores the differences between the mediator's role and that of an attorney or judge. While the facilitative style engages skills historically not taught in law school, there has been a noticeable shift towards teaching those skills as mediation courses and clinics have gained greater popularity in legal academia. Second, the facilitative style is the presumptive approach used by mediators in many settings; even some of the most evaluative mediators acknowledge that their first efforts in a mediation are usually facilitative and that they move into an "evaluative" framework only if the parties desire that type of intervention. Finally, the mediation process, from a foundational perspective, has been used across multiple disputing contexts, and the standard orientation in those settings is facilitative. The examples used in this chapter to illustrate the mediator's role and skills are drawn primarily from the general civil litigation context. Consider how executing the mediator's role would differ by adopting the evaluative, transformative, or other approaches to mediation when used in these cases as well as in other practice contexts discussed in Chapter 1.

In this chapter, for ease of identification, we have used the term "party" or "parties" when referring to the "principals" in a mediation. Other common ways to refer to such individuals are "participants" or "disputants." Consider how each of these terms convey different concepts of mediation.

B. The Mediator and Mediator Functions

The materials below target the functions that define the mediator's role and those personal qualities that contribute to one's effectively executing them. Though various mediation programs, statutes, and local practice define the mediator's role, their definitions differ. According to one state statute, "the role of the mediator includes, but is not limited to, assisting the parties in identifying issues, fostering joint problem solving, and exploring settlement alternatives." Section 44.1011(2), Florida Statutes. By contrast, the Uniform Mediation Act (Appendix D) defines a "mediator" as "an individual, of any profession or background, who conducts a mediation." Such definitions do not capture the wide range of dynamics, strategies, and techniques a mediator employs when attempting to assist parties in negotiating their dispute. In discussing the mediator's role below, the performance skills, abilities, and attributes required to execute it effectively are explored.

A mediator assumes such commonly listed roles as a: chairperson, facilitator of communication, educator, resource expander, inspirer of creativity, agent of reality, guardian of the process and of durable solutions. To perform these various roles, a mediator, at a minimum, should be a good listener, humble, flexible, creative, culturally competent, honoring of participant self-determination, and impartial. (Note that practitioners and academics have raised concerns about how impartiality could create conditions that overlook power dynamics and preserve the status quo, *See* Chapters 7 and 8 for further discussion.)

The mediator's tasks are very much tied to the goals and expectations of the parties, the particular mediation program, the substantive context in which the mediation takes place, and the mediator's style. To underscore this point, the 1995 Test Design Project Report, written by a diverse group of mediators working collaboratively for five years to provide mediation programs, courts, and other interested parties with improved tools for selecting, training, and evaluating mediators, stated in bold print "The resulting lists [of mediator tasks and KSAOs (knowledge, skills, attributes, and other attributes)] are not exhaustive, and they do not reflect reality for every program. They are intended merely as a starting point to encourage any given program to prepare a modified list that reflects its actual practices." The Report identified seven major tasks, which each involved several sub-tasks:

Gathering Background Information

Facilitating Communication

Communicating Information to Others

Analyzing Information

Facilitating Agreement

Managing Cases

Documenting Information

Notes and Questions

(1) What characteristics do you think would be important for a mediator to possess? Which are the most important to the mediation process? How do these correspond to the ethical duties of a mediator?

(2) Some claim that anyone can be a good mediator, if suitably trained. Do you agree?

(3) The Test Design's publication noted that the terms used "arise out of the predominant North American culture and may not apply to another society or even to indigenous or minority cultures within North America." What cultural assumptions are made in identifying a list of attributes and tasks? Are there other attributes which may be important in other cultural contexts?

C. The Mediation Process

It is easier to learn the skills of a mediator by considering the mediation process in a linear format, *i.e.*, the mediator begins the session, gathers information, develops a negotiating agenda, assists the parties in generating movement and, finally, the mediation reaches a conclusion. In actuality, these components are often cyclical, rather than linear. Each mediation may loop back and forth among these constructed stages. Further, some scholars, program administrators, and mediation trainers offer differing accounts concerning the number of steps within the mediation process, ranging from three, four or six stages to twelve or more; other scholars and practitioners, such as those subscribing to the transformative school of mediation, reject this "stage model" format. *See* Chapter 4.

1. Beginning the Mediation Process

The beginning stage of a mediation includes any review the mediator makes of preliminary information about the facts and circumstances of the mediation, planning for the location and set-up of the mediation, and the mediator's opening remarks. We begin with what happens prior to the convening stage.

a. Preliminaries: Prior to Convening

i. Locale and Physical Arrangement

There are no restrictions on where a mediation can be held. Mediation can take place in a conference room — either the mediator's or one of the attorney's or on Zoom or another electronic format. Mediation may take place in a courthouse or in a community dispute resolution center. As with traditional negotiation practices, a mediator must give thought to the location (neutrality of the setting, accessibility, comfort, etc.) and, if meeting in-person, the room set-up for the mediation. When conducting online mediation, mediators should be mindful of the digital tools embedded in and enabled by the underlying platform.

When mediating in-person, typically the mediator will identify for the parties and participants where they should sit (either verbally or by motioning to a particular grouping of chairs on one side of the table). The seating should reflect a structure conducive to the process of communication which the mediator is trying to create; if one party sits at the table but the other sits in the corner, the process is skewed. A mediator will often sit so that, from the parties' perspective, the mediator is "in the middle." Parties often bring other people with them to mediation, such as an attorney, their spouse or best friend. If other people are in the mediation room, they should sit with the persons whom they are accompanying. Here are some options:

Possible Seating Arrangements (mediator and two parties)

D = Disputant; **M** = Mediator

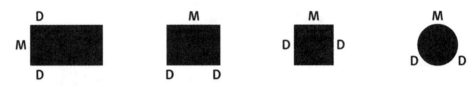

Possible Seating Arrangements (mediator, two parties and an attorney)

P = Parties; **M** = Mediator; **A** = Attorney

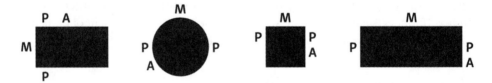

Note that there are many different possibilities; to some extent, the decision depends on the mediator's own personal style and preference as well as the shape of the available conference table or desk. Some mediators prefer not to use any table at all or to use only a low coffee table in a "living room" type setting; this practice is most common in divorce, family, and similar cases. When determining the seating arrangement, it is important to consider the following general principles:

- the mediator should be equidistant between the parties (and everyone should be seated on similar chairs);

- the parties should be able to look at each other and the mediator comfortably;

- the parties should be far enough apart that they are not bumping into each other, nor able to read each other's notes, but close enough that the mediator can see everyone, even while providing focused attention on one.

When mediating on-line, mediators do not have to concern themselves with how people are seated but will want to be sure that they use "gallery" mode rather than speaker mode so they can see everyone and not just the person speaking. Mediators should also set expectations about whether it is permissible for parties and attorneys to have their camera off or not, keeping in mind that some people may not be able to have their camera on due to bandwidth or hardware issues.

ii. Mediation Participants

How does a mediator decide whether someone should be in the mediation room or not? And, if the mediation is being conducted remotely, how does a mediator know who is "off-camera" in the mediation room?

Typically, the following persons are "entitled" to be in the room:

- the mediator;
- the people in dispute (if there is a court case, this will usually be defined as the "named parties");
- attorneys for the parties (if applicable) *Note*: in a state which has adopted the Uniform Mediation Act, this is expanded to include "an attorney or other individual designated by a party";
- a sign language interpreter or other representative necessitated under the Americans with Disabilities Act (if applicable);
- foreign language interpreter (if necessary).

Other individuals often "appear" at mediation; these include family members, bailiffs, members of the media, friends, moral supporters, observers, and witnesses. Whether these individuals are admitted into the mediation is usually dependent upon agreement of the parties. Since mediation is a voluntary process, any of the parties have a right to object to "others" participating in a mediation. The mediator may wish to discuss with the parties the ramifications of such a disagreement by noting that mediation requires active participation by the parties, that participation in mediation is voluntary, and that if one or more of the parties are unwilling to proceed because of someone's presence or absence, the mediation will not take place.

Whether to permit such persons into the mediation session is a decision for the parties to make. However, the extent of their participation, once admitted, is strongly influenced by the mediator's responsibility for conducting a constructive dialogue. How these decisions are made and by whom is dependent on the mediator's style and orientation. For example, mediators with more evaluative orientations would view these decisions as the sole responsibility of the mediator, while those who practice from a transformative perspective would view these decisions to be the sole responsibility of the parties. *See* Chapter 4, *infra*.

iii. Pre-Meeting Information Review

Determining whether to review pre-mediation session information by seeking summaries or memos from the attorneys or the case file is an individual mediator's decision and varies by context. In some instances, there will not be any pre-session information; in a court-ordered case, the mediator may not have the right to access the court file or there simply may not be any time to do so prior to beginning the mediation. In complex cases, mediators will often ask the attorneys to produce confidential pre-session statements which may include the theory of the case, negotiation efforts to date, and areas of concern for the attorneys and parties. If the mediation is conducted either "pre-suit" or under the auspices of a mediation program, an intake person or the mediator may have had some preliminary conversations with the parties, and their attorneys, if the parties are represented.

If pre-session information is available, it may be useful, in advance of the first meeting, for the mediator to review it in order to obtain an orientation to the context within which the contested issues might be discussed. For example, if mediating a divorce, the mediator might want to be aware, in advance, of the length of the marriage and the number and ages of any children. A mediator may also wish to conduct some pre-screening to ensure that mediation will be appropriate, for example, to determine if there is a history of domestic violence that could compromise the mediation process. If the mediator chooses to review pre-session information, the mediator must remember that the information provided only represents the issues from one party's perspective. Secondly, reliance on documents should not replace the opportunity for the parties to describe in their own words (or their attorney's) what has brought them to mediation.

Since the COVID-19 pandemic and the subsequent increase of mediations through video conferencing, there has also been an increased use of pre-mediation sessions. Practicing mediators have found that pre-mediation sessions increase trust and other important relationship building aspects.

In a study published by Roselle Wissler and Art Hinshaw in 2022, they found that 66% of the mediators surveyed in civil cases and 39% in family cases held pre-session discussions about non-administrative matters with the parties and/or their lawyers in their most recent cases. Some additional results of this study are included below.

What Happens Before the First Mediation Session? An Empirical Study of Pre-Session Communications

23 Cardozo J. Conflict Resol. 143, 144–46, 148, 169, 179, 181 (2022)*
By Roselle L. Wissler and Art Hinshaw

Mediator preparation in advance of the first formal mediation session is widely seen as important for the effectiveness of the mediation, as are party and lawyer preparation. Two primary means of information exchange are thought to aid each group in their preparation: pre-session communications between the mediator and the mediation participants, and party submission of case information and documents to the mediator.

The most common goals for pre-session communications are for: (1) the media-tor to develop a basic understanding of the dispute; (2) the mediation participants to gain an understanding of the mediator's approach and the mediation process; (3) the mediator and the mediation participants to discuss how to structure the mediation process for the particular dispute; and (4) the mediator and the media-tion participants to begin to build rapport and trust. Accomplishing these goals would enable the mediator and the mediation participants to plan how they can most productively approach the first mediation session and would also help reduce the parties' stress before and during the mediation. To help accomplish these goals, mediators and lawyers generally recommend the following topics be discussed or explored during pre-session communications: (1) the mediation process, the role of the participants, and the mediator's approach; (2) the background of the dispute, the main issues to be addressed, the parties' interests, and any non-legal issues; (3) the status of settlement negotiations and the offers that have been exchanged, the obstacles to settlement, whether the parties need additional information, and possible settlement options; (4) the procedural status of the case; (5) the parties' per-sonalities and emotional dynamics, issues of violence or coercion, who should or should not attend the mediation, and the specifics of how the mediation process should proceed in this case (*e.g.*, opening presentations, the role the parties will play, or topics to be avoided in joint sessions); (6) giving the parties a chance to vent and work through emotions before the formal mediation session; (7) establishing the ground rules, encouraging a civil tone, and coaching on more productive opening presentations and communications; and (8) the particular documents that should be submitted to the mediator before the first session and whether these documents should be exchanged between the parties.

Whether pre-session communications are held and which of these topics are discussed are said to depend on a number of factors, including the mediator, the case, and whether written case information has been or will be submitted. These communications can take place prior to or on the same day as the first mediation session. . . .

. . . [T]he findings of the few empirical studies that have been conducted, taken together, suggest that practices regarding pre-session communications and document submissions might vary considerably in different case and mediation contexts. . . .

During pre-session communications held prior to the day of the first session, mediators in civil cases were less likely than those in family cases to explain the mediation process, explain mediation confidentiality, assess the parties' capacity to mediate, and explore whether the parties would be okay being together in the same room. By contrast, mediators in civil cases were more likely than those in family cases to explore who should or should not attend the mediation, explore options for how the opening session might be structured and, marginally, discuss the informa-tion that should be submitted before the first session. During pre-session commu-nications held on the same day as the first mediation session, there were differences between civil and family cases in only three process actions: mediators in civil cases were less likely than those in family cases to assess the participants' ability to communicate civilly, assess the parties' capacity to mediate, and explore whether the parties would be okay being together in the same room. . . .

There were few differences between mediators who had only a legal background and those who had a non-legal background (instead of or in addition to a legal background) in the process actions in which they engaged. . . .

During pre-session communications held prior to the day of the first mediation session, neither party (*i.e.*, the disputants themselves) was present in approximately three-fourths of civil cases and one-fourth of family cases. And when the parties were present, they did not talk at all in around one-third of civil cases but in only a few family cases . . . .

The lack of the disputants' presence and participation during pre-session communications, especially in civil cases prior to the day of the first session, indicates that the exchange of information directly between the mediators and the disputants themselves is quite limited. . . . And that lack of direct personal contact with the disputants in civil cases means that many mediators are unable to develop rapport or trust with the disputants themselves before the first mediation session — one of the four main goals for holding pre-session communications. . . .

These findings demonstrate that some mediators explored issues that could help them work with the mediation participants to customize the mediation process to the needs of the individual case — another goal of pre-session communications. However, because a majority of the disputants in civil cases were not present and did not actively participate during pre-session communications held prior to the day of the first session, many civil mediators were not able to assess the disputants directly, get their input on how the initial mediation session should be structured and who should attend, or coach them on a less adversarial presentation and tone for the mediation. Instead, mediators in civil cases would largely obtain this information from the lawyers' perspective, which might be vastly different than that of their clients. . . .

Notes and Questions

(1) The illustrated seating arrangements when an attorney is representing one of the parties suggest that attorneys sit next to their clients and that the parties sit between the attorney and the mediator. What are the pros and cons of such an arrangement from the perspectives of the parties, the mediator, and the attorneys?

(2) Identify additional people who may participate in the mediation and how you would set up the room to accommodate their participation (*e.g.*, interpreters, co-mediators, moral supporters, etc.).

(3) Note that the people who have been identified as "entitled" to be in the room is based in part on the dominant (white) U.S. culture norms. In some cultures, it is expected that members of the extended family, clergy or community will attend the

mediation. What are the pros and cons for including extended family members in the mediation session? Where else do dominant cultural assumptions show up in the mediation procedures discussed above?

b. Mediator's Opening Remarks

A mediation typically begins with the mediator making some opening remarks to the participants (often referred to as the mediator's opening statement). Even if all parties have previously participated in a mediation, a mediator does not bypass this step. Whether the mediation is in-person or remote, there are several reasons for beginning the mediation in this fashion. By making this opening statement, the mediator can:

- establish the procedures and clarify the mediator's role;
- put people at ease;
- convey to the participants, by talking in a fluent manner and using language that is inclusive and personal, a sense of mediator competence and skill, thereby inviting trust and comfort with both the process and the mediator;
- reconcile any conflicting expectations regarding what might happen in mediation;
- satisfy ethical or procedural requirements (if applicable).

Typically, there are seven basic components to the mediator's opening, typically addressed in the following sequence:

Introducing the mediator, parties, and others present. This should also include clarifying how people will be addressed and their pronouns.

Establishing credibility and impartiality of the mediator.

Explaining the process of mediation and the role of the mediator.

Explaining the procedures that will govern the process (including, if applicable, the possibility of meeting separately with the parties).

Explaining the extent to which the process is confidential or privileged and/or inviting parties to set terms of confidentiality.

Establishing norms and expectations for the use of online communication tools, when available.

Asking the parties if they have any questions.

The mediator's opening remarks should be clear and concise. A mediator should try to avoid using technical words that the disputants are unlikely to understand (*e.g.*, plaintiff, defendant, claimant, respondent, pro se, cause of action) or "jargon" phrases of the mediation world ("I will facilitate this conversation" or "We'll try to reach a win-win outcome.") Even when the parties are represented by attorneys and those attorneys are present, most mediators focus delivering their opening statement to the parties, talking directly to them and ensuring their understanding of the process. Although delivering an opening should not consume a lot of time, a mediator should not rush through it. The mediator's opening is important — it must be long enough to cover all of the elements clearly and completely but short enough not to lose the interest of the parties. Some jurisdictions require parties to sign an agreement to mediate prior to beginning a mediation; this written agreement to mediate typically contains the content of a mediator's opening statement. If this is the case, mediators must complete this task during the preliminary portion of the mediation and should consider how to combine their "conversational" opening remarks with the more formal agreement to mediate. Some mediators use an electronic signing program like DocuSign for the agreement to mediate so they must think about when to have parties complete the electronic signature: some may want parties to sign before the session begins while others want parties to sign it only after they have logged onto the mediation session, listened to the mediator's opening statement and have asked any questions.

Delivering the mediator's opening is deceptively difficult. One cannot underestimate the importance of starting the mediation in an articulate, informative, and calming manner. This is the one part of the mediation that can be practiced in advance.

A mediator's opening statement's tone and content should reflect the context of the mediation session. Its sequence should flow and its language should be authentic to the mediator's style and practice. With these caveats in mind, a mediator should consider the following subtleties and choices.

i. Introductions

Mediators should decide how they want to be addressed. For example, are first names appropriate? ("I'm Jana Smith. Call me Jana.") What about titles or degrees? ("I'm Dr. Smith" or "I'm Colonel Smith.") The choice obviously impacts the degree of formality and comfort experienced in the session. In addressing the parties, generally, the mediator will use last names; however, this is not a firm rule. For example, if the parties are on a first name basis and request that the mediator use first names, it would be appropriate to do so. Other mediators might ask the parties how they would like to be addressed. Whatever choice is made, the mediator must be certain to pronounce the parties' names correctly and use the pronouns that have been requested by the parties. When mediating on-line, these details can be handled quite easily: mediators can include their pronouns in parentheses along with their name, thereby inviting participants to identify their own pronouns if they are so inclined.

ii. Establishing Credibility and Impartiality

A mediator, through communication and conduct, hopes to establish credibility in order to give everyone present the confidence that both the mediator and the mediation process may be helpful to them. To do that, mediators address two matters: their biography and their familiarity with the situation. Parties have confidence in a person the more they know about the individual, so mediators must decide how much biographical information it is useful to share. Should one reference one's experience? ("I've mediated cases like this for 20 years" or "I was a trial lawyer for 20 years and then became a full-time mediator.") Is it sufficient to communicate simply: "I have been certified as a mediator by the X Court"? In some mediation settings, mediators maintain websites describing their practice and experience. By contrast, for the party who appears at a small claims court expecting a trial but is then encouraged to try mediation with a person who is immediately available, the party or their counsel may have no biographical information about the mediator who has been assigned to work with them, so sharing a limited amount of one's biography in the opening statement might be valued.

A mediator must give parties confidence that the mediator will act impartially. The most concise, credible way to do this is to provide the participants with information regarding the mediator's previous experience and knowledge about the dispute and then let the parties draw their own conclusion. This can be accomplished with this simple sentence: "I have not met either of you before and may have no previous knowledge of the events which brought you to mediation today." Most people will conclude that the mediator is impartial if the mediator does not know either of them and has no preconceived notion about the dispute. This approach works best when mediating community or small claims disputes. For more complex disputes, the mediator may have been chosen by the parties or their attorneys based on their previous experience with the mediator or have received information in advance from them to review. This requires a modified approach. Mediators who practice in a more evaluative or directive style may have been chosen for their subject matter expertise, and therefore should disclose this information.

In situations in which mediators know one or more of the parties or attorneys, mediators should conduct a two-part analysis. First, mediators should assess how well they know the individual and if this relationship raises any concerns regarding their ability to remain impartial. If mediators believe that their impartiality might be compromised in a manner detrimental to the process, or perceived to be so, then they should not conduct the mediation. Mediators should attempt to make this assessment as soon as possible in order to create the least disturbance for the parties. When in doubt, it is better to err on the side of caution and decline the mediation. If the mediator concludes after an analysis of the prior relationship that it does not jeopardize the integrity of the process, then the mediator moves to the second part of the test, namely disclosing the contact to the parties. If either party expresses opposition to proceeding in light of that information, the mediator withdraws. While the exact requirements of ethical rules vary, a mediator is often prohibited from mediating any case in which one of the parties express concern regarding previous contact or in some cases if the relationship is "too close." Such ethical constraints placed on the mediator are examined in greater detail in Chapter 8, *infra*.

iii. Explaining Mediation and the Role of the Mediator

The mediator must explain what mediation is and what the parties and participants can expect in this process. The mediator should try to place this explanation early in their opening remarks. In defining mediation, the mediator strives to use the simplest terms possible. It is often helpful to explain mediation by highlighting the difference between mediation and the traditional court process since most people are familiar with litigation as a form of dispute resolution. A mediator tries to explain both the mediator's and the parties' roles in the process, and. if one or more of the parties are represented by counsel, include an explanation regarding the role of the party's (or parties') attorney(s).

Here is one example of how one might explain the mediation process and roles:

> Mediation provides you with an opportunity to talk with one another with the help of another person, a mediator, who is not involved in the dispute. As mediator, my job is to assist you in talking to each other so that you can gain a better understanding of what happened. It is not my job, nor am I permitted, to decide who is right or wrong or to tell you how to resolve your conflict. Rather, in mediation you have the ability to develop a resolution that makes sense to each of you, if you wish. If you develop options that each of you find acceptable, you may wish to write them into an agreement that each of you can sign and I can help you do so. If you are unable to reach an agreement, you will [return to the judge who will make a decision for you — if court-ordered] or [need to choose another means of handling your dispute — if private].

iv. Explaining the Procedures That Will Guide the Process

The mediator should discuss the following procedural guidelines for in-person mediations:

• *Speaking Order*: If the mediation involves a case already filed in court, the mediator will often invite the plaintiff to speak first. Typically, the person who filed the claim has the obligation to let the other person know why the case was filed. If the mediation is taking place prior to or in lieu of a case having been filed in court, the mediator may ask the person who requested mediation to begin; if it seems appropriate, a mediator may ask the disputants who would like to begin. The person who begins has an advantage in framing the dispute; therefore, whoever speaks second should be given latitude to share not only a response, but also to describe concerns which the disputant has. See Chapter 10, *infra*, for a further discussion of how an attorney might divide these responsibilities with a client.

• *Separate Sessions (Caucus)*: Sometimes it is helpful for the mediator to meet with the parties/disputants (and their attorneys, if represented) separately during the mediation. If the mediator might do so, they should discuss this during the opening statement so that no one is alarmed if it later occurs. Since there may not be a separate session, the mediator should not spend too much time in the opening statement discussing its procedural aspects. Mediators often refer to this separate session as a caucus but since most people do not regularly use that term, good practice prompts a mediator to refer to it simply as a separate session.

• *Note-Taking*: If the mediator plans to take notes, the mediator should let everyone know. If mediating in person, it is helpful to provide pen and paper for the disputants and encourage them to listen for new information and to take notes, if necessary, while the other is talking. This enables them to remember issues they want to discuss without having to interrupt each other.

• *Explaining the Confidentiality of the Process*: The mediator should be well-versed in the level of confidentiality and privilege which applies to the mediation and review this with the parties. Some mediators have a confidentiality agreement prepared for the parties (and attorneys) to sign prior to beginning a mediation so that everyone is clear on the level of confidentiality that attaches. Others provide an opportunity for parties (and their attorneys) to discuss and agree upon the level of confidentiality they want. *See* Chapter 5, *infra*.

The following is an example of the portion of a mediator's opening statement that addresses the procedural aspects of the in-person process. When possible, a mediator should use the parties' names and invite their responses and commitment to the procedures suggested by the mediator.

> Let me explain how this process will work today. When I finish speaking and have answered any questions you may have, we will begin. [I see that each of you are here with your attorney. It has been my experience that mediation works best when the parties themselves actively participate in the process. Mr. Green, have you and your attorney discussed your respective participation? . . . Ms. Kodly, have you and your attorney discussed your respective participation?]

> Since Mr. Green sought this mediation [or brought this case to the attention of the court], we will begin by having you [and your attorney] describe the concerns that brought you here today. Ms. Kodly, you will then have an opportunity to share your concerns [which I understand will be through your attorney] and please feel free to add additional information or concerns. At some point, I may find it useful to meet with each of you individually. If such a situation arises, I will explain the process in greater detail. [You each will have an opportunity to share your concerns and perspectives on the situation that brings you here today.]

> I have found it best if each of you treat the other with courtesy and respect during this mediation, so that when one of you is speaking, I would ask that the other listen carefully. Is that guideline acceptable to each of you? [I have provided each of you with paper and pen.] Feel free to jot down any new information you may hear, as well as any issue you wish to discuss and are afraid you may forget while the other person is speaking. I, too, may be taking some notes. This is merely to help me keep information straight.

At the end of this mediation, I will discard my notes and encourage you to do the same because the discussions we have here are confidential. [NOTE: this will need to be tailored to the specific circumstances under which the mediation is conducted, see Chapter 5, *infra*.]

If the mediation is conducted remotely, the mediator should still review procedures but there will be differences. For example, the mediator will have the same considerations for speaking order and separate sessions and may have some additional suggested guidelines, such as when you are not speaking, please place yourself on mute. Another aspect of remote mediation is that it is very difficult to hear anything if two people are speaking at the same time. It can be helpful if you share that with the parties that it would be best to have one person speak at a time due to this limitation.

v. Checking in for Questions and Clarifications

The parties have just received a lot of information, so it is important to pause and let them ask any questions about the information which has been provided.

After answering any questions or determining that there are none, the mediator should be ready to hear from the parties. Begin by asking the party who brought the claim (or the party's attorney) to describe the events that led to the mediation, or alternatively, by asking the participants who would like to begin.

2. Accumulating Information

In order to assist parties in mediation, mediators need to learn what the issues are that brought them to mediation. This is true regardless of whether they have come to mediation voluntarily, by contract, or by order of the court in which they filed their dispute. In addition to listening to parties' descriptions of the actual circumstances surrounding their dispute, mediators observe the behavior of the parties toward one another before, during, and after their presentations — non-verbal cues, posture, and tone of voice — as a means of accumulating helpful information.

A mediator should try to establish an atmosphere in which the possibility of constructive dialogue is enhanced. Frequently, the parties have let their concerns simmer, exchanged heated words, and then avoided each other. Assisting the parties' communicate with one another constitutes an important first step toward building a resolution.

The mediator's role in the information gathering process combines structure and patience. With the mediator's assistance, the parties may be able to reorient their perspectives from an adversarial posture to one of collaboration. The mediator's role, while not that of a decision-maker, need not be passive. The mediator listens for many things, including (a) the interests of the parties; (b) the issues in dispute; (c) proposals that the parties may have as to how the issues may be resolved;

(d) principles and values that each party holds; and (e) emotions or feelings associated with the conflict. It is important to note that the parties usually do not clearly identify each of these items, and thus the mediator must listen carefully in order to "hear" them. The mediator's role is not to endorse each person's perception as "right or wrong" but to acknowledge their concerns as ones which they possess and which constitute the benchmarks of settlement possibilities.

a. The Parties' Opening Statements

The parties or their attorneys will articulate their concerns. The mediator must listen carefully. What they say, the manner in which the information is shared, and the order of presentation are all important pieces of information. The mediator should usually let each disputant take as much time as needed without interruption from the other party or the mediator.

When the first party is finished, the mediator should not ask the other to "respond," but rather should invite a description or explanation of that party's issues and concerns. The second party to speak often feels defensive, as if they need to respond to or rebut what the party sitting across the table has said. It is the mediator's role to put the parties at ease enough to share what is important to them.

Mediators should consider refraining from asking any questions until all the parties and/or their attorneys have spoken. While it may be tempting to ask "just a quick question" before each party has spoken, one never knows how long the answer may be to even a quick question. Further, if the first person's opening statement was long, a significant amount of time may have elapsed from the point the mediation began. By the time the second or third party has an opportunity to speak, they may have already given up any hope of this being a fair process, so a mediator asking questions of the first party simply reinforces that disengagement. Finally, the comments of the remaining parties usually help clarify matters, thereby answering questions before the mediator asks them.

After each party has spoken, the parties often will look to the mediator to identify the next step in the process and to provide some structure. A helpful intervention is for the mediator to reflect a joint narrative of what the parties have shared as having happened and to identify the parties' issues or "agenda items." To perform that important task requires a mediator to organize the information accurately and constructively. Taking good "mediator notes" can be most helpful for executing that task, and a discussion of their role follows.

b. Notes

A mediator's notes serve three important purposes:
- identification of the issues which the parties wish to address;
- clarification of statements/issues for the mediator;
- record of "movement" with regard to offers and solutions.

The mediator's notes *should not* be a transcript of the mediation. Notes should be selective. Three practical dangers arising from taking too many notes are:

- If the parties observe the mediator taking voluminous notes, they may become more cautious in what they say. If they are represented by counsel, questions may be raised about future use of those notes.

- In taking copious notes, the mediator must look at what is being written rather than devote eye contact, concern, and attention to the person who is speaking. This undermines the rapport that the mediator wants to establish.

- If a mediator takes too many notes, it will be difficult for the mediator to locate helpful information and follow up questions the mediator may have.

In general, mediators should trust their memories for the larger details. A mediator's notes are an organizational tool and should permit the mediator to recall a particular issue by a quick glance.

In addition to using notes as an organizational tool, notes can help mediators assure the parties that they have been heard. This is particularly useful when one party is repeating a thought over and over. The mediator can read the areas of concern which the mediator has noted and then ask if there is anything other than what the mediator has already captured in the notes which the party wishes to discuss at the mediation. This approach assures the party that the mediator has heard the concerns and allows the party to add anything which has not yet been included. When attorneys present the issues, it is generally easier to identify clearly and concisely the legal areas of discussion; however, the mediator may need to delve deeper into some of the other interests of the parties. For example, attorneys may focus on monetary issues and potential outcomes in court, while omitting other concerns, such as relationships or acknowledgements of wrong-doing, that are important to the parties.

It is also important in taking notes that the information be recorded in neutral, simple terms. When in-person, it is probable that the parties will be able to see the mediator's notes during the mediation. One of the problems in recording the exact words used by a party is that the mediator is confirming that person's characterization of the issue. For example, one person may describe activities as "noise," while the other may describe it as "music." A mediator needs to use a neutral term to describe it which both can accept: for example, "drum playing."

The following paragraph summarizes the information that the parties shared with the mediator during their opening statements in a small claims action:

> Upon meeting with two parties, the mediator learned from Mr. Watkins that he is a landlord and is suing Mr. Goodwin for back rent of $1750; the lease allows tenants to keep only "small" pets; Mr. Goodwin has obtained a large dog; and Mr. Watkins has had frequent complaints from other tenants regarding Mr. Goodwin's late evening, early morning parties on the weekends. Mr. Goodwin has responded that the rent has not been paid as the oven has been broken for two months; Mr. Watkins has not fixed the oven

despite requests by Mr. Goodwin to do so; and he objects to Mr. Watkins' unannounced presence in his apartment several times in the past month.

The mediator's notes may look something like this:

Mr. Watkins	Mr. Goodwin
rent ($1750)	oven (two months)
dog	landlord visits
parties	

Accumulating information and taking effective notes depends heavily upon the mediator's ability to listen. In the following excerpt, Joseph Stulberg and Lela Love detail these required listening skills for the mediator.

c. Listening Skills

The Middle Voice: Mediating Conflict Successfully
64 (Carolina Academic Press, 2019)*
By Joseph B. Stulberg & Lela P. Love

Listening effectively to what someone is saying consists of more than just hearing sounds. One listens to understand the message the speaker is trying to communicate. To listen well is to capture the entire message. Listening skills prevent one from short-circuiting or contaminating that message-sending process. Here are some guidelines that a mediator can follow to insure he receives all that is sent:

Concentrate. Minimize distractions. . . .

Maintain Focus. People cannot talk as fast as others can listen. A mediator should not use the overlapping time to daydream or worry about something else. . . .

Be patient. One cannot hear, let alone be certain he has captured what someone else is saying, if that person is not given a chance to complete his statements. Sometimes parties repeat themselves. Some speakers are hard to understand. A patient listener allows a speaker the freedom to tell his story — even if the telling is less than perfect.

Don't interrupt. One cannot listen while talking. It is tempting to interrupt a party by asking questions or providing information, but such behavior both disrupts a speaker's chain of thought and exhibits unhelpful conduct that other participants might copy.

Understand without judgment. . . . A mediator cannot argue mentally with the speaker. Understand first; evaluate later — much later. . . .

A mediator actively seeks to ensure he understands the parties' communications and to demonstrate that understanding to them. In doing so, he displays a level of interest and respect that encourages disclosure and further communication.

A mediator can ask questions in order to clarify previous statements. . . . .

———————

Listening is hard work. It appears easy because there is not much physical activity involved. But the parties will know whether the mediator is listening to them; the following signs confirm it:

- Effective and appropriate eye contact
- Appropriate facial gestures
- Appropriate affirmative head nods (Remember that the nod of the head can be interpreted as agreement or acknowledgment. A mediator should try to be consistent with any nods to avoid concerns regarding lack of impartiality.)
- Avoidance of actions or gestures that suggest boredom (such as yawning and leaning on your hand)
- Asking clarifying questions
- Reflecting using neutral words
- Not interrupting the speaker
- Not talking too much
- Acknowledging and validating feelings and thoughts (having empathy)

d. Questioning

Part of accumulating information may take place through the mediator's use of questions. A mediator must pay attention to the forms in which they phrase the questions as well as the contexts in which they ask them. Consider how a mediator's use of questions is similar to and distinct from that of a lawyer.

Open: This question is designed to get or keep the disputants talking because it generally cannot be answered with a simple "yes" or "no." This form of question should be used predominantly in the early stages of the mediation when the mediator is gathering information. Asking open questions gives the parties the opportunity to share their experiences and shape the dialogue.

Examples:

Can you please elaborate on that statement?

The mediator usually will begin by asking broad questions which require explanations. As the session progresses, the mediator can ask narrower questions, such as:

How do you see the situation being resolved?

Clarifying: Commonly used to gather a clearer understanding or to confirm a piece of information. Clarifying questions are typically used at the beginning of mediation when the mediator is gathering information to understand the issues for discussion.

Examples:

Mr. Stockmeyer, can you explain in greater detail the injuries you suffered?

OR

Ms. Jones and Ms. Stoon, how would you like that payment to be made?

Closed or leading: These questions have two features: the question can be answered with only a "yes" or "no" response and the answer itself is contained in the question. While this technique may extract some information, it should be used infrequently and with discretion because it does not elicit a complete response. The best use of closed questions is toward the end of a mediation or with parties who volunteer a lot of information and the mediator is trying to limit their domination of the mediation.

Examples:

I have noted that your daughter Terry's religious upbringing and participation are important concerns for you. Would you be satisfied with the proposal that she attend a religious camp this summer?

OR

Does this written agreement completely satisfy your original claim?

Justification: This type of question usually begins with "Why" and calls on individuals to justify their position (*e.g.*, past behavior, actions, feelings). Since this type of question tends to make people feel defensive and is often judgmental in nature, mediators should try to avoid using it. Often the question can be asked in another way to obtain the same useful information.

Example:

Instead of "Why did you fire Ms. Benk?" try, "What were the reasons for Ms. Benk's discharge?"

Compound: This is typified by multiple questions being asked as one question. The problem with using a compound question is that it is confusing to the person who has been asked the question and thus leads to a confusing answer. Mediators should try to avoid using these questions.

Example:

Were you wearing your seat belt and talking on your cell phone at the time of the accident?

Using good questioning techniques can help the mediator learn and clarify information. More importantly, it can assist the parties gain a more enriched understanding about the dispute from each other's perspective. A mediator's deft use of questions can foster a rich information exchange and joint problem solving effort by the parties. A mediator should use questions to clarify, to help parties better understand their own interests and risks, to explore possibilities and to confirm movement or agreement. Mediators should not use questions merely to satisfy their own curiosity. Facilitative and evaluative mediators differ over whether a mediator should use questions to judge the situation. *See* Chapter 4, *infra*.

e. Non-Verbal Communication

Non-verbal communication is a vital part of our overall communication. Experts estimate that 55% of the information we gather is from non-verbal behavior; 38% from the tone and sound of the speaker's voice and only 7% from the actual words that the speaker uses. Paying attention to the silent cues and observing the communication between the parties is valuable for the mediator. These cues help the mediator to identify such matters as priorities, deeply held values, and areas that might be negotiable.

Non-verbal cues serve as guideposts and indicators, but a mediator should be careful not to make assumptions based on a single non-verbal action. For example, traditionally, body language experts identified standing with one's arms crossed in front as a "closed" posture that indicates that individual's unwillingness to participate or hostility to the person or issue being discussed. Today, we understand that there might be many different reasons for assuming such a posture — *e.g.*, one is cold, one is comfortable like that, one is missing a button and trying to cover it up, and so on. Experts currently suggest that one look at the total package of behaviors that an individual exhibits and, more importantly, at changes in behaviors.

The meaning or significance of a non-verbal communication may not be obvious, so the mediator must be careful not to assume too much. The mediator should be especially sensitive to and aware of the impact that culture has on nonverbal reactions to conflict. In addition, when mediating online, permitting the use of emojis may create or remove some of the ambiguity from the parties' exchange. It is important to confirm the desired meaning.

Mediators also need to be sensitive to their own non-verbal cues. A party may conclude that a mediator whose arms are folded is simply not interested in what the parties have to say, rather than someone who has simply achieved a comfortable physical position.

3. Developing an Agenda

The parties have told their respective versions of the events that brought them to mediation. They may have shared their reaction and evaluation of the other party's stated version of the events. The mediator should now lend a degree of structure to the discussion of the issues. The agenda is always subject to revision as the mediation proceeds and additional information is shared.

a. Characterizing the Issues

As opposed to the traditional way lawyers and law students think about "issues," — viz., identifying legal causes of action — in mediation, an issue is some matter, practice, or action that enhances, frustrates, alters, or in some way adversely affects some person's interests, goals, or needs.

Mediation then focuses on discussing "negotiating issues," which are issues that people are capable of, and have the resources for, resolving. By definition, not all issues — e.g., homelessness — can be negotiated because the negotiating parties themselves do not have all the resources necessary to resolve it.

As the parties and/or their attorneys speak, the mediator listens carefully to what is said, notes what is not said, and records the issues which the parties (or their counsel) have identified as needing to be discussed in order for them to resolve the dispute which brought them to mediation.

Unrepresented parties to a dispute will typically speak in plain English and not in the language commonly referred to as "legalese." They will relate a series of events and it is the mediator's task to cull through it and then succinctly state what the mediator has heard as the negotiating issues. It is important to realize the range of flexibility that the mediator possesses when characterizing the dispute.

Examples:

Fred Student housed his German Shepherd puppy at Al's House of Pets for 60 days over the summer and incurred a bill of $360. Fred has not made any payments on the bill, and it is past due by six months. Fred has promised to drop off payments twice in the last two months to Al and has not done so.

What are the issues in this dispute?

A mediator, particularly one who is legally trained, might be tempted to characterize the issues as: "bad debt and breach of contract (broken promises)." That is a mistake, for it simply invites parties to become defensive in arguing the merits of their claims. The more constructive approach is to characterize the issues as: "payment due and method of payment." By framing the issue in more neutral, future-oriented terms, the mediator reduces party defensiveness, invites party communication, and assists the parties to think creatively about possible resolutions.

When parties are represented in mediation, the parties or their representative may frame issues in legalistic terms similar to how a cause of action would be presented to a court. In these circumstances, a mediator's challenge is to help the parties and their attorneys identify the interests behind these issues, as well as, where appropriate, non-legal issues that are important to them.

A mediator shapes not only the way in which the parties talk with each other but also the range of their discussion. If one is mediating a case that has already been filed in court, it may be tempting to limit the mediated discussion to the legal issues or the "four corners of the complaint." However, often when people are embroiled in conflict, they get stuck. They keep talking about the same issues and ignore the fact that previous difficulties may have an impact on the current dispute. Sometimes, the greatest assistance a mediator can provide is to help the parties expand their discussion. A common misconception about negotiation and mediation is that the most difficult disputes to resolve are those that involve a lot of money and multiple issues; in fact, frequently, the most difficult conflicts to resolve are those that involve a single issue and very little money, for in these situations, there is little room for the parties to maneuver and there are few concessions to offer.

b. Structuring the Discussion

As human beings, we are limited by the fact that we can only talk about one thing at a time. Hence, the order in which issues are discussed in a mediation is an important element of the process. The parties and their attorneys will talk about many things. By definition, some will be more important to them than others, so assisting them identify what matters most and what matters least to them establishes an environment which invites negotiation. Note that parties will often discuss what is most important to them first and then repeat it several times in different ways. Listening carefully may reveal the attachment an individual has to an issue, and tactful questioning can confirm the level of interest on a particular topic.

Generally, the guiding principle when setting an agenda is that a mediator wants to propose an order of discussing the issues that will assist parties to move toward resolution. (Note, however, that mediators who practice from a transformative perspective view setting the agenda as a decision for the parties to make, not the mediator.)

Some mediators listen to the parties' opening statements with an ear toward identifying the "easy" issues. The mediator could then suggest one of these "easy" issues as a place to begin. The theory at work here is that individuals in dispute tend to feel frustrated and believe that their dispute will never be resolved — certainly not by talking with the other person. By helping parties experience success rapidly, even if it is only a relatively minor matter, they become more optimistic and develop some momentum for productively discussing the more difficult issues.

By contrast, other mediators listen to the parties' opening statements with the goal of identifying what is perceived as the core issue. Their theory is that by having the parties first discuss on the issue that they view as central to the dispute, the smaller (and easier) issues then fall into place. Finding a good place to start will come with practice and often will be driven by the preferences of the individuals involved in the mediation and the specific circumstances of the mediation.

Here are some guides mediators may use to find a starting place and structure the discussions.

Categories: Often the issues can be divided according to various subject matters or principles. Typical categories are: economic matters and non-economic matters, or financial and behavioral. Appropriate categories vary according to the nature of the dispute. By dividing multiple issues into a limited number of categories, the mediator assists the parties organize the discussion of their dispute into manageable parts.

Nature of Remedies: Some concerns raised by the parties invite remedies which are mutual, *e.g.*, require both to do something for the other. Other concerns require one party to do something and the other party merely to accept it, *e.g.*, one party pays the other party a sum of money. Often, mutual remedy issues are easier for the parties to discuss and agree to than are those for which one party has the burden of compliance.

Time: Sometimes a mediator might suggest sequencing the discussion of issues according to their time sequence. For example, the disputants could discuss the issues in chronological order (what happened first) or reverse chronological order (what happened last). In addition, sometimes an issue has a time constraint attached to it — *e.g.*, a child's birthday or the due date for a financial payment. The parties might find that discussing first those issues most constrained by time is constructive because there are outside interests pushing them toward resolution.

Relationship of the Party to the Issues: Some issues will be particularly difficult to resolve if the party or parties have a strong philosophical or personal attachment to them. It may be best to defer discussion of these matters until other issues are resolved and the parties have built some momentum toward resolution.

Logic: In some instances, issues will arise that are logically related to each other, so proceeding in their "logical" order might be helpful (*e.g.*, discussing if a tenant owes money under the lease before discussing payment amounts). Of course, it is important for a mediator to be careful not to focus unduly on past events instead of future possibilities.

There are many ways, not one "right way," to structure the discussion agenda. But, one of the mediators' greatest contributions to the mediation is their ability to create structure and develop a process to assist the parties' communication, if the parties do not do so for themselves. If the parties or mediator neglect to create an agenda, the possibility increases that the discussion will degenerate into impasse not because the parties necessarily disagree on all matters, but rather because no one focused on separating those items on which the parties might agree from those about which they remain in substantial disagreement.

4. Generating Movement

Establishing an agreed-upon agenda for discussion and the first issue to discuss only sets up the discussion. The parties may still be stuck, with, for instance, a landlord demanding payment of rent arrears and the tenant refusing to pay anything.

At this point, the mediator's job is to assist the parties think about their dispute in other ways to help them move forward. It is important to keep in mind that disputants and their attorneys may not want to resolve their dispute in mediation. They may believe it is in their (or their client's) best interest to pursue litigation, some other means of resolution, or no resolution at all. The mediator's job is not to make sure that every situation is resolved in mediation, but rather to help the parties consider their options and make an informed decision as to whether a proposed settlement in mediation presents their best alternative to other possibilities.

In addition to the possible negotiator strategies and tactics examined in Chapter 2, *supra*, there are additional ways a mediator may be helpful to the parties in generating movement. The following sections present some options to consider for keeping the mediation discussions moving. These techniques can help trigger flexibility. There is no assurance that the use of any technique at a given moment will succeed, but the mediator recognizes that at least some efforts can be tried before concluding the parties are currently at impasse.

a. Procedural Items

Alternate Discussion of Issues. Each party to a conflict may have raised issues. A repair person, for instance, may be demanding payment for work being performed to renovate a client's kitchen and that the client remove adverse comments about his work that were posted on Facebook; the client might be upset, in part, because the repair person continues to perform the work at odd times of a weekend day without notice, disrupting the children's routine. The mediator might invite discussion of payment for work already completed and then examine the work scheduling before addressing the posts to social media. Alternating the discussion of issues in this manner helps forestall parties becoming recalcitrant because they believe that the other person is the only one who needs to make concessions, or conversely, that they are the only one who is making concessions.

Focus on the Future. It is helpful to remind parties that while it is important for everyone, including the mediator, to understand what has happened, since that will help shape the future, they cannot change what happened in the past; what they can decide, however, is how they want things to be in the future. Understandably, and appropriately, the parties will need to express their concerns about what has occurred in the past before they will be ready and willing to consider and develop settlement terms for going forward. To compare processes on this crucial matter, the litigation process requires that parties submit and portray past events to a trier of fact, have the decision-maker weigh and evaluate the credibility of the proffered evidence, determine what happened, and decide who was wrong or right — i.e., who is liable; once that retrospective analysis is completed, if there is a finding that the defendant is liable, the adjudicator entertains and awards a prescribed set of financial damages. By contrast, in mediation, disputing parties may have an ongoing relationship and desire or need to sustain it, so that what happened in the past — one parent provided economic resources and the other was a stay-at-home parent of the children — may provide a foundation for helping parties determine how they want to behave in the future.

Be Positive. When disputants come to a mediation, they are often frustrated, nervous about being in mediation, and stressed about having a dispute which has not been resolved. As mediator, you may be the only one who remembers that conflict can be positive — that it can offer an opportunity for the parties to learn from each other and bring meaningful change. By maintaining a positive atmosphere in the mediation, the mediator can help the parties view their dispute as a learning endeavor.

Use of Silence. Periods of silence, whether for only a few seconds or longer, can be very powerful in helping parties and their attorneys reflect on the effect of a particular proposal or statement. Most people are not comfortable with silence; a mediator must be neither uncomfortable with nor afraid of it. Using silence can be deliberate: when a party or attorney has made an offer or counteroffer and silence ensues, for instance, the mediator should not be the person who breaks that silence — give the other party or attorney an opportunity to respond.

Reflection. A surprisingly effective way to assist parties in conflict is to use well-timed and appropriate reflections. Reflection is when the mediator tries to clarify and restate what the party is saying in a way that both the person who said it and the other party can hear and understand what was said. Often, parties hearing a reflection of what they have communicated will either add more to explain what they were thinking or recognize that what they said was much harsher than what they intended. This opens the door to movement.

Mindfulness. Mindfulness can help mediators respond to expected and unexpected tensions between parties. In *Managing Conflict Mindfully*,[1] Leonard Riskin describes mindfulness as "paying attention to your present-moment experience, deliberately and without judgment." As conflict can trigger physiological tension that disrupts a mediator's response to parties, mindfulness strategies that increase a mediator's awareness can increase their effectiveness in a tense environment.

Use of Humor. People become more flexible when they are laughing because laughter often reveals some comfort with oneself and the situation. Feel comfortable to use it, but never at the expense of anyone involved in the mediation.

b. Informational Items

Create Doubts. A great question for the mediator to pose to the parties and their attorneys is: "Is it possible . . . ?" If the parties acknowledge that something is possible, even if they say it is unlikely, they already are less rigid in their position and may then be able to consider other options. A corollary to this technique is to challenge assumptions. Often, a person assumes the worst about those with whom one

---

1. L. Riskin, *Managing Conflict Mindfully* (West Academic Publishing, 2023).

is in conflict. By asking them to consider whether their assumptions may not be accurate, a mediator might helpfully assist the parties and their attorneys remove a stumbling block to progress.

Integrative Solutions. If the mediator helps the parties and their attorneys to identify their interests (not just their positions) and generate multiple options for addressing them, they may be able to identify issues in which they both can achieve the "win-win" solution that they want.

Use of Facts. Often the disputants have not spoken for a significant period of time prior to the mediation, or perhaps ever. It is often helpful for the mediator to encourage the parties to listen to their counterpart for "new information" about the situation and to consider that as a possible rationale for adopting a different "position."

Establish Priorities and Trade-Offs. Not everything that the parties or their attorneys present at mediation will be of equal importance to them. Helping them identify which items are most important enables them see that other items are less crucial. This may yield greater flexibility and ideas regarding items to "trade-off." For example, if one person puts a high value on its position for one issue — *e.g.*, the amount of the payment sought for money owed must be complete — while the other puts a high value on its position on a different issue — the form of any payment must not be one lump sum transmission — these individuals may be able to reach an agreement which results in full payment over time, thereby addressing both of their "high priority" issues.

Use Role Reversal. Helping parties and attorneys see the situation from the other person's perspective is often helpful in piercing perceptions that the other person is being selfish, mean or uncooperative. This technique is most useful when meeting separately with the parties and they are able to react with greater honesty.

Point Out Possible Inconsistencies. A mediator should never embarrass or berate a party, attorney, or other person involved in the mediation, but sometimes a mediator can note gently that there may be inconsistencies within comments or proposals that have been made and request clarification..

Identify Constraints on Others. Everyone operates under some constraints — be they time, resource, psychological, or political (*e.g.*, proposed settlement must be ratified by one's constituents). Proposed solutions must account for these constraints or the solution will not be acceptable. Assisting the disputants and their attorneys to see each other's constraints may help them understand the dynamics at work in reaching an agreement and lead to greater creativity.

Be the Agent of Reality. The mediator should never force the parties to settle their dispute or any portion of it in mediation. The mediator may, however, help the parties to think through the consequences of not resolving the dispute in mediation (what is the party's BATMA, *i.e.*, best alternative to reaching a mediated agreement). The parties may want to consider monetary costs, time lost, relationship issues, and the uncertainty of a court outcome when evaluating the acceptability of the proposed negotiated settlement terms so that their decision as to whether or not they should embrace a settlement proposed in mediation is as informed as possible.

c. Relationship Issues

Appeal to Past Practices. Sometimes the parties have had a prior good relationship. In such cases, it may be useful for the mediator to explore with the parties how they have resolved similar issues in the past.

Appeal to Commonly Held Standards and Principles. Sometimes both parties express a common theme, for example, to be treated respectfully or that they are concerned about the "best interest of their child." While acknowledging this theme will not "solve" their issues, it is often helpful for the mediator to point out to the parties (and their attorneys) that they do agree on some matters. A corollary to this technique is to utilize "peer pressure" (what would the general public do in a situation) as a way of helping parties to identify commonly held standards.

Sometimes the mediator will want to meet with the parties separately. This can be another effective way of generating movement. Because there are many issues to consider when using this technique, it warrants separate discussion.

5. The Separate Session (Caucus)

At some point during a mediation, the mediator, a party, or an attorney, may decide that it would be useful for the mediator to meet separately with each of the parties. These separate meetings are referred to as caucuses, although, depending on how familiar individuals are with mediation, it is often better for the mediator to refer to these as separate sessions. Caucusing might also be used to facilitate a private meeting between an attorney and client, or for a conversation between co-mediators. For the purpose of this section, we focus on the separate meetings a mediator conducts with the parties.

The extent to which caucuses are used varies tremendously. Some mediators believe that it is more desirable to use joint sessions, whenever possible, to allow the disputants to communicate directly with one another. They are reluctant to use caucuses for fear of breaking the flow of the joint session, increasing distrust between the parties, or decreasing perceptions about each party's ability to work with one another. Other mediators rely on the technique extensively, and only use joint sessions at the very beginning and perhaps the end of a mediation, or not at all. Some mediators do not declare an impasse unless they have had an opportunity to meet with the parties separately. As a generalization, evaluative mediators tend to be more enthusiastic about caucuses than facilitative mediators. Similarly, attorney mediators tend to use caucuses more frequently than non-attorney mediators. However, many mediators break with these generalizations and vary their use of caucus depending on the nature of the particular mediation. In any event, mediators' varied approaches to caucus are neither inherently right nor inherently wrong.

When mediating online, if there is more than one person on one or both "sides" of the dispute, it is highly likely that each side will need some time to confer by themselves or with the assistance of the mediator. This is another use of the separate session.

Regardless of mediation style, there is general agreement that a mediator should have a reason and a purpose in calling a caucus. What follows are some reasons why the mediator might decide to meet privately with each party.

a. Rationale and Sequence of Separate Sessions

Explore Settlement Options. Sometimes the mediator will sense that the parties may be more open to discussing potential options if the other party is not present. In this situation, the mediator will usually begin with the party who appears to be willing to negotiate.

Signal Warning Signs. During the session, one party may exhibit behaviors which threaten any possibility of agreement. For example, one party may be continuing to refer to the other in an insulting manner or not allowing the other to finish a thought without interrupting. If a party is represented, the unhelpful behavior may be that of the attorney. If the mediator senses that such conduct is occurring and it appears to be detrimental to making progress, the mediator should meet first with the party (and attorney, if represented) who is exhibiting the behavior to discuss the mediator's observations.

Confirm Movement: At the start of the session, one party — for example, a landlord — may have indicated that the only acceptable resolution is for the other party — the tenant — to move out. As the discussion progresses, the landlord appears to signal a change in that position, but the mediator is not certain; the mediator needs to know if there is flexibility but does not want to explore that directly with the landlord while in the presence of the tenant for fear that the landlord would try to "save face" by immediately denying any willingness to adjust. The mediator would declare a caucus and meet first with the party who had signaled possible movement to learn if the signal was accurate or a misstatement.

Address Recalcitrant Party. Every so often, one party will take a position early in the session and not move from it. It may become apparent to the mediator that the session will quickly conclude unless the other party is willing to meet the demand or the recalcitrant party is willing to consider movement. In such instances, the mediator should meet first with the "recalcitrant" party to get a better understanding of what is happening for this party. As used here, the term "party" is not limited to named parties. A "recalcitrant party" may be an attorney or other representative.

Pause. At times, emotions run high and the mediator may sense that the parties need a break to collect themselves, stop crying, or calm down. Separate meetings can provide this opportunity. Mediators should use their judgment as to whether to meet first with the person who is upset or to meet first with the other party, thereby allowing the distraught individual an opportunity to calm down privately.

Evaluate. A caucus may be deemed necessary for the parties to evaluate the proposals that are currently being discussed. A private session affords the parties the opportunity to take a few moments to assess the impact of accepting or rejecting a potential resolution without the pressure of having the other party in the room. It also provides private time for reflection when the mediator is meeting with the other party. In situations in which there are multiple parties with shared interests or a party is represented, meeting alone enables them to consult with one another, either with or without the mediator, before making decisions. Generally, in this situation, the mediator can meet with either party first.

b. Why Not Meet Separately?

Some mediators follow a set sequence in their mediation conference. They start by making opening remarks, ask each party to make their opening remarks, and then immediately call for caucus sessions. But there are important reasons why a mediator might decide not to meet separately with the parties, so the better practice is for the mediator to assess each situation and proceed accordingly. Set out below are reasons why the mediator might not want to meet separately with the parties:

It is Unnecessary. If the parties are making progress and working together, there may be no need to stop them and meet separately. In fact, doing so might disrupt the momentum that has developed and have the effect of interrupting rather than assisting the process.

Low Level of Trust Between the Parties. Sometimes the parties have developed a very low level of trust between them. There will be no resolution to the dispute unless each party sees and hears from one another exactly why they accept particular settlement terms. Negotiating breakthroughs that happen while one party is out of the room will be viewed with suspicion and not accepted. In such circumstances, it might be best to keep the parties together.

Physical Arrangements. Sometimes the physical set-up of the mediation does not lend itself to meeting separately with the parties. For example, if there is no place for the parties and their attorneys to wait while the mediator is meeting with the others, calling a caucus might not be prudent.

c. Principles and Mechanics of the Separate Session

The Mediator Should Have an Identifiable Reason for Meeting Separately with the Parties. Non-agreement between the parties and "not knowing what else to do" are not reasons to meet separately. It seems overly simple to point out that the parties will not be in agreement from the outset of mediation. However, one of the most common misuses of caucus occurs when the parties state in their opening statements that they do not agree, so the mediator immediately, or very soon after the mediation begins, calls for separate sessions. Many mediators believe that when the caucus is called so early in the process, each party will simply repeat in caucus what was said in joint session. By calling an early caucus, the mediator has not provided the parties the opportunity to negotiate for themselves, and thereby has not fostered joint problem solving. However, as noted above, some mediators (often those who use a more evaluative approach) believe in the early use of caucus.

If the mediator decides to use a caucus, the mediator should state the intention to meet separately with each party, indicate the meeting sequence and the approximate length of time of the meeting, and then, presuming there are not separate physical rooms to which each party could be assigned to meet with the mediator, excuse one party and counsel from the "mediation room" — physical or virtual. When using online breakout rooms, consider using permissions that control when parties can join a breakout room.

In mediations involving unrepresented individuals, such as small claims mediation, a mediator should strive to keep separate meetings to no more than 10-15 minutes apiece. In complex cases, or those in which the party is represented by an attorney, a caucus may last considerably longer. One reason the length is less problematic when a party is represented is that the "waiting time" will not seem as long if the party has someone with whom to talk and plan strategy when the mediator is meeting with the other parties. Mediators should be mindful of how different allotted times for caucusing may impact a party's perception of mediator partiality.

If the parties are represented, the mediator will typically meet with the attorneys and their clients together. In some circumstances, the mediator might choose to meet with the attorneys without their clients. It would be unusual for the mediator to meet with represented parties without their counsel; however, a mediator could do so if such a meeting were requested by a party.

Confidentiality. Many mediators take the approach that unless the caucusing party (and their attorney) authorizes the mediator to share the content of what was said with the other party, the mediator must keep all information gained in a separate session private. Other mediators take the reverse approach, indicating to the party with whom they are caucusing that the mediator will presume that they are permitted to share, if helpful, all information that they learn in caucus *except* if instructed otherwise by the caucusing party. A third approach is to inform the parties at the beginning that nothing said in caucus would be considered confidential. Therefore, the parties would be on notice not to share any information they were unwilling to tell the other party. While any of these approaches may be acceptable, depending on applicable ethical and procedural standards, it is crucial that the mediator adequately explain what the parties should expect in terms of confidentiality prior to asking the party to share information and then, crucially, record their notes in a manner such that they know what was learned in joint session and what was learned in caucus.

The Mediator Meets with Each Party Every Time a Separate Session Is Called. Meeting with each party every time a caucus is called serves two purposes. First, it reduces the level of suspicion about what happened during the caucus in which one party participated and the other did not. Second, it provides each party an opportunity to share information with the mediator. There are many reasons why parties may be reluctant to share full information in the presence of the other party; a caucus allows them to speak freely.

The Amount of Time a Mediator Spends with Each Party in Caucus Need Not Be Identical. The mediator should promise *equal opportunity* to meet separately, *not equal time.* In fact, it is rarely equal. If, after meeting with one party, the mediator discovers that there is no strategic reason for meeting with the other party, the mediator should still meet with the waiting party, or that party's attorney, because the party or attorney may have a reason for wanting to meet with the mediator. In this example, a mediator would begin the second meeting by indicating that they do not have anything to ask or share but before reconvening, would willingly discuss anything the party or their attorney would like to share. Thus, the second meeting might last only a minute or two if the party (and attorney) has nothing to say. Nonetheless, since the mediator provided the opportunity to meet separately with the mediator and it was the party's decision to end the meeting, the mediator preserves the appearance of impartiality, and the party will be less likely to be concerned that the other caucus was longer.

Separate sessions may be conducted in virtual mediations by using "break-out" rooms or other similar options. Getting familiar with the technology before the mediation begins is important, and creating the breakout rooms before the mediation, if possible, is also advisable. Moving from one caucus to another is seamless using virtual technology and may actually increase the speed and efficiency of the mediation.

d. Second Caucus

To begin the second caucus, the mediator should proceed to the waiting area to invite and escort the other party (and attorney) to the mediation room. Once settled, the mediator begins the second meeting in the same fashion as the first (separate notes, record the time, and invite the party's and attorney's confidence). The difference in this setting is that the mediator has just spent time alone with the "other side," presumably has gained some additional information or insight, and everyone knows it. The mediator must fight the temptation to immediately reveal information which was learned in caucus, even if the mediator has permission to do so. The mediator's role has not changed. After the first separate meeting, the mediator should not become an advocate for settlement options proposed by one side or compromise a party's position by immediately revealing that party's concerns and interests. The mediator's focus in the second caucus is to invite the second party and attorney to share their perspectives and concerns on the topics under review. It is also useful to remember that negotiation principles, such as "reactive devaluation," may be at work in this situation.

A mediator technique frequently used in caucus is to ask questions as hypotheticals. For example, a mediator might ask, "If the other party were willing to do X, would you be willing to do Y?" This allows the mediator to assume the scapegoat role if a suggestion is unacceptable. The party or attorney can reject the "hypothetical" without getting angry at the other side for proposing the idea. It also protects offers of movement made by one side.

The second caucus, like every caucus, concludes by establishing with the party (and attorney) what information may be shared. Sometimes when caucus discussions generate additional developments or proposals regarding negotiating issues that warrant exploration or require clarification, the mediator continues meeting with the parties in separate sessions, Many mediators, however, after meeting once with each party, reconvene all parties and counsel in joint session to continue the discussion.

Sometimes as a result of information shared and developed in separate sessions, the parties and their attorneys may be in substantial agreement; at other times, the parties may still be very far apart. Regardless of where the parties are on that continuum, the mediator should begin the joint session with some encouraging words. Specifically, the mediator should thank the parties and the attorneys for the opportunity to meet with them separately. If the parties are still far apart, indicate that is the case but that this does not mean that the session needs to end immediately. The parties and attorneys may want to add additional information or ideas.

If the parties are close together or even in substantial agreement, the mediator might continue (after thanking them) with a statement along the lines of, "As a result of my individual conversations with each of you, it appears that you may be close to reaching an agreement on the following issues, but the precise terms need to be worked out."

Even if the mediator is certain the parties and attorneys are at the same point, the mediator must decide how to reveal this potential consensus. Basically, there are three options:

(1) The mediator announces the terms of the agreement: "After speaking with each of you, there appears to be agreement regarding the matter of rent arrears. Both Ms. Jones and Mr. Smith agree that payment by Mr. Smith to Ms. Jones of $1250 will constitute complete satisfaction of the claim for rent arrears. Is that correct?"

(2) The parties/attorneys reveal the agreement to each other: "Ms. Jones, will you please share with Mr. Smith your proposal for resolving the rent issue?"

(3) Some combination of (1) and (2), above.

If the parties are unrepresented, it is usually preferable to allow the parties to reveal the agreement to each other since it is their agreement. This allows the parties to assume greater ownership and commitment to it. However, if the parties are highly emotional or extremely angry at one another, or the agreement is very complicated, the mediator may choose to reveal some or all of the terms in the manner noted in (1), above. If the agreement is conveyed by the mediator, the mediator should check with each party after each term is revealed to ensure that there is agreement. At a minimum, the parties should at least be nodding their affirmation as the mediator speaks. If the parties are represented, the attorneys may want to take a more active role in discussing the settlement terms.

6. Concluding the Mediation

a. Possible Endings

It is the mediator's responsibility to end the session, whether or not the parties have settled their dispute. There are four ways in which a mediation session might end:

The Parties Do Not Reach Any Agreement. If the case was ordered by the court to mediation, the mediator will probably be required to file a report of "impasse" with the court. Most courts will accept a report from the mediator which states the date and time at the mediation occurred, who appeared at the mediation, and that no agreement was reached. While some judges may want to know why no agreement was reached, rules of confidentiality will often prevent mediators from providing this information. See Chapter 5, *infra*, for a more detailed discussion. If the case was mediated voluntarily or pursuant to an agreement of the parties, there is normally no need for the mediator to write a report. The parties will merely decide on another means of resolving their dispute.

The Parties Request to Continue Mediation After a Specific Period of Time. A continuation is usually requested when one or both of the parties want to resolve their dispute, but need additional time to gather information that has bearing on their decisions and actions. Typically, the mediator who began the mediation will complete the mediation.

The Parties Have a Partial Agreement, Meaning That They Have Resolved Some Issues but Need Some Other Type of Dispute Resolution to Help Them Address Issues Which They Were Unable to Settle. In this situation, the parties may draft an agreement in which they identify both the substantive settlement terms they have reached as well as the procedural agreements they have developed for addressing the unresolved issues. Any item included in the signed mediation agreement is typically not confidential, and thus, could be discussed with a judge or other dispute resolver.

The Parties Reach Agreement on All the Issues. Generally, if an agreement is reached, it is reduced to writing in order to preserve the parties' ability to enforce the agreement. *See* Chapter 6, *infra*. When attorneys are present at mediation, typically one of the attorneys will draft the mediated agreement. If attorneys are not involved, the mediator will typically provide to the parties a document outlining their settlement terms. In some states, it is the mediator's ethical responsibility in a court-ordered mediation to ensure that the terms of agreement are memorialized (written and signed). However, the potentially critical issue of unauthorized practice of law (UPL) has been raised against some non-lawyer mediators who have drafted written agreements. See Chapter 8, *infra*, for a more detailed discussion. Regardless of who writes the final agreement, the parties often leave with a signed "Memorandum of Understanding."

b. Closing When There Is No Agreement

Some parties will decide not to resolve their dispute in mediation because they believe their case was not suitable for mediation, they need more time to reflect, or there are strategic reasons for wanting to take a case to trial or another form of dispute resolution. If the parties do not reach an agreement in mediation, the mediator should still try to end the session in an upbeat manner. Many times, disputes which do not resolve at mediation do settle at some point before trial, with or without the further assistance of the mediator.

Before concluding, mediators typically do the following:

- Review with the parties and attorneys any issues that were resolved and explore the possibility of a partial agreement outlining what issues have been resolved and which issues are still unresolved.

- Encourage post-mediation communication between the parties by asking the parties or attorneys if they wish to exchange contact information (assuming that the parties' addresses are not confidential for some reason). Absent such an exchange, unrepresented parties often lack the ability to contact one another even if they wanted to reach out after the mediation.

- Encourage the parties and attorneys to consider returning to mediation (with the same or different mediator) if they think it would be helpful.

- End on a positive note by thanking the parties for their time and effort at the mediation. The mediator often accepts the scapegoat role by saying, "I regret that I was not able to assist you in resolving your dispute today," thereby encouraging the parties to have confidence that it is still within their capacity to end their controversy in a mutually satisfactory way.

- If the mediation is conducted in person, provide a comfortable exit for the parties. After a long or emotional mediation session, parties (and their attorneys) may desire space to grapple with the concerns expressed during the session. Consider having the parties leave one at a time so that they do not find themselves stuck in the same elevator as they depart.

c. Drafting an Agreement

Regardless of who writes the agreement (the parties, attorneys, or mediator), it must be done carefully and accurately, for the agreement most likely will become legally binding and enforceable. The parties also need to understand it and be able to refer back to it. And if the mediation itself had been court-ordered, a judge may have to review and enforce the settlement terms.

The written agreement should be clear and concise. Here are some guidelines:

- Separate the different elements of the agreement, assign a number to each and list them sequentially. Do not write a long narrative.

- Do not include "confessions."

- Use the names of the parties, not legal jargon (*e.g.*, complainant or respondent) and make certain the names are spelled correctly. The first time a name is referenced, write it out completely, and then when referring to the parties later in the agreement, use just the first or last names (depending on the context of the dispute).

- Write out dates rather than use the numerical equivalents (*e.g.*, March 4, 2035 rather than 3/4/35). In addition, be precise; avoid using ambiguous phrases such as bi-weekly, monthly, at the end of the month, the end of the week, in the summer, etc.

- When the agreement involves a monetary settlement, write out the dollar amount. This may appear old-fashioned, but it is easy to misread numbers or misplace a decimal. In addition, specify the place, method (*e.g.*, by means of cash with receipt, bank check, money order, Venmo, etc.) and timing of payments. If there is a payment schedule agreed to of less than five payments, write out each payment date and amount.

- Keep the tone positive and prospective. A mediation agreement should not retell the dispute's history nor contain admissions of wrongdoing. Make it forward looking. A useful phrase to include is "in the future" particularly if parties have agreed to do (or not do) something in the future but are unwilling to acknowledge that they did not (or did) do it in the past.

- If unrepresented, the mediator should invite the parties to assist in writing the document by reading each element of the agreement as it is written. Ask them if the words used accurately capture their agreement. Pride of authorship belongs to the parties, not the mediator.

- When writing the terms of the agreement, the mediator should never change the substantive settlement terms the parties have adopted. If related issues come up during the drafting of the agreement which were not previously discussed, the mediator should raise those matters with the parties for their negotiation and decision as to how they wish to handle the issues.

- Just as the mediation must be conducted in a neutral manner, the agreement or memorandum of understanding must be written in a fair and balanced manner. It is useful to start with those items which are mutual obligations, alternating, where possible, whose name appears first in each sentence. The goal is for the agreement to reflect an appropriate sense of balance between the parties. If the mediation is successful, everyone should feel as though they achieved something from it, and the written agreement should reflect that fact.

d. Enforcement

One advantage of a mediated agreement is in compliance. Since the parties have worked out the settlement terms themselves, they are more likely to understand them, believe they are fair and workable, and feel compelled to honor them.

But what happens if performance of the agreement is not fulfilled? If the case was mediated pursuant to a court order, the parties can often enforce their mediated agreement in the same manner as any court order. For the court to enforce the agreement, the performance terms must be clear and unambiguous. In addition, the court most likely can only enforce monetary terms. Settlement provisions such as, "The parties agree to treat each other respectfully in the future" are often helpful and fundamental in mediation agreements but are not ones that a court can effectively enforce. Parties may wish to include such terms, but they should understand that a court cannot enforce such specific performance obligations.

If the mediation is the result of a voluntary submission, the parties still have an enforceable agreement. If there is alleged non-compliance, then one party must take the additional step of filing a court case to enforce the mediation agreement as a contract.

If the parties are expressing significant concern about enforcement, the mediator may want to explore with them whether there are issues which remain unresolved in the mediation. See Chapter 6, *infra*, for a more complete discussion of enforcement issues.

Chapter 4

Mediator Roles, Orientations, and Styles

A. Introduction

Building on the discussion regarding mediator skills presented in Chapter 3, the materials in this chapter examine multiple perspectives regarding the mediator's role and alternative mediation styles and approaches. Section B contains excerpts from theorists and commentators offering different philosophical accounts of the mediator's proper *role*. Section C explores whether a mediator should be *accountable* for the outcome of a mediation, focusing on neutrality. In viewing the mediator's role from a practice perspective, the materials in Section D review mediator *orientations* that have been recommended or identified by commentators. Section E presents a foundational study of mediator *style* and a modern empirical analysis of techniques for mediator intervention.

With respect to a theory of mediation, consider carefully how these various *roles*, *orientations*, and *styles* interrelate. Which ones are consistent with one another? Which are inconsistent? When focusing on mediation practice, consider how the use of technology and remote mediation services intersect with your understanding of roles, orientations, and styles.

B. Mediator Role Conceptions

In the following excerpts, Lon Fuller and Robert A. Baruch Bush develop their conceptions of the mediator's role by first emphasizing the unique character of mediation. They then argue for a conception of the mediator's role that is most consistent with mediation's true character. Fuller sees mediation's "central quality" as "its capacity to reorient the parties toward each other." He thus views the mediator's role (or "function") as that of assisting the parties "to free themselves from the encumbrance of rules and of accepting, instead, a relationship of mutual respect, trust and understanding." Similarly, Bush examines "the special powers of mediation" in developing his "empowerment-and-recognition" conception of the mediator's role. He rejects two popular conceptions of the mediator's role — the "efficiency" conception and the "protection-of-rights" conception — because they are not in line with mediation's unique character.

Mediation — Its Forms and Functions

44 S. Cal. L. Rev. 305, 307–08, 315, 318, 325–26 (1971)*
By Lon L. Fuller

. . . [O]f mediation one is tempted to say that it is all process and no structure.

Casual treatments of the subject in the literature of sociology tend to assume that the object of mediation is to make the parties aware of the "social norms" applicable to their relationship and to persuade them to accommodate themselves to the "structure" imposed by these norms. From this point of view the difference between a judge and a mediator is simply that the judge orders the parties to conform themselves to the rules, while the mediator persuades them to do so. But mediation is commonly directed, not toward achieving conformity to norms, but toward the creation of the relevant norms themselves. This is true, for example, in the very common case where the mediator assists the parties in working out the terms of a contract defining their rights and duties toward one another. In such a case there is no pre-existing structure that can guide mediation; it is the mediational process that produces the structure.

It may be suggested that mediation is always, in any event, directed toward bringing about a more harmonious relationship between the parties, whether this be achieved through explicit agreement, through a reciprocal acceptance of the "social norms" relevant to their relationship, or simply because the parties have been helped to a new and more perceptive understanding of one another's problems. The fact that in ordinary usage the terms "mediation" and "conciliation" are largely interchangeable tends to reinforce this view of the matter.

. . . When we perceive how a mediator, claiming no "authority," can help the parties give order and coherence to their relationship, we may in the process come to realize that there are circumstances in which the parties can dispense with this aid, and that social order can often arise directly out of the interactions it seems to govern and direct.

. . . Where the bargaining process proceeds without the aid of a mediator the usual course pursued by experienced negotiators is something like this: the parties begin by simply talking about the various proposals, explaining in general terms why they want this and why they are opposed to that. During this exploratory or "sounding out" process, which proceeds without any clear-cut offers of settlement, each party conveys — sometimes explicitly, sometimes tacitly, sometimes intentionally, sometimes inadvertently — something about his relative evaluations of the various items under discussion. After these discussions have proceeded for some time, one party is likely to offer a "package deal," proposing in general terms a contract that will settle all the issues under discussion. This offer may be accepted by the other party or he may accept it subject to certain stipulated changes.

Now it is obvious that the process just described can often be greatly facilitated through the services of a skillful mediator. His assistance can speed the negotiations, reduce the likelihood of miscalculation, and generally help the parties to reach a sounder agreement, an adjustment of their divergent valuations that will produce something like an optimum yield of the gains of reciprocity. These things the mediator can accomplish by holding separate confidential meetings with the parties, where each party gives the mediator a relatively full and candid account of the internal posture of his own interests. Armed with this information, but without making a premature disclosure of its details, the mediator can then help to shape the negotiations in such a way that they will proceed most directly to their goal, with a minimum of waste and friction.

[T]he central quality of mediation ... [is] its capacity to reorient the parties toward each other, not by imposing rules on them, but by helping them to achieve a new and shared perception of their relationship, a perception that will redirect their attitudes and dispositions toward one another.

This quality of mediation becomes most visible when the proper function of the mediator turns out to be, not that of inducing the parties to accept formal rules for the governance of their future relations, but that of helping them to free themselves from the encumbrance of rules and of accepting, instead, a relationship of mutual respect, trust and understanding that will enable them to meet shared contingencies without the aid of formal prescriptions laid down in advance.

Efficiency and Protection, or Empowerment and Recognition?: The Mediator's Role and Ethical Standards in Mediation

41 Fla. L. Rev. 253, 259–73 (1989)*
By Robert A. Baruch Bush

... [U]nder the common definition of mediation, a neutral third party works with the disputing parties to help them reach a mutually acceptable resolution. This definition might itself appear to answer the question of what the mediator's role should be. However, this standard definitional language can be read in different ways, and it does not reflect in practice any common conception of the mediator's role in the process. On the contrary ... many different conceptions exist. Among these, however, two call for special and critical discussion. Both the efficiency and protection-of-rights conceptions of the mediator's role are quite popular today; both have greatly influenced the operation of mediation programs and the articulation of mediation standards. Nevertheless, neither merits such popularity or influence. Despite their prevalence, both conceptions are deeply flawed, and for similar reasons.

... The efficiency conception holds that the mediator's primary role, and the main value of the mediation process, is to remove litigation from the courts by facilitating settlement agreements in as many cases as possible. This reduces court congestion, frees scarce judicial time, and economizes on public and private expense. Sometimes this conception is framed more narrowly by saying that the mediator's role is simply to facilitate agreements. However, this characterization is usually only a surrogate for the efficiency conception, since the value of agreements in this view is that they represent conservation of public and private resources. Therefore, the efficiency conception usually is accompanied by a focus on mediators' settlement rates and time-and-cost figures. This conception is advanced most commonly by judicial administrators and planners, and by the business-law community, as part of the search for "alternatives to the high costs of litigation."

By contrast, the protection-of-rights conception holds that the mediator's primary role, and the main value of the mediation process, is to safeguard the rights of the disputing parties and potentially affected third parties by imposing various checks for procedural and substantive fairness on an otherwise unconstrained bargaining process. This prevents settlement agreements from compromising important rights. Sometimes, this conception is expressed by saying that the mediator's role is to ensure that agreements are based on informed consent and that they are not fundamentally unfair to either side. This characterization, however, is really only a surrogate for the protection-of-rights conception, for the primary concern is avoiding unknowing waivers of legal rights, including the right to fundamental fairness inherent in legal doctrines such as unconscionability. Therefore, the protection-of-rights conception usually engenders a focus on mediator duties, especially on the duty to advise and urge parties to obtain independent legal counsel and the duty to terminate a mediation that threatens to produce an unreasonably unfair agreement. Advocates of disadvantaged groups and the trial practice segment of the bar are among those advocating this conception. It has heavily influenced most of the mediation practice codes proposed in recent years.

. . .

The first flaw in both conceptions is that efficiency and protection of rights are both interests that third parties other than mediators can promote much more effectively than mediators themselves. Therefore, why give either of these jobs to mediators in the first place? If efficiency is the concern, an arbitrator can be more effective than a mediator in removing cases from court and disposing of them expeditiously and finally. The greater structure of the arbitration process, and the arbitrator's decisional authority, make speedy and final disposition much more likely in arbitration than in mediation. On the other hand, if protection of rights is the primary concern, a judge can do so far more effectively than a mediator. As many have observed, the informality and privacy of mediation, and its de-emphasis on substantive rules of decision, inevitably place rights and fairness at risk. By contrast, adjudication's emphasis on procedural formality, substantive rules, and neutral supervision of zealous advocates assures greater protection of rights and fairness than mediation could possibly afford. In short, if the concern is efficiency or protection of rights, mediation can be dismissed altogether as superfluous, because other processes can perform both these functions much more effectively.

One answer to this criticism is that mediation can accomplish something else of value that these other processes cannot. If so, however, then this value and not the two in question should define the mediator's role. . . . Another answer is that, while other processes can more effectively promote either efficiency *or* protection of rights, mediation somehow can combine both functions as those other processes cannot . . . [I]n practice these two functions are bound to conflict with one another. Thus, it is difficult to see how mediation, or any process, could effectively serve both.

In fact, this leads to the second flaw common to both the efficiency and protection-of-rights conceptions. Not only are mediators incapable of serving *both* these roles simultaneously, they actually are incapable of serving *either* of them separately. Indeed, the attempt to serve either will render the mediation process either useless or abusive.

If we adopt the efficiency conception, under which the mediator's primary role is simply to reach agreements as expeditiously as possible, the effect is to create a role devoid of any clear ethical constraints on mediator behavior. Mediators become little more than case-movers; the only performance standards are their agreement rates and time/cost figures. Such a conception creates perverse incentives; it opens the door to, and indeed encourages, manipulative and coercive mediator behavior, especially in a process unconstrained by procedural or substantive rules or fear of publicity. Mediation becomes the "forced march to settlement" that many of its critics have rightly decried. . . .

On the other hand, if we adopt the protection-of-rights conception, mediators cannot effectively serve this role without undermining their usefulness altogether. As Professor Stulberg has argued, mediators who try to protect substantive rights and guarantee that agreements are fair must adopt substantive positions that inevitably compromise their impartiality, either in actuality or in the parties' eyes.[31] Yet impartiality is crucial to the mediator's many tasks. . . .

To summarize, the mediator cannot effectively and coherently fulfill the role envisioned by either the efficiency or the protection-of-rights conception. On the other hand, neutral third parties in other processes, such as arbitration and adjudication, *can* fulfill these roles. Therefore, neither the efficiency nor the protection-of-rights conception offers a sound basis for establishing uniform standards for mediator qualifications, training, and practice. For this reason, it is important to resist the tendency to gravitate toward either conception, both of which remain

---

31. *See* J. Stulberg, Taking Charge/Managing Conflict 141–49 (1987); Stulberg at 87, 96–97 [J. Stulberg, *The Theory and Practice of Mediation: A Reply to Professor Susskind*, 6 Vt. L. Rev. 85, 88–91 (1981)]; *see also* McCrory, *Environmental Mediation — Another Piece for the Puzzle*, 6 Vt. L. Rev. 49, 80–81 (1981).

extremely influential despite their deficiencies. The only basis for resisting them, however, is the articulation of another conception of the mediator's role which is sounder, more fruitful, and more in touch with the positive essence of mediation. This is the . . . empowerment-and-recognition conception.

. . . The basis for a sounder conception of the mediator's role lies in examining what mediation *can* do that other processes cannot. In other words, what important powers or capacities are unique to mediation that are not found to the same degree, if at all, in other methods of dispute resolution? The mediator's role should then be to act in ways that fulfill these unique capacities.

. . . Thoughtful mediation theorists and practitioners have given much consideration to identifying mediation's unique powers. In their comments, two points consistently are expressed regarding the capacities of the mediation process.

The first special power of mediation, and what some call "[t]he overriding feature and . . . value of mediation," is that "it is a consensual process that seeks self-determined resolutions."[36] . . . Mediation places the substantive outcome of the dispute within the control and determination of the parties themselves; it frees them from relying on or being subjected to the opinions and standards of outside "higher authorities," legal or otherwise. Further, mediation not only allows the parties to set their own standards for an acceptable solution, it also requires them to search for solutions that are within their own capacity to effectuate. In other words, the parties themselves set the standards, and the parties themselves marshal the actual resources to resolve the dispute. When agreement is reached, the parties have designed and implemented their own solution to the problem. Even when the parties do not reach an agreement, they experience the concrete possibility, to be more fully realized in other situations, that they can control their own circumstances. They discover that they need not be wholly dependent on outside institutions, legal or otherwise, to solve their problems. I call this the empowerment function of mediation: its capacity to encourage the parties to exercise autonomy, choice, and self-determination.

. . . Mediated outcomes empower parties by responding to them as unique individuals with particular problems, rather than as depersonalized representatives of general problems faced by classes of actors or by society as a whole.

The second special power of mediation was described classically by Professor Lon Fuller. . . . Fuller sees mediation as evoking in each party recognition and acknowledgment of, and some degree of understanding and empathy for, the other party's situation, even though their interests and positions may remain opposed. Of course, such mutual recognition often will help produce concrete accommodations and an ultimate agreement. But even when it does not, evoking recognition is itself an accomplishment of enormous value: the value of escaping our alienated

---

36. J. Folberg & A. Taylor at 245. [J. Folberg & A. Taylor: Mediation: A Comprehensive Guide to Resolving Conflicts Without Litigation (1984).]

isolation and rediscovering our common humanity, even in the midst of bitter division. Professor Leonard Riskin observes accordingly that one of the great values of mediation is that it can "encourage the kind of dialogue that would help . . . [the disputants experience] a perspective of caring and interconnection."[45] Others also have stressed this special power of mediation to "humanize" us to one another, to translate between us, and to help us recognize each other as fellows even when we are in conflict. I call this the recognition function of mediation.

. . . Here, then, are the special powers of mediation: It can encourage personal empowerment and self-determination as alternatives to institutional dependency, and it can evoke recognition of common humanity in the face of bitter conflict. Both powers involve restoring to the individual a sense of his own value and that of his fellow man in the face of an increasingly alienating and isolating social context. These are valuable powers indeed. Further, they are unique to mediation. These are functions mediation can perform that other processes cannot.

As for evoking empathetic recognition of the other fellow, adjudication and arbitration at best treat such recognition as irrelevant. More often, they destroy the very possibility of empathy by encouraging strong, frequently extreme, adversarial behavior. While in negotiation, recognition may occur, but only haphazardly, for no one stands above the fray to encourage and help the parties rise above their own positions and acknowledge those of their opponents. As for empowerment, it is almost by definition impossible in adjudication and arbitration. Both disempower the parties in differing degrees, whether by their authoritative and legalistic character, or by their heavy reliance on advice and representation by professional advocates. Although empowerment is more of a possibility in negotiation, the difficulty of reaching settlement in unassisted negotiations often frustrates this possibility, and negotiation through professional advocates again involves disempowerment in its own way.

Thus, what mediation can do that other processes cannot is to encourage empowerment of the parties and evoke recognition between them. These are its unique and valuable capacities. The mediator's role is to act so as to fulfill these unique capacities. Accordingly, in general terms, the mediator's role is: (1) to encourage the empowerment of the parties — i.e., the exercise of their autonomy and self-determination in deciding whether and how to resolve their dispute; and (2) to promote the parties' mutual recognition of each other as human beings despite their adverse positions. I emphasize here that this role can and should be performed successfully whether or not the parties reach an agreement, and whether or not any agreement reached satisfies some external standard of right or fairness. In other

---

45. Riskin at 354 [Riskin, *Toward New Standards for the Neutral Lawyer in Mediation*, 26 Ariz. L. Rev. 329 (1984)]; *see also id.* at 332, 347–49, 352, 359 (*referring to the value of caring and interconnection*); *Riskin, supra* note 6, at 56–57 (*relating mediation* to the shift in public values from self-fulfillment to the ethic of commitment) [Riskin, *Mediation and Lawyers*, 43 Ohio St. L.J. 29, 30–34 (1982)].

words, it is not the mediator's job to guarantee a fair agreement, or *any* agreement at all; it *is* the mediator's job to guarantee the parties the fullest opportunity for self-determination and mutual acknowledgment. Mediators who ignore this job have not fulfilled their professional responsibilities, even if the parties reach an agreement. Conversely, mediators who do this job *have* fulfilled their responsibilities, even if the parties reach *no* agreement.

Notes and Questions

(1) Bush was obviously influenced by Fuller in developing his "empowerment and recognition" conception of the mediator's role. When Fuller was writing in the early 1970s, mediation was most widely used in the field of labor-management relations. Arguably, that field is less bound by rules of law and therefore, a mediator may be more inclined to eschew a protection of rights conception of the mediator's role and to assist the parties during the mediation to create their own norms defining their rights and duties. Does the rejection of a protection of rights conception become more difficult as mediation is used: (a) in substantive areas that are more traditionally defined by the parties' legal rights or (b) in areas in which a dispute has been transformed into a lawsuit filed in court and that case has been referred by a judge to mediation to be conducted by a lawyer-mediator?

(2) Writing in the context of collective bargaining, where representatives from a union meet with company management to negotiate a contract governing the terms and conditions of employment for an employee bargaining unit, Fuller suggests mediation is an opportunity for parties to create their own norms rather than submit to the guideposts of codified law or administrative rule. In Chapter 2, Ariel Eckblad urged negotiators to re-consider the norms used in a negotiation setting, asking negotiators to interrogate how norms were developed, and who (and for whom) norms were created. Would Eckblad agree with Fuller's suggestion that mediation is an opportunity to create new norms? Would Eckblad critique the institutionalization of mediation (*i.e.*, labor mediation, court-connected mediation) and its connection to potentially problematic institutional norms? For more discussion on the institutionalization of mediation, see Chapter 9.

(3) As dispute resolution processes transition to digital platforms, how might a mediator's role and orientation shift? Will a mediator's focus on efficiency, fairness, or self-determination be influenced—or even dictated—by the technology or the design of the technology?

C. Mediator Accountability

Should the mediator feel a sense of responsibility or accountability for the outcome of a mediation? Should the mediator seek to ensure that a mediation is fair or just? Lawrence Susskind and Joseph Stulberg present a now classic debate over mediator accountability. In focusing on the role of the environmental mediator,

Susskind expresses concern not only for the rights of the disputants but also for those persons unrepresented at the table. Building on this protection-of-rights conception of the environmental mediator's role, Susskind argues that the mediator must feel responsible not only for the mediation *process*, but also for the *outcome* of the mediation. Stulberg challenges such a conception of the mediator's role. He argues that Susskind's notion that a mediator should be accountable for the fairness of the outcome of a mediation is inconsistent with the essential functions and qualities of a mediator, particularly that of mediator neutrality. Three decades later, Stulberg and Susskind re-engage in this debate with Bernie Mayer in an excerpt from a Marquette Law symposium.

Environmental Mediation and the Accountability Problem

6 Vt. L. Rev. 1, 14–16, 18, 42, 47 (1981)*

By Lawrence Susskind

One analysis of environmental mediation suggests nine steps that must be completed for mediation to be successful: (1) all the parties that have a stake in the outcome of a dispute must be identified; (2) the relevant interest groups must be appropriately represented; (3) fundamentally different values and assumptions must be confronted; (4) a sufficient number of possible solutions or options must be developed; (5) the boundaries and time horizon for analyzing impacts must be agreed upon; (6) the weighting, scaling, and amalgamation of judgments about costs and benefits must be undertaken jointly; (7) fair compensation and mitigatory actions must be negotiated; (8) the legality and financial feasibility of bargains that are made must be ensured; and (9) all parties must be held to their commitments. Although these steps will ensure a fair and efficient process, the success of a mediation effort must also be judged in terms of the fairness and stability of agreements that are reached. From this standpoint, a mediator should probably refuse to enter a dispute in which the power relationships among the parties are so unequal that a mutually acceptable agreement is unlikely to emerge. In addition, environmental mediators should probably withdraw from negotiations in which any of the parties seek an agreement that would not be just from the standpoint of another participant or from the standpoint of a party not at the bargaining table.

To achieve just and stable agreements, mediators may have to find ways of enhancing the relationships among the parties so they will be better able to reconcile future differences (that threaten implementation) on their own. Mediators may also have to build the basic negotiating capabilities of one or more of the parties to ensure more equal bargaining relationships.

Agreements are sometimes reached because one party with substantial power holds out for what it wants while other parties, with less leverage, realize that they can either accept a small gain or wind up with nothing at all. Under these circumstances,

---

all sides may sign such agreements but with unequal degrees of enthusiasm. This result sends a message to the community-at-large that it is acceptable for the most powerful interests to pressure opponents into accepting less than completely fair outcomes. Mediators should avoid setting such precedents, if only because they undermine the chances of attracting less powerful but obstructionist parties to the bargaining table in the future.

It is also quite possible that short-term solutions with which the parties to an environmental dispute are quite pleased can generate new and different problems for other groups outside the bargaining process. It would be irresponsible to ignore these problems if they are indeed foreseeable, if only because implementation may be obstructed by those outside groups later on.

The classic model of labor mediation places little emphasis on the mediator's role as a representative of diffuse, inarticulate, or hard-to-organize interests. All the appropriate parties to a labor-management dispute are presumed to be present at the bargaining table. Thus, the problems of protecting unrepresented segments of the society or reducing impacts on the community-at-large receive little, if any, attention. Joint net gains are presumed to be maximized through the interaction of the parties and their ability to know for themselves how best to achieve their objectives. No effort is made to bolster the claims or abilities of the weaker stakeholders. Precedent is not a concern; indeed, one of the presumed strengths of labor mediation is that parties are free to devise agreements of their own design. Finally, spillovers, externalities, and long-term impacts are, for the most part, ignored since the time frame for implementing most labor-management agreements is relatively short. The parties will usually face the same adversaries again in a few years which makes it easier for them to hold each other to their agreements.

Although procedural fairness and ethical behavior on the part of labor mediators and self-interest maximizing behavior on the part of the participants in labor-management negotiations are presumed to be sufficient to ensure just and stable agreements, these assumptions are inappropriate in the environmental field. Just and stable agreements in the environmental field require much closer attention to the interests of those unable to represent themselves. Joint net gains can be achieved only if the parties attempt to understand the complex ecological systems involved and to generate appropriate compromises that go beyond their self-interests. In short, self-interested negotiation must be replaced by "principled negotiation."

. . . [E]nvironmental mediators ought to accept responsibility for ensuring (1) that the interests of parties not directly involved in negotiations, but with a stake in the outcome, are adequately represented and protected; (2) that agreements are as fair and stable as possible; and (3) that agreements reached are interpreted as intended by the community-at-large and set constructive precedents.

. . . Environmental mediators, to the extent that they adopt the broader view of their responsibilities suggested in this article, will probably need to possess substantive knowledge about the environmental and regulatory issues at stake. Effective environmental mediation may require teams composed of some individuals with technical background, some specialized in problem solving or group dynamics and some with political clout.

... An environmental mediator should be committed to procedural fairness — all parties should have an opportunity to be represented by individuals with the technical sophistication to bargain effectively on their behalf. Environmental mediators should also be concerned that the agreements they help to reach are just and stable. To fulfill these responsibilities, environmental mediators will have to intervene more often and more forcefully than their counterparts in the labor-management field. Although such intervention may make it difficult to retain the appearance of neutrality and the trust of the active parties, environmental mediators cannot fulfill their responsibilities to the community-at-large if they remain passive.

The Theory and Practice of Mediation: A Reply to Professor Susskind

6 Vt. L. Rev. 85, 86–87, 96–97, 114, 115–16 (1981)*
By Joseph B. Stulberg

The basis of this article is that Susskind's demand for a non-neutral intervenor is conceptually and pragmatically incompatible with the goals and purposes of mediation. The intervenor posture that Susskind advocates is not anchored by any principles or obligations of office. The intervenor's conduct, strategies or contribution to the dispute settlement process is, therefore, neither predictable nor consistent. It is precisely a mediator's commitment to neutrality which ensures responsible actions on the part of the mediator and permits mediation to be an effective, principled dispute settlement procedure.

Susskind maintains, in four distinct ways, that a mediator of environmental disputes should not be neutral. Environmental mediators ought to be concerned about:

1. The impacts of negotiated agreements on under-represented or unrepresentable groups in the community.

2. The possibility that joint net gains have not been maximized.

3. The long-term or spillover effects of the settlements they help to reach.

4. The precedents that they set and the precedents upon which agreements are based.

At a substantive level, Susskind argues that the mediator must ensure that the negotiated agreements are fair.

... [A] mediator must be neutral with regard to outcome. Parties negotiate because they lack the power to achieve their objectives unilaterally. They negotiate with those persons or representatives of groups whose cooperation they need to achieve their objective. If the mediator is neutral and remains so, then he and his

---

office invite a bond of trust to develop between him and the parties. If the mediator's job is to assist the parties to reach a resolution, and his commitment to neutrality ensures confidentiality, then, in an important sense, the parties have nothing to lose and everything to gain by the mediator's intervention. In these two bases of assistance and neutrality there is no way the mediator could jeopardize or abridge the substantive interests of the respective parties.

How is this trust exemplified in practice? Suppose a party advocates certain proposals because of internal political divisions which might impede discussions. For tactical reasons, however, the party does not want to reveal these internal divisions to the other parties. A mediator to whom such information is entrusted can direct discussions so that such a dilemma can be overcome. The mediator's vigorous plea made in the presence of all parties to remove the proposal from further discussions, for example, might provide a safe, face-saving way for that party to drop its demand.

There is a variety of information that parties will entrust to a neutral mediator, including a statement of their priorities, acceptable trade-offs, and their desired timing for demonstrating movement and flexibility. All of these postures are aimed to achieve a resolution without fear that such information will be carelessly shared or that it will surface in public forums in a manner calculated to embarrass or exploit the parties into undesired movement. This type of trust is secured and reinforced only if the mediator is neutral, has no power to insist upon a particular outcome, and honors the confidences placed in him. If any of these characteristics is absent, then the parties must calculate what information they will share with the mediator, just as they do in communicating with any of the parties to the controversy.

. . . If we were to accept the obligations of office that Susskind ascribes to the environmental mediator with regard to insuring Pareto-optimal outcomes, then the environmental mediator is simply a person who uses his entry into the dispute to become a social conscience, environmental policeman, or social critic and who carries no other obligations to the process or the participants beyond assuring Pareto-optimality. It is, in its most benign form, an invitation to permit philosopher-kings to participate in the affairs of the citizenry.

. . . A final note is in order regarding the propriety of a mediator having a substantive commitment to a particular outcome or range of outcomes for a given dispute. It appears that the impetus for Susskind's prescription, that an environmental mediator not be neutral, emanates from the understandable reluctance to accord conclusive weight to the preferences of the parties in every conceivable situation. For example, if parties to a collective bargaining session agree to adopt a racially-discriminatory hiring policy, the mediator, Susskind would argue, should object. Although the stated principle is correct, the mediator's role is not thereby converted into that of an advocate, even if the parties find acceptable an arrangement that is contrary to important principles of public policy or morality.

How should the mediator respond to such a situation? The answer seems relatively straightforward. The mediator should press the parties to examine whether or not they believe that (1) they would be acting in compliance with the law or with principles they would be willing, as rational agents, to universalize; (2) their activities will be acceptable to their respective constituencies and not overturned by public authorities; and (3) in the short and long run, their proposed actions are not contrary to their own self-interest. If the parties listen to these arguments and still find the proposed course of action acceptable, then the mediator can simply decide as an individual that he does not want to lend his personal presence and reputation, or the prestige of the mediation process, to that agreement and he can withdraw. That judgment is one for the mediator *qua* moral agent, not mediator, to make. It is comparable to the dilemma faced by a soldier who is given an order to commit a morally heinous act.

It is certainly the case that each of us is not neutral with regard to everything. Each of us has preferences, interests, commitments to certain moral principles and to an evolving philosophy of life which, when challenged or transgressed, will prompt us into advocating and acting in a manner that is faithful to these dictates. There is clearly no reason to be apologetic or hesitant about defending or advocating such considered judgments. It is also true, however, that mediation as a dispute settlement procedure can be used in a variety of contexts, not all of which would meet approval with everyone's considered judgments. What is important is that one keep distinct his personal posture of judgment from the rule defined practice of the mediator and act accordingly.

Core Values of Dispute Resolution: Is Neutrality Necessary?*

95 Marq. L. Rev. 805, 809-813, 816–820 (2012)**

PANELISTS

. . .

Bernard ("Bernie") Mayer
Joseph ("Josh") B. Stulberg
Lawrence ("Larry") Susskind

. . .

LARRY SUSSKIND: . . . If the institutional context that tees up the mediation doesn't define who is or who isn't a party, whether they come with advocates, what the responsibilities of those advocates might be, whether the product of the discussion is binding, whether it sets a precedent, etc. — if all these things aren't defined by the system you're in, what are the mediator's responsibilities?

Don't look to me if the parties don't show up; don't look to me to be responsible if there are enormous inequalities among the parties; don't look to me to

---

* The following discussion is an edited version of a panel discussion that occurred at Marquette University Law School on September 23, 2011.

be responsible if the parties have a hard time representing themselves or the category of stakeholders they're supposed to represent; don't look to me if the parties don't understand the scientific, technical, or other complexities surrounding the decisions they're making; I'M NEUTRAL!

In my world, you must be responsible, or at least accountable, for how these considerations get addressed. If the parties start to talk, and it's clear from the way they're talking that someone not present is going to be adversely affected, I would say, *Gee don't you think that group should be represented at the table?* And for each of the points I'm raising, I'm interested in what it means to have a theory of practice — a way of answering these different questions on a case-by-case basis.

To bring it back to today's discussion, maybe the system that you're mediating in, which has taken care of all this for you, ought to be questioned. Maybe it's not doing what it should do relative to who gets to the table, what their negotiating capacities are, whether they are prepared to pursue their own interests effectively, what other parties should be there, what other information they might need, what kind of accountability they ought to have to the community at large, whether an informal precedent is being set, etc. Maybe you should be asking yourself these questions. Maybe it is the mediator's responsibility to be highly attentive in every case to issues like these and not just say, *I'm in a court-connected context, the system is the way it is, it just tees up the cases for me, and I don't have to worry about any of that.*

JOSH STULBERG: . . .

Let me try to come at the question . . . in a slightly different way than the way in which Larry has set it up. At a conceptual level, I think of mediation as embracing the following elements. First, mediating is a justice event. It is not a casual conversation; it is not a conversation to create a business deal. It is a justice event, and so needs to be conducted with those values in mind. Second, participants are members of the political community. While I certainly want to support the central value of personal autonomy, that value cannot skew or escape the fundamental fact that we are all members, in an important sense, of a political community. How I want and choose to live my life is, to some extent, clearly and appropriately shaped and constrained by how others want to live their lives. It is simply not true that one's "self-determination" licenses him or her to do whatever she wants. Third, at least at a conceptual level, there is an important difference between concepts of impartiality, objectivity, and neutrality. My argument years ago — and I still believe it — is that neutrality is distinctive. It is neutrality with respect to outcome, not process. Being neutral means adopting an unswerving commitment to structure and guide a conversation that simultaneously embraces the values of a justice event and that encourages and cultivates disputing parties to work out matters in a way that they want to live their lives as members of a political community. That may sound like an abstract or "highfalutin" theory, but I am confident that it plays out in practice. I think if I were rewriting what I wrote thirty years ago, I would emphasize more strongly that mediation's central values systematically support not only party self-determination, but also, crucially, party responsibility.

The mediator's posture, then, must be congruent with promoting each of those central values. . . . With characteristic elegance, Larry talks about mediators who are working in public policy contexts. The image portrayed there, of course, is that parties are making decisions that foreclose options both for people not at the table and as well as for members belonging to future generations. If someone bulldozes a particular plot of land, it is hard, if not impossible, to recapture it. Given that substantive context, Larry argues in our *Vermont Law Review* exchange that a mediator should be held accountable for the negotiated outcomes in the ways that he prescribes. But he also claimed that mediators working in other contexts, particularly those who mediated labor-management collective bargaining impasses, did not confront that same challenge. I tried to argue that he was incorrect factually about that claim; I believe that disputes involving labor — management collective bargaining matters, as well as other explosive community disputes, share the feature that the parties' collective decision at a particular moment in time significantly forecloses some (though not all) future possibilities. But that fact, I argued, does not change the core values of the mediator's role, including the duty to be neutral.

. . .

BERNIE MAYER: . . . I think the real question here is about what our intentionality is and what our social responsibility is. In whatever role we play, we have to be clear about our intentions and how we see our responsibilities. And in most mediation structures I've seen, there is room for a lot of variation in how people view their role and responsibility. The key is that mediators are clear and transparent about this.

My specific concern about the way this debate has been framed is two-fold. First, I don't think mediators have the power to affect the outcome in the way you talk about, Larry. It's fine to say we should, but it's unrealistic. What we can do is help design the structure of the interaction. That structure for interaction can have a number of safeguards built in, and then we can implement that structure in a number of ways. Larry talks about the system teeing things up. Well, I think that's exactly the relevance of how the system tees things up — it determines in many ways whether what we are engaged in is a responsible approach to dealing with cases or not. I think some of the most important things we do are not what we do when we are sitting at the table. I think the most important thing that we do to insure a socially responsible outcome is how we design the system to make that happen and to insure that the right parties are at the table and that process is structured so as to give them a meaningful voice.

Second, when we are sitting at the table and we see the system hasn't worked right, then we can intervene in many ways, from within a neutral stance — in other words, we can insure that participants are provided an effective voice and that important issues are not avoided without intentionally trying to benefit one side at the expense of the other.

. . .

LARRY: Let me put a finer point on the kinds of choices that I think mediators have to make, whether in well-structured processes or less well-structured processes. I think most mediators believe that a good process almost always yields a good outcome. At the heart of what we do as mediators is trying to structure a good process — whether we gin it up ourselves or let the system tee it up. But notice, that means we are taking responsibility for a good outcome by ensuring that the process is organized and managed properly. So, if a good process yields a good outcome — if we believe that — then we are obligated to say what we mean by a good outcome.

So, what would a good outcome be in a mediated case? I argue that (1) the outcome must be viewed as fair by the parties; and (2) the process and outcome ought to be as *efficient as possible* — that is the parties ought to think that whatever time and money was spent, was well-spent. Now, I'm not sure that the parties are the only ones who have a right to assess the outcome. The system managers might want to say something about that as well. So a good outcome is fair and efficient, and then Bernie mentions that the result should be stable — we don't want unhappy participants to shun their negotiated commitments. This doesn't mean results can't be revised, but if an outcome is not stable, it probably wasn't a good process because the outcome wasn't one that people were willing to abide by.

Fair, efficient, stable, and now I would suggest a fourth indicator of the quality of a mediated outcome — and that is, it ought to be *wise*. Now what is a wise outcome? In retrospect, you could say that if the parties used the information available to them they probably reached as wise an outcome as they could. What a pity if they reached an outcome that didn't work well because they didn't bother to take account of the information or resources available to them. Fair, efficient, stable, wise — for me, these are the four qualities of a good mediated outcome.

As mediators, we need to be prepared to say what we think a good outcome is. If I take responsibility for a good outcome — or these four qualities of an agreement — then I've got to do something during the process to try to help the parties produce such outcomes. I have to remain impartial, but I can take responsibility in various ways for the management of the process. I can do this without taking sides, but I can make clear my commitment to helping the parties reach a high-quality outcome. I don't think that's a contradiction. I think I can ask questions that cause participants to think about choices they are making and whether those choices will lead to a "high quality" outcome.

. . .

JOSH (interrupting Larry): But, Larry, there is no requirement to be impartial in order for someone to help disputing parties promote a fair outcome that is efficient and wise. . . . So when you say that you, the intervener, need to remain impartial in order to promote "the good outcome," I can challenge that by saying, "no, you, the intervener, do not need to be impartial. You need to be really smart; you need to be savvy in terms of how to facilitate a conversation that yields a good outcome." We don't disagree that a good process generates a good outcome . . . Let me restate my point. On those criteria you cite — fair, efficient, stable, wise — I don't think the intervener being impartial is a necessary condition for effectively serving the parties' goals that fare well on those standards. As a practical matter, it might be prudent to be impartial so people work with you, but there is nothing in principle that requires the mediator, the intervener, to be, in your words, "impartial," and in mine, "neutral," in order to help them reach such outcomes. You and I agree that good process generates good outcomes, where good process reflects just that — it is fair, efficient, and stable; but the standard of "wise" introduces a substantive, not process, criterion — you accept it but I reject it.

Just one final point . . . I understood your earlier comments — both those in the Vermont article and what you said today — to be that one of the real challenges is who the parties are. And if not all the parties — people affected by the outcome — are in the room, you don't have a good process, even though everybody who actually is there does view it as "fair." I'm not sure how —

LARRY (interrupts): Substitute "stakeholders" for "parties."

JOSH: Okay. My question can be stated: *If all the stakeholders are not in the conversation, then is it the mediator's duty — in terms of being responsible for the outcome, accountable for the outcome — that the intervener in some sense represents those interests?*

LARRY: I don't think the neutral can represent those interests. I think that the neutral, in an effort to take responsibility for the quality of the outcome, can do a number of things to help ensure that all the appropriate stakeholding interests are represented, not by representing them but by saying, *Do you think a draft of this agreement ought to be reviewed before it's finalized by a group that hasn't been at the table? Aren't you worried that those groups that have been left at the sidelines might try to block implementation of the agreement? Let's at least give them a chance to review it before you finalize it. Maybe you want someone else sitting in, not in the same role as everyone else, but in some other related role. Maybe you want to make transparent what it is you're doing while you're doing it, so those groups can at least have a say.*

I never imagined the mediator saying: *For the next half hour I'm going to represent a hard-to-represent group that isn't here. Watch me transform myself chameleon-like into that group and speak for them.* That's not what I'm saying. But there are a whole variety of ways in which I can take responsibility for the quality of an outcome without speaking for a missing group: a mediator can ask leading questions, suggest ideas and options, or offer to carry a draft of an agreement to others who are not present and try to incorporate their reactions into a final version of the agreement.

JOSH: So what should a mediator do if a fourteen-year-old single child doesn't want to participate in the mediation of a divorce between her parents, though she will clearly be affected by the outcome?

LARRY: I can suggest that a [guardian ad litem] be appointed for them and I could say to the parents, "Don't you think the interest of your child should at least be discussed here, through eyes other than yours and you have the option of a proxy to represent your child?"

JOSH: And the mother says, "No, I know exactly how my daughter feels."

LARRY: If both of them say that and I say, "Well it's my obligation to try and point this out to you, and if I can't convince you, then I can't convince you." But my responsibility for trying to ensure a fair outcome goes as far as aggressively trying to think of ways to suggest that interests not represented at the table could be represented — not to represent them myself.

. . .

BERNIE: . . . I think it's misleading to say good process equals good outcome. . . .

Instead, I think we should view and articulate our primary purpose in bringing people together as being about helping them have the conversation that they need to have at that time, and to have that conversation go where it has the potential to go. And that's what I want, and my assumption is — and this actually works across many different kinds of disputes that I have been involved with — that if I am so focused on trying to get a good outcome, I will ultimately lose my capacity to help disputants have the kind of engagement they need to have and the result will not be a good outcome. The results of that will be that I will become an officer of the court trying to force an agreement on people that is not necessarily what they think is fair, efficient, stable, and wise — but what the court is advocating for. What really protects us against falling into this trap is remaining clear about what our fundamental ethical obligations are, regardless of the court's desire for us to come up with agreements and outcomes.

Notes and Questions

(1) In *The Neutrality Trap: Disrupting and Connecting for Social Change* (2022), Bernard S. Mayer and Jacqueline Font-Guzman leverage their collective experience as "conflict interveners and social activists" to highlight the tension between neutrality and social activism. They explain: intractable "problems will not simply disappear by reaching an agreement or enacting a new policy. As important as improved relationships, resolved conflicts, and good policies are, they are not the same as changing systems embedded in values, identity, power, and privilege." The following excerpt illustrates the core tension between neutrality and social change:

> When there is a significant difference in power, as between police and an African American community, even well-intended dialogue can easily reinforce the inequality that exists. The process itself tends to have both implicit and explicit rules of engagement that favor the most powerful. For example, the expectations that only one person speak at a time, that the focus be on the future, not the past, and that emotions, particularly anger, be toned down are most congruent with the norms of those in power. As a result, everyone may listen to each other but then return to their relative positions of power and powerlessness, and little will change.

Those of us who organize and conduct these events can easily think that something important has happened, abetted by our commitment to hearing everybody in an open-minded way. But what won't have happened is an effort to genuinely challenge power differentials and the systems that reinforce these. Instead, we may well have misdirected the energies of the disempowered from organizing for change to understanding the privileged — something they are likely to have had considerable experience in doing. We have fallen into the neutrality trap.

... Neutrality, impartiality, objectivity, and independence are values that many of us proclaim as a sign of our professionalism. But these are really the devil's bargain we make to maintain our privileged position in exchange for supporting the status quo. We confuse these with fairness, transparency, competence, moral clarity, and authenticity, which is what the people we work with are most likely to want from us. By substituting neutrality for a commitment to promoting justice and equality, we fall into the neutrality trap.

Mayer and Font-Guzman suggest conflict resolution practitioners cannot maintain neutrality *and* a commitment to social justice. Does their advice apply to mediators as well? If so, how would this work for a mediator in practice?

(2) Transformative mediators (discussed later in this chapter) believe that outcome and process are one and the same — that all process choices affect, or have the potential to affect, outcome. As discussed in Chapter 7, in *Mediation: Embedded Assumptions of Whiteness?*, 22 Cardozo J. Conflict Resol. 453 (2021), Professors Sharon Press and Ellen Deason suggest that a mediator's process-focused choices (tone policing, reframing, agenda setting, maintaining a focus on the future) devalue the experience of underrepresented racial groups. How would Stulberg respond to these arguments?

(3) In *Public Values and Private Justice: A Case for Mediator Accountability*, 4 Geo. J. Legal Ethics 503 (1991), Judith Maute writes that "the extent of mediator accountability for fairness varies by whether or not the mediator is a lawyer, and by whether the parties are independently represented by counsel." Expressing concern about disparities of bargaining power and knowledge, Maute suggests "the mediator must intervene to avoid a patently unfair agreement at odds with the probable outcome of adjudication."

Although a lawyer-mediator may possess general legal knowledge that may suggest to them that the unrepresented disputants are considering settlement terms that would be an unlikely outcome if the dispute were adjudicated in court, how might the lawyer-mediator assure themself during the mediation that their legal assessment is correct? That is, aside from the theoretical concerns that Bush and Stulberg would have with Maute's position, are there practical concerns?

(4) In *Informed Consent in Mediation: A Guiding Principle for Truly Educated Decisionmaking*, 74 Notre Dame L. Rev. 775, 812 (1999),* Jacqueline Nolan-Haley argues for acceptance of a principle of informed consent in mediation that would promote fairness:

> A robust theory of informed consent requires that parties be educated about mediation before they consent to participate in it, that their continued participation and negotiations be voluntary, and that they understand the outcomes to which they agree. Informed consent serves the values of autonomy, human dignity, and efficiency. It guards against coercion, ignorance, and incapacity that can impede the consensual underpinnings of the mediation process.

Nolan-Haley points out that she is not advocating an adversarial model for mediation sessions nor is she suggesting that mediation outcomes approximate likely adjudicated outcomes. Rather, she argues for a "sliding-scale model of informed consent disclosure," where mediators would owe a greater duty of informed consent disclosure to unrepresented parties than to those parties represented by counsel. Recognizing the value of neutrality in mediation, she considers the research of Cobb and Rifkin (*See* Sara Cobb & Janet Rifkin, *Practice and Paradox: Deconstructing Neutrality in Mediation,* 16 Law and Social Inquiry 35 (1991)). and others:

> Perhaps the real question should be: when is absolute neutrality called for and when is a modified approach preferable? I argue that when court programs require unrepresented parties to enter the mediation process, fairness demands that these parties know their legal options before making final decisions in mediation. A modified approach to mediator neutrality permits mediators to employ an *informative* decisionmaking model and give unrepresented parties such information.

Id. at 837.

But how is this legal information to be supplied to the parties? Will the mediator simply make a threshold decision that one or both parties need legal information and then suggest that they consult a lawyer? Although such an approach would be less likely to compromise a mediator's neutrality than having the mediator supply the information, is it realistic to expect that many unrepresented parties will be able to afford lawyers? Can ODR be helpful in this area? Will AI or websites with information provided by the court be able to fill the gaps in order to ensure informed decision making? For example, Michigan's court-sponsored online dispute resolution platform, MI-Resolve, enables parties to engage in asynchronous text-based conversations which engage a trained mediator to see if they can resolve disputes. The platform shares links to sources of legal information for pro se litigants including MichiganLegalHelp.org. Would such a system assist in informed decision making?

D. Mediator Orientations

As mediation and court processes become increasingly intertwined, the orientation of the mediator has been subject to more rigorous scrutiny. Because lawyer-mediators possess substantive legal knowledge and often have considerable litigation experience, there is a temptation to apply this knowledge and experience during the mediation and offer the mediator's personal evaluation of the case. Many have argued that an *evaluative* orientation is inconsistent with a mediator's focus on facilitating communication and therefore a mediator's orientation should be a strictly *facilitative* one. Moreover, as the contemporary practice of mediation has developed, alternative orientations have emerged. In Part 1, we share foundational articles in the facilitative-evaluative debate. In Part 2, we highlight other developed mediation modes or styles: transformative, inclusive, and understanding.

As you read, consider how the following descriptions and arguments for these various orientations are consistent or inconsistent with the mediator *roles* previously discussed.

1. Facilitative & Evaluative Mediation

The original debate comparing the efficacy of facilitative and evaluative mediator orientations was sparked in large part by the publication of the "Riskin Grid." In this foundational article, Leonard Riskin sought to "propose a system for classifying mediator orientations." Riskin's system is based on the answers to two questions: "1. Does the mediator tend to define problems *narrowly* or *broadly*? 2. Does the mediator think she should *evaluate* — make assessments or predictions or proposals for agreements — or *facilitate* the parties' negotiation without evaluating?" Riskin explains this classification scheme in the following excerpt from his longer article on the same subject. Note that Riskin is not advocating for either style, but simply seeking to describe the mediator orientations he observed among practitioners. The subsequent excerpt from Lela Love presents arguments against a mediator embracing an evaluative orientation, claiming that while evaluation might be a service valued by the parties, evaluation is inconsistent with the role and values of a mediator. In the final excerpt, Dwight Golann and Marjorie Aaron argue that mediator evaluation, when used as last resort, has a vital place in the repertoire of mediator techniques.

Understanding Mediators' Orientations, Strategies, and Techniques: A Grid for the Perplexed

1 Harv. Negot. L. Rev. 7, 24–32, 34–38 (1996)*
By Leonard L. Riskin

. . . Most mediators operate from a predominant, presumptive or default orientation (although, as explained later, many mediators move along continuums and among quadrants). For purposes of the following explication of mediator orientations, I will assume that the mediator is acting from such a predominant orientation. For this reason, and for convenience, I will refer to the "evaluative-narrow mediator" rather than the more precise, but more awkward, "mediator operating with an evaluative-narrow approach."

MEDIATOR ORIENTATIONS

Role of Mediator

EVALUATIVE

Problem Definition NARROW	EVALUATIVE NARROW	EVALUATIVE BROAD
	FACILITATIVE NARROW	FACILITATIVE BROAD

Problem Definition BROAD

FACILITATIVE

A mediator employs strategies — plans — to conduct a mediation. And a mediator uses techniques — particular moves or behavior — to effectuate those strategies. Here are selected strategies and techniques that typify each mediation orientation.

1. Evaluative-Narrow

A principal strategy of the evaluative-narrow approach is to help the parties understand the strengths and weaknesses of their positions and the likely outcome of litigation or whatever other process they will use if they do not reach a resolution in mediation. But the evaluative-narrow mediator stresses her own education at least as much as that of the parties. Before the mediation starts, the evaluative-narrow mediator will study relevant documents, such as pleadings, depositions,

---

reports, and mediation briefs. At the outset of the mediation, such a mediator typically will ask the parties to present their cases, which normally means arguing their positions, in a joint session. Subsequently, most mediation activities take place in private caucuses in which the mediator will gather additional information and deploy evaluative techniques, such as the following, which are listed below from the least to the most evaluative.

a. *Assess the strengths and weaknesses of each side's case....*

b. *Predict outcomes of court or other processes....*

c. *Propose position-based compromise agreements....*

d. *Urge or push the parties to settle or to accept a particular settlement proposal or range....*

2. Facilitative-Narrow

The facilitative-narrow mediator shares the evaluative-narrow mediator's general strategy — to educate the parties about the strengths and weaknesses of their claims and the likely consequences of failing to settle. But he employs different techniques to carry out this strategy. He does not use his own assessments, predictions, or proposals. Nor does he apply pressure. He is less likely than the evaluative-narrow mediator to request or to study relevant documents. Instead, believing that the burden of decision-making should rest with the parties, the facilitative-narrow mediator might engage in any of the following activities.

a. *Ask questions....*

b. *Help the parties develop their own narrow proposals....*

c. *Help the parties exchange proposals....*

d. *Help the parties evaluate proposals....*

The facilitative nature of this mediation approach might also produce a degree of education or transformation. The process itself, which encourages the parties to develop their own understandings and outcomes, might educate the parties, or "empower" them by helping them to develop a sense of their own ability to deal with the problems and choices in life. The parties also might acknowledge or empathize with each other's situation. However, in a narrowly-focused mediation, even a facilitative one, the subject matter normally produces fewer opportunities for such developments than does a facilitative-broad mediation.

3. Evaluative-Broad

It is more difficult to describe the strategies and techniques of the evaluative-broad mediator. Mediations conducted with such an orientation vary tremendously in scope, often including many narrow, distributive issues....

In addition, evaluative-broad mediators can be more-or-less evaluative, with the evaluative moves touching all or only some of the issues.

The evaluative-broad mediator's principal strategy is to learn about the circumstances and underlying interests of the parties and other affected individuals or groups, and then to use that knowledge to direct the parties toward an outcome that responds to such interests. To carry out this strategy, the evaluative-broad mediator will employ various techniques, including the following (listed from least to most evaluative).

a. *Educate herself about underlying interests.* . . .

b. *Predict impact (on interests) of not settling.* . . .

c. *Develop and offer broad (interest-based) proposals.* . . .

d. *Urge parties to accept the mediator's or another proposal.* . . .

If the mediator has concluded that the goal of the mediation should include changing the people involved, she might take measures to effectuate that goal, such as appealing to shared values, lecturing, or applying pressure.

4. Facilitative-Broad

The facilitative-broad mediator's principal strategy is to help the participants define the subject matter of the mediation in terms of underlying interests and to help them develop and choose their own solutions that respond to such interests. In addition, many facilitative-broad mediators will help participants find opportunities to educate or change themselves, their institutions, or their communities. To carry out such strategies, the facilitative-broad mediator may use techniques such as the following.

a. *Help parties understand underlying interests.* . . .

b. *Help parties develop and propose broad, interest-based options for settlement.* . . .

c. *Help parties evaluate proposals.* . . .

Figure 3 highlights the principal techniques associated with each orientation, arranged vertically with the most evaluative at the top and the most facilitative at the bottom. The horizontal axis shows the scope of the problems to be addressed, from the narrowest on the left to the broadest on the right.

ROLE OF THE MEDIATOR

Problem Definition NARROW	**Urges/pushes parties** to accept narrow (position-based) settlement **Proposes** narrow (position-based) agreement **Predicts** court or other outcomes **Assesses** strengths and weaknesses of each side's case	**Urges/pushes parties** to accept broad (interest-based) settlement **Develops and proposes** broad (interest-based) agreement **Predicts** impact on interests of not settling **Educates self** about parties' interests
	Helps parties evaluate proposals **Helps parties** develop & exchange narrow (position-based) proposals **Asks** about consequences of not settling **Asks** about likely court outcomes **Asks** about strengths and weaknesses of each side's case	**Helps parties** evaluate proposals **Helps parties** develop & exchange broad (interest-based) proposals **Helps parties** develop options that respond to interests **Helps parties** understand interests

Problem Definition BROAD

Figure 3

D. Movement along the Continuums and Among the Quadrants: Limitations on the Descriptive Capabilities of the Grid

Like a map, the grid has a static quality that limits its utility in depicting the conduct of some mediators.

It is true that most mediators — whether they know it or not — generally conduct mediations with a presumptive or predominant orientation. Usually, this orientation is grounded in the mediator's personality, education, training, and experience. For example, most retired judges tend toward an extremely evaluative-narrow orientation, depicted in the far northwest corner of the grid. Many divorce mediators with backgrounds or strong interests in psychology or counseling — and who serve affluent or well-educated couples — lean toward a facilitative-broad approach. Sometimes, the expectations of a given program dictate an orientation; for example, narrow mediation tends to dominate many public programs with heavy caseloads.

Yet many mediators employ strategies and techniques that make it difficult to fit their practices neatly into a particular quadrant. First, some mediators deliberately try to avoid attachment to a particular orientation. Instead, they emphasize flexibility and attempt to develop their orientation in a given case based on the participants' needs or other circumstances in the mediation.

Second, for a variety of reasons, some mediators who have a predominant orientation do not always behave consistently with it. They occasionally deviate from their presumptive orientation in response to circumstances arising in the course of a mediation. In some cases, this substantially changes the scope of the mediation. A mediator with a facilitative-broad approach handling a personal injury claim, for instance, normally would give parties the opportunity to explore underlying interests. But if the parties showed no inclination in that direction, the mediator probably would move quickly to focus on narrower issues.

In other cases, a mediator might seek to foster her dominant approach using a technique normally associated with another quadrant. Thus, some mediators with predominantly facilitative-broad orientations might provide evaluations in order to achieve specific objectives consistent with their overall approach. [For example,] Frances Butler, who mediates child-custody disputes for a New Jersey court, . . . uses a mixture of facilitative and evaluative techniques in the service of a broad, facilitative agenda: she asks questions (a facilitative technique) to help her understand the situation, then makes proposals (an evaluative technique), and then solicits the parties' input (a facilitative technique) in order to modify the proposals.

A narrow mediator who runs into an impasse might offer the parties a chance to broaden the problem by exploring underlying interests. This might lead to an interest-based agreement that would enable the parties to compromise on the distributive issue as part of a more comprehensive settlement. Similarly, a broad mediator might encourage the parties to narrow their focus if the broad approach seems unlikely to produce a satisfactory outcome.

For these reasons it is often difficult to categorize the orientation, strategies, or techniques of a given mediator in a particular case. . . .

The Top Ten Reasons Why Mediators Should Not Evaluate
24 Fla. St. U. L. Rev. 937, 937–946, 948 (1997)*
By Lela P. Love

. . . The debate over whether mediators should "evaluate" revolves around the confusion over what constitutes evaluation and an "evaluative" mediator.

. . . .

An "evaluative" mediator gives advice, makes assessments, states opinions — including opinions on the likely court outcome, proposes a fair or workable resolution to an issue or the dispute, or presses the parties to accept a particular resolution. The ten reasons that follow demonstrate that those activities are inconsistent with the role of a mediator.

I. The Roles and Related Tasks of Evaluators and Facilitators are at Odds

Evaluating, assessing, and deciding for others is radically different than helping others evaluate, assess, and decide for themselves. Judges, arbitrators, neutral experts, and advisors are evaluators. Their role is to make decisions and give opinions. To do so, they use predetermined criteria to evaluate evidence and arguments presented by adverse parties. The tasks of evaluators include: finding "the facts" by properly weighing evidence; judging credibility and allocating the burden of proof; determining and applying the relevant law, rule, or custom to the particular situation; and making an award or rendering an opinion. The adverse parties have expressly asked the evaluator — judge, arbitrator, or expert — to decide the issue or resolve the conflict.

In contrast, the role of mediators is to assist disputing parties in making their own decisions and evaluating their own situations. A mediator "facilitate[s] communications, promotes understanding, focuses the parties on their interests, and seeks creative problem solving to enable the parties to reach their own agreement."[9] Mediators push disputing parties to question their assumptions, reconsider their positions, and listen to each other's perspectives, stories, and arguments. They urge the parties to consider relevant law, weigh their own values, principles, and priorities, and develop an optimal outcome. In so doing, mediators facilitate evaluation by the parties.

These differences between evaluators and facilitators mean that each uses different skills and techniques, and each requires different competencies, training norms, and ethical guidelines to perform their respective functions. Further, the evaluative tasks of determining facts, applying law or custom, and delivering an opinion not only divert the mediator away from facilitation, but also can compromise the mediator's neutrality — both in actuality and in the eyes of the parties — because the mediator will be favoring one side in his or her judgment.

Endeavors are more likely to succeed when the goal is clear and simple and not at war with other objectives. . . . "No one can serve two masters." Mediators cannot effectively facilitate when they are evaluating.

II. Evaluation Promotes Positioning and Polarization, Which are Antithetical to the Goals of Mediation. . . .

When disputing parties are in the presence of an evaluator — a judge, an arbitrator, or a neutral expert — they act (or should act) differently than they would in the presence of a mediator. With an evaluator, disputants make themselves look as good as possible and their opponent as bad as possible. They do not make offers of compromise or reveal their hand for fear that it weakens the evaluator's perception of the strength of their case. They are in a competitive mind-set seeking to capture the evaluator's favor and win the case.

---

9. John Feerick et al., *Standards of Professional Conduct in Alternative Dispute Resolution*, 1995 J. Disp. Resol. 95 app. at 123.

While adversarial confrontations between parties are helpful to a neutral who must judge credibility and clarify the choices he or she must make, such confrontations are not helpful to collaboration. Adversarial behaviors run counter to the mediator's efforts to move parties towards a different perception of their own situation and of each other. While parties typically enter the mediation process in a hostile and adversarial stance, the mediator seeks to shift them towards a collaborative posture in which they jointly construct a win-win solution. An atmosphere of respectful collaboration is a necessary foundation for creative problem-solving.

III. Ethical Codes Caution Mediators — and Other Neutrals — Against Assuming Additional Roles. . . .

IV. If Mediators Evaluate Legal Claims and Defenses, they Must Be Lawyers; Eliminating Nonlawyers Will Weaken the Field. . . .

V. There are Insufficient Protections Against Incorrect Mediator Evaluations

. . . Even assuming that mediators could be governed by and held to appropriate standards when they evaluate, growing concerns about the quality of justice that disputants receive when they are diverted from courts into private alternative dispute resolution (ADR) processes argue for leaving evaluation to adversarial processes where due process protections are in place. In the courts, disputants can appeal decisions they feel are wrong. In arbitration, disputants pick arbitrators based on the arbitrator's substantive expertise or wisdom and consciously waive the right to appeal.

In mediation, little protection exists from a mediator's inadequately informed opinion. Confidentiality statutes, rules, and agreements keep sessions private. Quasi-judicial immunity in some cases can shield mediators from liability for careless opinions. . . . Mediators are not in the best position to make those sorts of evaluations because, if they are doing their facilitative job, they have not completed the necessary preliminary tasks of an evaluator. Additionally, unless a mediator has separate training as a judge, arbitrator, or neutral evaluator, he or she may not be competent to serve as an evaluator. Service as a mediator does not qualify a mediator to be a judge any more than service as a judge qualifies a judge to mediate.

VI. Evaluation Abounds: The Disputing World Needs Alternative Paradigms. . . .

The processes of litigation, "rent-a-judge," arbitration, early neutral evaluation, and summary jury trial are all available for parties who want opinions or decisions. Evaluative models and service providers abound. We need a genuine alternative to the adversarial paradigm of disputants who fight and a neutral who assesses.

The collaborative paradigm of mediation, in which mediator evaluation does not play a part, offers a dispute resolution process through which parties are taught how to resolve their own disputes, listen to each other differently, broaden their own capacities for understanding and collaboration, and create resolutions that build relationships, generate more harmony, and are "win-win." The lesson, "Give a man a fish and you feed him for a day, teach him to fish and you feed him for a lifetime," highlights the importance of teaching people how to solve their own dilemmas. . . .

VII. Mediator Evaluation Detracts from the Focus on Party Responsibility for Critical Evaluation, Re-evaluation and Creative Problem-Solving. . . .

If Einstein's insight is true that "[t]he significant problems we face today cannot be solved at the same level of thinking we were at when we created them," then we, as a society, are called on to nurture ways to achieve higher levels of thinking and creativity. Mediation is the one dispute resolution process in which the neutral's role is to assist the parties to collaborate creatively and resolve the issues they face.

Frequently, for the individuals, communities, or institutions involved, conflicts represent true crises, holding the potential for doing extreme harm and, at the same time, holding the potential for creative change and restructuring. The mediator's task of elevating the dialogue from recriminations and blame to the generation of possibilities and breakthrough ideas is a task we are just beginning to understand. If we allow mediation and mediators to slip into the comfortable (because it is the norm) adversarial mind-set of evaluation, we kill the turbo-thrust of the jet engine of idea generation. So-called "evaluative mediation" pulls mediation away from creativity and into the adversarial frame. If we are to continue to survive and evolve as a species, we need to nurture the processes that tap our affinity to create and imagine.

VIII. Evaluation Can Stop Negotiation. . . .

IX. A Uniform Understanding of Mediation is Critical to the Development of the Field . . . .

X. Mixed Processes Can be Useful, But Call them What they Are! . . .

Parties sometimes request that neutrals assume a variety of roles. "Mixed processes" abound: med-arb, arb-med, mini-trials, summary jury trials, and mediation and neutral evaluation. These mixed processes can address particular needs of a situation and can be very helpful.

Mediators are not foreclosed from engaging in some other process or helping parties design a mixed process. Whatever the service being provided, however, it should be requested by the parties and accurately labeled. When a process is "mixed" and the neutral has multiple roles, he or she is bound by more than one code of ethics and is charged with separate goals and tasks. A properly labeled process — or, conversely, a label that has a clear meaning — promotes integrity, disputant satisfaction, and uniform practice.

Mediators who regularly give case assessments and expert opinions should continue those practices only if they are requested by the parties, properly advertised, and accurately labeled . . . .

Beyond Abstinence: The Need for Safe, Impartial Evaluation in Mediation

25 Disp. Resol. Mag. 22–25 (2019)*
By Dwight Golann and Marjorie Corman Aaron

For too long there's been enormous division and vigorous debate in our field about the wisdom, value, and ethics of a mediator providing an evaluation of issues involved in a dispute. Most of this debate has concerned a mediator stating how he or she thinks a judge, jury, or arbitrator might rule if a case is adjudicated. Many academics and trainers argue that this kind of evaluation is improper. Some courts prohibit it outright or at least discourage it. Ethical standards waffle on the topic. But many lawyers and parties consistently say they want their mediator to evaluate.

We are concerned that this argument has distracted us from carefully examining the effects of evaluation in mediation practice. We believe that, at least in cases where all parties are represented by lawyers (pro se litigants, we recognize, pose special concerns), everyone involved can benefit from a mediator's evaluation — but only when done well.

A Working Definition

To "evaluate," dictionaries tell us, means to assess, analyze, consider, value, weigh, judge, size up, or form an opinion. Applying this definition, we believe that most mediators evaluate constantly, from the moment of their first contact with a dispute. They assess parties, lawyers, issues, options, and potential avenues for agreement, forming opinions not only about legal issues and likely case outcomes but also about personalities, bargaining tactics, and the conflict's impact on peoples' lives and businesses.

Evaluation, in this broad sense, is essential to a mediator's role. Parties and lawyers don't hire mediators to be "potted plants"; they expect them to use their wisdom, judgment, and experience to facilitate settlement. And mediators act on their opinions, whether expressed or not. Every question or comment by an experienced neutral reflects her assessment of the best next step in the process. Thus, to us, whether mediators should evaluate is not the question. The question instead is how to evaluate effectively. That leads to two related questions: what should mediators do with their evaluative views, and how does what they do affect the participants and the process?

We think mediators handle evaluations in three general ways: they express them directly; suggest them implicitly or "leakily"; or keep them unspoken and hidden. . . .

Direct Evaluation

Because it has been the subject of so much controversy, our analysis starts with and focuses substantially on direct evaluation: a clearly and explicitly communicated analysis or prediction that focuses on legal issues. We understand that direct evaluation can be risky, but we also believe it can be a useful tool in bringing parties to agreement.

First, however, a few clarifications. In our opinion, good evaluation does not include a mediator voicing his personal opinion about what is "right" or "fair" or a "just" outcome in a dispute. This is for two reasons: relevance and impartiality. A mediator's view of fairness or justice is irrelevant because he will not be the one deciding the case if it is adjudicated. More important, once a mediator suggests to a disputant that a claim or defense is less than "just," the listener may see him as biased. Even if a mediator can put his personal viewpoint aside, disputants may not believe he has done so. We understand that some mediators convey their personal views about fairness or justice, but we do not defend the practice.

We think direct evaluation, done well, should be an assessment and prediction about someone else's viewpoint: how a judge, jury, or arbitrator is likely to decide a specific issue or the entire case if it does not settle. Good evaluation, then, is akin to a professional weather forecast, except that the mediator is predicting the atmosphere in a future courtroom or arbitration. Such predictions are relevant because parties almost always see adjudication as their most likely alternative to settlement.

We fail to see how predicting the likely outcome of a trial inevitably compromises a mediator's impartiality. A weather forecaster's prediction of rain on a day chosen for an outing does not make the listener think the meteorologist wants her to get soaked, and listeners understand that. In the same way, a mediator's prediction that a jury may not respond well to a certain fact or argument, if communicated thoughtfully and skillfully, does not make the listener conclude that the mediator is partial to the other side.

We also don't believe that an evaluation diminishes parties' self-determination. Our weather forecaster's prediction of the likelihood of rain doesn't impinge on the family's ability to decide whether to rent a tent for their wedding reception; it simply provides useful information for the planner (or litigant) to consider. If anything, a mediator's offering a neutral view of the value of the parties' likely alternative to agreement may actually enhance their ability to exercise self-determination.

What are the Benefits?

Simply put, a mediator's explicit evaluation can help parties overcome impasses caused by divergent views of the likely outcome in adjudication of a single legal issue or the entire case. . . . But even if a mediator's evaluation doesn't persuade someone to change his assessment entirely, it can infuse uncertainty or reduce confidence that a future adjudicator will see it his way. Sometimes a party recognizes the flaws in his case but hopes to hide them. A mediator's assessment warns him that those flaws can unfortunately still be seen.

A mediator evaluation can also influence the views of individual parties. Lawyers often admit that their efforts to convey a realistic evaluation to a client have fallen on deaf (or at least resistant) ears. When the mediator's evaluation matches the lawyer's, a client may finally see the handwriting on the wall. If a lawyer had avoided raising doubts to a client for fear of being perceived as disloyal or insufficiently zealous, she might use a mediator's evaluation as "cover" to introduce uncomfortable topics. A lawyer might also choose to talk only about best-case outcomes, letting the mediator articulate less pleasant possibilities. Later, after the mediator has left, the lawyer may suggest the client consider the mediator's evaluation, even while maintaining that it's overly pessimistic.

Evaluation can have other useful effects. A nonbinding opinion from a respected person who has listened carefully to arguments can give a litigant the feeling of a "day in court." Given the small proportion of cases that go to formal adjudication, this is as close as most litigants will ever get to traditional justice—and much safer. A neutral opinion can also help a party deflect criticism from a spouse or advisor or get approval from a corporate supervisor, whether or not those individuals are present at mediation.

What about Risks?

No doubt, evaluation is risky. We see it as the "surgery" of mediation, a tool to use carefully and sparingly, to the minimum extent needed, and only when disagreement about legal issues is the barrier blocking agreement. If the barrier is something other than a legal issue—for instance, strong emotions or poor bargaining techniques—offering an evaluation is the equivalent of prescribing antibiotics to cure a viral infection. It's an ineffective treatment that carries the risk of side effects.

The largest, most obvious risk is that a disputant receiving an unfavorable evaluation will then perceive the mediator as aligned with the other side, no longer neutral, and may withhold confidential information and mistrust the mediator's actions from that point on. . . .

A closer look at evaluation reveals other, less often-acknowledged risks. One is that the mediator's prediction of the likelihood of success at trial may not reflect the way the judge or jury will look at it. Unless a specific case—or at least one with similar fact patterns and issues—has been tried many times, no one can know whether a single prediction is right or wrong. Research suggests that non-partisan evaluations are less subject to cognitive distortion and thus more accurate, but this doesn't mean that all mediator forecasts are correct or that every mediator would make the same prediction. Indeed, when one of us asked lawyer-mediators to evaluate likely outcomes in a simulated case, their responses varied widely. No mediator should think his evaluation is the only reasonable one.

Evaluation can also be dangerous if the disputant takes it as a signal that he cannot achieve his goals in a negotiation. This could trigger loss aversion, one of the strongest influences on human decisionmaking. Disputants do not always react to mediators' evaluations with respectful appreciation; often they express denial, disappointment, even anger, and this may trigger strong feelings in the evaluator. Having put forward a thoughtful forecast, the mediator may react defensively to criticism of her work, putting her in opposition to the parties or lawyers — not a place where a mediator should ever be.

A final risk is that mediators will treat evaluation as an end, rather than what it should be: a useful but limited tool to overcome specific obstacles. Even the best evaluation, in other words, should not conclude or unduly narrow the process. It can help get a settlement process moving when it is stalled but should not be used to steer the negotiation toward any particular outcome.

Notes and Questions

(1) In *Decisionmaking in Mediation: The New Old Grid and the New New Grid System*, 79 Notre Dame L. Rev. 1 (2003), Professor Riskin sought to revise the "Riskin Grid", writing

> [B]oth the structure and terminology of the facilitative-evaluative/role-of-the-mediator continuum have caused confusion. . . . [T]he narrow-broad/problem-definition continuum remains useful, even though it may not be capable of describing certain kinds of mediation behaviors, and even though many commentators have ignored or misunderstood it. In addition . . . the grid misses important issues because it: fails to distinguish between the mediator's behaviors with respect to substance and process; has a static quality that ignores both the interactive nature of mediation decisionmaking and the elements of time and persistence; is grounded on the idea of overall mediator orientations — an unrealistic notion that excludes attention to many other issues in mediator behavior, obscures much about what mediators do, and ignores the role and influence of parties.

Riskin's revised grid maintained the "narrow" and "broad" axis, changed the term "facilitative" to "elicitive," and changed the term "evaluative" to "directive." Professor Riskin explains some of his rationale for shifting this language:

> This "New Old Grid" of mediator orientations can better help us understand a range of mediator behaviors by focusing on the extent to which almost any conduct by the mediator directs the mediation process, or the participants, toward a particular procedure or perspective or outcome, on the one hand or, on the other, elicits the parties' perspectives and preferences — and then tries to honor or accommodate them. Thus, it gets much closer to the fundamental nature — and intent and impact — of various kinds of mediator behaviors, especially as they affect party self-determination.

> I do not mean to assert that all elicitive behavior enhances party autonomy and all directive behavior undermines it. Directive mediator behavior almost always impairs party autonomy in the very short run; however, sometimes it also may be essential for fostering party autonomy. For example, a mediator may have to be directive in establishing and enforcing

certain ground rules and pursuing particular lines of inquiry in order to protect one or more of the parties' ability to exercise their influence. Using the terms "directive" and "elicitive" also can help us recognize that mediators can direct (or push) the parties toward particular outcomes through "selective facilitation"—directing discussion of outcomes the mediator favors, while not promoting discussions of outcomes the mediator does not favor—without explicitly evaluating a particular outcome.

Which framing of the Riskin grid more accurately describes the practice of mediation? While Riskin's revised grid is known and taught in the academic community, the facilitative-evaluative dichotomy prevails in the practitioner community. Recent empirical studies, however, use alternative terms, including Riskin's "new" directive-elicitive framework.

(2) Since its initial publication in 1994, the "Riskin grid" has provoked considerable commentary and controversy which continues until today. In addition to Love, Golann and Aaron, others have weighed in. James Stark has argued that "case evaluation, performed competently, has a useful place in certain forms of mediation practice." James Stark, *The Ethics of Mediation Evaluation: Some Troublesome Questions and Tentative Proposals, from an Evaluative Lawyer Mediator*, 38 S. Tex. L. Rev. 769 (1997). John Bickerman takes the position that the parties often want and expect an evaluative mediator: "Without sacrificing neutrality, a mediator's neutral assessment can provide participants with a much-needed reality check. . . . Sophisticated parties ought to have the freedom to choose the mediation style that best suits their needs." John Bickerman, *Evaluative Mediator Responds*, 14 Alternatives to High Cost of Litigation 70, 70 (1996). More recently Donna Erez-Navot suggests "the mediation marketplace, which is directed by lawyer consumers of mediation, have led us to accept diverse mediator orientations (including evaluative ones)." *The Riskin Grid: A Mixed Legacy, in* Discussions in Dispute Resolution 196 (Schneider, Hinshaw, Cole, eds. 2022).

(3) In *In Praise of Party Empowerment—And of Mediator Activism*, 33 Willamette Law Review 501, 503, 532 (1997), Professor Donald T. Weckstein suggests a mediator's evaluation is a form of informed consent which enhances party self-determination. He explains:

> The key to self-determination is informed consent. A disputant who is unaware of relevant facts or law that, if known, would influence that party's decision cannot engage in meaningful self-determination. A mediator generally should encourage parties to seek such information from other sources. However, if a party cannot or will not do so and looks to the mediator for guidance, it should not be considered improper for the mediator to serve as a source of pertinent information. Likewise, if the mediator's style is to offer that information unless the parties decline it, the mediator should be free to do so ethically. Self-determination extends to the disputants' willingness or unwillingness to be exposed to a mediator's educational efforts or evaluations. Accordingly, when consistent with the parties' expectations

and the mediator's qualifications, activist intervention by the mediator should be encouraged rather than condemned. . . .

The decision of whether and how to use this information are determinations for the parties to make. If they choose to ignore it, it will be their intentional choice and not a default made in ignorance. Accordingly, the relevant inquiry should not be *whether* to inform the parties but *how* to inform them.

Do you believe that all parties should have access to a mediator's evaluation if a mediator is competent to give one? What about *pro se* parties?

(4) Does the context of a mediation make a difference? Consider the following scenarios: is evaluation appropriate: a) in court-connected mediation where all parties are represented? b) if the mediator is a non-lawyer working with parties to resolve a neighborhood dispute at a community mediation center? c) when determining payouts for individuals in connection with the Congressionally established September 11th Victim Compensation Fund of 2001 or the privately established Deepwater Horizon Oil Spill Trust?

(5) Reflecting on the Riskin Grid, Professor Alyson Carrel considers the role of technology, inquiring, "will the phrase 'evaluative mediator' become an anachronism with technology advances such as predictive analytics? Predictive analytics rely on vast databases of information to glean trends, gain insights, and predict outcomes. . . . [W]here on the grid would a mediator be placed if she refuses to give an evaluation, but offers parties the use of [artificial intelligence or a technology platform] to receive case insights and evaluation through predictive analytics?" Professor Carrel suggests technology may permit mediators to maintain a facilitative approach while urging the parties to consider the use of technology to secure an evaluation. Alyson Carrel, *Dismantling the "Facilitative/Evaluative" Dichotomy: Reflecting on the Future, in* Discussions in Dispute Resolution 188, 190 (Hinshaw, Schneider, Cole, eds. 2021).

2. Additional Mediation Orientations

This text focuses on the "traditional" mediation orientation taught in law school classrooms, court mediation programs, and community mediation centers — namely, the facilitative, problem-solving, or North American mediation model. Scholars and practitioners alike have developed alternative orientations which — from their perspective — are focused on one or more of mediation's core values or better meet party and community needs and concerns. Set out below is a brief overview of three alternative mediation orientations: transformative, inclusive, and understanding.

a. Transformative Mediation

In *The Promise of Mediation*, co-authored by Robert A. Baruch Bush and Joseph Folger, empowerment and recognition form the basis for a theory of understanding conflict and the role of mediators in helping parties in conflict. A transformative mediation offers the parties opportunities for personal empowerment and fosters parties giving and receiving recognition of each other's interests, concerns, and needs. Bush and Folger distinguish transformative mediation from problem-solving mediation. They argue that the focus of the mediator's activities in a problem-solving mediation are on achieving an outcome that will satisfy the parties rather than providing the parties with opportunities for empowerment and recognition. As you read the following excerpt from *The Promise of Mediation*, consider how the transformative orientation compares to the facilitative or evaluative orientations. Is it consistent with one or both?

The Promise of Mediation: The Transformative Approach to Mediation
45–46, 49–56, 62, 64–72 (2d ed. 2005)*
By Robert A. Baruch Bush & Joseph P. Folger

The Transformative Theory of Conflict

The transformative theory of conflict starts by offering its own answer to the foundational question of what conflict means to the people involved. According to transformative theory, what people find most significant about conflict is not that it frustrates their satisfaction of some right, interest, or pursuit, no matter how important, but that it leads and even forces them to behave toward themselves and others in ways that they find uncomfortable and even repellent. More specifically, it alienates them from their sense of their own strength and their sense of connection to others, thereby disrupting and undermining the interaction between them as human beings. This crisis of deterioration in human interaction is what parties find most affecting, significant—and disturbing—about the experience of conflict.

Negative Conflict Interaction: A Case in Point

The transformative theory starts from the premise that interactional crisis is what conflict means to people. And help in overcoming that crisis is a major part of what parties want from a mediator. . . .

. . . [R]esearch suggests that conflict as a social phenomenon is not only, or primarily, about rights, interests, or power. Although it implicates all of those things, conflict is also, and most importantly, about peoples' interaction with one another as human beings. . . .

The Picture of Negative Conflict Interaction— and the Evidence Behind It

. . . Conflict, along with whatever else it does, affects people's experience both of self and other. First, conflict generates, for almost anyone it touches, a sense of their own *weakness* and incapacity . . . [C]onflict brings a sense of relative weakness, compared with their preconflict state, in their experience of self-efficacy: a sense of lost control over their situation, accompanied by confusion, doubt, uncertainty, and indecisiveness. This overall sense of weakening is something that occurs as a very natural human response to conflict; almost no one is immune to it, regardless of his or her initial "power position." At the very same time, conflict generates a sense of *self-absorption*: compared with before, each party becomes more focused on self alone — more protective of self and more suspicious, hostile, closed, and impervious to the perspective of the other person. In sum, no matter how strong people are, conflict propels them into relative weakness. No matter how considerate of others people are, conflict propels them into self -absorption and self -centeredness.

. . .

[T]he experiences of weakness and self-absorption do not occur independently. Rather, they reinforce each other in a feedback loop: the weaker I feel myself becoming, the more hostile and closed I am toward you; and the more hostile I am toward you, the more you react to me in kind, the weaker I feel, the more hostile and closed I become, and so on. This vicious circle of *disempowerment* and *demonization* is exactly what scholars mean when they talk about *conflict escalation*. The transformative theory looks at it more as *interactional degeneration*. Before conflict begins, whatever the context, parties are engaged in some form of decent, perhaps even loving, human interaction. Then the conflict arises, and propelled by the vicious circle of disempowerment and demonization, what started as a decent interaction spirals down into an interaction that is negative, destructive, alienating, and demonizing, on all sides.

. . . When nations get caught up in that spiral, the outcome is what we've seen all too often in the last decades — war, or even worse than war, if that's possible. For organizations, communities, or families who get caught up in the conflict spiral, the result is the negative transformation of a shared enterprise into an adversarial battle. . . .

What Parties Want from a Mediator: Help in Reversing the Negative Spiral

Taking the transformative view of what conflict entails and means to parties, one is led to a different assumption, compared with other theories of conflict, about what parties want, need, and expect from a mediator. If what bothers parties most about conflict is the interactional degeneration itself, then what they will most want from an intervenor is help in reversing the downward spiral and restoring constructive interaction. Parties may not express this in so many words when they first come to a mediator. More commonly, they explain that what they want is not just agreement but "closure," to get past their bitter conflict experience and "move on" with their lives. However, it should be clear that in order to help parties achieve closure and move on, the mediator's intervention must directly address the interactional crisis itself.

The reason for this conclusion is straightforward: if the negative conflict cycle is not reversed, if parties don't regenerate some sense of their own strength and some degree of understanding of the other, it is unlikely that they can move on and be at peace with themselves, much less each other. In effect, without a change in the conflict interaction between them, parties are left disabled, even if an agreement on concrete issues is reached. The parties' confidence in their own competence to handle life's challenges remains weakened, and their ability to trust others remains compromised. The result can be permanent damage to the parties' ability to function, whether in the family, the workplace, the boardroom, or the community. . . .

From the perspective of transformative theory, reversing the downward spiral is the primary value that mediation offers to parties in conflict. That value goes beyond the dimensions of helping parties reach agreement on disputed issues. With or without the achievement of agreement, the help parties most want, in all types of conflict, involves helping them end the vicious circle of disempowerment, disconnection, and demonization — alienation from both self and others. Because without ending or changing that cycle, the parties cannot move beyond the negative interaction that has entrapped them and cannot escape its crippling effects.

This is transformative theory's answer to the question posed previously: What kind of help do people want from a mediator? As transformative theory sees it, with solid support from research on conflict, parties who come to mediators are looking for — and valuing — more than an efficient way to reach agreements on specific issues. They are looking for a way to change and transform their destructive conflict interaction into a more positive one, to the greatest degree possible, so that they can move on with their lives constructively, whether together or apart. . . .

The Theory of Mediation as Conflict Transformation

. . . [T]ransformative mediation can best be understood as a process of *conflict transformation* — that is, changing the quality of conflict interaction. In the transformative mediation process, parties can recapture their sense of competence and connection, reverse the negative conflict cycle, reestablish a constructive (or at least neutral) interaction, and move forward on a positive footing, with the mediator's help.

Party Capacity for Conflict Transformation: Human Nature and Capacity

. . . The critical resource in conflict transformation is the parties' own basic humanity — their essential strength, decency, and compassion, as human beings. As discussed earlier, the transformative theory of conflict recognizes that conflict tends to escalate as interaction degenerates, because of the susceptibility we have as human beings to experience weakness and self-absorption in the face of sudden challenge.

However, the theory also posits, based on what many call a *relational theory* of human nature, that human beings have inherent capacities for *strength* (agency or autonomy) and *responsiveness* (connection or understanding) and an inherent *social* or *moral impulse* that activates these capacities when people are challenged by negative conflict, working to counteract the tendencies to weakness and self-absorption. . . . The transformative theory asserts that when these capacities are activated, the conflict spiral can reverse and interaction can regenerate, even without the presence of a mediator as intervenor. In fact, the same research that documents the negative conflict cycle also documents the power of the human capacities for strength and understanding to operate in the face of challenge and conflict, and ultimately to transform conflict interaction. . . .

CHANGING CONFLICT INTERACTION

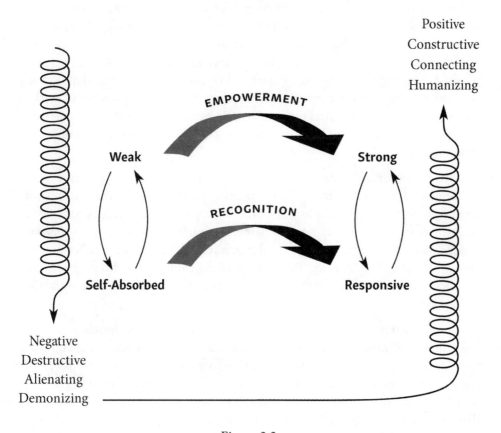

Figure 2.2

Figure 2.2 expands the picture presented earlier and illustrates this positive potential of conflict interaction. It is true, as we have seen with hundreds of parties in all of the different contexts that we've worked in, that people in conflict tend to find themselves falling into the negative cycle of weakness and self-absorption. But it is equally true that people do not necessarily remain caught in that cycle. Conflict is not static. It is an emergent, dynamic phenomenon, in which parties can — and do — move and shift in remarkable ways, even when no third party is involved. They move out of weakness, becoming calmer, clearer, more confident, more articulate, and more decisive — in general, *shifting from weakness to strength*. They move away from self-absorption, becoming more attentive, open, trusting, and understanding of the other party — in general, *shifting from self-centeredness* to *responsiveness to other.* Just as studies document conflict's negative impacts and the downward conflict spiral, they also document the dynamics of these positive shifts and the upward, regenerative spiral they engender.

The arrows moving from left to right in Figure 2.2 represent these shifts: the movements parties make from weakness to strength and from self-absorption to understanding of one another. In transformative theory, these dynamic shifts are called *empowerment* and *recognition.* Moreover, as the figure suggests, there is also a reinforcing feedback effect on this side of the picture. The stronger I become, the more open I am to you. The more open I am to you, the stronger you feel, the more open you become to me, and the stronger I feel. Indeed, the more open I become to you, the stronger I feel in myself, simply because I'm more open; that is, openness not only requires but creates a sense of strength, of magnanimity. So there is also a circling between strength and responsiveness once they begin to emerge. But this is not a vicious circle, it is a "virtuous circle" — a virtuous circle of conflict transformation.

Why conflict transformation? Because as the parties make empowerment and recognition shifts, and as those shifts gradually reinforce in a virtuous circle, the interaction as a whole begins to transform and regenerate. It changes back from a negative, destructive, alienating, and demonizing interaction to one that becomes positive, constructive, connecting, and humanizing, even while conflict and disagreement are still continuing. This reversal of the conflict cycle from negative and destructive to positive and constructive is what the spiral line ascending at the right of Figure 2.2 represents.

The keys to this transformation of conflict interaction are the empowerment and recognition shifts that the parties themselves make. No matter how small and seemingly insignificant, as these shifts continue and accumulate, they can transform the entire interaction. Is it hard for those shifts to occur? It most certainly is, especially for parties who have been overcome by the sense of weakness and self-absorption that conflict first brings. It's hard, but it's eminently possible.

. . .

The Role of the Mediator in Conflict Transformation: A Case in Point

Mediators provide important help and support for the small but critical shifts by each party, from weakness to strength and from self-absorption to understanding....

[T]he mediator . . . offer[s] specific forms of support that help the parties make empowerment and recognition shifts, when and as they choose, and thereby change the quality of their conflict interaction. This is perhaps the central claim of the transformative theory — that mediators' interventions can help parties transform their conflict interaction....

Mediation as Conflict Transformation: Definitions and Guiding Principles

The previous discussion brings us to the definition of mediation itself, and the mediator's role, in the transformative model. Both of these definitions differ markedly from the normal definitions found in training materials and practice literature — in which mediation is usually defined as a process in which a neutral third party helps the parties to reach a mutually acceptable resolution in some or all of the issues in dispute, and the mediator's role is defined as establishing ground rules, defining issues, establishing an agenda, generating options, and ultimately persuading the parties to accept terms of agreement....

By contrast, in the transformative model:

- Mediation is defined as a process in which a third party works with parties in conflict to help them change the quality of their conflict interaction from negative and destructive to positive and constructive, as they explore and discuss issues and possibilities for resolution.

- The mediator's role is to help the parties make positive interactional shifts (empowerment and recognition shifts) by supporting the exercise of their capacities for strength and responsiveness, through their deliberation, decision-making, communication, perspective taking, and other party activities.

- The mediator's primary goals are (1) to support empowerment shifts, by supporting — but never supplanting — each party's deliberation and decision-making, at every point in the session where choices arise (regarding either process or outcome) and (2) to support recognition shifts, by encouraging and supporting — but never forcing — each party's freely chosen efforts to achieve new understandings of the other's perspective.

[I]t is important to introduce here a few important principles that should guide the mediator in supporting empowerment and recognition shifts — all of which grow out of a proper understanding of the dynamics through which these shifts occur.

First, these are shifts that the parties, and the parties alone, can make. No mediator can "get" parties to shift out of weakness or self-absorption, nor should he try. Parties gain strength and openness by making decisions by and for themselves, in their own way and at their own pace. A mediator who tries to "get" shifts to happen actually impedes this process by removing control of the interaction from the parties' hands. In other words, this mediator violates the defined goal of supporting empowerment by *supplanting* party decision-making.

Second, the mediator should expect that parties do not normally begin to shift out of self-absorption until they have first shifted out of weakness and gained strength in some degree. Simply put, people are likely to extend themselves to others when they are still feeling vulnerable and unstable. Empowerment shifts are therefore usually the first to occur, as the desire and capacity for strength reasserts itself, and supporting them is where the mediator's help is likely needed first. When such shifts do occur, however, they are often followed quickly by recognition shifts, as the desire and capacity for connection reasserts itself. Thus gains in strength often lead directly and quickly to gains in responsiveness. . . .

Third, even though there is likely to be a dynamic interplay of empowerment and recognition, the move toward conflict transformation is unlikely to be smooth and even. Rather, empowerment and recognition shifts are often followed by retreats back into weakness and self-absorption, as the interaction reaches new or deeper levels; and the retreats are then followed by new shifts into strength and openness, and so on. In pursuing the goal of supporting shifts, the mediator has to be prepared for this back and forth, in order to follow along and be ready to provide support for new shifts as the opportunities for them arise. Ultimately, the cycling shifts and retreats tend to move forward, and the overall interaction changes in quality from negative to positive — but great patience is required of the mediator in *allowing* that movement rather than trying to "move" the parties forward.

Fourth, even though the mediator's job is to support empowerment and recognition shifts, the transformative model does not ignore the significance of resolving specific issues. Rather, it assumes that if mediators do the job just described, the parties themselves will likely make positive changes in their interaction and find acceptable terms of resolution for themselves where such terms genuinely exist. Consider the strong logic of this claim: if empowerment and recognition shifts occur, and as a result the parties are interacting with clarity and confidence in themselves (strength) and with openness and understanding toward each other (responsiveness), the likelihood is very high that they will succeed in finding and agreeing on solutions to specific problems, without the need for the mediator to do that for them. More important, they will have reversed the negative conflict spiral and will have begun to reestablish a positive mode of interaction that allows them to move forward on a different footing, both while and after specific issues are resolved and even if they cannot be resolved. . . .

Finally, it is important to point out that to focus on and successfully pursue the goal of supporting interactional shifts, two fundamental things are required of the mediator. . . . The first requirement is that the mediator never lose sight of the overall point of his or her mission: to help the parties transform their conflict interaction from destructive and demonizing to positive and humanizing. Maintaining this clear perspective is not all that easy in a professional culture that generally views attainment of agreement or settlement as all important. One thing that can help is to have a firm mental anchor that keeps the mediator on course. . . .

The other requirement is a deep acceptance of the premises about human motivation and capacity that constitute the ultimate foundation of the transformative theory. It will be very difficult for a mediator to stop trying to get the parties to make shifts, unless the mediator is firmly convinced that doing so is not only impossible but *unnecessary* — because the parties have both the desire and the capacity to make those shifts for themselves. Indeed certain hallmarks of transformative practice show how a transformative mediator's approach reflects the premises about human nature that underlie the model, including these: leaving responsibility for outcomes with the parties, refusing to be judgmental about the parties' views and decisions, and taking an optimistic view of the parties' competence and motives. . . .

Holding in mind clearly both the picture of the conflict transformation mission and the premises about human nature that underlie it, the mediator can steer clear of a few serious missteps that are easy to make. First, she is reminded that empowerment is independent of any particular outcome of the mediation. If a party has used the session to collect herself, examine options, deliberate, and decide on a course of action, significant empowerment shifts have occurred, regardless of the outcome. Whether the outcome is a settlement that the mediator finds fair and optimal or unfair or even stupid, or a decision not to settle at all, the goal of supporting empowerment shifts has been achieved. And as a result, the party has gained increased strength of self from the process of self-awareness and self-determination enacted in the mediation session.

So even if a mediator is tempted to think, "Perhaps steering the party to what I know is a better outcome is really more empowering," the clear understanding of empowerment as a shift from weakness to strength reminds the mediator that even a "poor outcome" produced by the party's own process of reflection and choice strengthens the self more than a "good outcome" induced by the mediator's directiveness or imposition. That is, such "good outcomes" do not engender strength of self, unless accompanied by the process of empowerment. Solving problems *for* parties is not transformative mediation, because it fails to support — and probably undermines — genuine party empowerment. It is the concrete steps toward strengthening the self within the session that constitute empowerment, not the nature of the outcome or solution.

In addition, we put "good outcome" in quotation marks in the foregoing discussion, because even beyond the empowerment effects of the process, the quality of an outcome must itself be measured not only by its material terms but also by the process through which it was reached. Outcomes that are reached as a result of party shifts toward greater clarity, confidence, openness, and understanding are likely to have more meaning and significance for parties than outcomes generated by mediator directiveness, however well-meant. . . .

b. Inclusive Mediation

In the mid-1990s, the Community Mediation Program (in urban Baltimore, Maryland) led the development of the "inclusive mediation" model in collaboration with other community mediation programs and community members. With the idea that "community members should identify and bring conflicts to light, not bury them in bureaucracies," inclusive mediation was designed to include "all participants' ideas and experiences, in whatever messy, real form they take" while "working on understanding those ideas and experiences in a deeper way" in order to build "a lasting resolution to conflict."

Inclusive mediators follow a five-step process in a direct "linear" fashion: 1) explaining mediation; 2) listening; 3) listing topics; 4) developing solutions; and 5) agreement writing. As you review the following excerpt, consider what it means to be a "radically inclusive" mediator. While some models allow for a flexible approach in executing the stages of mediation, the inclusive mediation model urges co-mediators to strictly follow this sequence.

Defining Inclusive Mediation: Theory, Practice, and Research

37 Conflict Resol. Q. 305, 306-307, 309-311, 323 (2020)*
By Caroline Harmon-Darrow, Lorig Charkoudian, Tracee Ford,
Michele Ennis & Erricka Bridgeford

Like the alternative dispute resolution movement generally, Inclusive mediation is rooted in conflict theory. . . . [C]onflict theory held, variously, that conflict was itself a neutral force, which could cause positive (*e.g.*, social change . . .) or negative (*e.g.*, violence) results, through cooperation or competition. . . .

Like the community mediation movement generally, Inclusive mediation has its roots in principles of community justice, where conflict belongs to the people and communities involved, not to an impersonal state. This model held that community members should identify and bring conflicts to light, not bury them in bureaucracies. Police, courts and corrections were not being overburdened, they were being misused to handle many issues that were between neighbors, coworkers, family members. Victims were erased in this system, both as actors, and as recipients of restitution, as in ancient systems of justice. . . . [T]hrough the community mediation movement . . . self-determined communities are empowered to resolve their own disputes through conflict resolution sessions facilitated by community members. . . .

The practice of Inclusive mediation is deeply rooted in community mediation structures and values. In many ways the macro-level core values of the community mediation delivery system are borne out on the micro-level at the mediation table through Inclusive mediation. . . . Those values have long included a radical inclusion of any person, place, time, or problem.

Community mediation and the Inclusive mediation model are also closely aligned with theories of collective efficacy and neighborhood cohesion as protective factors against crime and blight. . . . Out of the community mediation movement's roots in conflict theory, community justice theory, and collective efficacy theory, the

---

development of Inclusive mediation has been a process of bringing these core values to the mediation table through adjustments to mediation process and mediator skills.

Inclusive mediation holds that including all participants' ideas and experiences, in whatever messy, real form they take, and working on understanding those ideas and experiences in a deeper way, has the best chance of building a lasting resolution to conflict. Mediators practice radical inclusion of all ideas and forms of expression. In listening to stories about the past, this means mediators do not establish any communication guidelines, creating space for insults, screaming and cursing to occur, if needed. Inclusive mediators will hear cutting insults and reflect back the emotion and fury in it, but also the positive value that is not being fulfilled for that person. In brainstorming about solutions in the future, radical inclusion means that all ideas, the soberly considered, the outlandish, and the insulting, are given equal attention by the mediators, without filtering or editing. Illegal ideas and plans are also treated without judgment by Inclusive mediators. Child abuse, abuse of a vulnerable adult, and credible threat of future bodily harm are exceptions to confidentiality, and Inclusive mediators are scanning for whether participants feel they can meet without fear of retaliation, but beyond those ethical boundaries, illegal ideas are not excluded from Inclusive mediations. This is critical to the effort to uphold participant self-determination, and to the overall effort to apply mediation to resolve social problems such as violence, since the most dangerous conflicts that need peace may have some illegal aspects. Inclusive mediators are radically accepting of participants, greeting them exactly where they are, and doing all they can to build understanding at the table.

> Inclusive Mediation Framework: The goal of inclusive mediation is to support the participants in having difficult conversations and to guide a problem-solving process to develop solutions that meet everyone's needs, with all content decisions made by the participants. . . . Inclusive mediators would use listening, reflecting, and some summarizing [techniques], and do not use reframing, providing information, making suggestions, or persuading strategies.

To further define Inclusive mediation, what follows is a clear description of what Inclusive mediators do, as a rule. While much of this has evolved from facilitative practice, significant changes have been made such that Inclusive mediation can be considered a distinct approach.

Inclusive mediators are devoted to the use of joint session in mediation, and many have never used a private session, or caucus in two decades of practice. First, because communication and understanding are the core values of Inclusive mediation, it is only natural that Inclusive mediators would protect joint session as the norm. . . . Second, secrets and side conversations, and all the anxiety and bitterness they can engender, were often characteristics of the interpersonal conflicts being mediated. . . . Third, private sessions, and the confidentiality offered as they begin, can bring out new information that mediators may not share in the joint session (some of which might create an ethical quandary for a mediator). . . . Finally, when information is shared in private session, the mediator then has the power and responsibility to interpret the information, determine whether it should influence the direction the mediation takes, and decide what is shared back in the joint session, all of which should be choices made by participants in mediation.

Co-mediation is another defining practice of Inclusive mediators, for a number of philosophical and practical reasons. First, if mediators are being radically inclusive of all participants, ideas, and all types of communication, and foregoing communication guidelines, two mediators are needed to hear all views, keep pace, and capture all topics to be resolved. Second, in the solutions stage, all ideas are written on the board in real time, with no editing or filtering by mediators (as described below in greater detail). Depending on the nature of the ideas, number of participants, and level of adversarial thinking that still remains at the table, ideas may come very quickly, and two mediators are needed to catch all of them. Third, Inclusive mediation is happening in a community mediation setting where demographic matching of mediators and participants is known to be effective and is a major priority. Matching the race of the mediator and participant, for example, has been shown to increase participants' perception that mediators listened without judgment, and their sense of control of the conflict; as well as positive case outcomes in court-referred mediation. Co-mediation allows for this to occur to a much greater degree. Fourth, co-mediation is essential to the practice of Inclusive mediation because it provides a framework for continuous improvement and quality control in this high-demand, high-skill practice. Inclusive mediators in Maryland have designed a system of mutual support, structured feedback, basic training, apprenticeship, in-service training, advanced training, performance-based evaluation, and more to develop excellence. Most critical in that list is the 30 min[utes] of structured feedback that all Inclusive mediators give each other after every mediation session, only possible due to co-mediation. Finally, co-mediation allows mediators to model collaboration and facilitate transparently, increasing the capacity-building potential of mediation, so that its mediation table strategies can be used later at the kitchen table.

Case Vignettes by Michele Ennis. #1: Parenting Plan

". . . There were two parents who had been married and were going through the process of divorce. We were handling the two mediations separately, the divorce and the parenting plan. We had let people know that we were going to write all the possible ideas down, that they could be as creative as they like, and that there would be time later to evaluate those ideas. As we were capturing ideas, there was concern that had come up repeatedly from one of the participants about the possibility of the other one becoming involved with someone else. We had reflected those concerns consistently, and ultimately, they had chosen to shift their focus back to the parenting plan. However, it was painful, so there were times that it would still come back up. So we were in the throes of the brainstorm, and one of the participants looked at the other and said 'I know you're doing it, I heard that your vehicle was at her house, why would it be there at 2:00 in the morning? Just tell me, just tell me the truth!'

And so I wrote 'Jim tells Ashley the truth.' Then Jim turns to Ashley and says 'I am not doing it, I swear to God I can wait, I can wait the year. I tell you what: you can cut my dick off and put it in a Ziploc bag, and put it in the freezer for all I care, and I'll get it reattached in a year. I can wait the year.' And I captured each of those: 'Ashley cuts Jim's dick off. Ashley puts Jim's dick in a Ziploc bag. Ashley puts the dick in the freezer. Jim has his dick reattached in one year. Jim waits a year.' As I read through them, the participants were aghast, and looked at one another, and said 'she really is gonna write everything absolutely everything up there! She's crazy! We've gotta get serious. Alright, we need to focus.' So then there was this amazing moment of honoring their self-determination, honoring the process, when we're saying that we're going to be non-judgmental, and we're going to capture all of the ideas and we fulfill all of those ethical commitments. It also meant honoring that when people are ready to get serious and shift their focus, they will. Not as a result of being judged or shamed, or policed by us as mediators, who've ethically made a commitment not to do so, but because they're concerned about their own productivity, or efficiency, but they also get to express whatever they need to express. The shift and gift of this process was clear to all of us."

c. Understanding-Based Mediation

Another approach to mediation is the understanding-based mediation orientation. This orientation was developed by Gary Friedman and Jack Himmelstein and set out in detail in their book, *Challenging Conflict Mediation Through Understanding* (2008). Understanding-based mediation focuses on supporting the development of parties' increased understanding of the situation and resolving the conflict together. As you read the following article excerpt, consider the positive and negative impacts of not using caucuses during mediation, as was also discussed in the inclusive mediation model.

Resolving Conflict Together: The Understanding-Based Model of Mediation

2006 J. Disp. Resol. 523, 524–526, 553 (2006)*
By Gary Friedman & Jack Himmelstein

Four interacting principles guide this work:

1. Developing Understanding: The overarching goal of this approach to mediation is to resolve conflict through understanding. Deeper understanding by the parties of their own and each other's perspectives, priorities, and concerns enables them to work through their conflict together. With an enhanced understanding of the whole situation, the parties are able to shape creative and mutually rewarding solutions that reflect their personal, business, and economic interests.

We therefore rely heavily on the power of understanding rather than the power of coercion or persuasion to drive the mediation process. We want everything to be understood, from how we will work together, to the true nature of the conflict in which the parties are enmeshed, where it came from, how it grew, and how they might free themselves from it. We believe the parties should understand the legal implications of their case, but that the law should not usurp or direct our mediation. We put as much weight on the personal, practical, or business related aspects of any conflict as on the legal aspect. In finding a resolution, we want the parties to recognize what is important to them in the dispute, and to understand what is important to the other side. We strive for a resolution to satisfy both.

2. Going Underneath the Problem: Experience has shown us that conflicts are best resolved by uncovering what lies underneath them. Conflict is rarely just about money, or who did what to whom. It also has subjective dimensions: the beliefs and assumptions of the individuals caught in its grasp, their feelings, such as anger and fear, the need to assign blame, and the desire for self-justification. There are also assumptions about the nature of conflict itself, which support the conflict and keep it going — like the theory of the exclusivity of right and wrong. And there are ideas about how conflicts must be resolved, such as the belief that the other person must change his position or that an authoritative third party must decide the outcome.

We need breadth and depth of understanding to hope to break out of such a complex and multilayered situation, what we call a "Conflict Trap." Repeatedly, we find that the basis for resolution comes from discovering together with the parties what lies at the very heart of their dispute, which is often a surprise to the parties, and which often has a profound effect on their work together.

3. Party Responsibility: This approach is also grounded in the simple premise that the person in the best position to determine the wisest solution to a dispute is not a third party, whether a court or judge or mediator, but the individuals who created and are living the problem. Therefore, we ask the disputants to assume the primary responsibility for working things through, and we ask that they work things through together. As we like to think about it: Let the parties own their conflict.

4. Working Together: When we promote working together, we mean that all meetings with the mediator occur with all parties present (including lawyers if they have a role). There is no caucusing, no shuttling back and forth; no secrets to keep from one party or the other; and no private meetings, except for those between the parties and their counsel. Instead of being responsible for fashioning an acceptable solution, the mediator's job is to enable the parties to reach a mutually agreeable solution together.

We believe the impulse to work through conflict together is a natural part of the human condition, though it may be nascent, buried, or blocked. It is hardly recognized in the legal community, but we have seen it, waiting to be tapped and given room for expression. We have seen it succeed for many thousands of individuals and organizations . . . .

B. Parties' Responsibility and Non-Caucus Approach

. . .

Many other approaches to mediation recommend that the mediator shuttle back and forth between the parties (caucusing), gaining information that he or she holds confidential. Our central problem with caucusing is that the mediator ends up with the fullest picture of the problem and is therefore in the best position to solve it. The mediator, armed with that fuller view, can readily urge or manipulate the parties to the end he or she shapes. The emphasis here, in contrast, is on understanding and voluntariness as the basis for resolving the conflict rather than persuasion or coercion.

We view the mediator's role in the Understanding-Based Model as assisting the parties to gain sufficient understanding of their own and each other's perspective so as to be able to decide together how to resolve their dispute. The parties not only know first hand everything that transpires, but they have control over fashioning an outcome that will work for both. They also participate with the mediator (and counsel) in designing a process by which they can honor what they each value and help them reach a result that reflects what is important to both of them. As mediators, our goal is to support the parties in working through their conflict together, in ways that respect their differing perspectives, needs, and interests, as well as their common goals.

To work in this way is challenging for both the mediator and the parties. The parties' motivation and willingness to work together is critical to the success of this approach. Mediators often assume that the parties (and their counsel) simply do not want to work together, and therefore keep the parties apart. In our experience, many parties (and counsel) simply accept that they will not work together and that the mediator will be responsible for crafting the solution. But once educated about how staying in the same room might be valuable, many are motivated to do so. If the parties (and the mediator) are willing, working together throughout can be as rewarding as it is demanding.

C. Role of Law and Lawyers

. . . [I]n this model, we welcome lawyers' participation, and we include the law. But we do not assume that the parties will or should rely solely or primarily on the law. Rather, the importance the parties give to the law is up to them. Our goals are: 1) to educate the parties about the law and possible legal outcomes, and 2) to support their freedom to fashion their own creative solutions that may differ from what a court might decide. In this way, the parties learn that they can together reach agreements that respond to both their individual interests and their common goals while also being well informed about their legal rights and the judicial alternatives to a mediated settlement.

. . .

Through all of the above, mediators must maintain bifocal vision, with one eye on content and one eye on the impact that the legal conversation is having on the parties. Is it helping or not? Is the law "party-size?" Are the parties confused, overwhelmed, or frustrated? Are they losing focus on what is important to them that may be embodied in other reference points than law? Are they surrendering their own perspectives and responsibility to the lawyers or to the law? We tell by watching the parties' reactions, listening to their concerns, and inquiring of the parties with the shared goal of increasing their understanding. . . .

Notes and Questions

(1) The practice of transformative mediation gained heightened prominence in 1994 when the United States Postal Service (then the world's largest employer) adopted the transformative mediation model for its REDRESS (Resolve Employment Disputes Reach Equitable Solutions Swiftly) program, an agency initiative that provided postal service employees the opportunity to use mediation to address disputes among co-workers as an alternative to using the Equal Employment Opportunity (EEO) complaint process. In *Upstream Effects from Mediation of Workplace Disputes: Some Preliminary Evidence from the USPS*, 48 Lab. L.J. 601 (1997), Jonathan F. Anderson and Lisa Bingham reported the findings of their preliminary study of the use of the REDRESS program in three pilot cities: "Ninety-two percent of supervisors and 41% of employees experienced recognition of the other's perspective. Over two-thirds of all participants felt increased empowerment over their situation. There is evidence that mediation is having a transformative effect on participants." For other commentary and studies of the REDRESS program, see Antes, Folger & Della Noce, *Transforming Conflict Interactions in the Workplace: Documented Effects of the USPS REDRESS (TM) Program*, 18 Hofstra Lab. & Emp. L.J. 429 (2001); Bingham, Kim & Raines, *Exploring the Role of Representation at the USPS*, 17 Ohio St. J. on Disp. Resol. 341 (2002).

(2) In inclusive mediation, the mediators explicitly use the co-mediation model in order to allow for demographic matching between mediators and parties. In the foundational quantitative study conducted in New Mexico in 1996 comparing by gender and race the parties' experiences of having their Small Claims Court cases either adjudicated or mediated, Gary LaFree and Christine Rack found evidence of "ethnic and gender disparity in the treatment of minority claimants in mediation. Specifically, both minority male and female claimants received significant lower [monetary outcomes]," a disparity that "was only present in cases mediated by at least one Anglo mediator." Gary LaFree & Christine Rack, *The Effects of Participants' Ethnicity and Gender on Monetary Outcomes in Mediated and Adjudicated Civil Cases*, 30 L. & Soc. Rev. 767, 789 (1996).

In *Fairness, understanding, and satisfaction: Impact of mediator and participant race and gender on participants' perception of mediation*, Conflict Resol. Q., 23–52 (2010, Fall, Vol. 28, Issue 1), Lorig Charkoudian and E.K. Wayne found that "failing to match disputants and mediators by gender has negative effects on mediation satisfaction measures and that those effects increase when the mediator's gender also matches that of the other participant. In contrast, failure to match by racial or ethnic group has little effect, but when an unmatched participant faces both an opposing participant and a mediator who share a racial or ethnic identification, mediation satisfaction decreases in several respects."

How should these finding affect a mediator's planning in a particular case? In a court connected program where mediators are assigned to cases with no input from the parties, what responsibility should the program have with respect to the recruitment and assignment of mediators who match the racial, religious, or socio-economic demographics of their parties?

(3) In what types of conflict do you think transformative, inclusive, and under-standing, mediation would be most effective? How do you think transformative, inclusive, and understanding mediation address power imbalances?

(4) Other mediation orientations have been suggested by scholars and practition-ers. Some might be characterized as hybrids. In *Adapting Mediation to What Users Want*, 45 Md. B.J. 55 (2012), John Bickerman introduces an orientation he labels *analytical mediation*. In this orientation "the mediator adjusts his or her style based on needs of the parties." And the mediator "uses the style best suited to the dispute at each moment of the process." The style of mediation "should fit the circumstance of the moment and adapt as the circumstances change."

(5) In *Real Mediation Systems to Help Parties and Mediators Achieve Their Goals*, 24 Cardozo J. Conflict Resol. 347, 358–59 (2023), Professor John Lande suggests that mediators should replace the traditional models of mediation (facilitative, evalua-tive, transformative and others) with dispute system design ("DSD").

> ... [I]ndividuals and small practice groups also can use DSD principles and techniques to improve their case management and dispute resolu-tion procedures. A DSD framework provides a much more comprehensive understanding of mediation than the traditional theoretical models of mediation, which generally focus only on handling the ultimate issues in dispute during mediation sessions. Mediators and mediation programs reg-ularly perform many other significant tasks that are completely independent of traditional theories. . . .
>
> One can think of mediation systems as involving the combination of mediators' actions before, during, and after mediation sessions. Rather than deciding how to mediate every new case from scratch, mediators develop systems of default procedures that they adapt to fit the parties, issues, and circumstances of each case. These systems include routine procedures and strategies for dealing with challenging situations. Some mediators engage in pre-session activities to tailor the mediation process for each case. This may include educating parties about the process, soliciting submission of documents, and discussing specific aspects of the dispute. During media-tion sessions, mediators vary in the extent that they use joint opening ses-sions or caucuses, the focus of their questions (such as about expected court results and/or parties' intangible interests), role of parties (which may vary

depending on whether they are represented by lawyers), use of technological tools, seating arrangements, and even lunch breaks, among many other things. After mediation sessions, mediators may read relevant publications, take additional training, attend continuing education programs, reflect on their experiences, and plan how they might improve their techniques in future cases.

Is your style of mediation flexible to meet party needs and expectations or it is tailored to each meditation session? Do you think that dispute system design more accurately addresses the approaches to mediation than the formulaic styles posed by the Riskin Grid? For more on dispute system design, see Lisa Blomgren Amsler et al., Dispute System Design: Preventing, Managing and Resolving Conflict (2020), and Nancy H. Rogers et al., Designing Systems and Processes for Managing Disputes (2d ed., 2019).

(6) Donna Shestowsky's recent empirical work suggests that parties are wholly unaware of the ADR options that are available to them. "Litigants from three state courts were asked whether their court offered mediation or arbitration. Although all litigants had cases that were eligible for both procedures through their court, less than one-third of litigants correctly reported that their court offered either procedure. Represented litigants were not significantly more likely to know about their court's programs than their unrepresented counterparts." See Donna Shestowsky, *When Ignorance is Not Bliss: An Empirical Study of Litigants' Awareness of Court-Sponsored Alternative Dispute Resolution Programs*, 22 Harv. Negot. L. Rev. 189 (2017).

Given that parties know little about mediation generally, what information about the style of mediation should the parties have in advance of a mediation session? How should a mediator convey this information? In pre-mediation conversations? . . . during an opening statement? . . . at various points during the process? . . . or all of the above? If you are representing a client in an upcoming mediation, what questions will you ask your mediator about their style or technique? Would you do that in advance of the mediation?

E. Empirical Analysis of Mediator Style & Interventions

Unfortunately, empirical research on mediator style and interventions has not kept pace with the widespread adoption of mediation. Decades ago, there were several foundational studies of mediator style that sought to identify and characterize the varying styles employed by individual mediators and make clear the ubiquity of stylistic inclinations in the lives of practicing mediators (Kolb 1983; Silbey and Merry 1986; Alfini 1991). Although the settings for these studies varied widely by type of dispute and locale, the studies provide a starting point for conversation.

In her book, *The Mediators* (1983), Deborah Kolb reported on a study of public sector labor mediators working for the Wisconsin Employee Relations Commission and the Federal Mediation and Conciliation Service. Kolb identified two distinct mediator styles — *dealmakers* and *orchestrators*. The state mediators tended to adopt a *deal-maker* style that placed a heavy reliance on caucusing and having the parties communicate through the mediator rather than directly with each other. One *deal-maker* described the basic tactic used to develop a deal as "hammering." The federal mediators, on the other hand, tended to use an *orchestrator* style that emphasized flexibility and direct communication between the parties, putting the burden on the parties to come to an agreement.

Susan Silbey and Sally Merry studied mediators in three Massachusetts-based community and family mediation programs. In their article, *Mediator Settlement Strategies*, 8 Law & Pol'y 7 (1986), Silbey and Merry identified two modal styles of mediation, *bargaining* and *therapeutic*. The *bargaining* style tended to be more structured and controlling, employing caucuses and discouraging direct communication among the parties. It ignored emotions and concentrated on the bottom line. The *therapeutic* style, by contrast, encouraged the parties to fully and freely express their feelings to one another.

The first excerpt below features James J. Alfini's classic identification of three mediator styles — *trashing, bashing*, and *hashing it out* — that he developed based on interviews with lawyer-mediators handling relatively high stakes civil cases in the Florida court-connected mediation program.

More recent empirical research has shifted from analyzing the mediator's formal orientation (*e.g.*, facilitative, evaluative, transformative) towards examining individual mediator interventions. In the second excerpt, Deborah Thompson Eisenberg shares the results of one such study of court-connected mediation in Maryland that focused on mediator interventions.

Trashing, Bashing, and Hashing It Out: Is This the End of "Good Mediation"?
19 Fla. St. U. L. Rev. 47, 66–73 (1991)*
By James J. Alfini

... Our interviews with the circuit mediators and lawyers revealed three distinct styles. These three approaches to the mediation process are characterized as (1) trashing, (2) bashing, and (3) hashing it out.

1. Trashing

The mediators who employ a trashing methodology spend much of the time "tearing apart" the cases of the parties. Indeed, one of these mediators suggested the "trasher" characterization: "I trash their cases. By tearing apart and then building their cases back up, I try to get them to a point where they will put realistic settlement figures on the table."

To facilitate uninhibited trashing of the parties' cases, the overall strategy employed by these mediators discourages direct party communication. Following the mediator's orientation and short (five to ten minutes) opening statements by each party's attorney, the mediator puts the parties in different rooms. The mediator then normally caucuses with the plaintiff's attorney and her client in an effort to get them to take a hard look at the strengths and weaknesses of their case. One plaintiff's lawyer described the initial caucus:

> The mediator will tell you how bad your case is ... try to point out the shortcomings of the case to the parties and try to get the plaintiff to be realistic. They point out that juries aren't coming back with a lot of money anymore on these types of cases. They ask you tough questions to get you to see where you might have a liability problem or the doctor says you don't have a permanent injury so you may get nothing. They will try to get you to take a hard look at the deficiencies in your case that obviously I already know, but sometimes it enlightens the plaintiff to hear it from an impartial mediator.

Having torn down the case in this manner, the mediator will try to get the plaintiff and plaintiff's attorney to consider more "realistic" settlement options. The mediator then gives the plaintiff's lawyer and her client an opportunity to confer, while the mediator shuttles off to caucus with the defense.

The defense caucus is similar to that conducted with the plaintiff, except that the mediator may present the defendant with a new settlement offer if the plaintiff caucus has resulted in one. A defense attorney described the caucus:

> During the defense caucus, the mediator will usually say, "Well, you know they've asked for this figure and they think they have a strong case in this regard. Their figure is 'x.' They're willing to negotiate. They have told me that they'll take this amount which is obviously lower than the original demand" — if he has authority from the plaintiff to reveal that to you. If he doesn't, he won't say anything about that. He asks, "What do you think the case is worth? Why?"
>
> He'll then work through the case with us, pointing out outstanding medicals, lost wages and other special damages, then tallying them up and a certain percentage of pain and suffering and come up with a figure. And then they may discuss the strength of the case. I've had mediators say things to me in the caucus such as, "I was impressed by the plaintiff; I think they're going to be believable. Have you factored that into your evaluation of the case?"

If the trasher gets the defense to put a figure on the table that is closer to the plaintiff's current offer, the mediator will then shuttle back to the plaintiff.

Once the trasher has achieved the goal of getting both sides to put what she believes to be more realistic settlement figures on the table, she will shuttle back and forth trying to forge an agreement. If this is accomplished, the mediator may or may not bring the parties back together to work out the details of the agreement. One trasher explained that, once separated, he never brings the parties back together even at the final agreement stage.

. . . Mediators who employ a trashing methodology tend to draw on their own experiences with the litigation process to get the parties to take a hard look at their cases. Indeed, all of the trashers that were interviewed are experienced trial lawyers. They call upon their own experiences not only to expose procedural and substantive weaknesses on both sides, but also to get the parties to consider the costs of litigation. One defense attorney explained that once the mediator points out the weaknesses and has the party assess the costs of litigation, the mediator will say, "'Do you guys really want to spend all this money to take this case to trial?' I see a lot of that which, for your typical insurance company, is a very fruitful approach." This same lawyer, however, saw this approach as less effective when representing government agencies: "It's not nearly as fruitful because governmental agencies, especially the sheriff, are such easy targets for lawsuits that nuisance value doesn't really exist. If we don't think we have done anything wrong, we generally fight to the bitter end even if we get clobbered."

2. Bashing

Unlike the trashers, the mediators who use a bashing technique tend to spend little or no time engaging in the kind of case evaluation that is aimed at getting the parties to put "realistic" settlement figures on the table. Rather, they tend to focus initially on the settlement offers that the parties bring to mediation and spend most of the session bashing away at those initial offers in an attempt to get the parties to agree to a figure somewhere in between. Their mediation sessions thus tend to be shorter than those of the trashers, and they tend to prefer a longer initial joint session, permitting direct communication between the parties.

Most of the bashers interviewed were retired judges who draw on their judicial experience and use the prestige of their past judicial service to bash out an agreement. One of the retired judges explained that he emphasizes his judicial background during his opening statement to get them in the right frame of mind:

> I introduce myself and give them my background because I think that's very helpful to litigants to know they're before a retired judge with a lot of experience. . . . I tell them that even a poor settlement, in my judgment, is preferable to a long and possibly expensive trial together with all the uncertainties that attend a trial.

This mediator described the mediator's role as "one who guides," and explained why he believed that a retired judge makes an effective mediator: "If you're a retired judge you bring much more prestige to the mediation table than just an attorney because the people look at this attorney and say, 'I have an attorney; what do I need this guy for?' A 'judge' they listen to."

The notion that a mediator is "one who guides" suggests that the basher adopts a more directive mediator style than that employed by the trasher. The differences between the trasher and the basher in this regard were perhaps best revealed in their responses to a question we asked concerning the differences between mediation and a judicial settlement conference. The trashers tended to see the settlement conference judge as being much more aggressive than the mediator ("judges can lean on you, mediators I guess can, but they shouldn't"), while the bashers felt just the opposite. Another basher elaborated on his perception of the differences:

> The judge has to be very careful. Because if he expresses an opinion, the next thing he knows he's going to be asked to excuse himself because one side or the other will think he's taking sides. In mediation, you don't have to worry about that. You can say to the plaintiff, "there's no way the defendant is going to pay you that kind of money." You can say things as a mediator that you can't say as a judge.

As soon as the basher has gotten the parties to place settlement offers on the table, as one attorney explained, "there is a mad dash for the middle." One of the retired judges described a case he had mediated that morning:

> [T]he plaintiff wanted $75,000. The defendant told me he would pay $40,000. I went to the plaintiff and said to him, "They're not going to pay $75,000. What will you take?" He said, "I'll take $60,000." I told him I wasn't sure I could get $60,000 and asked if he would take $50,000 if I could get it. He agreed. I then went back to the defendant and told him I couldn't settle for $40,000, but "you might get the plaintiff to take $50,000" and asked if he would pay it. The answer was yes. Neither of them were bidding against themselves. I was the guy who was doing it, and that's the role of the mediator.

3. Hashing It Out

The third circuit mediation style can best be described as one involving a hashing out of a settlement agreement because it places greater reliance on direct communication between the opposing attorneys and their clients. The hashers tend to take a much more flexible approach to the mediation process, varying their styles and using techniques such as caucusing selectively, depending on their assessment of the individual case and the needs and interests of the parties. When asked to describe the mediator's role in one sentence, a hasher responded, "Facilitator, orchestrator, referee, sounding board, scapegoat."

The hasher generally adopts a much less directive posture than the trashers and bashers, preferring that the parties speak directly with one another and hash out an agreement. However, if direct communication appears counterproductive, the hasher acts as a communication link. One explained,

> If the parties are at war, they communicate through me. If the lawyers are not crazy, they communicate with each other through me. If the lawyers are crazy, and the parties can talk with each other, they talk with each other. If nobody can talk, they communicate through me. My preference is that they communicate with each other.

When asked how he gets the parties to communicate, the mediator elaborated:

> I may caucus with them to find out if they can. . . . If they don't want to, I don't force them. If they want to communicate, I put them together and say, "OK, tell them what you told me, if you want to." Or if it's a really complex thing like a long list of demands, I don't want to have to memorize it because I'm liable to misstate something. I simply say, "you tell them." . . . I may warn the other side not to respond, just to hear what they have to say, maybe ask questions, but don't get defensive. Then I'll take them out. Then I'll get with the other side and say, "How do you want to respond to this? Do you want me to bring them in?"

In addition to this more flexible orchestration of the process, the hasher is also unwilling to keep the parties at the mediation session if they express a desire to leave, unlike the trashers and bashers. When asked what he would do if the parties expressed a desire to leave the mediation session prematurely, a hasher responded, "Mediation is essentially a voluntary process even though they're ordered to show up. . . . If they don't want to go through the process or negotiate, they're basically free to walk out." None of the bashers and trashers was willing to give the parties this much latitude. They all expressed the view that it was the mediator's prerogative to decide when the mediation session was over. As one basher explained, "It's my decision to either declare it an impasse and have everybody go home or to continue. It's not their decision. You have to reassert control."

. . .

What We Know and Need to Know About Court-Annexed Dispute Resolution

67 S.C. L. Rev. 245, 258–262 (2016)*
By Deborah Thompson Eisenberg

. . . [T]he Maryland ADR study is the first to examine the impact of specific mediator interventions on the parties' attitudes and outcomes. Most ADR studies treat mediation as a "black box" and assume that all mediators use the same strategies. Prior studies have relied on mediator self-reports about what they did and how

---

* Copyright © 2016. Reprinted with permission.

it worked, which can be tainted by the mediator's own biases and perspectives. Many have debated the effectiveness and desirability of various "styles" of mediation, the most common being facilitative, evaluative, and transformative. Even within these mediation frameworks, mediators employ a variety of techniques, such as reflecting emotions and values, breaking the parties into separate private sessions or caucuses, and eliciting ideas from the parties about how the dispute should be resolved. Rather than focusing on a particular professed mediation style, the Maryland study isolated the impact of specific mediator strategies on the parties' attitudes and outcomes.

. . .

a. Reflections

Many mediators use reflections to acknowledge and validate the participants' emotions and values and clarify the issues that the parties would like to discuss during the mediation. The study found that reflections helped to promote party understanding and cooperation. Specifically, the more mediators used reflection strategies, the more likely parties were to say that the other person "listened to them and increased understanding of them through the process." In addition, reflective strategies resulted in "a decrease in the dismissal of the other participants' perspective." The use of reflections also led parties to agree that they believed they "could work together to resolve their conflicts and consider a range of options."

Reflections, standing alone, were found to be negatively associated with reaching an agreement. Nevertheless, if the parties reached an agreement in mediation, reflecting strategies resulted in more personalized or customized agreements. If the mediator combined reflecting strategies with eliciting techniques — such as asking participants to think of solutions, summarizing solutions, and asking the parties how solutions might work for them — the parties were more likely to report a positive shift in their ability to work together, say that the other person listened and understood them better, indicate that all of the underlying issues came out, and reach a personalized agreement. In other words, the study suggests that mediators who combine reflecting and eliciting strategies together are most likely to be successful in accomplishing the dual goals of (1) helping the parties better understand each other and (2) reaching a settlement agreement.

b. Caucusing

. . .

The Maryland study of child custody mediations found that private sessions caused the parties to have more positive attitudes toward the mediator but more negative attitudes about the other party and the conflict in general. Specifically, the longer the parties spent in caucus with the mediator, the more likely they were to report that the mediator respected them and did not take sides. This suggests that caucus can be a useful tool for mediators to establish a sense of trust and rapport with the parties, which some mediators have identified as an important factor in reaching a settlement.

On the flip side, mediators should be careful not to overuse caucus in custody cases. Specifically, the more time participants spent in caucus, the more likely they were to say that they felt hopeless about the situation, the less likely they were to believe that they could work with the other side, and the less likely they were to think there were a range of options to resolve the dispute. This finding occurred even holding constant other factors such as the history of the relationship and the participants' attitudes toward each other. In addition, the "sense of hope" variable was measured from before to after the mediation, with longer caucusing causing a decrease in parties' hopefulness for a resolution from the beginning to end of the mediation. The study therefore suggests that caucus may not be the most effective strategy to overcome impasse, and, if overused, may worsen party attitudes towards each other. If the parties remain separated throughout most of the mediation—talking only to the mediator rather than to each other—it makes sense that the parties may develop a better relationship with the mediator, but not with each other.

. . .

c. Telling

The dispute resolution community often debates the use of evaluative mediator strategies, such as sharing opinions or predictions about the case, offering potential solutions, assessing legal options, or introducing topics for discussion. The Maryland ADR study labeled these as "telling" strategies. Telling strategies did not have any statistically significant impact—positive or negative—on the parties' attitudes or on the outcome of the process in child custody mediations. In short, the Maryland study suggests that mediator telling strategies are a bit innocuous in child custody cases—not necessarily helpful or harmful in changing party attitudes or facilitating settlement.

d. Directing

The Maryland ADR study found that directing strategies harmed the parties' perception of the mediator. Directing strategies include introducing and enforcing process guidelines (such as "don't interrupt" or "respect each other"), explaining one participant to another, or advocating for one participant's ideas. The more mediators used directing strategies, the less likely parties were to report that the mediator listened to and respected them.

e. Eliciting

Mediators frequently use eliciting strategies to encourage creative problem-solving by the parties. These eliciting strategies include asking the participants to think of potential solutions, summarizing solutions mentioned by the parties, or asking the parties how various solutions might work for them. The Maryland ADR study found that the more the mediator used eliciting strategies, the more likely it was that the parties would settle in mediation, report that the other person listened and understood them during the mediation, become clearer about their desires, and say that the underlying issues came out during the mediation. Eliciting was the *only* mediator intervention positively correlated with reaching an agreement. When the mediator combined eliciting with reflecting strategies, the parties were more likely to reach personalized agreements. This finding suggests that mediators should spend more time listening, reflecting emotions, values, and issues, and asking the parties how they want to resolve the case — rather than telling them what to do (which does not have a significant impact), or directing them to something (which can harm the parties' perception of the mediator).

Notes and Questions

(1) In a follow-up to her 2017 South Carolina Law Review Article, Eisenberg and co-authors Lorig Charkoudian and Jamie L. Walter discuss the strategy of "eliciting" in the context of small claims mediations:

> The neutral strategy of eliciting participant solutions had the broadest impacts immediately and in the long term. This strategy involves asking participants for their ideas and solutions, brainstorming, summarizing the solutions offered by the parties, and exploring with the parties whether and how those ideas might work for them. In the short term, eliciting participant solutions was associated positively with parties reporting that they listened and understood each other in the ADR session and jointly controlled the outcome and that the other person took responsibility and apologized. Eliciting participant solutions was associated negatively with parties reporting that the neutral controlled the outcome, pressured them into solutions, and prevented issues from coming out. Of all behaviors studied, eliciting participant solutions was the only neutral strategy positively associated with the parties reaching a settlement during the ADR session.
>
> In the long term, eliciting participant solutions associated positively with parties' reports that they changed their approach to conflict and negatively with parties returning to court for an enforcement action within the subsequent 12 months. In other words, parties are less likely to return to court if the neutral uses more eliciting participant solution strategies.

Lorig Charkoudian, Deborah T. Eisenberg & Jamie L. Walter, *What Works in Alternative Dispute Resolution? The Impact of Third-Party Neutral Strategies in Small Claims Cases*, 37 Conflict Resol. Q. 101 (2019). In light of Charkoudian and her colleague's findings, should the dispute resolution community re-consider adoption of Riskin's revised grid?

(2) How does Eisenberg and Charkoudian's use of "eliciting" and "telling" mesh with Alifini's "trashing," "bashing," and "hashing"?

(3) Some mediation researchers have reviewed whether one mediator orientation is more effective than another. For example, describing his analysis of mediator self-reporting and post-mediation party surveys of employment law cases mediated with the Equal Employment Opportunity Commission, E. Patrick McDermott explained that regardless of mediator orientation, when parties reach agreement, they rate the process and mediator higher. When comparing facilitative and

evaluative orientations, McDermott's findings suggest "mediators describing them-selves as using the facilitative style attained higher participant satisfaction ratings" when compared to evaluative mediators. Further, McDermott reports that "when asked whether the disputants had obtained what they wanted, those who were in a facilitative mediation were more likely to report that they had obtained it than were those in the evaluative process." Yet, with respect to monetary outcome, "the high-est and the lowest monetary outcomes for charging parties were found where evalu-ative conduct was used. Thus, facilitative mediation had a more leveling effect on the amount received, while evaluation provided a wider range of settlement with higher payouts." E. Patrick McDermott, *Discovering the Importance of Mediator Style—An Interdisciplinary Challenge*, 5 Negotiation and Conflict Management Research 340–53 (November 2012).

Given Dwight Golann and Marjorie Aaron's advocacy for use of evaluation in their excerpt, *Beyond Abstinence*, in Section D(1) above, does the research refer-enced in this section give mediators pause—or enhance the case—for the use of evaluative techniques?

(4) In 2017, the ABA Section of Dispute Resolution issued the *Report on the Task Force on Research on Mediator Techniques*, the culmination of the rigorous review of forty-seven studies, a majority of which involved court-connected mediation and a single mediator. Convened to "learn what existing empirical evidence tells us about which mediator actions enhance mediation outcomes and which have detrimental effects," the Task Force cautiously concluded:

> [four] mediator actions appear to have a greater *potential* for positive effects than negative effects on *both* settlement ... *and* disputants' relationships and perceptions of mediation: (1) eliciting disputants' suggestions or solu-tions; (2) giving more attention to disputants' emotions, relationship, and sources of conflict; (3) working to build trust and rapport, expressing empa-thy or praising the disputants, and structuring the agenda; and (4) using pre-mediation caucuses focused on establishing trust.

The Task Force urged further research and collaboration to develop a "body of empirically derived knowledge about which mediator actions and approaches enhance mediation outcomes, and to use that knowledge to improve mediation practice."

(5) Reviewing three separate studies (a survey of mediation practitioners, obser-vations of live mediations and coding behaviors, and reports on the effectiveness of mediator styles) in *Just My Style: The Practical, Ethical, and Empirical Dangers of the Lack of Consensus about Definitions of Mediation Styles*, 5 Negotiation and Conflict Management Research 325, 367 (2012), Lorig Charkoudian suggests two possibilities for further research on mediator style:

> ... One option is to prioritize research on understanding and develop-ing consensus on definitions of mediator styles. This would involve drilling down into mediator strategies, not assuming that labels uniformly mean the

same thing, and taking self-reported strategies with some skepticism. This could involve working with the practitioner community toward consensus on labeling various mediator approaches and will likely require developing more detailed divisions than the classic dichotomies of facilitative versus evaluative or problem-solving versus transformative. This approach would certainly benefit the practitioner community, where there would be great value to having agreement on a series of labels to identify the various mediation styles.

Another option is to ignore labels altogether, leaving that issue to the practitioner community, and focus on mediator behaviors. Ultimately, the practitioner community and the agencies that use mediation need to know the short- and long-term effects of mediator strategies (or combination of strategies). , , , [A]n important contribution the research community can provide is an understanding of what mediators actually do and the impact of those actions.

Should those seeking to identify what works, or what works "best" in mediation seek to define and categorize mediator "styles" or "orientations," focus on mediator "interventions," or explore a more effective way to study what works best in mediation?

Chapter 5

Confidentiality

A. Introduction

Confidentiality is generally considered to be an essential ingredient in mediation. Policy concerns and legal issues arise, however, over both the means that may be used to ensure that the confidentiality of a mediation session is maintained and the scope of its protection. Some jurisdictions, for example, extend the confidentiality of mediation communications to the entire world, while others limit the protection to subsequent legal or administrative proceedings. The materials in this chapter represent the various approaches to maintaining the confidentiality of mediation communications and explore legal issues that arise in cases that challenge the application of confidentiality provisions, invoke a statutory privilege, or seek to compel a mediator to testify. Excerpts from these cases, scholarly articles, and provisions of the Uniform Mediation Act are reproduced to illuminate salient legal issues.

A popular way to address the interests in providing confidentiality in mediation is by adopting a mediation privilege provision that enables any party to a mediation or the mediator to assert the right not to share information developed during the mediation process with a different audience. In 2001, the National Conference of Commissioners on Uniform State Laws approved the Uniform Mediation Act (UMA) (Appendix D) that sets out such a privilege provision; by 2022, the UMA, or various provisions in it, had been adopted in twelve states and the District of Columbia. But there are several other approaches that are used to establish confidentiality in mediation, such as by private contracting or by statutory evidentiary exclusionary provisions.

In Section B, the policy rationales supporting mediation confidentiality are discussed. Section C provides a sample contract that mediators may use to establish confidentiality, followed by a discussion of the enforceability of such contracts. Section D contains material regarding evidentiary exclusions of settlement discussions. Section E discusses the use of a mediation privilege created by statute, particularly the Uniform Mediation Act, and Section F covers exceptions to confidentiality and the implications of those exceptions. Finally, Section G examines confidentiality in online mediation.

B. Purpose and Policy

As discussed in Chapter 1, mediation has taken hold during the past half century as an integral part of the dispute resolution landscape. During this period, the legal status of mediation communications — *viz.*, are they confidential or not — has received significant attention as an important policy matter.

Consider the policy reasons offered by the ABA Ad Hoc Committee on Federal Government ADR Confidentiality in its *Guide to Confidentiality Under the Federal Administrative Dispute Resolution Act* (2005):

> Confidentiality enables parties in [mediation] to focus on their interests, as opposed to positions. It assures parties that they may raise sensitive issues and discuss creative ideas and solutions that they would be unwilling to discuss publicly. A party may be willing to accept something less or different than he is advocating but could fear that revealing that willingness in an assisted negotiation would be used to his harm in the event that negotiations do not succeed completely. Without assurance that their confidences will not be disclosed, the parties would be far less willing to discuss freely their interests and possible settlements.

In the following article, Professor Ellen Deason discusses these policy rationales for mediation confidentiality and considers the additional element of *trust*:

The Need for Trust as a Justification for Confidentiality in Mediation: A Cross-Disciplinary Approach
54 U. Kan. L. Rev. 1387, 1387–1389, 1393, 1406, 1413–1418 (2006)*
By Ellen E. Deason

The need for confidentiality in mediation is almost axiomatic in the United States. It is also the primary focus of the legal rules that have been developed to support the process of mediation. All fifty states have statutes or rules designed to protect mediation communications from disclosure in legal proceedings . . . .

. . .

But despite this evidence that confidentiality in mediation is accepted wisdom, confidentiality is, and should be, controversial. It can hinder accurate decision making by excluding salient information. It can run counter to democratic principles of transparency and participation in public processes. In the context of mediation, confidentiality may compete with other important values that are served by reporting certain mediation conduct or statements. To cite a few examples, disclosures may be important in preventing or punishing crime, attorney misconduct, or child abuse. These competing values mean that the appropriate scope of confidentiality is not a matter of absolute protection or absolute disclosure. It is instead a matter of balance between protection and disclosure that requires difficult policy choices.

. . .

This balance is an issue that will come up repeatedly. On a policy level, state legislatures will face it as they consider whether to adopt the approach to confidentiality of the Uniform Mediation Act (UMA). Courts also face the need to balance disclosure and confidentiality, with or without legislative guidance.

. . .

Research on mediator approaches and techniques confirms the emphasis in mediation on building trust between the disputing parties. A study[1] designed to identify key features of professional mediation found that building trust between the parties is one of the major activities reported by mediators. Even untrained subjects placed in the role of mediator respond to their sense that trust between disputing parties is low by attempting to build rapport. Mediators try to build trust among parties through techniques such as creating situations in which the parties perform a joint task, clarifying the needs and perceptions of the other party, identifying common interests, and praising progress. They also coach the parties and encourage actions that demonstrate trust in the other party — such as taking a step that involves some risk — or actions that invite trust from the other party — such as demonstrating an understanding of the other side's concerns.

. . .

Mediation is characterized by both of the factors that create a need for trust: interdependence and risk. Interdependence is inherent in negotiation and mediation settings in that each of the parties seeks something it needs or wants from the other party. The degree of interdependence varies based on the relationship and can affect the negotiating process and the exchange of information. For example, researchers maintain that when parties have a positive working relationship built on mutual dependence, their negotiation is more efficient and more likely to result in a mutually beneficial agreement.

. . .

. . . [R]evealing information in negotiation creates a number of important risks, but is also central to the process of reaching an agreement, especially an integrative or optimal agreement. It is trust that makes it possible for negotiators, and participants in mediation, to share information in the face of the risks of doing so. "Without trust, negotiators are unlikely to engage in problem-solving behaviors . . . that enable them to coordinate their actions and find mutually beneficial solutions."[2] . . .

---

1. Peter J.D. Carnevale et al., *Contingent Mediator Behavior and Its Effectiveness, in Mediation Research: The Process and Effectiveness of Third-Party Intervention* 213, 220 (Kenneth Kressel & Dean G. Pruitt eds., 1989).

2. Mara Olekalns & Philip J. Smith, *Moments in Time: Metacognition, Trust, and Outcomes in Dyadic Negotiations*, 31 Personality & Soc. Psychol. Bull. 1696, 1698 (2005).

[M]ediation procedures, and in particular confidentiality protections, both provide trust and foster the growth of trust during mediation.

Parties to a conflict are likely to come to mediation with a relationship characterized by the vigilance of mutual distrust, especially if the conflict has a long history. . . . [P]arties with a developed relationship may find that their dispute threatens, or has already triggered, a decline in trust and an increase in distrust. Thus it is common that rebuilding or maintaining trust becomes an important part of the mediation process.

Given the risks involved in negotiation, how can individuals in conflict transcend low trust and high distrust to reach a mutually acceptable agreement? I propose that mediation procedures in general, and protections for confidentiality of mediation communications in particular, can provide enough trust — in the form of institutional trust — for parties to take negotiating risks. . . . In mediation, that situation is bounded by mediation norms and confidentiality rules. The mediation process and confidentiality protections can function to reduce the risks and uncertainties associated with trusting and generate a form of confidence that mitigates distrust. They can even provide a foundation on which the parties can build interpersonal trust.

. . .

Simply by using mediation rather than unfacilitated negotiation, parties can greatly reduce the risk that what they reveal will be disclosed outside the process or will allow the other party to use those revelations for competitive advantage (information loss) within the process. To the extent they can avoid providing sensitive information directly to each other, parties eliminate the risk that their sensitive information will be disclosed by their opponents. In mediation, they can accomplish this by communicating information solely to the mediator during caucuses. The same caucus mechanism can reduce the risk that disclosures in mediation will be used to exploit a party's weaknesses. Because sharing information with the mediator is often enough to move the process forward, the parties need not share it directly and explicitly with the opposing party.

. . . Ideally, the parties can then build interpersonal knowledge-based trust in the mediator and in the mediation process on this foundation. That more robust trust could stem from the parties' experience of the safety of the process and of the mediator's consistently evenhanded, impartial behavior.

. . .

While reducing risks of loss and their associated vulnerability is a central strength of mediation, without adequate information it is much harder for a mediator to reduce these risks effectively. A party who is worried about the risks of disclosure may not communicate sufficiently with the mediator to allow this to happen. Therefore . . . I contend that the legal mechanisms that protect the confidentiality of the information a party reveals in mediation are key to his ability to proceed in the face of risks of loss and disclosure.

. . .

Legal rules and norms that provide confidentiality for mediation communications lower risk and uncertainty by creating predictability. They reduce the available options for disclosing communications made during mediation and they standardize the situations in which disclosures may take place. As such, confidentiality rules are a form of institutional trust. With risk lowered through confidentiality provisions, the parties can then participate more fully in mediation even if their levels of interpersonal trust are low and their levels of distrust are high.

Within a mediation, confidentiality is based on the mediator's professional norms, a common source of institutional trust. Mediators typically assure parties that information they reveal in private will not be conveyed to the other party without authorization. It is a good practice for a mediator to follow up by confirming confidentiality at the end of each caucus and asking the party to identify communications to be kept confidential. Adhering to these norms of confidentiality is one of the most important ways that a mediator can establish her trustworthiness in the eyes of the parties.

Outside the mediation, a privilege or other statutory mechanism can provide a means of preventing disclosures of mediation communications in legal proceedings. Merely having a confidentiality rule standardizes the treatment of mediation communications within the relevant jurisdiction, and to the extent jurisdictions adopt a uniform approach, standardization will increase this predictability on a wider scale. Through standardization, confidentiality rules create predictability by reducing the options for the other party to disclose mediation communications and by establishing confidentiality as the routine.

Rules in the form of privileges generate an additional assurance of predictability. They eliminate any need to believe in good intentions on the part of the mediator and, more importantly, on the part of the opponent, because they vest control over disclosures in the party. In sum, legal requirements that protect confidentiality provide institutional trust by reducing the risk that one's adversary will expose sensitive information revealed in the course of mediation.

Contracts are another method of reducing disclosure risks through legal means. They are a classic form of institutional trust by which the parties mutually limit their actions. In agreeing to mediation, the parties can use a contract to prevent disclosures outside the context of legal proceedings to the public, press, or others. By entering a confidentiality agreement, the parties can designate desirable disclosures or prevent disclosures altogether, thus again reducing the options available for use of information revealed in mediation.

. . .

If confidentiality rules can reduce risks enough to permit one party to engage in risk-taking behavior by sharing information, that behavior has the potential to stimulate the other party to reciprocate in kind. This response, when repeated, creates a small sense that the other party's reaction can be predicted. With enough positive exchanges, this sense can grow to a "confident expectation" that the other party will continue to cooperate. When her confidence is strong enough, the party may be "willing to be vulnerable." This is the definition of trust. That trust may then enable the party to cooperate through actions that are not protected by confidentiality rules, such as by making a concession that would give the other party the power to take advantage. The party's trust is no longer merely institutional trust; it has become trust between the parties themselves that may expand in an upward spiral that continues by way of reciprocity. In this way, trust grounded in predictions enforced by confidentiality rules may provide a seed for trust that grows with and reinforces a new or renewed relationship during mediation.

. . .

Analyzing information exchange in mediation in terms of risk and the need for trust suggests a mechanism by which mediation procedures and confidentiality protections function to stimulate those exchanges and hence improve the likelihood of a quality agreement. The theory of institutional trust further suggests the potential for confidentiality rules to create a context that allows interpersonal trust to develop between the parties in mediation. When courts and legislatures weigh the need for confidentiality, they should consider the high levels of risk entailed in mediation, the importance of trust in overcoming those risks, and the value of confidentiality as a mechanism supporting trust in the mediation process.

National Labor Relations Board v. Macaluso

United States Court of Appeals for the Ninth Circuit
618 F.2d 51 (1980)

WALLACE, CIRCUIT JUDGE:

The single issue presented in this National Labor Relations Board (NLRB) enforcement proceeding is whether the NLRB erred in disallowing the testimony of a Federal Mediation and Conciliation Service (FMCS) mediator as to a crucial fact occurring in his presence. We enforce the order.

I

In early 1976 Retail Store Employees Union Local 1001 (Union) waged a successful campaign to organize the employees of Joseph Macaluso, Inc. (Company) . . . Several months of bargaining between Company and Union negotiators failed to produce an agreement, and the parties decided to enlist the assistance of a mediator from the FMCS. Mediator Douglas Hammond consequently attended the three meetings between the Company and Union from which arises the issue before us. . . .

During the spring and summer of 1976 the Company engaged in conduct which led the NLRB to charge it with unfair labor practices. At this unfair labor practice proceeding the NLRB also found that the Company and Union had finalized a collective bargaining agreement at the three meetings with Hammond, and that the Company had violated NLRA sections 8(a)(5) and (1) by failing to execute the written contract incorporating the final agreement negotiated with the Union. The NLRB ordered the Company to execute the contract and pay back-compensation with interest, and seeks enforcement of that order in this court. In response, the Company contends that the parties have never reached agreement, and certainly did not do so at the meetings with Hammond.

The testimony of the Union before the NLRB directly contradicted that of the Company. The two Union negotiators testified that during the first meeting with Hammond the parties succeeded in reducing to six the number of disputed issues, and that the second meeting began with Company acceptance of a Union proposal resolving five of those six remaining issues. The Union negotiators further testified that the sixth issue was resolved with the close of the second meeting, and that in response to a Union negotiator's statement "Well, I think that wraps it up," the Company president said, "Yes, I guess it does." The third meeting with Hammond, according to the Union, was held only hours before the Company's employees ratified the agreement, was called solely for the purpose of explaining the agreement to the Company accountant who had not attended the first two meetings, and was an amicable discussion involving no negotiation.

The Company testimony did not dispute that the first meeting reduced the number of unsettled issues to six, but its version of the last two meetings contrasts sharply with the Union's account. The Company representatives testified that the second meeting closed without the parties having reached any semblance of an agreement, and that the third meeting was not only inconclusive but stridently divisive. While the Union representatives testified that the third meeting was an amicable explanatory discussion, the Company negotiators both asserted that their refusal to give in to Union demands caused the Union negotiators to burst into anger, threaten lawsuits, and leave the room at the suggestion of Hammond. According to the Company, Hammond was thereafter unable to bring the parties together and the Union negotiators left the third meeting in anger.

In an effort to support its version of the facts, the Company requested that the administrative law judge (ALJ) subpoena Hammond and obtain his testimonial description of the last two bargaining sessions. The subpoena was granted, but was later revoked upon motion of the FMCS. Absent Hammond's tie-breaking testimony, the ALJ decided that the Union witnesses were more credible and ruled that an agreement had been reached. The Company's sole contention in response to this request for enforcement of the resulting order to execute the contract is that the ALJ and NLRB erred in revoking the subpoena of Hammond, the one person whose testimony could have resolved the factual dispute.

II

Revocation of the subpoena was based upon a long-standing policy that mediators, if they are to maintain the appearance of neutrality essential to successful performance of their task, may not testify about the bargaining sessions they attend. Both the NLRB and the FMCS (as amicus curiae) defend that policy before us. We are thus presented with a question of first impression before our court: can the NLRB revoke the subpoena of a mediator capable of providing information crucial to resolution of a factual dispute solely for the purpose of preserving mediator effectiveness? . . . We must determine . . . whether preservation of mediator effectiveness by protection of mediator neutrality is a ground for revocation consistent with the power and duties of the NLRB under the NLRA.

The NLRB's revocation of Hammond's subpoena conflicts with the fundamental principle of Anglo-American law that the public is entitled to every person's evidence. . . . The facts before us present a classic illustration of the need for every person's evidence: the trier of fact is faced with directly conflicting testimony from two adverse sources, and a third objective source is capable of presenting evidence that would, in all probability, resolve the dispute by revealing the truth. Under such circumstances, the NLRB's revocation of Hammond's subpoena can be permitted only if denial of his testimony "has a public good transcending the normally predominant principle of utilizing all rational means for ascertaining truth." The public interest protected by revocation must be substantial if it is to cause us to "concede that the evidence in question has all the probative value that can be required, and yet exclude it because its admission would injure some other cause more than it would help the cause of truth, and because the avoidance of that injury is considered of more consequence than the possible harm to the cause of truth." 1 Wigmore, Evidence 296 (1940). We thus are required to balance two important interests, both critical in their own setting.

We conclude that the public interest in maintaining the perceived and actual impartiality of federal mediators does outweigh the benefits derivable from Hammond's testimony. This public interest was clearly stated by Congress when it created the FMCS: "It is the policy of the United States that (a) sound and stable industrial peace and the advancement of the general welfare, health, and safety of the Nation and of the best interests of employers and employees can most satisfactorily be secured by the settlement of issues between employers and employees through the processes of conference and collective bargaining between employers and the representatives of their employees; (b) the settlement of issues between employers and employees through collective bargaining may be advanced by making available full and adequate governmental facilities for conciliation, mediation, and voluntary arbitration to aid and encourage employers and the representatives of their employees to reach and maintain agreements concerning rates of pay, hours, and working conditions, and to make all reasonable efforts to settle their differences by mutual agreement reached through conferences and collective bargaining or by such methods as may be provided for in any applicable agreement for the settlement of disputes. . . ." 29 U.S.C. § 171. [F]ederal mediation has become a substantial contributor to industrial peace in the United States. The FMCS, as amicus curiae, has informed us that it participated in mediation of 23,450 labor disputes in fiscal year 1977, with approximately 325 federal mediators stationed in 80 field offices around the country. Any activity that would significantly decrease the effectiveness of this mediation service could threaten the industrial stability of the nation. The importance of Hammond's testimony in this case is not so great as to justify such a threat. Moreover, the loss of that testimony did not cripple the fact-finding process. The ALJ resolved the dispute by making a credibility determination, a function routinely entrusted to triers of fact throughout our judicial system.

. . .

Public policy and the successful effectuation of the Federal Mediation and Conciliation Service's mission require that commissioners and employees maintain a reputation for impartiality and integrity. Labor and management or other interested parties participating in mediation efforts must have the assurance and confidence that information disclosed to commissioners and other employees of the Service will not subsequently be divulged, voluntarily or because of compulsion, unless authorized by the Director of the Service. No officer, employee, or other person officially connected in any capacity with the Service, currently or formerly shall . . . produce any material contained in the files of the Service, disclose any information acquired as part of the performance of his official duties or because of his official status, or testify on behalf of any party to any matter pending in any judicial, arbitral or administrative proceeding, without the prior approval of the Director. 29 C.F.R. § 1401.2(a), (b) (1979) . . . . To execute successfully their function of assisting in the settlement of labor disputes, the conciliators must maintain a reputation for impartiality, and the parties to conciliation conferences must feel free to talk without any fear that the conciliator may subsequently make disclosures as a witness in some other proceeding, to the possible disadvantage of a party to the conference. If conciliators were permitted or required to testify about their activities, or if the production of notes or reports of their activities could be required, not even the strictest adherence to purely factual matters would prevent the evidence from favoring or seeming to favor one side or the other. The inevitable result would be that the usefulness of the (FMCS) in the settlement of future disputes would be seriously impaired, if not destroyed. The resultant injury to the public interest would clearly outweigh the benefit to be derived from making their testimony available in particular cases.

During oral argument the suggestion was made that we permit the mediator to testify, but limit his testimony to "objective facts." . . . We do not believe, however, that such a limitation would dispel the perception of partiality created by mediator testimony. In addition to the line-drawing problem of attempting to define what is and is not an "objective fact," a recitation of even the most objective type of facts would impair perceived neutrality, "for the party standing condemned by the thrust of such a statement would or at least might conclude that the (FMCS) was being unfair."

We conclude, therefore, that the complete exclusion of mediator testimony is necessary to the preservation of an effective system of labor mediation, and that labor mediation is essential to continued industrial stability, a public interest sufficiently great to outweigh the interest in obtaining every person's evidence. No party is required to use the FMCS; once having voluntarily agreed to do so, however, that party must be charged with acceptance of the restriction on the subsequent testimonial use of the mediator. We thus answer the question presented by this case in the affirmative: the NLRB can revoke the subpoena of a mediator capable of providing information crucial to resolution of a factual dispute solely for the purpose of preserving mediator effectiveness. Such revocation is consonant with the overall powers and duties of the NLRB, a body created to implement the NLRA goals of "promot(ing) the flow of commerce by removing certain recognized sources of industrial strife and unrest" and "encouraging practices fundamental to the friendly adjustment of industrial disputes. . . ." 29 U.S.C. § 151.

Notes and Questions

(1) The ABA Committee statement, the Deason article, and the *Macaluso* case focus on the policy reasons for protecting confidentiality in mediation. Are the policy reasons mentioned in the ABA Committee statement and the *Macaluso* opinion consistent with those enumerated by Deason?

(2) Do these policy rationales for protecting confidentiality in mediation suggest that mediation adds value to the negotiation process? How?

(3) Would the affirmative answer to the legal question presented in *Macaluso* — *can the NLRB revoke the subpoena of a mediator capable of providing information crucial to resolution of a factual dispute solely for the purpose of preserving mediator effectiveness?* — be supported more strongly if the parties had contracted for confidentiality through an agreement such as the one reprinted in the next section below?

(4) Note that *Macaluso* holds only that the *mediator* cannot be compelled to testify and does not impose a broader confidentiality restriction (the parties did testify). Does it make sense to prohibit the mediator from testifying but allow the parties to do so? If so, what might be the policy reasons supporting such an approach.

(5) In the following excerpt from *Cassel v. Superior Court*, 244 P.3d 1080 (Cal. 2011), the Supreme Court of California adopted a very strict reading of California's mediation confidentiality statute and disallowed the reporting of mediation statements in Cassel's malpractice lawsuit against his attorneys. As you read the excerpt, consider whether there are any policy arguments for a more flexible interpretation.

Cassel v. Superior Court

Supreme Court of California
244 P.3d 1080 (2011)

Baxter, J.

In order to encourage the candor necessary to a successful mediation, the Legislature has broadly provided for the confidentiality of things spoken or written in connection with a mediation proceeding. With specified statutory exceptions, neither "evidence of anything said," nor any "writing," is discoverable or admissible "in any arbitration, administrative adjudication, civil action, or other noncriminal proceeding in which . . . testimony can be compelled to be given," if the statement was made, or the writing was prepared, "for the purpose of, in the course of, or pursuant to, a mediation. . . ." (Evid. Code, § 1119, subds. (a), (b).) "All communications, negotiations, or settlement discussions by and between participants in the course of a mediation . . . shall remain confidential." (*Id.*, subd. (c).) We have repeatedly said that these confidentiality provisions are clear and absolute. . . .

The issue here is the effect of the mediation confidentiality statutes on private discussions between a mediating client and attorneys who represented him in the mediation. Petitioner Michael Cassel agreed in mediation to the settlement of business litigation to which he was a party. He then sued his attorneys for malpractice, breach of fiduciary duty, fraud, and breach of contract. His complaint alleged that by bad advice, deception, and coercion, the attorneys, who had a conflict of interest, induced him to settle for a lower amount than he had told them he would accept, and for less than the case was worth.

. . .

A pretrial mediation of the . . . suit began at 10:00 a.m. on August 4, 2004. Petitioner attended the mediation, accompanied by his assistant . . . and by . . . lawyers Steve Wasserman, David Casselman, and Thomas Speiss. Petitioner and his attorneys had previously agreed he would take no less than $2 million to resolve the . . . suit by assigning his [global master label] rights to [the respondent]. However, after hours of mediation negotiations, petitioner was finally told VDO would pay no more than $1.25 million. Though he felt increasingly tired, hungry, and ill, his attorneys insisted he remain until the mediation was concluded, and they pressed him to accept the offer, telling him he was "greedy" to insist on more. At one point, petitioner left to eat, rest, and consult with his family, but Speiss called and told petitioner he had to come back. Upon his return, his lawyers continued to harass and coerce him to accept a $1.25 million settlement. They threatened to abandon him at the imminently pending trial, misrepresented certain significant terms of the proposed settlement, and falsely assured him they could and would negotiate a side deal that would recoup deficits in the . . . settlement itself. They also falsely said they would waive or discount a large portion of his $188,000 legal bill if he accepted . . . [the respondent's settlement] offer. They even insisted on accompanying him to the bathroom, where they continued to "hammer" him to settle. Finally, at midnight, after 14 hours of mediation, when he was exhausted and unable to think clearly, the attorneys presented a written draft settlement agreement and evaded his questions about its complicated terms. Seeing no way to find new counsel before trial, and believing he had no other choice, he signed the agreement.

. . .

We . . . conclude that the evidence the trial court ruled nondiscoverable and inadmissible by reason of the mediation confidentiality statutes was not, as a matter of law, excluded from coverage by those statutes on the mere ground that they were private attorney-client communications which occurred outside the presence or hearing of the mediator or any other mediation participant. Instead, such attorney-client communications, like any other communications, were confidential, and therefore were neither discoverable nor admissible — even for purposes of proving a claim of legal malpractice — insofar as they were "for the purpose of, in the course of, or pursuant to, a mediation...." (§ 1119, subd. (a).) By holding otherwise, and thus overturning the trial court's exclusionary order, the Court of Appeal erred. We must therefore reverse the Court of Appeal's judgment.

Conclusion

The Court of Appeal's judgment is reversed.

WE CONCUR: KENNARD, ACTING C.J., WERDEGAR, MORENO, CORRIGAN, JJ., and GEORGE, J.

CHIN, J.

[Justice Chin concurred in the California Supreme Court's judgment but said that he did so "reluctantly"]:

The court holds today that private communications between an attorney and a client related to mediation remain confidential even in a lawsuit between the two. This holding will effectively shield an attorney's actions during mediation, including advising the client, from a malpractice action even if those actions are incompetent or even deceptive.... This is a high price to pay to preserve total confidentiality in the mediation process.

I greatly sympathize with the Court of Appeal majority's attempt to interpret the statutory language as not mandating confidentiality in this situation. But, for the reasons the present majority gives, I do not believe the attempt quite succeeds.

...

Notes and Questions

(1) The *Cassel* decision, and cases relied on by the *Cassel* court, demonstrate that the Supreme Court of California has been very strict in interpreting California's statutory framework for protecting mediation confidentiality. As Justice Chin points out in the concurrence to *Cassel*, there are policy arguments for a less strict interpretation of a mediation confidentiality statute. One of those, as this case demonstrates, is legal malpractice. Are there any other situations where confidentiality in mediation may compromise a party's interests?

(2) In her article, *Musings on Mediation, Kleenex, and (Smudged) White Hats*, 33 U. La Verne L. Rev. 5, 14, 18 (2011), Professor Nancy A. Welsh criticizes the decision in *Cassel* and warns that a stringent approach to confidentiality in mediation can lead to exploitation of the non-discoverability and inadmissibility of mediation communications to keep disputants from reaching resolutions or accessing the courts if something goes awry:

... I cannot help but notice the emergence of a line of cases involving allegations of misbehavior in mediation—particularly misbehavior by lawyers. Further, I cannot help but notice the defendant-lawyers asserting the mediation privilege against their own clients, in order to keep them from introducing evidence that might help to prove claims of legal malpractice. In other words, these lawyers are using mediation to prevent potential litigants from accessing the very forum that lawyers are supposed to hold most dear—the public courtroom. ...

... [I]t seems indisputable that mediation is sometimes being used inappropriately: to shield lawyers from potential claims of malpractice; to force parties to settle when they would rather go to trial; and even to find a back door means to fund the staff that courts can no longer afford to hire themselves. ... We are inviting scandal—and then "reform" by those who may not be friends of our process.

Are Professor Welsh's concerns well founded?

C. Contract

Many mediators seek to establish confidentiality by having the parties sign an agreement prior to the mediation session. A sample agreement is reproduced below. Beyond the potential legal benefits of having contracted for confidentiality, are there other advantages to having the parties sign an agreement? Does it assist in educating the parties about the importance of keeping mediation communications confidential?

Minnesota Department of Human Rights (MDHR)

Mediation Program
Agreement to Mediate

Case No.: XXXXX

By signing below, you understand the terms of this Agreement to Mediate, and you agree to them.

1. Mediation is voluntary. Anyone may stop the mediation at any point if they need to. Also, at any time during the mediation session, you or the mediator may request that the mediator(s) meet(s) separately with you.

2. Mediation is self-determinative. You decide whether you come to an agreement and if you do, what is in your agreement.

3. Mediators are neutral. Mediators do not take sides or represent or advocate for anyone or any possible solution, before, during or after the mediation session.

4. Mediators do not offer legal advice, decide who is right or wrong, or decide what you should do next. Mediators must end a mediation session if they determine that anyone is using mediation for any purpose other than a good faith attempt to resolve the dispute.

5. Mediation is a confidential process. Mediators will not discuss information shared by anyone during the mediation process to anyone outside of mediation.

6. All communications and documents made during mediation are confidential unless all mediation participants expressly agree otherwise. You retain all legal rights to pursue this matter in other ways, but you will not be able to use mediation discussions or notes in subsequent judicial or administrative proceedings. Minn. Stat. §595.02, subd. 1(m), states that testimony regarding any communications and documents made or used, in the course of, or because of, mediation is inadmissible at subsequent legal or administrative proceedings. Mediators and/or their files cannot be subpoenaed on behalf of any party.

7. Exceptions To Confidentiality: Mediators are not required to keep confidential information disclosed during mediation regarding child abuse and/or abuse of a vulnerable adult, threats of serious bodily injury, or the substantial likelihood of serious bodily harm. Mediators also may debrief their experience with MDHR's mediation staff for the purpose of improving the MDHR Mediation Program and the mediators' skills, and MDHR retains and reserves the right to share de-identified, aggregate data on settlement terms.

8. According to Minn. Stat. §572.35, subd. 1, by signing this Agreement to Mediate, you acknowledge you have been advised in writing that: mediators have no duty to protect your interests or provide information about legal rights; signing a mediated settlement agreement may adversely affect your legal rights; and you should consult an attorney before signing a mediated settlement agreement if you are uncertain about any of your rights.

9. Any mediated settlement agreement is not binding unless there is a provision in the written agreement stating that the agreement is binding.

Charging Party's Signature

Charging Party's Representative

Respondent's Signature

Respondent's Representative

Mediator's Signature

Date

Note

Although many mediators have the parties sign confidentiality agreements, the courts may be somewhat timid if asked to enforce a confidentiality agreement. Enforcement is generally sought to preserve the confidentiality of a mediation communication, thus preventing the introduction of evidence that may be seen as crucial to deciding a particular case. However, such a result would go against the general policy that frowns on agreements to exclude evidence, as discussed in the previous section. Consider how this policy intersects with Rule 408 of the Federal Rules of Evidence, discussed in the next section.

D. Evidentiary Exclusions

1. Introduction

As the court pointed out in the *Macaluso* case discussed in section B above, the mediator was "the one person whose testimony could have resolved the factual dispute." Yet, the court upheld the revocation of the subpoena of the mediator because "the complete exclusion of the mediator testimony is necessary to the preservation of an effective system of labor mediation." Thus, the court found that the strong policy reasons for preserving mediation confidentiality overrode the similarly strong policy that one is entitled to "every person's evidence." Similarly, Rule 408 of the Federal Rules of Evidence, as reproduced below, excludes from evidence certain communications made during settlement negotiations, reflecting a strong policy of encouraging the settlement of court cases. Most states have similar provisions in their evidence codes. As you read the materials below, consider how far Rule 408 protections extend. For example, would the testimony excluded by the *Macaluso* or *Cassel* courts have been excluded by Rule 408?

2. Federal Rules of Evidence, Rule 408. Compromise Offers and Negotiation

(a) **Prohibited Uses.** Evidence of the following is not admissible — on behalf of any party — either to prove or disprove the validity or amount of a disputed claim or to impeach by a prior inconsistent statement or a contraction:

(1) furnishing, promising, or offering — or accepting, promising to accept, or offering to accept — a valuable consideration in compromising or attempting to compromise the claim; and

(2) conduct or a statement made during compromise negotiations about the claim — except when offered in a criminal case and when the negotiations related to a claim by a public office in the exercise of its regulatory, investigative, or enforcement authority.

(b) Exceptions. The court may admit this evidence for another purpose, such as proving a witness's bias or prejudice, negating a contention of undue delay, or proving an effort to obstruct a criminal investigation or prosecution.

Confidentiality, Privilege and Rule 408: The Protection of Mediation Proceedings in Federal Court
60 La. L. Rev. 91, 102–08 (1999)*
By Charles W. Ehrhardt

Most modern commentators argue that the justification for the rule excluding offers of compromise is not relevance, but one of evidentiary privilege. This rationale recognizes the strong public policy favoring negotiated dispute resolution requires that offers of compromise be made without fear the offer will be used against the offeror.

. . .

No specific statute or court rule is necessary for Rule 408 to be applicable in mediation proceedings, regardless of whether the mediation is voluntary or court-ordered. Mediations involve statements made during attempts to settle or compromise a claim. However, some district court local rules as well as some states have specifically adopted a provision which applies Rule 408 to mediation proceedings, probably as a reminder to counsel and the parties.

B. Inapplicability

Rule 408 precludes the admission at trial of evidence of settlement negotiations which are offered to prove liability for the underlying claim. The second sentence of Rule 408 cautions that documents presented during settlement negotiations are not protected simply because they were so presented. In other words, the rule is not a shield behind which one can divulge pre-existing documents during settlement discussions or negotiations and have them protected from admissibility during trial.

The rule does not prohibit discovery of matters pertaining to the settlement negotiations. However, because a party is aware of the statements made by the opponent during the negotiations or the joint sessions, the availability of discovery is not as significant as it is when the party is unaware of the evidence. Although Rule 408 does not prohibit discovery of an opponent's communications regarding negotiation strategies, Rule 26(c) of the Rules of Civil Procedure as well as the attorney-client privilege and the work product doctrine may be applicable to protect these discussions.

Rule 408 is only applicable when the offer of compromise is offered to prove liability. The final sentence of Rule 408 provides that the rule does not require the exclusion of evidence relating to settlement offers when it is offered for another purpose, "such as proving bias or prejudice of a witness, negativing a contention of undue delay, or proving an effort to obstruct a criminal investigation or prosecution." This sentence illustrates some of the purposes for which the rule would not exclude evidence; it is not an exclusive listing.

1. Bias or Prejudice

If a witness testifies during a trial, the cross-examining counsel may attack the credibility by showing a relevant bias, prejudice or interest. Evidence of a settlement agreement involving the witness is admissible when it is relevant to show the bias of the witness when testifying in the instant case. The language of Rule 408 does not prohibit admission of the evidence since it is not offered to show the validity or invalidity of the underlying claim. The second sentence of Rule 408 specifically recognizes that evidence of the prior settlement may be admitted to show bias. The details of the settlement agreement are subject to a Rule 403 balancing, as are the details of other evidence being offered to attack credibility by showing bias.

2. Act or Wrong Committed During Settlement Negotiations

When the question is not the validity or invalidity of the underlying claim, but rather a material issue of an act which occurred during the negotiations, Rule 408 does not prohibit the admission of evidence. For example, when an alleged wrong is committed during the negotiations; *e.g.*, libel, assault, breach of contract, or unfair labor practice, the evidence of statements made during negotiations is not being offered to prove the liability for the underlying claim and is not prohibited. Wrongful acts are not protected simply because they occurred during settlement discussion. The rule excluding settlement offers and discussions was not intended to be a shield for the commission of independent wrongs. So too, if a suit alleging that an insurance company failed to make a reasonable settlement within the policy limits, either the insured or the insurance company can offer evidence of the settlement offers that were made during the negotiations.

3. Impeachment

If a party testifies during the trial, a statement of fact made by the party during settlement negotiations may be offered as a prior inconsistent statement to impeach credibility. Applying the literal language of Rule 408, the evidence is not barred because the evidence of the prior statement is not offered to prove the validity or invalidity of its claim. This interpretation is bolstered by the policy that the rules of evidence should not be a shield to commit perjury. On the other hand, if a party's statements made during settlement negotiations are admissible to impeach whenever they are inconsistent with the party's trial testimony, the freedom of discussion in settlement negotiations will be inhibited. The few cases facing this issue are not in agreement. Most commentators assume that there are, at least, some cases where the interests of justice compel the introduction of prior inconsistent statements made during settlement discussions.

... In at least a few cases, statements made during a mediation may be admissible as prior inconsistent statements to impeach a witness who testifies during a trial to material facts which are inconsistent with what the party stated during the mediation. Even though Rule 408 does not protect certain statements made during mediation, a district court's local rule may protect confidentiality.

Notes and Questions

Professor Ehrhardt points out that Rule 408 is only applicable to communications that are offered to prove liability and discusses some of the other evidentiary purposes for which a particular communication would not be shielded by Rule 408. Professor Alan Kirtley describes these limitations as a "weakness" of Rule 408: "Since mediation discussions tend to be free flowing and often unguarded, revelations later serving as impeachment, bias or 'another purpose' evidence are likely. The 'another purpose' clause in the hands of creative counsel leaves little in mediation definitely exempt from disclosure." Kirtley also points out that Rule 408 offers no protection against *discovery* of mediation discussions or against their admission in proceedings that are not governed by the rules of evidence, such as administrative hearings and criminal cases. He thus concludes that Rule 408 is no substitute for a mediation privilege: "A mediation privilege should be of broad, unambiguous scope, bar discovery, and exclude evidence in all types of proceedings." Alan Kirtley, *The Mediation Privilege's Transition from Theory to Implementation: Designing a Mediation Privilege Standard to Protect Mediation Participants, the Process and the Public Interest*, 1995 J. Disp. Resol. 1, 11–14.

E. Privilege

While the federal government and many states have enacted numerous laws to protect the confidentiality of mediation communications from use in subsequent proceedings, this legislative activity has resulted in a hodgepodge of statutory formulations. To ensure that confidentiality will be handled uniformly across all U.S. jurisdictions, the National Conference of Commissioners on Uniform State Laws (NCCUSL) and the American Bar Association (ABA) undertook the drafting of a Uniform Mediation Act. The drafting committee of the NCCUSL/ABA Uniform Mediation Act chose an *evidentiary privilege* as the means of assuring confidentiality. The relevant UMA provisions are reprinted below.

The cases discussed following the UMA provisions illustrate that the federal cases seeking to determine whether there is a federal mediation privilege have been inconsistent at best. Similarly, the cases interpreting mediation privilege statutes have not always been in accord with regard to the scope of the privilege.

Uniform Mediation Act

National Conference of Commissioners on Uniform State Laws and the American Bar Association*

SECTION 4. PRIVILEGE AGAINST DISCLOSURE; ADMISSIBILITY; DISCOVERY.

(a) Except as otherwise provided in Section 6, a mediation communication is privileged as provided in subsection (b) and is not subject to discovery or admissible in evidence in a proceeding unless waived or precluded as provided by Section 5.

(b) In a proceeding, the following privileges apply:

(1) A mediation party may refuse to disclose, and may prevent any other person from disclosing, a mediation communication.

(2) A mediator may refuse to disclose a mediation communication, and may prevent any other person from disclosing a mediation communication of the mediator.

(3) A nonparty participant may refuse to disclose, and may prevent any other person from disclosing, a mediation communication of the nonparty participant.

(c) Evidence or information that is otherwise admissible or subject to discovery does not become inadmissible or protected from discovery solely by reason of its disclosure or use in a mediation.

Legislative Note: The Act does not supersede existing state statutes that make mediators incompetent to testify, or that provide for costs and attorney fees to mediators who are wrongfully subpoenaed. See, e.g., Cal. Evid. Code Section 703.5 (West 1994).

SECTION 5. WAIVER AND PRECLUSION OF PRIVILEGE.

(a) A privilege under Section 4 may be waived in a record or orally during a proceeding if it is expressly waived by all parties to the mediation and:

(1) in the case of the privilege of a mediator, it is expressly waived by the mediator; and

(2) in the case of the privilege of a nonparty participant, it is expressly waived by the nonparty participant.

(b) A person that discloses or makes a representation about a mediation communication which prejudices another person in a proceeding is precluded from asserting a privilege under Section 4, but only to the extent necessary for the person prejudiced to respond to the representation or disclosure.

(c) A person that intentionally uses a mediation to plan, attempt to commit or commit a crime, or to conceal an ongoing crime or ongoing criminal activity is precluded from asserting a privilege under Section 4.

SECTION 7. PROHIBITED MEDIATOR REPORTS.

(a) Except as required in subsection (b), a mediator may not make a report, assessment, evaluation, recommendation, finding, or other communication regarding a mediation to a court, administrative agency, or other authority that may make a ruling on the dispute that is the subject of the mediation.

(b) A mediator may disclose:

(1) whether the mediation occurred or has terminated, whether a settlement was reached, and attendance;

(2) a mediation communication as permitted under Section 6; or

(3) a mediation communication evidencing abuse, neglect, abandonment, or exploitation of an individual to a public agency responsible for protecting individuals against such mistreatment.

(c) A communication made in violation of subsection (a) may not be considered by a court, administrative agency, or arbitrator.

SECTION 8. CONFIDENTIALITY.

Unless subject to the [insert statutory references to open meetings act and open records act], mediation communications are confidential to the extent agreed by the parties or provided by other law or rule of this State.

Notes and Questions

(1) Do the UMA confidentiality provisions extend to a broad range of subsequent proceedings? Are the right persons identified as the holders of the privilege? Are the waiver provisions sensible?

(2) Does the UMA privilege extend confidentiality protection to all the areas discussed by Professor Ehrhardt as not shielded by Rule 408?

(3) Although there currently is no federal statute recognizing a general mediation privilege, a number of federal acts provide for a mediation privilege in specific types of proceedings. Most prominently, Congress created a mediation privilege in the Administrative ADR Act that prohibits the disclosure of communications made *pursuant* to the Administrative Procedure Act. Even then, it is not clear that the federal courts will interpret these congressional acts as providing broad confidentiality protection. In *In re Grand Jury Subpoena*, 148 F.3d 487 (5th Cir. 1998), the federal appeals court refused to uphold the district court's ruling that a federal mediation privilege protected against a federal grand jury subpoena for records of a mediation conducted under a state agricultural loan program. Although the relevant federal act (the Agricultural Credit Act) requires mediations to be "confidential," the Fifth Circuit ruled that it was not clear that Congress had intended to create a privilege that was so broad

that it would protect mediation communications from a federal grand jury. In the following excerpt of the *Facebook* case, consider Judge Kozinski's refusal to find that Congress had provided for a "mediator privilege" in the Alternative Dispute Resolution Act of 1998 that would extend to the mediation communications at issue.

(4) Although widely considered a "confidentiality act," note that the bulk of the UMA focuses on creating a privilege, defining who holds the privilege, and exceptions to the privilege (*see* Section F). Compare UMA Section 8 with Florida Statutes 44.405(1):

> 44.405(1) Except as provided in this section, all mediation communications shall be confidential. A mediation participant shall not disclose a mediation communication to a person other than another mediation participant or a participant's counsel. A violation of this section can be remedied as provided by s. 44.406. If the mediation is court ordered, a violation of this section may also subject the mediation participant to sanctions by the court, including but not limited to, costs, attorney's fees, and mediator's fees.
>
> . . .
>
> 44.406 (1) Any mediation participant who knowingly and willfully discloses a mediation communication in violation of s. 44.405 shall, upon application by any party to a court of competent jurisdiction, be subject to remedies, including:
>
> (a) equitable relief.
>
> (b) compensatory damages.
>
> (c) attorney's fees, mediator's fees, and costs incurred in the mediation proceeding.
>
> (d) reasonable attorney's fees and costs incurred in the application for remedies under this section.

What do you think were the reasons that the drafters of the UMA would adopt a broader statement of confidentiality? Do you think the Florida statute strikes the correct balance to provide protection while also limiting frivolous suits?

———————

Consider how the United States Court of Appeals for the Ninth Circuit analyzes the confidentiality issue in the case involving Facebook's action to enforce a mediation settlement agreement.

Facebook, Inc. v. Pacific Northwest Software, Inc.

United States Court of Appeals, Ninth Circuit
640 F.3d 1034 (2011)

Kozinski, Chief Judge:

Cameron Winklevoss, Tyler Winklevoss and Divya Narendra (the Winklevosses) claim that Mark Zuckerberg stole the idea for Facebook (the social networking site) from them. They sued Facebook and Zuckerberg (Facebook) in Massachusetts.

Facebook countersued them and their competing social networking site, ConnectU, in California, alleging that the Winklevosses and ConnectU hacked into Facebook to purloin user data, and tried to steal users by spamming them. The ensuing litigation involved several other parties and gave bread to many lawyers, but the details are not particularly relevant here.

The district court in California eventually dismissed the Winklevosses from that case for lack of personal jurisdiction. It then ordered the parties to mediate their dispute. The mediation session included ConnectU, Facebook and the Winklevosses so that the parties could reach a global settlement. Before mediation began, the participants signed a Confidentiality Agreement stipulating that all statements made during mediation were privileged, non-discoverable and inadmissible "in any arbitral, judicial, or other proceeding."

After a day of negotiations, ConnectU, Facebook and the Winklevosses signed a handwritten, one-and-a-third page "Term Sheet & Settlement Agreement" (the Settlement Agreement). The Winklevosses agreed to give up ConnectU in exchange for cash and a piece of Facebook. The parties stipulated that the Settlement Agreement was "confidential," "binding" and "may be submitted into evidence to enforce [it]." The Settlement Agreement also purported to end all disputes between the parties.

The settlement fell apart during negotiations over the form of the final deal documents, and Facebook filed a motion with the district court seeking to enforce it. ConnectU argued that the Settlement Agreement was unenforceable because it lacked material terms and had been procured by fraud. The district court found the Settlement Agreement enforceable and ordered the Winklevosses to transfer all ConnectU shares to Facebook. This had the effect of moving ConnectU from the Winklevosses' to Facebook's side of the case.

The Winklevosses appeal.

. . .

B.

The Settlement Agreement envisioned that Facebook would acquire all of ConnectU's shares in exchange for cash and a percentage of Facebook's common stock. The parties also agreed to grant each other "mutual releases as broad as possible," and the Winklevosses represented and warranted that "[t]hey have no further right to assert against Facebook" and "no further claims against Facebook & its related parties."

. . .

The Settlement Agreement even specifies how to fill in the "material" terms that the Winklevosses claim are missing from the deal:

> *Facebook will determine* the form & documentation of the acquisition of ConnectU's shares [] consistent with a stock and cash for stock acquisition. (emphasis added).

. . .

C.

After signing the Settlement Agreement, Facebook notified the Winklevosses that an internal valuation prepared to comply with Section 409A of the tax code put the value of its common stock at $8.88 per share. The Winklevosses argue that Facebook misled them into believing its shares were worth four times as much. Had they known about this valuation during the mediation, they claim, they would never have signed the Settlement Agreement.

. . .

The Winklevosses are sophisticated parties who were locked in a contentious struggle over ownership rights in one of the world's fastest-growing companies. They engaged in discovery, which gave them access to a good deal of information about their opponents. They brought half-a-dozen lawyers to the mediation. Howard Winklevoss — father of Cameron and Tyler, former accounting professor at Wharton School of Business and an expert in valuation — also participated. A party seeking to rescind a settlement agreement by claiming a Rule 10b-5 violation under these circumstances faces a steep uphill battle.

. . .

The Winklevosses make two related claims: that Facebook led them to believe during the settlement negotiations that its shares were worth $35.90, even though Facebook knew that its shares were, in fact, worth only $8.88; and that Facebook failed to disclose material information, namely the $8.88 tax valuation, during the negotiations.

In support of these claims, the Winklevosses proffered evidence of what was said and not said during the mediation. The district court excluded this evidence under its Alternative Dispute Resolution (ADR) local rule on "confidential information," which it read to create a "privilege" for "evidence regarding the details of the parties' negotiations in their mediation." A local rule, like any court order, can impose a duty of confidentiality as to any aspect of litigation, including mediation. *See* N.D. Cal. ADR L.R. 6-12(a); *see also* 28 U.S.C. § 652(d). But privileges are created by federal common law. *See* Fed.R.Evid. 501. It's doubtful that a district court can augment the list of privileges by local rule. *Cf. In re Grand Jury Subpoena Dated Dec. 17, 1996*, 148 F.3d 487, 491–93 (5th Cir.1998) (examining whether a federal statute created an evidentiary privilege). In any event, the parties used a private mediator rather than a court-appointed one. *See* N.D. Cal. ADR L.R. 3-4(b) ("A private ADR procedure may be substituted for a Court program if the parties so stipulate and the assigned Judge approves."). Their mediation was thus "not subject to the . . . ADR Local Rules," including Local Rule 6-11. *Id.*

. . . Nevertheless, the district court was right to exclude the proffered evidence. The Confidentiality Agreement, which everyone signed before commencing the mediation, provides that:

> All statements made during the course of the mediation or in mediator follow-up thereafter at any time prior to complete settlement of this matter

are privileged settlement discussions . . . and are nondiscoverable and inadmissible for any purpose including in any legal proceeding. . . . *No aspect of the mediation shall be relied upon or introduced as evidence in any arbitral, judicial, or other proceeding.* (Emphasis added).

This agreement precludes the Winklevosses from introducing in support of their securities claims any evidence of what Facebook said, or did not say, during the mediation. . . . The Winklevosses can't show that Facebook misled them about the value of its shares or that disclosure of the tax valuation would have significantly altered the mix of information available to them during settlement negotiations. Without such evidence, their securities claims must fail. . . .

The Winklevosses argue that if the Confidentiality Agreement is construed to defeat their Rule 10b-5 claims, it is void under section 29(a) of the Exchange Act as an invalid waiver. But section 29(a) "applie[s] only to express waivers of non-compliance," *Levy v. Southbrook Int'l Invs., Ltd.,* 263 F.3d 10, 14, 18 (2d Cir.2001), with the "substantive obligations imposed by the Exchange Act," *Shearson/Am. Express, Inc. v. McMahon,* 482 U.S. 220, 228, 107 S.Ct. 2332, 96 L.Ed.2d 185 (1987). The Confidentiality Agreement merely precludes both parties from introducing evidence of a certain kind. Although this frustrates the securities claims the Winklevosses chose to bring, the Confidentiality Agreement doesn't purport to limit or waive their right to sue, Facebook's obligation not to violate Rule 10b-5 or Facebook's liability under any provision of the securities laws. *See McMahon,* 482 U.S. at 230, 107 S.Ct. 2332.

. . .

The Winklevosses are not the first parties bested by a competitor who then seek to gain through litigation what they were unable to achieve in the marketplace. And the courts might have obliged, had the Winklevosses not settled their dispute and signed a release of all claims against Facebook. With the help of a team of lawyers and a financial advisor, they made a deal that appears quite favorable in light of recent market activity. *See* Geoffrey A. Fowler & Liz Rappaport, *Facebook Deal Raises $1 Billion,* Wall St. J., Jan. 22, 2011, at B4 (reporting that investors valued Facebook at $50 billion — 3.33 times the value the Winklevosses claim they thought Facebook's shares were worth at the mediation). For whatever reason, they now want to back out. Like the district court, we see no basis for allowing them to do so. At some point, litigation must come to an end. That point has now been reached.

AFFIRMED.

Notes and Questions

(1) Note that the federal court has decided to enforce the mediation agreement. Enforceability of mediated agreements is covered more extensively in Chapter 6, Section E. Enforceability and confidentiality issues are often intertwined.

(2) The Ninth Circuit disagrees with the Federal District Court Judge's application of the confidentiality "privilege" to the District Court's local rules:

The district court excluded this evidence under its Alternative Dispute Resolution (ADR) local rule on "confidential information," which it read to create a "privilege" for "evidence regarding the details of the parties' negotiations in their mediation." A local rule, like any court order, can impose a duty of confidentiality as to any aspect of litigation, including mediation. . . . But privileges are created by federal common law. *See* Fed.R.Evid. 501. It's doubtful that a district court can augment the list of privileges by local rule.

In citing the federal evidence rules, which received congressional approval, is the court saying that privileges may only be created by the legislative branch?

(3) Note that although the court refuses to recognize a confidentiality privilege, it does enforce the parties' confidentiality agreement.

(4) The federal appellate courts have thus far been reluctant to find a federal mediation privilege when presented with the opportunity. For an excellent discussion and analysis of the caselaw relating to the recognition of a mediation privilege in the federal trial and appellate courts, *see* Sarah R. Cole *et al.*, Mediation: Law, Policy & Practice 410–16 (2021–2022 ed.). The authors conclude that, "[f]ew areas of mediation law are as uncertain as the existence and applicability of a federal mediation privilege. . . . Ad hoc adoption of a federal mediation privilege, to the extent courts are willing to do so, will take a long time and will not provide a clear definition of the breadth and limitations of such a privilege." Accordingly, Professor Ellen Deason has recommended that Congress adopt a federal mediation privilege similar to the UMA. Ellen Deason, *Predictable Mediation Confidentiality in the U.S. Federal System*, 17 Ohio St. J. on Disp. Resol. 239 (2002).

(5) In states where a mediation privilege has been recognized, questions remain about the nature and scope of the privilege, even in UMA states.

(6) In *Society of Lloyd's v. Moore*, 2006 U.S. Dist. LEXIS 80963 (S.D. Ohio Nov. 1, 2006), the federal district judge carefully considered various provisions of the Ohio Uniform Mediation Act in holding that the mediator's email (in an arb-med proceeding in which the mediator communicated his opinions about settlement) was a privileged mediation communication and therefore not admissible in a subsequent proceeding. The judge also considered legislative intent in ruling that the UMA provision that would exclude the mediation privilege in cases where the "mediation is conducted by a judge or magistrate who might make a ruling on the case" does not apply in this case, and therefore the mediation privilege does extend to a hybrid process such as arb-med.

(7) Some courts have supported limits to the extensions of the mediation privilege. In *Mutual of Enumclaw v. Cornhusker*, 2008 U.S. Dist. LEXIS 80266 (E.D. Wash. Sept. 16, 2008), for example, a federal district judge interpreted provisions of the Washington UMA to allow discovery of evidence of alleged bad faith conduct by an insurer during the mediation. The judge reasoned that the privilege only extends to communications narrowly related to the underlying dispute. Also, in *Hopes v.*

Barry, 2011-Ohio-6688 (Ohio App. Dec. 27, 2011), an Ohio appellate court held that the Ohio mediation privilege did not extend to an email sent by one of the attorneys several weeks after the mediation.

———————

In the following article, Sharon Press and Gregory Firestone present a novel approach to reconciling "the disconnect between the common understanding of the term confidentiality and how it is used in the context of mediation." Does their approach help to make the terms "confidentiality" and "privilege" less confusing? Can you think of other approaches to dealing with this problem?

Privadentiality: What Does It Mean and Why Do We Need It?

26 Disp. Resol. Mag. 24–26 (2022)*
By Sharon Press and Gregory Firestone

When a mediator tells parties that mediation is confidential, what do the parties actually think that word means? Do they expect that only the mediator will keep everything confidential (as would be the case when they talk privately with an attorney or psychologist) or that all mediation participants must maintain the confidentiality of mediation communications? Do they know whether they can disclose what they themselves said in mediation to a judge or anyone else without getting permission from the other parties? Do they think confidentiality means only that a judge cannot be told what was communicated — or that no one outside the mediation can be told anything about what was disclosed during the process?

Mediators have many good reasons for assuring parties that mediation is a confidential process. These include promoting candor and the sharing of different perspectives between the participants; protecting the integrity of the mediation process (by not requiring the mediator, the "neutral" in the room, to be the tie-breaker as to what was said during the mediation process if the dispute moves to a court setting); and enhancing procedural justice and confidence in the process by encouraging parties to accept responsibility, apologize, express sympathy, and feel heard. In addition, the concept of protecting communication is based on the longstanding tradition of protecting offers of settlement, whether these are made in the course of negotiation or mediation. That tradition, codified in the Federal Rules of Evidence (Rule 408), is based on the premise that settlements should be encouraged. In addition, settlement offers often are the result of a decision to end a dispute rather than an admission of wrongdoing.

———————

However, in most jurisdictions, absent a contractual agreement between the participants, describing a mediation as confidential can be both confusing and misleading. In most areas, including states that have adopted the Uniform Mediation Act, the most that the mediator can promise is that "mediation communications" are inadmissible (or can be prevented from being shared) in a future adjudicative proceeding. This typically takes the form of an evidentiary privilege or an incompetency statute (where the mediator is not "competent," or legally qualified, to offer testimony about what was said during a mediation in a future adjudicative proceeding). But these provisions do not protect the supposedly "confidential" information from being posted on a social media site, discussed with a reporter, or shared with a friend or family member. While some jurisdictions do provide that mediation is confidential and cannot be disclosed to almost anyone, there is little consistency as to what confidentiality actually means.

The problem ... is that "confidentiality" is often used as an umbrella term that includes a broad array of communication protections (privilege, incompetency, etc.) and also as a specific form of communication protection (nondisclosure to anyone). This problem is exacerbated by the fact that most people have the common understanding that confidentiality means that what is said is private and will not be shared — with anyone. As a result, there is a disconnect between the common understanding of the term confidentiality and how it is used in the context of mediation.

This lack of clarity creates ambiguity, which in turn can be a trap for participants who don't understand the nuances of what is protected and what is not. For example, participants in a mediation operating under the misconception that everything they say is protected both from disclosure broadly and also in a future court proceeding may disclose facts, perceptions, and interests that could later be posted on social media platforms without any recourse for the person who said it. This could be problematic in all settings, but it may be particularly damaging in the context of dissolution-of-marriage cases, in which individuals often are required to attend a dispute resolution process and often are unrepresented. The lack of clarity might also cause problems in the opposite direction. Individuals may assume that communications are protected only in the context of use in a future adjudicative proceeding and find themselves in trouble for having disclosed information to the public that was actually protected from disclosure in certain jurisdictions.

Another problem with the term "confidentiality" is that outside the dispute resolution field, the word generally restricts a professional from making disclosures — but not the person whom the professional is helping. For example, lawyers, doctors, psychotherapists, and priests typically are prohibited (except if an exception applies) from breaching client, patient, or penitent confidences. The client, patient, or penitent is not restricted from sharing this information him/herself. Mediation and dispute resolution processes are more complicated because many people are involved, and therefore restrictions typically apply to everyone.

In some cases, confidentiality protections may not even apply, depending on who attends a meeting. When a client brings an additional person to an attorney-client meeting, the attorney-client privilege may be inadvertently waived. Generally, in mediation, the presence of these individuals does not result in any inadvertent waiver of confidentiality.

We propose a new term — privadentiality — to be used as the umbrella term for mediation and other dispute resolution communication protections. Because no one will have a preconceived notion about what this word means or what it covers, using it will require mediators and neutrals in other dispute resolution processes to slow down and explain what communication protections exist in the given process.

The term "privadentiality" would include confidentiality, privilege, incompetency to testify, evidentiary exclusions, and privacy of dispute resolution proceedings. It also would encompass other variations of communication protections that might be established by contract, common law, or court or administrative rule. Privadentiality would not be inadvertently waived when adversary or other persons attend a dispute resolution proceeding.

. . .

In collaborative methods, such as mediation, collaborative law, and family group conferencing, the parties communicate and negotiate with each other in the hope of reaching a mutually agreeable resolution. . . .

. . .

In collaborative processes, the greatest privadentiality protections should apply because most of the rationales articulated for privadentiality are relevant.

. . .

We think coining a new term will help clarify, for practitioners and parties alike, exactly what can and cannot be held in confidence. Whatever words are used, however, in this time of fast-moving information, we hope everyone involved takes time and care to make sure that everyone understands exactly how information is and is not protected.

F. Exceptions

Recall that in the *Macaluso* case, *supra*, the mediator was "the one person whose testimony could have resolved the factual dispute." Yet, the court upheld the revocation of the subpoena of the mediator because "the complete exclusion of the mediator testimony is necessary to the preservation of an effective system of labor mediation." Should the court have carved out an exception to confidentiality and considered the mediator's testimony for the limited purpose of determining whether the Company and the Union had reached an agreement? Similarly, as noted in the *Cassel* decision, the Supreme Court of California has consistently refused to carve out exceptions to the mediation confidentiality statute. As you read the Uniform Mediation Act provision dealing with exceptions to confidentiality and the related materials below, consider the policies that are served by each confidentiality exception and whether they are consistent with, or erode, the policies that protect the confidentiality of mediation communications.

The Mediation Privilege's Transition from Theory to Implementation: Designing a Mediation Privilege Standard to Protect Mediation Participants, the Process and the Public Interest

1995 J. Disp. Resol. 1, 39–52*
By Alan Kirtley

. . .

Mediation occurs after the events precipitating a dispute. During mediation pre-existing facts, statements, documents and tangible objects are often presented. The availability of such information to the mediation process is critically important. A privilege rule covering such preexisting information encourages party candor. However, other policy considerations weigh in favor of not extending the privilege to otherwise discoverable facts and documents.

While the mediation process needs privilege protection to function effectively, the privilege should not permit mediation to become a black hole into which parties can purposefully bury unhelpful evidence. For example, a party's admission during mediation that he falsified accounting records would be privileged, but his placing the records on the mediation table should not make the records privileged. Allowing discovery of preexisting facts and documents that are presented in mediation is consistent with traditional privilege and evidence law. The Washington statute contains a representative example of an exception for "otherwise discoverable" evidence found in several state privileges. These statutes follow the correct course by leaving the litigation discovery process undisturbed.

This approach, however, causes concern for unwary parties who tell or show "it all" during mediation. Such persons are unlikely to understand the distinction between privileged communications and the later discoverability of disclosed facts and preexisting documents. The concern is that unscrupulous parties will use mediation, where candor is urged and confidentiality promised, as an informal discovery device. But barring discovery based on clues obtained during mediation would entwine former mediation parties in litigation to determine whether the source of the discovery lead came from or was independent of the mediation. The benefit is not worth the cost. Moreover, such a policy would be inconsistent with other

---

privileges that do not protect facts, but only confidential communications. By carefully explaining the nuances of confidentiality, mediators can reduce the chances that mediation will become an informal discovery device for unscrupulous parties. Nonetheless, mediation disputants and their counsel need to be aware of the consequences before divulging discovery tips during mediation discussions.

One form of otherwise discoverable mediation information merits privilege protection. In anticipation of mediation, parties may solicit preliminary appraisals, financial statements or expert opinions. This material is obtained to provide "ballpark" information for mediation negotiations. Washington and a few states maintain the privileged status for materials "prepared specifically for use in mediation and actually used in the mediation proceeding." Such statutes are consistent with the attorney-client privilege and the work-product doctrine. Only on very narrow grounds does the work-product doctrine allow discovery of the facts and opinions of consulting experts. Mediation's goals of encouraging informal, prompt and cost-effective settlement are served if parties are not yoked with these preliminary estimates in later litigation.

b. Party Agreements and the Privilege

Parties usually begin a mediation by entering into a written agreement to mediate. Among other things, an agreement to mediate outlines the process, describes the mediator's role and sets forth the participants' understanding regarding confidentiality. Without an exemption to the privilege, such agreements remain confidential communications. This is despite the fact that mediation participants may need access to the agreement to mediate in order to demonstrate that the privilege was triggered, to evidence participation in a mandated mediation, to establish the terms of the mediator's undertaking or to prove a prior agreement to disclose otherwise privileged material. The Washington statute and a few other statutes have an exception for the agreement to mediate.

Settlement agreements present special considerations. Some parties are attracted to mediation out of the desire to preserve the privacy of their settlements. Yet, in certain cases, such as product liability and environmental cases, secret settlement agreements may do harm to third parties or the public at large. Also, parties may need access to their settlement agreement for enforcement purposes.

. . .

c. Subject Matter Exceptions

Among the most difficult policy choices in crafting the mediation privilege is deciding what particular classes of information should be excepted from the privilege in all instances. The process mirrors the analysis involved as to whether a mediation privilege is warranted. As to each type of information, the cost of the loss of evidence to the justice system must be weighed against the benefit of a broad-based mediation privilege.

A "laundry list" of subject matter exceptions has been enacted in various states or suggested. Examples include: (1) admission of threats to commit child abuse, a crime, a felony, physical/bodily harm, and damage to property; (2) information pertinent to a crime, an action claiming fraud or suits against the mediator; (3) information relating to the commission of a crime during mediation, and (4) use of mediation information for research purposes or non-identifiable reporting. In addition, some privilege statutes permit disclosure when mandated by another statute or a court. For purposes of the analysis that follows, the various exceptions have been organized in the categories of past criminal activity, ongoing or future crimes and threats of harm, and breakdowns in the mediation process and enforcement of mediated agreements.

i. Past Criminal Activity

[I have] argued that the mediation privilege ought to apply in all criminal cases. For the same reasons, admissions of past criminal activity made during mediation should not be excepted from the privilege. . . . [E]xcepting admissions of past criminal activity would eliminate programs mediating criminal cases and stifle mediation communications in other types of disputes.

Admissions of past criminal activity do not necessarily present current or future risks of harm. Such an approach is consistent with the treatment of confidential disclosure of past criminal activity under traditional privileges. Undoubtedly, because of that body of law, most mediation privilege statutes do not exclude disclosures regarding past criminal activity. Mediation disclosures involving ongoing or future plans to do crime and threats of harm require separate analysis.

ii. Ongoing and Future Crime; Threats of Harm

The few mediation statutes providing for disclosure of criminal activity generally limit the exception to ongoing or future crime. Such exclusions are consistent with some views of the attorney-client privilege; society does not wish to allow individuals to seek out the assistance of a lawyer in planning or carrying out a crime. However, the other privileges generally do not have an exception for ongoing or future crimes. In mediation, where the context is a meeting of persons in conflict, there is substantial risk of retaliatory reporting of mediation information. For example, an exception that allows a party to report, and the mediator to be compelled to testify to, the other party's use of drugs, illegal gambling, welfare misreporting or not paying income taxes is not warranted. The risks such offenses present to individuals or society do not justify penalizing mediation candor. On the other hand, an exclusion aimed at "serious physical harm" is a justified policy choice.

Public policy favoring disclosure of otherwise privileged information is nowhere stronger than in the area of abuse of vulnerable persons such as children, the aged and persons with a disability. In most states statutes exist requiring the reporting of knowledge of abuse or neglect of vulnerable persons to a designated governmental agency, even if learned during a confidential interview. That position is consistent with the law governing traditional privileges where the risk of injury is serious. The interests of mediation confidentiality are not so unique as to justify a different result. It is not surprising that the most common exclusion in mediation privilege statutes is for information relating to child abuse. The same result is reached in states, including Washington, with an exception allowing for disclosure of information "when mandated by statute."

Few mediation privilege statutes allow for disclosure of threats of physical harm made during mediation. Most of these statutes limit the exception to credible threats of serious bodily harm or violence. Such exceptions allow a mediation participant who is so threatened to take protective measures. A more troublesome question arises when the threat is directed toward a nonparticipant of the mediation. Does the mediator have a duty to warn the third party or notify the police of the threat?

Applying the reasoning of *Tarasoff v. Regents of the University of California*[351] to the mediation process, mediators may have an independent duty to report threats against third persons. In that case, a psychologist and others were sued for failing to inform a third person of death threats made by the psychologist's client during confidential treatment sessions. The client killed the threatened person. The court held the risk of serious physical injury or death to an identifiable person created a duty for the professional to warn the intended victim. Important to the case was the fact that both the applicable psychotherapist-patient privilege and professional ethics standards permitted disclosure by the psychologist under the circumstances presented.

In response to *Tarasoff*-like risks in mediation, several mediation privilege statutes have an exception eliminating confidentiality for threats of serious physical harm. The absence of such an exception is a weakness of most mediation privilege statutes, including Washington's. A *Tarasoff* exception for mediation would eliminate the privilege "when the mediator or a party reasonably believes that disclosing the mediation communications or materials is necessary to prevent a mediation party from committing a crime likely to result in imminent death or substantial bodily injury to an identifiable person." Adding a *Tarasoff* exception would implicate few mediations, resolve the *Tarasoff* dilemma for mediators and potentially save lives.

iii. Breakdowns in the Mediation Process; Enforcement of Mediation Agreements

As with any dispute resolution mechanism, there will be breakdowns in the mediation process. Mediators may commit malpractice. Parties may fail to bargain in good faith. Mediation agreements may be tainted with fraud, or may be ambiguous or unfair. The mediation privilege should not provide a safe haven for participant wrongdoing or injustice. However, in allowing for disclosure of mediation

---

351. 551 P.2d 334 ([Cal.] 1976).

information to deal with serious process breakdowns, care must be taken not to eviscerate the mediation privilege with exceptions that are too easily called upon.

A party claiming mediator misconduct must have access to mediation information and the mediator's testimony. A privilege that bars access to such information results in de facto immunity for malpracticing mediators. For that reason, and because the few claims of malpractice likely to arise will not greatly impact the operation of the privilege, a clear-cut exception to the privilege for mediator malpractice is appropriate. The Washington statute and a few other statutes address this obvious need. The Washington statute provides an exception to the privilege "in a subsequent action between the mediator and a party to the mediation arising out of the mediation." Exceptions for malpractice by mediators would be improved by explicit language permitting disclosure to mediator licensing authorities as well. Mediators also need access to mediation information to defend themselves against claims and charges, and to bring suit against parties, usually to collect agreed upon fees. Several exceptions accommodate such mediator needs for disclosure.

Good faith bargaining is the pathway to mediated settlements. However, providing an exception to the mediation privilege based on a claim of bad faith bargaining, short of fraud, is problematic. Most parties undertake mediation voluntarily. While such parties often negotiate under a mediator's entreaty to bargain in good faith, they may discontinue negotiations at will. When parties mediate voluntarily, mediation discussions should not be revealed based on a claim of bad faith negotiations. Negotiating in bad faith is often in the eyes of the beholder. Stonewalling or moving in small increments may be justified in particular mediations. Parties who become frustrated by their opponents' bargaining tactics have the option of withdrawing from the mediation and pursuing other means of resolving the dispute.

A different approach is justified when mediation parties come to the table involuntarily and under a statutory obligation to bargain in good faith, such as in labor mediation, farmer/creditor mediation and mandatory child custody mediation. In such cases, mediation communications are essential evidence to prove or defend against a claim of bad faith bargaining. Mediation communications should be available in contexts when parties have a statutory obligation to bargain in good faith, established standards of good faith bargaining exist and bargaining in bad faith is actionable. For example, in a school district/teachers' union mediation, if one side bargains in bad faith, mediation communications must be revealable to an administrative judge or court in order to obtain or oppose the requested relief. For that reason, some mediation privilege statutes eliminate confidentiality for claims of bad faith bargaining in mandatory mediations or simply exclude mediations in which negotiating in good faith is a legal obligation. While in this context parties should be free to introduce mediation communications to enforce good faith bargaining laws, the mediator should not be compelled to testify. It was on precisely that issue that the *Macaluso* and other court decisions provided the genesis of the mediation privilege.

Most would agree that mediation settlements tainted by fraud, obtained through duress or deemed unconscionable should not be enforceable. Yet relatively few mediation privilege statutes address these issues, and those that do mostly contain only fraud exceptions. This deviation from what might be expected may reflect the conclusion that fraud, duress and unconscionability are present in few mediations, and may reflect the concern that exceptions dealing with those ills will open the mediation privilege to wide-spread misuse by parties suffering from "bargainer's remorse." For example, a stated fraud exception to the privilege could be cited by those unwilling to abide by their mediation agreements, whether justified or not. Undoubtedly, states without fraud, duress or unconscionability exemptions, such as Washington, recognize that courts are likely to be willing to set aside the privilege when presented with viable contract defenses to the enforcement of a mediation settlement agreement. Once in court, mediation participants who wish to make out a case of fraud, for example, could seek *a priori* approval from the judge to present mediation information. By hearing the competing claims *in camera*, the court could preserve confidentiality unless disclosure was held to be necessary and appropriate. Since the parties will be able to present evidence related to fraud, duress or unconscionability, mediators should not be compelled to testify as the "tie-breaking" witness. A similar approach is appropriate when interpretive issues arise regarding the meaning of a settlement agreement.

Uniform Mediation Act

National Conference of Commissioners on Uniform State Laws and the American Bar Association*

SECTION 6. EXCEPTIONS TO PRIVILEGE.

(a) There is no privilege under Section 4 for a mediation communication that is:

(1) in an agreement evidenced by a record signed by all parties to the agreement;

(2) available to the public under [insert statutory reference to open records act] or made during a session of a mediation which is open, or is required by law to be open, to the public;

(3) a threat or statement of a plan to inflict bodily injury or commit a crime of violence;

---

(4) intentionally used to plan a crime, attempt to commit or commit a crime, or to conceal an ongoing crime or ongoing criminal activity;

(5) sought or offered to prove or disprove a claim or complaint of professional misconduct or malpractice filed against a mediator;

(6) except as otherwise provided in subsection (c), sought or offered to prove or disprove a claim or complaint of professional misconduct or malpractice filed against a mediation party, nonparty participant, or representative of a party based on conduct occurring during a mediation; or

(7) sought or offered to prove or disprove abuse, neglect, abandonment, or exploitation in a proceeding in which a child or adult protective services agency is a party, unless the

[Alternative A: [State to insert, for example, child or adult protection] case is referred by a court to mediation and a public agency participates.]

[Alternative B: public agency participates in the [State to insert, for example, child or adult protection] mediation].

(b) There is no privilege under Section 4 if a court, administrative agency, or arbitrator finds, after a hearing *in camera*, that the party seeking discovery or the proponent of the evidence has shown that the evidence is not otherwise available, that there is a need for the evidence that substantially outweighs the interest in protecting confidentiality, and that the mediation communication is sought or offered in:

(1) a court proceeding involving a felony [or misdemeanor]; or

(2) except as otherwise provided in subsection (c), a proceeding to prove a claim to rescind or reform or a defense to avoid liability on a contract arising out of the mediation.

(c) A mediator may not be compelled to provide evidence of a mediation communication referred to in subsection (a)(6) or (b)(2).

(d) If a mediation communication is not privileged under subsection (a) or (b), only the portion of the communication necessary for the application of the exception from nondisclosure may be admitted. Admission of evidence under subsection (a) or (b) does not render the evidence, or any other mediation communication, discoverable or admissible for any other purpose.

Legislative Note: If the enacting state does not have an open records act, the following language in paragraph (2) of subsection (a) needs to be deleted: "available to the public under [insert statutory reference to open records act] or."

Notes and Questions

(1) Does the Uniform Mediation Act section dealing with exceptions to a mediation privilege provide for all of the exceptions delineated by Professor Kirtley? Would Kirtley agree with the wording of the UMA exception "a threat to inflict bodily injury"?

(2) Considering what you now know about confidentiality and its exceptions, reexamine your mediator's opening statement. How would you describe confidentiality to the parties so that they would feel comfortable sharing information while also ensuring that you are accurate about the degree to which that information might not be confidential. Would your explanation to mediation parties who are *pro se* differ from what you would say if the parties are represented and their lawyers are present?

(3) In the following case, a federal appellate court wrestles with the application of mediation privilege exceptions. As you read this case, consider how well the court considers the policy concerns raised by Professor Kirtley and the UMA provision.

Olam v. Congress Mortgage Company

United States District Court for the Northern District of California

68 F. Supp. 2d 1110 (1999)

WAYNE D. BRAZIL, UNITED STATES MAGISTRATE JUDGE.

The court addresses in this opinion several difficult issues about the relationship between a court-sponsored voluntary mediation and subsequent proceedings whose purpose is to determine whether the parties entered an enforceable agreement at the close of the mediation session.

As we explain below, the parties participated in a lengthy mediation that was hosted by this court's ADR Program Counsel—an employee of the court who is both a lawyer and an ADR professional. At the end of the mediation (after midnight), the parties signed a "Memorandum of Understanding" (MOU) that states that it is "intended as a binding document itself. . . ."

Contending that the consent she apparently gave was not legally valid, plaintiff has taken the position that the MOU is not enforceable. She has not complied with its terms. Defendants have filed a motion to enforce the MOU as a binding contract.

One of the principal issues with which the court wrestles, below, is whether evidence about what occurred during the mediation proceedings, including testimony from the mediator, may be used to help resolve this dispute. Before we address the merits of these issues, we must decide whose law to apply (state or federal).

[The court discussed the factors surrounding the choice of federal or state (California) law, ultimately deciding to follow California law on the issue of mediator testimony.]

Having decided, for reasons set forth below, that fairness required the court to take evidence from the mediator in this case, I elected to call the mediator to the witness stand after the other principal participants in the September 10, 1998, mediation had testified. But, importantly, I also decided to take the testimony from the mediator in closed proceedings, under seal. After hearing his testimony in this protected setting, and after considering all the other evidence adduced during the hearing, I was positioned to determine much more reliably whether, or to what extent, overriding fairness interests required me to use and publicly disclose testimony from the mediator in making my decision about whether the parties had entered an enforceable settlement contract.

Pertinent California Privilege Law

The California legislature has crafted two sets of statutory provisions that must be addressed by courts considering whether they may use in a subsequent civil proceeding any evidence about what occurred or was said during a mediation.

Section 703.5 of the California Evidence Code states, in pertinent part: "No person presiding at any judicial or quasi-judicial proceeding, and no arbitrator or mediator, shall be competent to testify, in any subsequent civil proceeding, as to any statement, conduct, decision, or ruling, occurring at or in conjunction with the prior proceeding, except as to a statement or conduct that could [give rise to contempt, constitute a crime, trigger investigation by the State Bar or the Commission on Judicial Performance, or give rise to disqualification proceedings]."

. . .

The other directly pertinent provision from the California Evidence Code is § 1119. It states, in pertinent part: "Except as otherwise provided in this chapter: (a) No evidence of anything said or any admission made . . . in the course of, or pursuant to, a mediation . . . is admissible or subject to discovery, and disclosure of the evidence shall not be compelled, in any . . . noncriminal proceeding . . . (b) No writing . . . prepared in the course of, or pursuant to, a mediation . . . is admissible or subject to discovery, and disclosure of the writing shall not be compelled in any . . . noncriminal proceeding . . . (c) All communications . . . by and between participants in the course of a mediation . . . shall remain confidential."

Of the other provisions that expressly qualify the prohibitions set forth in section 1119, the most important for our purposes is § 1123. It states that "[a] written settlement agreement prepared in the course of, or pursuant to, a mediation, is not made inadmissible, or protected from disclosure . . . if the agreement is signed by the settling parties and . . . (b) The agreement provides that it is enforceable or binding or words to that effect."

As noted above, the "Memorandum of Understanding" that the parties executed at the end of the mediation session in this case states expressly that it "is intended as a binding document itself." No party contends that this MOU is inadmissible.

Waivers by the *Parties* (But *Not* the Mediator) of their Mediation Privilege

As we noted earlier, the plaintiff and the defendants have expressly waived confidentiality protections conferred by the California statutes quoted above. Both the plaintiff and the defendants have indicated, clearly and on advice of counsel, that they want the court to consider evidence about what occurred during the mediation, including testimony directly from the mediator, as the court resolves the issues raised by defendants' motion to enforce the settlement agreement.

Faced with a document that on its face appears to be an enforceable settlement contract, and contending that her apparent consent was not legally valid because of serious temporary impairments in her mental, emotional, and physical condition, plaintiff's waiver reaches not only perceptions by other participants of her appearance, demeanor, condition, and conduct during the mediation, but also their recollections of what she said and what others said in her presence. Her waiver expressly covers testimony about such matters not only by opposing counsel and parties, but also by the mediator and by her then lawyer, Ms. Voisenat. It covers group sessions as well as private caucuses.

. . .

The Mediator's Privilege

California law confers on mediators a privilege that is independent of the privilege conferred on parties to a mediation. By declaring that, subject to exceptions not applicable here, mediators are incompetent to testify "as to any statement, conduct, decision, or ruling, occurring at or in conjunction with [the mediation]," section 703.5 of the Evidence Code has the effect of making a mediator the holder of an independent privilege. Section 1119 of the Evidence Code appears to have the same effect — as it prohibits courts from compelling disclosure of evidence about mediation communications and directs that all such communications "shall remain confidential." As the California Court of Appeal recently pointed out, "the Legislature intended that the confidentiality provision of section 1119 may be asserted by the mediator as well as by the participants in the mediation." It follows that, under California law, a waiver of the mediation privilege by the parties is not a sufficient basis for a court to permit or order a mediator to testify. Rather, an independent determination must be made before testimony from a mediator should be permitted or ordered.

In the case at bar, the mediator (Mr. Herman) was and is an employee of the federal court (a "staff neutral"). He hosted the mediation at the behest of the court and under this court's ADR rules. These facts are not sufficient to justify ordering him to testify about what occurred during the mediation — even when the parties have waived their mediation privilege and want the mediator to testify. Mr. Herman is a member of the California bar — and no doubt feels bound to honor the directives of California law. He also is a professional in mediation — and feels a moral obligation to preserve the essential integrity of the mediation process — an integrity to which he believes the promise of confidentiality is fundamental.

Out of respect for these feelings, the court chose not to put Mr. Herman in an awkward position where he might have felt he had to choose between being a loyal employee of the court, on the one hand, and, on the other, asserting the mediator's privilege under California law. Instead, the court announced that it would proceed on the assumption that Mr. Herman was respectfully and appropriately asserting the mediator's privilege and was formally objecting to being called to testify about anything said or done during the mediation.

Regardless of whether Mr. Herman invoked the mediator's privilege, the wording of section 703.5 can be understood as imposing an independent duty on the courts to determine whether testimony from a mediator should be accepted. Unlike some other privilege statutes, which expressly confer a right on the holder of the privilege to refuse to disclose protected communications, as well as the power to prevent others from disclosing such communications, section 703.5 is framed in terms of competence to testify. In its pertinent part, it declares that (subject to exceptions not applicable here) a mediator is not competent to testify "in any subsequent civil proceeding" about words uttered or conduct occurring during a mediation. This wording appears to have two consequences: it would not empower a mediator to prevent others from disclosing mediation communications, but it would require courts, on their own initiative, to determine whether it would be lawful to compel or permit a mediator to testify about matters occurring within a mediation.

So the issue of whether it was appropriate under California law in these circumstances to compel the mediator to testify was squarely raised both by the court's assuming that Mr. Herman invoked the applicable statutes and by the court's understanding of its independent duty to address this question.

. . .

We turn to the issue of whether, under California law, we should compel the mediator to testify — despite the statutory prohibitions set forth in sections 703.5 and 1119 of the Evidence Code. The most important opinion by a California court in this arena is *Rinaker v. Superior Court*, 62 Cal. App. 4th 155 (Third District 1998).

. . .

In essence, the *Rinaker* court instructs California trial judges to conduct a two-stage balancing analysis. The goal of the first stage balancing is to determine whether to compel the mediator to appear at an *in camera* proceeding to determine precisely what her testimony would be. In this first stage, the judge considers all the circumstances and weighs all the competing rights and interests, including the values that would be threatened not by public disclosure of mediation communications, but by ordering the mediator to appear at an *in camera* proceeding to disclose only to the court and counsel, out of public view, what she would say the parties said during the mediation. At this juncture the goal is to determine whether the harm that would be done to the values that underlie the mediation privileges simply by ordering the mediator to participate in the *in camera* proceedings can be justified — by the prospect that her testimony might well make a singular and substantial contribution to protecting or advancing competing interests of comparable or greater magnitude.

The trial judge reaches the second stage of balancing analysis only if the product of the first stage is a decision to order the mediator to detail, *in camera*, what her testimony would be. A court that orders the *in camera* disclosure gains precise and reliable knowledge of what the mediator's testimony would be — and only with that knowledge is the court positioned to launch its second balancing analysis. In this second stage the court is to weigh and comparatively assess (1) the importance of the values and interests that would be harmed if the mediator was compelled to testify (perhaps subject to a sealing or protective order, if appropriate), (2) the magnitude of the harm that compelling the testimony would cause to those values and interests, (3) the importance of the rights or interests that would be jeopardized if the mediator's testimony was not accessible in the specific proceedings in question, and (4) how much the testimony would contribute toward protecting those rights or advancing those interests — an inquiry that includes, among other things, an assessment of whether there are alternative sources of evidence of comparable probative value.

So we turn now to a description of that balancing analysis.

As indicated in an earlier section, the product of the first stage of the analysis was my decision that it was necessary to determine (through sealed proceedings) what Mr. Herman's testimony would be. Reaching that determination involved the following considerations. First, I acknowledge squarely that a decision to require a mediator to give evidence, even *in camera* or under seal, about what occurred during a mediation threatens values underlying the mediation privileges.

. . .

While this court has no occasion or power to quarrel with these generally applicable pronouncements of state policy, we observe that they appear to have appreciably less force when, as here, the parties to the mediation have waived confidentiality protections, indeed have asked the court to compel the mediator to testify — so that justice can be done.

. . .

This is not a matter of time and money only. Good mediators are likely to feel violated by being compelled to give evidence that could be used against a party with whom they tried to establish a relationship of trust during a mediation. Good mediators are deeply committed to being and remaining neutral and non-judgmental, and to building and preserving relationships with parties. To force them to give evidence that hurts someone from whom they actively solicited trust (during the mediation) rips the fabric of their work and can threaten their sense of the center of their professional integrity. These are not inconsequential matters.

Like many other variables in this kind of analysis, however, the magnitude of these risks can vary with the circumstances. Here, for instance, all parties to the mediation want the mediator to testify about things that occurred during the mediation — so ordering the testimony would do less harm to the actual relationships developed than it would in a case where one of the parties to the mediation objected to the use of evidence from the mediator.

. . .

The magnitude of the risk to values underlying the mediation privileges that can be created by ordering a mediator to testify also can vary with the nature of the testimony that is sought. Comparing the kind of testimony sought in *Rinaker* with the kind of testimony sought in the case at bar illustrates this point. In *Rinaker*, one party wanted to use the mediator's recollection about what another party said during the mediation to impeach subsequent trial testimony. So the mediator was to serve as a source of evidence about what words a party to the mediation uttered, what statements or admissions that party made.

As the Court of Appeal appeared to recognize, this kind of testimony could be particularly threatening to the spirit and methods that some people believe are important both to the philosophy and the success of some mediation processes. Under one approach to mediation, the primary goal is not to establish "the truth" or to determine reliably what the historical facts actually were. Rather, the goal is to go both deeper than and beyond history — to emphasize feelings, underlying interests, and a search for means for social repair or reorientation. In this kind of mediation, what happened between the parties in the past can be appreciably less important than why, than what needs drove what happened or were exposed or defined by what happened, than how the parties feel about it, and than what they can bring themselves to do to move on.

Moreover, the methods some mediators use to explore underlying interests and feelings and to build settlement bridges are in some instances intentionally distanced from the actual historical facts. In some mediations, the focus is on feelings rather than facts. The neutral may ask the parties to set aside pre-occupations with what happened as she tries to help the parties understand underlying motivations and needs and to remove emotional obstacles through exercises in venting. Some mediators use hypotheticals that are expressly and intentionally not presented as accurate reflections of reality — in order to help the parties explore their situation and the range of solution options that might be available. A mediator might encourage parties to "try on" certain ideas or feelings that the parties would contend have little connection with past conduct, to experiment with the effects on themselves and others of expressions of emotions or of openness to concessions or proposals that, outside the special environment of the mediation, the parties would not entertain or admit. All of this, as mediator Rinaker herself pointed out, can have precious little to do with historical accuracy or "truth."

Given these features of some mediations, it could be both threatening and unfair to hold a participant to the literal meaning of at least some of the words she uttered during the course of a mediation. And testimony from the mediator about what those words were during the mediation might constitute very unreliable (actively misleading) evidence about what the earlier historical facts were.

For these reasons, a court conducting the kind of balancing analysis called for by the *Rinaker* court should try to determine what kind of techniques and processes were used in the particular mediation in issue. The more like the processes just described, the more harm would be done by trying to use evidence about what was said or done during the mediation to help prove what the earlier historical facts really were. On the other hand, if the mediation process was closer to an adjudicate/ evaluative model, with a clear focus (understood by all participants) on evidence, law, and traditional analysis of liability, damages, and settlement options, use of evidence from the mediation in subsequent civil proceedings might be less vulnerable to criticism for being unfair and unreliable.

Regardless of which approach or methods the mediator used, however, the kind of testimony sought from the mediator in this case poses less of a threat to fairness and reliability values than the kind of testimony that was sought from the mediator in *Rinaker*. During the first stage balancing analysis in the case at bar, the parties and I assumed that the testimony from the mediator that would be most consequential would focus not primarily on what Ms. Olam said during the mediation, but on how she acted and the mediator's perceptions of her physical, emotional, and mental condition. The purpose would not be to nail down and dissect her specific words, but to assess at a more general and impressionistic level her condition and capacities. That purpose might be achieved with relatively little disclosure of the content of her confidential communications. As conceded above, that does not mean that compelling the testimony by the mediator would pose no threat to values underlying the privileges — but that the degree of harm to those values would not be as great as it would be if the testimony was for the kinds of impeachment purposes that were proffered in *Rinaker*. And in a balancing analysis, probable degree of harm is an important consideration.

. . .

The interests that are likely to be advanced by compelling the mediator to testify in this case are of considerable importance. Moreover, as we shall see, some of those interests parallel and reinforce the objectives the legislature sought to advance by providing for confidentiality in mediation.

The first interest we identify is the interest in doing justice. Here is what we mean. For reasons described below, the mediator is positioned in this case to offer what could be crucial, certainly very probative, evidence about the central factual issues in this matter. There is a strong possibility that his testimony will greatly improve the court's ability to determine reliably what the pertinent historical facts actually were. Establishing reliably what the facts were is critical to doing justice (here, justice means this: applying the law correctly to the real historical facts). It is the fundamental duty of a public court in our society to do justice — to resolve disputes in accordance with the law when the parties don't. Confidence in our system of justice as a whole, in our government as a whole, turns in no small measure on confidence in the courts' ability to do justice in individual cases. So doing justice in individual cases is an interest of considerable magnitude.

When we put case-specific flesh on these abstract bones, we see that "doing justice" implicates interests of considerable importance to the parties — all of whom want the mediator to testify. From the plaintiff's perspective, the interests that the defendants' motion threatens could hardly be more fundamental. According to Ms.

Olam, the mediation process was fundamentally unfair to her — and resulted in an apparent agreement whose terms are literally unconscionable and whose enforcement would render her homeless and virtually destitute. To her, doing justice in this setting means protecting her from these fundamental wrongs.

From the defendants' perspective, doing justice in this case means, among other things, bringing to a lawful close disputes with Ms. Olam that have been on-going for about seven years — disputes that the defendants believe have cost them, without justification, at least scores of thousands of dollars. The defendants believe that Ms. Olam has breached no fewer than three separate contractual commitments with them (not counting the agreement reached at the end of the mediation) — and that those breaches are the product of a calculated effort not only to avoid meeting legitimate obligations, but also to make unfair use, for years, of the defendants' money.

Defendants also believe that Ms. Olam has abused over the years several of her own counsel — as well as the judicial process and this court's ADR program (for which she has been charged nothing). Through their motion, the defendants ask the court to affirm that they acquired legal rights through the settlement agreement that the mediation produced. They also ask the court to enforce those rights, and thus to enable the defendants to avoid the burdens, expense, delay, and risks of going to trial in this matter. These also are matters of consequence.

And they are not the only interests that could be advanced by compelling the mediator to testify. According to the defendants' pre-hearing proffers, the mediator's testimony would establish clearly that the mediation process was fair and that the plaintiff's consent to the settlement agreement was legally viable. Thus the mediator's testimony, according to the defendants, would reassure the community and the court about the integrity of the mediation process that the court sponsored.

That testimony also would provide the court with the evidentiary confidence it needs to enforce the agreement. A publicly announced decision to enforce the settlement would, in turn, encourage parties who want to try to settle their cases to use the court's mediation program for that purpose. An order appropriately enforcing an agreement reached through the mediation also would encourage parties in the future to take mediations seriously, to understand that they represent real opportunities to reach closure and avoid trial, and to attend carefully to terms of agreements proposed in mediations. In these important ways, taking testimony from the mediator could strengthen the mediation program.

In sharp contrast, refusing to compel the mediator to testify might well deprive the court of the evidence it needs to rule reliably on the plaintiff's contentions — and thus might either cause the court to impose an unjust outcome on the plaintiff or disable the court from enforcing the settlement. In this setting, refusing to compel testimony from the mediator might end up being tantamount to denying the motion to enforce the agreement — because a crucial source of evidence about the plaintiff's condition and capacities would be missing. Following that course, defendants suggest, would do considerable harm not only to the court's mediation program but also to fundamental fairness

. . .

In sum, it is clear that refusing even to determine what the mediator's testimony would be, in the circumstances here presented, threatens values of great significance. But we would miss the main analytical chance if all we did was identify those values and proclaim their importance. In fact, when the values implicated are obviously of great moment, there is a danger that the process of identifying them will generate unjustified momentum toward a conclusion that exaggerates the weight on this side of the scale. Thus we emphasize that the central question is not which values are implicated, but how much they would be advanced by compelling the testimony or how much they would be harmed by not compelling it.

We concluded, after analysis and before the hearing, that the mediator's testimony was sufficiently likely to make substantial contributions toward achieving the ends described above to justify compelling an exploration, under seal, of what his testimony would be. While we did not assume that there were no pressures or motivations that might affect the reliability of the mediator's testimony, it was obvious that the mediator was the only source of presumptively disinterested, neutral evidence. The only other witnesses with personal knowledge of the plaintiff's condition at the mediation were the parties and their lawyers — none of whom were disinterested. And given the foreseeable testimony about the way the mediation was structured (with lots of caucusing by the mediator with one side at a time), it was likely that the mediator would have had much more exposure to the plaintiff over the course of the lengthy mediation than any other witness save her lawyer.

. . .

In short, there was a substantial likelihood that testimony from the mediator would be the most reliable and probative on the central issues raised by the plaintiff in response to the defendants' motion. And there was no likely alternative source of evidence on these issues that would be of comparable probative utility. So it appeared that testimony from the mediator would be crucial to the court's capacity to do its job — and that refusing to compel that testimony posed a serious threat to every value identified above. In this setting, California courts clearly would conclude the first stage balancing analysis by ordering the mediator to testify *in camera* or under seal — so that the court, aided by inputs from the parties, could make a refined and reliable judgment about whether to use that testimony to help resolve the substantive issues raised by the pending motion.

As noted earlier, we called the mediator to testify (under seal) after all other participants in the mediation had been examined and cross-examined — so that the lawyers (and the court) would be able to identify all the subjects and questions that they should cover with the mediator. With the record thus fully developed, we were well situated to determine whether using (and publicly disclosing) the mediator's testimony would make a contribution of sufficient magnitude to justify the level of harm that using and disclosing the testimony would likely cause, in the circumstances of this case, to the interests that inform the mediation privilege law in California. As our detailed account, later in this opinion, of the evidence from all sources demonstrates, it became clear that the mediator's testimony was essential to doing justice here — so we decided to use it and unseal it.

[The court went on to conclude, based in part on the mediator's *in camera* testimony, that plaintiff had failed to present adequate evidence that the agreement she entered into was unenforceable.]

In re Teligent, Inc.

United States Court of Appeals for the Second Circuit
640 F.3d 53 (2011)

[A law firm had moved to lift two protective orders that would have prohibited disclosure of communications made during mediation. The federal bankruptcy judge denied this motion, and a related motion concerning the validity of provisions of the settlement agreement.]

. . .

In this case, the bankruptcy court denied K & L Gates's motion to lift the confidentiality provisions of the Protective Orders based on the court's conclusion that K & L Gates failed to demonstrate a compelling need for the discovery, failed to show that the information was not otherwise available, and failed to establish that the need for the evidence was outweighed by the public interest in maintaining confidentiality. The district court affirmed these conclusions. There was no error in this conclusion.

Confidentiality is an important feature of the mediation and other alternative dispute resolution processes. Promising participants confidentiality in these proceedings "promotes the free flow of information that may result in the settlement of a dispute," and protecting the integrity of alternative dispute resolution generally. We vigorously enforce the confidentiality provisions of our own alternative dispute resolution, the Civil Appeals Management Plan ("CAMP"), because we believe that confidentiality is "essential" to CAMP's vitality and effectiveness.

A party seeking disclosure of confidential mediation communications must demonstrate (1) a special need for the confidential material, (2) resulting unfairness from a lack of discovery, and (3) that the need for the evidence outweighs the interest in maintaining confidentiality. All three factors are necessary to warrant disclosure of otherwise non-discoverable documents.

We draw this standard from the sources relied upon by the learned bankruptcy court, which include the Uniform Mediation Act ("UMA"), the Administrative Dispute Resolution Act of 1996 ("ADRA 1996"), 5 U.S.C. §§ 571 *et seq.*, and the Administrative Dispute Resolution Act of 1998 ("ADRA 1998"), 28 U.S.C. §§ 651 *et seq.* Each of these recognizes the importance of maintaining the confidentiality of mediation communications and provides for disclosure in only limited circumstances. For example, ADRA 1996, which applies to federal administrative agency alternative dispute resolution, prohibits disclosure of confidential mediation communications unless the party seeking disclosure demonstrates exceptional circumstances, such as when non-disclosure would result in a manifest injustice, help establish a violation of law, or prevent harm to the public health or safety. Relatedly, under the UMA, the party seeking disclosure of confidential mediation communications must demonstrate that the evidence is not otherwise available and that the need for the communications substantially outweighs the interest in protecting confidentiality. The standards for disclosure under the UMA and the ADRAs are also consistent with the standard governing modification of protective orders entered under Federal Rule of Civil Procedure 26(c). . . .

Here, as the bankruptcy court observed, K & L Gates has sought a blanket lift of the confidentiality provisions in the Protective Orders. However, K & L Gates failed to demonstrate a special or compelling need for *all* mediation communications. Indeed, the law firm failed to submit any evidence to support its argument that there was a special need for disclosure of any specific communication. There was, therefore, no error in the bankruptcy court's conclusion that K & L Gates failed to satisfy prong one of the standard governing disclosure of confidential mediation communications.

Likewise, the bankruptcy court committed no error in holding that K & L Gates failed to satisfy prong two of the test. As the bankruptcy court explained, the law firm failed to demonstrate a resulting unfairness from a lack of discovery, because the evidence sought by K & L Gates was available through other means, including through responses to interrogatories or depositions. Accordingly, the law firm failed to show that "extraordinary circumstances" warrant disclosure.

Finally, because K & L Gates failed to demonstrate a special need for the mediation communications, the law firm did not satisfy prong three of the test, which requires a party seeking disclosure of confidential material to show that its need outweighs the important interest in protecting the confidentiality of the material. As we explained in the context of litigation, if "protective orders have no presumptive entitlement to remain in force, parties would resort less often to the judicial system for fear that such orders would be readily set aside in the future." It follows that similar concerns arise in the context of mediation. Were courts to cavalierly set aside confidentiality restrictions on disclosure of communications made in the context of mediation, parties might be less frank and forthcoming during the mediation process or might even limit their use of mediation altogether. These concerns counsel in favor of a presumption against modification of the confidentiality provisions of protective orders entered in the context of mediation. Accordingly, we conclude that there was no error in the denial of K & L Gates's motion to lift the confidentiality provisions of the Protective Orders in this case.

. . .

Conclusion

For the reasons stated herein, we AFFIRM the order of the district court.

Notes and Questions

(1) In taking the mediator's testimony "in closed proceedings, under seal" in the *Olam* case, was Judge Brazil, in effect, carving out a "manifest injustice" exception? Judge Brazil's lengthy commentary on the need for confidentiality displays a sensitivity to important policy concerns. Was his decision to go forward with the mediator's testimony largely influenced by the fact that he had been responsible for his court's ADR programs for 15 years and had never before encountered the issue? Was the fact that both parties agreed to waive confidentiality critical to his decision?

(2) In *Teligent*, the United States Court of Appeals for the Second Circuit takes a firm stand in protecting the confidentiality of mediation communications by establishing a restrictive, three-part test for granting an exception. For a discussion of the *Teligent* test, see Sarah R. Cole, *et al.*, Mediation Law, Policy & Practice 492–93 (2021–2022 ed.). In *Avocent Redmond Corp. v. Raritan Americas, Inc.*, 2011 U.S. Dist. LEXIS 109596 (S.D.N.Y. Sept. 23, 2011), a federal trial court applied the *Teligent* exceptions in ruling that the party seeking disclosure had "not satisfied any one of the three prongs." Do you think the *Teligent* test is likely to be followed in other courts?

(3) With regard to the confidentiality of mediation communications, Professor Richard Reuben describes Texas law as: "Mediation communications are confidential unless a court wants to hear them." Do the following Texas appellate court decisions support Professor Reuben's description of Texas law? In *Avary v. Bank of America, N.A.*, 72 S.W.3d 779 (Tex. App. 2002), otherwise confidential information was sought from a party concerning a tort (breach of fiduciary duty) that was allegedly committed during the mediation. The appellate court remanded to the trial court to determine whether disclosure of the information was warranted in light of the "facts, circumstances, and context." The trial court ordered disclosure, and the appellate court denied a subsequent request for a protective writ of mandamus. In *Alford v. Bryant*, 137 S.W.3d 916 (Tex. App. 2004), the trial court refused to allow the mediator to testify in an action for attorney malpractice as to disclosures allegedly made by the attorney during mediation. The appellate court reversed and remanded, ruling that the mediator's outcome determinative testimony was erroneously excluded at trial.

(4) Is evidence compiled for use in the mediation process subject to the same confidentiality protection as mediation communications? The high courts in two non-UMA states have taken somewhat different approaches in addressing this issue. In *Rojas v. Los Angeles County Superior Court*, 93 P.3d 260 (Cal. 2004), the Supreme Court of California ruled that the state's confidentiality statute not only protects the substance of communications in mediation, but also "raw evidence" exchanged

at the mediation, if it was compiled specifically to be used in the mediation. On the other hand, the Supreme Court of Alabama ruled in *Alabama Department of Transportation v. Land Energy Ltd.*, 886 So. 2d 787 (Ala. 2004), that tables prepared by a state agency were not protected and could be admitted in subsequent litigation, because they were not prepared solely for the mediation and were provided after the mediation in response to pre-existing discovery requests.

(5) Does confidentiality protection extend to matters following the mediation that relate to the substance of the mediation? The Supreme Court of Montana responded in the negative in *In re Estate of Stukey*, 100 P.3d 114 (Mont. 2004). The court ruled that a letter written after the mediation by the estate's attorney to the attorney for the decedent's daughter clarifying the scope of the settlement reached in mediation was not part of the mediation process, and thus not subject to the protection of the state's confidentiality statute.

G. Confidentiality in Online Mediation

In recent years, mediations have often been conducted online. Indeed, during the pandemic, online dispute resolution (ODR) was widespread. A number of commentators have suggested that online mediation requires an adjustment of mediation standards of practice, particularly with regard to confidentiality. Professor Susan Nauss Exon has argued that "[t]he biggest problem is that confidentiality and security in an online environment is beyond the sole responsibility of the mediator."[3] And Professor Noam Ebner counsels online mediators: *"Do not promise what you cannot keep.* Be explicit about what you can promise and what you cannot . . . refrain from promising 'We will all be keeping this secret.'"[4] Ebner explains:

> In online processes . . . parties never know who is "in the room" with them. Will my counterpart forward my message to their boss or colleagues? Is my counterpart alone in the room, or is someone listening in, off-camera? Beyond immediate privacy issues is that of privacy over time. Messages transmitted via email are recorded, forever archived on your counterpart's computer, beyond your control. Similarly, there is no way for one party to prevent another from recording a videoconference session without their knowledge or consent. Both records might even be tampered with, altering what you wrote or said. Private information might become public — due to the other's bad intentions, or just a technical mishap.[5]

---

3. Susan Nauss Exon, *Ethics and Online Dispute Resolution: From Evolution to Revolution*, 32 Ohio St. J. Disp. Resol. 609, 648 (2017).

4. Noam Ebner, *The Human Touch in ODR: Trust, Empathy and Social Intuition in Online Negotiation and Mediation*, Ch. 4, *in* Rainey, Katsch, and Wahab (eds.), Online Dispute Resolution: Theory and Practice 115 (2d ed. 2021).

5. *Id.* at 114.

In Section C above, an example of a contractual Agreement to Mediate document appears. It contains provisions outlining the scope of and exceptions regarding the confidentiality of the mediation. The presumed setting was that the mediation would be conducted in person. But are the provisions adequate if the mediation is to be conducted online? What follows is a proposed addendum to that agreement to address the online environment.

Minnesota Department of Human Rights (MDHR)

Mediation Program
Addendum For Online Mediation

Case No.: XXXXX

In addition to the terms set forth in the Agreement to Mediate, by signing below, you understand the terms of this Addendum for Online Mediation, and you agree to them.

1. In this mediation, Zoom will be used as the Online Platform, (OP). The mediator has reviewed and tested the OP and is comfortable using the OP for purposes of this mediation. Mediation participants agree that they will use this OP, and should they have a problem with the OP during the mediation, they will raise any questions or concerns to the mediator. If needed, all mediation participants agree to utilize voice conferencing by telephone as a substitute for the OP.

2. Mediation participants understand that because online applications will be used during this mediation, complete security of information may not be ensured. MDHR has reviewed the security protocols of the OP and is making this OP available for today's mediation. The state of Minnesota and the mediator make no representation that this OP is secure. MDHR and the mediator have taken reasonable measures to ensure a secure mediation, however, risks including but not limited to: data breach, illicit recording, or unknown parties attending the mediation, exist. Neither MDHR nor the mediator can guarantee the security or privacy of the OP. Mediation participants understand and accept these risks.

3. No mediation participant shall make any recording of this mediation or share information exchanged during this mediation with any unauthorized parties. Mediation participants shall protect the information shared during this mediation from being viewed or used by anyone, not a party to this agreement.

4. Mediation participants agree this mediation is confidential. Mediation participants shall take reasonable steps to ensure that they are in a secure and private environment. Mediation participants shall disclose the presence of any other persons present in the room, or with whom they are communicating remotely during the mediation.

5. The mediator shall show no bias toward any mediation participant concerning their comfort or familiarity with the OP and process used during this mediation.

The mediator shall maintain neutrality and communicate with both parties in a neutral manner. If mediation participants have any concerns with the use of the OP during this mediation, they will discuss these concerns with the mediator.

Charging Party's Signature

Charging Party's Representative

Respondent's Signature

Respondent's Representative

Mediator's Signature

Date

Note

Do you think that the addendum to the mediation agreement adequately deals with the concerns raised by Professors Exon and Ebner? Can you think of additional concerns with online mediation that should be addressed? For a proposed framework to protect confidentiality in online mediation, see Christopher R. Meltzer, *From Conference Rooms to Chat Rooms: The Need to Protect Confidentiality in Online Mediation*, 5 Appalachian L.J. 275 (2006).

Chapter 6

Legal Issues in Mediation

A. Introduction

This chapter examines some of the more prominent legal issues, in addition to the confidentiality issues explored in the previous chapter, that have arisen in the mediation process. Chief among these are matters relating to pre-dispute mediation clauses (Section B), the power to compel mediation (Section C), the requirement of "mediation in good faith" (Section D), and the enforceability of mediated agreements (Section E). While mediation is often touted as a flexible, non-legal process, unfettered by rigid procedures and rules, it is perhaps inevitable that with its more frequent use by legal professionals, attempts would be made to make the mediation process more regularized and uniform. Over the past several decades, there has been a rapid growth in the number of statutes and cases dealing with mediation. In addition to the legal issues discussed in this chapter and the previous chapter, other topics include those facing the mediator, such as conflicts of interest, the unauthorized practice of law, and mediator liability and immunity (Chapter 8, *infra*) and those governing a lawyer's participation in mediation, including the lawyer's duty to inform a client of dispute resolution alternatives (Chapter 10, *infra*).

B. Agreements to Mediate and Statutory Requirements to Mediate

What are the consequences of a party's unwillingness to mediate if they have a contractual agreement to mediate or are required to mediate pursuant to a federal or state statute? If it were arbitration rather than mediation that was in question, it is now well established that the courts will enforce the parties' written agreement-to-arbitrate contractual provisions, subject to such statutory exceptions as the arbitration clause was fraudulently induced or otherwise invalid as a matter of contract law. These clauses appear in multiple settings, including those governing service delivery for mobile phones and executing medical and hospital procedures. Pursuant to these provisions, courts compel parties to participate in the contracted-for-arbitration or, minimally, deny a party's petition to adjudicate the controversy in court. Additionally, some statutory schemes require that parties negotiate in good faith with a mediator's assistance as a condition-precedent to scheduling a trial on the matter.

While contractual agreements to mediate and statutory requirements to mediate are now commonplace, their enforceability is seen by some as more problematic than the enforcement of arbitration contracts and statutory mandates. Some argue that a court's enforcement of an agreement or requirement to mediate would be futile because, although parties may be forced to the mediation table, they cannot be forced to settle. Others assert that public policy now favors mediation as a means of resolving disputes and that courts should further this policy by enforcing obligations or requirements to mediate. As you read the following cases, consider the policy rationales presented by the courts as they confront issues over whether to enforce mediation agreements or statutory requirements to mediate. Note also the remedies chosen by the courts if they choose to enforce the mediation provision.

Brosnan v. Dry Cleaning Station

United States District Court for the Northern District of California
2008 U.S. Dist. LEXIS 44678 (June 6, 2008)

Elizabeth D. Laporte, United States Magistrate Judge.

On March 17, 2008, Plaintiffs Timothy Brosnan and Carla Brosnan filed this action in San Mateo County Superior Court alleging state law claims relating to fraud and breach of contract against Defendants Dry Cleaning Station, Inc. and John Campbell. Plaintiffs' claims arise from a Franchise Agreement executed by the parties for operation of a Dry Cleaning Station store. On April 18, 2008, Defendants removed this case to federal court alleging diversity jurisdiction pursuant to 28 U.S.C. §1332.

On April 23, 2008, Defendants filed a motion to dismiss Plaintiffs' complaint based on Federal Rule of Civil Procedure 12(b) (6) on the grounds that Plaintiffs failed to engage in mediation of this dispute prior to filing their lawsuit as required by the Franchise Agreement. The Franchise Agreement states in relevant part:

> Except to the extent that the Company believes it is necessary to seek equitable relief as permitted in Section 20.1, or to recover royalties or other amounts owed to it by the Franchisee, the Company and the Franchisee each agree to enter into mediation of all disputes involving this Agreement or any other aspect of the relationship, for a minimum of four (4) hours, prior to initiating any legal action against the other.

Plaintiffs do not dispute that they failed to engage in mediation prior to filing their lawsuit, but in their opposition seek a stay of this matter rather than dismissal. Because this matter is appropriate for decision without oral argument, the Court vacated the June 3, 2008 hearing.

Failure to mediate a dispute pursuant to a contract that makes mediation a condition precedent to filing a lawsuit warrants dismissal. *See B & O Mfg., Inc. v. Home Depot U.S.A., Inc.*, 2007 U.S. Dist. LEXIS 83998, (N.D.Cal. Nov. 1, 2007) ("A claim that is filed before a mediation requirement, that is a condition precedent to the parties' right to sue as set forth in an agreement, is satisfied shall be dismissed.") (citing *Gould v. Gould*, 240 Ga. App. 481, 482, 523 S.E.2d 106 (1999)). California state law so holds. *See Charles J. Rounds Co. v. Joint Council of Teamsters No. 42*, 4 Cal.3d 888 (1971) (affirming trial court's dismissal of a breach of contract action based on a collective bargaining agreement on the grounds that the dispute was covered by an arbitration clause in the agreement); *see also Johnson v. Seigel*, 84 Cal.App.4th 1087 (2000) (relying on *Rounds* and affirming the trial court's grant of summary judgment on the ground that the plaintiff failed to pursue arbitration as required by the real estate contract prior to filing the lawsuit). The *Rounds* Court provides specific instruction on the effect of a plaintiff's failure to pursue alternative dispute resolution as provided in a contract:

> Specifically, where the only issue litigated is covered by the arbitration clause, and where plaintiff has not first pursued or attempted to pursue his arbitration remedy, it should be held that (1) plaintiff has impliedly waived his right to arbitrate, such that defendant could elect to submit the matter to the jurisdiction of the court; (2) defendant may also elect to demur or move for summary judgment on the ground that the plaintiff has failed to exhaust arbitration remedies; and (3) defendant may also elect to move for a stay of proceedings pending arbitration if defendant also moves to compel arbitration.

Rounds, 4 Cal.3d at 899. By contrast, where a plaintiff has "attempted to exhaust its arbitration remedy or raises issues not susceptible to arbitration or not covered by the arbitration agreement," a stay rather than dismissal of the lawsuit is appropriate. *Id.*

Here, there is no dispute that Plaintiffs did not pursue mediation prior to filing this lawsuit. Defendants have not elected to submit to the jurisdiction of the Court, nor have they moved to stay this action. Instead, they seek dismissal, to which they are entitled under *Rounds*. Although Plaintiffs prefer a stay, they cite no authority supporting the grant of a stay when Defendants opted for dismissal under these circumstances.

The Franchise Agreement states that if an action is commenced prior to seeking mediation, and if the court dismisses the action, the party against which the lawsuit was brought is entitled to fees and costs "in an amount equal to the attorneys' fees and costs the party seeking dismissal incurred." . . . Because this Court grants Defendants' motion to dismiss, Defendants may be entitled to fees and costs under the Franchise Agreement. However, the Court has dismissed this matter without prejudice, so a fee award may be premature. Further, it appears that Plaintiffs may not have been represented when they entered into the Franchise Agreement, which may raise the question as to whether or not the fees provision is enforceable. *See, e.g., Armendariz v. Foundation Health Psychcare Servs, Inc.*, 24 Cal.4th 83, 113 (2000).

IT IS SO ORDERED.

Notes and Questions

(1) The decision of the federal court in *Brosnan v. Dry Cleaning Station*, dismissing the claims for failure to engage in mediation prior to filing a lawsuit as required by the parties' contract, is consistent with the current tendency of courts nationwide to enforce contractual mediation agreements as a condition precedent to allowing the parties to proceed to litigation. *See, e.g., Santana v. Olguin*, 208 P.3d 328 (Kan. Ct. App. 2009) (mediation clause in a real estate contract created a condition precedent to litigation requiring dismissal of purchaser's lawsuit against vendor); *Cohen v. Cohen*, 2007 N.J. Super. Unpub. LEXIS 271 (July 23, 2007) (child support payments resulting from divorce settlement could not be changed without first attempting negotiation or mediation as required by the contract). In *DeValk Lincoln Mercury, Inc. v. Ford Motor Co.*, 811 F.2d 326 (7th Cir. 1987), compliance with a "mediation clause" in a commercial agreement was a condition precedent to pursuing other legal remedies. See also *HIM Portland LLC v. DeVito Builders, Inc.*, 317 F.3d 41 (1st Cir. 2003), where the U.S. Court of Appeals for the First Circuit ruled that a party could not compel arbitration absent a request by either party for mediation where the arbitration clause in the parties' agreement stated that disputes between the parties were subject to mediation as a condition precedent to arbitration. Similarly, in *Tinnerman v. TecStar*, 2012 U.S. Dist. LEXIS 49984 (E.D. Wis. Apr. 10, 2012), the court dismissed the lawsuit over Tinnerman's objection that mediation would be futile, stating that: "the parties' contract requires that they at least try to work out a compromise through mediation, and until that mediation occurs, Tinnerman cannot proceed with a lawsuit."

(2) Note the *Brosnan* court's reliance on the *Rounds* case, which involved an arbitration clause rather than a mediation clause. Does this suggest that the courts will now be giving as much deference to mediation clauses as they have been giving to arbitration clauses? What if the contract clause called for "mediation or arbitration" and the parties disagreed over which process should be used? What if the clause required a "multilayered" (negotiation, mediation, and arbitration) approach to dispute resolution and one of the parties opted to jump forward to arbitration, skipping negotiation and mediation? For an excellent discussion and analysis of the use of mediation clauses in contracts and related caselaw, see Cole, McEwen, Rogers, Coben & Thompson, Mediation: Law, Policy & Practice (2011).

(3) Professor Thomas Stipanowich does not believe that mediation clauses and contracts should be held to the same standard as agreements to arbitrate. Stipanowich, *Contract and Conflict Management*, 2001 Wis. L. Rev. 831, 863. He notes that parties in mediation, unlike arbitration, are not required to settle, even if required to mediate. Mediators also do not have the same quasi-judicial immunity as arbitrators. According to Stipanowich, these two processes are too distinctive to be treated so comparably. If agreements to mediate are not considered enforceable, why would parties include the language in contracts? What should be the consequence for failing to mediate if it was agreed to?

(4) In *Klinge v. Bentien*, 725 N.W.2d 13 (Iowa 2006), a statute required a "farm resident" to file a request for mediation with the farm mediation service and obtain a mediation release before filing suit if the matter involved a livestock "care and feeding contract." Because Klinge failed to satisfy these requirements before filing suit, the Supreme Court of Iowa ruled that the small claims court lacked subject matter jurisdiction to hear his claim and Bentien's counterclaim, such that both the decision of the small claims court and that of the district court on review were declared void. But at least two other state's high courts have refused to view statutory requirements to mediate as absolute. In *Walsh v. Larsen*, 705 N.W.2d 638 (S.D. 2005), the Supreme Court of South Dakota ruled that the statutory mediation requirement was not jurisdictional but more like an affirmative defense that has to be pled and established. Similarly, the Supreme Court of Maine in *Twomey v. Twomey*, 888 A.2d 272 (Me. 2005), ruled that the statutory mediation requirement in child support disputes would be deemed to be waived where a father's motion for a continuance to allow mediation might be viewed as a delaying tactic. Are these decisions consistent?

C. Judicial Power to Compel Mediation

Initially, some courts had questioned whether they had the power to require parties to participate in ADR processes. In *Strandell v. Jackson County*, 838 F.2d 884 (7th Cir. 1987), for example, the United States Court of Appeals for the Seventh Circuit ruled that a federal district judge did not have the inherent authority to order the parties to participate in a summary jury trial. However, the increasing number of statutes and court rules authorizing judges to manage and control their caseloads by compelling the use of ADR has established court-ordered mediation as an essential part of the litigation landscape in many jurisdictions. The cases in this section clearly demonstrate that courts have the power to require parties to participate in mediation. In *In re Atlantic Pipe Corp.*, the United States Court of Appeals for the First Circuit traces the sources of a federal trial judge's inherent power to compel mediation even in the absence of a specific local rule and over a party's objections.

In re Atlantic Pipe Corporation

United States Court of Appeals for the First Circuit
304 F.3d 135 (2002)

SELYA CIRCUIT JUDGE.

This mandamus proceeding requires us to resolve an issue of importance to judges and practitioners alike: Does a district court possess the authority to compel an unwilling party to participate in, and share the costs of, non-binding mediation conducted by a private mediator? We hold that a court may order mandatory mediation pursuant to an explicit statutory provision or local rule. We further hold that where, as here, no such authorizing medium exists, a court nonetheless may order mandatory mediation through the use of its inherent powers as long as the case is an appropriate one and the order contains adequate safeguards. Because the mediation order here at issue lacks such safeguards (although it does not fall far short), we vacate it and remand the matter for further proceedings.

In January 1996, Thames-Dick Superaqueduct Partners (Thames-Dick) entered into a master agreement with the Puerto Rico Aqueduct and Sewer Authority (PRASA) to construct, operate, and maintain the North Coast Superaqueduct Project (the Project). Thames-Dick granted subcontracts for various portions of the work, including a subcontract for construction management to Dick Corp. of Puerto Rico (Dick-PR), a subcontract for the operation and maintenance of the Project to Thames Water International, Ltd. (Thames Water), and a subcontract for the fabrication of pipe to Atlantic Pipe Corp. (APC). After the Project had been built, a segment of the pipeline burst. Thames-Dick incurred significant costs in repairing the damage. Not surprisingly, it sought to recover those costs from other parties. In response, one of PRASA's insurers filed a declaratory judgment action in a local court to determine whether Thames-Dick's claims were covered under its policy. The litigation ballooned, soon involving a number of parties and a myriad of issues above and beyond insurance coverage.

On April 25, 2001, the hostilities spilled over into federal court. . . . Thames-Dick asked that the case be referred to mediation and suggested Professor Eric Green as a suitable mediator. The district court granted the motion over APC's objection and ordered non-binding mediation to proceed before Professor Green. The court pronounced mediation likely to conserve judicial resources; directed all parties to undertake mediation in good faith; stayed discovery pending completion of the mediation; and declared that participation in the mediation would not prejudice the parties' positions vis-à-vis the pending motion or the litigation as a whole. The court also stated that if mediation failed to produce a global settlement, the case would proceed to trial.

After moving unsuccessfully for reconsideration of the mediation order, APC sought relief by way of mandamus. Its petition alleged that the district court did not have the authority to require mediation (especially in light of unresolved questions as to the court's subject-matter jurisdiction) and, in all events, could not force APC to pay a share of the expenses of the mediation.

. . .

There are four potential sources of judicial authority for ordering mandatory non-binding mediation of pending cases, namely, (a) the court's local rules, (b) an applicable statute, (c) the Federal Rules of Civil Procedure, and (d) the court's inherent powers. Because the district court did not identify the basis of its assumed authority, we consider each of these sources.

A district court's local rules may provide an appropriate source of authority for ordering parties to participate in mediation. In Puerto Rico, however, the local rules contain only a single reference to any form of alternative dispute resolution (ADR). . . . The respondents concede that the mediation order in this case falls outside the boundaries of the mediation program envisioned by Rule V. It does so most noticeably because it involves mediation before a private mediator, not a judicial officer. Seizing upon this discrepancy, APC argues that the local rules limit the district court in this respect, and that the court exceeded its authority thereunder by issuing a non-conforming mediation order (*i.e.*, one that contemplates the intervention of a private mediator). The respondents counter by arguing that the rule does not bind the district court because, notwithstanding the unambiguous promise of the CJR Plan (which declares that the district court "shall adopt a method of Alternative Dispute Resolution"), no such program has been adopted to date.

This is a powerful argument. APC does not contradict the respondents' assurance that the relevant portion of the CJR Plan has remained unimplemented, and we take judicial notice that there is no formal, ongoing ADR program in the Puerto Rico federal district court. Because that is so, we conclude that the District of Puerto Rico has no local rule in force that dictates the permissible characteristics of mediation orders. Consequently, APC's argument founders.

There is only one potential source of statutory authority for ordering mandatory non-binding mediation here: the Alternative Dispute Resolution Act of 1998 (ADR Act), 28 U.S.C. §§ 651–658. Congress passed the ADR Act to promote the utilization of alternative dispute resolution methods in the federal courts and to set appropriate guidelines for their use. The Act lists mediation as an appropriate ADR process. *Id.* § 651(a). Moreover, it sanctions the participation of "professional neutrals from the private sector" as mediators. *Id.* § 653(b). Finally, the Act requires district courts to obtain litigants' consent only when they order arbitration, *id.* § 652(a), not when they order the use of other ADR mechanisms (such as non-binding mediation).

Despite the broad sweep of these provisions, the Act is quite clear that some form of the ADR procedures it endorses must be adopted in each judicial district by local rule. *See id.* § 651(b) (directing each district court to "devise and implement its own alternative dispute resolution program, by local rule adopted under [28 U.S.C.] section 2071(a), to encourage and promote the use of alternative dispute resolution in its district"). In the absence of such local rules, the ADR Act itself does not authorize any specific court to use a particular ADR mechanism. Because the District of Puerto Rico has not yet complied with the Act's mandate, the mediation order here at issue cannot be justified under the ADR Act.

. . .

We add, however, that although the respondents cannot use the ADR Act as a justification, neither can APC use it as a nullification.

. . .

The respondents next argue that the district court possessed the authority to require mediation by virtue of the Federal Rules of Civil Procedure. They concentrate their attention on Fed.R.Civ.P. 16, which states in pertinent part that "the court may take appropriate action[] with respect to . . . (9) settlement and the use of special procedures to assist in resolving the dispute when authorized by statute or local rule. . . ." Fed.R.Civ.P. 16(c)(9). But the words "when authorized by statute or local rule" are a frank limitation on the district courts' authority to order mediation thereunder, and we must adhere to that circumscription. . . .

Even apart from positive law, district courts have substantial inherent power to manage and control their calendars. This inherent power takes many forms. *See* Fed.R.Civ.P. 83(b) (providing that judges may regulate practice in any manner consistent with federal law and applicable rules). By way of illustration, a district court may use its inherent power to compel represented clients to attend pretrial settlement conferences, even though such a practice is not specifically authorized in the Civil Rules. *See Heileman Brewing Co. v. Joseph Oat Corp.*, 871 F.2d 648, 650 (7th Cir.1989) (en banc).

Of course, a district court's inherent powers are not infinite. There are at least four limiting principles. First, inherent powers must be used in a way reasonably suited to the enhancement of the court's processes, including the orderly and expeditious disposition of pending cases. Second, inherent powers cannot be exercised in a manner that contradicts an applicable statute or rule. Third, the use of inherent powers must comport with procedural fairness. And, finally, inherent powers "must be exercised with restraint and discretion."

. . .

We begin our inquiry by examining the case law. In *Strandell v. Jackson County*, 838 F.2d 884 (7th Cir. 1987), the Seventh Circuit held that a district court does not possess inherent power to compel participation in a summary jury trial. In the court's view, Fed.R.Civ.P. 16 occupied the field and prevented a district court from forcing "an unwilling litigant [to] be sidetracked from the normal course of litigation." *Id.* at 887. But the group that spearheaded the subsequent revision of Rule 16 explicitly rejected that interpretation. *See* Fed.R.Civ.P. 16, advisory committee's note (1993 Amendment) ("The [amended] rule does not attempt to resolve questions as to the extent a court would be authorized to require [ADR] proceedings as an exercise of its inherent powers."). Thus, we do not find *Strandell* persuasive on this point.

The *Strandell* court also expressed concern that summary jury trials would undermine traditional discovery and privilege rules by requiring certain disclosures prior to an actual trial. 838 F.2d at 888. We find this concern unwarranted. Because a summary jury trial (like a non-binding mediation) does not require any disclosures beyond what would be required in the ordinary course of discovery, its principal disadvantage to the litigants is that it may prevent them from saving surprises for the time of trial. Since trial by ambush is no longer in vogue, that interest does not deserve protection. Relying on policy arguments, the Sixth Circuit also has found that district courts do not possess inherent power to compel participation in summary jury trials. *See In re NLO, Inc.*, 5 F.3d 154, 157–58 (6th Cir.1993). The court thought the value of a summary jury trial questionable when parties do not engage in the process voluntarily, and it worried that "too broad an interpretation of the federal courts' inherent power to regulate their procedure . . . encourages judicial high-handedness. . . ."

The concerns articulated by these two respected courts plainly apply to mandatory mediation orders. When mediation is forced upon unwilling litigants, it stands to reason that the likelihood of settlement is diminished. Requiring parties to invest substantial amounts of time and money in mediation under such circumstances may well be inefficient.

The fact remains, however, that none of these considerations establishes that mandatory mediation is always inappropriate. There may well be specific cases in which such a protocol is likely to conserve judicial resources without significantly burdening the objectors' rights to a full, fair, and speedy trial. Much depends on the idiosyncrasies of the particular case and the details of the mediation order.

In some cases, a court may be warranted in believing that compulsory mediation could yield significant benefits even if one or more parties object. After all, a party may resist mediation simply out of unfamiliarity with the process or out of fear that a willingness to submit would be perceived as a lack of confidence in her legal position. In such an instance, the party's initial reservations are likely to evaporate as the mediation progresses, and negotiations could well produce a beneficial outcome, at reduced cost and greater speed, than would a trial. While the possibility that parties will fail to reach agreement remains ever present, the boon of settlement can be worth the risk.

This is particularly true in complex cases involving multiple claims and parties. The fair and expeditious resolution of such cases often is helped along by creative solutions — solutions that simply are not available in the binary framework of traditional adversarial litigation. Mediation with the assistance of a skilled facilitator gives parties an opportunity to explore a much wider range of options, including those that go beyond conventional zero-sum resolutions. Mindful of these potential advantages, we hold that it is within a district court's inherent power to order non-consensual mediation in those cases in which that step seems reasonably likely to serve the interests of justice.

Our determination that the district courts have inherent power to refer cases to non-binding mediation is made with a recognition that any such order must be crafted in a manner that preserves procedural fairness and shields objecting parties from undue burdens. We thus turn to the specifics of the mediation order entered in this case. As with any exercise of a district court's inherent powers, we review the entry of that order for abuse of discretion.

As an initial matter, we agree with the lower court that the complexity of this case militates in favor of ordering mediation. At last count, the suit involves twelve parties, asserting a welter of claims, counterclaims, cross-claims, and third-party claims predicated on a wide variety of theories. The pendency of nearly parallel litigation in the Puerto Rican courts, which features a slightly different cast of characters and claims that are related to but not completely congruent with those asserted here, further complicates the matter. Untangling the intricate web of relationships among the parties, along with the difficult and fact-intensive arguments made by each, will be time-consuming and will impose significant costs on the parties and the court. Against this backdrop, mediation holds out the dual prospect of advantaging the litigants and conserving scarce judicial resources.

In an effort to parry this thrust, APC raises a series of objections. Its threshold claim is that the district court erred in ordering mediation before resolving a pending motion to dismiss for lack of subject-matter jurisdiction (or, alternatively, to abstain). . . . [E]ven if it were error to enter the mediation order before passing upon the motion to dismiss, the error was harmless: it would be an empty exercise to vacate the mediation order on this ground when the lower court has already rejected the challenges to its exercise of jurisdiction.

Next, APC posits that the appointment of a private mediator proposed by one of the parties is per se improper (and, thus, invalidates the order). We do not agree. The district court has inherent power to "appoint persons unconnected with the court to aid judges in the performance of specific judicial duties." In the context of non-binding mediation, the mediator does not decide the merits of the case and has no authority to coerce settlement. Thus, in the absence of a contrary statute or rule, it is perfectly acceptable for the district court to appoint a qualified and neutral private party as a mediator. The mere fact that the mediator was proposed by one of the parties is insufficient to establish bias in favor of that party.

We hasten to add that the litigants are free to challenge the qualifications or neutrality of any suggested mediator (whether or not nominated by a party to the case).

. . .

APC also grouses that it should not be forced to share the costs of an unwanted mediation. We have held, however, that courts have the power under Fed.R.Civ.P. 26(f) to issue pretrial cost-sharing orders in complex litigation. Given the difficulties facing trial courts in cases involving multiple parties and multiple claims, we are hesitant to limit that power to the traditional discovery context. *See id.* This is especially true in complicated cases, where the potential value of mediation lies not only in promoting settlement but also in clarifying the issues remaining for trial.

The short of the matter is that, without default cost-sharing rules, the use of valuable ADR techniques (like mediation) becomes hostage to the parties' ability to agree on the concomitant financial arrangements. This means that the district court's inherent power to order private mediation in appropriate cases would be rendered nugatory absent the corollary power to order the sharing of reasonable mediation costs. To avoid this pitfall, we hold that the district court, in an appropriate case, is empowered to order the sharing of reasonable costs and expenses associated with mandatory non-binding mediation.

The remainder of APC's arguments are not so easily dispatched. Even when generically appropriate, a mediation order must contain procedural and substantive safeguards to ensure fairness to all parties involved. The mediation order in this case does not quite meet that test. In particular, the order does not set limits on the duration of the mediation or the expense associated therewith.

We need not wax longiloquent. As entered, the order simply requires the parties to mediate; it does not set forth either a timetable for the mediation or a cap on the fees that the mediator may charge. The figures that have been bandied about in the briefs — $900 per hour or $9,000 per mediation day — are quite large and should not be left to the mediator's whim. Relatedly, because the mediator is to be paid an hourly rate, the court should have set an outside limit on the number of hours to be devoted to mediation. Equally as important, it is trite but often true that justice delayed is justice denied. An unsuccessful mediation will postpone the ultimate resolution of the case — indeed, the district court has stayed all discovery pending the completion of the mediation — and, thus, prolong the litigation. For these reasons, the district court should have set a definite time frame for the mediation.

The respondents suggest that the district court did not need to articulate any limitations in its mediation order because the mediation process will remain under the district court's ultimate supervision; the court retains the ability to curtail any excessive expenditures of time or money; and a dissatisfied party can easily return to the court at any time. While this might be enough of a safeguard in many instances, the instant litigation is sufficiently complicated and the mediation efforts are likely to be sufficiently expensive that, here, reasonable time limits and fee constraints, set in advance, are appropriate.

A court intent on ordering non-consensual mediation should take other precautions as well. For example, the court should make it clear (as did the able district court in this case) that participation in mediation will not be taken as a waiver of any litigation position. The important point is that the protections we have mentioned are not intended to comprise an exhaustive list, but, rather, to illustrate that when a district court orders a party to participate in mediation, it should take care to assuage legitimate concerns about the possible negative consequences of such an order.

To recapitulate, we rule that a mandatory mediation order issued under the district court's inherent power is valid in an appropriate case. We also rule that this is an appropriate case. We hold, however, that the district court's failure to set reasonable limits on the duration of the mediation and on the mediator's fees dooms the decree.

We admire the district court's pragmatic and innovative approach to this massive litigation. Our core holding — that ordering mandatory mediation is a proper exercise of a district court's inherent power, subject, however, to a variety of terms and conditions — validates that approach. We are mindful that this holding is in tension with the opinions of the Sixth and Seventh Circuits in *NLO* and *Strandell*, respectively, but we believe it is justified by the important goal of promoting flexibility and creative problem-solving in the handling of complex litigation.

That said, the need of the district judge in this case to construct his own mediation regime ad hoc underscores the greater need of the district court as an institution to adopt an ADR program and memorialize it in its local rules. In the ADR Act, Congress directed that "[e]ach United States district court shall authorize, by local rule under section 2071(a), the use of alternative dispute resolution processes in all civil actions. . . ." 28 U.S.C. § 651(b). While Congress did not set a firm deadline for compliance with this directive, the statute was enacted four years ago. This omission having been noted, we are confident that the district court will move expediently to bring the District of Puerto Rico into compliance.

We need go no further. For the reasons set forth above, we vacate the district court's mediation order and remand for further proceedings consistent with this opinion. The district court is free to order mediation if it continues to believe that such a course is advisable or, in the alternative, to proceed with discovery and trial.

Vacated and remanded.

Notes and Questions

(1) The various sources of judicial authority for federal judges to compel mediation discussed in *Atlantic Pipe* parallel those available to state court judges. Note that while the court ruled that the trial judge had the power to require mediation, it stated that the court should set reasonable limitations on the length of the mediation and the mediator's fees. Do you think it is appropriate for the court to limit the parties' self-determination regarding these issues? If so, do you think the court offered sufficient guidance regarding the parties' ability to choose who will mediate? Some courts have denied motions to compel mediation, often citing futility. *See, e.g., Wells Fargo Bank Minnesota v. Kobernick*, 2009 U.S. Dist. LEXIS 81703 (S.D. Tex. Aug. 26, 2009) (court reasoned that the parties had already tried to reach agreement but failed). Cases often take multiple negotiation sessions or mediations before settlement is reached. Do you think that simply failing to reach an agreement is reason enough to decline to mandate mediation again? Denying compulsory mediation is not an abuse of discretion when the court determines that the mediation would not be fruitful (so long as a local rule doesn't require mediation). *Pieczenik v. Bayer Corp.*, 474 Fed. Appx. 766 (Fed. Cir. 2012). Parties often declare that they have no interest in mediation, but may mediation still be fruitful despite the parties' aversion? Should a court seek to decide when a mediation will be helpful or simply a waste of time?

(2) In *Liang v. Lai*, the Supreme Court of Montana refused to grant the appellant's motion to dispense with mediation even though it was unopposed. Liang v. Lai, 2003 MT 281, 317 Mont. 524, 78 P.3d 1212. The court insisted that the Montana rule requiring mediation by parties to an appeal be followed. The rule required that the mediation be completed within 75 days. Do you think the arguments for mandatory mediation at the appellate court level differ from those at the trial court level? If one party moves to dispense with mediation, doesn't that imply they have no interest

in mediation? Some states have local rules requiring mediation even if mediation would be futile. The court in *Liang* stated there is no "futility" exception to their rule. Oftentimes, mediation yields beneficial results such as streamlining issues and offering parties realistic expectations of the case. Do some local rules overstep by forcing unwilling parties to mediate in good faith? Chief Judge Kozinski and Judge Gould of the Ninth Circuit dissented in *Nordyke v. King*, where the parties were ordered to attempt settlement of their dispute before a Circuit Mediator. "The parties have not asked for mediation; they have said nothing that suggests mediation would be fruitful. . . . This delay serves no useful purpose; it only makes us look foolish." 676 F.3d 828 (9th Cir. 2012) (Chief Judge Kozinski dissenting).

(3) Courts have upheld compulsory mediation as not violating a party's constitutional right to a jury trial. *See Lynch v. City of Jellico*, 205 S.W.3d 384 (Tenn. 2006) (holding that compulsory mediation did not have to end in an agreement, and the parties were able to proceed to court).

D. Mediation in "Good Faith"

Although mediation is considered a consensual, voluntary process, is a party in a mediation under some obligation to treat the mediation with a certain degree of seriousness, particularly where the mediation is court-ordered? The preceding section explored the consequences of a party's refusal to participate in mediation when required to do so by contract or statute. What if the party participates in the mediation but does so half-heartedly or strategically — so much so that the party is arguably not making a "good faith" effort to settle the case? The materials below address the arguments and policy concerns over imposing a "good faith" participation requirement in mediation.

Pitts v. Francis

United States District Court for the Northern District of Florida
2007 U.S. Dist. LEXIS 93047 (Dec. 19, 2007)

RICHARD SMOAK, DISTRICT JUDGE.

Plaintiff Brittany Pitts has sued Defendant Joseph R. Francis and Defendant business entities operating under the name "Girls Gone Wild." Pitts alleges that in April 2003, while on her spring break vacation in Panama City Beach, Florida, Francis and another Girls Gone Wild employee approached her on the beach and coerced her into exposing her breasts on film. Pitts contends that she did not consent to be filmed and was sixteen years of age, a sophomore in high school, at the time of the alleged incident. Pitts' image was displayed on the cover of a Girls Gone Wild video and DVD, which were sold and distributed throughout the United States. The five-count First Amended Complaint asserts claims for unjust enrichment; violations of the Florida Deceptive and Unfair Trade Practices Act; unauthorized publication of

likeness under *Fla. Stat. § 54.08;* commercial misappropriation of one's likeness; and
false light doctrine of invasion of privacy.

. . .

On March 23, 2007, the plaintiffs in *Doe v. Francis* filed a motion requesting sanctions against Joe Francis. The motion alleged that Francis had behaved in a threatening and abusive manner toward the plaintiffs and their attorneys at a court-ordered
mediation. Because of the seriousness of those allegations, I held a hearing to determine whether a more formal, evidentiary hearing on the motion was warranted. . . .
Mr. Dickey, Joe Francis' attorney, agreed that the behavior of his *own* client at a
court-ordered mediation was so incredibly abusive and inappropriate as to justify
plaintiffs and their counsel to simply *leave* the mediation. Relying on Mr. Dickey's
representation, I found it appropriate to schedule an evidentiary hearing on the
motion for sanctions to afford Francis the opportunity to defend himself.

. . . [T]he sole purpose of the hearing, per my written order, was to consider
whether Francis had violated my standard order requiring all litigants in this Court
to attempt to resolve their cases through mediation.

At the evidentiary hearing, Francis was represented by Michael Burke, general
counsel for Girls Gone Wild, and by Mr. Dickey. The testimony and evidence presented at the evidentiary hearing and in the written documents filed on the docket
were shocking:

To report that Francis arrived late at the mediation is an understatement. Francis
arrived *four hours* late, keeping the out-of-town plaintiffs and their attorneys waiting.

Francis' tardiness did not result from time spent primping; rather, Francis arrived
at the mediation wearing sweat shorts, a backwards baseball cap, and was barefoot.
He was playing on an electronic devise [*sic*— misspelled "device"].

As plaintiff's counsel began his presentation, Francis put his bare, dirty feet on
the table, facing plaintiff's counsel. Plaintiff's counsel said four words before Francis
interrupted him.

Francis then erupted into a tantrum, yelling repeatedly: "Don't expect to get a
fucking dime — not one fucking dime!"

Francis shouted: "I hold the purse strings; I will not settle this case at all. I am
only here because the court is making me be here!"

Reasonably concluding that mediation was futile, the plaintiff's attorneys began
to leave the room. As if he had not made his point, Francis threatened: "We will bury
you and your clients! I'm going to ruin you, your clients, and all of your ambulance-
chasing partners!"

As they exited the room, Francis, without provocation, charged plaintiffs' counsel, "got in his face," and appeared as though he was going to physically assault
plaintiff's counsel. "I thought he was going to slug me," plaintiffs' counsel testified.

. . .

Francis' own attorney had to position himself between Francis and plaintiffs' counsel to prevent a brawl.

Francis' goodbye wish to plaintiffs' counsel was "Suck my dick."

. . .

Simply put, Francis' behavior was not mediation. It was not posturing. It was *violent.* Anyone attending that mediation, including Joe Francis himself, could have been injured. I will not permit a litigant in this *federal* court to exploit an order issued by me for the sole purpose of abusing and threatening another party. As judge, it is my responsibility to ensure the orderly administration of justice in the cases over which I preside. *Code of Conduct for United States Judges*, Canon 3A(2) ("A judge . . . should maintain order and decorum in all judicial proceedings.") To Joe Francis, my mediation order was apparently a conduit through which he could threaten and assault the other party and its attorneys under the cloak of confidentiality:

> THE COURT: [U]nder no stretch of the imagination can Mr. Francis' comments and his conduct be construed as being part of the mediation process. I think, to the contrary, he made it clear unequivocally and graphically that he was not there to mediate.
>
> I would characterize Mr. Francis' comments not of anything deserving or intended to foster the purposes of mediation, but rather something you might expect from a drunk fight in the parking lot of a bar at 3:00 in the morning.
>
> I find that his conduct and his statements were extreme, they were hostile, they were vulgar, they were obscene, and they are unacceptable, not only in just about every setting of our everyday life, Mr. Francis, but they are unacceptable in this court and in any activity required by this court . . .

If Francis had simply mediated in good faith and an impasse had resulted, he would not have been sanctioned. Indeed, many cases on this Court's dockets do not result in settlement, and parties are not sanctioned. Francis, however, failed to make an attempt at mediation. Worse, he exploited the mediation process for abusive purposes.

It is important to note that neither Francis nor his attorneys filed a motion to dispense with the mediation. Even at the evidentiary hearing on the motion for sanctions, Francis' attorneys expressed hope that settlement was a possibility. Had Francis filed a motion to dispense with mediation, I would have considered the reason stated in the motion, like any other motion filed on the dockets of this court, and rendered an appropriate ruling. Certainly, had Francis moved to dispense with mediation on the grounds that he would threaten and abuse the other party, I would have taken appropriate measures to prevent that. This Francis and his attorneys failed to do. Instead, Francis chose to attend the "mediation" and waste the time and money of his adversaries. He made a mockery of himself and of the alternative dispute resolution process . . .

. . .

In weighing the propriety of each sanction, I determined that financial sanctions alone would not be effective in forcing Francis to obey my order:

> And because of the financial situation of Mr. Francis and his totally controlled enterprises, thoroughly documented before this court, and the related criminal case, financial sanctions alone may not be sufficient and are unlikely to cause Mr. Francis to comply with the order this court . . .

I then concluded that

> Therefore, coercive incarceration is an appropriate sanction for this situation. Mr. Francis can cure his contempt and have this sanction of incarceration removed upon his proper participation in mediation . . .

Notes and Questions

(1) The judge in the *Girls Gone Wild* case (*Pitts v. Francis*) pointed out that the defendant (Francis) had not moved to dispense with mediation, but instead, "he exploited the mediation for abusive purposes." If Francis had sought to dispense with mediation, but the judge had denied his motion, would the judge's decision to sanction Francis for his egregious conduct and refusal to mediate in good faith be less justified? Do you think the judge would have reacted so strongly if Francis was merely "uncooperative" or just unwilling to reach an agreement? State court judges in Florida have consistently refused to find a "good faith" obligation beyond appearance at the mediation. The leading state court case on this topic is *Avril v. Civilmar*, 605 So. 2d 988 (Fla. Dist. Ct. App. 1992), in which the court reversed sanctions which were imposed on a party for "failure to negotiate in good faith." In *Avril*, attending mediation satisfied the good faith requirement, but making an offer was not required. In any event, is incarceration too extreme a sanction for even Francis' egregious behavior?

(2) Unilaterally ending mediation has been found to be a tell-tale sign of a lack of good faith. In *Brooks v. Lincoln National Life Ins. Co.*, the plaintiff immediately discounted the defendant's initial offer and said, "tell them that they had five minutes to put a 'serious' settlement offer on the table, or that [he] and his client were leaving." 2006 WL 2487937, *2 (D. Neb. 2006). The plaintiff did not allow the mediator to explain the initial offer, then relayed the plaintiff's statement. The defendant in response offered to raise its offer if the plaintiff would lower their original formal demand at which point the plaintiff left the mediation. The court held that the plaintiff's conduct was not indicative of good faith because refusing to negotiate, not allowing the mediator to explain offers, and unilaterally terminating the mediation was in violation of the court order, thus warranting sanctions. The court noted that unilateral termination creates an unfair situation for the other party and for their own client: "By refusing to participate further, [counsel] may have in fact entrenched his opponents' position. His action robbed his client of possibly her best opportunity to convince defendants they should re-evaluate her claims, to learn her opponents' side of the dispute, to negotiate a settlement, or even to be heard, perhaps, it may turn out, to her considerable detriment."

However, courts have held that simply ending a mediation does not always rise to the level of unilateral termination. In *In re Bolden*, 719 A.2d 1253 (D.C. App. 1998), the Court of Appeals of the District of Columbia ruled that ending mediation after requesting rescheduling, did not warrant sanctions because even though the other party did not consent to either rescheduling or termination of the session, there was a valid reason for the need to reschedule. The mediator had refused to allow an expert to attend the session, so the party needed to acquire an expert report in the absence of the expert. Terminating mediation and seeking to reschedule under these circumstances does not rise to the level of unilateral termination.

(3) Does failure to send a representative with settlement authority or failure to submit a memorandum amount to bad faith and therefore sanctionable? In *Nick v. Morgan's Foods*, 99 F. Supp. 2d 1056 (E.D. Mo. 2000), the defendant did not comply with the court's pre-mediation submission requirement and sent a representative with only 500 dollars' worth of settlement authority and no knowledge of the case. The federal judge stated: "Morgan's Foods' contention that a mediation memorandum is a waste of time is simply wrong. The memorandum would have permitted the neutral to prepare for the ADR conference. At a minimum the memorandum might have alerted the neutral that Morgan's Foods' corporate representative was not an appropriate participant in the ADR conference. It is even possible that Morgan's Foods' memorandum would have compelled the neutral to delay or even cancel the conference. When a corporate representative with the authority to reconsider that party's settlement position is not present, the whole purpose of the mediation is lost, and the result is an even greater expenditure of the parties' resources, both time and money, for nothing." Defendant Morgan's Foods was ordered to compensate not only the plaintiff and plaintiff's counsel for failure to participate in good faith, but also the clerk of the federal court for "vexationally increasing the costs of the litigation."

The Florida Supreme Court has attempted to remedy this situation by adding another requirement, a certificate of authority. Ten days prior to the mediation, the parties must submit a certificate of authority, "a written notice identifying the person or persons who will be attending the mediation conference as a party representative or as an insurance carrier representative and confirming that those persons have the [required] authority." Rule 1.720(e), Florida Rules of Civil Procedure. Do you think that this rule balances the interests of those who seek participation and those who want to preserve parties' rights not to settle in mediation?

(4) In the modern era, technology and travel can cause delays or make attendance impossible. If a party makes an effort to attend but fails to appear, should they be found to have violated their duty of good faith? In *Romero v. Diaz-Fox*, 2021 WL 3619677, at *1 (S.D. Fla. Aug. 16, 2021), the plaintiff was experiencing internet issues during a court-ordered mediation via Zoom. The plaintiff unsuccessfully attempted to resolve the issues but was available to continue via telephone. The mediator decided to reschedule the mediation. The court found that the plaintiff met the good faith attendance requirement because of her efforts and telephonic availability. Are

there other situations where the use of online dispute resolution (ODR) might raise good faith issues?

What if parties lie about technical or travel difficulties? In *Jones v. A Buyer's Choice Home Inspections, Ltd.*, the defendant claimed he could not fly across the country for a settlement conference due to his doctor's orders and he was confined to driving locally. 2020 WL 774356, *1 (C.D. Cal. 2020). At the show cause hearing for his failure to comply with the court order, the defendant was unable to show proof of why he could not attend and refused to contact his doctor. The court also discovered that the defendant had attempted to fly before and after the scheduled conference date, and he had competed in a half triathlon two days prior. The court held that the defendant, following another show cause hearing, should be held in contempt and sanctioned for failing to attend the conference in good faith. Is requiring proof of every excuse a slippery slope and potentially might slow litigation? To what extent should courts consider economic hardship factors when traveling to a mediation proceeding?

(5) In *Procap S.A. v. Patheon Inc.*, the court held that sanctions cannot be based on subjective criteria. Courts can only sanction a party based on objective criteria including: failure to attend, lack of settlement authority, failure to submit pre-mediation documents, leaving only minutes into mediation, or failure to give notice of non-participation. 2015 WL 3539737, *1 (S.D. Fla. 2015).

Good Faith Mediation in the Federal Courts

26 Ohio St. J. on Disp. Resol. 363 (2011)*
By Peter N. Thompson

For the most part, the pretrial process works well. Occasionally, however, adversarial zeal, or plain lack of professionalism, causes parties to refuse to follow orders or rules, or otherwise attempt to use the process improperly to obtain an unfair adversarial advantage. Courts respond with an elaborate enforcement system of judicial oversight and sanctions to assure that the rules are followed, parties are protected, and court orders are upheld.

The mediation process, on the other hand, is not designed to be adversarial. Mediation is championed as a private, confidential process centered on party autonomy and self-determination, where a neutral third party "facilitates communication and negotiation between parties to assist them in reaching a voluntary agreement regarding their dispute." Confidentiality, self-determination, and conciliation are lauded as essential features of the traditional mediation session. Superimposing this private, facilitative process in the midst of the public adversarial pretrial process is not an easy matter, and as many commentators have remarked, creates a "process dissonance" or clash of cultures.

This clash of cultures is apparent when assessing the role of the court in supervising or compelling mediation conduct in light of mediation values of confidentiality and self-determination. If self-determination and voluntary agreement are key mediation values, how can a court compel parties to mediate in good faith in circumstances where the parties do not want to settle? If confidentiality is a core value, how can a court police the mediation process and assure good faith participation without breaching the confidentiality of that process? What is required of parties who do not want to settle but are ordered to participate in mediation in good faith?

. . .

What are the expectations of the parties when a party who does not want to settle is ordered to go to mediation? In the context of court-mandated mediation, the substance of any good faith requirement must emanate from the expectations of the judge or from the text of the governing rules. What is it that the judge expects the parties to do when she orders them to mediation? Is this an order to plunge downstream toward settlement?

Courts and court rules repeatedly assure parties that there is no duty to settle a case and forego the right to trial. There also is no obligation to make a settlement offer and forego the right to trial. Yet, some court rules and pronouncements come sufficiently close, so that it may feel to the parties that they are being ordered to settle and forego their right to trial or suffer sanctions. Thus, there is ambiguity in terms of expectations in court-compelled mediation.

. . .

. . . Several commentators have attempted to provide a definition of good faith in the context of mediation. Kimberlee Kovach suggests various factors in a model rule that she proposes, including such requirements as complying with applicable law, court orders, the contract to mediate, and the mediator's rules.[131] In addition, parties should prepare for the mediation, attend the mediation with settlement authority, and participate in meaningful discussions. Included in the obligation is a duty not to affirmatively mislead the mediator or the adverse party. Kovach also includes an obligation not to file any new motions in the proceedings until the mediation is completed.

[Roger] Carter provides a more generalized standard. He argues bad faith occurs when a participant "uses the mediation process primarily to gain strategic advantage in the litigation process; uses mediation to impose hardship rather than to promote understanding and conflict resolution; or neglects an affirmative material obligation owed to another participant, the mediator, or the court."[135]

---

131. Kimberlee K. Kovach, *Good Faith in Mediation — Requested, Recommended, or Required? A New Ethic*, 38 S. Tex. L. Rev. 575, 616–17, 620–23 (1997) . . . .

135. Roger L. Carter, Oh, Ye of Little (Good) Faith: Questions, Concerns and Commentary on Efforts to Regulate Participant Conduct in Mediations, 2002 J. Disp. Resol. 367.

[Edward] Sherman advances a more limited definition that would require meaningful participation or participation that is necessary to prevent frustration of ADR process objectives. This would include a duty for parties and representatives with settlement authority to attend, listen, present positions, and pay for the mediator.[137] Sherman, however, argues against broader "good faith" requirements that focus on the quality of bargaining.

At the very least, good faith participation in mediation requires that parties prepare for and attend the mediation with settlement authority. Imposing sanctions for these "objective" requirements usually does not involve a deep intrusion into mediation communications and parties' litigation strategies. While even these issues can give rise to some indeterminacy, the more controversial issues surround questions relating to the court's power to police the quality of the bargaining.

. . .

The crux of the dispute over court enforcement of any obligation to participate in good faith centers on questions of whether, consistent with principles of confidentiality, the court can:

(1) compel the parties to actually listen to and communicate with the adverse party or mediator about the issues in the case.

(2) require that the parties actually bargain with each other and exchange offers to settle;

(3) police the mediation process to protect parties from offensive, abusive conduct, or efforts to misuse the mediation process for unfair adversarial advantage.

Several recent federal court decisions shed some light on these questions.

In *In re A.T. Reynolds & Sons*, the bankruptcy judge had little difficulty addressing the confidentiality rules since the local rules specifically provided that the "mediator shall report any willful failure to attend or participate in good faith."[203] Consequently, the judge concluded that the mediator was free to file a report and provide testimony about the mediator's perceptions of what went on during the mediation. The judge provided no explanation of what justified testimony from both parties about the bargaining communications at the mediation. Allowing parties to testify to mediation communications is an anathema to the mediation community. Allowing a mediator to testify is worse.

. . .

The concern with permitting or requiring a mediator report on what transpired at the mediation, however, raises additional issues. There is a concern that this practice may impair the role of the mediator as an impartial, neutral facilitator. Perhaps

---

137. Edward F. Sherman, Court-Mandated Alternative Dispute Resolution: What Form of Participation Should Be Required?, 46 SMU L. Rev. 2079 (1993).

203. *In re A.T. Reynolds & Sons*, 424 B.R. 76, 80-82 (Bankr. S.D.N.Y. 2010).

the leading case expressing this concern is *NLRB v. Macaluso*, a federal labor case in which the court precluded the mediator's testimony on the issue of whether the parties had reached an agreement in mediation. The court reasoned, "the public interest in maintaining the actual or perceived impartiality of federal mediators outweighs the benefits of relevant and decisive testimony on the issue at hand."

. . .

If the mediator is required to assess whether the parties are bargaining in good faith, however, the mediator may be acting more in an adjudicative role than as a facilitator. It is possible that parties might take a different approach with a mediator who purely facilitates the dispute as opposed to a mediator who has a responsibility or right to judge whether the parties are mediating in good faith. It is also possible that it makes no difference at all to most parties whether they are mediating in a jurisdiction with an obligation to mediate in good faith. The hope, of course, is that parties will be deterred from acting in bad faith if they are accountable to the mediator. Numerous districts allow, or require, a mediator to report bad faith conduct in mediation. This right or duty to report bad faith mediation conduct has been in place in many jurisdictions for many years.

. . .

Resort to mediator evidence should be avoided, unless necessary to resolve the legitimate issue of compliance with court duties. There is a strong interest in preserving mediation confidentiality and easing the burden on mediators. Where mediator testimony is necessary, it should be limited. The concern about neutrality may arise when the courts ask the mediator to go beyond reporting on what the mediator observed and seek the mediator's subjective views about the motivations of the parties. This assessment function is better left to adjudicators and not mediators. To the extent that it is essential to have full input about what transpired at the mediation to enforce court orders, to protect parties from abusive practices and to "preserve the integrity of the judicial process," it is rarely necessary for the court to hear the mediator's opinions about the subjective motivations of the parties.

Notes and Questions

(1) In Professor Thompson's article, he refers to Kimberlee Kovach's proposed statute, which places the responsibility on the court rather than the mediator, in court-annexed mediations, to "make the final determination of whether good faith was present in the mediation." Although placing responsibility on the court may initially overcome concerns over compromising confidentiality and mediator neutrality, how will a court make this determination absent input from the mediator?

(2) Other commentators have contributed to this debate. Professors Carol L. Izumi and Homer C. La Rue surveyed the debate and argue that good faith requirements strike at the heart of the mediation process by undermining core mediation values of party self-determination, confidentiality, and third-party neutrality. *Prohibiting "Good Faith" Reports Under the Uniform Mediation Act: Keeping the*

Adjudication Camel out of the Mediation Tent, 2003 J. Disp. Resol. 67. Izumi and La Rue assert that the Uniform Mediation Act (UMA) strikes the correct balance by rejecting arguments in favor of mediator reports to judges and others about the sanctions and statements of parties during the mediation for the purpose of assessing and sanctioning "bad faith" behavior, and that for the rare and extreme case, the UMA provides a mechanism to address egregious party behavior such as lying and fraudulent inducements causing another party to settle. Would imposing a good-faith requirement deter and punish bad faith conduct in a few truly egregious cases at the expense of overall confidence in the system of mediation?

(3) In *Using Dispute System Design Methods to Promote Good-Faith Participation in Court-Connected Mediation Programs,* 50 UCLA L. Rev. 69 (2002), Professor John Lande argues that enforcing a good-faith requirement would subject all participants to uncertainty about the impartiality and confidentiality of the process and could heighten adversarial tensions and inappropriate pressures to settle cases. Lande proposes using less risky means to achieve some of the ends being pursued by proponents of imposing a generalized "good-faith" requirement (by proposing the use of system design principles to promote desired conduct). In *Oh Ye of Little Good Faith: Questions, Concerns and Commentary on Efforts to Regulate Participant Conduct in Mediations,* 2002 J. Disp. Resol. 367, Roger L. Carter, as mentioned in the Thompson article, responds to Professor Lande by proposing narrowly tailored rules for mediation participants to reduce bad faith conduct and preserve party autonomy. Carter suggests that mediation's high aspirations will only be met if parties are free to shape outcomes unburdened by the fear of retributive sanctions. Even if courts were to provide litigating parties and their attorneys with clear rules, would the concerns expressed by Professor Sherman as described in the Thompson article remain? No matter how clear the rules are, might they impose requirements that compromise mediation's core values?

The ABA Section of Dispute Resolution issued a policy statement on mediation in good faith; excerpts appear below:

ABA Section of Dispute Resolution on Good Faith Requirements for Mediators and Mediation Advocates in Court-Mandated Mediation Programs
Approved by Section Council, August 7, 2004

The ABA Section of Dispute Resolution ("Section") has noted the wide range of views expressed by scholars, mediators, judges, and regulators concerning the question of whether courts should have the authority to sanction participants in mediation for bad-faith conduct in court-mandated mediation programs. The Section has also noted court rules and statutes that require mediators in court-mandated programs to make reports to court administrators or specific judges concerning alleged bad-faith conduct of participants in mediation. The Section believes that the public interest, court systems, and the practice of mediation would benefit from a re-examination and revision of some of these statutes and rules to preserve the core values of the mediation process, namely, party self-determination, mediator impartiality, and mediation confidentiality. These values are integral to the public's perception of the legitimacy of mediation as a consensual, flexible, creative, party-driven process to resolve disputes.

. . .

The Section has concluded that, in order for the core values of the mediation process to be honored and preserved, the appropriate approach to be taken by court-mandated mediation programs should address three policy areas: (1) what conduct should be sanctionable; (2) what conduct or other information may mediators be required to report to court administrators or judges; and [(3) what actions court-mandated mediation programs should take to promote productive behavior in mediation]. The Section emphasizes that all of these elements are needed to create an effective policy.

The rules must comply with statutes and rules protecting the confidentiality of mediation communications, which generally limit reports and disclosures about alleged bad-faith conduct. Rules authorizing sanctions may be necessary but not sufficient to promote productive behavior in mediation and thus additional measures may be needed.

. . .

A. Sanctions.

Sanctions should be imposed only for violations of rules specifying objectively-determinable conduct.

. . .

Such rule-proscribed conduct would include but is not limited to: failure of a party, attorney, or insurance representative to attend a court-mandated mediation for a limited and specified period or to provide written memoranda prior to the mediations. These rules should not be labeled as good faith requirements, however, because of the widespread confusion about the meaning of that term. Rules and statutes that permit courts to sanction a wide range of subjective behavior create a grave risk of undermining core values of mediation and creating unintended problems. Such subjective behaviors include but are not limited to: a failure to engage sufficiently in substantive bargaining; failure to have a representative present at the court-mandated mediation with sufficient settlement authority; or failure to make a reasonable offer.

. . .

B. Mediator Reports to the Court or Court Administrators.

The content of mediators' reports to the court or court administrators should be narrowly restricted.

. . .

Requiring mediators to report negotiating behaviors or alleged bad-faith conduct to the court imperils the confidentiality of the mediation process and the public's trust in it.

. . .

Under these statutes and rules, a negative report to a court from a mediator can cause a party to face the wrath of the court in the form of a tarnished reputation, adverse rulings, or the imposition of actual sanctions. In a sanctions hearing on allegations of a party's bad-faith conduct in mediation, the mediator is typically subpoenaed to testify, thereby further breaching the confidentiality of the mediation process. The lack of confidentiality protection creates uncertainty, engenders distrust of the mediation process, and impairs the public's full use of the process.

The Uniform Mediation Act ("UMA") precludes disclosure of mediation communications regarding alleged bad faith.... The official Reporter's Notes to Section 7 of the UMA state: "The provisions [of the UMA] would not permit a mediator to communicate, for example, on whether a particular party engaged in 'good faith' negotiation, or to state whether a party had been 'the problem' in reaching a settlement."

The Section believes that protecting mediation communications as provided in the UMA will foster the public's trust in the legitimacy and integrity of mediation as a useful process to resolve disputes. Especially in states adopting the UMA, statutes and rules should not require or permit disclosures about bad-faith conduct unless there is a valid waiver of the privilege. Given the ABA's approval of the UMA, the Section recommends that no states should adopt statutes or rules inconsistent with the UMA.

Notes and Questions

(1) The ABA warns against imposing sanctions for subjective reasons and to enforce sanctions only when the infraction is one that can be objectively determined. What about extreme cases like *Pitts v. Francis*? None of the objective rules laid out by the ABA were specifically broken, so should Francis' conduct have remained confidential? If a jurisdiction has adopted the ABA approach, how can a party still be punished for acting as Francis did when the objectively determinable rules were followed? Should sanctions be allowed for subjective conduct when a party exhibits such bad behavior?

(2) Courts tend to be reluctant to impose harsh sanctions such as dismissal of a case for failure to act in good faith In *Negron v, Woodhull Hosp.*, the court vacated a default judgment because the punishment was too harsh for simply failing to comply with the mediator's instructions. 173 Fed. Appx. 77 (2d Cir. 2006). *See also Robinson v. ABB Combustion Engineering Services*, 32 F.3d 569 (6th Cir. 1994) (holding that dismissal for nonattendance was too harsh of a sanction when "less drastic" sanctions were not considered first).

E. Enforceability of Mediated Agreements

Which legal principles should a court apply when asked to enforce a mediated agreement? In many jurisdictions, the answer to this question is unclear at present. In other jurisdictions, though, the courts or the state legislatures have decided that mediated agreements should be enforced in the same manner as a contract. Even in these jurisdictions, however, the enforceability issue may be complicated by there being other relevant laws that contradict the mediation enforcement provisions. Enforceability, for example, may also implicate confidentiality concerns. If the parties are fighting over the interpretation of certain terms in the mediation agreement, relevant evidence regarding the parties' intentions may be excluded because of confidentiality requirements. Indeed, the parties may even be disagreeing over whether an agreement was struck. Recall the *Macaluso* case excerpted in Chapter 5, where the court refused to hear testimony from the mediator even though the court stated that it would be the best evidence of the existence of a mediated agreement.

The cases excerpted or discussed below illustrate the range of policy concerns over whether and how to enforce a mediated agreement. The *Ames* case shows how problems of statutory interpretation may confront a court faced with an enforceability issue. In *Fidelity and Guaranty Insurance Co. v. Star Equipment Corp.*, the United States Court of Appeals for the First Circuit applies Massachusetts contract law in a diversity case to enforce a mediated settlement agreement based on mutual assent. In *Guthrie v. Guthrie*, the court elects to apply contract principles to enforce a mediated settlement agreement. In the *Silkey* case, the court wrestles with an issue of statutory interpretation revolving around the enforceability of an oral mediation agreement. The *Haghighi* litigation suggests that a legislature may create more problems than it solves when it seeks to address the enforcement issue head-on. Finally, *Del Bosque v. AT&T Adv.* and *Ferguson v. Ferguson* consider traditional defenses to contract enforcement such as duress and impossibility.

In re Marriage of Ames

Texas Court of Civil Appeals
860 S.W.2d 590 (1993)

H. BRYAN POFF, JR., J.

Appellant Raymond K. Ames appeals from the trial court's final decree granting him and his wife Nancy Jo Ames a divorce. In four points of error, Raymond contends the trial court erred in (1) not recognizing his repudiation of the mediated settlement agreement; (2) entering the decree of divorce without any evidence to support it; (3) modifying the settlement agreement; and (4) overruling his motion for new trial. We note that Raymond initially argues the settlement agreement is invalid; however, anticipating we might not agree, he alternatively argues that the agreement is inviolable and the court erred in modifying the agreement. His second argument compels us to reverse the judgment and remand the cause to the trial court.

Raymond filed suit to divorce his wife Nancy, appellee. Nancy answered Raymond's petition and filed a counter-petition for divorce. The parties were ordered to mediation which resulted in a community property settlement agreement reached on June 5, 1991. Both parties and their respective attorneys signed the settlement agreement. The record reflects that on June 20, 1991, Raymond attempted to withdraw his consent to the settlement agreement by means of a letter from his attorney to Nancy's attorney. On August 20, 1991, Nancy filed a "Motion For Entry of Decree of Divorce" based on the June 5 settlement agreement. On November 27, 1991, the trial court entered a decree of divorce.

In the first of four points of error, Raymond contends that the trial court erred in entering its decree of divorce on the basis of the settlement agreement because he had repudiated the agreement. We disagree. In its order of mediation, the trial court stated that "this case is appropriate for mediation pursuant to Tex. Civ. Prac. & Rem. Code §§ 154.001 *et seq.*" Chapter 154 of the Texas Civil Practice and Remedies Code is entitled "Alternative Dispute Resolution Procedures." Section 154.071(a) states:

> If the parties reach a settlement and execute a written agreement disposing of the dispute, the agreement is enforceable in the same manner as any other written contract.

Tex. Civ. Prac. & Rem. Code Ann. § 154.071(a) (Vernon Supp. 1993). We interpret this statute to mean, inter alia, that a party who has reached a settlement agreement disposing of a dispute through alternative dispute resolution procedures may not unilaterally repudiate the agreement.

While parties may be compelled by a court to participate in mediation, Tex. Civ. Prac. & Rem. Code §§ 154.021, 154.023 (Vernon Supp. 1993), "[a] mediator may not impose his own judgment on the issues for that of the parties." Tex. Civ. Prac. & Rem. Code § 154.023(b) (Vernon Supp. 1993). Put another way, a court can compel disputants to sit down with each other but it cannot force them to peaceably resolve their differences. *Decker v. Lindsay*, 824 S.W.2d 247, 250 (Tex.App. — Houston [1st Dist.] 1992, no writ). The job of a mediator is simply to facilitate communication between parties and thereby encourage reconciliation, settlement and understanding among them. Tex. Civ. Prac. & Rem. Code Ann. § 154.023(a). Hopefully, mediation will assist the parties in reaching a voluntary agreement that will serve to resolve their dispute and avoid the need for traditional litigation.

If voluntary agreements reached through mediation were nonbinding, many positive efforts to amicably settle differences would be for naught. If parties were free to repudiate their agreements, disputes would not be finally resolved and traditional litigation would recur. In order to effect the purposes of mediation and other alternative dispute resolution mechanisms, settlement agreements must be treated with the same dignity and respect accorded other contracts reached after arm's-length negotiations. Again, no party to a dispute can be forced to settle the conflict outside of court; but if a voluntary agreement that disposes of the dispute is reached, the parties should be required to honor the agreement.

Raymond argues strenuously, however, that section 154.071(a) does not apply in this case. Raymond maintains that section 154.071(a) conflicts with Tex. Fam. Code Ann. § 3.631(a) (Vernon 1993), and that the Family Code provision is controlling. Section 3.631(a) states:

> To promote amicable settlement of disputes on the divorce or annulment of a marriage, the parties may enter into a written agreement concerning the division of all property and liabilities of the parties and maintenance of either of them. The agreement may be revised or repudiated prior to rendition of the divorce or annulment unless it is binding under some other rule of law.

Raymond contends that section 3.613(a) controls over section 154.071(a) of the Texas Civil Practice and Remedies Code because section 3.613(a) deals with an agreement incident to divorce while section 154.071(a) concerns agreements in general. Raymond cites the well-known rule that a specific statute should control over a general statute and thus concludes that section 3.613 (a) is controlling.

We are not convinced, however, that the two statutes are in conflict. Even though section 3.613(a) is the more specific statute in this case, the Family Code provision expressly states that an agreement may be repudiated prior to rendition of the divorce "unless it is binding under some other rule of law." Pursuant to section 154.071(a) of the Practice and Remedies Code, the settlement agreement is binding. Raymond could not unilaterally repudiate the agreement. The trial court was empowered to consider the settlement agreement. Point of error one is overruled.

In his third point of error, Raymond, in the alternative, argues that if the agreement was not repudiated, the trial court erred in dividing the community property because the court's division differed significantly from the settlement agreement. Nancy contends that this argument is not properly before us because Raymond did not prepare and submit a proposed judgment to the court for signature as he was entitled to do under Tex. R. Civ. P. 305. While it is true that Raymond did not submit a proposed judgment, this does not preclude him from challenging the judgment entered by the court.

We agree with Raymond that there are several provisions of the divorce decree that are not found in the settlement agreement. First, while the settlement agreement is silent as to income tax liabilities, the divorce decree requires Raymond to pay all income tax liabilities of the parties through December 31, 1990. Second, the settlement agreement recites that Raymond will execute a $320,000 promissory note to Nancy; the divorce decree orders Raymond to execute the note and also orders him to pay a $320,000 money judgment. Third, the settlement agreement states that the stock of Raymond's company (Ridgmont Construction) is to be pledged as collateral for the promissory note if it will not impair Ridgmont's bonding capacity; the divorce decree contains no such conditional language.

Nancy contends that the divorce decree is "sufficiently representative of the agreement reached by the parties" to be upheld on appeal. We disagree. In *Vineyard v. Wilson*, 597 S.W.2d 21, 23 (Tex.Civ.App.—Dallas 1980, no writ), the court invalidated a judgment that did not embody the exact terms of the agreement on which it was based. "In order for a consent judgment to be valid, the parties must have definitely agreed to all the terms of the agreement. Nothing should be left for the court to provide." *Id.* In a judgment by consent, "the court has no power to supply terms, provisions, or essential details not previously agreed to by the parties." *Matthews v. Looney*, 132 Tex. 313, 317, 123 S.W.2d 871, 872 (1939). In fact, the court must accept the express terms of the agreement as binding "unless it finds that the agreement is not just and right." Tex. Fam. Code Ann. § 3.631(b) (Vernon 1993). The trial court made no such finding in this case. Therefore, the court was bound to accept the agreement. Because the trial court added terms to its decree of divorce that were not in the settlement agreement, the divorce decree cannot be allowed to stand. Point of error three is sustained.

In his second point of error, Raymond contends that the trial court erred in entering the decree of divorce because there is no evidence to support the decree. Clearly, the settlement agreement provides no evidence of the above-mentioned additional provisions of the decree. We also note that, contrary to the recitations in the decree of divorce, the parties never appeared before the trial judge at a hearing. The only evidence before the trial court was the settlement agreement. The record contains no evidence to support the court's modification of the agreement. The judgment and decree are therefore not supported by the evidence. Point of error two is sustained.

In his fourth point of error, Raymond contends that the trial court erred in refusing to grant his motion for new trial. We sustain this point of error. Inasmuch as one of the bases for a new trial was that "there are many provisions in the Decree of Divorce signed by the Court on November 27, 1991, contrary to or beyond the scope of, the agreement signed by the parties at the conclusion of the Mediation," a new trial should have been granted.

The judgment of the trial court is reversed and the cause is remanded to that court for proceedings not inconsistent with this opinion.

Fidelity and Guaranty Insurance Co. v. Star Equipment Corp.

United States Court of Appeals for the First Circuit
541 F.3d 1 (2008)

LIPEZ, CIRCUIT JUDGE.

This diversity case arises out of a dispute over a construction contract and an attempt to mediate that dispute through the district court's alternative dispute resolution program. Appellee Fidelity and Guaranty Insurance Company ("Fidelity") executed, as surety, a performance bond on behalf of Appellant Star Equipment Company ("Star") for work on a water main installation project that Star was to perform for Appellee Town of Seekonk, Massachusetts ("Seekonk"). Appellants Charlene and John Foran ("the Forans"), the principals of Star, executed a

General Agreement of Indemnity, promising to reimburse Fidelity for any losses, costs, and expenses, including attorney's fees, incurred by Fidelity as a result of the performance bond issued to Star.

After Seekonk declared Star to be in default on its construction contract with the town, Fidelity filed a declaratory judgment action to determine the rights and obligations of the parties under the performance bond. The parties entered mediation and emerged with a Settlement Memorandum of Understanding, signed by all the parties and their attorneys. When Star and the Forans refused to go forward with the settlement, Fidelity and Seekonk filed a motion to enforce the memorandum as a settlement of all claims in the case except the claim of Fidelity against Star and the Forans for indemnification, which had been explicitly reserved in the settlement agreement. The district court granted that motion, and subsequently granted Fidelity's motion for summary judgment on the indemnification claim. After a damage hearing, the court found that Star and the Forans were liable to Fidelity for $111,313.43, plus costs and interest. Star and the Forans appeal the enforcement of the settlement agreement, the summary judgment ruling, and the amount of the damage award. We affirm.

. . .

In this diversity case, we apply Massachusetts contract law. . . . The district court's determination that an enforceable settlement agreement existed is a mixed question of fact and law, which we review on "a sliding scale standard of review under the label of clear error review." . . . In other words, "[t]he more the district court's conclusions are characterized as factual conclusions, the more our review of those facts is for clear error; the more the district court's conclusions are conclusions of law, the more independent review we give."

Settlement agreements enjoy great favor with the courts "as a preferred alternative to costly, time-consuming litigation." . . . Thus, a party to a settlement agreement may seek to enforce the agreement's terms when the other party refuses to comply. . . . Where, as here, the settlement collapses before the original suit is dismissed, the party seeking to enforce the agreement may file a motion with the trial court. The trial court may summarily enforce the agreement, provided that there is no genuinely disputed question of material fact regarding the existence or terms of that agreement. When a genuinely disputed question of material fact does exist, the court should hold a hearing and resolve the contested factual issues.

On appeal, the Indemnitors argue that they were entitled to an evidentiary hearing as to whether the Settlement Memorandum of Understanding should be enforced as a settlement agreement. They claim that the Settlement Memorandum of Understanding was not binding because it had not settled all of the issues in the case. They explain that they signed the memorandum because of "explicit representations of Fidelity's representative at the mediation that she would 'work with the Forans' to resolve the Fidelity-Foran dispute in a manner that would be palatable to them; and, that their cooperation in the mediation would go a long way toward a favorable outcome in that resolution." However, these assertions are not sufficient to generate a genuine disputed question of material fact, entitling the Indemnitors to an evidentiary hearing. The Forans' subjective belief that the agreement was not "final" does not bar enforcement in the face of their assent — in writing — to the memorandum's unambiguous terms. . . .

The Indemnitors attempt to marshal the terms of the agreement in their favor on appeal, pointing to paragraph 3 of the memorandum, which states that the settlement was conditioned upon "[e]xecution of customary releases and settlement agreement." They argue that this paragraph reflected an understanding that no enforceable agreement would exist until an agreement settling all issues in the case, including the indemnification dispute, had been reached. However, the plain language of the memorandum does not support this interpretation. . . . Paragraph 2 of the memorandum explicitly states that the parties had agreed to settle all the claims in the case except those involving the indemnification agreement. Thus, the agreement reflects that the *other* issues in the case had been definitively settled, subject only to conditions in paragraph 3 — municipal approval and the execution of "customary releases and settlement agreement." A settlement of the indemnification dispute cannot be what is contemplated by those boilerplate conditions, given the language in paragraph 2 expressly excluding the indemnification claim from the scope of the agreement.

Moreover, the fact that the hand-written agreement contemplated execution of a more formal agreement does not preclude enforcement of the hand-written agreement. *Bandera [v. City of Quincy]*, 344 F.3d at 52. As we explained in *Bandera*, "[a]n agreement to make a further more detailed agreement could in some instances not be intended as a binding contract, or might be too indefinite; but neither is necessarily or even ordinarily so." *Id.* at 52 n. 2. Here, the language of the memorandum reflects a present intent by all the parties to settle all of the claims except the indemnification dispute. The terms of this settlement are clear and unambiguous. They are not contingent on the successful outcome of further negotiations to resolve the indemnification issue. Indeed, the Indemnitors do not argue that terms of the agreement were ambiguous or indefinite, nor do they claim that they were coerced into signing the agreement or that their counsel settled their claim without authority to do so. Accordingly, we find no error in the district court's order enforcing the Settlement Memorandum of Agreement as a settlement agreement that disposed of all the claims in the case except the indemnification dispute.

. . .

Affirmed.

Notes and Questions

(1) The memorandum of understanding in *Fidelity and Guaranty Insurance Co. v. Star Equipment Corp.* was clear that the settlement around specific issues was agreed upon and not dependent on the resolution of the indemnification issue, but what if

the MOU is not so clear? How does a court know if the agreement is final or just a tentative agreement to be used as a starting point for future negotiations? In *Habu v. Topcaio*, 12 Wash. App. 2d 1006, 2020 WL 533947, *1 (Div. 1 2020), the parties mediated for two days then signed a tentative agreement on several of the terms and they also included a statement that they would use best efforts to finalize an agreement within 30 days. After failing to finalize an agreement, one party moved to enforce the tentative agreement which the trial court granted. The appellate court reversed because some of the terms were missing from the term sheet, and the parties' intent to continue negotiating was shown by the terms being open to future resolution. The court then explained that there are three types of agreements:

> 1. An unenforceable agreement to agree that requires further meeting of the minds; 2. an enforceable agreement with open terms that could be supplied by a court or other authority where the parties intend to be bound by the key points agreed upon; and 3. a contract where the parties agree to negotiate in a certain manner (in good faith; for a specific period of time, etc.) but not necessarily to reach ultimate agreement.

What if a party's intent is unclear from the text of the tentative agreement? Should courts be able to look at other portions of the mediation to determine if the agreement was final or tentative? How can tentative agreements invite gaming the mediation process? When would such a gaming process lead to considerations of bad faith discussed in Section D?

(2) In *Guthrie v. Guthrie*, 594 S.E.2d 356 (Ga. 2004), the parties agreed to a mediated settlement agreement in a divorce proceeding and started performing under the agreement. One party later attempted to renounce the agreement but died before the court could rule on the motion. The estate asserted that the agreement was contingent upon divorce and should not be upheld. The court found that the language of the contract showed that the agreement was not contingent upon the court's approval of the divorce, so the agreement should be treated as a general contract. Is the Georgia Supreme Court's decision to apply contract principles in resolving the enforceability issue in *Guthrie v. Guthrie* convincing in light of the fact that the decedent had sought to repudiate the agreement prior to his death? Is the fact that the parties had begun to perform under the agreement relevant? For the application of contract principles to an oral settlement agreement in an environmental case, read the decision of the Supreme Court of Iowa in *Sierra Club v. Wayne Weber LLC*, 689 N.W.2d 696 (Iowa 2004).

(3) Note that the relevant Texas ADR statute in *Ames* makes written settlement agreements "enforceable in the same manner as any other written contract," but a provision of the relevant family law statute provides that a settlement agreement "may be revised or repudiated prior to rendition of the divorce or annulment unless it is binding under some other rule of law." Do you agree with the court's rationale in choosing the ADR provision over the family law provision? Texas appellate courts are split on this issue. *See Alvarez v. Reiser*, 958 S.W.2d 232 (Tex. App. 1997) (holding

in accord with *Ames*); *Cary v. Cary*, 894 S.W.2d 111 (Tex. App. 1995) (holding disagrees with *Ames*).

(4) The *Ames* divorce case involved a mediated property settlement. Should the law permit mediated agreements to be more open to repudiation if they involve the custody or support of minor children? In *Wayno v. Wayno*, 756 So. 2d 1024 (Fla. Dist. Ct. App. 2000), a Florida appellate court upheld a trial court's order setting forth different child support and custody arrangements than had been agreed to by the parties in a mediated, court-approved settlement agreement.

(5) Note that the *Guthrie* and *Ames* cases deal with family law. Are family cases more likely to raise enforceability issues? Why or why not? Consider the following case.

Silkey v. Investors Diversified Services, Inc.

Indiana Court of Appeals

690 N.E.2d 329 (1997)

Facts and Procedural History

In early 1983, the Silkeys received a capital gain of $650,000 from the sale of their farm land to a coal company. They sought investment assistance from Powers, who was a registered representative of IDS and possessed all the necessary securities licenses to qualify for that position. IDS is a securities dealer and brokerage firm with its principal offices located in Minneapolis, Minnesota, with an office located and doing business in Evansville, Indiana, and at other locations throughout the State of Indiana.

As a result of meetings and discussions, Powers recommended, and the Silkeys purchased, several investments, including a $100,000 investment in JMB Carlyle Real Estate Limited Partnership XII. This investment's performance did not meet the Silkeys' expectations, and on June 29, 1994, the Silkeys filed a complaint against IDS and Powers alleging misrepresentation, violations of the Indiana Securities Act, breach of fiduciary duty, and constructive fraud.

On August 16, 1995, the trial court ordered the parties to mediation. Mediation was held in Evansville, Indiana on January 17, 1996, five days before the scheduled trial date, with a mutually agreed-upon mediator. The mediator concluded the mediation with an oral recitation of the terms of the agreement and received verbal assent from all of the parties to the terms. This exchange was recorded on an audio tape. The tape was later transcribed by the mediator, and copies were sent to all parties. On January 18, 1996, the mediator filed with the trial court a Mediation Report which confirmed that a settlement had been reached, and the trial was removed from the court's calendar. On January 22, 1996, a typed transcription was sent to all parties by the mediator. On February 19, 1996, the Brokers forwarded to the Silkeys a Settlement Agreement and Mutual General Release (Agreement) which was prepared by counsel for the Brokers and signed by IDS and Powers. After receiving the Agreement, the Silkeys refused to sign it, and the Silkeys' counsel informed the Brokers of the repudiation. Subsequently, the Silkeys' counsel withdrew their representation, and the Silkeys obtained new counsel.

The Brokers filed a Motion to Enforce Agreement for Settlement on August 23, 1996. The trial court found that this was not a case where the parties were disputing whether the document accurately reflected the agreement, but rather the Silkeys were attempting to repudiate the agreement. The trial court concluded that an enforceable agreement was reached by the parties. The trial court ruled that the audio tape recording was a legally binding form of the agreement which set forth with reasonable certainty the terms and conditions and the parties' agreement to these terms and conditions. The trial court then directed that the terms of the audio tape recording be reduced to writing and that, when the writing fairly and accurately reflected the terms of the agreement, the parties would sign and file the agreement with the court.

Discussion and Decision

I. Effect of the Oral Agreement

The central question in this case is what effect, if any, should be given to the oral agreement reached by the parties at the conclusion of the mediation. The Silkeys argue that the Rules of Alternative Dispute Resolution control the disposition of this question. The rules provide that:

> (2) If an agreement is reached, it shall be reduced to writing and signed. The agreement shall then be filed with the court. If the agreement is complete on all issues, it shall be accompanied by a joint stipulation of disposition.

> (3) After the agreement becomes an order of the court by joint stipulation, in the event of any breach or failure to perform under the agreement, the court, upon motion, may impose sanctions, including costs, interest, attorney fees, or other appropriate remedies including entry of judgment on the agreement.

A.D.R. 2.7(E) (1996).

The Silkeys acknowledge that an agreement was reached and that it was reduced to writing. Appellant's Brief at 20. They also acknowledge that they have rescinded their verbal assent to the terms of the agreement. *Id.* They argue that because this agreement was neither signed by them nor filed with the court, there was no contract or breach; therefore, they argue neither enforcement nor sanction is appropriate. *Id.* We disagree.

The Silkeys present their appeal as one of statutory interpretation; therefore, we begin with consideration of the A.D.R. rules. The Indiana Supreme Court has noted in the preamble to the A.D.R. rules that the rules were "adopted in order to bring some uniformity into alternative dispute resolution with the view that the interests of the parties can be preserved" in non-traditional settings. A.D.R. Preamble. Mediation is a process to "assist[] the litigants in reaching a mutually acceptable agreement." A.D.R. 2.1. Although a court may order parties to participate in mediation and require that participation be in good faith, it cannot order them to reach agreement. *Id.* The ultimate goal of mediation is to provide a forum in which parties might reach a mutually agreed resolution to their differences. The A.D.R. rules provide a uniform *process* for negotiation, but they do not change the law regarding settlement agreements or their enforcement. Nothing in the text of the A.D.R. rules for mediation suggests the Indiana Supreme Court intended to change the trial court's role in enforcing settlement agreements. Thus, although the *process* of the mediation is controlled by the A.D.R. rules, the enforcement of any valid agreement is within the authority of the trial court under the existing law in Indiana.

"The judicial policy of Indiana strongly favors settlement agreements." *Germania v. Thermasol, Ltd.*, 569 N.E.2d 730, 732 (Ind. Ct. App. 1991). Courts retain the inherent power to enforce agreements entered into in settlement of litigation which is pending before them. *Id.* Settlement is always preferable to the action in the court, and the carrying out of the agreement should be controlled by that court.

The Silkeys argue that because no written agreement was ever signed, no joint stipulation was ever entered, and therefore, no breach occurred which could allow the court to enforce the agreement. The Silkeys misunderstand the rule. The text to which the Silkeys refer does, in fact, explain the manner in which the parties will present their agreement to the trial court in order to have it *transformed by the court* into an *order* of joint stipulation. This promotes judicial efficiency by assuring that the parties do not appear before the court in a later dispute over the same issue or action. Thus, the rule provides a uniform procedure by which parties dispose of an action in accordance with the terms of their agreement.

The Silkeys argue that they were never compelled to agree and so should not be held to an agreement about which they have changed their minds. Such a rule would clearly create a disincentive for settlement. Additionally, it would allow mediation to serve not as an aid to litigation, but as a separate and additional impetus for litigation. Neither the A.D.R. rules nor the law support such an interpretation.

The Silkeys are correct that a party has full authority over whether to settle his case or proceed to trial. Having decided to accept a settlement, however, the party is bound to that decision. "In the absence of fraud or mistake a settlement is as binding and conclusive of the parties' rights and obligations as a judgment on the merits." The Silkeys do not allege fraud or mistake in reaching this settlement agreement; in fact, they do not question the terms of the agreement at all. Instead, they assert that they "no longer agree" to the terms of the settlement. This is not a sufficient ground to rescind a contract.

The Silkeys argue that the agreement was not final or binding because it is oral. A settlement agreement is not required to be in writing. Whether a party has consented to particular terms is a factual matter to be determined by the fact-finder.

The trial court found that the terms of the agreement were not in dispute. In reaching this decision, it relied on the parties' affidavits, pleadings, and memoranda of law. At the hearing on the matter, the trial court admitted the tape recording of the recitation of agreement over the Silkeys' objection. It does not appear from the trial court's written findings that it relied on the tape recording of the agreement in reaching its decision, nor was it required to do so because neither the content nor the authenticity of the tape was in question. In fact, as noted, the Silkeys raise the issue that the agreement reached in the mediation was preliminary for the first time on appeal. Having failed to raise this issue before the trial court, it is waived.

The evidence before the trial court clearly supports its finding that the parties entered an agreement at the close of the mediation session. The trial court had available to it a tape and a transcript which clearly indicated the parties had agreed in substance to the terms of the mediation. The Silkeys did not argue to the trial court that there were any changes or defects in the terms as they were reduced to writing by the Brokers. Having found that a settlement agreement had been reached, the trial court acted within its authority under the A.D.R. rules and the case law in Indiana in directing the parties to reduce their agreement to writing and sign and file it with the court.

II. Statute of Frauds

The second issue raised by the Silkeys is that the verbal agreement is not in compliance with the Statute of Frauds and is, thus, unenforceable. They make three arguments on this issue: first, that the terms did not constitute the entire agreement; second, that the audio tape is insufficient to meet the requirements of a writing in order to take the agreement outside the Statute of Frauds; and third, that the agreement cannot be performed within one year of its making.

The Statute of Frauds provides:

> No action shall be brought in any of the following cases: . . .

> Fifth: Upon any agreement that is not to be performed within one (1) year from the making thereof. . . .

> Unless the promise, contract or agreement upon which such action shall be brought, or some memorandum or note thereof, shall be in writing, and signed by the party to be charged therewith, or by some person thereunto by him lawfully authorized. . . .

Ind. Code § 32-2-1-1. The Silkeys argue that the Statute of Frauds is applicable to this agreement due to the fact that it will not be performed within one year. They argue that this agreement will not be fully performed until January 31, 2001. However, the agreement is not this definite. The terms of the agreement guarantee that the Silkeys would receive an initial payment of cash immediately and a guarantee of a distribution of an additional fixed sum *on or before* January 31, 2001. If the investment pays a dividend equivalent to this additional sum before January 31, 2001, there is no further obligation on the part of the Brokers. The fact that this agreement *may not* be performed within one year is insufficient alone to make it subject to the requirements of the Statute of Frauds:

It must affirmatively appear by the terms of the contract, that its stipulations are not to be performed within a year after it is made, in order to bring it within the provisions of the statute of frauds. (*sic*) The Statute of Frauds has always been held to apply only to contracts which, *by the express stipulations of the parties*, were not to be performed within a year, and not to those which *might or might not*, upon a contingency, *be* performed within a year. The one year clause of the Statute of Frauds has no application to contracts which are *capable* of *being* performed *within* one year of the making thereof.

It is possible that the agreement could be fully performed within one year of its making if the underlying investment were to pay a distribution equal to or greater than the guarantee amount within the first year. There is no express stipulation between the parties that the agreement would not be performed within one year. Thus, the agreement falls outside the Statute of Frauds. Because the Statue of Frauds is not applicable to this settlement agreement due to the fact that it could be completed within one year, we need not address whether it meets the other requirements of the Statute of Frauds.

Conclusion

The trial court acted within its authority to enforce a settlement agreement in a case pending before it where the parties clearly agreed to the terms, but later attempted to rescind their assent. The oral settlement agreement is enforceable, and the parties may be ordered to reduce their agreement to writing and file it with the court. Additionally, because the oral agreement may be performed within one year and there is no express stipulation between the parties that it will not be performed, it is outside the Statute of Frauds.

Affirmed.

Notes and Questions

(1) What if one of the brokers in *Silkey* sought to disassociate himself from the agreement the other broker was seeking to enforce? For a discussion of a party's First Amendment right to disassociate himself or herself from a settlement agreement, see *Krystkowiak v. W.O. Brisben Companies, Inc.*, 90 P.3d 859 (Colo. 2004). In *Krystkowiak*, a member of a homeowner's association (Krystkowiak) sought to contest a development even after the homeowner's association (NECSNA) mediated an agreement to discontinue its opposition. The developer sued Krystkowiak for tortious interference with contract, contending that Krystkowiak contracted away his right to continue protesting the development when the homeowner's association president signed the proposed settlement agreement. Moreover, the developer argued that Krystkowiak tortiously interfered with its contract with NECSNA because he knew about the contract and intentionally induced NECSNA not to perform it by continuing to protest. In ruling in favor of Krystkowiak, the court explained that Krystkowiak had the right to disassociate from NECSNA once it no longer represented his individual viewpoint:

Forced inclusion of a member is no more acceptable when an association's expressive activity becomes inconsistent or incompatible with the member's viewpoint as an individual. If this occurs, the person is free to drop his or her membership and disassociate from the organization. . . . Once NEC-SNA's and Krystkowiak's viewpoints diverged, he was free to disassociate from the organization and continue to petition against the development in his individual capacity. The fact that Krystkowiak was initially acting in a representative capacity does not subsume his individual rights. . . . [W]e conclude that Krystkowiak's continued opposition to [the] development was not prohibited by contract, and that he was free to invoke the First Amendment to defend against [the] suit.

Does this First Amendment claim not to be bound by one's group agreement differ in principle or effect from a situation in which an interested stakeholder contests the negotiated settlement terms reached in an OSHA "reg-neg" process governing workplace practices, with settlement terms reached between a city government and protest group regarding police practices?

(2) What if a party to a settlement agreement argues that its enforcement would be unfair in light of subsequent circumstances? In *Walker v. Gribble*, 689 N.W.2d 104 (Iowa 2004), the Iowa Supreme Court affirmed the trial court's enforcement of a mediated settlement between former law partners regarding future division of contingency fee recoveries in overtime pay cases. The court found no violation of public policy based on professional responsibility rules and concluded that the lawyer could not now renegotiate fees simply because she ended up working more overall than she anticipated when she finalized the fee agreement in mediation. The court explained:

> The fact that one [(or both)] of the parties was wrong does not provide a basis for overturning a settlement agreement that was entered into as a result of arms-length negotiations by parties who are not only attorneys themselves but who were both also represented throughout the negotiations by other attorneys. . . . Walker must live with the bargain she freely entered into. . . . Even if it was a bad bargain, under general principles of contract law, she lives with that bargain. . . . We will not interfere with their agreement—fully performed with the exception of the payment of fees—simply because one party got the better end of the bargain.

(3) In *Silkey*, if the mediator had not recorded the agreement and transcribed it later, would the agreement still have been enforceable? In *National Union Fire Ins. Co. of Pittsburgh, PA v. Price*, 78 P.3d 1138 (Colo. Ct. App. 2003), the Court of Appeals of Colorado refused to enforce an alleged oral mediated settlement as contrary to the requirements of Colorado's Dispute Resolution Act, which mandates that settlements be reduced to writing, be approved and signed by all parties, and presented to the court for approval. Florida has a specific rule that contemplates the recording of agreements: "By stipulation of the parties, the agreement may be

transcribed or electronically recorded. In such event, the transcript may be filed with the court." Rule 1.730(b) Florida Rules of Civil Procedure.

(4) In *Ali Haghighi v. Russian-American Broadcasting Co.*, 577 N.W.2d 927 (Min. 1998), the Minnesota statute regulating the requirements of mediated settlement agreements required a clause stating that the agreement is binding on the parties. After the mediation, an agreement was drafted by both parties, and the binding clause was left out. On a motion to enforce the settlement agreement, the court found the settlement was unenforceable due to the clear noncompliance with the statute. The court reasoned that these statutes are binding and meant to protect the parties from a dispute over whether notes taken during a mediation are enforceable even though they were not meant to be. Is this too much of a hardline rule? The parties aided each other in drafting the agreement, so should it be presumed that they meant it to be binding even though the express language was missing? If this rule was softened, how could parties prove their intent that the agreement was to be binding?

The federal district court in *Haghighi* ruled that the Minnesota statute prevents the mediator's testimony. However, the court questioned the "appropriateness of such a limitation on testimony in circumstances where a dispute arises regarding the existence of a mediated settlement." Why? For an excellent analysis of the dilemma a court has to deal with when attempting to enforce mediated settlement agreements in the face of statutory confidentiality provisions, see Ellen E. Deason, *Enforcing Mediated Settlement Agreements: Contract Law Collides with Confidentiality*, 35 U.C. Davis L. Rev. 33 (2001).

The Eighth Circuit reversed the federal district court's decision in *Haghighi* and remanded the case for further proceedings in light of a Supreme Court of Minnesota decision on the certified question. *Ali Haghighi v. Russian-American Broadcasting Co.*, 173 F.3d 1086 (8th Cir. 1999). For a discussion and critique of the *Haghighi* litigation and the relevant Minnesota rule, see James R. Coben & Peter N. Thompson, *The Haghighi Trilogy and the Minnesota Civil Mediation Act: Exposing a Phantom Menace Casting a Pall over the Development of ADR in Minnesota*, 20 Hamline J. Pub. L. & Pol'y 299 (1999).

(5) In *Caballero v. Wikse*, 92 P.3d 1076 (Idaho 2004), the Supreme Court of Idaho upheld a trial court's order requiring specific performance of an oral settlement agreement in a wrongful discharge case. Moreover, the court enforced the agreement over the plaintiff's objection that his attorney did not have the authority to settle the case in the plaintiff's absence. The plaintiff had walked out prior to the end of the mediation and arguably authorized his attorney to settle. Clearly, the case would have had a different result if Idaho had a statute similar to that in Minnesota. Is this the mediation party that the Minnesota legislature was seeking to protect?

Del Bosque v. AT & T Advertising

United States Court of Appeals for the Fifth Circuit
2011 U.S. App. LEXIS 19280 (Sept. 16, 2011)

Before GARZA, SOUTHWICK, AND HAYNES, CIRCUIT JUDGES.

PER CURIAM

Sylvia Del Bosque filed suit against AT & T in the United States District Court for the Western District of Texas in May of 2008. Del Bosque's complaint, as amended, alleged that AT & T discriminated against her in her employment on the basis of race and sex and retaliated against her after she formally complained to AT & T's human resources staff, both in violation of Title VII of the Civil Rights Act of 1964.

The parties engaged in settlement discussions throughout the pretrial process, culminating in a mediation on November 18. The case did not settle on the day of mediation, but from November 18, 2010, until November 22, 2010, the parties continued efforts to attempt to resolve the case. Del Bosque was represented by counsel throughout this process. On November 22, 2010, Del Bosque and her attorney signed a settlement agreement after making certain handwritten changes on the face of the agreement that had been proposed by AT & T. On November 29, 2010, AT & T's attorney signed the agreement and initialed the changes Del Bosque had made.

On November 30, 2010, Del Bosque filed a pro se motion to revoke the settlement agreement. AT & T responded by filing motions with supporting affidavits to enforce the settlement agreement and to dismiss the case. Del Bosque filed a response without formal evidence. . . . [T]he district court conducted a hearing on December 13, 2010, at which Del Bosque, the attorney who represented Del Bosque at the mediation, and AT & T's attorney spoke. No witnesses were presented, but it appears that the district court considered the attendees' statements as evidence; the affidavits and exhibits presented with the motion to enforce were also considered as evidence. The district judge carefully and diligently listened to both attorneys and Del Bosque. At the conclusion of the hearing, the district judge advised Del Bosque that he intended to enforce the settlement agreement and to deny her motion to revoke the agreement; the district court entered an order to that effect the same day but deferred dismissal of the case until AT & T had paid Del Bosque according to the terms of the settlement. Del Bosque filed a notice of appeal following the entry of this order. After AT & T satisfied the court that it had paid Del Bosque, the district court entered an order and final judgment dismissing the case with prejudice on December 30, 2010. Del Bosque then filed a second notice of appeal, and the two appeals were consolidated before us.

. . .

We address only the issue of whether the district court erred in enforcing the settlement agreement.

As an initial matter, we conclude that the question of the enforceability of the settlement agreement is, under our precedent, to be determined by reference to federal law, not—as AT & T would have us hold—Texas law. . . . Del Bosque contends that the agreement—including the choice-of-law provision—is the product of incapacity or coercion. . . .

Under federal law, "'[o]ne who attacks a settlement must bear the burden of showing that the contract he has made is tainted with invalidity.'" The burden, therefore, lay with Del Bosque to establish before the district court that there was some basis for holding the agreement invalid. As the district court concluded, she has not met this burden; indeed, she offered virtually no basis for the court to rule in her favor.

First, although Del Bosque initially suggested that she had not in fact signed the settlement agreement that AT & T presented to the district court, she admitted at the hearing that she had, in fact, signed the agreement.

Second, Del Bosque asserted that she had been coerced into signing the settlement agreement. When the court inquired as to how and why Del Bosque felt coerced, she first stated that she had had insufficient time to review the agreement despite having reviewed it over a weekend and having consulted with counsel before signing. On further questioning, Del Bosque asserted only that "everybody wanted it done" and then asked the court for a recess. She offered no other evidence of coercion or even statements that would show coercion. The district court did not clearly err in finding that the facts did not support the defense of coercion. . . .

Third, Del Bosque argues that she lacked capacity to enter into the settlement agreement. Del Bosque gave the district court a signed, unsworn letter from Holli Esteban (the "Esteban Letter"), a nurse at an endocrinology practice, addressed "To Whom It May Concern" and expressing the opinion that "[d]ue to Ms. Delbosque's [*sic*] recent worsening condition, she may not have been in the best medical condition to enter into a legal agreement." Although the district court reviewed and considered the Esteban Letter, Del Bosque affirmatively refused to allow the court to receive the letter into evidence—nor is it at all clear that the district court could have accepted the letter as evidence even if Del Bosque had offered it. Even assuming arguendo that this Letter constituted medical evidence, it falls far short of proving "incapacity." Other than telling the court that she was "distraught" during the mediation, Del Bosque offered no other purported evidence to support her claim of incapacity. The district court's determination of the facts was not clearly erroneous, and the district court did not abuse its discretion in rejecting the defense of incapacity. . . .

Instead of being a case about incapacity or duress, this seems to be a case where Del Bosque expected the mediation to give her a feeling of closure that she did not get. Del Bosque argued to the district court (and on appeal) that there was no "meeting of the minds" as to the settlement agreement. On further questioning from the district court, Del Bosque explained that the basis for her argument was that the mediation did not resolve, and the settlement agreement was not predicated upon, the full resolution of certain fact questions that Del Bosque had wanted the court to resolve when she filed the lawsuit. For example, it did not resolve whether the circumstances of her departure from AT & T constituted termination, retirement, or a disability release. However, she expressed no misunderstanding or mistake about the terms of the settlement agreement *itself.* Instead, at the hearing, Del Bosque confirmed that she understood the amount of money that she would receive under the agreement but nevertheless argued that the agreement was invalid because it did not explain how the agreement arrived at that amount.

Del Bosque appears to have been under the misimpression that reaching an agreement on stipulated facts was somehow a required precursor to the mediation process. That is not so: as the district court explained, frequently the opposite is the case — a mediated agreement reaches an ultimate disposition that fundamentally avoids the resolution of disputed facts. "[S]ettlement is a process of compromise in which, in exchange for the saving of cost and elimination of risk, the parties each give up something they might have won had they proceeded with the litigation, rather than an attempt to precisely delineate legal rights. Ultimately, it seems that this misapprehension of the process, rather than any misunderstanding as to the terms of the agreement, drove Del Bosque's motion. A misunderstanding that does not "ha[ve] a material effect on the agreed exchange of performances" has no effect on the validity of the contract.

Del Bosque was represented when she negotiated and entered into the agreement. To the extent that Del Bosque's argument is predicated on an alleged misunderstanding of the legal effect of the contract, the fact that she was represented by retained counsel seriously undercuts that position. . . . We therefore perceive no abuse of discretion in the district court's decision to enforce the settlement agreement on this record. The district court acted within its discretion in refusing to set aside a facially valid settlement agreement on the basis of the sparse evidence offered by Del Bosque in support of her motion. The district judge very patiently gave her every opportunity to say whatever she wished at the hearing — even granting her request for a recess to allow her to consider what she wanted to say. The court then issued a ruling well-grounded in the facts (and lack of facts) presented. No more was required.

AFFIRMED. MOTIONS GRANTED in part, DENIED in part.

Notes and Questions

(1) In ruling against Ms. Del Bosque's defense of duress, was the Fifth Circuit panel less sympathetic than they would have been if they were considering enforceability of a contract rather than a mediated settlement agreement? For cases reaching similar outcomes to a duress defense, see *In re D.E.H.*, 301 S.W.3d 825 (Tex. App. 2009), where the court ruled that the pressure and anguish caused by the possibility of losing parental rights were not sufficient to deny enforcement of the agreement, and *Thomas v. Sandstrom*, 2012 U.S. App. LEXIS 1497 (3d Cir. Jan. 25, 2012), where a dog owner brought a lawsuit alleging civil rights violations in connection with confiscation of his dog and claimed he was coerced into signing the agreement "by

the broken bond of love for his dog." Although a duress defense is rarely successful, in *Cooper v. Austin*, 750 So. 2d 711 (Fla. Dist. Ct. App. 2000), a party was successful in claiming duress where his wife extracted a favorable settlement in mediation by threatening to deliver incriminating juvenile sex pictures to the prosecutor if he did not agree to her settlement terms.

Proving claims of duress, fraud, and other general contract defenses are often very difficult and tend to require evidence of something extreme, such as in *Everett v. Morgan*, 2009 WL 113262 (Tenn. Ct. App. 2009), where a friend impersonated the mediator during a child support dispute. Obviously, this constituted fraud, and the court set aside the agreement. Contrast this with the *Facebook* case in Chapter 5, where the Winklevosses claimed to have been misled as to the value of the Facebook stock. The court still enforced the agreement because they were sophisticated parties with talented lawyers, so they should have known the value of the stock. Is this a harsh result? Why are some courts imposing a seemingly high burden for defenses against enforcement?

(2) In *Ferguson v. Ferguson*, 54 So. 3d 553 (Fla. Dist. Ct. App. 2011), the parties accepted a mediated marital settlement agreement which included a home. The agreement was reached prior to the 2008 housing collapse; due to the drastic change in the market, the deal became very uneven in terms of monetary value, so one party attempted to void the settlement by arguing that the agreement should now be unenforceable because refinancing the home in his name was impossible given the current market conditions. The court upheld the contract because market conditions are a foreseeable variable at inception that could affect the contract. "A marital settlement agreement entered into by the parties and ratified by a final judgment is a contract, subject to the laws of contract. Because of the central importance placed upon the enforceability of contracts in our culture, the defense of impossibility (and its cousins, impracticability and frustration of purpose) must therefore be applied with great caution if the contingency was foreseeable at the inception of the agreement."

Did the Florida appellate court in *Ferguson v. Ferguson* set the bar fairly high in deciding to reverse the lower court and rule against Mr. Ferguson's impossibility defense?

(3) In *Atlantic Pipe* (Section C, *supra*), the judge refers to mediation as a "nonbinding" process. Given the cases in this section, is that an accurate description?

(4) In *Shuford v. Musashi Auto Parts*, 2022 WL 3716051 (W.D. Mich. Aug. 29, 2022), the defendant sought to enforce an agreement that had been reached during a Zoom mediation. Although the plaintiff and plaintiff's counsel were in different locations during the Zoom mediation and the plaintiff's counsel signed for the plaintiff the "Term Sheet" prepared by the mediator setting out settlement terms, the court found by clear and convincing evidence that a settlement had been reached and enforced the agreement. Are there potential circumstances or characteristics surrounding an online mediation that might be relevant in considering whether a court should enforce a settlement agreement reached in an online mediation?

Chapter 7

Diversity, Power, and Justice

A. Introduction

It is critical to be fully aware and cognizant of the social reality in which we are participating in conflict resolution. We live in a diverse, multicultural society in which the beautiful differences between human beings have been institutionalized according to a dominant, power-over model of resolving differences. When we talk about racism, sexism, homophobia, and so on, what are we referring to if not a model of dominance and chronic conflict? . . . [T]he Americanization process generates a tyranny of conformity that places people of color in the untenable position of being the "wrong" kind of American.

—Roberto M. Chené[1]

Mediation, when conducted well, promotes individual autonomy in the decision-making process; ideally, the result is that each person's values and aspirations assume a dominant role in how people discuss, develop, and shape their mediated outcomes. Chené's quote challenges mediators to consider the social reality and the institutional forces molding the context and power dynamics of each mediation session, the institutions and structures in which mediators operate, and the role of each individual involved in the mediation process.

Mediation participants (inclusive of the mediator) bring a range of cultural diversity to each conversation. Professor Carrie Menkel-Meadow writes that "Culture is a product of 'groupness' including practices, beliefs, norms, rules, behaviors, and customs which are often further identified with race, nationality, ethnicity, religion, gender, and social groups (*e.g.*, self-identifying non-binary, LGBTQ+) and even voluntary associations and affiliations (*e.g.*, political parties, gangs) and 'status' cultures (*e.g.*, student, academic, legal, professional, 'business' capitalist culture, working class)."[2] Cultures value things differently, and that leads to behavioral differences. In some cultures, for example, people show respect by not having direct eye contact with their discussion counterparts while others interpret a person's not maintaining

---

1. Roberto M. Chené, *Beyond Mediation — Reconciling and Intercultural World: A New Role for Conflict Resolution*, *in* Re-Centering Cultural Knowledge in Conflict Resolution Practice 33–34 (Mary Adams Trujillo et al., eds., 2008).

2. *Cross-Cultural Disputes and Mediator Strategies*, *in* The Routledge Handbook of Intercultural Mediation 30 (Dominic Busch, ed., 2023).

eye contact as a sign of disrespect. Similarly, in some religious traditions, a married man will not shake hands with a female who is not his wife; a woman raised in a different tradition may view that man's refusal to shake her hand as a deliberate act of disengagement or hostility. People from different cultures develop different habits regarding what constitutes a comfortable physical distance between persons talking to each other; if one person "invades the other's space," deliberately or accidentally, discomfort ensues. Similarly, the fact that some individuals speak more loudly or quickly than others might lead others to conclude that the person speaking loudly is disrespectful, or that the fast-talking individual is being deceptive.

What is the significance of such complexities for a mediator? The mediator must adopt procedural and conversational practices that enable all parties to feel that they are being treated with dignity and respect. The mediator, for instance, would try to place parties at the conference table at a distance comfortable for everyone; the mediator must consider the barriers and opportunities that use of a particular technology might pose for parties, particularly those who lack access to stable internet access or those with disabilities. The mediator should schedule meeting times in a manner that respected the participants' desire to celebrate particular holidays or religious events, or serve parties with food and beverages that reflected their differing cultures. By behaving in such a manner, the mediator displays fundamental sensitivity and respect to persons of varying backgrounds, and thereby enables all participants to feel included.

At the same time, a mediator cannot fall into the trap of interacting with disputants based on stereotypes. There is an important difference between one's being conscious of differences based on race, gender, ethnicity, or religion, and one's engaging in stereotyping. While group membership tends to create commonalities among members, each individual adopts particular views, behaviors, and values in their own way. It is obviously not the case, for instance, that "all male lawyers in the United States think the same way about effective or desirable parenting arrangements governing divorced spouses," that "all white male supervisors in employment settings harass female subordinates," or that "no clergy person would deceive or mistreat a parishioner." But licensed lawyers in the United States do undergo a common form of educational training; workplace supervisors regularly address similar challenges relating to disciplining or terminating workplace subordinates; and clergy of particular faiths embrace a theological creed integral to their calling. A mediator's challenge and responsibility is to be sensitive to blending a respect for group norms with awareness of how each individual embraces or rejects that norm. In this very fundamental way, a mediator takes seriously the belief that every case is different because each person is unique.

Diversity conflicts can reflect clashes not only of behavioral habits but also of fundamental values. Controversies regarding leadership succession in a family-operated business can pit one family member's belief about the priority of family cohesiveness against another person's desire to exercise autonomy by pursuing other life callings. Deep conflicts emerge when a group's cultural values might define gender roles in a manner that is sharply at odds with the dominant culture's public policy and the lived experiences of individual family members who are challenging those norms. In such situations, a mediator can encourage persons to engage in discussions to search for a workable, acceptable resolution; some efforts will succeed and others fail. While no mediator should be deterred from trying to assist parties to such a dispute, the mediator must recognize that more is at stake than simply trying to deploy an effective technique to help parties respect alternative practices; rather, one party may be asking the other to alter a web of their fundamental convictions. Such controversies, in particular, also raise the question of whether the mediator's own background enables them to act in a neutral fashion or be perceived and accepted by the parties as so acting.

In sum, there are many types of differences among parties. Minimally, the mediator wants to ensure that parties do not declare impasse by drawing incorrect inferences based on ignorance of one another's cultural practices or erroneous stereotyping. Affirmatively, the mediator, to the extent possible, wants to capitalize on the strengths of parties' differences to assist them design and shape imaginative, acceptable bargaining outcomes.

This chapter asks readers to grapple with considerations of diversity, power, and justice as they shape and inform mediation theory and practice. Part B presents theoretical considerations connected to bias and culture, and presents three ethnographic illustrations from culturally diverse mediators. Part C presents classic critiques of the mediation process tied to informality and gender, shares a modern perspective on the cultural influence of racism and whiteness, and concludes with a classic study which considers whether diverse parties receive lower monetary outcomes in mediation as compared to what they would have been awarded at trial. Part D examines questions about mediation's connection to the rule of law and poses sharp challenges to whether settlement through mediation is appropriate. Consider this chapter a mere starting point for grappling with these topics in our evolving world.

B. Interrogating Bias, Considering Culture

1. Considerations for Bias & Culture

Mediation practitioners, organizations, and trainers have embedded considerations related to bias and culture into their respective practices and training protocols. New mediators are often asked to reflect on their own biases — implicit and explicit — and consider how those biases influence the choices they make at the mediation table. Explicit biases are those which are openly held while implicit biases are those operating without conscious awareness, informed by society and our lived experience. In the first excerpt, Professor Carol Izumi identifies how implicit biases percolates in mediation and identifies strategies for countering them.

Cultural consideration often takes the form of "cultural competency," or gaining information about a culture's traditions, activities, and stereotypes. While cultural competence may be a valuable starting point for interacting with individuals from diverse cultures, scholars have noted that this framing is insufficiently narrow. Cultural humility is an alternative approach, designed to shift the expertise from those with cultural competency training to the individuals involved in a dispute. In the second excerpt, Shino Yokotsuka explains how cultural competency fails to empower mediation participants and urges mediators to consider the basic tenets of cultural humility in their practice.

Implicit Bias and Prejudice in Mediation

70 SMU L. Rev. 681, 685-693 (2017)*
By Carol Izumi

. . . Just as our brains help us categorize objects based on characteristics, our brains use schemas to sort people into groups, such as male or female, young or old. Mental processes that operate outside our conscious awareness are implicit, or unconscious. The big reveal of this research is that we do not always have conscious, intentional control over our mental associations, perceptions, and impressions.

Simply stated, implicit bias refers to automatic associations of stereotypes and attitudes with social groups. Implicit stereotypes and attitudes that result from repeated exposure to cultural stereotypes in our society form the basis for implicit racial, gender, ethnic, and other biases. Research shows that stereotypes are automatically activated merely by encountering a member of a social group. This "automaticity" of stereotype activation influences our judgments, actions, and decisions. Despite our best intentions and explicit beliefs, implicit biases can produce behavior that diverges from our endorsed principles. So, a mediator may espouse egalitarian beliefs, but her implicit biases produce discriminatory responses toward the parties.

. . .

Four main conclusions are drawn from implicit social cognition research: (1) there is variance, sometimes wide, between implicit and explicit cognition; (2) we show a pervasive and strong favoritism for our own social group, as well as for socially valued groups; (3) implicit cognitions predict behavior; and (4) implicit cognitions can be changed.

Significantly, implicit bias often predicts individually discriminatory behaviors more than explicit attitudes. Here are a couple of research examples. Doctors with stronger anti-black attitudes and stereotypes were less likely to prescribe a medical procedure for African Americans compared with white Americans with the same medical profiles. In another study, white subjects with stronger levels of implicit racial bias found a facial expression happy or neutral if the face was white, but angry

---

or neutral if the face was black. Nonverbal behaviors are also shaped by unconscious attitudes and stereotypes.

In mediation, well-meaning practitioners who hold explicit egalitarian attitudes and views experience automatic stereotype activation upon encountering parties. Mediators are highly likely to favor their own ingroup and be biased against out-group members, especially less socially valued ones. This bias can play out in spontaneous behaviors such as eye contact, seating distance, blinking, and smiling. White male mediators, the predominant racial and gender group in the field, may unconsciously ascribe negative traits to parties of color relating to work ethic, honesty, criminal propensity, and competence. A study about lawyers is instructive here. Partners at a law firm were given an identical memorandum written by "Thomas Meyer," identified as an associate who graduated from NYU Law School. Half of the partners were told Meyer was white; on average, they found 2.9 of the 7 spelling/grammar errors in the memo. The partners who were told that Meyer was black found 5.8 of the 7 errors. Qualitative evaluations of the memos were equally striking.

In-group bias or preference may not seem as pernicious as out-group discrimination, but the effect can be the same. Treating a favored group more positively still results in a discriminatory outcome. . . .

In addition, bias can cause racial anxiety. Social scientists have observed that we may feel more anxious when we interact with out-group members than with our in-group members. Research on racial anxiety shows that for some people interracial interactions may trigger physical and cognitive indicators of anxiety. People of color often fear discrimination and hostile treatment; white individuals may fear being perceived as racist and being treated with distrust. This can result in unsatisfactory interaction and a negative feedback loop — their respective fears seem to be confirmed by each other's behavior. People experiencing racial anxiety have shorter interactions, maintain less eye contact, use a less friendly tone, and feel more awkward. A 2014 report by The Perception Institute, a consortium of leading social scientists, documents the adverse effects of implicit bias and racial anxiety in education and health care. For example, patients of color may perceive discrimination on the part of white health care professionals, which leads to distrust and avoidance of health services.

Combined with implicit bias and racial anxiety, other phenomena may foster discrimination in mediation. Confirmation bias reinforces mediator judgments formed by implicit attitudes and stereotypes. By seeking and over-relying on evidence that merely confirms our beliefs, contradictory information is ignored. In other words, mediators may see more stereotype-congruent than counter-stereotypical evidence.

Also, the lack of normative certainty in mediation may play a role.[65] Studies show that "situations that include clear indications of right and wrong behavior . . . tend

---

65. Carol Izumi, [*Implicit Bias and the Illusion of the Mediator Neutrality*, 34 Wash. Univ. J.L. & Pol'y 71 (2010)] at 107–08 (citing Lu-in Wang, *Race as Proxy: Situational Racism and Self-Fulfilling Stereotypes*, 53 DePaul L. Rev. 1013, 1038 (2004)).

to lessen the likelihood of discrimination."[66] Normative ambiguity arises when appropriate behavior is not clearly defined in a particular context and where negative behavior can be justified on a basis other than race. With scant normative consensus in the ADR field regarding appropriate mediator behavior, mediators can rationalize discriminatory actions on neutrality or other grounds.

IV. Bias Reduction Strategies

The good news is that implicit biases are amenable to change. Suppression of stereotyped associations and engagement of non-prejudiced responses requires "intention, attention, and effort." What might this look like for mediators?

Intention requires *Awareness and Motivation.* Acknowledging one's own biases is a necessary first step. Court programs and service providers should require mediators to take the [Implicit Association Test] IAT and engage in other bias reduction efforts to receive case referrals. Once mediators become aware of their biases, they are more likely to muster the two kinds of motivation necessary to reduce their biases: external (appearing non-prejudiced to others) and internal (appearing non-prejudiced to oneself). Studies show that both types of motivation are important for bias reduction success.

Attention entails Salience and Cognitive Resources. While stereotypes are automatically activated, the application of those stereotypes in our judgments, decisions, and interactions may be moderated. By confronting their implicit biases, rather than ignoring them, mediators can actively monitor and inhibit stereotype-consistent responses. On this point, in August 2016, 250 immigration judges attended mandatory antibias training, and the United States Department of Justice announced that 28,000 more employees would take the training. Mediators should be required to undergo rigorous anti-bias training, much more than a one-hour Elimination of Bias class.

For example, mediators could be taught two effective debiasing strategies: (1) using discrepancy experiences to enhance motivation and inhibit prejudiced responses; and (2) goal-directed behavior. A discrepancy experience is when you become aware of a response or reaction that runs counter to your explicit beliefs and attitudes. Developing an "implementation-intention" plan for bias reduction is expressed as follows: "If I encounter X, I will do Y." Also, mediators can suppress stereotype application more effectively with sufficient cognitive resources. This means eliminating distractions, stress, fatigue, time-pressures, and other circumstances that lead to decision-making shortcuts and less thoughtful, deliberate responses.

Effort involves Exposure and Enhanced Practices. Implicit social cognition research shows that bias and racial anxiety can be attenuated through interpersonal

---

66. Wang, *supra* note 65, at 1038.

interactions with people of different social groups. A meta-analysis of studies found that intergroup contact correlates negatively with prejudice. Also, exposure to counter-stereotypical exemplars decreases implicit bias. People who increased their exposure to positive examples of social groups showed decreased implicit bias toward blacks, women, gays, and Asian Americans in various studies.

To this end, I urge use of a co-mediation model. Given the dismal level of mediator diversity, I would go so far as to require mixed race and gender mediator teams. I am rethinking my initial aversion to race matching in mediation because we need a way to mentor and employ more mediators of color. Studies show that minority mediators are underrepresented in the field and encounter significant barriers to gaining access. In an implicit bias presentation to the International Academy of Mediators last year, the co-presenter and I showed statistics obtained from seven mediation service providers. The percentage of mediators of color within these organizations ranged from a low of 3% to a high of 14%. Even when they are on lists, mediators of color report difficulty receiving appointments. While the use of mediation has increased, the use of minority mediators has not. At a minimum, if every court-connected mediation included at least one mediator of color on a two-person team, the diversity picture would change.

Having diverse mediators matters to participants. A recent study by the State Justice Institute of Maryland surveyed ADR participants in district court day-of-trial mediation. Of note, having at least one ADR practitioner's race match the race of the reporting participant was positively associated with: (1) parties feeling that they listened and understood each other and jointly controlled the outcome; (2) an increase in a sense of self-efficacy (*i.e.*, ability to speak and make a difference) and an increase in the sense that the court cares.

I would also require regular observations and evaluations of mediators. Having periodic oversight would offer some review of interactions with the parties. Official oversight of spontaneous actions and decisions has been shown to reduce implicit bias.

And finally, effective bias reduction practices include using protocols and tools to track evaluations, decisions, and outcomes. Data collection, checklists, rubrics, and the like are ways to detect and reduce discrimination. More consistent and granular data collection and analysis by courts, service providers, and mediators could reveal troublesome patterns or practices in mediation. As seen in the Maryland Court report and the New Mexico MetroCourt studies from the late 1990s, information on the race of the mediator and the participants can yield important information and help us see if racial disparities are evident.

Cultural Humility in Intercultural Mediation

in The Routledge Handbook of Intercultural Mediation 51, 53–56 (2023)*
By Shino Yokotsuka

The limitations of the cultural competency approach

The concept of culture is extremely complex. . . . More than . . . a half century ago, two American anthropologists . . . [discovered] more than 150 definitions for the concept. . . . [C]ulture has diversities even within the same cultural group. For example, Hispanic culture is often perceived to be homogeneous. However, not all Hispanic people share the same cultural traditions, interpret their cultures in the exact same way, and come from the same countries or same regions. Also, culture is fluid rather than static. Culture is constantly changing, adopting itself to new interpretations, environments, and challenges.

Even though culture is far more complex than one can imagine, the mediation field has a tendency of oversimplifying it. Today, a cultural competence approach instead of cultural humility has been a very popular strategy in the conflict resolution field to handle cultural diversity and inclusiveness. Cultural competence is defined as being capable of functioning effectively in the context of cultural difference. That is to say, developing cultural competency means to cultivate an ability to understand, communicate with, and effectively interact with people across cultures. While the cultural competency approach has the positive intention of deepening intercultural understanding, the problematic aspects of cultural competency are its lack of awareness of multidimensional identities/cultures and the existing power imbalances. The most serious concern of the cultural competency approach is that it assumes that cultural knowledge or skill is something people can 'master'.

The limitation of the cultural competence approach is well-illustrated by the example of the following African American nurse and Latino physician. There was an African American nurse who took care of a middle-aged Latino patient, and this patient had undergone surgery several hours ago. A Latino physician on a consult service approached this patient's bedside and commented to the nurse, saying that this patient seemed to have been in a great deal of postoperative pain. The nurse immediately responded to the physician and dismissed his/her comment, saying that the nurse took a cross-cultural medicine class in her nursing school and learned that Hispanic patients over-express pain that they are feeling, and therefore, there is no need to take it seriously. This Latino physician had a difficult time helping this nurse to see this from a different perspective from the one she already had through her education because the nurse was excessively focused on her self-proclaimed cultural expertise.

While this Latino physician could have been a great resource for the nurse in that moment, the nurse felt that she did not need it because of her notion of cultural

---

competence. This similar tendency can be observed in the community mediation field. Board members as well as mediation practitioners are often highly educated and middle-class people in a society. People, especially those who are providers of the services and are trained in academia, assume that they know 'everything.' This notion makes marginalized populations feel that their voices are not heard. Hence, another question arises: Considering all such limitations of the conventional approach to cultural differences, how should intercultural mediation be improved to better serve the needs of people of diverse cultural backgrounds?

The potential of cultural humility in intercultural mediation

Based on these facts, one can argue that the conversation surrounding intercultural mediation has not devoted sufficient efforts toward including culturally, ethnically, or racially distinct minority groups. . . . The cultural competency approach places more emphasis on self-proclaimed cultural expertise. . . .

. . . [T]here is a clear need for listening to and empowering those often-silenced communities so that intercultural mediation can be developed in a truly inclusive way. In this vein, intercultural mediation should incorporate the concept of cultural humility. . . . We should note the three core elements of cultural humility here. The first core element is "Lifelong learning and critical self- reflection"; then, "recognize and mitigate power imbalances"; and lastly, "institutional accountability."[3] In the process of learning culture and of developing intercultural mediation skills, there are no such achievable goals. As stated previously, culture is far more complex than one can imagine. Culture has not only been constantly changing, but it also has tremendous diversities within the same or different cultures. Rather than assuming that cultural knowledge is something one can "master," individual limitations in knowledge should be acknowledged with humility.

. . .

In addition, the existing power dynamics have a huge impact on cultural understandings. Although we all have unconscious assumptions and biases, many taken-for-granted social norms have been influencing people's belief, behaviors, and attitudes towards the so-called other cultures. Such taken-for-granted social norms are often intertwined with power. . . .

For example, Asian American people's voices are often overlooked in the United States because of the taken-for-granted idea in conflict resolution that people need to speak up and directly confront each other in order to receive the assistance they need. In many Asian cultures, conflicts are perceived negatively. Many Asian Americans tend to avoid direct confrontation because they see conflicts as negative and place an importance on relations and social harmony. Consequently, they tend not to raise their voices in a direct and explicit manner as many Westerners do, and

---

3. Melanie Tervalon & Jann Murray-Garcia, *Cultural Humility Versus Cultural Competence: A Critical Distinction in Defining Physician Training Outcomes in Multicultural Education*, Journal of Health Care for the Poor and Underserved 9 (2): 117-125 (1998).

perhaps this is one of the reasons they are largely overlooked. Many articles point out how Asians are often forgotten and are treated as if they are model citizens who have no need to receive assistance. Similarly, even trained intercultural mediators could overlook Asian Americans' needs because of how Asian Americans perceive conflicts and the way they communicate. Mediators' unconscious bias could silence culturally different others' voices. In addition, while many people believe that "culture is uniformly distributed among members of a group," this belief has risks of overlooking the rich dimensions of diversity contained within the same culture. For example, research found that three East Asian countries, namely, China, Korea, and Japan, have different conflict management styles. Additionally, Chinese, Korean, and Japanese cultures are also not homogenous, having diversities within. This explains the importance of treating the process of developing intercultural mediation skills as a life-learning and critical self-reflection process rather than achievable knowledge. It is almost impossible to master such knowledge, and therefore . . . mediation practitioners, need to continue humbly learning from community members because the community knows best. That is to say, they are the experts of themselves.

. . .

Notes and Questions

(1) *Project Implicit* offers free Implicit Association Tests (IATs) on topics ranging from Race and Disability to Weight and Presidents. Tests are available at implicit .harvard.edu. After completing a test, identify how the identified biases could impact a mediation. Consider strategies for addressing the identified biases.

Can you identify any additional strategies (beyond Professor Izumi's) for mitigating implicit biases?

Helen Winter and David Hoffman suggest individuals engage in "experiential learning about bias-reduction, including opportunities for sharing narratives of participants' experiences." Winter shares the following example:

> I can attest to this from my own experience and observations as a mediator. Offering a safe space for participants, such as refugees and locals, to address stereotypes and difficult topics with "the other side" without being afraid of losing face or asking something inappropriate to members of the outgroup, leads to a greater awareness of prejudice and self-reported decrease in bias. "Becoming sensitized to those stereotypes, as well as more conscious as a group that everyone has biases, is a first crucial step to their reduction." However, these findings largely relied on self-reporting. A story-sharing forum with the purpose of addressing prejudice directly with members of the outgroup should further explore other measuring mechanisms such as IAT scores.

David Hoffman & Helen Winter, *Follow the Science: Proven Strategies for Reducing Unconscious Bias*, 28 Harv. Neg. L. Rev. 1, 42–43 (2022).

(2) If the mediator's own values and individual characteristics prompt them to act in a way that undermines respect for the values and aspirations of the mediation parties, should they disqualify themselves from service? *See* Standard IV of The Model Standards of Conduct for Mediators (Appendix A, *infra*).

(3) You are mediating a dispute over the phone with Blake Smith and Cameron Davis. You have been provided with a file about the matter that contains minimal information. The submission to mediation form completed by a court clerk contains only the names and addresses of the parties and the phrase: "neighborhood dispute." While there is not clear evidence in the file, you suspect that there may have been some physical altercation between the parties. What assumptions have you made about the participant's respective race, gender, and other layers of diversity based only on knowing their names, location of their residence, and the reported nature of the dispute? How might these assumptions influence the mediation session? What can you do to mitigate any of your implicit or explicit biases?

(4) As part of its international competence qualifying assessment program, the International Mediation Institute (IMI) has identified six "Cultural Focus Areas . . . that mediators may want to give attention to when mediating inter-culturally." These areas include: relatedness and communication styles, mindset toward conflict, mediation process, orientation toward exchanging information, time orientation, and decision-making approaches. International Mediation Institute, Cultural Competency Criteria, https://imimediation.org/practitioners/competency-criteria/.

(5) Are the examples referenced by the authors at the beginning of this Chapter regarding culturally different practices and understandings regarding spatial distance, talking volume, and eye contact aligned with Yokotsuka's vision of cultural humility?

(6) Professor Dorcas Quek Anderson interrogates "whether intercultural differences in communication styles remain when the mediation process is shifted from the physical to the virtual environment" in her article *Interculturality in Online Dispute Resolution (ODR), in* The Routledge Handbook of Intercultural Mediation 67 (2023). Ultimately, she suggests that while the complexity of technology's interface with dispute resolution poses "challenges to ODR practitioners and ODR system designers, it provides an excellent opportunity to suspend pre-existing assumptions concerning intercultural mediation and to carefully observe and adapt to disputants' unique responses to the virtual environment." How is Yokotsuka's articulation of a cultural humility framework applicable to ODR?

2. Bias & Culture: Mediator Perspectives

This section features the experiences of three diverse mediators and the impact of culture and bias on their engagement. The first excerpt features Nadine Tafoya's first-person account of her path as an indigenous mediator-facilitator. In the second reading, Hasshan Batts shares his insights gained from having shouldered numerous program roles as the only Black mediator at a community mediation center in

North Carolina. In the final excerpt, Professor Sukhsimranjit Singh discusses his approach to working with parties immersed in conflict shaped by their deep-seated religious convictions. While reading these excerpts, consider how biases impact the author's work in individual mediations and within the organizations and institutions in which they operate.

Rage Is *Not* an Option: An Indigenous Woman's Path to Building Resiliency and Advocacy

in Beyond Equity and Inclusion in Conflict Resolution: Recentering the Profession at 18, 18-19, 21-22 (S.Y. Bowland *et al.*, eds., 2022)*

By Nadine Tafoya

I am a Native American woman living in the Southwest, a member of the Mescalero Apache Tribe. I have spent my entire life trying to read between the lines of my daily social interactions. When I enter a meeting room of my colleagues at work, I'm trying to "read" if they're welcoming me with respect and true camaraderie, or if they're oblivious to my very presence, as if I'm invisible, until I make a comment or interact with them first. When I go into a restaurant, I notice if the server glances at me and looks away or if a sales person in a store shouts out "How are you?" to me or to the person who entered behind me. Even though this type of thing may happen a hundred times a day, week after week, year after year, and I may not consciously be aware of it, my Spirit notices and keeps a running tally.

Conversely, I have a real physical reaction when I leave work and head home. My home, located on the reservation, is a refuge to me. I have a sense of comfort when I enter the boundaries of my home. I begin to feel a sense of relief and calm wash over me. Not only is it stressful to navigate the hustle and bustle of the city but it's also full of cues, signs, and images of a place that is not my world. As I leave the urban areas and make my way home to the reservation, I see the beautiful wide-open spaces that mark the entrance into the reservation. I see the markers that engulf me, the Sacred mountains (the Grandmothers) that tell me I'm protected; I see the crosses on one side of the road that mark the places of a funeral procession on its way to someone's final resting place, no doubt a relative of mine. I sense the blanket of the green hillsides that meet me at the entrance of my home. If I pass a fellow driver coming down the narrow dirt road as I'm making my way to my place, I casually nod or wave. I feel like I belong. I feel like I'm part of a larger group. I'm a known piece of this landscape. I am a piece of this vibrant quilt that makes up my community. I know my place and feel comforted. Everything is familiar and reassuring. I share the culture, the language, the ancestors.

This entire place speaks to me, marking my history and revealing the tales of my People's very beginnings.

This is what it's like being a Native person. We carry our history within us. Native people sometimes say we "live in two worlds" simultaneously. I feel like I'm always switching from hearing what the world is saying to me and feeling what I'm hearing. When I'm expressing myself, I'm speaking not only for myself but for my People, both present and past. I honor that lineage of the generations that have passed and those that will come after; as Maya Angelou said, "I speak as one, but I stand with thousands."

It is this perspective that led me into doing the work of an intercultural facilitator-mediator.

. . .

My experience is not unique among those of Black, Indigenous, or people of color (BIPOC). We have all struggled to be visible to the world around us. We have all strived to be seen and heard. At some point I came to realize that I can't afford to be angry all the time; I can't afford to be voiceless or be just okay with it all. So, it became my life's work to understand the dynamic of who gets to be heard and why, and to develop strategies that allow for people like me to get the same time and space as others. We deserve that much, and the opportunity will not be given or created unless we do it ourselves.

It has been important for me to work for that visibility for tribal voices. Our strategy includes creating processes that upset the status quo and thinking creatively about how best to allow for soft voices, long pauses, and wry humor — just a few of the qualities of Indigenous thought leaders.

As an "intercultural facilitator-mediator" I feel it is my job to set the tone of each session as we get started. I believe that I have been given a "sacred" responsibility to create a safe space for conversation to take place. I acknowledge to the participants that it is my responsibility to create that space, to ensure that all voices get heard, to listen with intent, to reframe issues as needed, and then to get out of the way. I am not the expert on every issue; instead, my responsibility is to create a process where various perspectives can be voiced. In addition, I feel that my most sacred obligation is to be cognizant of power dynamics. "Business as usual" is a paradigm ensuring those in power will control the conversation and the process. Some white people, for example, are accustomed to speaking in public forums. They come to the table with their titles, their credentials, and their privilege, and they feel that these characteristics allow them to speak freely and to speak often. The intercultural facilitator-mediator must notice these power dynamics and quickly assess the cultural mix of the group. Cultural nuances may come into play as culture may bump into the power dynamic. For example, some people of color, let's say Native Americans, may find it difficult to speak in a public forum. They may have to process what is being said on multiple levels. Sometimes the spoken word may need to be translated from English into a Native language, then translated back into English. This is happening in the moment, and they are also trying to muster up their response or their position. When a lively discussion is taking place, often the facilitator doesn't allow enough time or allow for silence for someone to respond as needed. Sometimes a person of color or an elder, for instance, needs to hear from someone who looks like them or speaks like them first for them to feel confident enough to voice their concerns. Being aware of this power dynamic, the intercultural facilitator or mediator may start a session by saying, "Today, we're leaving our credentials and titles at the door; today we're here to start a conversation, and we each will have an equal voice." Furthermore, the facilitator can also be explicit in letting the room know that they may be interrupted if they go on too long and that space will always be made for silent voices. In almost all instances, as an intercultural facilitator-mediator, I will always implore people to conduct the conversation with humility and awareness. It is of utmost importance to spend our time together speaking from the heart. I remind them that our time together is precious.

I have learned to be direct, to be deliberate, and to be aware of creating a sacred space for important work to be conducted. People know when the energy and the intent are to honor them and our time together. Indigenous people have gathered in this way since time immemorial and the time is now to revisit the wisdom of the elders.

A Conversation with Hasshan Batts

in Re-Centering Culture and Knowledge in Conflict Resolution Practice 215,
215–222, 224 (Mary Adams Trujillo *et al.*, eds. 2008)*

... [A community mediation center in North Carolina] asked me to be a board member; I was still somewhat young, and I was impressed, you know, with being a board member. Happy to be involved. I got involved and tried to bring a different perspective. There was no one black on the board. Not one black involved in the organization. And in a county that's probably ... I would say 13, 14 percent black.

So I'm on the board. And then they got a contract to go into the school system. And they needed some help. They needed a youthful perspective, as they said. That's what they considered me. So they brought me in because these were all middle-aged white women.

... They brought me in. These are thirty-five-, forty-five-year-old white women, I would say. And we did some work. We trained the whole ninth grade at [a high] school. ... And the kids were real receptive to me. The way that I approached them-I came dressed as myself. I brought who I was to the table. And the kids were receptive, and it impressed the director. So she later said, "Well, you need to be doing this

* "A Conversation with Hashan Batts," in *Re-Centering: Culture and Knowledge in Conflict Resolution Practice*, edited by Mary Adams Trujillo, S. Y. Bowland, Linda James Myers, Phillip M. Richards, and Beth Roy © Syracuse University Press 2008. Reproduced with permission from the publisher. Developed through the auspices of the Practitioners Research and Scholarship Institute (PRASI), www.prasi.org.

full-time." I was working at a psychiatric hospital. She said, "You need to be doing this full-time with us."

. . . . I started off as the coordinator of youth services, or something like that. And the center was relatively young. It was about three years old when I got involved. It had just splintered off from a parent organization. So I helped build the center . . . programming . . . networking with the community . . . funding. . . . And the center was really built around youth services. I mean, we had some court money coming in from the administrative offices of the courts here in North Carolina that all of the centers get. But our funding stream came to youth services. When I came on, the budget increased significantly. I was involved with so many different things. It got to the point at the center where the [executive director] was working maybe twenty hours, sixteen hours a week, I think. I was the only full-time employee. I was working forty hours a week.

The executive director at that time wanted me to become the executive director. This was after about three years. She presented it to the board. And for some reason that I can't explain the board disagreed with it. They didn't want me to be the executive director. They felt that we still needed her. She's an attorney. But her time had dropped so much that I was the one representing the center everywhere. I was writing grants. I was doing most of the workshops, in terms of youth and community and diversity. She was more involved with business mediations and facilitations — corporations and county employee stuff.

In the end they decided to go with a circular management model, where we had three directors-three co-directors, two of which were part-time. One was sixteen hours, one was maybe thirty hours, and I was forty hours. That was also an interesting experience for me. . . . And I was always out there alone. And the models that we would use were, from my point of view, always Eurocentric. They weren't reality based. They didn't take other cultural perspectives into consideration. They didn't take the spiritual needs of black people into consideration, the emotional needs of black people into consideration. It was all more centered on Europeans. And I saw that I was studying a lot and looking for an answer. All of this to make sense, to resolve problems I confronted in the job.

I had seen so much violence, and I had seen so much conflict that I was trying to find a way for people to peacefully work out their issues. But I was just discouraged, I guess you could say. A lot of our clients came in because of a court diversion contract, a juvenile court diversion contract. And one thing that I found real interesting occurred when the kids would get arrested. Very few of my clients were black. Very few of the people we mediated with were black, even when we did workshops, we got very few black referrals. Then when I looked at the boot camps, there were more blacks, but still the majority were not black youth.

Then when you go into the prisons and the jails, it was 80 or 90 percent of the kids are black. And when you're talking to these kids about what they are incarcerated for, a lot of it was the same stuff that these kids were coming to mediation with me for. I mean, one kid came to mediation one time because he shot another kid. That was the most difficult mediation I ever had, because of my stuff. He shot a twelve year old. He's in mediation. This kid is getting no time. And I had to catch myself. . . . I had a white co-mediator, and I told her we needed to write our different perspectives about this mediation because so many things were different, in terms of the racial issues involved in the mediation. Just him [the boy] sitting there upset me. Because he shot another kid. He was crippled, I mean, for life. And it was a hybrid of a victim-offender mediation, because the victim's family was present, and it was a terrible experience for me.

And it just represented the whole system to me. He seemed unaffected. Yet here was a kid who can't walk, who can't talk because of his actions. And society told him it was okay. How does the saying go? Young, white, and twenty-one, or something like that. And my co-mediator — though she was frustrated-she didn't feel what I felt. She didn't see what I saw in that mediation.

So that was kind of the climax of my experience as a mediator. I came to understand that mediation is just another tool of oppression. And it's used by the system to meet its needs. In the case of owner-tenant relations, you have first the relations between "have-nots" and people with power, an issue that nobody really wants to address. This is the case whether you have victim-offender situation — depending on the circumstances, whether you have community mediation or barking dogs. Especially once the court system is involved. Once the court system becomes involved, there's a power imbalance. And we go into the mediation with the goal being harmony. Perfection. A balance of honesty. As Doctor Jones [Bill Jones is a retired professor who teaches oppression theory] taught me: cuss and discuss. We don't allow people to truly put their concerns on the table.

One thing I find interesting about practicing is that black parties are relieved when they see black mediators. This fact is more important than any consideration of models: getting people to come to the table when they give black parties the authority. In my three years of experience, I have found that black people often will say that only a black mediator will understand their problem. . . . "Everything is a model" . . . .

There are models that we use that aren't models that we have tested in the field with communities of color. So we ask what do you do with models that work with black problems or black disputants versus the Eurocentric models that we have encountered. I have just found that black and white people are different in the way that they see things. Our Eurocentric models have ground rules: we bring parties to the table; one person speaks at a time; let's not get too boisterous; keep your voices down; and all those things that even precede any talk. Not to say that we are a pack of wolves, but I find that we as people of color are more animated; we speak more with our hands. We may even stand up and raise our voices in a session. And that in itself is a part of the conflict. I have been black for twenty-seven years and that may not be a long time but it is an eternity, I guess you can say, as far as my attitude is involved. Black people do not approach conflict resolution from a logical perspective; we are more emotional.

. . .

. . . [A]bout mediation being another tool of oppression. What I find is that often-times parties of color, blacks in particular, view mediation as a part of the system. And we have developed a lack of trust for the system because of historical circumstances. For whatever reason we have perpetuated this distrust from generation to generation, and I think a lot of time has to be spent in the field building that trust. . . .

Best Practices for Mediating Religious Conflicts
25 Disp. Resol. Mag. 12, 12–15 (Fall 2018)*
By Sukhsimranjit Singh

All across the globe, people are passionate about religion — both their own beliefs and those of others. Religion informs people's core values, codifies their morals, and inspires their actions. We have seen this throughout history, but we can also see it today, in people's day-to-day lives, in how they see themselves, what they care about, and how they treat others.

. . . Religious conflict requires me to think creatively, respectfully, and judiciously to work with disputes that revolve around people's most sensitive beliefs.

. . .

Past versus Future Orientation

When I started mediating, like most practitioners, I learned about the practice and importance of persuading parties to understand their past — and then urging them to use this understanding to move on and look toward their future. In church conflicts, however, I have learned to take a different approach: I spend much more time than usual on the parties' historic orientations.

In church conflicts, the central dispute often revolves around the clash of a shared worldview. . . . In religion, people learn to form patterns of behavior. With such patterns come expectations of what is right and what is wrong, which tends to raise differences above commonalities. Language is always important in discussing and resolving disputes, and this is even more true when religious beliefs are involved. When personal values are up for discussion, what someone says can take on great meaning and help bring people together — or drive them further apart. The more contact the parties have, the more focused they can become on their differences.

I recently mediated a dispute between two congregations in a large religious community. When they agreed to work with me, each group declared that its "religious orientation" was right and the other congregation's was wrong. All attempts at conversation and resolution had failed.

I started the mediation in a joint session with more than a dozen representatives from each side. After the two-hour joint session, I learned what so many mediators discover in working with many people who disagree on any topic: in this multi-party environment, the participants all expected to be heard, but none was willing to listen.

I spent days in caucus with the representatives from each congregation, listening to their stories, which (as so often happens) were intertwined with facts and emotional innuendo. During these caucus sessions, I began to understand the interests at play: each group was rejecting the other's religious worldview, and each was feeling deep disrespect and distrust due to the other's past comments and actions. What made this case especially complicated was the fact that several group members from both sides had suffered harm. In order for this mediation to succeed, I needed to convince everyone involved, not just the majority of the representatives, to listen to the other side.

In another dispute, I might have asked the parties to review their stories in an opening session and then immediately tried to help them move on in a private caucus. But in this case, as in so many involving religion, I knew that before I could help, I needed to understand more about the parties and their faiths.

To get to the core distrust, during each caucus I asked specifically about events that each side framed as the turning point in their relationship. One group talked at length about a specific day, six years in the past, and then the members of the other group, separately, described their own version of the same incident. While they focused on facts, I perceived crucial differences in value systems. They didn't understand that the center of their conflict was how differently each group interpreted the larger community's religious code of conduct. One group believed in strict adherence of the faith code, while the other inclined toward a more moderate application. Taking time and extending the information-gathering phase of mediation allowed me to get a clear view of what each group cared about and valued, and after providing feedback to both sides, it also allowed each side to understand more deeply the other's motivating core beliefs and values.

In other words, in working on cases involving religion and faith, even when I wish to fast-forward the mediation conversation to the future, I find that respecting history, specifically the pasts of parties' specific religious institutions and communities, has deepened my own understanding of the conflict, helped me create more trust and connection with parties, and been critical to motivating everyone to find a shared solution.

Religious Identity

For many people of faith, religion goes beyond a simple belief process or practice and extends to personal identity. "I am a Christian (or a Muslim or a Jew or a Sikh or a Buddhist or an atheist)," we say, by way of explaining ourselves to others. Because cultural identities are intertwined with our worldviews, divorcing our cultural identity from decision-making is not an easy process. Cultures, like religion, provide insights into how members of a particular group will behave — guidelines as to how a person should act in the world, what makes for a good life, how to interact with others, and which aspects of situations require more attention and processing capacity.

With this in mind, faith-based conflict resolution makes sense for many religious adherents, but for some, it might not be a comfortable choice because it represents something that goes against the essence of following the religious tenets of peace and peacemaking. In other words, just accepting the fact that a conflict exists may mean acceptance of the fact that the congregation has failed in maintaining order and in assisting others to maintain order. This internal inconsistency might challenge the basic cultural identity of the group and as a result, make the conflict more difficult to solve.

. . .

Addressing Emotion and Generosity

In my research, I have been particularly interested in the concept of generosity — where it comes from, how it manifests itself, and what it means. While studying the concept, I learned that every major religion, in its own way, promotes spirituality-based approaches to mediation and conflict resolution. I also found deep connections across such faiths: for example, the practice of generosity. . . . Each faith . . . has its own version of the Golden Rule: "Always treat others as you would wish to be treated yourself."

. . .

Flexibility, Respect, and Presence

Religions are complex, and within each religion, people have different levels of adherence, and these individual differences make practices and beliefs even more subjective. With such wide diversity of values and belief systems, one thing is for sure — no two mediations will be identical. You are bound to find differences, and they may be large or small.

Religious mediation has taught me humility — to approach each and every mediation situation with caution and respect. It has also taught me to not judge a party's belief system or a group's value system.

Notes and Questions

(1) Imagine taking a call from the Mayor of a mid-sized community which is also the home of a large university campus. The Mayor describes a thriving, diverse community experiencing significant racial tension connected to its city-sponsored farmers' market. The Mayor explains that Black Lives Matter-aligned community activists began peacefully protesting outside the Saturday morning farmers' market, targeting one farmer who was publicly aligned with a white nationalist movement. Protestors demanded that the farmer be removed from the market; the Mayor explained that the City's legal counsel had advised the Mayor that the farmer has a

First Amendment right to express her political views so that if the City embraced the protestors' demand, any litigation contesting that decision would result in a reversal of the City's decision—at significant cost to the City. The Mayor has asked you to provide advice regarding whether and how to mediate this dispute. What questions connected to bias, culture, and diversity would you consider regarding the background of a potential mediator? The composition of a mediator team? The relevant stakeholders? The manner and method of initiating contact? For a thoughtful discussion of how a mediator might advise the mayor or take on this matter, *see* William Froehlich, Nancy H. Rogers, and Joseph B. Stulberg, *Sharing Dispute Resolution Practices with Leaders of a Divided Community or Campus: Strategies for Two Crucial Conversations*, 35 Ohio St. J. on Disp. Resol. 781 (2020).

(2) Established pursuant to Title X of the Civil Rights Act of 1964, the Department of Justice Community Relations Service (CRS) provides mediation, facilitation, and conciliation services to communities facing conflict based on actual or perceived race, color, national origin, gender, gender identity, sexual orientation, religion, or disability. Serving as "America's Peacemaker," CRS services are provided on a voluntary basis and free of charge to communities. *See* Community Relations Service, https://justice.gov/crs. For a detailed history of CRS's work in communities, see Bertram Levine & Grande Lum, *America's Peacemakers: The Community Relations Service and Civil Rights* (2020). Conversations with former CRS conciliators are available through a Civil Rights Mediation Oral History Project. *See* Civil Rights Mediation Oral History Project, https://civilrightsmediation.org.

(3) In her co-authored article with long-time co-mediator and co-facilitator Frank Dukes, Selena Cozart grapples with the phrases "white supremacy" and "white supremacy culture":

> Frank was the first between the two of us to advocate for the use of the term "white supremacy" in our work as we described the forces at work that kept anti-Black racism alive in our country. I was reluctant because "white supremacy" at that point in my understanding conjured up images of well-heeled white men hidden in white robes terrorizing Black families and communities. To me, it was loaded and divisive. How could one possibly engage white people in conversations around race when they might conclude from our word choice that we were accusing them of being overt racists? Additionally, "white supremacy" seemed like, and was often used by some, as a statement to imply a measure of validity to the imagined hierarchy of human value which places people in the category of whiteness on the top. For me, the term needed to shift from a noun to an adjective.

> Once I warmed to the idea of using the term "white supremacy," the construct continued to evolve in my thinking. Continued reading and engagement shifted the use to include "culture" in the term. This shift allowed me to not focus on the people in the category of whiteness as the problem, but the culture created to advantage those people. The addition of the word "culture" indicated the systems, practices, and mindsets in operation to

perpetuate the mass illusion that there was something inherently superior about people in white skinned bodies.

Over the years, my definition of white supremacy culture has evolved. Currently I define white supremacy culture as the notion that a society, in all of its expressions, assigns significance to people based on the made-up category of race, placing the notion of whiteness at the top of this hierarchy of human value. White supremacy culture assigns value and roles to human beings based on their proximity to the standard of whiteness.

. . .

One of the most powerful ongoing pernicious narratives has to do with how acceptable it is to be a passive passenger in this stream of white supremacy culture. This narrative would have people see that racism and other "-isms" are matters of personal behavior, and that simply making an effort not to personally discriminate against anyone constitutes a sufficient counter to racism writ large. Indeed, one of white supremacy culture's most invidious effects is its ability to whisper "I don't exist" in a world so dominated by its impacts.

Frank Dukes & Selena Cozart, *Rethinking Systems Design for Racial Justice & Equity "We Don't Want Any of That Neutrality" and Other Lessons from Mediating Race and Equity*, 38 Ohio St. J. on Disp. Resol. 341, 350–55 (2023).

Batts uses the term "Eurocentric." Are Eurocentric culture and white supremacy culture distinct? How do these cultures impact the practice and institutionalization of mediation? For a thorough discussion *see* Sharon Press & Ellen E. Deason, *Mediation: Embedded Assumptions of Whiteness*, 22 Cardozo J. of Conflict Resol. 453 (2021) (discussed section C below).

(4) Deborah Kolb and Gloria Coolidge explore whether and how one's gender shapes a participant's negotiating effectiveness. Notably, they suggest women have a "relational view of others", writing:

. . . [W]omen are expected to do the emotional work in a group. In negotiation contexts, they often carry the burden for attending to relationships and the emotional needs of those involved. While such a burden might be consistent with a voice she might like to speak in, a woman who has trained herself to negotiate from a different premise might find that these expectations frequently constrain her ability to maneuver for herself or those she represents. Learning how to use their strengths and manage the dual impressions of femininity and strategic resolve are important aspects of negotiating tactics for women.

. . .

There seem to be two major ways that a relational view of self is potentially manifest in negotiation. The first is the conception a woman has of herself as a party negotiating. She conceives of her interests within a constellation of responsibilities and commitments already made. That is, she is always aware of how her actions in one context impact on other parts of her life and on other people significant to her.

The second implication is that relational ordering in negotiation may be a prerequisite for interaction. Relational ordering means creating a climate in which people can come to know each other, share (or do not share) values, and learn of each other's modes of interacting. Expressions of emotion and feeling and learning how the other experiences the situation are as important, if not more important, than the substance of the discourse. In other words, separating the people from the problem is the problem. Negotiation conducted in a woman's voice would, we predict, start from a different point and run a different course than either a purely principled or purely positional model.

Deborah M. Kolb & Gloria C. Coolidge, *Her Place at the Table: A Consideration of Gender Issues in Negotiation, in* Negotiation Theory and Practice 261–71 (William Breslin & Jeffrey Z. Rubin, eds., 1991).

Written more than three decades ago, does the "relational view of others" thesis remain applicable to women engaged in a mediation?

C. Power Prejudice and the Resolution of Conflict

People and organizations possess power, and some have more than others. When persons or groups interact with one another, they start from different initial positions with respect to their capacity to influence what the other can or will do.

Power inequalities can arise at an interpersonal level or institutional level. Whereas mediation advocates identify process informality as one of mediation's distinctive strengths, critics assert that mediation's informality permits bargaining behavior to reinforce or exacerbate power disparities. To prevent or minimize such inequities, these critics suggest adopting one of two strategies: reshape the mediation process to incorporate rules and procedures that reduce inequalities, or impose obligations on the mediator to ensure fair outcomes. However, other observers assert that rules (like tone policing) diminish the voice and engagement of the parties. As you review the excerpts below, consider how these arguments might be addressed in your mediation sessions.

In their widely-cited article, Richard Delgado and his colleagues suggest that the informality of mediation and other dispute resolution processes may increase the risk of prejudice, particularly for members of marginalized groups. Trina Grillo addresses how mediation (specifically mandatory mediation) might diminish the female voice in a manner antithetical to the promise of mediation. In the third article — *Mediation: Embedded Assumptions of Whiteness* — Professors Sharon Press and Ellen Deason question some of mediation's foundational assumptions through a modern lens. To develop their work, they engaged with one another by jointly undertaking Layla Saad's 28-day challenge for confronting racism and white supremacy (Saad's, *Me and White Supremacy*). Drawn from their insights gained from their daily journaling and discussion regarding ways in which they observed, benefited from, or engaged in acts of white supremacy, Press and Deason re-examine mediation practices that emerge from the confluence of anti-black bias and western culture. The section concludes with a classic empirical study that evaluated the connection between monetary outcomes, party compliance, and participant satisfaction with the gender and ethnic identities of both the parties and the mediator.

Fairness and Formality: Minimizing the Risk of Prejudice in Alternative Dispute Resolution

1985 Wis. L. Rev. 1359, 1360–01, 1367–74, 1387–91, 1402–04 (1985)*
By Richard Delgado, Chris Dunn, Pamela Brown, Helena Lee & David Hubbert

... [W]e [raise] a concern that has seemingly been overlooked in the rush to deformalize — the concern that deformalization may increase the risk of class-based prejudice. ADR has been promoted, in large part, with the rhetoric of egalitarianism. Moreover, it is aimed at serving many groups whose members are particularly vulnerable to prejudice. Thus, if our criticism is correct — if rhetoric is untrue or if ADR injures some of those it is designed to help — society should proceed cautiously in channeling disputes to alternative mechanisms.

. . .

II. Procedural Safeguards in Formal Adjudication

Virtually absent from previous discussions of ADR is consideration of the possibility that ADR might foster racial or ethnic bias in dispute resolution. Before turning ... to that question, [we survey] the main elements of formal adjudication that operate to reduce prejudice at trials.

. . .

The American legal system strives to provide litigants a fair trial: to this end, it has developed an array of rules. To secure their intended purpose, however, the rules must be applied even-handedly. That task falls, in the first instance, to the trial judge.

Both internal and external constraints are designed to keep a judge from exhibiting bias or prejudice. Internal constraints stem from a judge's professional position. Many judges are appointed for lengthy terms, in some cases for life, and are to that extent freed from having to be politically responsive in their decisions. Moreover, when a judge is appointed, he or she agrees to apply an existing system of rules. The simple act of applying rules reduces bias. Furthermore, the repetitive nature of their caseloads disposes judges to perceive a case not in terms of the parties in dispute, but of the legal and factual issues presented — for example, as a pedestrian-intersection

---

accident case, rather than one of a black victim suing a white driver. The doctrine of *stare decisis* is intended to produce consistent results in similar cases, and anomalous results can be subjected to appellate review.

External constraints also operate to control bias. The Code of Judicial Conduct requires judges to disqualify themselves from cases in which their impartiality is in question; it specifically requires disqualification if a judge feels any animus or prejudice towards a party. If a judge should disqualify himself or herself, but does not do so, recusal statutes enable parties to request a new judge. . . .

. . .

In addition to rules that limit prejudice by circumscribing the role of judge or jury, modern procedural systems contain rules that limit prejudice by prescribing the events that occur in the course of litigation. Some of these rules promote fairness and discourage prejudice more or less directly. Others promote fairness indirectly by equalizing the parties' knowledge or by requiring public trials. . . .

. . .

One group of rules lessens the scope for bias in adjudication by requiring notice of the suit to all parties and timely filing of pleadings, motions, and responses. Early notice enables defendants to move to eliminate duplicative lawsuits, possibly filed to harass, or suits that have no foundation in fact. The rules requiring pleadings and motions to be filed with the court and opposing counsel enable parties to learn about and respond promptly to significant events in the action. . . .

Other rules specify that pleadings need only give a brief, plain statement indicating the basis of a claim or defense and provide for liberal amendment. These rules encourage resolution of lawsuits on their merits, rather than on the basis of the traditional complex pleading rules that benefited wealthy or experienced parties. The rules require that the complaint state the basis of the claim. That disclosure may warn a party and the court that the claim is groundless and motivated by prejudice, enabling appropriate action to be taken.

Another rule requires counsel to sign all papers filed in a case. The signature certifies that the attorney, after reasonable inquiry, believes that the paper is grounded in fact and either warranted by existing law or by a good faith argument for modification of current law. The attorney's signature also certifies that the paper is not filed for an improper purpose such as bias or prejudice. . . .

If scandalous or indecent matter, a possible indication of prejudice, appears in any paper filed, the rules provide for sanctions against the attorney who filed it, and that portion of the paper may be stricken. These provisions confine pleadings and other papers to material issues and punish those who inject matter for the purpose of embarrassing or harassing the adversary.

The use of pretrial orders also serves to reduce prejudice. A federal rule requires the parties to consider and define the issues for trial. Once agreement is reached, a pretrial order is entered which guides the course of trial. This order may only be modified to prevent manifest injustice. . . . If an extraneous issue, motivated by bias or prejudice, arises later it may be excluded based on the pretrial order.

The requirement that the court state its findings and opinions further limits bias. It puts judges' reasoning into the public record, allows for appellate review, and encourages judges to find the facts in an unbiased manner. Finally, the rules provide for a new trial if it can be shown that the proceedings were affected by prejudice, bias or improper influence of the jury.

Rules of evidence also serve to reduce prejudice. These rules are intended to facilitate introduction of all relevant evidence. . . . Evidence which is not relevant but rather is offered to induce prejudice should be excluded. Even when relevant, evidence may be excluded if its probative value is outweighed by the danger of prejudice, confusion of the issues, or misleading the jury.

. . .

. . . [M]odern rules of procedure and evidence contain numerous provisions that are intended to reduce prejudice in the trial system by defining the scope of the action, formalizing the presentation of evidence, and reducing strategic options for litigants and counsel. ADR, to date, has very few such safeguards; indeed, the absence of formal rules of procedure and evidence is often touted as an advantage — it enables ADR to be speedy, inexpensive, and flexible. ADR decisionmakers or other third parties are rarely professional, and there is rarely a decision-making body similar to a jury. Rules of evidence are absent or open-ended; the inquiry is wide-ranging, probing, "therapeutic." The proceedings are often conducted out of the view of the public; in an intimate setting; and with little, if any, provision for review.

. . .

III. Theories of Prejudice and ADR

. . .

The selection of one mode or another or dispute resolution can do little, at least in the short run, to counter prejudice that stems from authoritarian personalities or historical currents. Prejudice that results from social-psychological factors is, however, relatively controllable. Much prejudice is environmental — people express it because the setting encourages or tolerates it. In some settings people feel free to vent hostile or denigrating attitudes towards members of minority groups; in others they do not.

Our review of social-psychological theories of prejudice indicates that prejudiced persons are least likely to act on their beliefs if the immediate environment confronts them with the discrepancy between their professed ideals and their personal hostilities against out-groups. According to social psychologists, once most persons realize that their attitudes and behavior deviate from what is expected, they will change or suppress them.

Given this human tendency to conform, American institutions have structured and defined situations to encourage appropriate behavior. Our judicial system, in particular, has incorporated societal norms of fairness and even-handedness into institutional expectations and rules of procedure at many points. These norms create a "public conscience and a standard for expected behavior that check *overt* signs of prejudice." They do this in a variety of ways. First, the formalities of a court trial—the flag, the black robes, the ritual—remind those present that the occasion calls for the higher, "public" values, rather than the lesser values embraced during moments of informality and intimacy. In a courtroom trial the American Creed, with its emphasis on fairness, equality, and respect for personhood, governs. Equality of status, or something approaching it, is preserved—each party is represented by an attorney and has a prescribed time and manner for speaking, putting on evidence, and questioning the other side. Equally important, formal adjudication avoids the unstructured, intimate interactions that, according to social scientists, foster prejudice. The rules of procedure maintain distance between the parties. Counsel for the parties do not address one another, but present the issue to the trier of fact. The rules preserve the formality of the setting by dictating in detail how this confrontation is to be conducted.

. . .

V. Prejudice in ADR—Assessing and Balancing the Risks

. . .

. . . [We] showed that the risk of prejudice is greatest when a member of an in-group confronts a member of an out-group; when that confrontation is direct, rather than through intermediaries; when there are few rules to constrain conduct; when the setting is closed and does not make clear that "public" values are to preponderate; and when the controversy concerns an intimate, personal matter rather than some impersonal question . . .

It follows that ADR is most apt to incorporate prejudice when a person of low status and power confronts a person or institution of high status and power. In such situations, the party of high status is more likely than in other situations to attempt to call up prejudiced responses; at the same time, the individual of low status is less likely to press his or her claim energetically. The dangers increase when the mediator or other third party is a member of the superior group or class . . .

ADR also poses heightened risks of prejudice when the issue to be adjudicated touches a sensitive or intimate area of life, for example, housing or culture-based conduct. Thus, many landlord-tenant, interneighbor, and intra-familial disputes are poor candidates for ADR. When the parties are of unequal status and the question litigated concerns a sensitive, intimate area, the risks of an outcome colored by prejudice are especially great. If for reasons of economy or efficiency ADR must be resorted to in these situations, the likelihood of bias can be reduced by providing rules that clearly specify the scope of the proceedings and forbid irrelevant or intrusive inquiries, by requiring open proceedings, and by providing some form of higher review. The third-party facilitator or decisionmaker should be a professional and be acceptable to both parties. Any party desiring one should be provided with an advocate, ideally an attorney, experienced with representation before the forum in question. To avoid atomization and lost opportunities to aggregate claims and inject public values into dispute resolution, ADR mechanisms should not be used in cases that have a broad societal dimension, but forward them to court for appropriate treatment.

Would measures like these destroy the very advantages of economy, simplicity, speed, and flexibility that make ADR attractive? Would such measures render ADR proceedings as expensive, time-consuming, formalistic, and inflexible as trials? These measures do increase the costs; but, on balance, those costs seem worth incurring. The ideal of equality before the law is too insistent a value to be compromised in the name of more mundane advantages. Continued growth of ADR consistent with goals of basic fairness will require two essential adjustments: (1) It will be necessary to identify those areas and types of ADR in which the dangers of prejudice are greatest and to direct those grievances to formal court adjudication; (2) In those areas in which the risk of prejudice exists, but is not so great as to require an absolute ban, checks and formalities must be built into ADR to ameliorate these risks as much as possible.

The Mediation Alternative: Process Dangers for Women

100 Yale L.J. 1545, 1547–51, 1555–59, 1563–65, 1567–76, 1610 (1990)*
By Trina Grillo

The western concept of law is based on a patriarchal paradigm characterized by hierarchy, linear reasoning, the resolution of disputes through the application of abstract principles, and the ideal of the reasonable person. Its fundamental aspiration is objectivity, and to that end it separates public from private, form from substance, and process from policy. This objectivist paradigm is problematic in many circumstances, but never more so than in connection with a marital dissolution in which the custody of children is at issue, where the essential question for the court is what is to happen next in the family. The family court system, aspiring to the ideal of objectivity and operating as an adversary system, can be relied on neither to produce just results nor to treat those subject to it respectfully and humanely.

There is little doubt that divorce procedure needs to be reformed, but reformed how? Presumably, any alternative should be at least as just, and at least as humane, as the current system, particularly for those who are least powerful in society. Mediation has been put forward, with much fanfare, as such an alternative. The impetus of the mediation movement has been so strong that in some states couples disputing custody are required by statute or local rule to undergo a mandatory mediation process if they are unable to reach an agreement on their own. Mediation has been embraced for a number of reasons. First, it rejects an objectivist approach to conflict resolution, and promises to consider disputes in terms of relationships and responsibility. Second, the mediation process is, at least in theory, cooperative and voluntary, not coercive. The mediator does not make a decision; rather, each party speaks for himself. Together they reach an agreement that meets the parties' mutual needs. In this manner, the process is said to enable the parties to exercise self-determination and eliminate the hierarchy of dominance that characterizes the judge/litigant and lawyer/client relationships. Third, since in mediation there are no rules of evidence or legalistic notions of relevancy, decisions supposedly may be informed by context rather than by abstract principle. Finally, in theory at least, emotions are recognized and incorporated into the mediation process. This conception of mediation has led some commentators to characterize it as a feminist alternative to the patriarchally inspired adversary system.

. . .

. . . I conclude that mandatory mediation provides neither a more just nor a more humane alternative to the adversarial system of adjudication of custody, and, therefore, does not fulfill its promises. In particular, quite apart from whether an acceptable result is reached, mandatory mediation can be destructive to many women and some men because it requires them to speak in a setting they have not chosen and often imposes a rigid orthodoxy as to how they should speak, make decisions, and be. This orthodoxy is imposed through subtle and not-so-subtle messages about appropriate conduct and about what may be said in mediation. It is an orthodoxy that often excludes the possibility of the parties' speaking with their authentic voices.

Moreover, people vary greatly in the extent to which their sense of self is "relational"—that is, defined in terms of connection to others. If two parties are forced to engage with one another, and one has a more relational sense of self than the other, that party may feel compelled to maintain her connection with the other, even to her own detriment. For this reason, the party with the more relational sense of self will be at a disadvantage in a mediated negotiation. Several prominent researchers have suggested that, as a general rule, women have a more relational sense of self than do men, although there is little agreement on what the origin of this difference might be. Thus, rather than being a feminist alternative to the adversary system, mediation has the potential actively to harm women.

Some of the dangers of mandatory mediation apply to voluntary mediation as well. Voluntary mediation should not be abandoned, but should be recognized as a powerful process which should be used carefully and thoughtfully. Entering into such a process with one who has known you intimately and who now seems to threaten your whole life and being has great creative, but also enormous destructive, power. Nonetheless, it should be recognized that when two people themselves decide to mediate and then physically appear at the mediation sessions, that decision and their continued presence serve as a rough indication that it is not too painful or too dangerous for one or both of them to go on. . . .

. . .

II. The Betrayal of Mediation's Promises

. . .

Persons in the midst of a divorce often experience what seems to them a threat to their very survival. Their self-concepts, financial well-being, moral values, confidence in their parenting abilities, and feelings of being worthy of love are all at risk. They are profoundly concerned about whether they are meeting their obligations and continuing to be seen as virtuous persons and respectable members of society. They are especially vulnerable to the responses they receive from any professional with whom they must deal. Against this backdrop, mediation must be seen as a relatively high-risk process. To begin with, for most people it is a new setting. Its norms are generally not understood by the parties in advance, with the result that the parties are extremely sensitive to cues as to how they are supposed to act; they will look to the mediator to provide these cues. Mediators are often quite willing to give such cues, to establish the normative components of the mediation, and to sanction departures from the unwritten rules. The informal sanctions applied by a mediator can be especially powerful, quite apart from whatever actual authority he might have. These sanctions might be as simple as criticizing the client for not putting the children's needs first, or instructing her not to talk about a particular issue. That these informal sanctions might appear trivial does not mean they will not be as influential in changing behavior as sanctions that might on their face appear more severe; "the micro-sanctions of microlegal systems to which we are actually susceptible may be much more significant determinants of our behavior than conventional macrosanctions which loom portentously, but in all likelihood will never be applied to us."[41]

. . .

Traditional western adjudication is often criticized for its reliance on abstract principles and rules rather than on subjective, contextualized experience. . . .

Of course, under the common law some context, in the form of the facts of an individual case, is also to be considered. The concern for the particular facts of a dispute has been characterized as a feminine search for context, while the pursuit of applicable legal principles has been viewed as a masculine search for certainty and abstract rules. To the extent that its issues are framed merely as questions of law, simply involving precedents and rights, the result in a case may be insensitive to the particular facts of the dispute. The invocation of *stare decisis* to establish the broad rules of a decision also serves to minimize the importance of the factual context to the resolution of a particular case. Finally, a primary focus on questions of law masks many underlying social and political questions.

Where child custody is being determined, a system that ostensibly brings context — *this* mother, *this* father, *these* children — into the process of dispute resolution,

---

41. Reisman, *Looking, Staring and Glaring: Microlegal Systems and Public Order*, 12 Den. J. Int. L. & Pol'y 165, 177 (1983).

and renders a decision based on the lives of those actually involved in the dispute rather than on the basis of a general rule, has much to offer. There is, however, a cost to this change in emphasis; for although the language of legal rights may divert public consciousness away from the real roots of anger, the assertion of rights may also clarify and elucidate those roots. The process of claiming rights, by itself, can be empowering for people who have not shared societal power. Thus the risk of mediation is that if principles are abandoned, and context is not effectively introduced, we end up with the worst of both worlds. . . .

A series of attempts has been made to make the court system more responsive to the actual situation of persons undergoing a divorce and to their children by deemphasizing claims of right and principle. The first of these attempts consisted of reduced reliance on the notion of fault. Before this change, the principles shaping the legal process of divorce were not difficult to discern. In the absence of flagrant misconduct on the part of the spouse, one was to stay in one's marriage. One was not to engage in adultery. A man was to support his wife and children. A mother was to be the primary caretaker of her children.

. . .

With the advent of "no-fault" divorce, these rules changed, signaling an as yet undefined departure from the principles upon which they had been based. It is now typical for states to allow divorce on grounds that do not require fault by either spouse. For the most part, one spouse need only show that the marital relationship is irreparable. These changes have increased the individual autonomy of married persons and given husbands and wives freedom to extricate themselves from unhappy relationships. They have reduced the oppressiveness of principles which, although written into the law, did not fit the manner in which many persons choose to lead their lives.

But there have been other consequences of these changes. For example, results were once much more predictable than they are now, both in terms of the availability of support and the likelihood of the father's being able to obtain custody of the children. This lack of predictability generally harms the party who has the lesser amount of power in the relationship, or who is most risk-averse. . . .

. . .

The chief means by which mediators eliminate the discussion of principles and fault is by making certain types of discussion "off-limits" in the mediation. Mediation experts Jay Folberg and Alison Taylor propose the following as one of the "shared propositions" upon which nearly all mediators agree:

> *Proposition 5.* In mediation the past history of the participants is only important in relation to the present or as a basis for predicting future needs, intentions, abilities, and reactions to decisions.[74]

---

74. J. Folberg & A. Taylor, Mediation 14 (1984).

It is typical for mediators to insist that parties waste no time complaining about past conduct of their spouse, eschew blaming each other, and focus only on the future. For example, one of the two essential ground rules mediator Donald Saposnek suggests a mediator give to the parties is the following:

> There is little value in talking about the past, since it only leads to fighting and arguing, as I'm sure you both know. . . . Our focus will be on your children's needs for the future and on how you two can satisfy those needs. . . . [U]nless I specifically request it, we will talk about plans for the future.[75]

Thus, while one of the principal justifications for introducing mediation into the divorce process is that context will be substituted for abstract principles, in fact, by eliminating discussion of the past, context — in the sense of the relationship's history — is removed. The result is that we are left with neither principles nor context as a basis for decision making.

. . .

Felstiner, Abel and Sarat note that some people are apparently able to tolerate substantial amounts of distress and injustice.[77] This "tolerance," they posit, comes from a failure to perceive that they have been injured. They describe a three-step process by which (1) injurious experiences are perceived (naming), (2) are transformed into grievances (blaming), and, (3) ultimately, become disputes (claiming). "Naming" involves saying to oneself that a particular experience has been injurious. [An] acquaintance who called me could barely go this far. "Blaming" occurs when a person attributes fault to another (rather than to an impersonal force, such as luck or the weather). One cannot arrive at "claiming," that is, the assertion of rights, without passing through "blaming." By making blaming off-limits, the process by which a dispute is fully developed — and rights are asserted — cannot be completed. Short-circuiting the blaming process may fall most heavily on those who are already at a disadvantage in society. Whether people "perceive an experience as an injury, blame someone else, claim redress, or get their claims accepted . . . [is a function of] their *social position* as well as their individual characteristics."[81]

The cultural commitment to access to justice has focused on the last stage of disputing — claiming. The more critical place at which inequality is manifested, however, is before experiences are transformed into disputes, that is, at the naming and blaming stages. One adverse consequence of deemphasizing discussion of principle and fault is that some persons may be discouraged from asserting their rights when they have been injured. Even more troubling, some persons may cease to perceive injuries when they have been injured, or will perceive injuries but those injuries will remain inarticulable, because the language to name them will not be easily available.

---

75. D. Saposnek, Mediating Child Custody Disputes 70 (1983).

77. *See* Felstiner, Abel & Sarat, *The Emergence and Transformation of Disputes: Naming, Blaming, Claiming . . .* , 15 L. & Soc'y Rev. 631, 633 (1980–81).

81. Felstiner, Abel & Sarat, *supra* note 77, at 636.

My acquaintance whose husband had an affair and left her did not trust her sense that she had been injured, treated in a way that human beings ought not to deal with each other. She did not have the support of a clear set of legal principles to help her define her injury; rather, she had been exposed to a discourse in which faultfinding was impermissible, so that she ended up unable to hold her husband responsible for his actions, and instead felt compelled to share his fault. To the extent that there is something to be gained by the assertion of rights, especially for women and minorities, this is unacceptable.

   . . .

Rights assertion cannot take place in a context in which discussion of fault and the past are not permitted, for recognition and assertion of rights are ordinarily based on some perceived past grievance, as well as on some notion of right and wrong. From the point of view of the courts, minimizing conflict is always a good thing: less litigation means less expenditure of court time and resources. From the point of view of the individual, however, conflict sometimes must occur. Conflict may mean that the individual has realized he has been injured, and that he is appropriately resisting the continuation of that injury. The perception of injury arises from a sense of entitlement, which in turn is "a function of the prevailing ideology, of which law is simply a component."[95] If mediation creates a sense of disentitlement, it will interfere with the perception and redress of injuries in cases where they have in fact occurred. . . .

Context is also destroyed by a commitment to formal equality, that is, to the notion that members of mediating couples are, to the extent possible, to be treated exactly alike, without regard for general social patterns and with limited attention to even the history of the particular couples. Thus, it becomes close to irrelevant in determining custody that the mother may have been home doing virtually all the caretaking of the children for years; she is to move into the labor market as quickly as possible. It is assumed that the father is equally competent to care for the children. In fact, it frequently is said that one cannot assume that a father will not be as competent a caretaker as the mother just because he has not shown any interest previously:

> Many women have told me, "He never did anything with the children. If he is given even part-time responsibility for them, he'll ignore them, he won't know what to do."

> Research has shown, however, that little correlation exists between men's involvement with the children before and after divorce. . . . When they gain independent responsibility for the children, many men who were relatively uninvolved during the marriage become loving and responsive parents after divorce.[98]

---

95. Felstiner, Abel & Sarat, *supra* note 77, at 643.
98. R. Adler, Sharing the Children 33 (1988).

In mediation, insistence on this sort of formal equality results in a dismissal of the legitimate concerns of the parent who is, or considers herself to be, the more responsible parent. Such concerns are often minimized by characterizing them as evidence of some pathology on the part of the parent holding them. The insistence of a mother that a young child not be permitted to stay overnight with an alcoholic father who smokes in bed might be characterized as the mother needing to stay in control. Or the mediator might suggest that it is not legitimate for one party to assume that the other party will renege on her obligations, simply because she has done so in the past.... The point is not that mothers never inappropriately desire to stay in control, or that people who have not fulfilled their obligations once will continue to fail to do so, but rather that by defining the process as one in which both parties are situated equally, deep, heartfelt, and often accurate concerns either are not permitted to be expressed or are discounted.

Equating fairness in mediation with formal equality results in, at most, a crabbed and distorted fairness on a microlevel; it considers only the mediation context itself. There is no room in such an approach for a discussion of the fairness of institutionalized societal inequality. For example, women do not have the earning power that men have, and therefore are not in an economically equal position in the world. All too often mediators stress the need for women to become economically independent without taking into account the very real dollar differences between the male and female experience in the labor market. While gaining independence might appear to be desirable, most jobs available for women, especially those who have been out of the labor market, are low-paying, repetitious, and demeaning. Studies show that women in such dead-end jobs do not experience the glories of independence, but rather show increased depression.

. . .

The notion of equality, used so effectively to remove control of children from women by treating men as equally entitled to custody regardless of their prior childcare responsibilities, is not nearly so effective when it comes to requiring men to assume responsibility for their children should they choose not to. One rarely hears of joint custody's being used to mandate that a father participate in the raising of his child although many women might desire that help. But fathers who wish to participate even marginally in childrearing are given full rights, and even special privileges to enable them to do so. These privileges are paid for by the mother in terms of inconvenience and instability in her own life. Fathers who do not want to be concerned with raising their children need only pay support, and many do not even do that. Despite the presumption in favor of joint custody, it is assumed, by and large, that the mother will be available to care physically and emotionally for the children for as much or as little time as she is granted.

Western wage labor is based on the availability of an "ideal" worker with no childcare responsibilities. Joan Williams has written that in this system men are raised to believe they have the right and responsibility to perform as ideal workers.

Women are raised to believe that they should be able to spend some time with their small children and, upon return to outside employment, must shape their work around the reality that they have continuing childcare responsibilities.

The laws governing custody are now, in theory, gender neutral. Mediators, however, are as likely as others in society to assume that women's work commitments are secondary to those of men, and to give more credence to the work obligations and ambitions of fathers. Women may be encouraged in mediation not to think of themselves as ideal workers so that they will be able to take on primary responsibility for the children.

The result of assuming that one parent will make herself available in this way is that disproportionately more attention is paid to ensuring the access of the parent without physical custody (usually the father) to his children than to meeting the needs of the parent who, in all likelihood, will bear the primary responsibility for these children.

Custody decrees frequently specify joint legal or physical custody, or both, when in fact the children are with one parent — generally the mother — as much or more than children who are living under a sole custody arrangement. The result of such a discrepancy under a joint custody arrangement is that the caretaking parent may be subject to the control of the noncaretaking parent without being relieved of any sizable amount of day-to-day responsibility for the children.

. . .

Another criticism of the traditional adversary method of dispute resolution is that it does not provide a role for emotion. Decisions by adversarial parties are posited as rational, devoid of emotion, self-interested, and instrumental (result-oriented). Some proponents of mediation and other methods of alternative dispute resolution believe these characteristics should be retained in mediation to the extent they permit parties to serve their self-interests efficiently. Others have argued that mediation and other forms of alternative dispute resolution provide an opportunity to bring intuition and emotion into the legal process.[117] This latter group of proponents points out that family conflicts in particular often involve a combination of emotional and legal complaints, so that the "real" issues are often obscured in the adversarial setting. Thus, "there may be a great need for an open-ended, unstructured process that permits the disputants to air their true sentiments."

Although mediation is claimed to be a setting in which feelings can be expressed, certain sentiments are often simply not welcome. In particular, expressions of anger are frequently overtly discouraged. This discouragement of anger sends a message that anger is unacceptable, terrifying and dangerous. For a person who has only recently found her anger, this can be a perilous message indeed. This suppression

---

117. *See, e.g.*, S. Goldberg, E. Green & F. Sander, Dispute Resolution 313 (1985) ("Family disputes are also well suited to alternative forums because the conflicts often involve a complex interplay of emotional and legal complaints.").

of anger poses a stark contrast to the image of mediation as a process which allows participants to express their emotions.

Women undergoing a divorce, especially ones from non-dominant cultural groups, are particularly likely to be harmed by having their anger actively discouraged during the dissolution process. Women have been socialized not to express anger, and have often had their anger labeled "bad." A woman in the throes of divorce may for the first time in her life have found a voice for her anger. As her early, undifferentiated, and sometimes inchoate expressions of anger emerge, the anger may seem as overwhelming to her as to persons outside of it. And yet this anger may turn out to be the source of her energy, strength, and growth in the months and years ahead. An injunction from a person in power to suppress that anger because it is not sufficiently modulated may amount to nothing less than an act of violence.

. . .

People are necessarily angry at divorce, in two senses. First of all, anger is inevitable in ending a marriage; almost everyone who obtains a divorce becomes angry sooner or later. This anger may have many different causes: it may be a result of anticipated losses, wrongful treatment, or the myriad compromises of self that may have been made along the way to the marriage's end. Second, some anger is necessary for the disengagement which is essential to the completion of the divorce. It is thus critical that any system of marital dissolution take anger into consideration and establish a means by which it is permitted to enter into the divorce process.

. . .

Some mediation literature suggests that mediators should proceed by discouraging the expression of anger. This literature evinces a profound lack of respect for the anger that divorcing spouses feel. For example, Donald Saposnek suggests that "[i]n many ways, the mediator must act as a parent figure to the parents, since their struggles are often not unlike those of siblings squabbling over joint possessions."[129] Saposnek's depiction of divorcing parents suggests that their struggles are devoid of content. He characterizes their anger and conflict as "squabbling" rather than as arising from substantively important conflicts or as a necessary and important step in the divorce process.

Saposnek suggests that the mediator ask questions of the parties that will imply to them that elaboration of their feelings during conflicts with each other is "irrelevant and counterproductive" and that the mediator is "interested in . . . ideas for solutions to these problems." Saposnek thus views the expression of feelings as antithetical to problem-solving; a mediator must choose one or the other.

. . .

Even when mediation literature does approve of bringing anger into the process, it often recommends doing so in a way that subtly undercuts the legitimacy of the

---

129. D. Saposnek, Mediating Child Custody Disputes 176 (1983).

anger. Mediators are encouraged, where necessary, to permit parties to "vent" their anger, after which the parties can move on to discuss settlement. This view does not take anger seriously enough. Because it treats expressed anger as having no long-range impact on the party who is exposed to it, it is not necessarily seen as objectionable to require one party to be present and endure the other party's "venting" — even where the party enduring the venting has been the subject of abuse in the marriage. The effects of exposure to anger in such a case can be devastating. If the privilege of expressing anger has not been distributed equally in the relationship prior to mediation, then the mediator should not grant that privilege equally during the mediation.

Second, and equally critically, the view of anger as something to be "vented" does not take anger seriously as a path to clarity and strength. Anger that is merely vented has lost its potential to teach, heal, and energize; it is ineffective anger, anger that "maintains rather than challenges" the status quo.

Not all writers suggest that anger be suppressed or vented in the service of eventual suppression. Some mediators, however, especially those in mandatory settings, do advocate that parties suppress their anger. The mediator's personal antagonism toward anger and conflict may lead her to urge clients to keep their angry feelings to themselves.

At the same time, there are other forces which may intensify this dynamic of suppression. Mediators working under time pressures recognize that it takes time to express anger, and its full expression might, indeed, jeopardize a quick settlement. More significantly, there are substantial societal taboos against the expression of anger by women, taboos which have particular force when the disputant is a woman of color. For a woman who has just found her anger, anger which has enabled her to free herself from an oppressive relationship and involve herself and her family in a divorce proceeding, the suppression of the very force that has driven her forward is a devastating message.

. . .

Conclusion

Although mediation can be useful and empowering, it presents some serious process dangers that need to be addressed, rather than ignored. When mediation is imposed rather than voluntarily engaged in, its virtues are lost. More than lost: mediation becomes a wolf in sheep's clothing. It relies on force and disregards the context of the dispute, while masquerading as a gentler, more empowering alternative to adversarial litigation. Sadly, when mediation is mandatory it becomes like the patriarchal paradigm of law it is supposed to supplant. Seen in this light, mandatory mediation is especially harmful: its messages disproportionately affect those who are already subordinated in our society, those to whom society has already given the message, in far too many ways, that they are not leading proper lives.

Of course, subordinated people can go to court and lose; in fact, they usually do. But if mediation is to be introduced into the court system, it should provide a better alternative. It is not enough to say that the adversary system is so flawed that even a misguided, intrusive, and disempowering system of mediation should be embraced. If mediation as currently instituted constitutes a fundamentally flawed process in the way I have described, it is more, not less, disempowering than the adversary system — for it is then a process in which people are told they are being empowered, but in fact are being forced to acquiesce in their own oppression.

Mediation: Embedded Assumptions of Whiteness?

22 Cardozo J. Conflict Resol. 453, 459–70, 472–73, 475–79 (2021)*
By Sharon Press & Ellen E. Deason

III. Mediation and Tone Policing

One of the dimensions of white supremacy that first made us think of a connection to mediation is "tone policing." [Layla] Saad defines tone policing as a "tactic used by those who have privilege to silence those who do not by focusing on the tone of what is being said rather than the actual content."[41] Consider these examples from her list of ways in which tone policing is expressed:

- "If you would just calm down, then maybe I would want to listen to you."

- "You are bringing too much negativity into this space, and you should focus on the positive."[43]

Can you hear the mediator? Here are some echoes of Saad's examples:

- I can understand you better if you don't interrupt and speak so loudly.

- What is past is past and we are not here to assess blame; you need to focus on the future and building a positive outcome.

. . . We think that tone policing by the mediator shows up in two related dimensions. The first is in terms of the type of communication that mediators at a minimum endorse, and often require. The second is in how many mediators treat anger.

A. Communication

The setting of communication norms happens at the beginning of most mediations when the mediator delivers what is commonly referred to as the mediator's opening statement. Training manuals (and trainers) often encourage the mediator to set "ground rules" for the mediation. These ground rules tend to include such items as: treat each other with "common courtesy" and respect; "do not interrupt each other;" "speak calmly" or "no use of inflammatory" language." It should be obvious that how one defines "courtesy," "inflammatory," and "respectful" communication,

---

41. Layla F. Saad, Me and White Supremacy: Combat Racism, Change the World, and Become a Good Ancestor (2020). [Editors' note: subsequent references to Saad are to the same text.]
43. Susan S. Silbey & Sally E. Merry, *Mediator Settlement Strategies*, 8 L. & Pol'y 7, 14 (1986).

and even what one considers to be an interruption, are inherently ambiguous and certainly informed by one's culture and upbringing.

Why is this control harmful? After all, it is merely intended to foster a productive conversation. From a person of color's perspective, when a white person insists that they speak in an approved tone that suits the white person, then the white person is imposing the idea that their standards are superior. Worse, in controlling "how BIPOC are supposed to talk about their lived experiences with racism and existing in the world," the white person is "reinforcing the white supremacist ideology that white knows best."

We also wonder about disparities in enforcement of the ground rules on communication. In the opening statement, ground rules are directed equally to all participants. But are they enforced more often against Black participants in mediation because their interruptions are seen as more "scary" or aggressive? There is no data to support, or refute, this speculation, and it would depend on the narratives about race that the mediator carries into the process. But it would not be inconsistent with unexamined prejudices and implicit biases.

Finally, in an effort to avoid tone policing by others, BIPOC often will preemptively tone police themselves. This might be most likely to occur in mediation when BIPOC parties work with a white mediator. . . . If a BIPOC participant avoids a difficult subject because it would elicit an "inappropriate" tone from them, then this topic (obviously an important one) would not factor explicitly into exchanges of views or discussions of the shape of an agreement. It would likely, however, remain in the background where it could act as a barrier to a resolution or result in an incomplete resolution. . . .

B. Expressions of Anger

Controlling the tone of communication is closely linked to controlling expressions of anger; often interruptions and loud exclamations are triggered by anger or other strong emotions. As with interruptions and volume, one's perception of anger may have a racial dimension. Saad makes the point that "[s]o much about tone policing has to do with anti-Blackness and racist stereotypes (often intersected with sexism) . . . . A white person's expression of anger is often seen as righteous, whereas a Black person's anger is seen as aggressive and dangerous." There is a deep-seated societal fear of anger on the part of racial minorities, especially Blacks, and we speculate that Black men are especially likely to be seen as dangerous when they are angry because of common stereotypes about them. There are also strong social taboos against women expressing anger, and these taboos have particular force in the case of Black women. The effect of this fear and these taboos is to delegitimate anger expressed by Blacks.

. . .

Not all conflicts involving BIPOC are explicitly about racist behavior, but the suppression of emotion, and hence emotional topics, is likely also damaging in other disputes (perhaps even more damaging). For BIPOC, many negative interactions have their roots in racism. Even if there is no racist intention for the behavior underlying a dispute, the effect on a person of color may be felt as racist. Yet tone policing may submerge this aspect of a dispute beneath a veneer of adherence to the mediation ground rules. . . . [D]enying this anger may remove a source of strength and growth for resolving the dispute at issue and for dealing with conflicts going forward.

IV. Mediation and Color-Blindness

Saad defines color-blindness as the idea that one does not "see" color or notice race. Taken literally, the phrase would be an obviously false denial of actual perception. However, many whites use it instead to characterize their attitudes and actions, asserting that they do not treat people differently based on differences in race. On the surface, that sounds admirable. They aspire to live in a society where, in Dr. Martin Luther King, Jr.'s words, people "will not be judged by the color of their skin, but by the content of their character."

Yet scratch the surface and the reality of the world is that color does matter. Saad describes how, even to a child, colorblindness is not neutral. Failure to recognize racial differences in skin tone creates the impression that being Black is somehow synonymous with "bad" and should be a source of shame. Why else, she queries, would someone deny the difference? And if color does not matter, why do BIPOC continue to experience oppression? There are differences that correlate with race: in wealth, rates of incarceration, death from COVID-19, education, infant mortality, and on many other measures.

Color-blindness surely does not cause these discrepancies by itself, so what is the harm in aspiring to a better world? The answer is that "[c]olor blindness is a particularly insidious way for people with white privilege to pretend that their privilege is fictitious." Saad identifies three ways in which color-blindness is harmful. First, it is "an act of minimization and erasure." Second, it is an act of gaslighting — an attempt to make BIPOC "believe they are just imagining they are being treated the way they are being treated because of their skin color." And third, it allows whites to avoid looking at their own race. This reenforces the assumption that to be white is to be "raceless" and "normal" and allows whites to refuse to look at themselves as persons with white privilege. In this way, color blindness helps perpetuate the discrepancies associated with race.

We have identified several ways in which we think color-blindness is expressed in mediation practices in ways that can be harmful. . . . First, we contend that the practice of reframing, the mediator's guidance in developing narratives, and the common admonition to take a forward-looking perspective can foster blindness to BIPOC's life experiences and thus minimize or erase the relevance of those experiences to the resolution of the dispute. Second, a mediator who is color blind is also likely blind to stereotypes and microaggressions — their own and those of participants. Third, color blindness is coupled with white silence through the way that many mediators apply the principle of neutrality. And fourth, Western mediation assumptions are largely blind to the diversity of cultures and wide variety of approaches to conflict in the United States. This blindness is of special concern for court mediation programs that serve diverse populations. All these aspects of color blindness shape the narrative that develops in mediation, and hence the content of the discussion and the outcome.

A. Blindness to BIPOCs' Life Experiences

One implication of color-blindness is a minimization of, or failure to hear and appreciate, the differences in BIPOC experiences from the experiences of those who are white. . . .

. . .

The role of narration and narratives is very important in mediation. At its core, mediation allows participants to tell their story in their own words. This provides the opportunity for "voice" that is an essential element of a sense of procedural justice, and that can support self-determination when the stories reflect the perceptions of the participants.

While this all sounds good in the abstract, the problem is that to encourage settlement, mediators reconstruct the language, and along with it the experience, of the parties. This represents a form of control by the mediator over the substantive aspects of the interaction. It increases the prospect of resolution through the "construction of an account that both parties will accept." Mediators regulate this account as it develops by "interpretation and reinterpretation of disputants' statements, determinations of relevance and irrelevance of statements, and styles of discourse."[77] The process has been characterized as the "rephrasing" of a dispute.

In fact, mediators literally rephrase what parties say. They are taught to use active listening to reflect back what a participant says when they tell their story at the start of the mediation process. This serves to confirm that the mediator understands correctly, to demonstrate to the participant that they have been heard, and to help the other participants hear what is said. As a mediator reflects back a party's statements, a common approach is to "reframe," to neutralize the language used by the party. Although mediators are also taught to acknowledge emotion, reframing often has the effect of stripping all the emotion out of the story. In a sense, the mediator is projecting a new reality onto the participant. For BIPOC, this may feel as if their story is being taken from them and recast using the white gaze.

. . .

In addition, mediators often engage in what many call "reality testing" or, perhaps more accurately, "assumption testing" with the parties. Often this is an attempt to get the parties to realistically assess their alternative(s) to reaching a settlement. But it can also take the form of questioning a participant's inferences by stressing the underlying facts and asking if the participant's conclusion from those facts is the only possible interpretation. Consider how it might feel to a person of color if they

77. Silbey & Merry, at 15.

had asserted that a particular action represented racism, only to have it questioned in this way (perhaps by someone with no experience of racism).

Finally, mediators restrict the narrative that a participant may express by emphasizing a forward-looking focus. Among the touted benefits of mediation is that participants need not agree on the facts; nor will a decision-maker determine what "actually" happened. Rather than focusing on the past, the mediator will assist the participants in figuring out how they want to approach the future. The goal is to avoid getting stuck in an argument about blame that cannot be resolved in mediation.

But this forward-looking emphasis has costs. In curtailing the expression of anger and blame, it short-circuits the "naming, blaming, claiming" sequence through which a dispute develops from a perception of injury (naming), into a grievance (blaming), and ultimately becomes a demand (claiming).[86] Without the key step of blaming, the process cannot be completed. In other words, one cannot effectively look forward and formulate demands and proposals without first looking back. . . .

. . . [W]ithout a discussion of a BIPOC's lived experience, a mediation will be left in a color-blind state where the participants cannot understand, and thus cannot respond, to the full dimension of the dispute.

. . .

C. Blindness Coupled with White Silence

While tone policing is a mechanism by which white people silence BIPOC, white silence describes the way that many white people stay silent about racism. Saad asserts that this silence may be born of discomfort with the topic, but it serves to defend the status quo of white supremacy; it is a way "of holding onto one's white privilege through inaction." One of Saad's examples, which we think sometimes applies to mediation, is "[s]taying silent by not holding those around you accountable for their racist behavior." This silence flows from one of the foundational concepts of mediation — namely, mediator impartiality/neutrality.

. . .

Neutrality has been described as, "the antidote against bias."[122] Yet serious critiques have been raised as to whether it is possible for a mediator to be truly impartial or neutral; and mediators have reported feeling like a failure because of their inability to live up to the expectation of neutrality by keeping their reactions to parties at bay. Furthermore . . . there is a disconnect between mediators' aspirations of neutrality/impartiality and common practices, which frequently involve influencing parties to obtain a settlement. This influence does not show an indifference to the outcome. Moreover, purging bias requires that "mediators be conscious of their

---

86. William L.F. Felstiner, Richard L. Abel & Austin Sarat, *The Emergence and Transformation of Disputes: Naming, Blaming, Claiming . . .*, 15 L. & Soc'y Rev. 631, 633–36 (1980–81).

122. Sara Cobb & Janet Rifkin, *Practice and Paradox: Deconstructing Neutrality in Mediation*, 16 L. & Soc. Inquiry 35, 35 (1991).

assumptions, biases, and judgments about the participants."[126] But because of the operation of implicit bias, this level of consciousness is unattainable and illusory. This means that the principles of impartiality and neutrality are ineffective as an antidote to racial bias on the part of the mediator, both in terms of attitudes toward the parties and toward the outcome.

. . .

The principle that a mediator should not favor or disfavor any party to a mediation is often interpreted as a command to treat them evenhandedly or to remain equidistant. That injunction is inconsistent with intervening in the face of expressions of racism. As a result, the principles of neutrality and impartiality may contribute to a racist effect for a BIPOC participant by silencing a mediator who sees a racist dynamic.

. . .

Outcome neutrality is similarly fraught. This principle has generated significant debate, not only about the degree to which it is achievable, but also about the degree to which it is desirable. But the standard advice for a mediator who thinks that an agreement is unfair is to withdraw from the mediation. That could be interpreted as an extreme form of white silence that elevates the value of neutrality above the values of fairness and justice.

. . .

D. Blindness to the Limitations of Western Cultural Assumptions about Negotiation/Mediation

Finally, one must acknowledge that the commitment to impartiality and neutrality are based on Western (white) ideology. As Wing explains:

> *These values are imbedded in a Western ideology of positivism that assumes it is possible for the observer to be separate from the observed; that one can conduct an intervention (whether it be as a scientist leading an experiment or as a judge, jury, or mediator engaged in a proceeding) without having one's own experiences or values permeate the process. This outlook does not take into account that valuing distance between a conflict intervener and disputing parties is a cultural belief; it does not consider the impact the intervener has on the course of a mediation as he guides the process by asking certain questions and not others.*[130]

. . .

. . . Culture affects both how individuals experience conflict and how they approach it. It creates "the mental and emotional structures through which people

---

126. Carol Izumi, *Implicit Bias and Prejudice in Mediation*, 70 S.M.U. L. Rev. 681, 684 (2017).

130. Leah Wing, *Whither Neutrality?: Mediation in the Twenty-First Century*, in Recentering: Culture and Knowledge in Conflict Resolution Practice 93, [95] (Mary Adams Trujillo et al. eds., 2008).

understand their actions and those of others in the conflict." . . . The framing of mediation as "negotiation with assistance" embeds the Western, rational, linear approach to negotiation and conflict in the mediation process. Certainly, these white assumptions about conflict manifest themselves in mediation as generally practiced in court-connected programs.

. . .

Notes and Questions

(1) Professor Deborah Eisenberg describes a comparative analysis of Maryland small claims cases. In one set of cases, parties engaged in dispute resolution; in the second, cases were resolved through trial. Eisenberg noted the parties who participated in dispute resolution were "more likely than those in the litigation group to report that 'they could express themselves, their thoughts, and their concerns.'" She explained in greater detail:

> There were a few notable exceptions when controlling for different party demographics: plaintiffs were more likely to report that they expressed themselves in court rather than ADR and, conversely, defendants were more likely than plaintiffs to report that they expressed themselves in ADR. When one considers that many of the plaintiffs in small claims court are creditors collecting debts or landlords collecting rent, these findings may inform the question of whether mediation benefits litigants who have less money or power. Perhaps defendants — who may have less power and fewer viable defenses to non-payment in a traditional trial — find greater voice and empowerment in a mediation process that allows them to explain why the payment was not made. In a trial, only recognized legal defenses may be asserted for non-payment of rent or a contractual debt. Mediation allows defendants to explain special circumstances and negotiate more flexible and creative outcomes, such as payment plans.

Deborah Thompson Eisenberg, *What We Know and Need to Know about Court-Annexed Dispute Resolution*, 67 S.C. L. Rev. 245, 257 (2016).

Professor Delgado concludes that the risk of mediated outcomes being influenced by prejudice is especially great in many landlord-tenant, inter-neighbor, and intra-familial disputes. Yet, beginning with mediation's foundational years of 1969–89 to the current time, these types of cases have constituted the typical caseload in many mediation programs, and those program advocates believe mediation is particularly well suited to handle those matters. Do Eisenberg's conclusions about empowerment and voice address Delgado's concern or are mediation advocates ignoring a fundamental problem?

(2) Another concern that Delgado's thesis references is whether persons participating in mediation are being afforded "second class" justice; the literature refers to this topic as "access to justice." For a thoughtful, contemporary analysis of access to justice issues connected to dispute resolution, and to online dispute resolution,

consider the 2020 symposium *Achieving Access to Justice through ADR: Fact or Fiction*, 88 Fordham L. Rev. 2111–2500 (2020).

(3) If Delgado's concerns are well placed, what are their implications for the structure and practice of mediation? If one introduces into the mediation process the types of formalities that Delgado proposes, would that advance or undermine mediation's core values? What capacities or protections, if any, does the mediation process afford to minimize the adverse impact of prejudice influencing the dialogue and outcome? Does the digital environment shift your consideration? Many of these questions are explored in the excerpts on justice in mediation, appearing in Section D, below.

(4) The late Trina Grillo was herself an active mediator. The concerns she discusses arise, she believed, with particular urgency when parties are mandated to use mediation. Do you agree that the impact of mediation on women would be substantially different depending on whether the process was mandatory or voluntary? Others believe that the force of Grillo's critique stems not from its conceptual account but rather from identifying, and properly criticizing, multiple examples of poor mediating. For a thoughtful response to Grillo's article, see Joshua D. Rosenberg, *In Defense of Mediation*, 33 Ariz. L. Rev. 467 (1991).

(5) In *Mediation: Embedded Assumptions of Whiteness*, Press and Deason discuss anger at the mediation table. They connect "the way whites perceive Black anger" to Grillo:

> ... [T]he way mediation treats anger has a racist effect. The argument here is parallel to the one that Trina Grillo made in an important article written in 1991, in which she explored the process dangers for women who were court-ordered to mediation. She posited that while mediation promised to include an opportunity to express emotion, instead, there was a systematic suppression of anger.

> Grillo claimed that discouraging anger sends a message that anger is unacceptable, and dangerous. . . .

> The situation for BIPOC dealing with a dispute tinged with racism is similar. Their experiences with racism are painful. Insisting that they discuss these experiences in mediation without expressing rage or grief is dehumanizing. Some mediators will allow parties to "vent" their anger as a prelude to moving on to discuss settlement. Grillo argues that this does not take anger seriously as a "path to clarity and strength. Anger that is merely vented has lost its potential to teach, heal, and energize; it is ineffective anger, anger that 'maintains rather than challenges' the status quo."

(6) Grillo's classic article was published a generation ago, long before the legalization of same-sex marriage. How do Grillo's concerns apply in this context?

An Empirical Study of the Effects of Race and Gender on Small Claims Adjudication and Mediation

Institute of Public Law, University of New Mexico, xiii–xxxii (Jan. 1993)*
By Michelle Hermann, Gary LaFree, Christine Rack & Mary Beth West

I. Introduction

A basic tenet of conflict theory is that socio-cultural factors influence decision-making processes. Applying this theory to the judicial system, scholars have asked whether informal processes, such as alternative dispute resolution, are more susceptible than adjudication to bias. In theoretical work and studies involving controlled experimental conditions, several authors have studied the differences between courts and alternative dispute resolution mechanisms in this context. The basic conclusions from these studies have been that the adversarial procedure of adjudication counteracts decision-maker bias, and that the risks of prejudice are greatest in informal settings involving direct confrontation where few rules exist to constrain conduct.

In addition, studies during the past 10 to 15 years have described the composition of parties, cases and outcomes in small claims courts and have tested the hypotheses that mediation is superior to adjudication in generating positive attitudes among litigants of small claims, that mediation is superior in altering post-dispute behavior (*i.e.*, in achieving compliance), and that the two types of dispute resolution lead to significantly different case outcomes.

We proposed empirically to test the conclusions of some of these studies in actual mediations and adjudications in the Bernalillo County Metropolitan Court in Albuquerque, New Mexico.[1] Our research hypotheses were as follows:

That women and minorities achieve less in both mediated and adjudicated small claims settlements than males and nonminorities achieve in similar cases.

That the disparity between outcomes achieved by women and minorities and the outcomes achieved by males and nonminorities is greater in mediated small claims settlements than in adjudicated decisions.

That disputes involving inherent power imbalances, such as landlord-tenant or creditor-lender disputes, are more subject to the effects of bias in small claims mediation.

That the participation of women or minority mediators or adjudicators in small claims disputes involving minority disputants reduces the effects of bias.

. . .

---

1. [Ed. Note: The final study sample consisted of 603 cases, 323 of which were adjudicated and 280 mediated.]

IV. Results

ĭ. Ethnicity

... [W]e sought to test the hypothesis that both minority and female claimants would do more poorly in the study cases. Moreover, because mediation is a less formal, less visible, and less controlled forum than adjudication, we hypothesized that effects of ethnicity and gender would be greater for mediated than adjudicated cases. Looking at objective monetary outcomes, our results confirmed our hypothesis for ethnicity, but not for gender. Measures of subjective satisfaction, however, were more complex and showed different patterns.

As measured by the objective Vidmar outcome ratio, minority claimants consistently received less money than nonminorities in our study cases, while minority respondents consistently paid more. These effects were stronger for mediated than adjudicated cases. When case characteristics were added to the model, claimant and respondent ethnicity was no longer statistically significant in the adjudicated cases. It is notable, however, that the most influential case character factors (being represented by a lawyer and being involved in a collection case) were both ethnically and sociologically related. For example, monetary outcomes were higher for collection cases involving individual respondents in which the claimant was either a lawyer or was represented by a lawyer. Whites were more likely to be claimants in collection cases, as well as to be lawyers or be represented by lawyers. Thus, monetary outcomes in adjudicated cases were due primarily to case characteristics and, secondarily, to the ethnicity of participants, with strong interrelationships between the two. In contrast, ethnicity remained significantly more important for predicting outcomes of mediated cases, even with the addition of the case characteristic variables. Case characteristics (such as whether the case was a collection case, whether a counterclaim was involved, the size of the dispute, whether claimants and respondents were individuals or businesses and whether lawyers were involved) had relatively little effect on outcomes in mediation. The one exception to these results occurred when the mediated agreement created a payment plan. Payment plans did help to explain the differences between white and minority outcomes. White claimants were more likely to enter into payment plans than minority claimants and minority respondents were more likely to enter into payment plans than white respondents. Because payment plans typically exchange a long time to pay smaller incremental amounts for a larger total amount paid, they become a significant factor in increasing the amounts paid by minority respondents. The only additional characteristic of claimants and respondents which had a significant effect on monetary outcomes in either mediation or adjudication was education. Higher education worked to the disadvantage of the respondent in adjudicated cases and to the advantage of the claimant in mediated cases.

Having found that minority claimants received less and minority respondents paid more in mediation cases, we sought to explore whether these effects might be counteracted by the ethnicity of the mediators. Our results were quite startling, showing that having two minority mediators eliminated the negative impact on the size of monetary outcomes for minority claimants in mediation. The combination of one minority mediator and one white mediator, however, did not produce a similar result.

Our analysis of subjective outcome and procedural satisfaction by ethnicity produced interesting contrasts. In general, claimants were no more or less satisfied in mediation than in adjudication with regard to procedure, outcome or long-term outcome. Compared to claimants in adjudication, however, mediation claimants reported the outcome as being fairer and less biased. In contrast, respondents in mediation were far more satisfied with the procedure, outcome and long-term outcome, as well as with fairness. The tendency for claimant and respondent satisfaction to be inversely related in adjudication was not found in mediation.

Despite their tendency to achieve lower monetary awards as claimants and to pay more as respondents in mediation, minority claimants taken together were more likely than nonminority claimants to express satisfaction with mediation. Minority claimants and respondents were consistently more positive about mediation than they were about adjudication on all satisfaction and fairness measures. They also reported process satisfaction significantly more often than nonminorities in mediation.

Minority claimants were more likely to be satisfied with the procedure when the two mediators were also minorities.[2] In fact, white as well as minority claimants were more likely to report procedural satisfaction when the mediation involved a minority respondent and two minority mediators. . . .

2. Gender

The effects found for minority participants were generally not replicated when the data were analyzed for gender. Gender of claimant and respondent had no direct effect on monetary outcomes for either adjudicated or mediated cases. The only statistically reliable tendency we found was for female respondents to pay lower monetary outcomes in mediation than adjudication.

Looking at measures of satisfaction, we found that as claimants and respondents, compared to all other ethnic/gender groups, white women report relatively greater satisfaction with adjudicated outcomes. While white female respondents achieved significantly better (*i.e.*, lower) monetary outcomes than the other three groups in mediation, they also reported the lowest rates of satisfaction. Furthermore, compared to other mediation respondents, white women were less likely to see the mediation process as fair and unbiased. Minority women, on the other hand, reported higher satisfaction with mediation, despite their tendency to receive less as claimants and to pay more as respondents.

Female mediators had a significantly greater likelihood of having their disputants reach agreement in mediation. Mediations with two male mediators had the lowest agreement rate. Mediations with mixed gender pairs fell in the middle. Testing for

---

2. [Ed. Note: The mediation format used in the New Mexico program assigned two persons to act as co-mediators for each case.]

disputant/mediator gender interactions, we found that female claimants were less likely to express procedural satisfaction and reported a lack of fairness more often in cases where the two mediators were women. Conversely, respondents in those cases with a female claimant and two female mediators were somewhat more likely to report satisfaction with the outcome.

Both claimant and respondent groups in mediation were more likely to respond favorably to the procedure with a mixed gender pair of mediators.

3. Long-term Satisfaction and Compliance

The higher frequency of respondent satisfaction in mediation remained unchanged over time. Approximately six months after initial interviews, mediation respondents still reported higher levels of satisfaction than adjudication respondents. . . .

Although we found few effects by ethnicity or gender, minority claimants tended to report higher long-term satisfaction levels in mediation than nonminority claimants. Women respondents in general, and minority women in particular, were more likely to comply with mediated agreements and non-monetary obligations. In contrast, white men were most likely to comply with court rulings.

V. Discussion

It is apparent that among the rich variety of data we gathered about mediation and adjudication of small claims cases in Albuquerque, New Mexico, two findings are especially provocative. One is the finding that white women tend to do as well or better than others in mediation, yet are less satisfied with the outcome. The other is the finding that ethnic minorities achieve relatively poorer monetary outcomes than do whites, especially in mediation, yet are more satisfied with the outcome.

The findings for women are interesting from at least two perspectives. First, many scholars have argued that mediation is unfair to women because they are likely to achieve poorer outcomes in the process. Our study shows this fear to be unfounded, at least in the types of small claims dispute that we have examined here. . . .

Second, the gender findings are interesting because they show that white women are relatively less satisfied with the outcome of mediation and perceive it to be less fair, even though they achieve objectively more positive results. An examination of the open-ended responses of women in mediation shows a significant number who expressed anger. A number of white women also reported that they thought that the mediation process was unfair or biased. Surprisingly, unfairness was reported by female claimants and respondents most frequently when there were two female mediators. . . .

The data involving minorities raise substantial concerns about the fairness of the mediation process. This study demonstrates that the fears of scholars who have postulated that the invisible, informal, nonreviewable forum of mediation produces worse results for minority disputants may be well founded. What is particularly telling is that the presence of two minority mediators largely erases the disadvantage, so that the outcomes of minority disputants in mediation becomes nearly equal to those achieved by white disputants.

What is far less clear about these unequal results is what causes them and what their implications are for mediation.

Notes and Questions

(1) One research challenge in this area is definitional: what is meant by a "successful" outcome in mediation and can each element be quantitatively measured? In the Hermann study, outcome comparisons relate to elements of legally defined issues and remedies. But if a Respondent apologized to a Claimant for improper or insensitive behavior and that apology led the Claimant to agree to a lower financial settlement, does that mean that the Claimant did "worse" than someone who received more money but no apology? How would an evaluator capture that sense of "fairness" that was so important to a party?

(2) Does Hermann's finding regarding the favorable impact of a minority mediator team on mediated outcomes constitute evidence to support Delgado's claim that parties alter their behavior to conform to what is expected of them in the social context? If so, does that suggest, contrary to Delgado's conclusion, that nonminority claimants might behave constructively when participating in a mediation with parties of differing ethnicities, races, or religions?

(3) Some authors argue that it is the mediator's responsibility to address and rectify power imbalances. *See, e.g.,* Jacqueline M. Nolan-Haley, *Informed Consent in Mediation: A Guiding Principle for Truly Educated Decision Making*, 74 Notre Dame L. Rev. 775 (1999). One California statute converts this sentiment into a statutory duty for a mediator: "Mediation of cases involving custody and visitation concerning children shall be governed by uniform standards of practice adopted by the Judicial Council. The standards of practice shall include, but not be limited to, all of the following . . . *the conducting of negotiations in such a way as to equalize power relationships between the parties.*" Cal. Fam. Code § 3162(b)(3) (emphasis added). Scott Hughes, in his article entitled *Elizabeth's Story*, 8 Geo. J. Legal Ethics 553 (1995), combines a superb narrative of his client's divorce mediation experience with a penetrating analysis of the dangers of using mediation in a matrimonial dissolution setting when there are both explicit and subtle power disparities among the divorcing partners.

D. Re-Examining Justice: Mediation and the Rule of Law

Mediation advocates thoughtfully argue that mediation's primary strength is that it empowers participants to decide for themselves what priority to accord to conflicting legal, business, prudential, and personal principles. For many individuals, knowing the answer to the question: "what am I legally entitled or obligated to do?" does not conclusively answer the question: "what should I do to resolve this dispute?" The dialogue over what role public rules play in the dispute resolution process raises fundamental jurisprudential and policy questions.

To justify the use of mediation philosophically requires an account of how the rule of law is compatible with supporting mediation's commitment to promoting participant decision-making. Legal positivists, most eloquently through the writings of H.L.A. Hart, offer a simple, compelling distinction: what the law is can differ from what the law ought to be. So, if mediation participants develop settlement terms that constitute, from their perspective, their shared vision of what ought to be, should their resolution be supported if it conflicts with what the law requires? Does it matter if the disputants have equal power and resources, or whether the system was designed to advantage some at the expense of others? Probing such questions requires one to examine complex theories of legal obligation, legal legitimacy, and the concept of change in a democratic society.

Although investigating these more abstract philosophical concepts significantly enriches policy analysis, important practical questions about mediation's use, regrettably, often cannot await their answers. So persons examine these matters by analyzing concrete practices. Professor Fiss, in his celebrated article excerpted below, maintains that privatizing justice by using a structured, facilitated negotiated settlement process—i.e., mediation—erodes important public values; he argues that having parties approve settlement terms should not be the decisive standard for determining if the controversy has been resolved. Professor Menkel-Meadow takes issue with Fiss by highlighting competing considerations between those who advocate settlement and those supporting adjudication. Embedded in their respective accounts are assumptions about the relationship, if any, between the mediation process and considerations of justice.

The chapter's two concluding excerpts consider justice in mediation. Professors Jonathan M. Hyman and Lela Love delineate the various dimensions that justice principles address and consider how consensual and adjudicatory processes secure them. Professor Isabelle Gunning discusses justice in the modern context, framed by American racial tension.

Against Settlement
93 Yale L.J. 1073, 1075–80, 1082–83, 1085–87 (1984)*
By Owen Fiss

. . .

In my view . . . the case for settlement rests on questionable premises. I do not believe that settlement as a generic practice is preferable to judgment. It should be treated instead as a highly problematic technique for streamlining dockets. Settlement is for me the civil analogue of plea bargaining: Consent is often coerced; the bargain may be struck by someone without authority; the absence of a trial and judgment renders subsequent judicial involvement troublesome; and although dockets are trimmed, justice may not be done. . . .

The Imbalance of Power

. . . [S]ettlement is . . . a function of the resources available to each party to finance the litigation, and those resources are frequently distributed unequally. . . .

The disparities in resources between the parties can influence the settlement in three ways. First, the poorer party may be less able to amass and analyze the information needed to predict the outcome of the litigation, and thus be disadvantaged in the bargaining process. Second, he may need the damages he seeks immediately and thus be induced to settle as a way of accelerating payment, even though he realizes he would get less now than he might if he awaited judgment. All plaintiffs want their damages immediately, but an indigent plaintiff may be exploited by a rich defendant because his need is so great that the defendant can force him to accept a sum that is less than the ordinary present value of the judgment. Third, the poorer party might be forced to settle because he does not have the resources to finance the litigation, to cover either his own projected expenses, such as his lawyer's time, or the expenses his opponent can impose through the manipulation of procedural mechanisms such as discovery. It might seem that settlement benefits the plaintiff by allowing him to avoid the costs of litigation, but this is not so. The defendant can anticipate the plaintiff's costs if the case were to be tried fully and decrease his offer by that amount. The indigent plaintiff is a victim of the costs of litigation even if he settles.

. . .

Of course, imbalances of power can distort judgment as well: Resources influence the quality of presentation, which in turn has an important bearing on who wins and the terms of victory. We count, however, on the guiding presence of the judge, who can employ a number of measures to lessen the impact of distributional inequalities. He can, for example, supplement the parties' presentations by asking questions, calling his own witnesses, and inviting other persons and institutions to participate as amici. These measures are likely to make only a small contribution toward moderating the influence of distributional inequalities, but should not be ignored for that reason. Not even these small steps are possible with settlement. There is, moreover, a critical difference between a process like settlement, which is based on bargaining and accepts inequalities of wealth as an integral and legitimate component of the process, and a process like judgment, which knowingly struggles against those inequalities. Judgment aspires to an autonomy from distributional inequalities, and it gathers much of its appeal from this aspiration.

The Absence of Authoritative Consent

The argument for settlement presupposes that the contestants are individuals. These individuals speak for themselves and should be bound by the rules they generate. In many situations, however, individuals are ensnared in contractual relationships that impair their autonomy. Lawyers or insurance companies might, for example, agree to settlements that are in their interests but are not in the best interests of their clients, and to which their clients would not agree if the choice were still theirs. But a deeper and more intractable problem arises from the fact that many parties are not individuals but rather organizations or groups. We do not know who is entitled to speak for these entities and to give the consent upon which so much of the appeal of settlement depends.

Some organizations, such as corporations or unions, have formal procedures for identifying the persons who are authorized to speak for them. But these procedures are imperfect. They are designed to facilitate transactions between the organization and outsiders, rather than to insure that the members of the organization in fact agree with a particular decision. Nor do they eliminate conflicts of interests. The chief executive officer of a corporation may settle a suit to prevent embarrassing disclosures about his managerial policies, but such disclosures might well be in the interest of the shareholders. The president of a union may agree to a settlement as a way of preserving his power within the organization; for that very reason, he may not risk the dangers entailed in consulting the rank and file or in subjecting the settlement to ratification by the membership. . . .

These problems become even more pronounced when we turn from organizations and consider the fact that much contemporary litigation involves even more nebulous social entities, namely, groups. Some of these groups, such as ethnic or racial minorities, inmates of prisons, or residents of institutions [for persons with intellectual disabilities], may have an identity or existence that transcends the lawsuit, but they do not have any formal organizational structure and therefore lack any procedures for generating authoritative consent. . . .

. . .

Going to judgment does not altogether eliminate the risk of unauthorized action, any more than it eliminates the distortions arising from disparities in resources. The case presented by the representative of a group or an organization admittedly will influence the outcome of the suit, and that outcome will bind those who might also be bound by a settlement. On the other hand, judgment does not ask as much from the so-called representatives. There is a conceptual and normative distance between what the representatives do and say and what the court eventually decides, because the judge tests those statements and actions against independent procedural and substantive standards. The authority of judgment arises from the law, not from the statements or actions of the putative representatives, and thus we allow judgment to bind persons not directly involved in the litigation even when we are reluctant to have settlement do so.

. . .

The Lack of Foundation for Continuing Judicial Involvement

... [D]ispute-resolution ... trivializes the remedial dimensions of lawsuits and mistakenly assumes judgment to be the end of the process. It supposes that the judge's duty is to declare which neighbor is right and which wrong, and that this declaration will end the judge's involvement. ... Often, however, judgment is not the end of a lawsuit but only the beginning. The involvement of the court may continue almost indefinitely. In these cases, settlement cannot provide an adequate basis for that necessary continuing involvement, and thus is no substitute for judgment.

The parties may sometimes be locked in combat with one another and view the lawsuit as only one phase in a long continuing struggle. The entry of judgment will then not end the struggle, but rather change its terms and the balance of power. One of the parties will invariably return to the court and again ask for its assistance, not so much because conditions have changed, but because the conditions that preceded the lawsuit have unfortunately not changed. This often occurs in domestic-relations case, where the divorce decree represents only the opening salvo in an endless series of skirmishes over custody and support.

The structural reform cases that play such a prominent role on the federal docket provide another occasion for continuing judicial involvement. In these cases, courts seek to safeguard public values by restructuring large-scale bureaucratic organizations. The task is enormous, and our knowledge of how to restructure on-going bureaucratic organizations is limited. As a consequence, courts must over-see and manage the remedial process for a long-time — maybe forever. This, I fear, is true of most school desegregation cases, some of which have been pending for twenty or thirty years. It is also true of antitrust cases that seek divestiture or reorganization of an industry.

The drive for settlement knows no bounds and can result in a consent decree even in the kinds of cases I have just mentioned, that is, even when a court finds itself embroiled in a continuing struggle between the parties or must reform a bureaucratic organization. The parties may be ignorant of the difficulties ahead or optimistic about the future, or they may simply believe that they can get more favorable terms through a bargained-for agreement. Soon, however, the inevitable happens: One party returns to court and asks the judge to modify the decree, either to make it more effective or less stringent. But the judge is at a loss: He has no basis for assessing the request. He cannot, to use Cardozo's somewhat melodramatic formula, easily decide whether the "dangers, once substantial, have become attenuated to a shadow," because, by definition, he never knew the dangers.

. . .

Justice Rather Than Peace

The dispute resolution story makes settlement appear as a perfect substitute for judgment ... by trivializing the remedial dimensions of a lawsuit, and also by reducing the social function of the lawsuit to one of resolving private disputes. In that story, settlement appears to achieve exactly the same purpose as judgment — peace between the parties — but at considerably less expense to society....

In my view, however, the purpose of adjudication should be understood in broader terms. Adjudication uses public resources, and employs not strangers chosen by the parties but public officials chosen by a process in which the public participates. These officials, like members of the legislative and executive branches, possess a power that has been defined and conferred by public law, not private agreement. Their job is not to maximize the ends of private parties, nor simply to secure the peace, but to explicate and give force to the values embodied in authoritative texts such as the Constitution and statutes: to interpret those values and to bring reality into accord with them. This duty is not discharged when the parties settle.

In our political system, courts are reactive institutions. They do not search out interpretive occasions, but instead wait for others to bring matters to their attention. They also rely for the most part on others to investigate and present the law and facts. A settlement will thereby deprive a court of the occasion, and perhaps even the ability, to render an interpretation. A court cannot proceed (or not proceed very far) in the face of a settlement. To be against settlement is not to urge that parties be "forced" to litigate, since that would interfere with their autonomy and distort the adjudicative process; the parties will be inclined to make the court believe that their bargain is justice. To be against settlement is only to suggest that when the parties settle, society gets less than what appears, and for a price it does not know it is paying. Parties might settle while leaving justice undone. The settlement of a school suit might secure the peace, but not racial equality. Although the parties are prepared to live under the terms they bargained for, and although such peaceful coexistence may be a necessary precondition for justice, and itself a state of affairs to be valued, it is not justice itself. To settle for something means to accept less than some ideal....

. . .

The Real Divide

To all this, one can readily imagine a simple response by way of confession and avoidance: We are not talking about those lawsuits. Advocates of ADR might insist that my account of adjudication, in contrast to the one implied by the dispute-resolution story, focuses on a rather narrow category of lawsuits. They could argue that while settlement may have only the most limited appeal with respect to those cases, I have not spoken to the "typical" case. My response is twofold.

First, even as a purely quantitative matter, I doubt that the number of cases I am referring to is trivial. My universe includes those cases in which there are significant distributional inequalities; those in which it is difficult to generate authoritative consent because organizations of social groups are parties or because the power to settle is vested in autonomous agents; those in which the court must continue to supervise the parties after judgment; and those in which justice needs to be done, or to put it more modestly, where there is a genuine social need for an authoritative interpretation of law. I imagine that the number of cases that satisfy one of these four criteria is considerable; in contrast to the kind of case portrayed in the dispute-resolution story, they probably dominate the docket of a modern court system.

Second, it demands a certain kind of myopia to be concerned only with the number of cases, as though all cases are equal simply because the clerk of the court assigns each a single docket number. All cases are not equal. The Los Angeles desegregation case, to take one example, is not equal to the allegedly more typical suit involving a property dispute or an automobile accident. The desegregation suit consumes more resources, affects more people, and provokes far greater challenges to the judicial power. The settlement movement must introduce a qualitative perspective; it must speak to these more "significant" cases, and demonstrate the propriety of settling them. Otherwise it will soon be seen as an irrelevance, dealing with trivia rather than responding to the very conditions that give the movement its greatest sway and saliency.

. . .

Notes and Questions

(1) Do commentators such as Professors Fiss and Delgado make the mistake that Legal Positivists accuse lawyers of making — *viz.*, assuming that whatever is legal is also morally desirable? Is Fiss accurate when he states, as his final challenge, that the mediation process might be irrelevant because it deals with "trivial" rather than "significant" cases? Revisit Chapter 1's account of mediation's use even during its foundational years to examine the types of controversies in which it was used.

(2) Professor Fiss observes that persons with power may have no incentive to talk to others if they believe their interests are secure. In such settings, the use of the legal system by parties who seek to challenge existing arrangements constitutes a crucial resource for triggering change in a non-violent manner. For example, without the Ohio Supreme Court declaring that the state's system for funding public elementary and secondary education was unconstitutional, there appears to be no compelling incentive for residents of wealthier school districts to support reallocating their tax dollars to financially poorer districts. *See DeRolph v. Ohio*, 728 N.E.2d 993 (Ohio 2000). Yet, once parties are in litigation, participating in mediated negotiations might create opportunities for creative problem-solving. The simultaneous interplay of multiple dispute resolution processes, which is the realistic context for most dispute resolution efforts, creates significant challenges. For a more thorough discussion of the interrelationship between law and mediation, see Chapter 6, *infra*.

(3) During the course of a mediation conference involving a claim by the landlord for rent arrears, the mediator learns that the landlord is renting the basement area of their home in violation of the zoning ordinance governing single-family-home-use in that neighborhood; the mediator also learns that the tenant is an immigrant who is not lawfully in the U.S. Both parties develop mutually acceptable settlement terms to pay the rent arrears and continue the tenancy. What should the mediator do? For a discussion of similar dilemmas, see the portion of Chapter 8, *infra*, dealing with Mediator Ethics.

Whose Dispute Is It Anyway? A Philosophical and Democratic Defense of Settlement (In Some Cases)

83 Geo. L.J. 2663, 2664–71, 2692 (1995)*
By Carrie Menkel-Meadow

. . .

. . . For me, the question is not "for or against" settlement (since settlement has become the "norm" for our system), but *when, how, and under what circumstances* should cases be settled? When do our legal system, our citizenry, and the parties in particular disputes need formal legal adjudication, and when are their respective interests served by settlement, *whether public or private?*

. . .

In this essay, I hope to explore . . . how can we decide which settlements to be for and which to be against? In other words, how can we tell good settlements from bad ones, and when should we prefer adjudication to settlement? . . . . In the words of current academic cachet, much depends on the context — of disputes, of disputants, and of the system being considered. . . .

Those who criticize settlement suffer from what I have called, in other contexts, "litigation romanticism," with empirically unverified assumptions about what courts can or will do. More important, those who privilege adjudication focus almost exclusively on structural and institutional values and often give short shrift to those who are actually involved in the litigation. I fear, but am not sure, that this debate can be reduced to those who care more about the people actually engaged in disputes versus those who care more about institutional and structural arrangements. I prefer to think that we need both adjudication and settlement. These processes can affect each other in positive, as well as negative ways, but in my view, settlement should not be seen as "second best" or "worst case" when adjudication fails. Settlement can be justified on its own moral grounds — there are important values, consistent with the fundamental values of our legal and political systems, that support the legitimacy of settlements of some, if not most, legal disputes. Those values include consent, participation, empowerment, dignity, respect, empathy and emotional catharsis, privacy, efficiency, quality solutions, equity, access, and yes, even justice.

Though some have argued that compromise itself can be morally justified, I . . . argue . . . that compromise is not always necessary for settlement and that in fact, some settlements, by not requiring compromise, may produce better solutions than litigation. . . .

. . . [I]t seems to me that the key questions implicated in the ongoing debate about settlement vs. adjudication are:

---

1. In a party-initiated legal system, when is it legitimate for the parties to settle their dispute themselves, or with what assistance from a court in which they have sought some legal-system support or service?

2. When is "consent" to a settlement legitimate and "real," and by what standards should we (courts and academic critics) judge and permit such consent?

3. When, in a party-initiated legal system, should party consent be "trumped" by other values — in other words, when should public, institutional, and structural needs and values override parties' desire to settle or courts' incentives to promote settlement? In short, when is the need for "public adjudication" or as Luban suggests, "public settlement" more important (to whom?) than what the parties may themselves desire?

. . .

. . . I have here tried to make the following arguments on behalf of the "best" aspects of settlement:

1. Settlements that are in fact consensual represent the goals of democratic and party-initiated legal regimes by allowing the parties themselves to choose processes and outcomes for dispute resolution.

2. Settlements permit a broader range of possible solutions that may be more responsive to both party and system needs.

3. What some consider to be the worst of settlement, that is, compromise, may actually represent a moral commitment to equality, precision in justice, accommodation, and peaceful coexistence of conflicting interests.

4. Settlements may be based on important nonlegal principles or interests, which may, in any given case, be as important or more important to the parties than "legal" considerations. Laws made in the aggregate may not always be appropriate in particular cases, and thus settlement can be seen as yet another "principled" supplement to our common law system.

5. Settlement processes may be more humanely "real," democratic, participatory, and cathartic than more formalized processes, permitting in their best moments, transformative and educational opportunities for parties in dispute as well as for others.

6. Some settlement processes may be better adapted for the multiplex, multiparty issues that require solutions in our modern society than the binary form of plaintiff-defendant adjudication.

7. Despite the continuing and important debates about discovery and information exchange in the litigation process, some settlement processes (mediation and some forms of neutral case evaluation and scheduling) may actually provide both more and better (not just legally relevant) information for problem-solving, as well as "education" of the litigants.

8. When used appropriately, settlement may actually increase access to justice, not only by allowing more disputants to claim in different ways, but also by allowing greater varieties of case resolutions.

. . .

Notes and Questions

(1) Professor Menkel-Meadow criticizes Fiss and others for maintaining a romanticized vision of the adjudication process; she believes that party-facilitated settlements (mediation) can often secure more desirable outcomes than those obtained through adjudication. Do you agree? By contrast, can one criticize Menkel-Meadow for offering a romanticized vision of mediation? Lela P. Love and Cheryl B. McDonald's *A Tale of Two Cities: Day Labor and Conflict Resolution for Communities in Crisis*, provides a concrete setting in which competing visions of fairness collide.

(2) Commentators observe that many mediated negotiations are conducted "in the shadow of the law," so that failure to reach settlement might result in one party continuing to pursue their litigation options. Do the benefits of settlement dissipate if the negotiating context is divorced from this litigation fallback?

(3) Menkel-Meadow asserts that encouraging party settlement reflects one goal of democratic legal regimes. Do you agree? Does her account of the "best" aspects of settlement satisfactorily meet the concerns raised by commentators such as Delgado, Grillo, and Press and Deason, that power inequities may be reinforced through mediated negotiations rather than rectified?

(4) Consider racial tension in a community following a law enforcement-involved shooting. The community might be consumed with demonstrations and protests. Such demonstrations might draw the attention of the U.S. Department of Justice, which could investigate law enforcement practices, or file litigation against the community or law enforcement; alternatively, local actors could make allegations in federal or state court. Are disputes between law enforcement agencies and communities best resolved through litigation, mediation, or some other process? For illustrations of how a mediator might be involved following community unrest, see Jay Rothman, *Identity and Conflict: Collaboratively Addressing Police-Community Conflict in Cincinnati, Ohio*, 22 Ohio St. J. on Disp. Res. 105 (2006) (discussing Rothman's work leading to a "collaborative agreement" following court-ordered mediation); Sharon Press, *Using Dispute Resolution Skills to Heal a Community*, 25 Ohio St. J. on Disp. Res. 645 (2020) (discussing the process design for community conversations in Falcon Heights, Minnesota, after Philando Castile was killed by a police officer during a traffic stop). *See also* Divided Community Project, Virtual Toolkit, https://go.osu .edu/dcptoolkit (providing resources for dispute resolution practitioners, community leaders, and others engaging in proactive work to build community resilience or responding to community unrest).

If Portia Were a Mediator: An Inquiry into Justice in Mediation

9 Clinical L. Rev. 157, 159–62, 166–70, 172–73 (2002)*
By Jonathan M. Hyman & Lela P. Love

Introduction

Using mediation rather than adjudication to resolve disputes carries important implications for justice. How can an agreed-upon solution, crafted by disputing parties rather than by duly appointed arbiters, judges or juries, comport with ideals of justice? Critics claim that mediation and settlement sacrifice a just result . . . for mere efficiency or expedience. Such critiques neglect the multi-faceted nature of justice . . . [We examine] how a justice rationale undergirds the consensual resolution of disputes, while another justice rationale undergirds adjudication. Justice-seeking is a central component of all dispute resolution processes, and one that mediators, like judges and arbitrators, must attend to. Rather than abandoning justice, the unique attributes of mediation enable mediators to help those who ultimately have the most intimate understanding of the complexities of their situation achieve a resolution they find "just."

Justice in adjudicative systems comes from above, from the application by a judge, jury or arbitrator of properly created standards or rules to "facts" as determined by the adjudicator. Justice inheres in two aspects of that system—in the standards or rules that are applied, and in the process that is used to apply them. Mediation has parallel, but very different, aspects. The rules, standards, principles and beliefs that guide the resolution of the dispute in mediation are those held by the parties. The guiding norms in mediation may be legal, moral, religious or practical. In mediation, parties are free to use whatever standards they wish, not limited to standards that have been adopted by the legislature or articulated by the courts. Consequently, justice in mediation comes from below, from the parties. . . .

. . .

I. What We Mean when We Talk about Justice

. . .

. . . When parties talk about fairness and justice, without the overlay of the elaborate system of adjudicatory justice, they will most likely find themselves talking about the well-known Aristotelean categories of reparative justice, distributive justice, and procedural justice.

A. Reparative Justice

Parties in mediation may use claims of justice to seek repair of what they see as a wrongful deprivation or harm imposed on them by the other. They need not limit

---

their claims of injustice to acts that may have violated the law. A party who has taken more than is "fair" from the complaining party might have arguably committed an injustice that needs to be corrected, even if the law does not prohibit the taking. Treating someone disrespectfully, taking or diminishing their dignity, for example, might become part of a claim that an injustice was done even though there may be no cognizable "cause of action" for such a wrong. . . .

. . .

B. Retribution and Revenge

What if a party to a mediation seeks revenge for the wrong claimed to have been done? The notion of "an eye for an eye" is an ancient form of balancing that some experience as both just and "reparative." Frequently, mediated discussions result in the parties' recognition that the wrong they experienced may be counter-balanced by a wrong they sponsored. Or, the proverbial "eye" they wish to extract can be given in a more meaningful (and less costly) way than blinding the other side. In other words, mediated discussions of justice can be responsive to desires for revenge even though revenge, as it is normally conceived, is not usually the product of mediation. . . .

C. Distributive Justice

. . .

. . . The well-known concepts by which we can measure the justice of distributions are equality, equity, and need.

"Splitting the difference" between settlement demands, a common last step in a negotiated distribution, is a claim to equality, and has a powerful attraction to people's sense of fairness and common sense justice. Similarly, siblings, employees, or victims who must share resources in a common fund may be guided by understandable principles of equal treatment.

Equity, as distinct from equality, can support distributions other than an even split. A victim's feelings or a perpetrator's ability to pay can be more important for determining a just distribution than simply splitting the difference or precisely measuring actual losses. The concept of *Pareto efficiency* also carries implications for justice. That concept asks us to consider, for any given or proposed distribution of resources, whether there is another possible distribution that would make at least one party better off without making any other party worse off. . . .

The relative needs of the parties also play into questions of distributive justice. Such considerations make it acceptable for disparate treatment such as the rich being taxed at a higher rate than the poor. The precept *from each according to his ability, to each according to his need* can fuel claims of justice and lead to responsive settlement terms and sometimes acts of generosity which restore families and communities.

. . .

E. Procedural Justice

While mediation lacks the formality and elaborate rules of litigation, it nonetheless provides a rich opportunity to implement procedural justice. From a disputant's perspective, the perception of fairness is linked to having a meaningful opportunity to tell one's story, to feeling that the mediator considers the story, and to being treated with dignity and in an even-handed manner. Adherence to principles of procedural justice influences the parties' perceptions about the fairness of the process, as well as their perceptions of substantive justice and their willingness to comply with the outcome of the dispute resolution process. . . .

Justice for All in Mediation: What the Pandemic, Racial Justice Movement, and the Recognition of Structural Racism Call Us to Do as Mediators
68 Wash. U. J. L. & Pol'y, 36, 52–54 (2022)*
By Isabelle Gunning

. . .

. . . There has been a tension in mediation scholarship and practice between an idea of justice defined by the application of articulated laws, legal norms and accepted societal norms, and the kind of "justice-from-below"[60] that parties can provide for each other during and through mediation. On the one hand, there are mediation models, often characterized as "evaluative," that involve norm-educating as well as norm-advocacy, where mediators see their role to include providing information on the applicable legal norms to either ensure that all parties are fully informed of their legal rights (but leaving the parties free to accept or reject the law) or to not only educate but ensure that any agreement will conform to the prevailing legal requirements. On the other hand, there are mediation models that involve norm generation, where mediators see their roles as providing little to no information to the parties so that the parties can generate whatever norms will work best for them and their conflict. It is the norm generating models that have attracted the critics, myself included, who are concerned that disadvantaged groups — BIPOC and white women — will forfeit legal rights out of ignorance and/or pressure within the mediation context.

. . . The idea that civil rights laws designed to ensure equality for all regardless of race should be ignored when racial inequality clearly continues in deadly forms would seem to reveal an indifference to the facts and pain so publicly revealed over the past year. Still, the racial reckoning is also making clear . . . that our very laws have been defined only with the voices, views, and circumstances of a small and privileged few out of the white American populace and that the resultant legal

---

60. Jonathan M. Hyman & Lela P. Love, *If Portia Were a Mediator: An Inquiry into Justice in Mediation*, 9 Clin L. Rev. 157, 162 (2002).

definitions promote and preserve white supremacy. Civil rights laws which support or enhance equality for all — as an example, laws that expand voting rights for all voters rather than create barriers to restrict voting rights — ought to be encouraged and promoted while processes that allow for norm generation that includes the voices of people who have been excluded from positions of power are also encouraged and promoted. . . .

Justice or "social justice" must encompass individually experienced outcomes as well as societal structures that support just outcomes equally for all. . . .

Our work in mediation needs to recognize the societal and structural nature of inequality and thus the need to support and advocate for those social norms and laws that support individual and structural equality. And our work in bringing people together in a space that supports their self-determination and empathy can be a place of generation for norms that build and expand upon the equality-promotion laws and norms of other parts of society.

Mediation and mediation processes could be one place to encourage the voices of people left out of the formal legal or norm generating process. What we do in supporting parties in mediation is support their relationship with each other. People can only provide "justice" for each other when they are in relationship. The quality of that relationship and the respect within that relationship matters. Consequently, our definition of justice must also include how we support not only individual self-determination and empowerment but also how we support parties' relationship to each other. . . .

Notes and Questions

For probing accounts of the relationship between questions of procedural justice and mediation, see Nancy A. Welsh, *Disputant's Decision Control in Court-Connected Mediation: A Hollow Promise Without Procedural Justice*, 2002 J. Disp. Resol. 179. *See also* Welsh, *Do You Believe in Magic?: Self-Determination and Procedural Justice Meet Inequality in Court-Connected Mediation*, 70 SMU L. Rev. 721 (2017). For a contrary perspective on these matters, see Deborah R. Hensler, *Suppose It's Not True: Challenging Mediation Ideology*, 2002 J. Disp. Resol. 81.

Chapter 8

Ethical Issues for Mediators

A. Introduction

This chapter explores ethical issues for mediators, including the special concerns that may arise when the mediator is also a licensed attorney. Section B presents the components of typical mediator codes of conduct and the challenges associated with defining mediator behavior in the context of ethical standards. Where applicable, considerations for online dispute resolution are included. Section C examines enforcement options for breaches of ethical and professional standards, including civil suits and disciplinary procedures. Section D analyzes the intersection between the legal community and mediation, focusing specifically on the regulation of attorneys serving as mediators and the potential for allegations of the "unauthorized practice of law" for non-attorney mediators. As you read this chapter, consider the impact that the mediator roles, styles and orientations explored in Chapter 4, *supra*, have on what is considered to be ethical behavior.

B. Mediator Standards of Conduct

As the use of mediation expanded, there was increased interest in developing and codifying standards of conduct for mediators and, to a lesser extent, adopting disciplinary procedures to secure compliance with them. In 1986, Hawaii became the first state to adopt ethical guidelines for mediators, in the "Standards for Private and Public Mediators in the State of Hawaii." Since then, nearly every jurisdiction has adopted either its own set of ethical standards or some version of the Model Standards of Conduct for Mediators that were drafted and adopted by the American Arbitration Association, the American Bar Association, and the Association for Conflict Resolution. The Model Standards were initially adopted in 1995 and revised in 2005.[1] While there has been some discussion since that time among professionals about updating the Model Standards, the general consensus has been to treat them as foundational guidelines and if more specific guidance is required to govern mediator conduct in a particular area, such as the intersection of mediation and technology, those with subject-matter expertise should draft companion guidelines.

---

1. James Alfini was one of the drafters representing the ABA on the 1995 Model Standards. For the 2005 Model Standards, Sharon Press was one of the drafters representing the Association for Conflict Resolution and Joseph Stulberg served as the Reporter.

In theory, mediator standards of conduct should provide guidance on the ethical issues that arise for mediators. In 1992, Professor Robert A. Baruch Bush published a study of ethical dilemmas, *The Dilemmas of Mediation Practice: A Study of Ethical Dilemmas and Policy Implications.* Drawing on extensive interviews he conducted with practicing community, divorce and civil case mediators, he identified two major problems with the mediator standards that existed at that time:

> First, the codes and standards promulgated thus far almost always suffer from internal inconsistency. That is, where the mediator is confronted in a dilemma with the need to choose between two values, like fairness and self-determination, the codes typically contain provisions that, read together, tell her *to choose both.* For example, they tell her to protect and to leave alone, when she can't possibly do both. . . .

> The second problem . . . is, the codes and standards are framed at a level of generality that is not responsive to the mediator's need to know how to apply the principles in specific situations. They lack concreteness . . . [y]et clearly, given the kinds of problems mediators encounter, specific guidance is what they most need.

In the years since this critique was published, not much has changed.

While mediator standards of conduct vary in their language describing behavior that is condoned and sanctioned, there is general agreement as to the topics that should be included. In this section, we identify these consensus topics, citing the language of the relevant standard appearing in the 2005 Model Standards of Conduct to illustrate how it is expressed. Thereafter, we pose hypotheticals reflecting recurring practice dilemmas that require understanding a standard's purpose to enable a practitioner to resolve the dilemma in that moment. Online dispute resolution considerations have been added where applicable. In the Appendix, the complete version of the 2005 Model Standards of Conduct for Mediators (Appendix A) and its Reporter's Notes (Appendix B) appear, as do the Florida Disciplinary Procedures found in the Florida Rules for Certified and Court-Appointed Mediators (Appendix C).

An ethical dilemma arises for a mediator when there are two (or more) mediation values governing the situation but offer competing guidance. The mediator must choose which value takes precedence. Although the hypotheticals which follow are raised in the context of a single standard, consider how other standards relate to answering the issues that are raised. Finally, consider Professor Bush's critique as you read and resolve these dilemmas. Are the standards internally consistent? Are they written with a sufficient degree of specificity?

1. Self-Determination

This value enjoins a mediator from interfering with the parties' right of self-determination both in terms of substance and process. Interference with party self-determination often implicates other standards, such as impartiality and professional advice or opinions.

a. Model Standards of Conduct for Mediators

Standard I. Self-Determination

A. A mediator shall conduct a mediation based on the principle of party self-determination. Self-determination is the act of coming to a voluntary, uncoerced decision in which each party makes free and informed choices as to process and outcome. Parties may exercise self-determination at any stage of a mediation, including mediator selection, process design, participation in or withdrawal from the process, and outcomes.

1. Although party self-determination for process design is a fundamental principle of mediation practice, a mediator may need to balance such party self-determination with a mediator's duty to conduct a quality process in accordance with these Standards.

2. A mediator cannot personally ensure that each party has made free and informed choices to reach particular decisions, but, where appropriate, a mediator should make the parties aware of the importance of consulting other professionals to help them make informed choices.

B. A mediator shall not undermine party self-determination by any party for reasons such as higher settlement rates, egos, increased fees, or outside pressures from court personnel, program administrators, provider organizations, the media or others.

b. Online Dispute Resolution Considerations

1. In giving parties the choice between an in-person, remote, or hybrid mediation, a mediator should inform parties of the benefits and limitations of each option. At a minimum, no party should be given an option without the other party also receiving the same option. Not providing the options to all parties can impact not just their self-determination, but can also implicate other ethical concerns, such as the parties' perceptions of a mediator's impartiality.

2. Parties should be fully informed of the meeting options before the mediation begins. If a party participating in a remote mediation expresses discomfort with a particular technology, the mediator should provide parties with the option to change. Regardless of whether a party requests changing the technology being used, a mediator should always consider whether the quality of the process is being undermined by its use and how best to address a poor process.

c. Mediation Dilemmas for Discussion

1. The parties to a dissolution of marriage mediation are set to make an agreement regarding a parenting plan which would, in the mediator's opinion, be detrimental to the welfare of their young children; or one parent is ready to agree to an amount of child support which is significantly below the Court's

minimum guidelines. Neither party is represented. What are the competing values? How should the mediator handle this situation?

2. Party B appears to be emotionally intimidated by Party A. Party A, in a firm, authoritative tone, proposes a financial settlement that requires Party B to make a substantial monetary payment within a short period of time. Party B makes it clear that doing so will severely restrict their ability to meet other financial obligations but agrees to pay. What are the mediator's ethical obligations? Does the mediator have different obligations if Party A threatened Party B with a specific threat tied to the financial settlement, such as, "If you don't pay this amount immediately, I am going to beat the daylights out of you"?

3. After Party B chooses to join the mediation via Zoom, the mediator learns that Party B has never used Zoom. Party A joins the mediation in-person, making this a hybrid mediation. Party B struggles to use Zoom and doesn't know how to mute or unmute while accidentally appearing as a grizzly bear avatar, leading to challenges in non-verbal communication. What are the mediator's ethical obligations? What should the mediator do?

4. In a case that involves a high degree of animosity between the parties, the mediator is making extensive use of online breakout rooms. After meeting with each party once, the mediator returns to the plaintiffs who appear to be entirely different in demeanor from the initial joint session and their first caucus. They now are willing to resolve the dispute for a fraction of the proposal which they had adamantly stated earlier. No one has said what has caused this significant change, but the mediator suspects that their attorney has pressured them by implying that since mediation was court-ordered, they are unable to leave the mediation without resolving the case. What are the mediator's ethical obligations? What should the mediator do?

5. Is a mediator's obligation regarding self-determination any different depending on whether the parties are represented by legal counsel or not?

6. After a lengthy mediation in which both parties are represented by competent counsel, everyone agrees that they have reached an impasse. Given the time that the parties have invested in the mediation, and the high esteem to which they hold the mediator, the lawyers ask the mediator to become the arbitrator and render a binding decision. Can the mediator ethically do so? Does it make a difference if the request is made by the parties (not their attorneys)? How should a mediator balance ethical obligations to honor self-determination and a quality process (see below)?

Notes and Questions

(1) In Florida, a party filed a grievance after a 10-hour mediation. The party alleged that by the ninth hour, the party was emotionally and physically exhausted and reported just wanting to get out of the session. The party alleged that they were

unable to exercise self-determination due to their exhausted state. A similar griev-ance included the allegation that a party was hypoglycemic and had not been given sufficient opportunity to eat prior to signing a mediation agreement. Should there be a maximum time limit on the length of a particular mediation session? Can indi-viduals make good decisions if they are physically and mentally exhausted?

(2) What does party "informed decision-making" mean in terms of the media-tor's obligation? Imagine mediating a personal injury case where both parties are represented by counsel. A very experienced PI attorney represents the defendant while a family friend who is a transactional lawyer represents the plaintiff. Dur-ing the course of the mediation, it becomes clear that the plaintiff is receiving bad advice from their attorney who does not know the law in this subject area. How does this ethical obligation relate to the obligation for a mediator to maintain impartial-ity (*see* impartiality section below)?

(3) Standard I (regarding self-determination) in the Model Standards of Practice for Family and Divorce Mediation includes the following affirmative ethical obliga-tion for mediators. "A family mediator shall inform the participants that they may withdraw from family mediation at any time and are not required to reach an agree-ment in mediation." Do you believe that a similar provision should be in the Model Standards for Mediators? Why or why not?

(4) Professor Nancy Welsh, in *The Thinning Vision of Self-Determination in Court-Connected Mediation: The Inevitable Price of Institutionalization?*, 6 Harv. Negot. L. Rev. 1 (2001), explores the way courts are modifying the meaning of self-determination and analyzes their implications for mediation in the court context. Welsh concludes the article by suggesting that the best way to protect party self-determination is by modifying the presumption that a mediated settlement agree-ment is immediately binding:

> ... [T]he standards currently used to determine whether parties exer-cised their "free will" in reaching a negotiated agreement are likely to fall short in protecting the fundamental principle of self-determination. There-fore, we may be *required to embrace and advocate for* a protection that holds court-connected mediation to a higher standard than traditional negotia-tion. The [most effective] protection [would be] the imposition of a three-day non-waivable cooling off period before mediated settlement agreements (whether oral or written) become binding. ...

> ...

> ... [T]he benefits provided by this cooling-off proposal clearly outweigh the possible risks. First, a cooling-off period ... is relatively straight for-ward, easily-administrable, and unlikely to invite litigation and/or intru-sions upon the confidentiality of mediation.

> ... [T]his option would [importantly] reward mediators who view their role as primarily facilitative and penalize mediators who use techniques designed to force an agreement.

Do you believe Professor Welsh's proposal is desirable?

(5) Drawing the line between ethical mediator behavior that supports party self-determination and inappropriate manipulation of party conduct is sometimes difficult. As you analyze the suggestions offered below by Professors Coben and Love from their article, *Trick or Treat, The Ethics of Mediator Manipulation*, Dispute Resol. Mag. 18–19 (Fall 2010),* consider whether their proposal would help you to determine the appropriateness of intervening in the dilemmas presented above.

> ... [M]uch of what good mediators do can be characterized as "helpful interventions" that assist the parties toward legitimate goals such as a better understanding, a platform for developing options, and (where the parties choose) an agreement or settlement. In those senses ... failure to make certain interventions would be poor practice.
>
> The problem, of course, is that all such "helpful interventions" are inevitably manipulative, in the sense that the mediator is, often unilaterally, making "moves" with profound impact on the parties' bargaining.
>
> ... To evaluate the ethics of any individual move we propose asking two questions.
>
> First, to be "OK," a move should further or *help* a legitimate party or process goal and be in keeping with the Model Standards of Conduct for Mediators that advance party self-determination in decision making. ... In other words, does the move support self-determination?
>
> Second, a move should not be manipulative in such a way that it disadvantages one side or undermines the integrity of the mediator or the mediation process. ... Moves that, if discovered, would be considered "tricky" and underhanded would not pass the test we propose. Following this logic, we would ask of the move: Is it consistent with mediator and mediation process integrity (i.e., not "tricky" or devious)?
>
> If we can respond "yes" to the two questions, then the mediator move is more likely to be ethically sound.
>
> Of course, different mediator goals will drive different practices. ... Despite differences in strategies, we believe all mediation interventions should be both helpful to a legitimate party goal and to party self-determination. Interventions should also be nondevious so that mediators and mediation integrity remains intact.

(6) The Florida Rules for Certified and Court-Appointed Mediators highlight the connection between self-determination and competence in Rule 10.310(d) by requiring a mediator to cancel or postpone a mediation in the event that a party is "unable to exercise self-determination." The committee note to this standard

---

* Copyright © 2010. All rights reserved. Reprinted with permission.

suggests that a mediator should be mindful of such things as "the threat of domestic violence, existence of substance abuse, physical threat or undue psychological dominance" which might "impair any party's ability to freely and willingly enter into an informed agreement."

2. Impartiality/Conflicts of Interest

Mediation is universally understood as involving an "impartial" or "neutral" individual who serves as the mediator. Standards of conduct typically track this requirement that mediators maintain impartiality throughout the mediation process and that they do not mediate matters that present clear or undisclosed conflicts of interest.

a. Model Standards of Conduct for Mediators

Standard II. Impartiality

A. A mediator shall decline a mediation if the mediator cannot conduct it in an impartial manner. Impartiality means freedom from favoritism, bias or prejudice.

B. A mediator shall conduct a mediation in an impartial manner and avoid conduct that gives the appearance of partiality.

1. A mediator should not act with partiality or prejudice based on any participant's personal characteristics, background, values and beliefs, or performance at a mediation, or any other reason.

2. A mediator should neither give nor accept a gift, favor, loan or other item of value that raises a question as to the mediator's actual or perceived impartiality.

3. A mediator may accept or give *de minimis* gifts or incidental items or services that are provided to facilitate a mediation or respect cultural norms so long as such practices do not raise questions as to a mediator's actual or perceived impartiality.

C. If at any time a mediator is unable to conduct a mediation in an impartial manner, the mediator shall withdraw.

Standard III. Conflicts of Interest

A. A mediator shall avoid a conflict of interest or the appearance of a conflict of interest during and after a mediation. A conflict of interest can arise from involvement by a mediator with the subject matter of the dispute or from any relationship between a mediator and any mediation participant, whether past or present, personal or professional, that reasonably raises a question of a mediator's impartiality.

B. A mediator shall make a reasonable inquiry to determine whether there are any facts that a reasonable individual would consider likely to create a potential or actual conflict of interest for a mediator. A mediator's actions necessary to accomplish a reasonable inquiry into potential conflicts of interest may vary based on practice context.

C. A mediator shall disclose, as soon as practicable, all actual and potential conflicts of interest that are reasonably known to the mediator and could reasonably be seen as raising a question about the mediator's impartiality. After disclosure, if all parties agree, the mediator may proceed with the mediation.

D. If a mediator learns any fact after accepting a mediation that raises a question with respect to that mediator's service creating a potential or actual conflict of interest, the mediator shall disclose it as quickly as practicable. After disclosure, if all parties agree, the mediator may proceed with the mediation.

E. If a mediator's conflict of interest might reasonably be viewed as undermining the integrity of the mediation, a mediator shall withdraw from or decline to proceed with the mediation regardless of the expressed desire or agreement of the parties to the contrary.

F. Subsequent to a mediation, a mediator shall not establish another relationship with any of the participants in any matter that would raise questions about the integrity of the mediation. When a mediator develops personal or professional relationships with parties, other individuals or organizations following a mediation in which they were involved, the mediator should consider factors such as time elapsed following the mediation, the nature of the relationships established, and services offered when determining whether the relationships might create a perceived or actual conflict of interest.

b. Mediation Dilemmas for Discussion

1. An insurance company maintains a short list of mediators who it feels comfortable utilizing when a case is referred to mediation. These mediators have mediated hundreds of times for this company and are familiar with the insurance representatives and their attorneys. The plaintiffs typically are one-time players. Should the mediators have any ethical concerns?

2. A mediator who lives in a relatively small town is the only trained mediator in the area. A couple who knows the mediator very well is getting a divorce. They call the mediator to request a mediation. They tell the mediator that they do not wish to engage in an adversarial process and that they are "not worried about any conflicts of interest or inappropriate dual roles" that the mediator might experience in taking on their case. May the mediator accept this mediation? What constitutes the type of conflict of interest that "might reasonably be viewed as undermining the integrity of the mediation"? Given the importance of self-determination, should a mediator be obligated to withdraw "regardless of the expressed desire or agreement of the parties to the contrary"?

3. The mediator has a niece by marriage who is currently working as a paralegal for a large multi-office law firm. Is it a conflict of interest for the mediator to mediate cases involving a party who is represented by a lawyer affiliated with that law firm? What if the niece is an attorney (not a paralegal)? What if the person is the mediator's child?

4. If a mediator discovers a conflict of interest or issue related to their impartiality once the parties have arrived at mediation, can the mediator effectively obtain a waiver or will parties feel obligated to go forward since they have already taken the time to attend the mediation? How can mediators protect themselves and ensure that a waiver is legitimate? Can an attorney effectively waive the conflict for their client or must the named party also expressly waive the conflict?

5. What are the allowable limits of a mediator's marketing efforts? May a mediator take "prospective" attorney mediation participants to lunch at the mediator's expense, or host a luncheon for prospective attorney mediation participants or judges who will make referrals? May the mediator give or accept football tickets (or some other high value item) for the purpose of expanding their mediation practice?

6. What is the appropriate balance for building rapport and maintaining impartiality? For example, prior to mediation, should the mediator "google" the parties and their lawyers to find possible connections? What if the mediator did so not for the purpose of building rapport but to determine if there were any potential conflicts of interest? If the mediator discovers a connection, such as the mediator and one party grew up in the same town or attended the same undergraduate university, must the mediator disclose the connection? If disclosure is not ethically required, should the mediator, as a matter of best practice, disclose it anyway?

7. The virtual platform used for asynchronous mediation in a small claims court was designed by computer scientists who are primarily well-educated white men. Further, numerous concerns surfaced when the court mediation program tested the web platform for ADA accessibility. Could these design concerns impact the mediator's impartiality? What if one party is unsighted and struggles to use the platform? What should the mediator do?

Notes and Questions

(1) How do a mediator's obligations related to conflict of interest compare to those of an attorney?

(2) There are critics who suggest that "impartiality" is not only impossible but it is also undesirable. Professor Whitney Benns contends that mediators are "... always implicated in the substantive outcome and impact — period." In an interview in the Dispute Resolution Magazine Vol 27, No.1, she stated:

> The way neutrality gets claimed, asserted, and held up as the gold standard has a lot to do with the maintenance of power. It is asserted as a poor substitute for trust and accountability by equating neutrality and fair process and then equating fair process with a fair outcome. It is an assertion of legitimacy drawing on legal values and a rhetorical fiction that is false in the case of the courts and the legal systems and also false in the space of ADR. I have

seen that "neutral" really means alignment with the norms of white spaces, cis-gendered spaces, straight spaces — if you are protecting those norms, you are protecting the status quo. That is not neutral. The status quo is protecting a power paradigm that is causing all types of harm.

See also Leah Wing & Janet Rifkin, *Racial Identity Development and the Mediation of Conflicts, in* New Perspectives on Racial Identity Development (Charmaine L. Wijeyesinghe & Bailey W. Jackson III, eds., New York University Press 2001) (raising challenges to the possibility of mediator impartiality). Does the definition of impartiality in the standards of conduct address such challenges sufficiently? Do you agree that a standard that requires a mediator to be impartial favors preserving the status quo, thereby putting individuals with low power at risk during mediation? *See* Chapter 7.

(3) Some scholars suggest that the duty of impartiality, while important, should not be considered absolute and must be balanced with other mediator ethical obligations, such as promoting party self-determination and conducting a mediation in a manner that preserves the public trust. Omer Shapira provides the following example and conclusion:

> ... [I]f you realize that Party A inclines to accept an offer of Party B while unaware of a legal right that has decisive effect on his case, you cannot proceed with the mediation as usual, justifying your action with your obligation of impartiality. You might not want to favor Party A, but "doing nothing" and proceeding with the mediation would in effect favor Party B. . . .
>
> Moreover, if you stay passive and allow uninformed Party A to enter a mediated agreement, you risk violation of some other ethical obligations you owe. First, your duty to respect each party's right to self-determination. . . . Party A cannot exercise self-determination if he lacks relevant information and is unaware of its existence. Being the one in charge of the mediation, if you become aware of Party A's state of ignorance, you have responsibility to intervene and act, notwithstanding your obligation of impartiality. . . .
>
> [T]here is a second reason supporting your duty to act: your obligation to the profession. From a reasonable bystander's point of view, by allowing Party A to enter a mediated agreement, you and the mediation profession have at least some responsibility for the agreement and its implications on Party A. Depending on the degree of harm caused to Party A, your conduct might jeopardize the standing of the profession and public trust in the profession, thereby triggering a duty to take some action.
>
> Your obligation of impartiality must, therefore, allow you some room to treat parties differently, otherwise you will not be able to mediate ethically and keep your other obligations. . . . You must exercise professional discretion and choose that intervention that would be limited to the minimum necessary for Party A to make a self-determined, informed decision

whether to accept or decline the offer, and that would not result in a loss of public trust in the profession and process of mediation.

Omer Shapira, Chapter 1 *What Do Mediators Need to Know to Mediate Ethically?*, Mediation Ethics: A Practitioner's Guide (American Bar Association, 2021)

(4) Failure to maintain impartiality is the most common grievance filed against mediators. Examples of grievances filed include: (a) the mediator did not allow one of the parties to present information the party believed critical to the mediation; and (b) during a mediation caucus, the mediator first learned that his law partners had a business relationship with one of the parties to the mediation, an architect, and the subject of the mediation was the alleged misrepresentation of the architect's credentials.

3. Mediator Competence

This requirement takes many different forms, including provisions that require a mediator to acquire and maintain professional competence or that require a mediator, in a particular case, to withdraw if the facts or circumstances of that mediation are beyond that mediator's competence.

a. Model Standards of Conduct for Mediators

Standard IV. Competence

A. A mediator shall mediate only when the mediator has the necessary competence to satisfy the reasonable expectations of the parties.

1. Any person may be selected as a mediator, provided that the parties are satisfied with the mediator's competence and qualifications. Training, experience in mediation, skills, cultural understandings and other qualities are often necessary for mediator competence. A person who offers to serve as a mediator creates the expectation that the person is competent to mediate effectively.

2. A mediator should attend educational programs and related activities to maintain and enhance the mediator's knowledge and skills related to mediation.

3. A mediator should have available for the parties' information relevant to the mediator's training, education, experience and approach to conducting a mediation.

B. If a mediator, during the course of a mediation determines that the mediator cannot conduct the mediation competently, the mediator shall discuss that determination with the parties as soon as is practicable and take appropriate steps to address the situation, including, but not limited to, withdrawing or requesting appropriate assistance.

C. If a mediator's ability to conduct a mediation is impaired by drugs, alcohol, medication or otherwise, the mediator shall not conduct the mediation.

b. Online Dispute Resolution Considerations

A. 1. When mediating using Information Communication Technology (ICT) tools, a mediator should have a requisite understanding of how to effectively use these tools. A mediator should participate in ongoing training to ensure a requisite knowledge of ICT tools is maintained.

2. Using a particular ICT tool during mediations creates the expectations that the mediator can properly convey to parties how these tools are used in addition to common benefits and risks in using these tools.

3. A mediator should be prepared to convey to parties the extent that they have an adequate understanding of how relevant ICT tools operate.

B. 1. A mediator who identifies that they do not have requisite knowledge of relevant ICT tools after a remote mediation has commenced should discuss this observation with parties as soon as practical. If this lack of knowledge makes continuing the mediation impractical, a mediator should develop remediating alternatives, either through different ICT tools or through in-person options.

c. Mediation Dilemmas for Discussion

1. Having completed your mediation class, you are eligible to add your name to the court's roster (or to become certified), which you do. Amazingly, you are contacted by a party requesting that you serve as a mediator. From what you learn by reviewing the parties' statements, the case involves complicated legal issues and neither party is represented by counsel. What are your ethical obligations?

2. You are an attorney who has served for many years as in-house counsel for a major corporation. You completed family mediation training a few years ago but have not actually conducted any mediations. Today, you are contacted by a divorcing couple to mediate the matters involved in the dissolution of their marriage. What are your ethical obligations?

3. You have conducted more than one hundred mediations in your career, having completed 20 in the past year alone. All of your mediations have been in-person. You are now hired to mediate a dispute where both parties have agreed to use an ODR platform called Immediation. You have never used this platform, and, after an hour exploring it, are still unsure how it works. What are your ethical obligations? What should you do?

4. You are hired to conduct a mediation involving a dissolution of marriage which you feel competent to handle. The parties to the mediation appear pro se and reach a full agreement only after the woman makes some significant concessions. Following the mediation, the woman retains counsel and files a grievance against you (the mediator) for failure to identify that the woman was intimidated during the mediation by her now ex-husband due to long

standing domestic violence issues. Pursuant to Standard IV, did you have an ethical obligation to screen participant capacity in advance of this mediation or to have special training or expertise in identifying domestic violence dynamics? Does a mediator's ethical duty in this situation differ if the woman were represented by counsel at the mediation?

Notes and Questions

(1) How does mediator competence relate to mediator style? Should there be a different standard of competence depending on the style or orientation of mediation offered by a mediator? For example, if one is an evaluative mediator, must they have some particular expertise or be licensed to practice law?

(2) If a mediator finds that they are not competent to proceed with a mediation, what are the mediator's ethical obligations with regard to fees?

(3) This standard only addresses a mediator's competence. See Section 5, Quality of Process, for discussion of a mediator's ethical responsibility regarding party competence.

4. Confidentiality

Confidentiality parameters can be established by legal rules or developed through contractual commitments. Thus, the mediator's ethical obligations typically focus on the mediator's duty to ensure that the parties are aware of the extent to which a mediation communication would be considered confidential and address the mediator's obligations governing their use or disclosure of such information when executing their mediating tasks.

a. Model Standards of Conduct for Mediators

Standard V. Confidentiality

A. A mediator shall maintain the confidentiality of all information obtained by the mediator in mediation, unless otherwise agreed to by the parties or required by applicable law.

1. If the parties to a mediation agree that the mediator may disclose information obtained during the mediation, the mediator may do so.

2. A mediator should not communicate to any non-participant information about how the parties acted in the mediation. A mediator may report, if required, whether parties appeared at a scheduled mediation and whether or not the parties reached a resolution.

3. If a mediator participates in teaching, research or evaluation of mediation, the mediator should protect the anonymity of the parties and abide by their reasonable expectations regarding confidentiality.

B. A mediator who meets with any persons in private session during a mediation shall not convey directly or indirectly to any other person, any information that was obtained during that private session without the consent of the disclosing person.

C. A mediator shall promote understanding among the parties of the extent to which the parties will maintain confidentiality of information they obtain in a mediation.

D. Depending on the circumstance of a mediation, the parties may have varying expectations regarding confidentiality that a mediator should address. The parties may make their own rules with respect to confidentiality, or the accepted practice of an individual mediator or institution may dictate a particular set of expectations.

b. Online Dispute Resolution Considerations

1. A mediator should take proactive steps to ensure data shared from parties are protected from unwanted third parties. A mediator should consider proactive tools such as encryption, email security, and firewalls in order to ensure a remote process has an equivalent level of confidentiality as an in-person process.

2. A mediator should work to ensure that unwanted third parties are unable to access remote proceedings. A mediator should consider taking privacy-enhancing initiatives, such as password protected log-in credentials and control over who enters the online platform.

3. At the start of synchronous remote proceedings, a mediator should receive the express affirmation from both parties that there are no unwanted third parties in the same physical room as either of the parties and that no unwanted third parties are able to hear online communications.

4. Before remote proceedings begin, a mediator should provide parties with the privacy policy of any and all ODR platforms used. A mediator should receive parties' express consent before continuing with remote proceedings.

c. Mediation Dilemmas for Discussion

1. A party files a complaint against their attorney alleging that the attorney failed to advise the party of their rights relative to the mediated settlement of the case. The client in a complaint to the bar association alleges that the attorney spent too much time reminiscing with the mediator about "old times." Does the filing of the attorney complaint with specific references to what was said in the mediation remove the mediator's obligation to keep confidential personal knowledge about the mediation which would vindicate the attorney? Can the mediator volunteer to testify on behalf of the attorney or must the mediator be compelled to do so?

2. In an Equal Employment Opportunity Commission (EEOC) mediation related to workplace discrimination, an employee joins a remote mediation from a Starbucks where they are seated next to several patrons. The employee

says that they can no longer afford Wi-Fi after being fired by the employer. What should the mediator do?

3. In a court-ordered foreclosure mediation, the borrower is unrepresented and the lender is represented by counsel who is physically at the mediation and by a representative "with full settlement authority" who is not physically present but is participating in the mediation by speaker phone. Before the mediator completes their opening statement, the representative of the lender who is on speaker phone announces that the telephone conversation is being recorded for "compliance purposes." Should the mediator continue? What if the borrower objects?

4. In the mediator's opening statement, they state that while everyone may take notes, at the conclusion of the mediation, the mediator will collect the notes and dispose of them. One party states that they intend to keep their notes. How should the mediator respond? Does it make a difference whether the mediation is being conducted in-person or remotely?

5. Imagine you are the mediator in the "Girls Gone Wild" case (*Pitts v. Francis*) excerpted in Chapter 6. In that case, the judge issued an order for the parties to try mediation to resolve their case that included a specific requirement that the parties try mediation and "participate in good faith." Imagine you are the mediator and following the mediation, the judge asks you to describe the participation level of each party. How should you respond?

6. During the course of a mediation, one party discloses to you in caucus that they are severely depressed over the lawsuit and are seriously contemplating suicide. They describe to you in detail their plans to end their life and you believe that the party intends to follow through with those plans. What are the competing ethical considerations? What should you do?

7. You are serving as a mentor for a new mediator by observing that person conduct a mediation. During a caucus, a party shares sensitive information with the mediators, indicating that they do not authorize the information to be shared with anyone. When meeting with the other side, the mediator trainee discloses this information and asks the party not to let the other party know that they know this information. What are your ethical obligations?

8. If there is an applicable confidentiality statute in the jurisdiction in which the mediator is conducting their case and the mediator violates that statutory provision, is that act, by definition, also a breach of the mediator's ethical duty?

5. Quality of Process

Standards relating to quality of process include such matters as delivering appropriate opening statements, knowing when to terminate or postpone a mediation, mediating only when the mediator has sufficient time to commit to the mediation, and promoting honesty and candor between and among all participants. The analysis below divides these elements into four categories, with dilemmas, notes and comments for each category.

a. Timeliness

i. Model Standards of Conduct for Mediators

Standard VI. Quality of the Process

A. A mediator shall conduct a mediation in accordance with these Standards and in a manner that promotes diligence, timeliness, safety, presence of the appropriate participants, party participation, procedural fairness, party competency and mutual respect among all participants.

    1. A mediator should agree to mediate only when the mediator is prepared to commit the attention essential to an effective mediation.

    2. A mediator should only accept cases when the mediator can satisfy the reasonable expectation of the parties concerning the timing of a mediation.

ii. Mediation Dilemmas for Discussion

1. The day before a scheduled mediation, the mediator's 84-year-old mother falls and breaks her hip and wrist and has emergency surgery. The mediator is the primary caregiver and patient advocate for their mother. The mediation has been scheduled for several weeks, and the court hearing date for the parties is shortly after the scheduled mediation. Both parties are represented by counsel. The mediator believes that they can devote approximately three hours for mediation before going to see their mother. What ethical constraints and responsibilities does the mediator have? What should the mediator do?

2. You are a very popular mediator and your calendar fills quickly. You are contacted by an attorney to schedule a full day mediation. Your first available date is one month away but you are only available for a half day; in your mediation experience, a certain number of cases settle prior to the scheduled mediation so you are confident that you will be able to provide the full day for mediation. May you ethically accept the case?

Notes and Questions

The Florida Rules for Certified and Court-Appointed Mediators include the following provisions: "A mediator shall schedule a mediation in a manner that provides adequate time for the parties to fully exercise their right of self-determination" (Rule 10.430) and "A mediator shall . . . (2) adjourn or terminate any mediation which, if continued, would result in unreasonable emotional or monetary costs to the parties; (3) adjourn or terminate the mediation if the mediator believes the case is unsuitable for mediation or any party is unable or unwilling to participate meaningfully in the process." (Rule 10.420(b)). What are the challenges for a mediator in adhering to these provisions?

b. Participation and Candor

i. Model Standards of Conduct for Mediators

Standard VI. Quality of the Process

3. The presence or absence of persons at a mediation depends on the agreement of the parties and the mediator. The parties and mediator may agree that others may be excluded from particular sessions or from all sessions.

4. A mediator should promote honesty and candor between and among all participants, and a mediator shall not knowingly misrepresent any material fact or circumstance in the course of a mediation.

ii. Online Dispute Resolution Considerations

When parties opt for a remote mediation, a mediator should notify parties of any technological requirements and receive confirmation that parties have reliable access to the internet.

iii. Mediation Dilemmas for Discussion

1. An unrepresented party asks to have a friend join them in the mediation. May the mediator deny this request? . . . even if the other side does not object? What if the other side objects?

2. Party A is involved in a landlord-tenant mediation and joins a remote mediation session with their four-year-old on their lap. The child is crying loudly and asking their parent questions. When the mediator asks Party A if everything is okay, Party A says that their babysitter canceled the day before, but that they would like to continue the mediation. What should the mediator do?

3. In a mediation of a dissolution of a business partnership, the mediator learns in caucus with one party that that individual has been cheating the business by funneling money to an offshore bank account that the other partners know nothing about. The mediator does not have permission to share this information. What should the mediator do?

4. Before beginning a court-ordered mediation, one of the parties announces that they have no intention of participating in the mediation and requests that the mediator report an impasse to the court. What are the mediator's ethical obligations?

Notes and Questions

(1) The Model Standards of Practice for Family and Divorce Mediation Standard III states that before family mediation begins, a mediator

> . . . should provide the participants with an overview of the process and its purposes, including: . . . informing the participants that the presence or absence of other persons at a mediation, including attorneys, counselors or

advocates, depends on the agreement of the participants and the mediator, unless a statute or regulation otherwise requires or the mediator believes that the presence of another person is required or may be beneficial because of a history or threat of violence or other serious coercive activity by a participant.

How would a mediator implement this ethical obligation if there was no statute or regulation in place, but the mediator believed that the participation of a support person for one of the parties was necessary? What if that party wanted to go forward without the support person?

(2) According to the Reporter's Notes to the Model Standards (Appendix B), Standard VI(A)(4) was intended to reflect "the nuanced environment in which mediation occurs" by prohibiting a mediator from knowingly misrepresenting a material fact or circumstance to a mediation participant while acknowledging that resolving matters in mediation is not always predicated on there having been complete honesty and candor among those present. Is this balance consistent with or supported by other Standards?

(3) How, if at all, does an attorney's ethical obligations regarding truthfulness in negotiations support or undermine the mediator's ethical obligation set forth in Standard VI(A)(4)?

(4) Note that the language of the standard is "promote" rather than "ensure" honesty and candor. In what ways does a mediator "promote honesty and candor between and among all participants"? Does it matter if one or more of the parties are unrepresented?

c. Advice, Opinions, Information

i. Model Standards of Conduct for Mediators

Standard VI. Quality of the Process

5. The role of a mediator differs substantially from other professional roles. Mixing the role of a mediator and the role of another profession is problematic and thus, a mediator should distinguish between the roles. A mediator may provide information that the mediator is qualified by training or experience to provide, only if the mediator can do so consistent with these Standards.

6. A mediator shall not conduct a dispute resolution procedure other than mediation but label it mediation in an effort to gain the protection of rules, statutes, or other governing authorities pertaining to mediation.

7. A mediator may recommend, when appropriate, that parties consider resolving their dispute through arbitration, counseling, neutral evaluation or other processes.

8. A mediator shall not undertake an additional dispute resolution role in the same matter without the consent of the parties. Before providing such service, a mediator shall inform the parties of the implications of the change in process and obtain their consent to the change. A mediator who undertakes such role assumes different duties and responsibilities that may be governed by other standards.

ii. Mediation Dilemmas for Discussion

1. If the mediator concludes that the parties are at impasse, may the mediator, consistent with these standards, propose the following: if both sides are willing, each will privately reveal to the mediator their "bottom line." With this information, the mediator will determine if the bottom-line numbers overlap; if they do, the mediator will split the difference and inform the parties of the number and the case will settle at that number. If the numbers are close but do not overlap, the mediator will tell the parties "you are close and I suggest that we continue to mediate." If the mediator determines that the parties are "too far apart," the mediator will inform them that they are at impasse. Would you have a different response if the request came from a single party or their attorney or by all parties to the dispute?

2. An authorized agent for a financing company brings an action in small claims court against a party, alleging failure to make monthly payments pursuant to a legally executed contract and note. Both the contract and the note are standard documents used by the consumer lending company. The claim is for $1,250. At a pre-trial court session, the defendant admits to owing the money. The judge asks the defendant if there is a reason why she should not award a judgment to the plaintiff. The defendant states that she would like to work out a payment schedule, so the judge orders a session of mediation. At the mediation session, the mediator scans the agreements and notices a provision that obligates the defendant to pay interest at the rate of 29.5% per year if the payments are in arrears. In the mediation conversation, the mediator learns that the company representative had told the defendant in the hallway before the court session that the defendant should avoid a judgment because it would hurt their credit. The mediator is not an attorney but knows that interest on judgments accrues at the rate of 8% per year. With this context, the defendant proposes a payment schedule of $110 per month until the entire debt, including interest charges, is paid; the plaintiff quickly accepts the offer and requests that the agreement be written to reflect the contractual interest rate of 29.5% per year. Would it be permissible for the mediator to ask the defendant, "Are you aware that if a judgment were entered against you, the interest would be reduced from 29.5% to 8%?" Does your answer depend on whether the mediator is an attorney?

3. After mediating for a significant period of time, the parties are showing fatigue and frustration that they have been unable to arrive at a settlement. They turn to the mediator and request that the mediator render a decision that resolves each of the contested issues. Can the mediator do so ethically? Does it depend on whether your "decision" will be binding on the parties or just advisory? What if only one party makes the request?

Notes and Questions

(1) The Reporter's Notes to the Model Standards (*see* Appendix B) suggest that the language of Standard VI(A)(5) "recognizes the differing roles that a mediator as an individual assumes in his or her life and then supports the mediator sharing information that he or she is qualified by training or experience to provide only if it is done in a manner consistent with other Standards, most notably promoting party self-determination and sustaining mediator impartiality." As a practical matter, how does a mediator share information, which presumably favors one side, while "sustaining mediator impartiality"?

(2) Dilemma 2, *supra*, (regarding the finance company in mediation) is based on a request for an ethical opinion in Florida. The Mediator Ethics Advisory Committee (MEAC) responded:

> It is improper for a mediator to provide legal advice by any method within the scope of a mediation, whether such advice be by statement, question or any other form of communication. The mediator, while fulfilling the role of reality tester, must be aware of, and consciously avoid, crossing the line between partiality and impartiality, neutrality and non-neutrality. The mediator may, however, often obtain the desired information if the question is framed more generally. It appears to the panel that the mediator wishes to be certain that the party is aware of the alternatives available for satisfaction of the debt-fulfillment of the contracted payments or payment through a judgment. It is the opinion of the panel that the mediator can obtain that information by asking the following: "Is interest levied on a judgment? Does either of you know?" These two questions set the stage for the parties to provide information to the mediator and to each other without placing the mediator in the position of providing that information. In so doing, the mediator assists in maximizing the exploration of alternatives, and adheres to the principles of fairness, full disclosure, self-determination, and the needs and interests of the participants while honoring the commitment to all parties to move toward an agreement.

Professor Jeffrey W. Stempel took issue with this MEAC opinion in *Beyond Formalism and False Dichotomies: The Need for Institutionalizing a Flexible Concept of the Mediator's Role*, 24 Fla. St. U. L. Rev. 949 (1997). Specifically, he stated:

> Although the issues of interpreting the law and the Rules are reasonably close, I believe the [Committee] opinion was in error and took an excessively restrictive view of mediator discretion under Florida law. The [rule] prohibits a mediator's giving of "legal advice," an admittedly malleable term, but hardly one that requires the expansive definition placed upon it by the [Committee]. As a law professor, like most lawyers, I am frequently asked about legal problems by students and friends. Although I have yet to agree to represent any of them (and could not do so in Florida without obtaining

pro hac vice admission because I am a member of the Minnesota bar), I feel compelled as a teacher or friend to at least alert them to the apparent legal issues and to inform them of sources of information, potential counsel, and so on. Am I practicing law? Not at all (although some older vintage lawyers might assert it). Am I giving legal advice? Only in the broadest sense.

Do you agree with Professor Stempel? How does this relate to prohibitions against the Unauthorized Practice of Law (see Section D, *infra*)?

(3) Do these standards suggest that one style of mediation is preferable? Can one mediate in an evaluative manner and still adhere to the ethical guidelines?

(4) Should an attorney-mediator be accountable for the outcome? Professor Judith Maute argues:

> [W]hen mediated settlement supplants public adjudication, the mediator is accountable for procedurally fair process and minimally fair substantive outcome. Procedural intervention to insure access to relevant information and independent advice is consistent with neutrality.... As to substantive fairness, the probable litigated outcome should serve as a reference point; the parties are free to find a solution that better serves their personal values and concerns. The mediator, however, should refuse to finalize an agreement when one party takes undue advantage of the other, when the agreement is so unfair that it would be a miscarriage of justice, or when the mediator believes it would not receive court approval. Completed agreements failing this standard should be vulnerable to rescission for a limited period of time on request of a party or during public review. If rescission is not possible, the disadvantaged party should have recourse against a mediator for malpractice.

Judith Maute, *Public Values and Private Justice: A Case for Mediator Accountability*, 4 Geo. J. Legal Ethics 503 (1991). How does Maute's position compare to the Susskind/Stulberg debate that you read in Chapter 4? You should consider these mediator ethical standards when reviewing Section (D)(1) Is Mediation the Practice of Law?, later in this chapter.

(5) In a survey conducted by the ABA Section of Dispute Resolution, 96% of mediation users (mostly lawyers) surveyed rated "making suggestions" as important, very important or essential characteristics of a mediator. In that same survey, 50% of the parties thought that mediator comments such as "I think this is the best offer you're going to get" were inappropriate and 73% objected to mediators "telling them what to do." *The ABA Section of Dispute Resolution Task Force on Improving the Quality of Mediation Final Report*. Sharon Press recommended caution for mediators who choose to provide "mediator proposals" in order that they do so consistent with the ethical standards for mediators — namely, competence for providing a proposal, honoring party self-determination, maintaining confidence

of caucus information, and ensuring mediator impartiality, quality of process, and integrity. Specific guidance includes:

- Only [provide a mediator proposal] upon request of "sophisticated" parties. . . .

- Before offering a proposal, a mediator should be sure that [they] possess the knowledge and expertise to provide an appropriate proposal and that doing so is not considered to be . . . in violation of Unauthorized Practice of Law provisions.

- . . . [M]ediators should only entertain [providing] mediator proposals "late in the process" or as an 'end game.' . . . Mediators also need to be careful about providing the option of a mediator proposal after mediation fatigue has set in . . . and parties should be given a reasonable period of time for determining its acceptability and delivering their confidential response to the mediator.

- . . . The final phase of ethically providing a mediator proposal is to be clear with the parties as to the procedure for accepting or rejecting a proposal and protecting the confidentiality of the responses.

Sharon Press, Chapter 7 *Making Proposals, in* Mediator Ethics (Omer Shapira ed., 2021).

The Maryland Court system found that when a mediator offered "opinions and solutions" in mediation, parties are less likely to report, six months after the conclusion of a matter, "that the outcome was working, they were satisfied with the outcome, they would recommend ADR" and that participants "changed their approach to conflict." https://www.mdcourts.gov/sites/default/files/import/courtoperations /pdfs/districtcourtstrategiesfullreport.pdf, at 7; *see* Chapter 9.

d. Adjournment or Termination

i. Model Standards of Conduct

Standard VI. Quality of the Process

9. If a mediation is being used to further criminal conduct, a mediator should take appropriate steps including, if necessary, postponing, withdrawing from or terminating the mediation.

10. A. If a party appears to have difficulty comprehending the process, issues, or settlement options, or difficulty participating in a mediation, the mediator should explore the circumstances and potential accommodations, modifications or adjustments that would make possible the party's capacity to comprehend, participate and exercise self-determination.

B. If a mediator is made aware of domestic abuse or violence among the parties, the mediator shall take appropriate steps including, if necessary, postponing, withdrawing from or terminating the mediation.

C. If a mediator believes that participant conduct, including that of the mediator, jeopardizes conducting a mediation consistent with these Standards, a mediator shall take appropriate steps including, if necessary, postponing, withdrawing from or terminating the mediation.

ii. Mediation Dilemmas for Discussion

1. What is the mediator's ethical obligation if all the parties want to continue with the mediation, but the mediator is concerned with regard to one party's capacity to participate for any of the reasons detailed above? If the mediator decides to terminate a mediation, as a practical matter, how should they do it?

2. You are the mediator for a community mediation. The dispute is between two neighbors; the Complainant alleges that members of Respondent's family damaged the roof on the Complainant's home. One proposed settlement option they identify is for the Respondent to perform the required repair work; this would result in considerable financial savings for the Complainant because the Respondent is not a licensed contractor. Do you have any ethical obligations to intervene?

3. Party A, a former employee of Party B, files a claim seeking severance pay; the matter is referred to mediation. During the course of the discussion, Party B offers a cash settlement that is "off the books" so that various federal, state, and city taxes will not have to be paid. Party A immediately accepts the offer and they both ask that you, the mediator, assist them in drafting the agreement for their signature. Assuming that neither party is represented by counsel, how should you respond? Does it matter if you are a licensed lawyer?

4. As you escort the parties to the room for mediation, the attorney for Party A informs you that their client will not sit in the same room as Party B and requests that the mediation be conducted exclusively by means of caucus. Party B adamantly rejects that proposed approach, asserting that they will not participate unless they get to "confront the lies" that Party A is spreading. What are your ethical obligations? How should you respond? Does it depend on whether Party B is represented by an attorney at the mediation?

5. You are the mediator who has been hired for this case. When you greet the parties and their attorneys, you detect a strong odor of alcohol which you believe is emanating from one of the parties. What should you do? What if the parties are unrepresented? What if you are fairly certain it is not the party but their attorney from whom the alcoholic odor emanates? What if you did not detect anything at the start of the mediation, but as the mediation has continued, you come to believe that one of the parties appears to be under the influence of drugs or alcohol and does not appear to be tracking the conversation. What should you do? Would your response differ if the party was unrepresented?

Notes and Questions

(1) The Reporter's Notes to the Model Standards (Appendix B) explain that there were public comments that suggested that the mediator's duty in situations where mediation is "being used to further criminal conduct" should be to affirmatively report such conduct to appropriate legal authorities.

> The Joint Committee rejected that suggestion for two reasons. First, the subtlety of such matters — including there being multi-issue cases in which only one issue raised a specter of criminal conduct — requires that a mediator be firm but flexible in addressing such a situation; second, confidentiality laws or agreements may prevent it, such that unless there were an exception in the confidentiality agreement for this situation or a mediator had a duty to report such conduct, a mediator might expose himself or herself to liability by reporting such conduct.

Do you believe that the standard was appropriately crafted? Does an attorney who is an officer of the court have a higher duty?

(2) Guardianship cases are sometimes mediated. If the presenting issue in the case is the capacity of one of the parents or responsible parties, can mediation be ethically offered? If so, how?

(3) One in five Americans will experience a mental illness or mental health issue in a given year. That equates to tens of millions of people. Mediators, then, are likely to confront situations in which they are challenged to decide what their obligations are in such circumstances. In *Mental Health and Mediation*, Dispute Resolution Magazine, Vol. 28, p. 32, Nikki Knisley and Sharon Press raise questions as to how to understand Standard XI.10.A. in the following situation:

> [In a] court-ordered mediation, [t]he parties and their counsel are present and anxious to speak.... [T]hey have not provided any premediation information.... [T]he first hour is spent unravelling the complexities of plaintiff's completed work tasks, which were never documented by the employer ... [and then] plaintiff's counsel [announces] that [their] client has a traumatic brain injury (TBI), and cannot remember signing documents ten minutes after doing so. Counsel assures [the mediator that the] plaintiff is more than capable of managing [their] own affairs and can proceed with the case.

> Questions include: is the mediator obligated to inquire further about the plaintiff's condition? Is the plaintiff or their counsel required to answer such questions, and if so, to what extent? If plaintiff's counsel indicates that there are no concerns, is it appropriate for the mediator to rely on that assurance? What if the mediator feels otherwise? What constitutes an appropriate accommodation, modification, or adjustment? Should the modification suggestion come from the mediator, the party, or the party's counsel? ... Does a mediator have a different obligation if the party is

pro se, as opposed to represented by counsel or accompanied by another representative?

Dan Berstein, cofounder of Dispute Resolution in Mental Health Initiative, cautions mediators from becoming "inadvertent perpetrators of discrimination" by, for example, asking inappropriate questions. Instead of asking questions related to the nature or severity of a person's disability, mediators should "offer accommodations to all parties . . . ." Mediators should not "screen out cases based on a party's identity characteristics." Instead, "look for a party's difficulty with comprehension, reasoning, appreciating consequences, or expressing a choice. . . ." Instead of treating people in different, unrequested ways, "focus on presenting process options to the parties, in furtherance of their own self-determination." Dan Berstein, *Preventing Unintentional Discrimination in Dispute Resolution*, Dispute Resolution Magazine, Vol 29, No. 1, 30.

(4) The Model Standards of Practice for Family and Divorce Mediation contain standards specifically devoted to situations involving child abuse and neglect (Standard IX) and domestic abuse (Standard X). Standard X(D) states that "the mediator shall consider taking measures to insure the safety of participants and the mediator." Does "shall consider" provide sufficient guidance to a mediator? Should a similar provision be included in the Model Standards of Conduct for Mediators?

6. Advertising/Solicitation

In general, mediators are not restricted from advertising. They must, however, ensure that their advertising is truthful and not misleading. Given the confusing status regarding certification, qualification and licensure of mediators, the requirement to represent one's qualifications accurately can pose subtle, but significant challenges.

a. Model Standards of Conduct for Mediators

Standard VII. Advertising and Solicitation

A. A mediator shall be truthful and not misleading when advertising, soliciting or otherwise communicating the mediator's qualifications, experience, services and fees.

   1. A mediator should not include any promises as to outcome in communications, including business cards, stationery, or computer-based communications.

   2. A mediator should only claim to meet the mediator qualifications of a governmental entity or private organization if that entity or organization has a recognized procedure for qualifying mediators and it grants such status to the mediator.

B. A mediator shall not solicit in a manner that gives an appearance of partiality for or against a party or otherwise undermines the integrity of the process.

C. A mediator shall not communicate to others, in promotional materials or through other forms of communication, the names of persons served without their permission.

b. Mediation Dilemmas for Discussion

1. Is the following advertisement ethically permissible: *Want Your Case Settled? Hire Larry Settle, Certified Mediator — 95% settlement rate.* What if there was no mediator certification scheme in the locale in which the advertisement ran?

2. May a mediator describe mediation as "a dispassionate evaluation by a neutral third party"?

Notes and Questions

(1) In 2010, the Florida Supreme Court revised the mediator standard of conduct relating to advertising. The basic provision is: "A mediator shall not engage in any marketing practice, including advertising, which contains false or misleading information." In addition to re-titling the standard from "Advertising" to "Marketing Practices," the court added the following provisions:

(c) Other Certifications. Any marketing publication that generally refers to a mediator being "certified" is misleading unless the advertising mediator has successfully completed an established process for certifying mediators that involves actual instruction rather than the mere payment of a fee. Use of the term "certified" in advertising is also misleading unless the mediator identifies the entity issuing the referenced certification and the area or field of certification earned, if applicable.

(d) Prior Adjudicative Experience. Any marketing practice is misleading if the mediator states or implies that prior adjudicative experience, including, but not limited to, service as a judge, magistrate, or administrative hearing officer, makes one a better or more qualified mediator.

. . .

(f) Additional Prohibited Marketing Practices. A mediator shall not engage in any marketing practice that diminishes the importance of a party's right to self-determination or the impartiality of the mediator, or that demeans the dignity of the mediation process or the judicial system.

Commentary

2010 Revision. . . . The roles of a mediator and an adjudicator are fundamentally distinct. The integrity of the judicial system may be impugned when the prestige of the judicial office is used for commercial purposes. When engaging in any mediation marketing practice, a former adjudicative officer should not lend the prestige of the judicial office to advance private interests in a manner inconsistent with this rule. For example, the depiction of a mediator in judicial robes or use of the word "judge" with or without modifiers to the mediator's name would be inappropriate. However, an accurate representation of the mediator's judicial experience would not be inappropriate.

7. Fees and Expenses

Most standards contain provisions regarding fees that a mediator may charge for services. Minimally, they require that a mediator disclose the basis of fees to be charged.

a. Model Standards of Conduct

Standard VIII. Fees And Other Charges

A. A mediator shall provide each party or each party's representative true and complete information about mediation fees, expenses and any other actual or potential charges that may be incurred in connection with a mediation.

    1. If a mediator charges fees, the mediator should develop them in light of all relevant factors, including the type and complexity of the matter, the qualifications of the mediator, the time required and the rates customary for such mediation services.

    2. A mediator's fee arrangement should be in writing unless the parties request otherwise.

B. A mediator shall not charge fees in a manner that impairs a mediator's impartiality.

    1. A mediator should not enter into a fee agreement which is contingent upon the result of the mediation or amount of the settlement.

    2. While a mediator may accept unequal fee payments from the parties, a mediator should not use fee arrangements that adversely impact the mediator's ability to conduct a mediation in an impartial manner.

b. Mediation Dilemmas for Discussion

1. Presume that there is a highly publicized dispute in a community. The parties have not been willing to pay for a mediator because they do not think "more talking" will help to resolve it. Can a mediator encourage the parties to use mediation by offering to mediate pro bono?

2. A large employer has found using mediation to be useful and cost-effective in handling employment disputes. In order to encourage employees to use mediation rather than pursue litigation, the employer offers to pay the costs for these mediations. May a mediator ethically work under such an arrangement?

3. An insurance company maintains a short list of two or three mediators whom it will agree to utilize if a case in which it is a party is referred to mediation. As a result of the volume of work this insurance company generates, these mediators earn most of their annual income from mediating cases involving this one insurance company. If the plaintiff/plaintiff's counsel agrees to the mediator, does this arrangement raise any concerns about the mediator's impartiality as required by Standard VIII(B)?

4. The mediation unexpectedly extends through the dinner hour. In order to maintain momentum, the mediator orders food for the participants and the attorneys to be delivered to the mediation office. If the mediator's initial fee statement did not include any information about meals, must the mediator cover the costs?

5. Your normal fee for mediation is $250/hour. You are contacted by a large company to handle a mediation. You know that it would be no problem for the company to pay a mediator's fee of $500/hour or more. Is it ethically permissible for you to charge more for the large company case?

Notes and Questions

The propriety of the use of contingency fees in mediation received spirited attention and public discussion during the 2003-05 revision process of the Model Standards. Some argued that any contingent fee puts the mediator in the position of having a vested interest in the outcome of the mediation, and therefore permitting it compromises a mediator's impartiality. Others suggested that mediators should be entitled to a "success fee" or a "bonus" — especially in very large cases in which all of the parties are represented by counsel and are very sophisticated. For a more detailed discussion of contingency fees in the context of mediation, see Scott Peppet, *Contractarian Economics and Mediation Ethics: The Case for Customizing Neutrality Through Contingency Fee Mediation*, 82 Tex. L. Rev. 227, 239 (2003). Proponents of such arrangements contend that the mediator should be working for a settlement, so there is no conflict regarding a mediator's impartiality — such an arrangement simply enables the mediator to share in the value created by a settlement. Do you believe mediators should be restricted from all contingent fee arrangements?

8. Obligations to the Profession

Many standards include aspirational provisions, in addition to ethical duties that resolve particular practice dilemmas. These provisions encourage a mediator to help to mentor/train less experienced mediators, support research, foster diversity within the field, and strive to make mediation accessible to all.

a. Model Standards of Conduct

Standard IX. Advancement of Mediation Practice

A. A mediator should act in a manner that advances the practice of mediation. A mediator promotes this Standard by engaging in some or all of the following:

1. Fostering diversity within the field of mediation.

2. Striving to make mediation accessible to those who elect to use it, including providing services at a reduced rate or on a pro bono basis as appropriate.

3. Participating in research when given the opportunity, including obtaining participant feedback when appropriate.

4. Participating in outreach and education efforts to assist the public in developing an improved understanding of, and appreciation for, mediation.

5. Assisting newer mediators through training, mentoring and networking.

B. A mediator should demonstrate respect for differing points of view within the field, seek to learn from other mediators and work together with other mediators to improve the profession and better serve people in conflict.

Notes and Questions

(1) What is the relationship of standards of conduct to "best practices"?

(2) If a mediator never provides pro bono mediation services or assists new mediators as a mentor, should that mediator be subject to sanctions, such as removal from the court's roster of mediators? Does it matter if the mediator has never been asked to do so? Should the mediator only be subject to sanctions if someone files a complaint?

C. Enforcement of Ethical Standards

If standards of conduct govern mediator behavior, how are they enforced? In the following excerpt, Professor Michael Moffitt reviews the most common ways a mediator can be susceptible to a civil suit for malpractice, a disciplinary action for misconduct, a criminal proceeding, or a sanction by a professional association. As you read this excerpt, consider whether the standards of conduct referenced above, as written, would enable a harmed party to successfully sustain a misconduct or malpractice claim against a mediator.

Ten Ways to Get Sued: A Guide for Mediators
8 Harv. Negot. L. Rev. 81, 81–86, 89–90, 92–98, 102–05, 107–31 (2003)*
By Michael Moffitt

Mediators have practiced for decades without significant exposure to legal actions stemming from their mediation conduct. Despite the thousands, if not millions, of disputants who have received mediation services, instances of legal complaints against mediators are extraordinarily rare. Several factors likely contribute to the historical lack of litigation against mediators. Many parties are happy with mediators' services, making lawsuits irrelevant. In some practice contexts, mediators enjoy qualified or quasi-judicial immunity from lawsuits. Confidentiality protections and privileges often prevent public and, sometimes, even private examination of mediators' behaviors. Mediators and former mediation parties may also be inclined to

---

* Copyright © 2003. All rights reserved. Reprinted with permission.

settle post-mediation disputes out of court. Perhaps most significantly, the legal requirements of likely causes of action present considerable obstacles to any plaintiff seeking to recover from a former mediator.

. . .

Mediators confronted with complaints regarding their mediation services face sanctions from four basic sources. First, some mediator misconduct may create personal, civil liability under which the mediator would owe compensation to the complaining party for injuries caused by mediator misconduct. Most of the examples outlined in this article create at least a risk of private civil lawsuits alleging either contractual or tort-based liability. Second, certain mediator misconduct may constitute criminal behavior, subjecting the mediator to sanctions ranging from fines to imprisonment. Only a few of the behaviors listed below rise even to the level of criminal misdemeanors.

Third, mediators operating within formal referral programs risk exposure to the complaint mechanisms of the programs in which they serve. Not all mediators operate within the structure of a formal program. However, mediators who operate within referral structures such as court-annexed programs or community programs are almost always subject to a set of standards of conduct. In many circumstances, mediators operating in affiliation with a court-sponsored or court-annexed mediation program do not face civil liability because they will qualify for either quasi-judicial or qualified immunity. A mediator who fails to uphold the standards of most referral programs risks sanctions that could range from reprimands to disqualification from future service in the program to the imposition of the costs of the proceeding in which the misconduct took place.

Fourth, many mediators maintain membership in voluntary associations, most of which require their members to uphold certain principles or standards of conduct. A party complaining of mediator misconduct can seek sanctions within the voluntary association by demonstrating a violation of those standards. Many voluntary organizations have developed complaint or grievance procedures. A mediator who violates the terms of an organization's standards of conduct risks sanctions ranging from required apologies and additional training to suspension or revocation of membership. Some voluntary associations may even publish the names of mediators found to have engaged in improper behavior. In most circumstances, violations of voluntary association standards of conduct would not directly create the basis for legal action. If, however, the mediator's contract made reference to membership in the voluntary association, then the terms of the association's standards of conduct may be implied into the agreement to mediate, possibly creating a basis for legal action.

Technically, perhaps, the term "getting sued" applies only to sanctions creating personal civil liability through a contract or tort-based claim. Nevertheless, actions within each of these four categories may be significant to a mediator seeking to avoid sanction for misconduct.

I. Fail to Disclose a Conflict of Interest

Melissa Mediator is a member of a small consulting firm specializing in corporate dispute resolution. One of the firm's clients is a large, multi-national conglomerate. Unlike most of her colleagues, Melissa has never done work for the conglomerate. A dispute arises between one of the subsidiaries of the conglomerate and a local business. Melissa agrees to mediate the dispute and discloses nothing about the relationship between the conglomerate and her firm.

A mediator who holds an interest in opposition to one or more of the parties, and who fails to disclose that interest to the parties, opens the door to the prospect of legal action. . . .

Beyond the prospect of programmatic or organizational sanctions, a mediator faces the possibility of civil liability if he or she fails to disclose a conflict of interest. In some circumstances, failure to disclose a potential conflict of interest could amount to a breach of an express contractual term. . . .

Even in contracts lacking such express promises, impartiality may be implied as a term of the mediation contract. . . . No court has yet implied impartiality into a mediation contract, but the legal foundations of implied impartiality are sufficient to make such a ruling a genuine possibility. Mediators, therefore, may not necessarily avoid all potential legal consequences of conflicting interests merely by remaining contractually silent on the question.

A mediator faces significant liability for failure to disclose a conflict of interest only if the mediator's bias led him or her to take actions that resulted in injury to a mediation party. . . .

A mediator's obligations regarding conflicts of interest are not extinguished by initial disclosures. . . .

Perhaps even more significantly, a mediator's duty to avoid acquiring interests in conflict with parties may extend beyond the life of the mediation. For example, in *Poly Software International v. Su*,[34] a lawyer-mediator conducted a mediation involving a dispute between a corporation and two former employees. Following the mediation, a dispute arose between the former employees, one of whom sought to retain the mediator as legal counsel. Citing Utah's Rules of Professional Conduct, the court disqualified the mediator from representing one former mediation party against another former mediation party in the new lawsuit. The court drew on language in Model Rule 1.9 in concluding that the ban against subsequent adverse representations in a "substantially related matter" applied to this case because of the "confidential relationship" between mediators and mediation parties. Many voluntary associational standards of conduct have codified this result with provisions that require mediators to guard against subsequent professional relationships that may give rise to the appearance of partiality. No theory bars, in perpetuity, a mediator

---

34. 880 F. Supp. 1487 (D. Utah 1995)

from acquiring any interests in conflict with a former mediation party. Nevertheless, a mediator's obligation to avoid conflicts of interests does not extinguish at the moment when a mediation concludes.

II. Breach a Specific Contractual Promise Regarding Structure or Outcome

Marijke Mediator has the disputants sign her standard Agreement to Mediate. The agreement says, "In addition to talking together as a group, each party will have a chance to meet with the mediator privately." Marijke's standard agreement also states, "At the conclusion of the mediation, the mediator will assist the parties in writing up the terms of an agreement." The parties sign the agreement, and Marijke conducts the mediation. After several hours of joint session discussions, Marijke concludes that the mediation is unlikely to produce a useful result and terminates the mediation. . . .

One relatively common set of contractual promises that create exposure to liability involves pre-commitments regarding the mediation structure . . . For example, in the hypothetical contract described at the outset of this section, Marijke promises to meet with each of the parties separately . . . . [A] party might complain that Marijke failed to implement a specifically described step in the process and in so doing breached the mediation contract. Damages in such a claim would be difficult to establish, given the parties' voluntary participation in the mediation and the extraordinary degree of speculation required to determine what would have occurred if the mediator had undertaken the step in question. However, a mediator who describes a mediation process with specificity and then fails to implement that process risks civil liability for breach of contract.

A second potential risk in the structure of some mediation agreements comes from express, or even implied, promises of particular outcomes . . . . As a general matter, a mediator is at no liability risk merely because he or she presides over a mediation that produces no settlement. If, however, a mediator promises a particular result, he or she risks civil liability if the mediation fails to produce that outcome. . . .

Similarly, liability may result from contractual guarantees about the nature of any settlement . . . . [A] mediator is responsible only to assure that the parties' participation in the mediation is voluntary, and that any outcome is the product of an autonomous and informed decision. However, a mediator who contractually undertakes to assure the equity or efficiency of mediated settlement terms disrupts that baseline assumption in a way that may create subsequent liability. A mediator who promises to help the parties to reach, for example, a "fair outcome," risks a subsequent allegation that he or she failed to assure that a particular outcome was substantively and distributively fair.

III. Engage in the Practice of Law

After considerable efforts to facilitate an agreement, and at the request of the disputants, Marjorie Mediator examines the evidence each side has compiled and develops her best assessment of a court's likely disposition of the case. The parties then quickly agree to basic settlement terms. Again at the parties' request, Marjorie drafts a formal contract to capture the terms of the parties' agreement . . . .

In some states, a mediator who predicts the outcome of a disputed legal issue engages in the practice of law. . . . The practice of law is often defined as including drafting settlement documents whose terms go beyond those specified by the disputants. A mediator who advances one settlement option as more favorable than another may also be engaging in the practice of law. However, as the North Carolina Bar has admitted in their treatment of the topic, "there are no bright lines" in defining the practice of law.

IV. Engage in the Practice of Law Badly

Mortimer Mediator facilitates an agreement between disputing former business partners. The agreement includes a voluntary dismissal of certain pieces of litigation, a new licensing agreement on the partnership's intellectual property, and a division of the partnership's assets. Based on Mortimer's advice about a "tax smart" way to craft the deal, the parties agree to a novel agreement structure proposed and drafted by Mortimer. Later, a dispute arises over the interpretation of a poorly drafted clause in the agreement, and both parties find themselves stuck with substantial tax burdens that could have been avoided with a more standard agreement.

A mediator who negligently engages in the practice of law faces not only the kinds of complaints described in the section immediately above, but also the prospect of a professional negligence or legal malpractice suit. . . . The threat of legal malpractice applies equally to attorney-mediators and non-attorney-mediators whose behavior constitutes the practice of law. . . .

Any legal malpractice claim requires a demonstration that the attorney owed a duty to the plaintiff and caused injury to the plaintiff by breaching that duty. . . . Without answering, therefore, the question of whether a mediator owes a duty of loyalty to a particular client, the mediator owes at least a duty not to provide negligent legal services to the parties. A mediator who refuses to render legal services to a mediation party may be at no risk of subsequent legal action, but if he or she chooses to render legal services, the services must be at least minimally competent. . . .

[M]ediators who choose to pursue activities constituting the practice of law will be held responsible for conducting legal research to supplement their legal understanding. . . .

V. Breach Confidentiality Externally

To the surprise of the disputants, Marcus Mediator calls a press conference during a break in the mediation. At the press conference, Marcus reveals that the plaintiffs have indicated an intention not to pursue at least certain parts of their original lawsuit against the City. Marcus further says to the press, "Now, with a little flexibility from the City, we should be able to get the whole thing settled."

. . .

A mediator who breaches confidentiality externally . . . faces the prospect of civil liability for damages resulting from that breach. . . . A mediator who shares mediation information with non-participants in violation of those terms will be liable to a mediation party who can demonstrate an injury stemming from that breach of confidentiality. . . .

Under certain circumstances, a mediator could even be liable for breaches of confidentiality under the tort theory of privacy. . . . Public disclosure of private information may create tort-based liability if a person of ordinary sensibilities would find the information disclosed to be "highly offensive" and "objectionable." . . .

A mediator's duties regarding confidentiality do not extinguish at the termination of a mediation. . . . Most programs requiring [post-mediation] reports now strictly limit the information to be included in those reports. A mediator who supplements these reports with other information stands at risk of program sanction and civil liability.

VI. Breach Confidentiality Internally

Plaintiffs brought suit seeking injunctive relief to force a change in a particular policy at the defendant corporation and seeking modest monetary damages. During a private caucus, Marsha Mediator learns that the defendant has already decided to change the policies in question, in a way the plaintiffs will embrace. When Marsha asks defense counsel why they have not told the plaintiffs about the corporation's plans, they indicate that they hope to use the change in policies as a "trade-off concession" in order to minimize or eliminate any financial payment. In a subsequent private meeting with the plaintiffs, without the consent of the defendant, Marsha says, "Look, the defendants have already told me that they're going to make the policy change. The only issue is money."

. . . A mediator who receives private information faces considerable strategic and ethical decisions about how to handle the information. In some circumstances, a mediator who takes information privately shared by one party and improperly discloses it to other parties may face the prospect of sanction or civil liability. . . .

[A] mediator who makes explicit oral statements regarding confidentiality at the outset of a private caucus with a party creates at least the possibility of contract-based obligations regarding internal confidentiality.

Mediators violating internal confidentiality also face the possibility of tort liability under the theory of interference with prospective advantage. . . . A party whose information was leaked may reasonably believe that he or she is placed at a comparative disadvantage because of the breach of internal confidentiality. . . .

VII. Maintain Confidentiality Inappropriately

Maurice Mediator learns during a conversation with a divorcing couple that the children are regularly subjected to living arrangements tantamount to abuse or neglect. Maurice mentions his concern, but both of the parents swear that the circumstances will change once they can finalize the divorce. Maurice says nothing to anyone outside of the mediation and proceeds to assist the parties in finalizing the terms of the divorce.

. . .

The most obvious illustrations of conditions in which a mediator risks sanction for improperly maintaining confidentiality arise with so-called "mandatory reporting." Mandatory reporter laws hold certain individuals responsible for informing state authorities of incidences of misconduct such as child abuse, elder abuse, and abandonment. . . .

Mediators who fail to uphold the requirements of mandatory reporting face a range of sanctions. . . .

Failure to report in a mandatory reporting situation can also create grounds for civil liability. As with criminal prosecutions, actions in tort against persons who improperly fail to report abuse are rare. Nevertheless, mediators stand some risk of civil liability for failing to report instances of abuse.

Referral sources and voluntary associations typically provide standards of conduct either permitting or demanding a breach of confidentiality in conditions such as those under consideration here. . . .

Beyond the circumstance of mandatory reporting requirements, so-called *Tarasoff*[139] conditions may also create an obligation for mediators to breach confidentiality. The *Tarasoff* case involved a psychologist who learned that one of his patients intended to kill a woman in whom the patient had an unrequited romantic interest. The psychologist maintained confidentiality, and his patient murdered the woman. The woman's family brought a wrongful death action against the psychologist. The California Supreme Court ultimately ruled that the psychiatrist had a duty to prevent harm to the victim, even if that meant breaching patient confidentiality. States vary broadly regarding the existence or scope of *Tarasoff* disclosure obligations, with most retreating from any duty to warn. . . . Fortunately, *Tarasoff* conditions are extremely rare, but they create a second set of circumstances in which a mediator may be exposed to complaints for upholding confidentiality inappropriately.

VIII. Advertise Falsely

Mitchell Mediator's website touts his mediation services as "expert." In part, it says, "Over 1,000 cases of experience. Certified and sanctioned by the State and by prominent national mediation organizations." Mitchell is a former judge who presided over more than a thousand civil cases during his years on the bench. He has formally mediated, however, only a few dozen cases. Furthermore, neither the state nor the national mediation organizations to which Mitchell belongs certifies or sanctions mediators. Mitchell is simply a member of the mediation rosters each body maintains.

. . .

---

139. *See* Tarasoff v. Regents of the University of California, 551 P.2d 334 (Cal. 1976)

The risk of civil liability for advertising falsely stems principally from a theory of fraudulent inducement. In order to prevail in a complaint against a mediator on this theory, a plaintiff needs to demonstrate that the mediator knowingly made a false representation about a material issue, that the plaintiff reasonably relied upon the representation, and that the plaintiff's reliance produced injury. . . .

In addition to facing private civil lawsuits for compensatory damages, a mediator who improperly advertises his or her credentials or services may also face the prospect of private actions under consumer protection laws. . . .

A mediator making false public statements about his or her credentials may also be subject to criminal charges. . . .

IX. Inflict Emotional Distress on a Disputant

During the mediation, Muriel Mediator adopts an aggressive approach to creating settlement. As always, she had told the parties, a divorcing couple, "Bring your toothbrushes when you show up to my mediation." The divorcing wife, unrepresented by counsel, is visibly worn down by Muriel's relentless efforts at "persuasion." When the wife protests and indicates a desire to leave, Muriel threatens to report to the judge that the wife did not participate in the mediation in good faith. Muriel further indicates that such a report would "all but guarantee that you'll lose your claim for custody of the children."

While mediators have no obligation to guarantee the comfort and happiness of mediation parties, mediators do not operate with carte blanche regarding their treatment of parties . . . . [I]f a mediator's conduct rises to the level of tortious infliction of emotional distress, the mediator is exposed to a threat of civil liability.

All jurisdictions provide for common law, tort-based claims against people who inflict emotional distress on others under certain circumstances. The most common construction of the tort of intentional infliction of emotional distress requires a plaintiff to demonstrate that the mediator intentionally or recklessly engaged in extreme or outrageous conduct, causing emotional distress in the plaintiff. Jurisdictions vary in the evidence required to demonstrate emotional distress. Some jurisdictions also recognize claims sounding in negligence rather than intentional tort. In most circumstances, however, a plaintiff must demonstrate that the mediator intentionally or recklessly inflicted the distress. Fortunately, few imaginable mediator behaviors are sufficiently outrageous to satisfy the elements of the tort of infliction of emotional distress. . . .

Disputants can enter mediations in fragile emotional states. Mediators' practices often encourage the parties to develop trust in the mediator, and some practices even encourage a degree of deference. In such a context, a mediator who recklessly disregards the psychological impacts of his or her mediation conduct risks creating actionable emotional distress.

X. Commit Fraud

In a private caucus, the plaintiffs tell Manuel Mediator that they would be able to break this case wide open if only they could get some cooperation from a few important executives in the defendant corporation. They admit, however, that they have had no luck so far in their efforts. Manuel then sits down privately with the general counsel for the defendant and says, "Look, I spoke with the plaintiffs. They have just lined up some key insider witnesses, including a couple members of your management team. It's time for you to end this." The general counsel looks surprised but increases the defendant's offer considerably. The mediator takes the new offer to the plaintiffs, who quickly agree to it.

. . . A mediator commits fraud if the mediator knowingly misrepresents a material fact and a mediation party reasonably relies on that misrepresentation to his or her detriment. . . .

A mediator's misrepresentation creates a risk of fraud only if the subject of the misrepresentation is material to the topic of the mediation. . . . In all but the most extraordinary cases, statements of opinion cannot constitute fraud. . . . For example, a mediator who merely tells one party, "I think this is a fair settlement offer" runs little risk of a subsequent complaint in which the party later accuses the mediator of fraud for having shared the opinion. On the other hand, a mediator who knowingly misrepresents the existence of witnesses and says, "I know that they have just secured cooperation from members of your management team and have uncovered a smoking gun memo," and then adds, "so I think this is a fair settlement offer" exposes himself or herself to a fraud claim. . . . A bright line does not always exist between what constitutes an opinion (not material) as opposed to a statement of fact (potentially material), leaving mediators who employ misrepresentations as part of their mediation practice exposed to liability.

. . .

Honorable Mention: Mediate Poorly

Michael Mediator misses an opportunity to improve the parties' understanding of each other and of the relevant issues. Michael creates an unhelpful agenda and refuses to adapt his approach. Michael misreads the parties' primary concerns. He makes inappropriate suggestions. Michael is unprepared. He listens horribly. Michael oversees a lengthy process that produces no agreement and worsens the parties' relationship.

. . . While mediators face a theoretical risk of a malpractice or negligence-based suit, the nature of mediation practice makes negligence an unlikely source of liability exposure.

. . . To establish negligence, a plaintiff must demonstrate that the mediator breached his or her duty of care toward the plaintiff. A successful negligence-based claim would also require a demonstration of causation and injury. . . .

The difficulty of defining a standard or customary set of practices against which to measure a mediator's performance creates a significant challenge to any plaintiff pursuing a negligence-based action against a mediator . . . For better or worse (and I largely think it is for the better), the diversity of mediation renders the articulation of an identifiable customary practice difficult.

The nearly ubiquitous principle of mediation confidentiality further complicates the issue of identifying customary mediation practice. . . . [T]he cumulative effect of confidentiality prevents outsiders from generating a clear picture of what actually takes place in an "ordinary" mediation. This generalized secrecy presents an extraordinary barrier for a plaintiff trying to demonstrate a customary mediation practice. . . .

Even if a plaintiff successfully establishes a breach of duty by the mediator, causation and damages pose additional hurdles. . . . Unless a party can demonstrate that his or her capacity to exercise autonomy was impaired in some way, it would be difficult to lay blame for the terms of the agreement at the feet of the mediator.

The complex question of establishing damages further clouds a negligence-based claim. . . . Proving what would have happened in settlement discussions but for the interventions of a mediator or any other party demands extraordinary speculation. . . .

In the second circumstance, involving allegedly improper non-settlement, a plaintiff will have similar difficulty proving that the disputants would have reached a settlement but for the mediator's negligence. Many mediation cases fail to settle for reasons entirely separate from the mediator's competence. . . .

Establishing damages further complicates the claim in a non-settlement circumstance. Mediation parties have no general obligation to remain in mediation, even in so-called mandatory mediation contexts. . . . The fact that parties can vote with their feet makes negligence claims in non-settlement circumstances even more difficult to sustain. . . .

. . . Complaints against mediators are unlike natural disasters in that they are neither random nor entirely beyond mediators' control. An understanding of the possible foundations of liability, coupled with some care in describing and dispensing mediation services will help a mediator avoid getting sued.

Notes and Questions

(1) Given the potential ways to get sued identified by Moffitt, what measures should a mediator routinely include? Discuss which of these would be useful: a) clarify the role of the mediator orally (as part of your opening) and in writing, in an agreement to mediate; b) immediately address any confusion by the parties, such as their referring to the mediator as "judge" or "your honor"; c) avoid marathon mediations; d) conduct an oral "voir dire" in combination with the execution of the settlement agreement to ensure that the parties have read and understand the

settlement terms and the implications of signing a mediated agreement; e) retain your notes; and f) maintain professional malpractice insurance coverage. *See Mediator Malpractice: A Proposed Defensive Path Through the Minefield*, Dispute Resolution Magazine Vol. 17, No. 1 (Fall 2010).

(2) For an overview of mediator regulatory schemes, and an in-depth analysis of mediator grievance programs for court-connected mediation programs in Florida, Georgia, Maine, Minnesota, and Virginia, *see* Paula Young, *Take It or Leave It, Lump It or Grieve It: Designing Mediator Complaint Systems That Protect Mediators, Unhappy Parties, Attorneys, Courts, the Process, and the Field*, 21 Ohio St. J. on Disp. Resol. 721 (2006).

(3) Attorney mediators often can obtain riders to their legal malpractice insurance coverage for their mediation activities. It is also possible for attorney and non-attorney mediators to obtain separate mediator malpractice insurance coverage. For a critical review of insurance coverage for mediators, *see* Paula Young's series of articles, *The Crisis in Insurance Coverage for Mediators — Part 1: Even Lawyer-Mediators are "Going Bare"*, 15 Appalachian J.L. 1 (2016); *The Crisis in Insurance Coverage for Mediators, Part 2: Coverage for Mediators Entering the Field from the Mental Health Professions — You May as Well be "Going Bare" Because "There's No There, There"*, 19 Appalachian J.L. 79 (2019–2020); *The Crisis in Insurance Coverage for Mediators, Part 3: Underwriters at Lloyds, London Offers a Meaningful Option for Mediators*, 20 Appalachian J.L. 191 (2021).

(4) In conjunction with the adoption of its standards of conduct in 1992, Florida adopted a disciplinary procedure to enforce them. By contrast, the Model Standards were not adopted with a related enforcement mechanism, although ACR utilizes the standards as part of the requirements for membership. Further, in the Standards themselves, the introduction states that "the fact that these Standards have been adopted by the respective sponsoring entities, should alert mediators to the fact that the Standards might be viewed as establishing a standard of care for mediators." What influence does the presence or absence of an enforcement scheme have on a mediator's compliance with the Standards' guidance? What would you expect to be some of the difficulties in attempting to enforce standards of conduct for mediators?

(5) In Florida, the standards as originally adopted contained the following provision: "A mediator shall withdraw from mediation if the mediator believes the mediator can no longer be impartial." The provision was later revised to read: "A mediator shall withdraw from mediation if the mediator is no longer impartial." Is the revised language more enforceable? If so, how? Review the Model Standards with a view toward enforcement. Are the standards objective? Are they clear?

D. Mediation and the Legal System

The first portion of this section examines the relationship between the mediation process and the mediator to legal practice. Is mediation the practice of law? Should it be?

The second section focuses on the special ethical and practical issues facing the lawyer serving as a mediator. When attorneys choose to work as mediators, they encounter special ethical constraints. In 1996, a Pennsylvania attorney mediator asked the local Bar Association whether, assuming compliance with the Model Standards of Conduct for Mediators, the attorney would also be deemed to have complied with the obligations under the Rules of Professional Conduct. The bar committee stated that the Rules of Professional Conduct may often impose additional burdens beyond the Model Standards. Pa. Bar Ass'n Comm. on Legal Ethics and Prof. Resp., Informal Op. No. 96-167, December 30, 1996. The ethical burdens are especially complex for those lawyer-mediators who attempt to offer a mediation practice while maintaining their traditional law practice. For some lawyers in this situation, continuing their law practice may be a short-term financial necessity as they build their mediation business into a full-time endeavor. Other lawyer-mediators, however, enjoy pursuing both practices simultaneously, and believe that they are supportive of one another. "Aside from representing clients in dispute-resolution processes, lawyers often serve as third-party neutrals." ABA Model Rules of Prof. Resp. Rule 2.4, cmt. 1.

One author has stated: "Nowhere is cross-professionalism as problematic as it is for lawyer-mediators." Maureen E. Laflin, *Preserving the Integrity of Mediation Through the Adoption of Ethical Rules for Lawyer-Mediators*, 14 Notre Dame J.L. Ethics & Pub. Pol'y 479, 479 (2000). The ABA Model Rules focus on two ethical problems relevant to lawyer-mediators. First, disputants in a mediation may experience "role confusion" if they are unsure whether a lawyer-mediator is acting only as a neutral or also has a duty to represent and protect their interests. Second, the ABA Model Rules recognize that lawyer-mediators must deal with distinctive conflict of interest issues. For example, if a lawyer-mediator mediates a dispute for a large company, have they created a conflict of interest that would prevent their representing anyone having a dispute with that company? The law in this area is still developing, and significant differences between various jurisdictions often exist. The lawyer-mediator must research the extant law and operative ethical opinions in order to ensure that their conduct complies with the duties imposed by the multiple professional standards. Finally, the combination of advocate and neutral practices raises challenging business concerns, such as how to handle advertisement and solicitation materials. Further, if the lawyer-mediator wishes to establish a mediation practice with non-attorneys, the lawyer confronts restrictions related to profit sharing between attorneys and non-attorneys.

1. Is Mediation the Practice of Law?

Mediation and the Legal System, Is Mediation the Practice of Law?

14 Alternatives 57 (May 1996)*

By Carrie Menkel-Meadow

One of the hottest questions in ADR ethics is whether mediating a case is the "practice of law."

. . .

How we answer the question . . . will determine the standards by which we judge the work — whether we rely on legal ethics codes, or those of "coordinate" professions. . . .

If mediation is the practice of law (or as Geoffrey Hazard has argued, it is the "ancillary" practice of law), we must refer to lawyers' ethics codes. Trouble is, they provide little, if any, guidance about issues like: confidentiality (among parties and with mediators), conflicts of interests, fees, and unauthorized practice (in co-mediating, for example, with a non-lawyer).

. . .

The risk, as with many ethical issues, is that the desired solution to one problem determines the conclusion. Most of us in the field are concerned about access to mediation — expanding the pool of capable mediators, and the choices for consumers of mediation services. Therefore, we would like to define mediation broadly, so that it doesn't involve the practice of law. To that end, we argue that mediation in its "pure" form of facilitation does not involve law, but communication and other skills.

One example of this approach is a proposal by the District of Columbia Bar to clarify and revise the local ethics rule dealing with the unauthorized practice of law. The proposed amendment expressly exempts mediation because "ADR services are not given in circumstances where there is a client relationship of trust and reliance and it is common practice for providers of ADR services explicitly to advise participants that they are not providing the services of legal counsel," Proposed Clarification and Revision of District of Columbia Court of Appeals Rule 49 Concerning the Unauthorized Practice of Law, Rule 49 Committee of the District of Columbia Bar.

Lawyer-Client Relationship

This approach to the issue, one of the more popular ones, treats the absence of a lawyer-client relationship as the governing test. It allows a broad range of individuals

---

to mediate, including non-lawyers and lawyers who are not members of the local or state bar.

Another route to the same result is to simply define away the problem. A report two years ago to the Tennessee Supreme Court Commission on Dispute Resolution by the state Board of Professional Responsibility illustrates this approach. It recommends a rule of professional responsibility that says: "A neutral shall give legal opinions to a party only in the presence of all parties, providing, however, that a prediction of litigation outcomes by a lawyer acting as a dispute resolution neutral shall not for purposes of this section constitute the provision of a legal opinion."

. . .

For people concerned about standards and quality control in mediation, here's the problem: to the extent that mediators, especially those who work within court programs or by court referral, "predict" court results or "evaluate" the merits of the case (on either factual or legal grounds), they are giving legal advice.

Mediators, courts and rules may disclaim responsibility for any information mediators give out, or treat it as not given by an agent, fiduciary, or "counsel." But as a practical matter, parties and others may rely on what the mediator tells them, in assessing their alternatives, suggesting other options, and agreeing to settlements.

Reliance on the Mediator

. . .

The current trend . . . is to grant quasi-judicial immunity to at least court-based third-party neutrals. . . . However, that means parties have virtually no recourse against a third-party neutral when they rely on a mediator's information or advice that is unfair, unjust, or just plain wrong . . . .

Ideally, we should analyze the work of third-party neutrals to see what they do, and then attempt to develop the appropriate regulatory models. I disagree with the argument that mediators can give neutral, unbiased "legal information" that is not the practice of law . . . .

. . .

While some ADR experts pin their analysis on "client representation," I prefer to look at reliance. . . .

When mediators engage in some prediction or application of legal standards to concrete facts — and especially when they draft settlement agreements, I think they are "practicing" law. That means neutrals who are not trained as lawyers need to be wary of evaluative mediation. They still have other options as mediators: they can limit their role to facilitation, co-mediate with lawyers, or ask the parties to release them from liability for bad legal advice. Non-lawyer mediators might still be subject to the . . . regulation against unauthorized practice of law. . . .

Giving legal predictions and evaluations is law work, whether or not there is a lawyer-client relationship. Within these boundaries, we need rules that permit qualified people without legal training to mediate . . .

Still there's clearly a quality control problem. Just because a mediator has a law degree — or even an up-to-date license to practice — does not mean that he or she will give accurate legal advice, prediction or evaluation.

Lawyers Who Mediate Are Not Practicing Law
14 Alternatives 74 (June 1996)*
By Bruce Meyerson

Generally speaking, to practice law, one must have a client. Assuming that mediators clarify with parties that no attorney-client relationship exists, engaging in a legal discussion would not be the practice of law. Specifically, in order for a mediator's conduct in advising parties about the legal aspects of a particular dispute to be considered the practice of law, the party to the mediation must view the mediator as her lawyer and therefore assume that she is receiving legal advice for her personal benefit. If the parties are represented by counsel, or if the mediator has carefully clarified that the unrepresented parties do not view the mediator as their lawyer, I cannot imagine a situation where parties to the mediation will be confused about the mediator's role and mistakenly assume that the mediator is functioning as a lawyer. . . .

If . . . mediators are practicing law any time they give evaluations or predict outcomes, a number of undesirable consequences will follow. First, lawyer-mediators would be subject to all of the duties and obligations under the Model Rules, and presumably would owe these duties to the parties in the mediation. Although it is possible that a lawyer can function as a neutral mediator on behalf of clients in certain limited circumstances, Ethics Rule 2.2, in most instances the role of a mediator is fundamentally incompatible with an attorney's role in representing a client. For example, a mediator is supposed to be impartial and evenhanded during the mediation. On the other hand, a lawyer representing a client owes that client a duty of undivided loyalty. Most certainly, this obligation is inconsistent with the neutral duties owed to all of the parties in mediation. . . .

Second, a conclusion that mediation is the practice of law would raise the specter that thousands of professionals in other disciplines are engaged in the unauthorized practice of law. Surely, this is casting the "practice of law" net too widely.

Third, if mediation is the practice of law, judges presiding over settlement conferences would be breaking ethical rules in many jurisdictions. That could happen in states that prohibit judges from practicing law while they serve on the bench. Under these rules, judges would be practicing law when, in an attempt to settle a case, they

---

discuss the legal merits of a case with disputing parties. A judge engaged in this common settlement technique would be engaged in unethical conduct. . . .

Clearly, we need a framework for regulating mediation. But we can develop that framework without labeling mediation as the practice of law.

Notes and Questions

(1) The Department of Dispute Resolution Services of the Supreme Court of Virginia adopted Guidelines on Mediation and the Unauthorized Practice of Law (UPL) in response to a UPL case filed in Virginia as an effort to "provide guidance and protection" particularly to the non-attorney mediator population. The Guidelines have sparked considerable debate. Some critics expressed concern that the Guidelines are overly restrictive and "rob mediation of its fluidity and flexibility." In the June 2000 edition of *Alternatives*, Geetha Ravindra, then-director of the Department of Dispute Resolution Services, explained the committee's actions in the following excerpt:*

> [The UPL committee] recognized by definition, the mediation process is not the practice of law. There are activities, however, that mediators engage in during the mediation process, that may constitute the practice of law. The committee aspired to identify a test by which activities could be measured to assess whether they fall within the definition of the practice of law. . . .
>
> As a result, the guidelines try to identify the extent to which evaluation may be provided in mediation without UPL concerns and when evaluation more clearly falls into the category of the practice of law. The guidelines . . . allow mediators to offer evaluation of, for example, strengths and weaknesses of a case, assess the value and cost of settlement alternatives, or barriers to settlement.
>
> The committee believed that mediators should not predict the specific resolution of legal issues because such activity is part of a lawyer's function as advisor and counselor and could give rise to an implicit lawyer/client relationship . . . [however] neutrals may be able to provide a range of possible outcomes under this definition.

Is this Guideline consistent with the Model Standards of Conduct for Mediators?

(2) In 2002, the American Bar Association Section of Dispute Resolution adopted a resolution on Mediation and the Unauthorized Practice of Law which contained the following statement: "Mediation is a process in which an impartial individual assists the parties in reaching a voluntary settlement. Such assistance does not constitute the practice of law. The parties to the mediation are not represented by the mediator." The resolution also contains the following principles: mediators'

---

* Geetha Ravindra, *The Response: The Goal Is to Inform, Not Impede ADR*, Alternatives to the High Cost of Litigation, Vol. 18 No. 6, pp. 124–25 (June 2000). Copyright © 2000. All rights reserved. Reprinted with permission.

discussions of legal issues do not constitute legal advice, whether or not the mediator is an attorney; the preparation of a memorandum of understanding or settlement agreement by a mediator, incorporating the terms of settlement specified by
the parties, does not constitute the practice of law (but, if the mediator drafts an
agreement that goes beyond the terms specified by the parties, he or she may be
engaged in the practice of law); and the mediator should inform parties that the
mediator is not providing them with legal advice, that a settlement agreement may
affect the parties' legal rights, and that each of the parties has the right to seek advice
of independent legal counsel throughout the mediation process.

(3) The Association for Conflict Resolution addressed this issue by adopting the
following resolution in 2006:

> ACR affirms that mediation is a distinct practice with its own body of knowl-
> edge, foundational principles, values and standards of practice. While ACR
> recognizes that the definition of and penalties associated with the unau-
> thorized practice of law are matters of state law, ACR affirms that mediators
> who practice mediation consistent with standards of conduct approved by
> ACR should not be considered to have engaged in the unauthorized prac-
> tice of law. If an ACR member is charged with unauthorized practice of law,
> ACR will provide assistance and/or support as may be appropriate.

What are the differences in the approaches taken by the ABA and ACR?

(4) What are the arguments supporting and opposing the statement that mediation is the practice of law? Is there a relationship between style of practice and the
validity of such a statement?

(5) *See* Paula Young, *A Connecticut Mediator in a Kangaroo Court?: Successfully
Communicating the "Authorized Practice of Mediation" Paradigm to "Unauthorized
Practice of Law" Disciplinary Bodies*, 49 S. Tex. L. Rev. 1047 (2008), for an interesting
discussion of what happened when a non-attorney mediator was charged with the
unauthorized practice of law.

2. Confusing the Role of Lawyer and Mediator

While recognizing that both lawyers and non-lawyers may serve as mediators,
the ABA Model Rules of Professional Conduct explain that lawyer-mediators face
a unique problem in that unrepresented parties may be confused as to the lawyer-
neutral's role and responsibilities. Thus, the Model Rule requires lawyer-mediators
to clarify their role to unrepresented clients.

Rule 2.4(b), and its accompanying comments, make clear that the nature and
extent of disclosure required depends on the factual context of the situation, including the subject matter at issue, who the parties are, and the nature of the dispute
resolution process. Lawyer-mediators are responsible for deciding precisely how
and when to make the required disclosure, and may in some cases choose to make

the disclosure in writing. Lawyer-mediators are well advised to include a statement describing their role in an agreement to mediate that is signed by the disputants.

Concerns about possible role confusion may also limit the tasks in which the lawyer-mediator may engage. The Utah State Bar opined that it is improper for a lawyer-mediator, after successfully assisted divorcing disputants resolve their issues in mediation, to draft a settlement agreement and necessary court pleadings on their behalf. Ethics Adv. Op. Comm. Op. No. 05-03, May 6, 2005 explains that drafting such documents is "the practice of law" and that it is improper in Utah to represent two adverse parties. However, the Opinion recognizes that a number of jurisdictions have reached contrary conclusions, and several committee members also dissented.

Rule 2.4 Lawyer Serving as Third-Party Neutral

(a) A lawyer serves as a third-party neutral when the lawyer assists two or more persons who are not clients of the lawyer to reach a resolution of a dispute or other matter that has arisen between them. Service as a third-party neutral may include service as an arbitrator, a mediator or in such other capacity as will enable the lawyer to assist the parties to resolve the matter.

(b) A lawyer serving as a third-party neutral shall inform unrepresented parties that the lawyer is not representing them. When the lawyer knows or reasonably should know that a party does not understand the lawyer's role in the matter, the lawyer shall explain the difference between the lawyer's role as a third-party neutral and a lawyer's role as one who represents a client.

Comments

[1] Alternative dispute resolution has become a substantial part of the civil justice system. Aside from representing clients in dispute-resolution processes, lawyers often serve as third-party neutrals. A third-party neutral is a person, such as a mediator, arbitrator, conciliator or evaluator, who assists the parties, represented or unrepresented, in the resolution of a dispute or in the arrangement of a transaction. Whether a third-party neutral serves primarily as a facilitator, evaluator or decisionmaker depends on the particular process that is either selected by the parties or mandated by a court.

[2] The role of a third-party neutral is not unique to lawyers, although, in some court-connected contexts, only lawyers are allowed to serve in this role or to handle certain types of cases. In performing this role, the lawyer may be subject to court rules or other law that apply either to third-party neutrals generally or to lawyers serving as third-party neutrals. Lawyer-neutrals may also be subject to various codes of ethics, such as the Code of Ethics for Arbitration in Commercial Disputes prepared by a joint committee of the American Bar Association and the

American Arbitration Association or the Model Standards of Conduct for Mediators (excerpted in this chapter).

[3] Unlike non-lawyers who serve as third-party neutrals, lawyers serving in this role may experience unique problems as a result of differences between the role of a third-party neutral and a lawyer's service as a client representative. The potential for confusion is significant when the parties are unrepresented in the process. Thus, paragraph (b) requires a lawyer-neutral to inform unrepresented parties that the lawyer is not representing them. For some parties, particularly parties who frequently use dispute-resolution processes, this information will be sufficient. For others, particularly those who are using the process for the first time, more information will be required. Where appropriate, the lawyer should inform unrepresented parties of the important differences between the lawyer's role as third-party neutral and a lawyer's role as a client representative, including the inapplicability of the attorney-client evidentiary privilege. The extent of disclosure required under this paragraph will depend on the particular parties involved and the subject matter of the proceeding, as well as the particular features of the dispute-resolution process selected.

[4] A lawyer who serves as a third-party neutral subsequently may be asked to serve as a lawyer representing a client in the same matter. The conflicts of interest that arise for both the individual lawyer and the lawyer's law firm are addressed in Rule 1.12.

[5] Lawyers who represent clients in alternative dispute-resolution processes are governed by the Rules of Professional Conduct. When the dispute-resolution process takes place before a tribunal, as in binding arbitration (*see* Rule 1.0(m)), the lawyer's duty of candor is governed by Rule 3.3. Otherwise, the lawyer's duty of candor toward both the third-party neutral and other parties is governed by Rule 4.1.

Notes and Questions

(1) Does Rule 2.4 adequately address all of the concerns raised by potential role confusion?

(2) Another approach was highlighted in the *Ali Haghighi v. Russian-American Broadcasting Co.* cases discussed in Chapter 6. The Minnesota Civil Mediation Act includes a provision (Minn. Stat. § 572.35, subd. 1 (1999)) that a mediated settlement agreement is not binding unless: "(1) it contains a provision stating that it is binding and a provision stating substantially that the parties were advised in writing that (a) the mediator has no duty to protect their interests or provide them with information about their legal rights; (b) signing a mediated settlement agreement may adversely affect their legal rights; (c) they should consult an attorney before signing a mediated settlement agreement if they are uncertain of their rights; or (2) the parties were otherwise advised of the conditions in clause (1)." In 2023, the Minnesota Supreme Court went a step further to require that mediators in civil and family

cases provide a Written Agreement for ADR Services prior to or "promptly" at the commencement of the mediation process. The language from Minn. Stat. §572.35, subd. 1(1)(a), (b), and (c) (1999), must be included. Rule 114.13 Subd. 7(b), Minnesota General Rules of Practice.

3. Conflict of Interest Issues Facing the Lawyer-Mediator

Lawyer-mediators must worry about the possibility of conflicts of interest stemming from their dual practice. May an attorney attempt to mediate a dispute between two parties if they have previously represented one or both parties? Are attorneys barred from mediating or litigating due to past representation by other members of their firm? Is the firm barred from litigating all disputes involving a particular company because a member of the firm mediated a dispute involving that company? Alternatively, once an attorney has served as a mediator in a dispute involving two clients, is the attorney forever precluded from representing either client as an advocate? The ABA Model Rules of Professional Conduct address many of these issues and are examined below.

Rule 1.12 Former Judge, Arbitrator, Mediator, or Other Third-Party Neutral

(a) Except as stated in paragraph (d), a lawyer shall not represent anyone in connection with a matter in which the lawyer participated personally and substantially as a . . . mediator . . . unless all parties to the proceeding give informed consent, confirmed in writing.

(b) A lawyer shall not negotiate for employment with any person who is involved as a party or as lawyer for a party in a matter in which the lawyer is participating personally and substantially as a . . . mediator . . . .

(c) If a lawyer is disqualified by paragraph (a), no lawyer in a firm with which that lawyer is associated may knowingly undertake or continue representation in the matter unless:

(1) the disqualified lawyer is timely screened from any participation in the matter and is apportioned no part of the fee therefrom; and

(2) written notice is promptly given to the parties and any appropriate tribunal to enable them to ascertain compliance with the provisions of this rule.

Notes and Questions

(1) Several aspects of this Rule warrant emphasis. First, as a general matter, lawyer-mediators are foreclosed from representing a party for whom they earlier mediated a dispute. This prohibition can be waived by the parties, but only in writing. Second,

the firm at which the lawyer works is *also* disqualified, but that disqualification can be overridden when the individual lawyer-mediator is "screened" from actual or financial participation in the new matter. Comment 4 to Rule 1.12 explains that while the screened lawyer may continue to receive their regular salary or partnership share established "by prior independent agreement," they may not be provided compensation "directly related to the matter in which the lawyer is disqualified."

It is also important to note two matters that are not covered by Rule 1.12. First, the Rule only covers a situation where the lawyer-mediator first mediates, and thereafter seeks to represent one of the disputants who had participated in a mediation that the lawyer-mediator had conducted. It does not govern situations where a lawyer represents a disputant as an advocate and thereafter is called upon to mediate a dispute in which that disputant is a party. That scenario is governed by mediation ethical rules and standards. Second, Rule 1.12 sets a floor rather than a ceiling for the ethics of lawyer-mediators. Comment 2 notes that "[o]ther law or codes of ethics governing third-party neutrals may impose more stringent standards."

(2) In addition to ethical concerns, the attempt to integrate mediation and litigation practices has raised practical concerns for some attorneys, particularly when they are part of a larger firm that provides substantial litigation services. For many reasons, lawyers acting as mediators often bring less revenue into the firm than lawyers acting as litigators. Lawyer-mediators typically do not need the assistance of associate attorneys or paralegals, thereby eliminating the firm's ability to bill for work performed by these additional personnel. Further, mediators use only a fraction of the overhead services that is often required by litigators. While lawyer-mediators may need greater than normal time for conference room bookings, they rarely require messenger assistance and typically need little, if any, secretarial support. The business reality is that it may be difficult for attorneys who decide they want to spend substantial time as mediators to work out an equitable financial arrangement with their own firms. These sorts of pressures, as well as others, may sometimes lead lawyer-mediators to leave their firms to establish an independent mediation practice.

(3) Do you believe the ABA Model Rules pertaining to lawyer-mediators are adequate? Do they need to be more stringent? Less stringent? Would you revise them in any respect?

(4) What rationale might be offered for preventing a person who had previously mediated a dispute involving a particular client from representing that client in future litigation in an unrelated matter?

(5) What rationale might be offered for preventing a person who had previously represented a particular client in litigation from subsequently serving as mediator in a dispute involving that client in an unrelated matter?

(6) The Virginia legal ethics committee considered a request for an opinion related to the following challenge. A lawyer who owned a mediation company was also "of counsel" to a law firm in which their spouse was a partner. After a mediation was terminated, having failed to resolve all the issues, one of the parties to the mediation asked an associate in the law firm (not the person who mediated) to file a divorce on their behalf. The Committee, consistent with rationales discussed above, found that the individual lawyer-mediator could not represent that disputant even if both clients consented. The Committee further explained that, while associates in the firm were not entirely disqualified, due to confidentiality concerns, an associate in the firm nonetheless could represent that client only with the consent of both parties. Va. Leg. Ethics Op. 1759 (Feb. 18, 2002).

(7) Courts have determined the ethicality of post-mediation representation of mediation parties by lawyer-mediators and those with whom they affiliate based on whether screening has been implemented. In *Pappas v. Waggoner's Heating & Air, Inc.*, 2005 OK CIV APP 11, 108 P.3d 9 (Div. 3 2004), the court approved subsequent representation in part because the law firm representing the former mediation party had screening procedures in place to avoid a perceived or real conflict of interest, whereas in *U.S. Bank Nat. Ass'n v. Morales*, 50 Conn. L. Repr. 212, 2010 WL 3025615 (Conn. Super. Ct. 2010), the defendant's law firm and attorney were disqualified because of lack of screening which was demonstrated by the fact that the attorney who had mediated the case later received a case file in the same case. In *Burkhardt v. Kastell*, 2018 WL 2921911, *1 (N.J. Super. Ct. App. Div. 2018), the court reversed an order that disqualified a firm from continuing to serve as counsel for a defendant because an attorney who mediated an earlier dispute in the matter later became affiliated with the firm.

(8) If an individual or a firm seeking to combine mediation and litigation practices solicited your advice, what steps would you suggest to them to avoid potential conflicts of interest?

(9) Conflict-of-interest rules developed to govern lawyer-mediators may also have an impact on other legal practices. In *Fields-D'Arpino v. Restaurant Assocs., Inc.*, 39 F. Supp. 2d 412 (S.D.N.Y. 1999), the court examined a situation in which the firm representing the defendant designated an attorney at the firm to meet with the plaintiff and try to settle the case. Calling this process "mediation," the court held that the defense firm must be disqualified from further representation, given a New York ethical rule stating that "[a] lawyer who has undertaken to act as an impartial . . . mediator should not thereafter represent in the dispute any of the parties involved." *Id*. at 414 (citing N.Y. Code of Prof. Resp. EC 5-20).

(10) For a discussion of potential legal malpractice issues facing lawyer-mediators, *see* David Plimpton, *Liability Pitfalls May Be Waiting for Lawyer-Neutrals*, 18 Alternatives 65 (Apr. 2000).

4. Fee Sharing Issues Facing the Lawyer-Mediator

The traditional rule barring lawyers from sharing fees with non-lawyers poses issues for mediation practices that seek to include both lawyers and non-lawyers. The ABA's Model Rule of Professional Conduct 5.4 is quite explicit in barring lawyers from sharing legal fees with non-lawyers. That rule also prohibits lawyers from practicing in the form of a professional corporation or association authorized to practice law for a profit if any non-lawyer owns an interest in that firm or has the right to control activities of the firm. Citing these rules, several jurisdictions have wrestled with the question of whether or how lawyers and non-lawyers may join together in a practice to offer mediation services. A Florida Opinion provides that "any non-lawyer mediators employed by the inquirer's law firm may not have an ownership interest in either the law firm or the mediation department. To do so would implicate rules prohibiting sharing fees with non-lawyers, partnership with non-lawyers, and assisting in the unauthorized practice of law." Fla. Ethics Op. 94–6, Apr. 30, 1995. A Rhode Island Opinion also seems to preclude such an arrangement, emphasizing that a lawyer who provides mediation services will nonetheless be perceived as an attorney, and stating that the rule barring a fee-sharing arrangement "avoids the possibility of a non-lawyer's interference with a lawyer's independent professional judgment and avoids encouraging non-lawyers from engaging in the unauthorized practice of law." RI Op. 95–1, Rep. No. 558, Mar. 6, 1995. By contrast, a Vermont Opinion states that so long as the partnership between a lawyer and non-lawyer does not include the "practice of law," in that legal advice will not be offered by the attorney or any members of the attorney's firm, lawyer and non-lawyer mediators may join together to form a business. Vt. Ethics Op. No. 93-05, *undated.*

Another fee-sharing issue is raised when lawyer-mediators seek to provide referral fees to others who provide them with mediation clients. An Illinois ethics opinion addressing this issue found that lawyer mediators were precluded from paying a 20% referral fee to an accounting firm that sent them mediation business, even though the lawyers sought to establish a separate mediation firm that, while containing some members of the law firm, would only provide mediation services. The Opinion found this "mediation firm" to be a "sham" that did not excuse lawyers from the usual rules barring sharing of fees with non-lawyers. Ill. St. Bar Assoc. Adv. Op. on Prof. Cond. No. 01-05, Jan. 2002.

Notes and Questions

(1) Why do ethical rules generally prohibit fee-sharing between lawyers and non-lawyers?

(2) Given the purpose of the rule prohibiting fee-sharing between lawyers and non-lawyers, does it make sense to prohibit lawyers and non-lawyers from sharing fees in a mediation practice? Does the distinction drawn in the Vermont opinion above make sense?

5. Advertising and Solicitation Issues Facing the Lawyer-Mediator

Lawyers face strict rules on advertisement and solicitation. *See, e.g.*, ABA Model Rules of Professional Conduct 7.1–7.3. Do these same rules apply to lawyers who choose to practice mediation exclusively or in combination with their advocacy practice? Opinions differ. Most jurisdictions provide that lawyers who mediate are nonetheless governed by the rules relating to attorney advertising. Thus, a Kansas Opinion states that the same restrictive advertising rules apply, even though "mediation may be a new addition to the 'forms' of practice." Kan. Formal and Informal Op. No. 95-02, May 26, 1995. A New York opinion similarly states that even if mediation is not technically considered the "practice of law," a "lawyer's role as a neutral mediator may include rendering advice about legal questions or preparing a separation agreement." It further notes that even where a mediator "serves as a mediator outside of the law office, gives no legal advice or opinions, and does not draw up an agreement," participants would be aware that the mediator was an attorney. The committee concluded, therefore, lawyer-mediators should be proscribed from participating in a referral service that might mistakenly be thought by clients to be a disinterested agency. N.Y. St. Bar Ass'n Comm. on Prof. Ethics, Op. 678, (42–95) Jan. 10, 1996. By contrast, an Illinois Opinion states that "[i]f the advertising and promotional material for the mediation business does not amount to advertising for the lawyer's law practice, it is not subject to the rules on lawyer advertising." Ill. Op. No. 92-05, 10/92.

When considering promotional materials, however, most jurisdictions are permissive in letting lawyers tout their mediation background. Kansas, South Carolina, and Tennessee each state that lawyers may indicate on their letterhead that they are certified mediators, so long as the statement is truthful. Kan. Op. 95-02, May 26, 1995; SC Bar Advisory Op. 96-29; Tenn. Ethics Op. 98-F-142(a), Dec. 11, 1998. Several jurisdictions, though, seek to ensure that a mediator defines their status in a way that does not mislead the public. In Tennessee, a lawyer-mediator may state that they are a "Rule 31 Listed Mediator" but not an "Approved Rule 31 Mediator," because the latter does not indicate what body issued the approval. Tenn. Ethics Op. 98-F-142(a), Dec. 11, 1998. Similarly, in Minnesota, lawyer-mediators may state that they are a "qualified neutral under the Rules of the Minnesota Supreme Court for ADR Rosters and Training" but may not simply identify themselves as a "certified" mediator. Minn. Gen. Rule of Practice 114.13 Subd. 6, 2023. A Florida ethics opinion, in a related matter, proscribes the mediation department of a law firm from using the trade name "Sunshine Mediation," as it would be misleading unless applied to the entire law practice. Fla. Ethics Op. 94-6, Apr. 30, 1995.

A Vermont ethics panel faced an unusual issue. According to the practice of the Vermont Environmental Court, litigants are asked in a pretrial conference whether they would be willing to use mediation. If the litigants are undecided, a mediator from a court list may contact the party to discuss the benefits of mediation. The panel ruled that even when the mediators who make such contacts are attorneys, their conduct does not violate anti-solicitation rules in that "service as a mediator does not involve an attorney client relationship, and consequently does not implicate the ethical rules directed to such a relationship." Vt. Bar Assoc. Adv. Ethics Op. 2001-08.

Notes and Questions

(1) What are the rationales for restricting advertising and solicitation by attorneys?

(2) Do these rationales apply when a lawyer offers services as a mediator?

(3) Note that even where non-lawyer mediators are not governed by ethical rules restricting advertising, they do potentially face the risk of a civil lawsuit or even criminal liability if they advertise falsely. *See* Michael Moffitt, *Ten Ways to Get Sued: A Guide to Mediators*, 8 Harv. Negot. L. Rev. 81, 116–20 (2003) (excerpted above).

(4) Restrictions on advertisements or solicitation by mediators (regardless of whether they are attorneys) may sometimes be more stringent than those applied to non-mediator attorneys. Consider how the following rulings in opinions issued by the Florida Mediator Ethics Advisory Committee compare to constraints on attorney-advocate activity:

(1) 95-007: precluding a mediator from advertising that the mediator would provide "a dispassionate evaluation by a neutral party," reasoning that this activity was not consistent with Florida's definition of mediation.

(2) 99-013: prohibiting a law firm from listing Circuit Court Mediation as a specialty, where only one member of the two-person firm was so qualified.

(3) 2001-006: prohibiting mediators from giving away items of value such as embossed golf shirts and from treating prospective clients to lunches or golf outings.

(4) 2011-009: prohibiting a mediator from using the company name "Litigation Terminators" in advertising mediation services to members of the Florida Bar.

(5) 2010-013: prohibiting a former judge from using the terms "Judge Emerita" in the title of the mediator's company and other marketing materials.

Chapter 9

The Institutionalization of Mediation in the Courts

A. Introduction

This chapter focuses on the institutionalization of mediation. Although mediation's increased use in the United States can trace its roots to community programs, mediation today is closely tied to numerous societal institutions. Mediation is now established as part of many federal and state court programs, employed by many federal and state governmental agencies, embraced by many corporations, and used in schools, prisons, and other settings. By 1994, every state, the District of Columbia and Puerto Rico had enacted at least one statute relating to the use of mediation.

Not surprisingly, courts at the local, state and federal levels are the settings for the most extensive institutional use of mediation. In some jurisdictions, judges are required to order mediation in certain types of cases (*e.g.*, divorce actions in which children are involved). Judges in other state and federal courts have the discretion to refer (or order) parties to mediation in many or all civil cases. And, in other courts, the judge may suggest or recommend mediation or conduct a judicial settlement conference using mediation techniques. Although this chapter's materials closely examine the development of mediation within the court context, many of the challenges raised by institutionalizing mediation in the courts arise in other institutional settings.

While such institutionalization has certainly helped to increase the use of mediation dramatically, there may also be some drawbacks to this trend. As you read this chapter, consider the positive outcomes achieved through institutionalization, as well as the potential negative consequences of what happens when a flexible process is placed in a structured environment. Certainly, institutionalization raises some new issues that require substantial thought.

Section B highlights the development of mediation as an integrated feature within the court institution. Section C explores the policy choices made when institutionalizing it, including those related to certification of mediators. Section D examines empirical research findings regarding the operation of mediation in the court context. Finally, Section E presents critiques of embedding mediation within the court system.

B. Development of Institutionalization

The modern movement towards institutionalizing ADR in general, and mediation in particular, traces its roots to experimental court-related mediation programs in the 1960s and 1970s. A seminal event in the institutionalization of these programs was the Pound Conference in 1976, in which judges, court administrators, and legal scholars gathered to discuss the public's pervasive dissatisfaction with the administration of justice. At that conference, Professor Frank E.A. Sander delivered a paper in which he described a courthouse of the future where parties could go for a variety of services to assist them in resolving their disputes. His vision, subsequently coined the "multi-door" courthouse, was premised on the state providing the necessary financial support not only for judges but also for intake specialists, mediators, arbitrators, and other dispute resolvers.

For multiple reasons, mediation as an institution has not grown in that direction. In fact, the Pound Conference "Follow-Up" Committee did not endorse the "multi-door courthouse" and instead recommended that "the American Bar Association, in cooperation with local courts and state and local associations, invite the development of models of Neighborhood Justice Centers, suitable for implementation as pilot projects." The primary reason for not implementing the multi-door courthouse concept is that it is an extremely expensive undertaking for the sponsoring institution. Even as mediation has become more integrated into the court, many courts continue to rely on volunteers and private providers to serve mediation programs rather than court staff. A secondary challenge for implementing the "multi-door" courthouse is that researchers have not identified objective criteria that can be reliably used to sort out which cases are most likely to benefit from each process, noting that case dynamics significantly fluctuate based on the parties and their attorneys, the amount in controversy, the status of negotiations, and the state of the governing law.

In the following excerpt, Professor Frank E.A. Sander, twenty-four years after offering his seminal remarks at the Pound Conference, reflects on the history of the mediation movement and speculates on the future of mediation in light of institutionalization.

The Future of ADR
2000 J. Disp. Resol. 3, 3–8*
By Frank E.A. Sander

Because I've been fortunate to observe the ADR scene for much of its recent development, I'm often asked my views of where we stand now. My somewhat flip answer is, "On Monday, Wednesday and Friday, I think we've made amazing progress. On Tuesday, Thursday and Saturday, ADR seems more like a grain of sand on the adversary system beach." . . .

What are some of the signs that the glass is half full? What are the things that give me optimism . . . ? First, in 1998, the Congress of the United States enacted the Dispute Resolution Act, which directs each federal district to establish an ADR program by local rule [28 U.S.C. §§ 651–658 (Supp. IV 1998)]. There is also comparable state legislation in a large number of states, sometimes mandating referral of specific cases to ADR or authorizing judges to do so in their discretion.

Second, dispute resolution clauses, sometimes quite sophisticated, are increasingly being used in contracts of all kinds.

Third, some businesses and law firms systematically canvass cases for ADR potential. . . .

Fourth, the CPR Institute for Dispute Resolution, an impressive New York organization of representatives from 800 leading businesses and law firms, is dedicated to the goal of educating its members and others concerning better ways of resolving disputes. Its CPR pledge commits signers to explore ADR before resorting to court. . . .

Fifth, a number of states now require that lawyers discuss ADR options with clients or to certify on the pleadings that they have done so. . . .

Sixth, for disputes in the public sector, the Administrative Dispute Resolution Act of 1996 requires federal agencies to consider the use of ADR and to appoint an ADR specialist. And there have been some Executive Orders issued by the President to stimulate similar action in the U.S. Department of Justice.

Seventh, about half the states now have state offices of dispute resolution that seek to facilitate the resolution of public disputes by providing technical assistance or recommending competent dispute resolvers.

Eighth, virtually every law school as well as many schools of business and planning now offer one or more ADR courses. . . .

So those are a few of the positive indicators. What are the downsides and remaining challenges?

Let me pause briefly for a little historic summary. I think there have been three periods in the approximately twenty-five years of the modern ADR development. Obviously, we didn't invent mediation. . . . But, by common agreement, it was about 1975 that the current interest in ADR began. The first period . . . was about 1975 to 1982. I call it, "Let a thousand flowers bloom." There were many experiments. . . .

The second period, about 1982 to 1990 . . . I call "Cautions and caveats": Concerns about where we're heading, attempts to sort out the wheat from the chaff. . . .

The third period, starting about 1990, is what I call "Institutionalization." The question there is: How do we weave ADR into the dispute resolution fabric so that ADR options are systematically considered at various points along the life of a dispute rather than putting the onus on the party who wants to use ADR, which will often be construed as a sign of weakness? . . .

What are the present obstacles and impediments to institutionalization, and what are some of the hopeful signs? When you look at the situation from the disputant's perspective there is often a lack of knowledge of ADR . . . . [T]he prevailing assumption that the court is the place to resolve disputes is a major part of the problem.

Second, there is a lack of readily available public dispute resolution options — the absence of a public facility like a comprehensive justice center where someone can go to have access to mediation or arbitration — a place where the sign over the door says, "This is where disputes get handled. The experts here will help you decide which is the best process for your case." . . .

What if we look at the situation from the perspective of lawyers? What are the impediments there? . . .

. . . The fact is that in ADR [lawyers] lose control, particularly in flexible procedures like mediation. . . . So lawyers are sometimes reluctant to get involved with an unfamiliar, threatening procedure.

There are also economic incentives for lawyers to stay with litigation . . . .

There are also other perverse incentives. For example, in some companies a settlement is charged to the budget of that division, but litigation costs are not charged to a department. So in that company there's an incentive to litigate rather than settle a case. Attorney compensation also sometimes takes account of successful wins but not of money-saving settlements.

Finally, there is a public policy impediment, and that is the lack of adequate cost-benefit studies . . . . [I]t's very difficult to document the specific money savings of pursuing a case through mediation rather than court adjudication. We have some anecdotal data, but when you think about it, that kind of research is incredibly difficult to do. For example, one claim for mediation is that in cases of continuing relationships, it's often a more lasting solution. That is, it prevents future disputes because you get at the underlying concerns and it teaches the parties how to resolve disputes more effectively by themselves in the future. That means you have to have a longitudinal study, spanning over many years in order to document that kind of thing, quite aside from the difficult questions of how you measure the peace of mind that comes from an absence of future lawsuits. . . .

. . .

Let me end up with some promising future directions for overcoming these impediments and advancing the cause of institutionalization. In the short run, we need to strengthen some of the institutionalization devices such as . . . the duty of a lawyer to apprize a client about ADR options as part of professional consultation, coupled with early court consideration of ADR possibilities, and judicial power to refer cases to appropriate ADR processes. All these institutionalization devices have an important indirect effect. They not only teach clients about these possibilities, but they also get lawyers up to par.

. . .

. . . That is also why I favor mandatory mediation at the present time. There are some hot arguments in the literature with some people saying, "Mediation means voluntarily agreeing to a result. How can you force somebody to voluntarily agree to a result?" I think that confuses coercion *into* mediation with coercion *in* mediation. If you have coercion *in* mediation, it is not mediation . . . . [W]e have evidence that the process is very powerful, that it works for people who use it, but for some of the reasons I mentioned earlier, people don't seem to be using the process sufficiently voluntarily. So my view about mandatory mediation is about the same as affirmative action — that is, it's not the right permanent answer, but it is a useful temporary expedient to make up for inadequate past practices.

My basic view is that it is for the court, not the parties, to allocate the precious public resource that is the court. The courts and the legislature should decide how much use you should make of courts and in what kind of cases, not the parties or their lawyers. . . .

In the long run we need more education of lawyers and clients. . . .

Second, I am concerned about the long-term professional issues that are raised by ADR. At the moment we have a lot of people who have been trained in ADR, but there is insufficient paying work for them. . . . There are many places where ADR is done by volunteers, and that's a good thing. . . . But I get concerned about developing career paths by which talented graduates of law schools can become self-purporting ADR professionals . . . Increasingly over this period of twenty-five years, more and more people have made careers out of ADR, but it's still extremely difficult and there's no simple way to do it. . . . That's not a good way of developing a new profession.

C. Institutionalization of Mediation in the Court Context: Policy Development

The following section presents readings regarding policy considerations for the development of court-connected mediation. Professor Baruch Bush imagines that a judge has been given an opportunity to order cases to mediation and conducts a conversation with selected friends seeking guidance as to how best implement it. Through this conversation, Professor Bush highlights the underlying philosophical questions about mediation conceptions which must be considered before a judge institutionalizes its use. Professor Donna Shestowsky explores litigants' awareness of court sponsored ADR programs and subsequent policy considerations, and Professor Art Hinshaw discusses the importance of mediator certification and licensing schemes.

Mediation and Adjudication, Dispute Resolution and Ideology: An Imaginary Conversation

3 J. Contemp. Legal Issues 1, 1–10, 14–15, 18–21, 23–24 (1989)*
By Robert A. Baruch Bush

This essay started out as an informal talk to a number of dispute resolution colleagues concerning what I believe is a neglected and important perspective on our field. My goal here is to bring some attention to that perspective, at two levels. First, I want to show that there is an underlying ideological dimension to the ongoing controversy over adjudication and mediation that accounts for a lot of the heat, if not the light, that goes on in the discussion of these and other dispute resolution processes. Second, I want to dig a bit deeper than I think most of us have dug so far to try to say what that ideological dimension is. . . .

Instead of approaching these goals through a formal or abstract analysis, however, I intend to pursue them through imagining a story or conversation which, as it were, gives voices to the different positions taken in the controversy over mediation and adjudication. I invite the reader to listen and respond to this conversation. . . .

The setting for the conversation is as follows. A judge has been empowered by a state statute to refer cases from his civil docket to mediation. The statute says that he can, in his discretion, refer any and all cases; the decision is his, and the parties cannot refuse mediation without showing good cause. The judge can send all his cases to mediation on a blanket basis, or certain categories of cases, or individual cases on a case-by-case basis, whichever he decides. . . . The problem is that the judge is uncertain how to exercise this new power. . . .

So he picks six representative cases from his civil docket: a divorce case with a custody question, a complex commercial litigation, a landlord-tenant case, a discrimination suit, a consumer case, and a personal injury litigation. He sends copies of the case files, with names deleted, to four individuals who are friends or associates: his law clerk, his court administrator, his former law professor, and a practicing mediator. . . . The judge asks each of them for their advice. . . .

He is a bit startled when he gets back the results of this survey, because he gets four completely different recommendations. From the law professor, he gets the recommendation that he should send no cases to mediation; all the cases should stay in court. The law clerk . . . says that the discrimination case, the consumer case, and the personal injury case should be kept in court, but the divorce, the landlord-tenant, and the commercial cases should go to mediation. The court administrator says he should send them all to mediation, unless both parties to the dispute object; if both parties object, he shouldn't refer them to mediation, whatever the type of case. Finally, the mediator tells him that he should send all the cases to mediation, whether or not the parties object.

The judge is puzzled by this set of responses. . . .

[So] he calls all four advisors and says, "I'd like you to argue this out in front of me. I want to hear what you have to say in the presence of one another."

So the four advisors come together with the judge. . . . The court administrator goes first. ". . . As far as I'm concerned, the most important goal we have here is saving time and money. . . . The courts are heavily backlogged, delay is epidemic, and adding new judges and courtrooms appears fiscally — and politically — impossible. Settlements are the only solution . . . [S]ince all cases have some potential to settle," she continues, "and we don't know which ones will and which ones won't, it makes sense to refer them all to mediation, unless we have a clear indication in advance that there's no real settlement possibility. . . . That's the reason for my recommendation. Refer to mediation, unless it's clear that there's opposition on both sides to settlement."

The law clerk then is called upon. He says, ". . . In my view, the main goal is not saving time and money, regardless of what the legislature may have had in mind. There are goals of dispute resolution that are much more important."

". . . [P]rotecting individual rights and ensuring some kind of substantive fairness to both sides in the resolution of the dispute are the most important goals. And where rights and substantive fairness are most important, adjudication in court is the best tool we have to accomplish those goals. However, there are cases where rights and fairness are not the only or the most important goals. For example, if there is an ongoing relationship between the parties, preserving that relationship may be very important both to the parties and to the public. In that case, mediation would be desirable, because preserving relationships is something that mediation does better than the adjudication process. Therefore, I think that you can distinguish between cases on the basis of the ongoing relationship factor. When you have such a relationship, refer to mediation; otherwise, keep the case in court. . . ."

Next is the mediator's turn. "I both agree and disagree with the administrator and the law clerk. . . . Sometimes the best solution will be one that saves the parties time and money; sometimes it will be one that preserves the relationship. Sometimes it will be one that does neither of these. That will all depend on many details of the case."

"But whatever the details, there is plenty of evidence that in terms of achieving the best results for the individual case in question, mediation is a process that has tremendous advantages over adjudication. The process is flexible, issues can be framed more effectively and discussed more fully, a greater variety of possible solutions can be considered, and unique, innovative and integrative solutions are possible, even likely. Therefore, mediation ought to be tried first in all cases because the potential to arrive at superior substantive results is always greater in mediation than in adjudication. If mediation doesn't work . . . then the parties can go back to court. . . ."

Finally the law professor speaks. "Your Honor," he begins, "I'm sorry I have to disagree. But all of your other friends have missed the point. . . . A court is a public institution, and the goal of a court as a public institution is not to save time and money; nor is it to help private parties secure private benefits in individual cases. Your goal as a public institution is to promote important public values. That ought to be your primary concern: the promotion and the securing of important public values through the dispute resolution process. . . ."

"I submit to you, your Honor, that the most important public values at stake in dispute resolution are basically four. . . .[T]he public values a court must concern itself with are: protection of fundamental individual rights, provision of social justice, promotion of economic welfare, and creation of social solidarity."

". . . [T]he rule-based, public adjudication process is an excellent — an unparalleled — instrument for accomplishing these values. Mediation, on the other hand, weakens and undermines every single one of these values. . . ."

"This brings me to the heart of my argument . . . [f]irst, we can't sacrifice public values of this statute solely to save time and money . . . [T]o adopt a public policy saying that values like rights protection and social justice are less important than saving money and judicial economy would be inexcusable. Second, there's no way of neatly dividing up cases on the basis that some involve these public values and others do not. . . . All six of the kinds of cases that you submitted to us involve one or more of these public values . . . Therefore . . . 'channeling' of different cases to different processes is undesirable."

"Finally, you cannot, as the mediator suggested, consider the value of better results for the parties in the individual case superior to these public values. As a matter of public policy, we cannot put private benefit over the public good. Therefore, your Honor, I say all of these cases should remain in court, unless perhaps a petition is submitted by both parties to adjourn pending voluntarily initiated settlement discussions or mediation."

. . .

Before the judge has a chance to adjourn and consider the arguments more thoroughly, however, the mediator asks the judge for one more minute. . . . "When I say mediation ought to be used in all these cases, my reason is also based on promoting public values, public values which are important to all of the cases you sent us, public values different from and more important than the ones that the professor mentioned. In other words, like the professor's argument for adjudication, my argument for mediation is also a public values argument, but it is based on a different view of public values than the view he presented."

"Now my problem is that it is hard to articulate clearly what these different public values are. I think they're evoked or implied by concepts like reconciliation, social harmony, community, interconnection, relationship, and the like. Mediation does produce superior results, as I argued earlier. But it also involves a non-adversarial process that is less traumatic, more humane, and far more capable of healing and reconciliation than adjudication. Those are the kinds of concerns that make me feel that these cases ought to be handled in mediation, not for private benefit reasons and not for expediency reasons, but because of these reconciliatory public values promoted by mediation."

. . .

Let us pause for a minute from this story. The conversation to this point should be familiar to many readers as a parallel to the state of the adjudication/mediation debate today. . . .

Given the state of the debate right now, what are the prospects for the immediate future in the use of adjudication and mediation? What are judges like the one in the story likely to do? I think there are three possible scenarios. First — and most likely, despite the good intentions of the judge in our story — expediency and private interest may rule. Mediation will be used widely, and perhaps indiscriminately, to reduce court caseload and to satisfy private disputants' individual needs. Second, and less likely . . . the public values argument could lead to rejection of mediation generally and retrenchment back to adjudication in court as the primary way of resolving disputes . . . Third, and least likely, if a clear and persuasive public value argument can be articulated on behalf of mediation, then in all likelihood mediation will spread more widely — but perhaps in a different form than the private-benefit/ expediency version.

The present debate over adjudication and mediation therefore has two dimensions. One is the public-value versus private-benefit/expediency dimension . . . [I]t is a clash over whether the public good matters, not what the public good is. . . . The second dimension is the public-value versus public-value dimension, and it is reflected in the conflict . . . here, between the professor and the mediator. . . . In this dimension, both adjudication and mediation represent public values, and the question is which public values are more important. This is a clash over what the public good is, a clash of social vision or ideology. . . . This is the dimension of the debate . . . to which the conversation above is about to proceed.

. . .

The judge repeats his question to the mediator: "What exactly is this public value underlying mediation . . . ?"

. . .

". . . Simply put, it is the value of providing a moral and political education for citizens, in responsibility for themselves and respect for others. In a democracy, your Honor, that must be considered a crucial public value and it must be considered a public function. . . . It cannot be accomplished in adjudication. . . . In my view, this civic education value is more important than the values the professor is concerned about. . . . And . . . even if the parties had reached no agreement in mediation, that education could still have occurred anyway. The case could then have gone back to court where those other values could have been dealt with as secondary matters."

"Finally, I just want to clarify an important connection between my argument here and our earlier discussion. On reflection, I've realized that the 'superior results' argument . . . is also based, at least in part, on the public value I'm talking about here . . . [T]he 'superiority' of results we speak of is not only, or primarily, that the results better serve the individual interests of the parties — a private benefit — but that they express each individual's considered choice to respect and accommodate the other to some degree — a democratic public value. . . ."

. . .

Let us take another pause. What we have now in the story is a parallel of yet another debate that we see in a much larger field. . . .

Once the public-value argument for mediation is fully stated and set against the public-value argument for adjudication, it becomes clear that the adjudication/ mediation debate derives from a much deeper debate between the liberal/ individualist and the communitarian/relationalist visions of society . . . .

. . .

To return to and conclude our conversation . . . what additional advice does this reading suggest we might want to offer the judge in our story? In answer to this question, I want to exercise a little poetic license and jump into the conversation myself, to speak directly to this judge.

Based on what we have heard from the others so far, I would say, "Judge, you're asking what kind of choice you should make, as between keeping cases in court and referring them to mediation. But it's clear to me and I hope it's clear to you that you have a deeper choice to make here: a choice between different social visions. If you accept the prevailing individualist vision, Judge, then you should reject mediation completely, or limit it very severely, to ensure that public values like those advocated by the professor are not undermined. . . . On the other hand, if you accept the relational vision, then you should not merely use mediation; you should expand it to ensure the accomplishment of the most important public values under that vision. . . ."

"But whatever you do . . . as a public servant you should not use mediation at all, if you're going to use it simply as a tool for saving time and satisfying private litigants' individual interests. Because this will undermine both of the contending visions. . . ."

". . . [M]ediation — as the mediator presented it to you — is either being co-opted or rejected entirely. No real attention has been given to the relational vision, and the potential of mediation as a transformative instrument, a means of civic education."

. . .

"This sort of approach . . . — preference for mediation over adjudication across the board — means changing completely the terms of reference in this discussion. It means regarding mediation as a primary dispute resolution process, not an 'alternative' dispute resolution process. . . ."

"Finally . . . if you are going to explore this vision of mediation, it means making sure that mediation as practiced is in fact an opportunity for self-determination and self-transcendence on the part of the parties, and not simply a tool of expediency. . . ."

". . . Am I suggesting mandatory mediation for every case, absent good cause for exemption . . . ? . . . [Y]es, I advise you to use your mandatory mediation power fully; but in any event, do whatever you consider appropriate to encourage mediation in every case."

". . . If you're not prepared . . . to make sure mediation really provides an opportunity for self-determination and self-transcendence — then my advice to you is very different. Forget mediation. . . . Salvage what you can of the individualist vision. Improve the courts. . . ."

"Some people may ask: If I support mediation, then why should I care what the reasons are for expanding it? . . . Let's expand it first, and worry later about clarifying the reasons. . . . I disagree . . . I am afraid that publicly sponsored, court-connected mediation oriented towards efficiency and private benefits alone would crowd out other versions and reduce the chance for the educational vision to develop."

. . .

That is what I would say to the judge — for now, at least. And that is where I close this installment of the conversation. And I throw it open to you, reader. For other voices are surely needed to continue this conversation. After all this, what would you say?

When Ignorance Is Not Bliss: An Empirical Study of Litigants' Awareness of Court-Sponsored Alternative Dispute Resolution Programs
22 Harv. Negot. L. Rev. 189, 191–92, 194–95, 206, 218,
222, 224–26, 229, 231, 233 (Spring 2017)*
By Donna Shestowsky

. . . Considering the significant resources that many courts devote to their ADR programs, it is particularly important to examine how accurately litigants identify court-connected options. This Article presents a novel empirical investigation into litigants' awareness of their court's ADR programs.

Exploring how well litigants can identify court-connected procedures can help us shed light on important issues relating to litigation practices as well as the perceived institutional legitimacy of the courts. First, it can help us better understand whether lawyers and courts are adequately educating litigants about their procedural options. Second, and related, it can help us understand whether informed consent constitutes the basis of their participation in legal procedures. Absent such knowledge, consent cannot truly be informed and party self-determination cannot

---

be achieved. Third, exploring litigant awareness of court programs can provide a window into how litigants perceive the courts. . . .

. . .

A. Why Litigants Should Know about their Procedural Options

The reason that litigants with active cases should know about their procedural options is simple: their preferences should guide which procedures they use. Litigants' ability to exercise their preferences rests on the gateway issue of whether they know about (and then come to understand) the options that are available. As other scholars have argued, litigants should participate in decisions regarding procedural choice for philosophical and pragmatic reasons that implicate party self-determination and court efficiency. . . .

ADR options offer a more democratic form of dispute resolution compared to trial because they offer parties the opportunity to participate more directly in the process and craft outcomes that are more responsive to their needs and interests.

To the extent that courts value efficiency, they should also value educating litigants about their ADR programs so that they can make informed decisions about which procedures to use for their case. Research has found that litigants are more likely to comply with the outcome of their dispute when they are satisfied with their dispute resolution experience.

Thus, when litigants select procedures that subjectively appeal to them, we would expect courts to face fewer appeals when trial verdicts are at issue, and fewer breach-of-contract claims when outcomes derive from settlement procedures such as mediation. Either situation would result in less need for court intervention, and therefore greater efficiency. Moreover, as empirical research by Tom Tyler from Yale Law School has persuasively demonstrated, when people regard the government as offering subjectively attractive and fair procedures, they tend to better comply with even unrelated laws and regulations. Courts benefit from such voluntary compliance with the law. . . .

. . .

III. Method

STUDY COURTS AND THEIR PROGRAMS: We collected data from litigants from three state courts: the Third Judicial District Court, Salt Lake City, Utah ("Utah Court"), the Superior Court of California, County of Solano, ("California Court") and the Fourth Judicial District, Circuit Court of the State of Oregon for the County of Multnomah ("Oregon Court"). We selected these courts because they offered both mediation and non-binding arbitration, in addition to trial, for the *same* causes of action. . . .

V. Discussion

A. Most Litigants did not Correctly Identify their Court's Programs

Although all litigants participating in our study were eligible for both court-sponsored mediation and arbitration, only a minority of litigants correctly identified these offerings at their court—approximately 27% for arbitration and 24% for mediation. Roughly half of the litigants indicated uncertainty regarding whether their court offered arbitration or mediation, and the rest incorrectly believed that their court offered neither of them. . . .

In sum, our results suggest that discussions about procedure did not take place at all, were not flagged as important, or were not conducted in an in-depth or personalized enough way to trigger deep processing. To promote elaboration on the part of their clients, lawyers should emphasize why they should view information regarding procedural options as personally relevant. They might accomplish this goal by ensuring that clients know they have the power to participate in decisions regarding procedure, barring limitations such as those imposed by agreements, court rules, or the opposing party. They should also engage in collaborative learning strategies. For example, lawyers and clients could review information about the court's programs together with the aim of producing a list of questions relevant to applying the information to the client's specific case. Lawyers could then counsel their clients by answering these questions or, if needed, help them obtain such information from the court.

B. Represented Litigants were No Better than Unrepresented Litigants at Identifying Court Programs

What can be done to motivate lawyers to better educate their clients? Court rules could follow the informed consent models in other disciplines, such as medicine, by requiring parties to sign a disclosure indicating that their attorney provided them with information about their options. The protocol of United States District Court for the Northern District of California provides a useful example. The court requires parties and their lawyers to sign an "ADR Certification by Parties and Counsel" form whereby they confirm that they have read the court's handbook describing its ADR procedures, which is available online, discussed the procedures offered by the court as well as private entities, and considered whether their case might benefit from any of the options. . . .

Remedies that rely on attorneys to educate their clients will be effective only insofar as lawyers themselves are well-educated on the available options. In her research on the barriers to lawyer-client conversations about ADR, Roselle Wissler found that when attorneys were less familiar with ADR, they were less likely to discuss ADR with their clients. This finding underscores the important connection between attorney knowledge and litigant education. Wissler also investigated different forms of ADR education and experience and found that the strongest predictor of whether attorneys advised their clients to try ADR was their own past experience acting as counsel in a case that used ADR. . . .

More immediately, one implication of our findings is that courts should consider playing a more active role in litigant education. . . .

Recent research in the small claims context also suggests that more detailed and personalized education is key. In situations where mediation was optional, litigants were "more likely to choose mediation if an authority figure [gave] them a number of legitimate, easy- to-understand incentives for doing so." The researchers concluded that it is not enough for a judge to simply say, "I think you should go to mediation," or "want to try mediation?" as those kinds of statements did not include an explanation of what the procedure entailed. Instead, in order for litigants to seriously consider mediation as a plausible option, the judge should "literally or figuratively [step] down off the bench, [talk] with litigants in a casual way, [use] plain language to explain the incentives that mediation has over trial, and [ask] if litigants have any questions." In other words, court personnel must do more than simply name "mediation" or "arbitration" as options; they must also explain what these procedures involve and how the parties may or may not benefit from using them compared to alternative procedures. . . .

. . .

D. Procedures that Litigants Considered

The majority of our participants indicated that they considered using neither mediation nor arbitration. Negotiation was at the forefront of their minds: over 70% of them considered negotiation, and no procedure obtained a higher contemplation rate than that. Trial was the next most commonly contemplated procedure. And yet, still less than half of the litigants reported that they considered going to trial. When we break down these descriptive statistics further, we find that only half (49.57%) of the plaintiffs indicated that they considered going to trial. This finding resonates with earlier research observing that some disputants file lawsuits not to force the conflict to trial but to express their negative emotions or to motivate the opposing party to negotiate. . . .

E. Implications of Litigant Awareness for Court Programs: Procedures that Litigants Considered and How Litigants Viewed their Court

Litigants did, however, view their court significantly more favorably when they knew it offered mediation. Specifically, litigants who knew their court offered mediation thought more highly of their court than those who incorrectly believed it did not offer mediation or were unsure whether it did. One interpretation of this result is that litigants who think highly of their court are more inclined to learn about court procedures. Another interpretation is more intuitive: litigants are more pleased with their court when they know it offers mediation. . . .

If litigants favor mediation, they might think more highly of courts that clearly endorse it programmatically. Given that we found this relation between litigants' impressions of their court and their knowledge of court ADR offerings after their cases ended, our findings suggest that courts should market their mediation programs in ways that litigants will find memorable over the long run. Courts might even remind them at several intervals, including at the end of their case. The latter proposal might be accomplished through exit surveys or by providing litigants with a "in case you need our help again in the future" pamphlet that reminds them about their ADR programs once their case is closed.

Regulating Mediators

21 Harv. Negot. L. Rev. 163, 167–69, 172–73, 187–92, 194–97 (2016)*
By Art Hinshaw

Mediation has seen tremendous growth over the last thirty years, moving from an unconventional means of conflict resolution to a common step in the traditional litigation process. This growth has generated periodic calls for regulation that have been largely unanswered. Anyone in any state can hold herself out to the public as a mediator without any training or other demonstration of competence. . . .

This is not to say that mediators are always unregulated. Court-connected mediation programs exist in state and federal courts and serve a quasi-regulatory function. However, most of these programs are small, focusing only on mediators who mediate cases in that particular court, and only a handful of states operate a statewide court-connected mediation program out of a centralized office. But a strategy of relying on court-connected mediation programs to regulate mediators is problematic because a large number of mediations take place outside of court-connected programs. Even when mediators are removed from a court-approved list, there is no mechanism to discontinue their mediation practice outside the court system. This leaves the vast majority of mediators in the United States largely unregulated and subject only to market forces unless they engage in criminal activity.

One might expect civil litigation to be an important check against incompetent and dishonest mediators, acting as a substitute for regulation through breach of contract or professional malpractice. But several states protect mediators from civil liability, and some like Florida, Indiana, and North Carolina, provide mediators with absolute immunity from civil liability. . . .

. . .

B. Becoming a Mediator

Since the mediation field is unregulated, there are no general restrictions as to who can be a mediator or who can provide mediation services, and no requirements for what one has to do to become a mediator. To make things murkier, there is no established career path for becoming a mediator. As a result, people typically come to mediation as a secondary profession after being educated and employed in another field. This is because having substantive knowledge in particular fields helps mediators appear competent and qualified to do their job. For example, divorce mediators come to the field from a variety of backgrounds relating to domestic relations, including psychology, mental health, social work, and counseling as well as law. A large number of mediators come from the ranks of lawyers and judges, two careers focused on disputes and disputing, but one need not be a lawyer to succeed as a mediator.

Not surprisingly, there is a wide variation in the training and education of mediators. There is no standard curriculum for mediation training, although most mediation trainers agree that for the best results, mediation training should have a mix of lecture, skills, practice, and reflection. Forty-hour basic or introductory mediation training programs are widely held across the country, but some states like Missouri require "at least 16 hours of formal training" to be a mediator in the state court system. Upon completion of their training, mediators often casually refer to themselves as "being certified," implying that their skills have passed muster with a certifying entity, when they simply received a certificate indicating the completion of a training program.

Despite the lack of structure in becoming a mediator, most mediators indicate their competency using professional affiliations and mediation referral sources. Professional affiliation credentials are qualifications established by an organization to which a mediator belongs. Some organizations do membership screening, like requiring election into the organization or completion of a certain number of mediations, but for many the only hurdle for membership is the payment of dues. Mediation referral sources, on the other hand, are the organizations from which mediators receive disputes to mediate such as court systems, other governmental agencies, social service agencies, or mediation service provider organizations. To receive referrals from these organizations, mediators must meet or exceed organizational standards for training, education, and experience. As such, professional organization and mediation referral sources have the ability to influence the field in a number of ways, but their direct influence extends only to membership.

. . .

IV. Occupational Regulation

. . .

There are three basic forms of occupational regulation: registration, certification and licensing. Registration is the least restrictive. It requires individuals to give a governmental entity their names, contact information, and qualifications along with posting a bond or fee before practicing their occupation. Slightly more restrictive is a certification regime which allows any person to perform the relevant service, but only those who have met the certifying agency's knowledge and skill requirements are certified, presumably giving them a reputational advantage in the marketplace. Individuals without certification may perform the duties of the occupation, but may not claim to be certified. The most restrictive form of regulation is licensure, which is also known as the right-to-practice. Licensure laws typically make it unlawful to practice an occupation without first meeting the government's standards and obtaining a license. Presently, only a few states offer certification schemes for mediators, but in the majority of jurisdictions, none of these forms of regulation are used for mediators.

B. Attempts to Regulate Mediators

1. Legislative

Legislation impacting the mediation processes is proposed and adopted regularly, but legislation to regulate mediators is rarely promulgated. California has the most extensive history of attempts to regulate mediators but has never successfully done so. In 1995, State Senator Newton R. Russell introduced a bill to create a three-part mediator credentialing system administered by a new state agency. After the California mediation community voiced opposition to the bill, Senator Russell agreed to allow a year's worth of consideration before resuming the bill's progress through the legislature. Three subsequent hearings prompted him to introduce a revised bill based on a voluntary certification program with universities and mediation organizations conducting the certification process. Although this second bill enjoyed the widespread support of the California mediation community, it never made it out of the Senate Business and Professions Committee.

... [I]n 2012, the Bay Area Lawyers for Individual Freedom proposed legislation to the California Conference of Bar Associations (CCBA), a group of attorneys from specialized bar sections who attempt to improve California's laws. This legislation would have established minimum qualifications for mediators including: completing 40 hours of mediation training, conducting 20 separate mediations "as a solo mediator," and holding a law degree or specialized graduate degree in a field directly related to the subject matter of the controversy being mediated, such as medicine, psychology, or engineering. This proposal named the State Bar of California as the certifying and regulating body, and named the State Bar Court as the disciplinary tribunal. The CCBA rejected the proposal outright. . . .

. . .

2. National Professional Organizations

Mediation's two national professional organizations, the American Bar Association's Dispute Resolution Section (ABA DR Section) and the Association for Conflict Resolution (ACR) have worked for decades to protect the integrity of the field by providing expertise, advice, and guidance to legislative, judicial, and administrative bodies in drafting mediation related policies and best practices. And while these organizations favor mediator certification over licensure, they have refused to certify mediators.

In 1989, the Commission on Qualifications of one of ACR's predecessor organizations, the Society of Professionals in Dispute Resolution (SPIDR), adopted three central regulatory principles for mediators:

> No single entity .... should establish qualifications for [mediators]; The greater degree of choice the parties have over the dispute resolution process, program, or neutral, the less mandatory the qualification requirements should be; and qualification criteria should be based on performance rather than paper credentials.

In 1995, the Commission on Qualifications confirmed the conclusions of its 1989 report and recognized that formal certification would assure practitioner competence. It concluded that certification is only appropriate when: (1) certification standards are specific enough to serve as a basis to decertify a practitioner, (2) there is a mechanism in place for certification, (3) certification is tied to competence, and (4) the certification process is regularly reviewed and amended as needed.

In 2002, the ABA DR Section's Task Force on Credentialing made recommendations outlining the essential components of a credentialing program and the methods for assessing mediator competency. However, the Task Force only proposed undertaking a flexible, low-cost accreditation system for mediator training programs rather than individual mediators. In 2004 the ACR Mediator Certification Task Force recommended establishing a voluntary two-step certification program for mediators through a separate administrative entity, but for reasons that are unclear, ACR ended up abandoning the plan entirely.

In 2005, ACR and the ABA DR Section developed a survey for practicing mediators about a national certification program. . . . [L]ess than 40% of respondents thought a national certification program was necessary. Based on these survey results, the ABA DR Section determined that a national credentialing program was not feasible.

A 2008 ACR membership survey indicated broad support to establish a certification process. Instead, ACR promulgated Model Standards for Mediator Certification Programs in 2011. Along these lines, ACR's ongoing strategic plan includes developing a certification program for family mediators that would include a performance-based assessment. In 2012, the ABA DR Section's Task Force on Mediator Credentialing adopted a policy supporting credentialing efforts and established minimum standards for any credentialing process, but limited its support to an optional system. Since then, the ABA DR Section has not had a group study the question of occupational regulation.

. . .

4. Courts

Some jurisdictions regulate those who conduct court-ordered mediations. Known as either court-connected or court-annexed mediations, these mediation programs maintain rosters of approved mediators for judicial referral. Every state in the country has some form of a court-connected mediation program and each state runs its program differently. A few states such as Florida, Georgia, Maine, Maryland, Minnesota, North Carolina, and Virginia have well-developed and comprehensive state-wide mediation programs; other states' programs are run out of a trial courts' administrative offices or an individual judge's chambers.

The more comprehensive court-connected mediation programs were developed for a wide range of reasons, but all recognize that a successful program requires a pool of practitioners who will protect the legitimacy of the program and the integrity of the courts. When mediation becomes an integral part of a court's civil litigation system, the court assumes responsibility for protecting the public from bad mediators.

To meet their consumer protection objectives, these court-connected mediation programs require the following from their mediators:

A combination of minimal mediation training and experience;

Continuing education requirements;

Ongoing regular work as a mediator;

A formal ethics code; and

A complaint and disciplinary procedure to penalize mediators engaging in misconduct, including the possibility of removal from the approved mediator list.

In addition, some of these programs also mandate training by specific mediation trainers, training programs, or continuing education programs. Other programs provide their mediators with ethics advisory opinions.

Even though limited regulation through the courts has been successful, initial reactions to the concept were negative, ranging from open hostility to begrudging acceptance. Over time, however, this discomfort has been replaced with increased acceptance. Courts' ability to overcome the initial antagonism to regulation may stem from the development of effective administrators, the perception that court referrals may be a good source of business, the belief that having a court-related credential is good for marketing, or, perhaps, the reluctant acknowledgment that courts have the inherent authority to control all aspects of the litigation process. Despite the apparent success of court-connected mediation in states with comprehensive state-wide mediation programs, there appears to be no impetus to adopt similar systems in other states.

Notes and Questions

(1) Professor Bush intentionally presents the ideological debate as an either/or choice over which set of public values one adopts. Might they be integrated? If so, how?

(2) Do you agree with Bush that a person who adopts an individualist vision should reject mediation completely or limit it severely?

(3) For another view on the policy decisions involved in institutionalizing a mediation program, see Professor Sharon Press, *Building and Maintaining a State-wide Mediation Program: A View from the Field*, 81 Ken. L.J. 1029 (1992–93).

(4) In 2006, the Florida Supreme Court revised the qualification requirements for certified mediators from one based on professional education to a "point system" which recognized the variety of ways individuals may obtain competence. *See* Rules 10.100–10.105, Florida Rules for Certified and Court-Appointed Mediators. Do you believe that these revised requirements ensures a roster of competent mediators? Do you think that such a point system would help to address the issues raised by Professor Hinshaw in his article?

(5) The voluntary certification bills referenced in Hinshaw's article were not adopted but did provide opportunity for additional commentary on the topic of certification. An important challenge engendered by any certification process is how to ensure mediator competence while preserving diversity of mediator orientations and style. In her article *The Challenge of Certification: How to Ensure Mediator Competence While Preserving Diversity*, 30 U.S.F. L. Rev. 723, 724–25 (1996), Professor Ellen Waldman addresses this matter when analyzing proposed California S.B. 1428:

> The proposed Bill's overall sensitivity to the diverse professional mix which mediators bring to their work was laudable. However, the Bill displayed less sensitivity to the variety of mediator approaches prevalent in the field. SB 1428 failed to make clear that mediator training and performance evaluations must be implemented in ways that encourage the full panoply of regnant mediator styles. In so doing, the Bill threatened to establish credentialing machinery which constricted rather than enriched mediation practice.

Reflecting on the materials in Chapter 4, *supra*, when considering the operationalization of a credentialing scheme, is there a risk that mediators preferring a particular mediator style or orientation will dominate the certification process, leading to an undesirable homogenization of the mediation field? Waldman framed her criticism of the legislation in terms of diversity of style. Is there a similar concern regarding cultural, ethnic, and racial diversity? Consider how the empirical findings in the New Mexico study described in Chapter 7, *supra*, relate to the issues of qualifications, certification, and licensure of mediators.

Which approach to institutionalizing mediation is most desirable for the courts? The parties? The programs? In this excerpt, Sharon Press highlights the positive aspects of institutionalization, if managed appropriately.

Institutionalization: Savior or Saboteur of Mediation?
24 Fla. St. U. L. Rev. 903, 904–13, 917 (1997)*
By Sharon Press

. . . [O]ne of the most exciting and challenging developments for practitioners . . . has been the increased institutionalization of ADR particularly in relation to mediation within the court system. Spreading ADR processes has been a goal many who are committed to the field have pursued with great vigor. As the old cliché reminds us, however, "be careful what you wish for." The growth and development of mediation and other dispute resolution processes in institutional settings, while certainly producing more exposure and interest in these processes, has also brought with it a host of concerns I believe worthy of thought and discussion. . . .

. . .

... For purposes of this Article, I use the term "institutionalization" to refer to any entity (governmental or otherwise) which, as an entity, adopts ADR procedures as a part of doing business. Some examples include schools that develop peer mediation programs, courts that establish rules to govern referral to ADR procedures, and government agencies that incorporate ADR processes in developing rules and regulations. My discussion will focus primarily on the institutionalization of court mediation programs, with examples drawn from Florida's experience ... however, I believe that many of the same opportunities and concerns raised are readily transferable to other institutions. To me, Florida's experience with court-connected mediation can serve as a case study for how and why bureaucracies develop.

Institutionally, Florida entered the ADR movement in the mid-1970s with the establishment of "citizen dispute settlement" (CDS) centers. The CDS centers are similar to the neighborhood justice centers of other jurisdictions and handle disputes (mostly minor criminal, neighborhood-type disputes) that are voluntarily brought by the individuals involved in the disputes. The model pursued for the Florida CDS centers, after the initial ones came into being, centered around local development with strong support from the Office of the State Courts Administrator (OSCA) and the Chief Justice of the Florida Supreme Court. ...

Some argued that this development was not in keeping with the primary goal of the CDS movement, which was to empower those in the local community to resolve issues for themselves. On the other hand, these programs would not have spread as quickly or completely had it not been for the Florida Supreme Court's support. The research conducted by OSCA provided the data to show that the programs worked, the organizational manuals provided the step-by-step information on how to establish programs, and the training manuals and guidelines provided some measure of consistency and quality control that led to confidence in the program. Looking around the nation, one finds that programs have flourished primarily in those states in which the courts provided an institutional home, established institutional frameworks, and promoted the use of these processes. I believe there is a direct correlation. In Florida, the CDS programs thrived when the supreme court focused attention on the program. When attention shifted from the CDS programs toward the court programs, no new programs were established and many of those that were in existence expanded to include court cases. Within a few years, the bulk of the CDS centers' cases had shifted away from communities and towards courts. This shift is not surprising, based upon the difficulty CDS or neighborhood justice centers have in generating cases. Because the number of cases that a community center actually mediates is significantly lower than the number of cases that are scheduled (due to the inherent difficulty in getting both parties to attend a completely voluntary process), the centers face a continuing challenge, resulting in disappointingly low caseloads.

. . .

If we start from the premise that mediation and other alternative processes provide a positive means of resolving disputes, then it seems to follow that providing for the more rapid spread and more comprehensive use of these processes would also be a positive step. As practitioners, we have longed for more cases to be referred to mediation so more disputants can benefit from the empowerment possibilities of mediated disputes (and also so there is enough work for us to pursue our chosen field). Institutionalization certainly focuses attention on the processes, and it can be very instrumental in promoting its uses; yet increased institutionalization is not without its downside.

. . .

. . . Since 1987, Florida has experienced tremendous growth in the number of rules and laws surrounding the mediation program. From an administrative perspective, each additional rule has been necessary and important in the maturation of the program. Overall, however, I remain concerned about the ultimate effect that additional rules will have on the mediation process, *i.e.*, what will happen when a flexible process, like mediation, is incorporated into the traditional court process. Which process changes?

A description of some of the . . . revisions and additions to the Florida Statutes and the Florida Rules of Civil Procedure serves as an ideal way to illustrate this dilemma. In 1988, the Florida Supreme Court adopted qualifications for court mediators. To promote use of the qualifications and add to the comfort level of the judges and lawyers who would ultimately be the users of the process, the court relied heavily on previous experience and "paper credentials." The national mediation community was outraged by the development of mediator qualification requirements by an institution. Nevertheless, if an institution takes the step to order parties who file in court to participate in mediation prior to (or hopefully instead of) obtaining a trial before a judge, doesn't it logically follow that the court has an affirmative obligation to ensure that the individual to whom the case is referred has some expertise? To take it a step further, wouldn't it be irresponsible, if not negligent, for the courts not to develop some method of determining who should mediate for the courts and who should not? I do not see easy answers to these questions. While I am sympathetic to the view that the qualifications originally established by the Florida Supreme Court are not perfect, I do believe that the establishment of mediation as an alternative within the court system brought with it the obligation to provide some means for individuals ordered to mediation to have confidence in their mediator. I also believe, based on discussions I have had over the years with judges and attorneys, that mediation would not have succeeded in the court system if the early mediators in large cases were not attorneys.

This is not to say that the obligation of the court or institution that establishes the program ends with its initial rules and its ability to gain acceptance for the program. On the contrary, I am a strong proponent of the notion that if a court undertakes to institutionalize mediation, it has an ongoing obligation to routinely and systematically review the governing policies, rules, and procedures with an eye toward continual revision. To me, this is a crucial step in preventing the ossification of a flexible process.

. . .

. . . [T]he Florida Legislature has revised the statute governing mediation and arbitration several times since its adoption in 1987.

One of the legislative changes adopted provides for "judicial immunity in the same manner and to the same extent as a judge." . . . The passage of this legislation created a situation that led to the need for the next major set of rules, namely, the Florida Rules for Certified and Court-Appointed Mediators, which contain the standards of conduct and rules of discipline for supreme court-certified and court-appointed mediators.

The original legislation establishing the comprehensive mediation program contained a provision that the Florida Supreme Court would establish minimum standards and procedures for professional conduct and discipline. However, the adoption of the immunity for mediators provided the real impetus to adopt standards and a disciplinary procedure. Absent such adoption, parties to court-ordered mediation had no redress for inappropriate mediator behavior . . . with such a backdrop, one can readily appreciate the need for the development of standards of conduct. In 1992, the Florida Supreme Court adopted such a code of conduct and a means for enforcing the standards. . . . I remain concerned about the impact that these standards will have on the process. I come back again to the overriding concern that mediation is a flexible process and that adoption of a code of conduct will somehow rigidify the process. If the standards are written broadly to allow for the subtle nuances of an individual situation, might they then offer no real guidance to mediators in discharging their duties? If they are written very specifically, might they then inhibit a mediator's ability to handle each situation creatively?

. . .

. . . I believe that the institutionalization of mediation programs has served a worthwhile purpose. It is only with institutionalization that we are able to achieve the increased attention and high level of debate around these issues. I have seen firsthand . . . how helpful — and transforming — these programs can be. I know that most people are still not very sophisticated in thinking through their options for resolving disputes. In the school setting, students frequently view their options as limited to ignoring the situation, telling a teacher or other authority, or fighting it out. For adults, the choices are surprisingly similar: ignoring the conflict, appealing to the authority of the courts, or fighting it out. . . . Institutionalization provides necessary legitimacy and widespread utilization to a process that is only useful if one knows about it. One can only make informed decisions about whether to use mediation if one is aware that the process exists.

Notes and Questions

(1) In a more recent critique of the Florida program, *Institutionalization of Mediation in Florida: At the Crossroads*, 108 Penn St. L. Rev. 43 (2003), Press describes the sheer size and complexity of the Florida program in this excerpt:

> When I describe the Florida program, I often say that the program "may not be the best, but it probably is the most." What I mean by this is that the Florida court-connected mediation program is quantitatively large. The program encompasses a wide range of cases and is implemented statewide. This also means there are many implementing layers, including procedural rules for court-ordered mediation, qualification standards for certified mediators, and a process for certifying the mediators, which includes completing an initial Supreme Court of Florida certified mediation training program and obtaining the appropriate amount of continuing mediator education credits every two years. The fact that there are certified mediation training programs means that there also are rules governing the content and delivery of such mediation training programs and a procedure for filing a grievance or complaint against a certified training program. In addition, there are ethical standards for certified and court-appointed mediators, a grievance procedure to enforce these ethical rules, and an ethics advisory committee charged with providing advisory opinions to mediators who are subject to the rules. Along with the Mediator Qualifications Board (which handles the grievances against individual mediators), the Mediation Training Review Board (which handles the complaints against certified training programs), and the Mediator Ethics Advisory Committee, the Florida Supreme Court also has a standing committee on ADR, the Supreme Court Committee on ADR Rules and Policy. The existence of this committee ensures that the Florida mediation program engages in a process of continuous review and assessment for improvements.

(2) While the courts have been in the forefront of the move to institutionalize mediation, they are not unique. Federal and state agencies have also been using mediation and creating institutional mediation opportunities. In 1990, Congress passed the first Administrative Dispute Resolution Act ("ADRA" Public Law 101-552, 104 Stat. 2736, 5 U.S.C. §§ 581 *et seq.* (1990)). This statute required each federal agency to "adopt a policy that addresses the use of alternative means of dispute resolution," "designate a senior official to be the dispute resolution specialist of the agency," and "review each of its standard agreements for contracts, grants . . . [to] encourage the use of alternative means of dispute resolution." In 1996, the ADRA was reenacted and made permanent (*i.e.*, no sunset provision).

(3) Employee-grievance situations have proven to be particularly conducive to mediation. Here, the conflict is often between individuals who have an ongoing relationship which will often benefit from a private, informal process of resolution. For

a complete description of the U.S. Equal Employment Opportunity Commission's mediation program, see https://www.eeoc.gov/mediation.

Since the COVID-19 Pandemic, the EEOC has elected to mediate a majority of their employment discrimination cases online. In two recent studies involving EEOC-mediated cases, E. Patrick McDermott and Ruth Obar examined both the perceptions of the mediators and the litigants (in EEOC terminology, the Charging Parties ("CPs") and Employers) in how they experienced the online dispute resolution ("ODR") process and the in person mediation ("IPM") process.

In the research examining the mediator's perception, the researchers found that mediators reported:

- Twenty percent of mediators report a higher settlement rates for their ODR cases than for IPM, with 9% reporting lower rates. A majority (62%) of mediators report that their settlement rate for ODR is the same as IPM. Independent EEOC data confirms that ODR has a similar settlement rate (70.9%) as IPM (71.9%).

- ODR at the EEOC is more flexible than IPM. There is increased use of caucusing, increased sharing of important documents, a significant reduction of the time pressure element found in IPM, scheduling flexibility including the ability to extend the time of a mediation and/or quickly reconvene a mediation to maintain settlement momentum, the added value of physical separation of the parties' safe space, increased/varied communication lanes, the positive role played by insurance adjusters, and the real-time ability to invite other persons such as a key decision-maker into the mediation.

- Access to justice is enhanced by the EEOC ODR program by increased employer personnel and decision-maker participation, ease of participation of other key attendees, increased employee access, power balancing, removal of the CP's fear of being in the same location as the Employer for some cases, and related benefits to both parties.

E. Patrick McDermott & Ruth Obar, *Equal Employment Opportunity Commission Mediators' Perception of Remote Mediation and Comparisons to In-Person Mediation* (Feb. 18, 2022), https://www.eeoc.gov/sites/default/files/2022-06/508%20Final_Mediator_FINAL%20EEOC%20REPORT_3_4.pdf.

In the research based on litigant perception, the researchers found that:

- Ninety-two percent of CPs and 98% of Employers would use EEOC ODR mediation again.

- Procedural Justice measures show that 86% of Charging Parties "CPs" and 94% of Employers view the ODR procedures used by EEOC mediators as fair.

- The Distributive Justice measure of overall fairness shows that 82% of CPs and 91% of Employers view the overall ODR mediation as fair.

- The Distributive Justice measure of outcome satisfaction shows that 60% of CPs and 72% of Employers are satisfied with the results of the ODR mediation.

- Nearly 70% of the participants prefer ODR to IPM for a future mediation even where IPM is offered by the EEOC. Only 13% preferred IPM in the future.

E. Patrick McDermott & Ruth Obar, *The Equal Employment Opportunity Commission Mediation Participants Experience in Online Mediation and Comparison to In-Person Mediation* (Feb. 18, 2022), https://www.eeoc.gov/sites/default/files/2022-06 /508%20Final_PARTICIPANT%20FINAL_3_4_2022.pdf.

(4) In 1994, the United States Postal Service established a mediation program to service disputes among co-workers that operates within the transformative framework. *See* Chapter 4, *supra.* For a review of the initial evaluation of this program, *see Mediating Employment Disputes: Perception of Redress at the United States Postal Service*, 17 Rev. Pub. Personnel Admin. 20 (1997).

What similarities and differences are there between the institutionalization of mediating legal disputes through the court system and institutionalizing mediation's use in government agencies or private companies?

(5) Institutional uses of mediation can also be found in schools — from primary and pre-school through high school and universities — in the form of peer mediation programs for addressing school-related conflicts involving students, teachers and staff, or for alleged breaches of the student code of conduct. *See* the Education Section of the Association for Conflict Resolution for resources and additional information on programs.

(6) While small claims mediation in the court connected context has been popular for many years, mediation for landlord-tenant matters, particularly evictions, has been institutionalized more recently. Many practitioners, law makers and community advocates question its use in this area. In her article, *Mitigating Power Imbalance in Eviction Mediation: A Model for Minnesota*, 38(1) Law & Ineq. (2020), Rebecca Hare identifies the inherent power imbalance between the tenants and landlords in eviction mediations and offers some solutions to address it.

> Reducing the forced displacement of tenants supports both individual dignity and community prosperity — and can be achieved through mediation. However, for mediation to be effective in preventing eviction, it must be a tool of empowerment. This is not possible in a system that prioritizes the convenience and expediency of eviction. Effective mediation requires time, opportunity, and equal access to the protection of the law. To be an effective alternative to the eviction process, both parties must be incentivized and empowered to mediate. With reform of unlawful detainer classification and disclosure, systemic obstacles to negotiation are dismantled and tenants gain incentive to mediate. Instituting a notice period prior to filing an eviction encourages both parties to participate in mediation to negotiate an

agreement to allow tenants to remain in their homes and avoid an eviction filing. Finally, and most importantly, access to legal resources and representation are necessary for tenants to effectively represent themselves in mediation. A statutory eviction mediation process, modeled after the Farmer Lender Mediation Act, is necessary to ensure that the opportunity to mediate is extended to all tenants and that these strategies are incorporated into a comprehensive approach to reduce the power differential between landlords and tenants and achieve successful mediated agreements. Promoting successful mediation in eviction disputes enables both parties to negotiate mutually beneficial agreements, curtails ineffective and excessive use of the eviction process, and improves housing stability by preventing tenant displacement. By reducing this harmful displacement, we preserve homes, livelihoods, and communities.

Hare suggests adopting several procedural protections to correct power imbalances in eviction mediation. Can you think of eviction cases where some of these protections may not be necessary? Where other protections are needed?

D. Empirical Evaluations

In this section, we turn to empirical evaluations. Empirically evaluating the efficacy of mediation's use in the courts is controversial. From the courts' perspective, achieving significant settlement rates, thereby clearing its dockets, is an important focus for empirical evaluations. But practitioners worry that focusing exclusively on settlement as a success measure encourages mediators to push parties to settle rather than support their efforts to make decisions for themselves. Further, emphasizing settlement rates diminishes assessing other goals of court connected mediation, such as procedural justice, participant satisfaction with the process, and repairing party relationships.

Conducting empirical evaluations of court connected mediation has not accompanied its growing, widespread use. One recent robust and unique study was undertaken by the Maryland courts, with funding by the State Justice Institute in collaboration with Community Mediation Maryland, Salisbury University and University of Maryland. Lorig Charkoudian, Deborah Thompson Eisenberg and Jamie L. Walter describe the results of an aspect of Maryland's court ADR initiative.

What Difference Does ADR Make? Comparison of ADR[1] and Trial Outcomes in Small Claims Court

35 Conflict Resol. Q. 1, 7–9, 38, 39, 41 (2017)*

By Lorig Charkoudian, Deborah Thompson Eisenberg and Jamie L. Walter

Many courts offer alternative dispute resolution (ADR) processes, such as mediation and settlement conferences, but few rigorous studies have examined what difference ADR makes as compared to trial. This research is the first to compare the attitudes and changes in attitudes of litigants who participated in ADR to an equivalent comparison group who used the traditional court process, both immediately and three to six months later. The research measured a variety of litigant attitudes including: attitudes toward the other party, sense of empowerment and voice in the process, sense of responsibility for the dispute, belief that the conflict could be or had been resolved, and satisfaction with the judicial system. These attitudes were tracked from before to after the ADR session or trial as well as three to six months later. The study also tested whether experiences differed for various demographic groups. Finally, the study examined the predicted probability that the treatment and comparison groups would return to court for an enforcement action in the subsequent year.

Many ADR studies rely on the results of post-ADR participant evaluation forms, without conducting surveys prior to the intervention, using a comparison group that went to trial without ADR, or controlling for other variables that could affect the outcome. The present study measures the immediate and long-term attitudes and changes in attitudes of those litigants who participated in ADR as compared to those who went to trial without ADR. . . .

This study uniquely tests whether there is value in simply participating in the ADR process, regardless of whether the parties reach agreement. Many judicial assessments of ADR focus on settlement rates and trial avoidance as the main goals of ADR. To evaluate the impact of ADR participation beyond settlement, we included parties who reached agreement in ADR and those who did not. In addition, some commentators question the value of ADR because parties can negotiate directly with each other and settle on their own "on the courthouse steps." The comparison trial group therefore included those who reached "hallway" agreements before trial and those who did not. . . .

We report outcomes that are statistically significant at a 95 percent confidence level. Using this heightened benchmark, ADR has significant positive impacts in both

---

1. [While this empirical study compares ADR outcomes to trial outcomes, it is clear from the research design and methodology that a vast majority of the practitioners were providing mediation services. — Eds.]

* Used with permission of Conflict Resolution Quarterly, from Lorig Charkoudian, Deborah Thompson Eisenberg and Jamie L. Walter, Volume 35, Issue 1, 2017; permission conveyed through Copyright Clearance Center, Inc.

the short term and long term, regardless of whether the parties settle. In the short term, ADR improves the parties' attitudes toward each other, gives parties a greater sense of empowerment and voice in the process, increases their taking responsibility for the dispute, and increases their satisfaction with the judicial system more generally. In the long term, ADR participants are more likely than those who went to trial to report an improved relationship with and attitude toward the other party, satisfaction with the outcome, and satisfaction with the judiciary. Parties who reach agreement in ADR are less likely to return to court for an enforcement action than all other cases (including those in which the parties settled on their own without any ADR, ADR cases that did not settle, and cases with a court verdict).

Research Design and Methodology

The study compares the immediate and long-term attitudes and changes in attitudes of litigants who used day of trial ADR (the "treatment" group) to an equivalent group who proceeded to trial without ADR ("comparison" group). The study focused on civil cases in the District Court of Maryland, a statewide unified court that has jurisdiction over a variety of contract, tort, return of property (replevin and detinue), and landlord-tenant claims (tenant holding over, breach of lease, and wrongful detainer).

The District Court of Maryland ADR program offers mediation or settlement conferences at no charge to litigants on the day of their trials through a roster of volunteer mediators and settlement conference attorneys, collectively called "ADR practitioners." The type of process provided depends upon the expertise of the volunteer ADR practitioner present that day. Most ADR practitioners in the study indicated that they were providing mediation (88 percent) with the remaining 12 percent providing a settlement conference. Prior studies have shown that mediators who profess to practice a particular framework or orientation of mediation may vary in the strategies they use during the session. Thus, the actual techniques used by mediators or settlement conference attorneys may be similar in some ways.

Treatment cases were recruited from the small claims civil dockets in Baltimore City and Montgomery County. To control for selection bias, comparison cases were selected from these same dockets, on days when an ADR practitioner was not present, using the same criteria that would have been used to refer cases to ADR in that jurisdiction. . . .

Discussion

ADR has significant positive, immediate impacts on parties who participated in ADR as compared to those who went to trial without ADR. In the short term, ADR improves the parties' attitudes toward each other, gives parties a greater sense of empowerment and voice in the process, increases their taking of responsibility for the dispute, and increases their satisfaction with the judicial system more generally. In the long term, ADR participants are more likely than the trial group to report an improved relationship with and attitude toward the other party, satisfaction with the outcome, and satisfaction with the judicial system. In addition, cases that settled in ADR are less likely to return to court for an enforcement action within the next year.

Short-Term Impact

ADR participants were more likely than those who proceeded through the standard court process to indicate that: (1) they could express themselves, their thoughts, and their concerns; (2) all of the underlying issues came out; (3) the issues were resolved; (4) the issues were completely resolved rather than partially resolved; and (5) they acknowledged responsibility for the situation. Importantly, this was true for all ADR cases, including those that reached an agreement in ADR and those that did not settle.

ADR permits participants to discuss topics beyond the legal issues in the case. This study confirms the value of these discussions in ADR, even if the parties do not settle the legal case. As compared to those who proceeded to trial without ADR, participation in ADR shifted party attitudes about their own level of responsibility for the conflict. Specifically, ADR participants had an increase in their rating of their level of responsibility for the situation from before to after the intervention. ADR also increased their appreciation for the opposing party's perspective, with ADR participants more likely to disagree with the statement "the other people [in the conflict] need to learn they are wrong" from before to after the process. ADR participants were also less likely to report that no one took responsibility or apologized than litigants who went through the standard court process without ADR. This finding confirms that ADR helps parties gain a new perspective on the conflict that adversarial litigation cannot offer.

Again, all of these short-term findings applied uniformly to ADR, regardless of whether the parties settled in ADR. Including a variable for negotiated agreement held constant for the settlement impact of ADR and included the potential benefits of the negotiated "hallway" agreements for those in the trial group who did not use ADR. Parties who reached agreement in ADR were more likely to be satisfied with the judicial system than all others. Those parties in the trial group who negotiated an agreement on their own without any ADR were not more likely to be satisfied with the judicial system than those who did not settle at all. This suggests that it is the process of reaching an agreement through the ADR process—rather than simply the fact of settlement—that causes higher satisfaction levels.

This research shows that there are important short-term benefits of ADR for the parties beyond efficiency and settlement concerns. The ability to talk directly to the other side may explain many of the short-term findings. ADR allows the parties to express their thoughts and concerns more fully and discuss and potentially resolve all of the underlying issues. Judges must decide cases based only on the applicable law and can award only the legal remedies available.

If they reach agreement in ADR, participants are more satisfied with the judiciary overall than those who go to trial without ADR. This is consistent with prior research that ADR offers a sense of voice and procedural justice that increases public confidence in the judicial system more generally. . . .

Long-Term Impact of ADR

Several striking long-term benefits of ADR emerged. Regardless of settlement, ADR participants were more likely than the trial group to report an improved relationship with and attitude toward the other party measured from before the intervention to three to six months later. This finding confirms that ADR can have important long-term relational benefits.

ADR participants are also more likely than trial participants to report that the outcome was working and that they were satisfied with the outcome and the judicial system three to six months after the intervention. This was true for all ADR participants, although it was slightly stronger for those who settled in ADR. This is important for the broader public respect for the judiciary and rule of law. As Wissler writes, "Litigants' experiences in court, particularly their judgments of procedural fairness, have been found to affect their general views of the legal system and its legitimacy."

Finally, the long-term analysis found that parties who settled in ADR were less likely to return to court for an enforcement action in the twelve months following the intervention compared to all other cases, including those that reached an agreement on their own, ADR cases that did settle, and cases with a judge verdict. Specifically, reaching an agreement in ADR decreased the predicted probability of returning to court by 21 percent.

This finding suggests that courts should consider the durability of the ultimate resolution as well as immediate judicial efficiency and time savings. Although not all parties will settle in ADR, this study shows that parties who do are significantly less likely to consume court resources in the future as compared to cases with a judge verdict and cases with a negotiated "hallway" agreement developed with no ADR.

Limitations

The primary limitation of this study is the relatively small sample size. In several equations where ADR was not found to be statistically significant, it appeared to be close to a reportable level of significance. A larger sample size might permit conclusions about additional impacts of ADR and potential differences in outcomes for various subgroups. Despite these limitations, this research provides one of the most rigorous studies to date of the impact of ADR as compared to trial. The results confirm many benefits of small claims ADR programs for litigants and the judiciary.

Notes and Questions

(1) One of the most significant institutional implementations of mediation in the courts occurred as part of the Civil Justice Reform Act (CJRA) of 1990. Importantly, the implementation included an evaluation conducted by the prestigious RAND Institute for Civil Justice. The study's objectives were to assess implementation, costs, and effects of mediation and neutral evaluation programs in six pilot and comparison federal district courts. The Report, published in 1996, concluded that

there was "no strong statistical evidence that the mediation or neutral evaluation programs, as implemented in the six districts studied, significantly affected time to disposition, litigation costs, or attorney views of fairness or satisfaction with case management. . . . [The] only statistically significant finding is that the ADR programs appear to increase the likelihood of a monetary settlement."

The dispute resolution community was disappointed by the results of the RAND study. In a series of responses following the release of the RAND report, mediation proponents pointed out that there were significant quality issues in terms of education and training of the neutrals in the programs which were studied. Specifically, "one of the four mediation programs violated most of what is known about building successful court ADR programs. The court required no training for its lawyer-mediators, excluded settlement empowered clients and insurers from the mediations, and held short and often perfunctory mediation sessions." *Concerns and Recommendations*, 15 Alternatives 6, 72 (May 1997).

(2) In 1994, the National Center for State Courts conducted a National Symposium on Court Connected Dispute Resolution Research under a cooperative agreement with the State Justice Institute (SJI). SJI had a history of funding such research and desired to clarify what was then known about ADR effectiveness and, more importantly, determine what further evaluation and research was needed. Compiling and publishing the research that had been conducted to that date in the *National Symposium on Court-Connected Dispute Resolution Research: A Report on Current Research Findings — Implications for Courts and Future Research Needs* (NCSC Publication No. R-152), the National Center for State Courts noted the following themes, which highlight the challenges in executing this type of research:

- . . . courts need to know more about the dynamics of the litigation process and attorneys' expectations about how ADR fits into that scheme. . . .

- courts need more reliable findings on the benefits of ADR. . . . Future studies should use more consistent sets of measures in order to develop more comparable sets of findings across jurisdictions.

- . . . courts need significantly greater knowledge about the most effective methods for training, qualifying, and selecting ADR providers.

- innovative measures of participant satisfaction should be developed because most individual litigants are one-time users of the justice system and thus have no reference for comparing the dispute resolution process they experienced with other processes. In addition, research on satisfaction should address a broader array of factors and identify those that contribute to greater satisfaction with the dispute resolution process and its outcomes.

- courts need better access not only to research findings, but also to practical guides for implementing, operating and evaluating ADR programs.

(3) The 2004 Fall-Winter Issue of *Conflict Resolution Quarterly* was devoted to the topic, *Conflict Resolution in the Field: Assessing the Past, Charting the Future* (Vol.

22, No. 1–2). In that issue, Roselle L. Wissler reviewed the empirical research on mediation in small claims, general jurisdiction trial cases, and appellate cases. *See The Effectiveness of Court-Connected Dispute Resolution in Civil Cases*, 22 Conflict Resol. Q. 55, 80–82 (2004).* Wissler concluded:

> In small claims cases, a majority of studies find that compared to trial, mediation receives more favorable assessments from litigants, reduces the rate of noncompliance, and at least in cases that settle, has more positive effects on the parties' relationship. In general civil jurisdiction cases, a majority of studies find no differences between mediation cases and non-mediation cases in participants' assessments, transaction costs, the amount of discovery, and the number of motions filed. The findings are mixed with regard to whether mediation does or does not increase the rate of settlement or reduce the trial rate, reduce the time to disposition, and enhance compliance compared to the traditional litigation process. . . . In appellate cases, a majority of studies find that mediation reduces the rate of cases that go to oral argument and reduces the time to disposition compared to cases that are not assigned to mediation. Mediation does not, however, appear to reduce transactional costs in appellate cases.
>
> . . . The mode of referral to mediation does not affect the likelihood of settlement or participants' assessments in some studies, but in others the voluntary use of mediation has positive effects. Earlier sessions reduce the time to disposition and the number of motions filed, and in some studies also increase the likelihood of settlement; but in other studies, timing has no impact on settlement. With regard to mediator qualifications, a majority of studies find that more mediation experience is associated with more settlement, but mediation training and subject matter expertise do not affect settlement rates. . . . The impact of the neutral's approach on participants' assessments seems to vary depending on what the mediators do, when they do it, and what approach was expected. A majority of studies find that neither the general case type category nor the litigants' relationship is related to settlement, but some studies suggest that other case characteristics might play a role.
>
> . . . Our ability to draw clear conclusions about the relative effectiveness and efficiency of court-connected mediation, neutral evaluation, and traditional litigation is limited by the small, number of studies with reliable comparative data based on the random assignment of cases to dispute resolution processes and the use of statistical significance tests. The variation in findings across studies and across court levels also might reflect the use of different measures in different studies or differences in program design or

the court context in which different programs operate. . . . Future studies need to address these gaps in the research.

(4) In the same issue of *Conflict Resolution Quarterly* noted in (3), psychologist Joan Kelly, an experienced researcher who had examined children's adjustment to divorce, custody and access issues, and divorce mediation, analyzed family mediation research. *Family Mediation Research: Is There Empirical Support for the Field?*, 22 Conflict Resol. Q. 3, 28–30 (2004).* She concluded:

> In public and private sectors, in voluntary and mandatory services, and when provided both early and late in the natural course of these disputes, family mediation has been consistently successful in resolving custody and access disputes, comprehensive divorce disputes, and child protection disputes. Mediation has given evidence of its power to settle complex, highly emotional disputes and reach agreements that are generally durable.
>
> . . .
>
> Client satisfaction has been surprisingly high in all studies and settings on a large number of process and outcome measures. . . .
>
> . . . . When contrasted to parents in adversarial processes, parents using a more extended mediation process experience a decrease in conflict during divorce, and in the first year or two following a divorce, they are more cooperative and supportive of each other as parents and communicate more regarding their children, after controlling for any preintervention group differences. One astonishing result has been that twelve years following divorce, fathers in mediation remained more involved with their children compared to the litigation fathers.
>
> Cautions as well emerge from the literature. Consistently, 15 to 20 percent of parents of both sexes are dissatisfied with aspects of mediation process and outcomes. Although this represents half the rate of dissatisfaction of adversarial clients, it is important to know if this reflects a more rushed or coercive mediation process, untrained or inept mediators, or parents who are angry and dissatisfied with any divorce process and outcome that does not produce what they expected or wanted. With the trend to limit court custody mediation to one session, more difficult cases with multiple serious issues most likely will not be given sufficient opportunity to settle, and settlement rates may decline.
>
> . . . . To date . . . this research has not led to more complex second generation research, in part due to chronic lack of research funding for mediation, the complexity of what is required, and an apparent diminishing interest in research questions in the field.

E. Critiques of Institutionalization

The trend toward institutionalization of mediation has not been accepted universally or incorporated without criticism. Various authors highlight below the potential "dark side" to institutionalization. Professor Carrie Menkel-Meadow raises questions about the potential co-option of the flexible mediation process when it becomes institutionalized in the rule-bound legal system; and U.S. Magistrate Judge (Northern District of California) Wayne Brazil shares his perspective on court ADR, 25 years after the Pound Conference. Finally, Professor Nancy Welsh analyzes court-connected mediation programs in relation to procedural justice.

Pursuing Settlement in an Adversary Culture: A Tale of Innovation Co-Opted or "The Law of ADR"

19 Fla. St. U. L. Rev. 1, 1–2, 5, 7, 11, 25, 30–33, 36–44 (1991)*
By Carrie Menkel-Meadow

In this Article I tell a tale of legal innovation co-opted. Put another way, this is a story of the persistence and strength of our adversary system in the face of attempts to change and reform some legal institutions and practices. In sociological terms, it is an ironic tale of the unintended consequences of social change and legal reform. A field that was developed, in part, to release us from some — if not all — of the limitations and rigidities of law and formal legal institutions has now developed a law of its own. With burgeoning developments in the use of non-adjudicative methods of dispute resolution in the courts and elsewhere, issues about alternative dispute resolution (ADR) increasingly have been "taken to court." As a result, we are beginning to see the development of case and statutory law and, dare I say, a "common law" or "jurisprudence" of ADR.

. . .

. . . In this Article, I explore the larger institutional issues presented when lawyers, judges, and parties to a conflict come together to resolve disputes using new forms within old structures. As a proponent of a particular version of ADR — the pursuit of "quality" solution — I am somewhat troubled by how a critical challenge to the status quo has been blunted, indeed co-opted, by the very forces I had hoped would be changed by some ADR forms and practices. In short, courts try to use various forms of ADR to reduce caseloads and increase court efficiency at the possible cost of realizing better justice. Lawyers may use ADR not for the accomplishment of a "better" result, but as another weapon in the adversarial arsenal to manipulate time, methods of discovery, and rules of procedure for perceived client advantage. Legal challenges cause ADR "issues" to be decided by courts. An important question that must be confronted is whether forcing ADR to adapt to a legal culture or

---

environment may be counterproductive to the transformations proponents of ADR would like to see in our disputing practices.

. . .

. . . The major question I wish to explore here is whether, in a more likely scenario, the power of our adversarial system will co-opt and transform the innovations designed to redress some, if not all, of our legal ills. Can legal institutions be changed if lawyers and judges persist in acting from traditional and conventional conceptions of their roles and values?

. . .

. . . [O]utcomes derived from our adversarial judicial system or the negotiation that occurs in its shadows are inadequate for solving many human problems. Our legal system produces binary win-lose results in adjudication. It also produces unreflective compromise—"split the difference" results in negotiated settlements that may not satisfy the underlying needs or interests of the parties. Human problems become stylized and simplified because they must take a particular legal form for the stating of a claim. Furthermore, the "limited remedial imagination" of courts in providing outcomes restricts what possible solutions the parties could develop. Some of us have argued that alternative forms of dispute resolution, or new conceptualizations of old processes, could lead to outcomes that were efficient in the Pareto-optimal sense of making both parties better off without worsening the position of the other. In addition, the processes themselves would be better because they would provide a greater opportunity for party participation and recognition of party goals. Thus, the "quality" school includes both elements of process and substantive justice claims. Some of the arguments here have been supported by the jurisprudential and anthropological work of those studying the different structures that human beings have developed in response to different disputing functions.

. . .

Partly because of the institutionalization of ADR, some of its earlier proponents, including anthropologist Laura Nader, now oppose ADR because it does not foster communitarian and self-determination goals. Instead, it is used to restrict access to the courts for some groups, just at the time when these less powerful groups have achieved some legal rights. Indeed, some critics have argued that ADR actually hurts those who are less powerful in our society—like women or racial and ethnic minorities—by leaving them unprotected by formal rules and procedures in situations where informality permits the expression of power and domination that is unmediated by legal restraints. In other criticisms, proceduralists have argued that various forms of ADR compromise our legal system by privatizing law making, shifting judicial roles, compromising important legal and political rights and principles, and failing to grant parties the benefits of hundreds of years of procedural protections afforded by our civil and criminal justice rules.

From another quarter, where the claims are usually brought by non-parties to the litigation, one of the major critiques of the development of ADR techniques has been that ADR privatizes disputing. To the extent that mandatory settlement conferences, mediation, and summary jury trials result in settlements before a full public trial, they may rob the public of important information. Some critics charge that with so much private settlement there will not be enough public debate, or enough cases going through the traditional adversary system, to produce good law.

. . .

Public access and first amendment issues are only a few of the constitutional challenges that have been leveled against ADR. Invoking a first amendment claim, both litigants and the public may seek to open settlement processes that were designed to permit confidential and open exploration of options and possibilities for settlement.

I will not pursue in great detail the claims about the constitutionality of ADR because they have been well canvassed by others. As ADR proceeds in its various forms through the courts, advocates have raised issues about violations of the right to jury trial, due process, equal protection, and separation of powers. Most of these claims have failed, and it is clear that with certain protections like nonbinding results, rights to *de novo* hearings, and limited penalties, ADR can constitutionally be conducted in the courts. Thus, in the constitutional arena the key issue is how the particular ADR programs are structured. Nonbinding settlement devices have virtually all been sustained against constitutional challenges. Binding procedures, or those that tax too greatly the choice of process (such as cost or fee shifting penalties), are likely to be more problematic. Constitutional challenges are not likely to eliminate or abolish ADR in the courts, though they may have some role in shaping the particular forms that are used.

. . .

The use of settlement activity in the courts should be understood as the clash of two cultures. To the extent that settlement activity seeks to promote consensual agreement through the analysis of the point of view of the other side, it requires some different skills and a very different mind-set from those litigators usually employ. Thus, the issue is whether judges and lawyers in the courts can learn to reorient their cultures and behaviors when trying to settle cases or whether those seeking settlement continue to do so from an adversarial perspective. To the extent that we cannot identify different behaviors in each sphere, we may see the corruption of both processes. If one of the purposes of the legal system is to specify legal entitlements from which settlements may be measured, or from which the parties may depart if they so choose, then having the adjudicators engage in too much mediative conduct may compromise the ability of judges to engage in both fact-finding and rule-making. If courts fail to provide sufficient baselines in their judgments, we will have difficulties determining if particular settlements are wise or truly consensual. There is danger in the possibility that good settlement practice will be marred by over-zealous advocacy or by over-zealous desire to close cases that may require either full adjudication or a public hearing.

. . .

In an important sense, the ADR movement represents a case study in the difficulties of legal reform when undertaken by different groups within the legal system. At the beginning were the *conceptualizers*—academics and judicial activists who developed both the critique of the adversary system and, in some cases, the design of alternative systems of dispute resolution. The implementers developed the concrete forms these innovations took when they moved into the legal system. Some of the *conceptualizers*—Frank Sander and several of the judges—were also *implementers*. In addition, other judges and judicial administrators principally concerned about case load management, and about the quality of solutions or decisions, became *implementers*. Support for the implementation of these ADR programs came from the principal foundation and government funding sources, as well as from groups of change-oriented practicing lawyers who have played an important catalytic role in supporting and using some of the first alternative procedures.

Finally, the *constituents* of these ADR systems—lawyers and their clients as consumers—were "acted upon," sometimes somewhat consensually, by the force of court rules or judicial encouragement. We are just beginning to see some of their reactions in the litigation developing from ADR innovation and in evaluation research.

Each of these groups of actors within the ADR legal reform movement inhabit different cultural worlds—academia, the judiciary, law practice, the business world, and everyday life. Each group uses, transforms, and "colonizes" the work of the others. The research of academics is ignored or simplified; judges move cases along and adopt the language of case management rather than justice; lawyers "infect" clients with a desire for adversarial advantage, or in other cases clients do the same to lawyers; and professionals argue about credentialing and standards for the new profession.

Each of these actors in the dispute resolution arena may be serving different masters. As the ideas are institutionalized, they develop into new and different forms of dealing with problems. Those who work in the field have attempted to create environments for dialogues among and between these constituencies. Some of these meetings have been productive and have fostered "cross-class" understanding. Just as often, however, such meetings leave people confirmed in their views that their particular paradigm is most accurate. Others do not understand the particular reality that some may face—whether it be the crush of caseloads or the lack of "justice" in settlements.

In my view, productive discourse about ADR will have to transcend the language of these cultural differences. Academics, and particularly those who theorize about jurisprudential concerns, need to root their views in the practicalities of our empirical world. Occasionally, judges and legal practitioners need to step back and review the larger jurisprudential and policy issues implicated in "quick-fix" reforms. Practitioners and clients need to consider new forms of practice and process while diminishing their adversarial ways of thinking. A professional life should be one of re-examination, growth, and change. If we are really looking for new ways to process disputes — both to increase case-processing efficiency and to promote better-quality solutions — then we have to be willing to look critically at the innovations and their effects from all quarters. I believe that social innovation and transformation are possible here — the issues are whether conventional mind-sets will "infect" these innovations on the one hand, or whether the "cure" will be worse than the disease on the other.

In a sense, we are at a second stage in the development of alternative dispute resolution innovations. The bloom on the rose has faded as some experiments have been tried and now present their own problems or dilemmas. Some of us still aim for consciousness transformation and institutionalized forms of ADR and what can be done to make them work. Many of the issues raised by these developments require policy judgments for which we have an inadequate empirical data base; others require us to make normative choices based on what we value in a procedural system. If ADR is to meet the basic levels of fairness, then the following questions must be collected to prevent ADR from becoming totally swallowed by the adversarial system:

1. To what extent will courts lose their legitimacy as courts if too many other forms of case-processing are performed within their walls? If the "other" processes are not considered legitimate within public institutions, they will be legally challenged and transformed so that they will no longer be "alternatives," but only watered-down versions of court adjudication. These watered-down versions may be violative of the legal rights and rules our courts are intended to safeguard. Are theorists, practitioners, and citizens capable of changing our views of what courts should do?

2. Should some case types be excluded from alternative treatment?

3. What are the purposes for using particular forms of alternative dispute resolution? . . . If the goals and purposes of particular ADR institutions are clarified now, future problems based on overly abstract goals may be avoided.

4. What forms of ADR should be institutionalized? Not all ADR devices are the same. There is a tendency in the literature and in the rhetoric to homogenize widely different approaches to dispute resolution. A more thorough and careful consideration of each of the devices might lead to different conclusions about the utility and legitimacy of these devices. . . .

5. What are the politics of ADR? Does ADR serve the interests of particular groups? This is not an easy question to answer. Many have argued that "minor" disputes have been siphoned out of the public legal system, while "major" disputes have continued to receive the benefits of the traditional court system. Large corporations are also removing their cases from the court system. Through the increased use of private ADR, the economics of

dispute resolution are more subtle. Some may be "forced" out while others choose to opt out. What will this mean for payment and subsidies of dispute resolution? Will "free market" forces decide the fate of ADR? Who will control decision-making about ADR—judges, lawyers, clients, or legislators? If those with the largest stake in the system exit, who will supply the impetus and resources for court and rule reform? At the level of institutional decision-making, are these issues for individual judges, for the Congress, or for the United States Supreme Court to decide?

6. What are the cultural forces producing these legal changes at these particular times? Has the larger culture around us changed since particular legal innovations were adopted? If attempts to incorporate party participation in disputing were made in the "participatory" 1960s and 1970s, then does the 1980s era of privatization of public services dictate other considerations in the use of ADR? How has the rhetoric of quality justice been transformed into a rhetoric of quantity and case processing?

7. How are different forms of ADR actually functioning? . . .

. . . In order for ADR to develop in a way that enhances our trust in the American legal system, several important reforms should accompany our experimentation.

First, some forms of ADR should remain mandatory, but not binding. . . . Second, if some settlement processes are to be made mandatory, certain essential legal protections may have to flow from those processes. If they do not, then processes may have to be chosen consensually or voluntarily. . . .

Third, if settlement processes are to be conducted within the courts, they should be facilitated by those who will not be the ultimate triers of fact. Because I believe that good settlement practice frequently depends on the revelation of facts that would be inadmissible in court, the facilitator of settlement cannot be the same person who will ultimately find facts or decide the outcome of the case. . . .

Fourth, settlement facilitators must be trained to conduct settlement proceedings, particularly those that depart from conventional adjudication models. . . .

Fifth, we must provide the evidence for systematic evaluation of alternative dispute resolution devices. To accomplish this goal, I recommend the recording of proceedings, as well as more sophisticated data collection at the court level.

. . .

Sixth, different forms of ADR should be unbundled and separately evaluated. . . .

Finally, categorical judgments about particular processes are likely to be unhelpful. Mediation or summary jury trials *per se* do not violate our procedural rules or jurisprudential norms. More often, the issue is whether a particular process is carried out sensitively or "coercively."

Court ADR 25 Years After Pound:
Have We Found a Better Way?

18 Ohio St. J. on Disp. Resol. 93, 98–100, 104, 107–09, 111, 114–16,
120–21, 124–25, 128, 130, 132–33, 135, 141–45 (2002)*
By Wayne D. Brazil

. . .

"Has the addition of ADR to pretrial processes improved the administration of justice?"

Before responding to this . . . question, we must try to identify the criteria we should use to identify "improvements" in the "administration of justice." Hopefully, as we work through the issues, we will remain more concerned about justice than administration. It is simple-minded, however, to suggest that justice and administration are not related. So it is fair to ask, when we try to identify the criteria for identifying "improvements," whether we should focus primarily on efficiency values. If so, efficiency for whom? For the courts? For lawyers? For parties? Is efficiency for one necessarily efficiency for all? Or, when we determine what constitutes an improvement in the administration of justice, should we also look to a broader range of values: (1) party and lawyer feelings about fairness and about the utility of the process (taking into account the full range of parties' values), (2) the extent to which the process permits or encourages participation by parties (reducing levels of alienation from the system), (3) what the process contributes to the clarity of the parties' understanding of their situation and their options, and (4) the parties' feelings about the system of justice and our judicial institutions.

With respect to the last -mentioned criterion, we should take into account the impact the ADR process or program has on the inferences parties draw about what values and concerns animate the courts as institutions. We also should consider what effect the ADR programs have on how well served the parties feel by the system of justice and on whether their experience in the court system enhances or reduces their respect for and feeling of connection with their government. Because how people feel about their governmental institutions is so important in a democracy, when we ask whether the addition of ADR to the pretrial menu has improved the administration of justice, we need to give full and fair consideration to both objective and subjective measures.

. . .

We should take heart from the fact that in studies of the programs that I know best, the subjective data support, often strongly, a conclusion that the addition of ADR to court services has improved (in the all-important eyes of users) the administration of justice — regardless of the criteria we use to define improvement.

. . .

So one way to conceptualize our court now is as an institution that offers three kinds of processes: (1) traditional litigation, (2) ADR processes (arbitration, ENE, and some versions of evaluative mediation) that proceed within the context of traditional litigation but help parties combat some of its limitations and problems, and (3) ADR processes (variations of facilitative mediation) that enable and encourage parties to pursue goals and to behave in ways that are quite different from those associated with traditional adversarial litigation.

. . .

. . . I must acknowledge that despite the considerable progress and the many achievements described in the preceding sections, we have not realized many ambitions. A great deal remains to be done. There are many challenges and dangers on the road ahead for court ADR, and we disserve ourselves and the values we hold dear if we do not try to identify them accurately and face them squarely.

. . . My guess is that appreciably less than half of the civil cases filed in this country have real access to court-sponsored ADR services. In many courts, there are entire categories of civil matters that receive no ADR services at all. Perhaps the most disturbing and challenging example is pro se cases.

Moreover, in many jurisdictions no parties can secure ADR services unless they pay full market rates for a private neutral whose connection with the court often is tenuous, at best (and over whom the court, realistically, exercises virtually no "quality control"). The requirement of paying the neutral a substantial fee serves as a real barrier for some litigants and triggers difficult policy questions about why the courts offer litigation services for free, but ADR services only at a substantial price.

. . .

. . . We also have discovered occasions in which neutrals have misunderstood, sometimes fundamentally, the role they were to play or the specific characteristics of the process they were to host. We work hard to try to control what is being done by our neutrals under the auspices of our program, but we need to do more. We also worry about what happens in programs where the courts do less. Because of serious shortfalls in means to assure quality control in many programs there likely is considerable variability in the quality of the neutral services received in different cases.

There also is a distressing level of unevenness in ADR offerings between different jurisdictions. . . .

. . . In sum, there are great inequalities both in access to and in the character of court ADR products.

. . .

. . . I will close by identifying some internal sources of peril — matters about ourselves and our program design decisions that could become sources of danger for court ADR.

A. Sources of Peril in Our Relationships with Legislatures

. . .

There is a risk that perceived abuses . . . in the private sector would unfairly contaminate the standing of all ADR in the minds of influential lawmakers and the public. The risk of contamination is particularly great in courts that "outsource" some or all of the ADR services they sanction or that fail to adopt stringent conflict of interest requirements and quality control mechanisms. The more a court depends on professional service providers from the private sector, the greater the risk that legislators will paint court and corporate ADR programs with the same broad brush of suspicion.

. . .

Ironically, a second peril in our relationships with legislatures is animated by policy concerns that cut in the opposite direction. Legislatures can generate program-distorting pressures by insisting on using only efficiency criteria to assess the value of court ADR. . . .

. . . Those who would insist on using only efficiency criteria to assess the value of ADR programs jeopardize the courts' most precious and only necessary assets: public confidence in the integrity of the processes the courts sponsor and public faith in the motives that underlie the courts' actions. We must take great care not to make program design decisions that invite parties to infer that the courts care less about doing justice and offering valued service than about looking out for themselves as institutions (*e.g.*, by reducing their workload, or off-loading kinds of cases that are especially taxing or emotionally difficult or that are deemed "unimportant").

B. Sources of Peril From Our Relationship with Judges

. . .

The first of the concerns that can fuel judicial inhospitality to court ADR is fear that ADR threatens the vitality of the jury system as a critical tool of democracy — as an essential weapon to discourage and to discipline abuse of public or private power. There are judges who believe passionately that one of the most powerful and essential deterrents to misbehavior in our society is fear of the jury trial, the public exposure and humiliation it can generate, the great transaction costs it can impose, and the huge damage awards to which it can lead. . . .

. . . [A second] concern is about money, more specifically, budgets for courts. The financial resources available to the courts to perform their traditional core functions are already strained in many jurisdictions, and some judges and court administrators fear that supporting good ADR programs consumes resources that the courts simply cannot afford to divert. . . .

A very different source of judicial skepticism about the place of ADR in courts is concern that ADR processes, especially facilitative mediation, tend to be analytically sloppy. Some judges worry that there is considerable risk that decisions made by lawyers and clients in these settings will be based on unreliable data or inaccurate legal premises, or on a blurring of thinking and emoting about matters relevant under the law and matters irrelevant under the law. They fear all of this will increase the risk that important rights will not be protected and legal norms will not be followed.

. . .

An independent judicial concern at a very different level is that ADR threatens delay or disruption of traditional litigation — that it jeopardizes timeliness of dispositions by eroding the pressure that derives from early and firm trial dates. . . .

. . .

C. Sources of Peril From Our Relationships with Practicing Lawyers

. . . Lawyers could undermine or sabotage court ADR programs by failing to inform clients that they have ADR options, failing to accurately consider the pros and cons of those options with their clients, or by actively discouraging their clients from trying to use ADR or from participating in good faith in ADR events. Lawyers also may undermine ADR programs, more subtly but no less significantly, by failing to take full advantage of the potential in an ADR proceeding when they prepare for and attend it. Sometimes failings of these kinds are attributable to ignorance, sometimes to inertia, sometimes to fear of unfamiliar processes and fora, of loss of control over inputs to and from the client, and sometimes to greed.

. . .

D. Sources of Peril in Our Relationships with the Fourth Estate

. . .

There is one additional policy arena of potential tension between court ADR programs and the private ADR provider community that warrants mention here: compensation for neutrals. Some courts and parties will want neutrals to work at economy rates, or pro bono, while organizations of neutrals are likely to press for payment at professionals' market rates (agreeing to perform only limited work for free as a public service). While lobbying for higher levels of compensation may be vulnerable to cynical inferences about self-interest, organized mediators would contend that their real purpose is to protect against compromising the quality of mediator services. They would argue that if neutrals are not paid at market rates, the quality of neutrals will suffer, or the quality of the effort that neutrals are willing to commit to individual cases will suffer, thus harming the integrity and viability of mediation generally.

. . .

E. Perils with Sources in Ourselves

. . .

The first such peril arises from the temptation to impose on parties and their lawyers a generalized requirement to participate in "good faith" in our ADR processes . . . [S]uch a requirement could do considerable damage without yielding sufficient offsetting benefits.

. . .

Like the imposition of a generalized good faith requirement, the devolution of court ADR programs into one hybrid but largely evaluative process could have several dangerous consequences. . . .

. . . If we fail to maintain clear differences between processes and permit all court ADR to become some blur of evaluative mediation and a settlement conference, we will needlessly compromise our ability to be responsive to the full range of values and needs that litigants bring to our courts. We will reduce the occasions on which parties perceive the court as reaching out to them, trying to help them pursue the goals that are most important to them. Offering only an evaluative form of ADR also could increase the risk of parties inferring that the courts' only real interest in the program is getting cases settled, thus reducing occasions for parties to feel grateful to the court for providing a party-oriented service. Moreover, the more that "evaluation" pervades an ADR process, the greater the risk of the "litigization" of that process, which in turn, reduces the capacity of ADR to contribute in unique ways to problem solving.

. . .

The more like a smorgasbord an ADR process becomes, the greater the risk that the neutral will make poor judgments about which process route to follow or which techniques are appropriate. As these risks increase, so does the likelihood that neutrals in the same court program, hosting what is nominally the same kind of ADR process, would use different procedures in similar circumstances. If neutrals in the same program use different procedures and techniques in parallel settings, it becomes appreciably more difficult for parties and lawyers to predict what will occur in any particular ADR event.

As predictability of process declines, so does the parties' ability to prepare adequately, which not only jeopardizes the usefulness of the ADR event but also increases the risk that parties will feel that the program is unfair. Parties are more likely to be resentful when they encounter turns in the process which they did not anticipate. Turns in process that parties do not anticipate are more likely to be viewed as inconsistent with the court's rules and of dubious propriety, or as offending deeply rooted feelings about what the appropriate roles of lawyers, clients, and the court are. An ADR program that spawned resentment toward the court, instead of gratitude, could hardly be considered an improvement in the administration of justice.

Do You Believe in Magic?: Self-Determination and Procedural Justice Meet Inequality in Court-Connected Mediation

70 SMU Law Review 721, 723–25, 727–29, 732–52, 754, 756–58, 760–61 (2017)*
By Nancy A. Welsh

I. Introduction

Dreams and noble intentions, at least in part, inspired the "contemporary mediation movement." Many mediation advocates urged—and continue to urge—that mediation should be embraced and institutionalized because it is an inclusive process and can enable people to find paths that allow them to exercise meaningful self-determination in resolving their disputes. This promise of self-determination has dimmed, however, as courts and agencies have focused on efficiency as a primary reason to institutionalize mediation, as lawyers and repeat players have come to dominate the issue framing and negotiations occurring within mediation, and as research has revealed that a significant percentage of parties do not possess the temperament or desire to fashion their own unique resolutions.

As self-determination has lost luster, some mediation advocates have emphasized mediation's potential to provide an "experience of justice." Drawing on the vast social–psychological literature regarding procedural justice, these mediation advocates have urged that the process offers important opportunities for "voice," "trustworthy consideration," and "even-handed and respectful treatment," in marked contrast to the processes used to resolve the vast majority of litigated civil matters—*i.e.*, default, lawyers' bilateral negotiation, and dispositive motions. This Article, in part, represents a reminder regarding mediation's potential to provide self-determination and procedural justice and then considers the fate of proposals that have arisen to reclaim this potential.

But this Article also examines more recent research raising questions regarding the appropriateness of expecting mediation to deliver self-determination or procedural justice. In particular, the Article examines research indicating that people's societal identity and status can and does affect the likelihood that they will perceive procedural justice in mediation, their ability and willingness to exercise voice in mediation, and even their ability and willingness to demonstrate trustworthy consideration. Members of society who feel marginalized or isolated—or who know that they exercise no power due to their disadvantageous place within an extreme hierarchy—are less likely to be willing or able to embrace opportunities to express themselves in mediation. To do so represents an unacceptable risk. Meanwhile, members of society who are powerful—or who know that they exercise privilege due to their superior place within an extreme hierarchy—are less likely to be willing or able to embrace opportunities to hear and acknowledge what other parties have said in mediation. If mediation lacks participants' voice and trustworthy consideration, it is difficult to understand how the process can provide either procedural justice or a meaningful version of self-determination. In other words, as self-determination and procedural justice meet inequality in mediation, these noble intentions are found wanting.

. . .

"It depends" must be the appropriate response to the question of whether we should continue to believe in the potential power of mediation to foster dialogue, procedural justice, and self-determination. Therefore, this Article will *not* end with the conclusion that mediation represents a failed experiment, unable to overcome the negative effects of inequality, bias, and prejudice. Instead, this Article will call for more realistic expectations of the process, the establishment of conditions that make achievement of its potential more likely, and reforms to increase the inclusivity and safety of the process — thus fostering all people's ability to find and express their own voices, find and exercise their abilities to consider the voice of the other, and arrive at their own voluntary (self-determined) agreements. There is work to be done.

. . .

Largely due to concerns about declining access to justice — specifically, concerns that litigants were experiencing unacceptable delay and increased costs due to burgeoning civil and criminal court filings and litigation inefficiencies — federal and state courts institutionalized mediation for the resolution of all sorts of civil matters. Respect for parties' self-determination was not a guiding principle. When insufficient numbers of litigants voluntarily elected to try mediation to resolve their cases, courts began making mediation mandatory. As lawyers became more involved in the process, their voices and framing of issues dominated the discussions occurring in mediation, thus marginalizing their clients' participation. The lawyers also chose mediators who were experienced litigators or judges with relevant subject-matter expertise. They sought mediators who would provide reality testing. In some types of cases, lawyers counseled their clients not to attend the mediation. Increasingly today, lawyers urge mediators to avoid joint sessions that would allow the parties to talk directly with each other. Instead, many lawyers prefer private conversations with the mediator (caucuses) and shuttle diplomacy.

All of these adaptations have occurred while many courts continue to describe mediation in a manner that hearkens back to the early days of the contemporary mediation movement and as judges express a preference for mediation because they believe that it involves the parties more directly in the resolution of their disputes. . . .

When parties seek to set aside agreements they have reached in mediation, however, courts generally do not try to determine whether there was . . . the exercise of self-determination. Rather, courts look for the other extreme, trying to determine whether any participant in the process engaged in behaviors or threats so overwhelming that they could be classified as "coercion." Courts rarely find coercion in mediation. This standard of self-determination as "*not* coercion" represents a very thin vision of self-determination indeed. But it is important to recall that (1) the courts exist in order to produce resolution of disputes; (2) they do not exist to foster citizens' self-determination; (3) they have an interest in the disposition of cases; and (4) they are constantly facing legislative calls for increased efficiency, budget cuts, and competition from administrative courts, private dispute resolution, and even international tribunals. Nonetheless, over the years, there has been no shortage of proposals to reinvigorate self-determination in court-connected mediation.

Working under the assumption that courts will continue to mandate parties' participation in mediation, Leonard Riskin and I have urged that courts should provide for a pre-mediation consultation with the parties to determine the issues that the parties hope to address and their preferred mediation model. . . . Jaqueline Nolan-Haley has called long and consistently for parties to have access to information regarding their legal rights and remedies so that their consent to any agreements in mediation is sufficiently informed. . . . I have urged courts to establish mechanisms to monitor mediation or provide parties with post-mediation opportunities to submit feedback regarding their experience with the mediation process and the mediators. I have also advocated for a "cooling off" period to be applied to mediated settlement agreements, which would allow parties to rescind their agreements at will as long as such rescission occurred relatively promptly after the agreement was reached. I have urged that courts should be sure that court-connected mediation is supplemented with other alternatives so that parties are ordered to participate in the process that is most appropriate for their dispute — rather than expecting mediation to be all things to all people.

. . .

Most of these proposals have fallen on barren soil in American courts and thus have borne no or little fruit. The only real exception is the option of allowing parties to opt out, usually conditioned upon a sufficient showing. This exception exists primarily in court-connected family mediation and represents an acknowledgement of the unfortunately widespread reality and likely effects of intimate partner abuse.

At this point, then, it is difficult to muster up faith in the reality of the magic of self-determination as applied to court-connected mediation, especially mandatory court-connected mediation. The courts, certainly, are not going to act as the optimizers or guarantors of self-determination.

As a result, this Article will now turn from the concept of self-determination to the social-psychological concept of procedural justice. This is because assuring procedural justice in mediation may serve as a reasonable link between achieving the courts' mission of case disposition and providing a meaningful measure of self-determination in mediation.

. . . Many people use the social–psychological term "procedural justice," but a smaller number actually ground their understanding in the vast social–psychological empirical literature regarding the subject. This literature reveals that people tend to perceive a process as fair or just if it includes the following elements: (1) "voice" or the opportunity for people to express what is important to them; (2) "trustworthy consideration" or a demonstration that encourages people to believe that their voice was heard by the decision-maker or authority figure; (3) a neutral forum that applies the same objective standards to all and treats the parties in an even-handed manner; and (4) treatment that is dignified. If people believe that they were treated fairly in a decision-making or dispute resolution procedure (*i.e.*, the process was "procedurally just" or "procedurally fair"), they are more likely to (1) perceive that the substantive outcome is fair — even when it is adverse to them; (2) comply with the outcome; and (3) perceive that the sponsoring institution is legitimate. . . .

. . . [I]t is important to notice the potential relationship between a procedurally just process and one that provides some measure of self-determination. If a person truly has and takes advantage of the opportunity for voice — *i.e.*, if she truly says what she wants and needs to say — she has engaged in an act of procedural self-determination. Her expression of voice also makes it more likely that she will have significant input into the outcome (even though she cannot entirely control that outcome), and the opportunity to share this information may open up a new path toward both relational and instrumental resolution. It is important to notice as well the ways in which trustworthy consideration, a neutral forum, and even-handed and dignified treatment may create a greater likelihood that both parties will be able to *hear* and *share* information that may surprise or enlighten them, that such information may create new opportunities for resolution, that the parties may experience enhanced trust, and that this trust and the expanded exchange of information thus may produce both an integrative solution and a changed relationship.

. . .

. . . [U]nfortunately, something called "sham" procedural justice exists. A process may include all of the elements listed above — with the implicit message that people's voice has the potential to affect the outcome. However, the mediator or the parties may have absolutely no intention of allowing themselves to be affected by what they have heard or seen. This situation is most likely to occur when the mediator or the other party has a vested interest in the outcome. Under these circumstances, the mediator or the other party may be using the lessons of procedural justice research simply to seduce compliance. Not surprisingly, people's trust can plummet if they learn that they were misled and unwittingly participated in a sham procedure. They may perceive the outcome of this sham procedure to be *less* fair than the identical outcome of an *obviously* unfair process.

. . .

There is also research indicating that even if a process is authentic and conducted in a procedurally just manner, individuals' roles or social statuses affect the extent to which their judgments regarding procedural justice will influence their perceptions of substantive justice. Some of this research involves mediation directly. *The*

Metrocourt Project, for example, reported that Hispanic-American litigants were more likely than Whites to be satisfied with the mediation process and its outcomes, even though Hispanic-Americans' mediation outcomes were neither as favorable as Whites' mediation outcomes nor as favorable as the outcomes Hispanic-Americans received in adjudication. Interestingly, women of color expressed the highest level of satisfaction with mediation, while white women were the least satisfied and least likely to perceive the mediation process as fair even though they experienced the most favorable outcomes.

Recent research in the Netherlands regarding the mediation of labor disputes similarly indicates that people's place in a hierarchy affects the influence of their procedural justice perceptions upon their perceptions of substantive outcomes. In this study, researchers found that supervisors were more likely than subordinates to judge mediation as effective even when the supervisors perceived low levels of procedural justice. Meanwhile, subordinates' perceptions of mediation's procedural justice determined their perceptions of the process's effectiveness. Especially if subordinates perceived low levels of procedural justice, they perceived mediation to be ineffective. Supervisors also were more likely than subordinates to perceive mediation as procedurally just. Thus, in this research, those with higher status in the hierarchy of the workplace were *more* likely than those lower in the hierarchy to judge mediation as procedurally just and effective and *less* likely to find that low levels of procedural justice undermined the effectiveness of the mediation process.

Other research, not involving mediation, also suggests the relevance of status to procedural justice perceptions and their power. Substantial research has been conducted regarding the effect of procedural justice perceptions on people's perceptions of substantive justice when they interact with police. In general, that research has shown that when police behave in a manner consistent with procedural justice, people are more likely to perceive substantive outcomes as fair even when they are adverse. In other words, the provision of procedural justice can reduce the impact of outcome favorability on perceptions of substantive fairness. . . .

More recent research suggests that in interactions between lower status and higher status people in negotiations or the workplace, the lower status persons are more likely to desire future interactions with higher status persons if they perceive that the higher status persons behaved in a procedurally just manner — even when those interactions produced disappointing outcomes for the lower status persons. In contrast, the higher status persons (which would tend to include more powerful parties and dominant repeat players) were less likely to be influenced by procedural fairness. Indeed, when lower status persons treated them in a procedurally just manner, those with higher status were more likely to perceive outcomes as fair only if those outcomes were consistent with what they expected or knew themselves to be entitled to receive.

. . .

There is even biological support for the value of using the assessment of procedural justice as a coping mechanism. Being treated in a manner that is dignified, feels safe, and reduces stress has been shown to have a positive physiological effect that enhances people's cognitive ability and decision-making. Thus, it makes sense that procedural justice will be particularly important for those dealing with vulnerability or uncertainty. . . .

. . .

There is also an increasing amount of research focusing on the element of voice, and some of this research is particularly problematic in considering how inequality, bias, and prejudice may undermine the potential of mediation to offer procedural justice and a forum in which people's authentic voices and experiences can be expressed.

. . .

. . . [T]he expression of voice is central to both procedural justice and self-determination. It is important, however, to identify the particular aspects of voice that are valuable in mediation. Roselle Wissler . . . has found that people perceive that they have experienced the opportunity for voice and a procedurally just process in mediation if their lawyers speak on their behalf. Second, she has found that people's perceptions of voice are even stronger if they have the opportunity to "tell their stories" themselves. Third, Wissler has found a distinction between voice and "participation." In her research, while people's perceptions of procedural justice are strongly related to their perception that they had a sufficient opportunity for voice, their perceptions of procedural justice are much less strongly related to the extent of their direct participation in the mediation.[88] Indeed, Wissler found that those who spoke more in both domestic relations and civil mediation sessions were more likely to feel pressured to settle. This research suggests a disconnect between the voice that is important to procedural justice and the sort of participation that is often associated with self-determination — i.e., the opportunity to participate directly in the back-and-forth or bargaining of negotiation and mediation. . . .

Meanwhile, voice is not always pretty or easy to hear. Voice can be angry, aggressive, and cause discomfort, both for the person expressing it and the person listening to such expression. Such voice, with a strong emotional content, is often called "venting" in mediation. Although mediation commentators acknowledge venting as valuable when new information is being shared (including revealing emotional impacts and needs), they increasingly criticize the notion that venting is valuable for its own sake. There is physiological evidence, for example, that allowing a party to vent too much is not effective in helping with the release of difficult feelings and

---

88. *See* Roselle L. Wissler, *Representation in Mediation: What We Know from Empirical Research*, 37 Fordham Urb. L.J. 419, 447–52 (2010). Roselle L. Wissler, *Party Participation and Voice in Mediation*, Disp. Resol. Mag., Fall 2011, at 20 . . . .

instead has the opposite effect. Continued venting, particularly in the presence of the other party, can result in heightened cortisol levels, which can then lead to greater entrenchment in negative feelings such as anger, as well as distorted perceptions that can inhibit problem-solving and decision-making. Thus, unrestrained venting can chill communications that are likely to be productive in terms of producing settlement in mediation.

At the very least, this research regarding the physiological effects of venting suggests that there can be a "right" and a "wrong" sort of voice in mediation. At this point, it is not clear who is more likely to exercise the wrong sort of voice in mediation, but this research raises legitimate concerns that mediators who seek to place restrictions on venting ultimately could chill the expression of righteous anger and fear by those feeling the effects of inequality, bias, and prejudice.

. . .

Research also reveals that we cannot assume that those who perceive that they have been ignored, excluded, or disrespected will be willing or able to exercise their voice at all. Robert Rubinson has written quite passionately about the difficulties facing low-income participants who are required to participate in court-connected mediation. They may not be able to get childcare. Their reliance on public transportation could make it difficult for them to travel to the courthouse. They may have to forego hourly wages and may fear the loss of their jobs if they fail to turn up for work in order to participate in mediation.[99] These difficulties make it unlikely that people will be able to afford the luxury of voice.

Recent research also has demonstrated that people's willingness or ability to exercise their voice will depend, in large part, upon their identification with the relevant social group. In this research, the more people felt themselves to be part of a social group, the more they desired and expected voice in matters relevant to group membership. The less they identified with the social group, however, the less they desired and expected voice. Thus, despite the centrality of voice in the procedural justice literature, we cannot assume that everyone will always and uniformly have a high desire for voice. . . .

. . .

. . . [P]rocedural justice research generally reveals that while people care about the opportunity for voice, they also care about whether their voice has been heard — *i.e.*, whether their views were considered in a trustworthy manner. . . .

Trustworthy consideration is a concept that bears similarities to several others: active or reflective listening, "looping," perspective taking, open-minded listening, testing for understanding, and empathizing. There are three key questions here: "Did the authority (or other) *listen* to what I said?" "Did the authority (or other)

---

99. *See* Robert Rubinson, *Of Grids and Gatekeepers: The Socioeconomics of Mediation*, 17 Cardozo J. Conflict Resol., 873, 891–92 (2016).

understand what I said?" "Did the authority (or other) *care* to understand what I said?" Research indicates that people tend to judge accurate procedures — *i.e.*, those in which the decision maker or authority takes all relevant information into account in coming to a decision — as fairer than inaccurate procedures.

As with voice, there is research indicating that inequality, bias, and prejudice can get in the way of listening to someone else's perspective, accurately understanding what she has said, and caring to understand her perspective. Research regarding the fundamental attribution bias, for example, shows that when someone has hurt us and is not in our social group, we are more likely to over-attribute her bad behavior to her essential character and under-attribute it to the situation in which she found herself. We are more forgiving of those in our in-group and even more forgiving of ourselves. This psychological phenomenon is likely to impede our ability or desire to listen and really understand the voice of someone who is not in our social group.

There is also research showing that status can impede trustworthy consideration. Those who have higher status and greater power have been shown to be less likely to be trustworthy and thus less likely to provide consideration that is trustworthy. Worryingly, there is even research suggesting that people naturally associate the failure to provide procedural justice with power and assume that someone who has behaved in a procedurally just manner is less powerful. The failure of those with higher status and greater power to extend trustworthy consideration has been attributed to their reduced need for others' help. This phenomenon also may be self-protective.

. . .

The following potential responses represent just a beginning in trying to address the potential for inequality, bias, and prejudice to undermine mediation's potential to deliver procedural justice, substantive justice, and self-determination. . . .

. . . [I]ncreasing the diversity of the pool of mediators should enhance marginalized parties' willingness to perceive that they will be, and were, heard and understood, therefore increasing marginalized parties' willingness to exercise voice and increasing the likelihood of actual understanding and trustworthy consideration — which may then reduce the likelihood of unjustifiably disparate outcomes. There are hopeful signs that public and private dispute resolution providers and other organizations are moving in this direction.

. . .

. . . [T]argeted and careful use of caucus may have the effect of enhancing the voice of those who are hesitant to exercise it (*i.e.*, those who are of lower status or who do not identify with the "social group" being served by the mediation). Targeted and careful use of caucus also may increase the likelihood that people feel and believe that their views received trustworthy consideration and respect. Thus, used appropriately, caucusing has the potential to help parties gain the benefits of procedural justice.

. . .

. . . Other researchers have also recommended the use of pre-mediation caucuses in order to build trust and specifically *not* to develop settlement proposals. . . .

. . .

. . . [P]eople can learn the value of listening as a result of participating in mediation. People also can learn at least the rudimentary components of active or reflective listening — *e.g.*, allowing the other party to speak and then trying to summarize, accurately, what they believe the other party has said. . . .

. . .

Some have . . . suggested that those who are hesitant to exercise voice may be emboldened by the opportunity to participate in asynchronous online mediation. There certainly is plenty of research and personal experience demonstrating that people's online voice can be different from their in-person voice. Research has indicated that lower-status individuals, for example, are more willing to participate in "lean media" like email and that social influence bias is reduced. People can also take their time in composing messages, discerning the meaning of the messages they receive, and making decisions about how to respond. Indeed, a person's written facility with language under these circumstances may be quite different from her verbal facility with language in an in-person meeting.

Some dispute resolution organizations actually facilitate an online pre-mediation exchange of information between the parties by requesting that parties respond online to a series of questions and then allowing the parties to see each other's answers. Thus, these online providers facilitate a form of voice and trustworthy consideration.

. . .

. . . [E]ven if mediation sessions provide for voice, trustworthy consideration, even-handed treatment, and respect, they also have the potential to produce unconscionable outcomes. . . . [T]here is precedent for imposing some ethical obligation upon mediators to avoid extreme substantive unfairness in specified contexts. It is also relatively easy to understand how such an obligation would make it more likely that marginalized parties would perceive the mediation process as offering at least minimal assurance that they and their claims will be treated in an even-handed and dignified manner.

. . .

Notes and Questions

(1) Professor Menkel-Meadow uses the term "ADR" in her article. Are the concerns she raises generic to alternative processes? Are mediation and arbitration equally susceptible to such concerns?

(2) In 1991, Professor Menkel-Meadow raised the question of whether the adversarial system would co-opt ADR. Ten years later, James J. Alfini and Catherine G.

McCabe analyzed the emerging case law related to the requirement to mediate in good faith and the enforcement of mediation agreements. In particular, the authors focused on the tension between mediation's core values and principles and the general principles favoring settlement. *See* James J. Alfini & Catherine G. McCabe, *Mediating in the Shadow of the Courts: A Survey of the Emerging Case Law*, 54 Ark. L. Rev. 171, 173 (2001). The authors conclude with this caution:

> In general, the courts have demonstrated an understanding of the mediation process, a sensitivity to the core values and principles of mediation, and a clear desire to further the general policy favoring settlement in deciding cases involving mediation process issues. . . .
>
> On the other hand, the general policy favoring settlement, while advancing the goal of judicial economy, may not always be consistent with mediation principles and values. In particular, allegations of settlement coercion raise troubling issues relating to mediation's core values of party self-determination, voluntariness, and mediator impartiality that may not be easily discerned or correctable through the judge process.

How do these concerns compare with the "sources of peril" raised by Wayne Brazil?

(3) Professor Menkel-Meadow refers to the 1960s and 1970s as "participatory" and the 1980s as the era of "privatization." How would you describe the current era?

(4) Despite concerns surrounding the mandatory use of mediation, it has become the norm in many jurisdictions, including Florida and most recently New York. Do you believe that mandatory (court-ordered) mediation should be utilized only for a brief period of time to promote understanding of the process and then transition to being available only on a voluntary basis?

(5) Professor Welsh refers to the research done by Professor Robert Rubinson regarding the challenges facing low-income participants who are required to participate in court-connected mediation, including childcare and transportation constraints. Has the option for parties to participate remotely, on Zoom or video conferencing, lessened this concern? *See* Robert Rubinson, *Of Grids and Gatekeepers: The Socioeconomics of Mediation*, 17 Cardozo J. Conflict Resol. 873, 891–92 (2016).

Chapter 10

Mediation and the Lawyer as Advocate

A. Introduction

The materials in this chapter shift the focus from the perspective of the mediator and the parties to the special role that lawyers play as advisors and advocates in mediation. Although litigation and mediation are distinct processes, they are significantly related to one another. Even if no case has been filed with the court, lawyers assist their clients evaluate their dispute by considering their legal rights and obligations and the likely court outcome. For many cases, lawyers file pleadings and are then encouraged by both clients and court personnel, or required by court rules, to consider or participate in mediation. In such circumstances, lawyers must effectively manage their preparation and participation, with their clients, to ensure that they are operating compatibly rather than at cross purposes with one another. These advocate challenges were aptly portrayed by Mnookin and Kornhauser when they observed, in discussing negotiator conduct, that negotiations often take place in the "shadow of the law." *See* Robert H. Mnookin & Lewis Kornhauser, *Bargaining in the Shadow of the Law: The Case of Divorce*, 88 Yale L.J. 950 (1979).

Combining these processes requires lawyers to consider their obligations in new ways. What responsibility does a lawyer have to advise a client about the use of mediation? Should a lawyer participate in mediation? If so, how? How does a lawyer effectively protect a client in a non-adversarial process? Are advocacy skills in mediation comparable to or distinct from trial skills?

This chapter investigates these questions. Section B explores the interrelationship between litigation and mediation and the "evolution of the new lawyer." Section C examines the role attorneys do and should play as their client's representative prior to and during the mediation process and highlights tactics, strategies, and ethical issues that shape the lawyer's contributions.

B. The Relationship Between Mediation and Litigation

Mediation and litigation are often intertwined. When parties and their counsel file pleadings to advance a case, a state or federal court might order the participants to try to resolve some or all matters in mediation; or the parties and their counsel, before formally filing any pleadings, might themselves initiate efforts to secure a mediator to address their concerns, thereby possibly avoiding the need for a trial. It also is possible for attorneys and their clients to use mediation in complex cases to develop a plan for discovery and to manage other procedural aspects of the case. In such circumstances, all participants must skillfully navigate their conduct to ensure that their participation in one process supports or does not harm their effectiveness in the other. Sometimes, that is easier said than done.

Attorneys have responded in diverse ways to the rapid growth of mediation. Professor Len Riskin observed in 1982 that the lawyer's "standard philosophical map" can sometimes vary radically from the premises on which mediation is founded. *See* Leonard L. Riskin, *Mediation and Lawyers*, 43 Ohio St. L.J. 29, 43 (1982). Building on Riskin's insights, Professor Chris Guthrie has argued that even in a world mandating facilitative mediation, mediation with lawyer-mediators is unlikely to be a purely facilitative process because of the lawyer's philosophical map and the disputant's perceptual map. *See* Chris Guthrie, *The Lawyer's Philosophical Map and the Disputant's Perceptual Map: Impediments to Facilitative Mediation and Lawyering*, 6 Harv. Negot. L. Rev. 145, 148–50 (2001). While some litigators embrace the distributive bargaining theory's assumption that one party's gain is inevitably the other party's loss, mediation is dependent on creative problem solving which searches for mutual gains. Professor Robert Rubinson has similarly observed that mediation and litigation are dependent on very different "narratives," explaining that whereas litigation attempts to convince a decision maker as to what really happened and who was right, mediation seeks to reframe or expand negotiating issues, thereby transforming conflict through collaboration. *See* Robert Rubinson, *Client Counseling, Mediation, and Alternative Narratives of Dispute Resolution*, 10 Clinical L. Rev. 833 (2004).

Despite these potential philosophical differences in process values, many lawyers have embraced mediation's use, recognizing that it can offer a desirable solution for their clients in numerous situations. What elements must lawyers analyze as they proceed to engage in two processes in tandem? They examine such matters as: At what stage of the litigation process does it make most sense to mediate: early or just before trial? What discovery should or should not be sought prior to a pending mediation? Should the attorney file certain motions — *e.g.*, a motion for summary judgement — in order to further the chances of resolving the dispute in mediation or will doing so polarize the opposition? And if parties are participating in a mediation, whether pre-filing or post-filing, what disclosures should or should not be made during the mediation session in light of the possible or pending litigation? What documents must be prepared to orient and inform the mediator most constructively about the situation and are they compatible with the language, tone and content of documents prepared for litigation? Is the privacy of the mediation process — and potentially a confidential agreement — the most constructive environment for raising one's client's concerns?

In the following excerpt, Professor Julie Macfarlane describes how the changes in legal practice have led to a movement away from adversarial advocacy and toward the development of conflict resolution advocacy. Based on her empirical research, she asserts that a new professional identity for lawyers has emerged in response to a changing climate for disputes. These changes include the "vanishing trial" phenomenon, a dramatically altered business model, and an increase in institutional uses of mediation. *See supra,* Chapter 9.

As you read the excerpt, consider how mediation and litigation might blur into one another as fewer cases are resolved through trials. Is it desirable or possible to retain the uniqueness of each process?

The Evolution of the New Lawyer: How Lawyers Are Reshaping the Practice of Law[1]

2008 J. Disp. Resol. 61, 62–70, 73–75, 77–79*

By Dr. Julie Macfarlane

I. Times of Change

There have been seismic changes in the legal profession — especially in its internal structures and in legal disputing procedures — over the last thirty years. The "vanishing trial" phenomenon is just one aspect of this, but it is a vital one. A 98% civil settlement rate and the increasing use of negotiation, mediation, and collaboration in resolving lawsuits have dramatically altered the role of the lawyer. The traditional conception of the lawyer as "rights warrior" no longer satisfies client expectations, which center on value for money and practical problem solving rather than on expensive legal argument and arcane procedures.

At the same time, the business model of the profession has altered dramatically.... Both corporate and personal customers appear increasingly unwilling to passively foot the bill for a traditional, litigation-centered approach to legal services, preferring a more pragmatic, cost-conscious, and time-efficient approach to resolving legal problems.

. . .

Changes in procedure, voluntary initiatives, and changing client expectations are coming together to create a new role for counsel and a new model of client service. This role is moving away from the provision of narrow technical advice and strategies that center on litigation and fighting (*i.e.,* the "warrior lawyer") towards a more holistic, practical, and efficient approach to conflict resolution. The result is a new model of lawyering practice that builds on the skills and knowledge of traditional legal practice but is different in critical ways. The new lawyer is not completely unrelated or dissimilar to the warrior lawyer but an evolved, contemporary version....

---

1. Professor Macfarlane significantly expanded the development of this article in her book-length treatment of these matters. *See* The New Lawyer (2d ed. 2017).

* Copyright © 2008. All rights reserved. Reprinted with permission.

Both the emerging and the traditional models of lawyering place legal intelligence at their center as the primary and unique skill of the lawyer. Both approaches require excellent client communication skills, good writing skills, and, sometimes, persuasive oral advocacy skills. Both approaches require effective negotiation. However, the new lawyer realizes that she needs to utilize these skills in different ways and in new and different processes, designed to facilitate earlier settlement. The goals of these processes are almost always information exchange and the exploration of options. Sometimes they include the settlement of some peripheral issues, sometimes full resolution. The warrior lawyer is more familiar with processes that rehearse and replay rights-based arguments, look for holes in the other side's case, and give up as little information as possible. The new lawyer bases her practice on the undisputed fact that almost every contentious matter she handles will settle without a full trial, and some will settle without a judicial hearing of any kind. She assumes that negotiation, often directly involving her clients, is feasible in all but the most exceptional cases and that in this capacity she is an important role model and coach for her clients. The new lawyer understands that not every conflict is really about rights and entitlements and that these are conventional disguises for anger, hurt feelings, and struggles over scarce resources. The new lawyer recognizes that part of her role is to assist her clients to identify what they really need, while constantly assessing the likely risks and rewards as well as what they believe they "deserve" in some abstract sense. She also understands the purpose and potential of information in settlement processes. In adversarial processes, information is used to gain an advantage over the other side (information as "power over"); in settlement meetings, information is used as a valuable shared resource to broaden the range of possible solutions (information as "power with"). The new lawyer must develop the best possible outcome — often in the form of a settlement — for her client, using communication, persuasion, and relationship building. This is a different role than making positional arguments and "puffing" up the case. It moves beyond the narrow articulation of partisan interests to the practical realization of a conflict specialist role for counsel.

. . .

III. Conflict Resolution Advocacy

. . .

The new lawyer will conceive of her advocacy role more deeply and broadly than simply fighting on her clients' behalf. This role comprehends both a different relationship with the client — closer to a working partnership — and a different orientation towards conflict. The new lawyer must help her client engage with the conflict, confronting the strategic and practical realities as well as making a game plan for victory. The new lawyer can offer her client skills and tools for conflict analysis, an understanding of how conflict develops and evolves over time, and the experience of working continuously with disputants on (perhaps similar) disputes. Conflict resolution advocacy means working with clients to anticipate, raise, strategize, and negotiate over conflict and, if possible, to implement jointly agreed outcomes. . . .

. . . Conflict resolution advocacy understands rights-based strategies as important and useful but rarely exclusive tools for engaging with conflict and seeking solutions. As a result of broadening discussions to include non-legal issues and potential solutions, the role of the client in conflict resolution advocacy becomes more significant in both planning and decision making, modifying the simple notion of the lawyer as the expert who is "in charge." . . . Finally, conflict resolution advocacy does not deny or contradict justice as process, but it takes what lawyers already know about the importance of integrity in the processes and procedures of conflict resolution and applies this awareness to private ordering outside the legal system. As a consequence, the new lawyer will be deeply involved in, and knowledgeable about, the design of processes and procedures of negotiation, mediation, and other collaborative processes . . .

IV. Conflict Resolution Advocacy and Client Loyalty

There is no lessening of the lawyer's responsibility to achieve the best possible outcome for his client in client resolution advocacy. In fact, advocacy as conflict resolution places the constructive and creative promotion of partisan outcomes at the center of the advocate's role and sees this goal as entirely compatible with working with the other side. In fact, this goal can *only* be achieved by working with the other side. The new lawyer remains just as dedicated to achieving her clients' goals as the warrior or adversarial advocate. What changes is that her primary skill becomes her effectiveness and ability to achieve the best possible negotiated settlement, while she remains prepared to litigate if necessary. . . .

Counsel's loyalty and focus should be on achieving the client's best possible outcome(s). . . . A contradiction between client loyalty and creative consensus building only exists if counsel is convinced that the only effective way to advance the client's wishes is by using rights-based processes. Aside from these fairly exceptional cases, the goal of the conflict resolution advocate is to persuade the other side to settle — on her client's best possible terms.

Adversarial advocacy offers no frameworks to counsel to resolve classic dilemmas such as when and how to settle, or how to balance their own judgment with the clients' aspirations. Admitting a need to compromise in any way undermines the core of zealous advocacy. Conflict resolution advocacy both anticipates these dilemmas and makes them resolvable on a principled basis. Whereas adversarial advocacy tends to view settlement as capitulation, conflict resolution advocacy is committed to evaluating the pros, cons, and alternatives of any settlement option, which includes an evaluation of the legal, cognitive, and emotional dimensions because all of these are part of how clients appraise settlement.

V. Fact Gathering and Information in Conflict Resolution Advocacy

The dominant epistemology of litigation is that knowledge and information have the sole purpose of advancing the client's legal case. This approach means that only information that fits the legal argument is either sought or utilized, and ignores other information that may be important to realizing the client's goals. The adversarial advocate approaches fact-gathering and information as a competitive process, with information withheld from the other side even where it may be of little or no consequence, and often where it would be beneficial in clarifying the relative goals and expectations of each.

In a conflict resolution model, the purpose and uses of information are understood differently. First, the type of information that may be important is expanded. . . . If counsel takes seriously her responsibility to engage the client in the resolution of the conflict, she will seek out information that could be key to understanding how to advance the client's interests and needs, as well as his legal entitlements.

Second, conflict resolution advocacy regards information as a shared resource that may advance all party interests. This approach to information sharing requires significant reorientation, both conceptual and collegial. For a less aggressive and more collaborative approach to information sharing to work, lawyers need to be able to build trusting relationships with other counsel and other professionals. There is an obvious need for norms of reciprocity. . . .

VI. Re-Envisioning Outcomes in Conflict Resolution Advocacy

. . .

In envisioning and evaluating potential outcomes, conflict resolution advocacy will certainly include proximity to an "ideal" (*i.e.*, successful) legal outcome, but many other factors will also be important. For example, responsible counsel will always consider the issue of costs in planning a conflict resolution strategy. Conflict resolution advocates should consider how far any one outcome will meet client interests. Aside from "winning," these might include, for example, recognition and acknowledgment, business expansion or solvency, future relationships both domestic and commercial, vindication and justice, emotional closure, and reputation. These interests have both short-term and long-term elements. They reflect not only outcome goals but also the importance of procedural justice — feeling listened to, being taken seriously, and being fairly treated. In a conflict resolution model of advocacy, it is not only the final deal that matters but also how the client feels about how it was reached, which includes a sense that the outcome is fair and wise. . . .

Conflict resolution advocacy . . . does not mean abandoning rights-based advocacy and even trial work in appropriate cases. In fact, conflict resolution advocacy builds on some traditional skills and knowledge, notably information assimilation, legal research, effective oral communication, strategic planning, and insider knowledge, which are core elements of effective trial advocacy. Conflict resolution advocacy takes these familiar tools and applies them to a newly articulated and more realistic goal: the pursuit of acceptable, reasonable, and durable settlements that meet client interests.

VII. Placing Negotiation at the Center of Legal Practice

... [C]onflict resolution advocacy demands that negotiation planning be addressed even in the earliest stages of file development as a part of the process of canvassing goals, priorities, and alternatives with the client. An early and explicit focus on the potential for negotiated settlement requires the holistic framing of the problem rather than the selective use of information in a way that narrows the case to its generic legal issues. ...

Lawyers ... experienced in settlement advocacy settings identify a number of discrete negotiation skills — implicating both cognitive and emotional abilities and qualities — which enable them to be most effective. These include preparing an effective opening statement ... which adopts a firm yet not overly positional tone; matching the appropriate informal process to the case; displaying confidence and openness; and thinking outside the "box" of conventional, legal solutions ... Critical to being able to persuade the other side to settle on your client's best terms is an understanding of what the other side needs in order to be able to settle. ...

X. Decision Making and Control

... Reframing the lawyer-client relationship as a working partnership has profound implications for the balance of power in lawyer-client relationships. A partnership gives the client far greater power not only to review and critique decisions but also to participate in making them. ...

In anticipation of early mediation, there are many questions that the lawyer now needs to ask at the planning stage — questions that only the client can answer and that are not necessarily related to making the legal case. ...

[A] business client is likely to provide additional information on business needs and goals, both long-term and short-term. ... Issues that would not be apparent otherwise may surface. Instead of removing emotional and psychological issues from the negotiation, the inclusion of clients in planning may mean that important and otherwise unspoken barriers to settlement can be raised and discussed.

... Reconceiving lawyer-client relations in this way means that much of the weight of both moral and practical responsibility shifts from the lawyer to her client. Depending on the extent to which counsel embraces a working partnership with her client, this shift may be a significant one or it may be more marginal — but it will occur in some way. ...

. . .

XI. Client Participation

. . . In informal settlement procedures, lawyers have far less control over the proceedings and need to be able to understand how their client will behave and how to relate to him throughout the process. The new lawyer needs to not only be able to minimize any negative consequences of the client being present but also to maximize the benefits.

Counsel experienced in mediation and other convened settlement processes have learned that bringing a client with them who is not prepared and has not agreed in advance on how to present the issues (for example, how much and what information to disclose, or what options to canvass) may be a recipe for disaster. . . .

. . . A working partnership between lawyer and client aims to produce superior solutions — that is, superior to those solutions negotiated privately by lawyers or imposed by a judge. Involving clients in negotiation and mediation processes can significantly advance this goal. . . .

Notes and Questions

(1) Do you agree that mediation and litigation rely on different philosophical mindsets? If so, is it possible for a single person to be a competent advocate in the worlds of both litigation and mediation? Professor Rubinson's article, *Client Counseling, Mediation, and Alternative Narratives of Dispute Resolution*, 10 Clinical L. Rev. 833 (2004), provides advice to lawyers on how to properly counsel their clients regarding mediation. *See also* Jacqueline M. Nolan-Haley, *Lawyers, Clients, and Mediation*, 73 Notre Dame L. Rev. 1369, 1370–71 (1998) (arguing that "[m]ediation offers enormous potential for lawyers to recognize and honor the missing human dignity dimension in current versions of adversarial lawyering," and offering suggestions to lawyers on how to be good counselors with respect to mediation).

(2) In 1997, Professor John Lande, in *How Will Lawyering and Mediation Transform Each Other?*, 24 Fla. St. U. L. Rev. 839 (1997), coined the term "litimediation" to refer to the phenomenon that mediation would be the normal way to end litigation. At the time he wrote his article, he was to some degree predicting what the impact would be of blending litigation and mediation cultures. From what you know of the legal culture in your own area, how accurate were Lande's predictions? In a presentation to Professor Stulberg's mediation class, Lawrence Watson, a pre-eminent mediator and former chair of the Trial Lawyer's Section of the Florida State Bar Association, said: "When I was a trial lawyer in Florida (pre-1989), I was in court 40–42 weeks per year. A trial lawyer in the state of Florida today [2018] is in court 2 weeks per year — and spends the other 40 weeks per year representing clients in a mediation conference."

(3) Several studies have examined the attitudes of litigators toward ADR, including mediation. Their findings reflect diverging attitudes among attorneys and reveal that cultural differences exist among jurisdictions. *See* Dr. Julie Macfarlane & Michaela Keet, *Civil Justice Reform and Mandatory Civil Mediation in Saskatchewan: Lessons from a Maturing Program*, 42 Alberta L. Rev. 677 (2005); Roselle L.

Wissler, *Barriers to Attorneys' Discussion and Use of ADR*, 19 Ohio St. J. on Disp. Resol. 459 (2004) (focusing on Arizona); Bobbi McAdoo & Art Hinshaw, *The Challenge of Institutionalizing Alternative Dispute Resolution: Attorney Perspectives on the Effect of Rule 17 on Civil Litigation in Missouri*, 67 Mo. L. Rev. 473 (2002); Bobbi McAdoo, *A Report to the Minnesota Supreme Court: The Impact of Rule 114 on Civil Litigation Practice in Minnesota*, 25 Hamline L. Rev. 401 (2002).

(4) The changes in the legal system have implications for legal education. In *Separate and Not Equal: Integrating Civil Procedure and ADR in Legal Academia*, 80 Notre Dame L. Rev. 681 (2005) (Jean Sternlight), and *It's Time to Get It Right: Problem-Solving in the First-Year Curriculum*, 39 Wash. U. J. L. & Pol'y 39 (2012) (Bobbi McAdoo, Sharon Press, and Chelsea Griffin), the authors argue that given the interrelatedness of ADR and litigation (Sternlight) and the importance to all lawyers of the skills taught in ADR courses (McAdoo, Press, and Griffin), law schools err to the extent that they segregate the teaching of litigation/lawyering and ADR into totally separate courses. Do you agree?

(5) Mediation is not the only dispute resolution process that challenges lawyers' adopting an adversarial mindset. In 2009 (amended 2010), the National Conference of Commissioners on Uniform Laws promulgated a Uniform Collaborative Law Rules/Act. In a collaborative law practice, lawyers contract to try to resolve their clients' issues in a cooperative way, including a commitment to terminate their legal services to their clients if parties opt to pursue some or all matters in a traditional court process. The Uniform Law attempts to standardize the most important features of a collaborative law practice. *See* http://www.uniformlaws.org/Act.aspx?title =Collaborative%20Law%20Act. For debate regarding some of the ethical issues surrounding this approach, see James K.L. Lawrence, *Collaborative Lawyering: A New Development in Conflict Resolution*, 17 Ohio St. J. on Disp. Resol. 431 (2002); Sandra S. Beckwith & Sherri Goren Slovin, *The Collaborative Lawyer as Advocate: A Response*, 18 Ohio St. J. on Disp. Resol. 497 (2003); and Christopher M. Fairman, *Ethics and Collaborative Lawyering: Why Put Old Hats on New Heads?*, 18 Ohio St. J. on Disp. Resol. 505 (2003).

(6) Beginning in 2026, the NextGen Bar Examination identifies "Negotiation and Dispute Resolution" as one of the seven (7) pre-requisite Foundational skills that could be tested for those individuals seeking to secure their license to practice law.

C. Lawyers' Role in Mediation

It is well recognized that lawyers perform many roles for their clients in addition or as an alternative to representing them in litigation. The Preamble to the ABA Model Rules of Professional Conduct states:

> As a representative of clients, a lawyer performs various functions. As advisor, a lawyer provides a client with an informed understanding of the client's legal rights and obligations and explains their practical implications.

As advocate, a lawyer zealously asserts the client's position under the rules of the adversary system. As negotiator, a lawyer seeks a result advantageous to the client but consistent with requirements of honest dealing with others. As an evaluator, a lawyer acts by examining a client's legal affairs and reporting about them to the client or to others.

Model Rule 2.1 elaborates: "In rendering advice, a lawyer may refer not only to law but to other considerations such as moral, economic, social and political factors, that may be relevant to the client's situation." Since the Model Rules are silent regarding the lawyer's role as a representative in mediation, some questions surface as to their responsibilities in it.

In 1990, Professor Frank Sander and Attorney Michael Prigoff engaged in a debate (*A.B.A. Journal*, Nov. 1990) regarding whether attorneys do or should have a duty to advise their clients about mediation or other forms of ADR. Sander argued that the duty may already exist, and, if not, should be imposed. Prigoff agreed that it is often desirable, as a matter of good lawyering, to inform clients of ADR options, but suggested that it would be unwise to create an ethical duty requiring such conversations. Today, a number of jurisdictions *explicitly* impose such a requirement by court rule. *E.g.*, Minn. Gen. R. Prac. 114.03 (noting that the court administrator shall provide parties and attorneys with ADR information and stating that "attorneys shall provide clients with information about available ADR processes"); Mo. Sup. Ct. R. 17.02(b) (requiring attorneys to advise their clients of the availability of ADR programs). Alternatively, some jurisdictions have used their ethical codes or lawyers' creeds to impose such a duty. *E.g.*, S.D. Tex. L.R. 16.4.B ("Before the initial conference . . . in a case, counsel are required to discuss with their clients and with opposing counsel the appropriateness of ADR in the case."). It is important to note that some jurisdictions *require* attorney-client consultation while others *encourage* attorneys to advise clients about ADR. The hard rule would, theoretically, be enforceable, whereas the precatory rule or statute is not. Furthermore, some rules require attorneys merely to describe existing programs, whereas others require a more general discussion of all dispute resolution approaches. Finally, some rules and statutes prescribe a duty to inform clients, whereas others focus on a duty to discuss ADR with opposing counsel. As a practical matter, because an increasing number of courts mandate mediation in some or all cases (*see* Chapter 9), attorneys are increasingly finding it essential to discuss mediation with their clients.

Notes and Questions

(1) In addition to Sander's article referenced above, there are many authors who examine the question of whether attorneys already have an implicit duty to inform their clients of the benefits of mediation. For example, see Suzanne J. Schmitz, *Giving Meaning to the Second Generation of ADR Education: Attorneys' Duty to Learn About ADR and What They Must Learn*, 1999 J. Disp. Resol. 29 (arguing that they do have such a duty); Monica L. Warmbrod, *Could an Attorney Face Disciplinary Actions or Even Legal Malpractice Liability for Failure to Inform Clients of*

Alternative Dispute Resolution?, 27 Cumb. L. Rev. 791, 809 (1996–97) (concluding that they could); and Stuart M. Widman, *Attorneys' Ethical Duties to Know and Advise Clients About Alternative Dispute Resolution*, The Professional Lawyer 18 (1993 symposium issue) (arguing that attorneys have a duty to inform their clients about mediation where it might save them money). Do you believe attorneys have an implied duty to inform their clients about mediation under the ABA Model Rules of Professional Conduct? For an article discussing lawyers' duty to discuss ADR in the family law context, see Nicole Pedone, *Lawyer's Duty to Discuss Alternative Dispute Resolution in the Best Interest of the Children*, 36 Fam. & Conciliation Cts. Rev. 65 (1998).

(2) Presumably, the point of a duty to inform clients about mediation is to foster its consideration and potential use. Professors Rogers and McEwen note that corporate lawyers who were instructed to consider using mediation in their cases did not do so regularly until they had received more education on mediation and until other relevant incentives were changed. Nancy H. Rogers & Craig A. McEwen, *Employing the Law to Increase the Use of Mediation and to Encourage Direct and Early Negotiations*, 13 Ohio St. J. on Disp. Resol. 831, 862–63 (1998). A study of Arizona attorneys concluded that "[b]ased on the limited empirical evidence available to date, requiring attorneys to both assess ADR options with clients and confer about using ADR with opposing counsel seems to hold promise as a means to increase voluntary ADR use." Roselle L. Wissler, *Barriers to Attorneys' Discussion and Use of ADR*, 19 Ohio St. J. on Disp. Resol. 459, 506 (2004). *See also* Roselle L. Wissler, *When Does Familiarity Breed Content? A Study of the Role of Different Forms of ADR Education and Experience in Attorneys' ADR Recommendations*, 2 Pepp. Disp. Resol. L.J. 199, 237 (2002) (merely taking a CLE course or law school course on ADR has little or no correlation with attorneys' likelihood to recommend ADR to their clients).

(3) If there *should* be a duty for attorneys to inform their clients of the availability of mediation as an alternative to negotiation or litigation, when should such a duty arise: only if the opposing party is or might be amenable to participating in a mediation? . . . a court mediation program has been provided? . . . the case, in the attorney's opinion, is a "reasonable" candidate for mediation? And in what body of law should such a duty be contained: court rule? Statute? Code of Ethics? Can a meaningful sanction be applied against attorneys who fail to fulfill such a duty? For an argument that "[t]he ABA should amend the Model Rules to require lawyers to present the option of pursuing ADR to the client," see Robert F. Cochran Jr., *ADR, the ABA, and Client Control: A Proposal That the Model Rules Require Lawyers to Present ADR Options to Clients*, 41 S. Tex. L. Rev. 183, 200 (1999). *See also* Marshall J. Breger, *Should an Attorney Be Required to Advise a Client of ADR Options?*, 13 Geo. J. Legal Ethics 427, 460 (2000) (arguing that the ABA should adopt a rule providing that "[a] lawyer has a duty to inform his client about the availability and applicability of alternative dispute resolution procedures that are reasonably appropriate under the circumstances").

(4) Do attorneys have a duty to *learn* about mediation or other forms of ADR? If they have such a duty, where is it enunciated? Do you believe attorneys *should* have a duty to inform themselves about mediation?

———————

Once it has been decided that a particular dispute will be mediated, various issues arise regarding the appropriate role of the lawyer-representative in the mediation. Section 1 below examines what role a lawyer should play in selecting a mediator. Section 2 addresses the question whether lawyers ought to participate in the mediation. Section 3 looks at how lawyers should conduct themselves in mediation in order to provide their clients with effective representation. Finally, Section 4 examines ethical constraints on lawyers in mediation.

1. Lawyers' Role in Selecting a Mediator

Many jurisdictions allow disputants to choose their own mediator rather than accept the individual a court might appoint from its staff or roster of qualified mediators, even when the mediation is court-ordered. *See* Mo. Sup. Ct. R. 17.03 (allowing court to appoint neutral when parties cannot agree); Fla. R. Civ. P. 1.720(j)(1) (providing parties with 10-day period in which to appoint mediator of own choosing). When mediation is conducted pre-suit or voluntarily, the disputants have complete discretion to select a mediator.

When selecting a mediator is within the parties' discretion, it is their lawyers, not themselves, that routinely make the choice. Clients may believe that their attorneys are more qualified than themselves to identify both the traits desirable in a mediator and the individuals who possess such traits.

That attorneys, not clients, typically select the mediator has a significant impact on which persons are chosen most frequently to serve as mediators. For example, because attorneys tend to focus on the legal aspects of disputes, they are likely to believe that it is important that a mediator be knowledgeable regarding the relevant law, so they often select an attorney or a retired judge to serve as a mediator. Further, attorneys typically pick someone they know, such as an attorney who is now a practicing mediator but is someone with or against whom they have previously interacted when representing clients in litigation. If clients assumed more responsibility for selecting mediators, perhaps they would be more likely to select persons knowledgeable in areas such as psychology, communications, science, or accounting, not only attorneys. Greater client participation in selecting mediators might also increase the diversity among mediators in terms of race, gender, and ethnicity. As referenced in Chapter 7, *supra,* the overwhelming percentage of current mediators handling complex civil cases are white male attorneys.

The first reading by David Geronemus outlines factors attorneys ought to consider when selecting a mediator. In his account, Geronemus relies significantly on Professor Riskin's four-quadrant grid, which divides mediators along the dimensions of evaluative to facilitative and broad to narrow. *See* Chapter 4, Section D.1., *supra*. Geronemus suggests that the "grid" is a good starting point for selecting a mediator, but attorneys should also consider a variety of other factors relating to their expertise, style, and philosophy. He argues that attorneys should think through their decision carefully in each case, based on their perceptions of what barriers are precluding that case from settling, noting that a mediator suitable for assisting parties in resolving one dispute could be a poor match for helping in another.

The second reading, by Professor Jean Sternlight, briefly describes the professional responsibility literature on how attorneys and clients ought to more broadly divide decision-making responsibilities. After reading Sternlight's excerpt, consider whether attorneys, as a matter of professional ethics, have a duty to consult with their clients regarding the selection of mediators.

Mediation of Legal Malpractice Cases: Prevention and Resolution

609 PLI/Lit 847, 860–66 Practicing Law Institute Litigation and
Administrative Practice Course Handbook Series Litigation PLI
Order No. H0-003Q (June 1999)*
By David Geronemus

The issue of choosing the right mediator might best be phrased as finding the mediator who is most likely to be successful in helping to resolve the dispute. There are certain clear prerequisites. Obviously any mediator should be neutral and respected by both sides. In this regard, consider how one should react to a mediator proposed by an opponent — especially one that the opponent has used before. Although some litigants reflexively reject a mediator the other side has used before, it is interesting to note that such a mediator presumably has the respect of the opposition. If the mediator agrees with you on the merits of the case, it will be difficult for your opponents to walk away from the mediator's advice. Thus, it is often worth investing the time to determine whether you can become comfortable with the mediator's neutrality. If so, he or she may well be a serious candidate for your mediation. This analysis also leads to the proposition that picking a mediator because you believe he or she may be sympathetic to you on the merits can be hazardous. Even if you are able to convince the other side to use your candidate, unless the other side perceives the mediator as neutral and fair throughout the process, he or she will be able to have little impact.

. . .

One useful way of classifying mediators is to consider whether they rely principally on "evaluative" techniques or on "facilitative" techniques. *See* L. Riskin, *Mediator Orientations, Strategies and Techniques*, 12 Alternatives 111 (1994). [Ed. note: For the more complete article, see Leonard L. Riskin, *Understanding Mediators'*

Orientations, Strategies, and Techniques: A Grid For The Perplexed, 1 Harv. Neg. L. Rev. 7 (1996), in Chapter 4, Section D.1., *supra*.] Briefly stated, a purely evaluative mediator focuses on the strengths and weaknesses of the parties' cases, while a purely facilitative mediator will not offer an opinion on these issues, focusing his or her attention on clarifying communications and issues, defusing emotion, and curing any information deficiencies that may retard settlement. In addition, mediators differ in whether they focus only on parties' legal rights or whether they also attempt to find creative solutions that satisfy the parties' underlying needs or interests.

Even within these broad categories, mediators differ widely in their approaches. For example, some evaluative mediators tend to offer their views of the case early in the proceedings; others view evaluation as one of many impasse breaking techniques, and will offer evaluative feedback only as necessary to break an impasse — typically in the latter stages of the mediation. Indeed, this distinction can be crucially important to the success of the process, since the "right" evaluation at the wrong time can cause one of the parties to decide that the process is not worth pursuing. In addition, if a mediator evaluates the case before the parties have negotiated to impasse, there is always the risk that the evaluation will itself become a barrier to settlement. For example, assume that the opening positions before a mediation are $2 million demanded and $25,000 offered. Unbeknownst to the enthusiastically evaluative mediator, the plaintiff is really willing to settle for $250,000, not much more than the defendant would be willing to pay. I suspect that if the mediator produces an early evaluation of say $500,000, the mediator will have gone a long way towards making the case more difficult to settle. On the other hand, consider what might occur if the mediator withheld the evaluation until the parties had negotiated to impasse at, say, $275,000 demanded and $200,000 offered. A well-reasoned statement by the mediator that the defendant should add to her offer may well be effective in breaking the impasse.

Mediators also differ in the extent to which they will want to work with the parties in structuring the process and in the kind of process that they prefer. For example, some mediators will want to work with the parties as soon as they are retained to discuss what kind of process makes sense. Others leave the process structure entirely to the parties. Some mediators will talk to the parties or counsel prior to the mediation to gain an understanding of the problems and opportunities that they may face at the mediation; others rely on the impressions that they gain in the mediation. Some mediators rely extensively on joint sessions, others do most of their work in private caucuses. And, of course, mediators differ in the substantive legal expertise that they bring to the process. Finally, some mediators have worn a judge's robes; others have not.

These differences among mediators lead to two points about choosing the right mediator for a case. First, given the extent of these differences, at least for cases with relatively high stakes, it is important to spend time learning in some detail about prospective mediators. Relying on a mediator's general reputation for having a high settlement rate, being a distinguished and fair member of the legal community, or being a highly skilled mediator is a useful start, but operates at too great a level of generality to provide the best answers. Talking with parties who have used the mediator before is one useful tool in learning in detail about a mediator's approach. Another approach that is underutilized is a joint interview of the mediator by both parties. Most mediators are in my experience willing to be interviewed about significant cases. There is probably no better way to learn about the approach that a mediator will take than to ask him or her about it. Indeed, to at least some extent lawyers will want to determine whether the prospective mediator has the right personality to interact in a productive way with the parties to the dispute, and to a great extent an interview provides a useful forum to find out.

Second, the choice of the mediator ought to be made with reference to the barriers to the settlement of the case and to your goals in the dispute. For example, if restoration of a damaged relationship is an important goal, it will be important to choose a mediator with strong interpersonal skills. By contrast, if there are widely divergent views of the merits that are making it difficult to settle the case, a mediator with strong evaluative skills will be important. Of course, in many cases both strong evaluative and facilitative skills will be required. And, the extent to which the mediation will require evaluation should determine the extent to which the mediator need have at least some specialized substantive experience.

Following these guidelines should enhance your chances of choosing the best possible mediator for your dispute. Making sure that you design the right sort of mediation process — preferably in conjunction with the mediator — is an equally important next step in utilizing mediation effectively.

Lawyer's Representation of Clients in Mediation: Using Economics and Psychology to Structure Advocacy in a Nonadversarial Setting

14 Ohio St. J. on Disp. Resol. 269, 349–52 (1999)*
By Jean R. Sternlight

A vast professional responsibility literature discusses the appropriate division of responsibilities in a case between lawyer and client. This literature attempts to fill in the gaps left by the rather vague strictures of both the Model Rules of Professional Conduct and the Model Code of Professional Responsibility. While both sets of rules essentially require the lawyer to defer to her client on major matters (ends) while allowing the lawyer leeway on tactical choices (means), [see Rule 1.2(a) of the Model Rules of Professional Conduct and Ethical Canon 707 of the Model Code of Professional Responsibility], this distinction leaves plenty of room for argument. One school of thought, which some have called "traditional," contends that expert attorneys should behave very directively toward their typically passive clients. The other model, which some have called "participatory," urges that because many strategic decisions involve important choices on ultimate objectives, attorneys need to work closely and consultatively with their clients. As Professor David Luban has observed:

> [The ends-means rule] assumes a sharp dichotomy between ends and means, according to which a certain result (acquittal, a favorable settlement, *etc.*) is all that the client desires, while the legal tactics and arguments are merely routes to that result. No doubt this is true in many cases, but it need not be: the client may want to win acquittal *by* asserting a certain right, because it vindicates him in a way that matters to him; or he may wish to obtain a settlement without using a certain tactic, because he disapproves of the tactic. In that case, what the lawyer takes to be mere means are really part of the client's ends.[269]

In short, current rules, codes, cases, and commentary provide some guidance but do not provide crystal clear guidance on how, in general, lawyers and clients ought to divide decision-making responsibilities.

Nor do existing ethical provisions or commentary provide clear guidance on the specific question of how lawyers and their clients ought to divide negotiation and mediation responsibilities. While it is well recognized that lawyers have an obligation to convey settlement offers to their clients and to allow their clients to make the decision as to whether or not to accept a particular offer, few decisions or commentators have addressed the further questions of how lawyer and client should divide responsibilities beyond that bare minimum. One exception is Professor Robert Cochran, who has argued eloquently that lawyers ought to be required to consult with their clients extensively both as to the nature of the negotiation and as to whether a dispute would best be handled through litigation or rather through some form of alternative dispute resolution.[271] Cochran argues that such consultation is desirable to preserve parties' individual autonomy, to ensure better results, and to protect against attorney conflicts of interest.

Notes and Questions

(1) Do you believe that attorneys have an ethical obligation to consult with their clients regarding the choice of a mediator? *Should* attorneys have such an obligation? Note that some mediators say that they view their client as the attorney, rather than the attorney's client. Does this perspective raise any concerns?

---

269. David Luban, *Paternalism and the Legal Profession*, 1981 Wis. L. Rev. 454, 459 n.9; *see also* Robert F. Cochran, Jr., *Legal Representation and the Next Steps Toward Client Control: Attorney Malpractice for the Failure to Allow the Client to Control Negotiation and Pursue Alternatives to Litigation*, 47 Wash. & Lee L. Rev. 819, 827–828 (1990); Mark Spiegel, *Lawyering and Client Decisionmaking: Informed Consent and the Legal Profession*, 128 U. Pa. L. Rev. 41, 57 (1979). [Ed. note: parentheticals omitted.]

271. *See* Cochran, *supra* note 269, at 823–24.

(2) As a matter of "good practice," should attorneys consult with their clients regarding the choice of a mediator?

(3) Whether alone or in consultation with a client, what criteria should an attorney use to select a mediator for a particular dispute?

(4) Once a lawyer and client have decided on the relevant criteria for selecting a mediator, how do they actually find a mediator who meets them? Many not-for-profit and for-profit organizations, including the American Arbitration Association, the CPR International Institute for Conflict Prevention and Resolution, and JAMS, maintain lists of mediators and will provide biographical information about the mediators on their list to inquiring parties. As noted previously, some courts or administrative agencies provide training and/or "certify" mediators in their jurisdiction (*see, supra,* Chapter 9) and may make information about the mediators on their lists available to parties and counsel. Extensive information about a mediator or mediation firm, much of it in a marketing format, is available through the Internet.

2. Does the Participation of Lawyers Benefit or Harm the Mediation Process?

In civil litigation cases — ranging from catastrophic tort claims, employment discrimination charges, and complex business contract disputes to personal injury claims and insurance controversies — attorneys actively participate in a mediation session.

But particularly for some categories of mediated cases, there is a policy debate as to whether attorneys should be allowed to be present. Some court rules bar attorneys from representing their clients in the mediation of small claims disputes, and parties involved in neighborhood-based cases often participate in mediation pro se. Perhaps not surprisingly, the policy question of whether an attorney/advocate's presence and participation in mediation is helpful or harmful has been raised most frequently for marital dissolution cases. In these cases, the mediator may be a mental health professional (as opposed to an attorney); the issues discussed have long-term impact on the parties and their children; and the conversations can be emotionally volatile. Given these features, some jurisdictions bar attorney presence at a mediation, concerned that an attorney's traditional adversarial training would systematically undercut mediation's problem-solving approach.

In response to such concerns, commentators, such as Mark Rutherford, *Lawyers and Divorce Mediation: Designing the Role of "Outside Counsel,"* 12 Mediation Q. 17 (June 1986), have suggested that attorneys may be helpful to the mediation process: (1) during the pre-mediation referral period; (2) as an expert adviser during the mediation process; or (3) after the mediation, as a reviewer of the final mediated agreement and as a drafter of a legally binding marital agreement. He contends that to the extent that the attorney participates at all, he or she should do so non-adversarially.

Craig A. McEwen, Nancy H. Rogers, and Richard J. Maiman, in their excerpt below, suggest that it is important for lawyers to participate in mediation to protect the rights and interests of their clients. Though its focus relates to attorney participation in divorce mediation, its insights can be readily generalized to most civil litigation disputes. The second reading, Section 10 of the Uniform Mediation Act (Appendix D), prohibits excluding attorneys from mediation; while states do not necessarily adopt uniform acts in their entirety, all six jurisdictions that first adopted the UMA adopted Section 10.

Bring in the Lawyers: Challenging the Dominant Approaches to Ensuring Fairness in Divorce Mediation

79 Minn. L. Rev. 1317, 1322, 1376–77, 1394–95 (1995)*
By Craig A. McEwen, Nancy H. Rogers & Richard J. Maiman

. . . [W]e argue that the debate about fairness in divorce mediation, as well as the resulting legal schemes based on either the "regulatory" or "voluntary participation" approaches, results from the view that one must choose between a "lawyered" process ending in the courtroom, and an informal, problem-solving process involving parties but not lawyers in the mediation room. In our view, this dichotomy has unnecessarily narrowed the policy choices underlying mediation schemes, because it assumes that lawyers either cause conflict or act as mouthpieces for clients with a cause; that the divorce process is one in which, absent mediation (where lawyers do not appear), aggressive lawyers contest custody cases at hearings; and that mediators either protect parties' interests or pressure them toward a particular (and sometimes unjust) settlement.

We challenge these assumptions and the two approaches in statutes and court rules that follow from them — the "regulatory" and the "voluntary participation" approaches. We argue that the mediation scheme in Maine, where attorneys participate regularly and vigorously in mandated divorce mediation, provides a third avenue — one we call the "lawyer-participant" approach. Research evidence about this third approach undermines the assumptions that have confined the debate about fairness. . . .

. . .

Most fairness concerns evaporate if lawyers attend mediation sessions with the parties or if the parties opt out of the process when unrepresented. Less intrusive regulations, such as judicial review of agreements, prohibition of settlement pressures, and provisions for unrepresented parties, may moderate the remaining fairness issues. The detailed rules of the "regulatory approach" largely become unnecessary to preserve fairness if lawyers are present.

By encouraging lawyer presence and permitting modification of the mediation ground rules, this scheme is more flexible and certain in responding to the problems of bargaining imbalances and mediator pressures. Especially given the unpredictability and changing situational character of these challenges to fairness, the presence of lawyers in the process can assure necessary help in those unpredictable circumstances. The Maine research shows that with lawyers present as advisors and potentially as spokespersons, the risks of unfairness decline, even in the most unbalanced situations. By permitting adjustment of the mediation process (for example, allowing shuttle mediation), mediation can be tailored to fit particular relationships and issues in each case.

Lawyers prevent or moderate the effects of a face to face encounter with an abuser, thus diminishing the likelihood of unfairness in domestic violence cases. Maine lawyers attending mediation sessions with their clients report arranging separate sessions, time-outs, and other measures to protect their clients. Past violence, which may be a key factor in determining whether the parties will submit to an unfair settlement or will be forced into a frightening situation, becomes less of a bargaining factor if the parties attend with their lawyers. Lawyers can advise clients to avoid settlements that will allow further opportunities for abuse, or that are unlikely to be obeyed, or that are bad deals. Lawyers can also advise their clients to terminate mediation sessions. . . .

Issue limitations also become unnecessary if lawyers attend and can advise on economic trade-offs and legal issues. There is no more danger in combining the issues in mediation than exists if disposition of all issues occurs outside of mediation.

So, too, an assumption that lawyers will be absent underlies reliance on mediator qualifications as a means to ensure fairness. Absent lawyers, mediators must have at least some of the skills and knowledge that lawyers would otherwise provide. In fact, Maine divorce lawyers acknowledge that they sometimes get poor mediators. In these cases, the lawyers simply take charge and use the sessions as four-way negotiation sessions. Although mediator qualifications involving advanced educational degrees may help increase settlements or party confidence, they are unnecessary to protect against unfairness under the "lawyer-participant" approach, because mediators need not substitute their knowledge for that of lawyers. Lawyers can intervene (as discussed above) to compensate for inferior mediators and can request their removal.

Mediator duties to appraise [sic] parties of various legal rights, to terminate mediation, and to moderate bargaining imbalances also rest on the assumption that lawyers are absent in mediation. Obviously, requirements for post-mediation review of settlements by lawyers rest on the assumption that the lawyer does not take part in the give-and-take of negotiations.

In other words, lawyer participation reduces substantially the need for regulation. . . .

. . .

With lawyers present and participating, the concern for fairness no longer justifies heavy regulation or confining mediation to voluntary participants. Lawyer participation in the mediation sessions permits intervention on behalf of clients and buffers pressures to settle. Lawyers may also counsel clients to moderate extreme demands. In addition, once lawyers become accustomed to mediation, lawyer involvement in mandated mediation does not appear to prevent the meaningful participation of parties or inhibit emotional expression between spouses.

With mediation covering a broad scope of issues and with lawyers in attendance, the parties probably will pay more for lawyers and less for mediators. Overall costs, however, will probably remain unchanged because settlements are more likely to be comprehensive and less likely to fall victim to negative reviews by a non-participating lawyer. In addition, mediation with lawyers may reduce discovery costs. What the parties will get is likely to be a fair process in which lawyers intervene to protect against pressures from the other party, the process, or the mediator. They are also likely to get a more spontaneous mediation, unfettered by a web of regulation or defensive mediators. They will enjoy, as compared with parties in a system without mandatory mediation, a greater likelihood of having the opportunity to express themselves and to listen to discussions regarding matters of utmost concern. About one-half the time, they can expect to secure a settlement earlier in the process than would otherwise be the case.

Bringing the lawyers into mandatory mediation will permit the repeal of numerous statutes and a reduction in court rules. Furthermore, it will ease fairness concerns as a reason not to compel participation in mediation. The revised regulatory approach preserves the widespread use and flexibility of the mediation process without undue risk of unfairness.

Uniform Mediation Act, Section 10

An attorney or other individual designated by a party may accompany that party to and participate in a mediation. A waiver of participation given before the mediation may be rescinded.

Comments

The fairness of mediation is premised upon the informed consent of the parties to any agreement reached . . . Some statutes permit the mediator to exclude lawyers from mediation, resting fairness guarantees on the lawyer's later review of the draft settlement agreement . . . At least one bar authority has expressed doubts about the ability of a lawyer to review an agreement effectively when that lawyer did not participate in the give and take of negotiation. Similarly, concern has been raised that the right to bring counsel might be a requirement of constitutional due process in mediation programs operated by courts or administrative agencies. Richard C. Reuben, *Constitutional Gravity: A Unitary Theory of Alternative Dispute Resolution and Public Civil Justice*, 47 UCLA L. Rev. 949, 1095 (April 2000).

Some parties may prefer not to bring counsel. However, because of the capacity of attorneys to help mitigate power imbalances, and in the absence of other procedural protections for less powerful parties, the Drafting Committee elected to let the parties, not the mediator, decide. Also, their agreement to exclude counsel should be made after the dispute arises, so that they can weigh the importance in the context of the stakes involved. . . .

Notes and Questions

(1) Do you agree with the principle set out in Section 10 of the UMA? Do you think it is important for a jurisdiction to have a uniform approach on whether or not attorneys are permitted to participate in any type of mediation? Why do you suppose that attorneys are less likely to participate in family mediations than in mediations involving other subjects?

(2) For another view on how lawyers can assist in the settlement process, see Robert H. Mnookin, Scott R. Peppet & Andrew S. Tulumello, *Beyond Winning: Negotiating to Create Value in Deals and Disputes* (2000).

(3) Should states be permitted to require disputants to mediate their disputes without the assistance of an attorney? Do you believe that such a restriction would raise constitutional concerns, as has been suggested by Professor Reuben? See Richard Reuben, *Constitutional Gravity: A Unitary Theory of Alternative Dispute Resolution and Public Civil Justice*, 47 UCLA L. Rev. 949 (2000).

3. How Lawyers Advocate for Their Clients in Mediation

Professor Macfarlane advanced the thesis that the changes in the legal profession have resulted in the need for a new conception of lawyering — namely a move away from adversarial advocacy and toward conflict resolution advocacy. *See* Section B, *supra*. Many commentators have analyzed how lawyers ought to participate in mediations. Virtually all agree that good preparation by both attorney and client is essential for a productive session but note that many attorneys either fail to prepare or do so using the same adversarial mindset as though preparing for a deposition or a court appearance. Instead, the commentators urge lawyers to prepare themselves and their clients for a very different kind of process, one that combines aspects of litigation and negotiation. To be effective in this distinctive setting, lawyers must understand their clients' underlying needs and interests, anticipate the projected interests of the opposing party, begin to brainstorm possible solutions, consider settlement ranges and limits, and map out a settlement strategy; further, and crucially, attorneys must prepare their clients for this engagement, explaining how it differs from litigation, what the various stages of the mediation will be, and what roles the client and the client's attorney will play in presenting the narrative, the dialogue interaction, and the decision-making process.

Commentators differ in their advice regarding the respective roles that an attorney and client should play when an attorney accompanies the client to a mediation.

Should the attorney sit quietly and let the client do most of the talking? Should the attorney dominate the mediation conversation, making the client a silent observer?

In their excerpts below, Professors Jackie Nolan-Haley, Harold Abramson, and Jean Sternlight offer their views regarding the appropriate stance of advocacy in mediation. As you review these readings, remember and consider that how lawyers should approach mediation is a subset of larger professional responsibility questions such as how lawyers can best represent their clients' interests and whether lawyers have duties to persons or interests (justice) other than their clients. *See, supra*, Chapter 7.

In the readings thereafter, the authors identify particular behaviors or strategies that support effective advocate conduct. Professor Sternlight, drawing upon social science literature regarding barriers to negotiation, identifies the respective roles attorneys and clients ought to take in order to capitalize on the possibility that mediation offers for resolving a dispute. Tom Arnold discusses 20 errors a lawyer might make in preparing for and handling a mediation and offers practical tips for avoiding them. And Professor Golann provides specific suggestions on how lawyers can advocate effectively during mediation.

Lawyer Representation in Mediation

in Mediation Ethics: A Practitioner's Guide 187, 188–189, 200–202, 204
(ed. Omer Shapira, ABA 2021)*
By Jacqueline Nolan-Haley

. . .

The standard conception of the lawyer's traditional role has been characterized by scholars as one that honors partisanship and nonaccountability. Translated into practice, this has meant zealous advocacy with little moral responsibility for helping clients achieve their goals. Existing models for lawyers who represent clients in mediation are based largely on the dominant ethic of the zealous advocate, and this raises a question of fit. What does zealous advocacy require in mediation? Is the traditional zealous advocate, sometimes "hired gun," model of the adversarial system consistent with the primary participatory and dignitary values of mediation? The short answer is no. Representational lawyering in mediation is different from adversarial-style lawyering, and it should be grounded in a deliberative and problem-solving process. As noted wisely by Professor Harold Abramson, the zealous advocate should be replaced by the zealous problem solver.

The transition to zealous problem solving has not been a smooth one for the legal profession. In many cases, lawyer-controlled mediation still has the appearance of a muscle settlement conference, and negotiation in mediation resembles aggressive trial advocacy. Meanwhile, many clients are kept in the dark. The problem is largely a conceptual one. Many lawyers lack an authentic understanding of the mediation process, the premises and values that drive it, and the creative outcomes that are possible. As a result, when engaging with clients in representational mediation practice, too many lawyers are pouring new wine into old wineskins. This explains why human dignity, mutuality of respect, and responsible client decision making, values that have been absent from much of traditional adversarial practice, are frequently missing in representational mediation practice.

Mediation is a client's process, and a conceptual understanding of the mediation process as a client's process based on informed consent is essential in developing and sustaining an ethical theory of representational mediation practice.

. . .

Client counseling is a critical component of representational mediation practice. Too often, lawyers' involvement in mediation is not preceded by any meaningful deliberation with clients. Some lawyers do not listen to their clients but presume to know their goals and then dictate what should occur in mediation. Unfortunately, this behavior has the potential to sabotage the mediation process. Instead, the ethical responsibilities of attorneys who represent parties in mediation should be grounded in what I have described as a "deliberative model" of client counseling based on informed consent.

. . . In general, the principle of informed consent in the lawyer-client relationship requires that clients be educated about their choices and that they participate in decision making. . . .

. . . The first precondition for deliberation is that lawyers understand their clients' perspective — the facts as well as the clients' emotional state. . . . As a general matter, the content of attorney-client deliberation takes into account the totality of the clients' circumstances and may include the cultural, economic, social, psychological, moral, political, and religious consequences of actions.

Second, lawyers must attempt to understand and not presume to know their clients' initial goals. . . .

Third, lawyers should ensure that clients have a general understanding of what will occur in the counseling interaction. . . . They should be advised of the roles that both attorney and client will have in this relationship. Clients must also be educated about the mediation process and understand its essential differences from litigation.

Finally, clients should have a general knowledge about the relevant law governing their case, so that during deliberation they may meaningfully evaluate alternative courses of action and give informed consent, not only to their participation in mediation, but also to any agreement that is reached in mediation.

. . .

Lawyers' professional conduct is governed by the Model Rules of Professional Conduct of the jurisdiction in which they are licensed. The rules in all U.S. states are based on the ABA Model Rules of Professional Conduct, which do not specifically address the role of the representational lawyer in mediation. Nevertheless, representational lawyering in mediation encompasses the functions that lawyers perform generally for clients: counseling, negotiation, evaluation, and advocacy. As a general matter, therefore, the rules governing lawyer representation of parties in negotiation also apply in mediation.

These rules include the duties to provide competent representation, to avoid conflicts of interest in representing parties, to inform clients of ADR options, to keep clients informed about their case, to exercise candor toward the mediator and refrain from engaging in any material misrepresentation, to participate in good faith, to protect confidentiality, and to avoid the unauthorized practice of law.

... According to Model Rule 1.1, lawyers have a duty to "provide competent representation to a client. ... Competent representation in mediation requires specific knowledge and skill with which the lawyer might be unfamiliar. To provide adequate representation at the premediation stage, the lawyer has to consider the agreement to mediate, prepare the client for mediation, select the appropriate mediator, prepare premediation submissions, and decide upon a course of bargaining behavior. In the case of online mediation, lawyers must also be prepared to engage with new technologies and to navigate the ethical issues that arise.

... Effective client preparation is achieved through a deliberative process of client counseling. ... Clients need to understand the mediation process, be clear on their goals, understand their options and BATNA, and be clear on the extent of their settlement authority. There are a number of practical and strategic decisions to be considered, including (a) the timing of mediation (b) choosing the right mediator (c) deciding who should attend the mediation (d) deciding what documentary evidence and witnesses should be produced (e) determining the client's role in the mediation—would an active role be helpful for this client, or would she benefit more by assistance from an attorney?

... In accordance with Model Rule 1.4(a)(2), a lawyer shall "reasonably consult with the client about the means by which the client's objectives are to be accomplished." Thus, prior to the beginning of the mediation, lawyers should consult with their clients about what strategic approach they will take. ... [T]here is no free license to engage in hostile or negative behavior. In *Brooks v. The Lincoln National Life Insurance Co.,* [2006 WL 2487937 (D. Neb. 2006),] sanctions were imposed upon an attorney who engaged in highly aggressive behavior and left the mediation. Sanctions included an order to apologize to all the participants, to take a course on mediation representation within six months and file a certificate of completion, and to inform his client of these sanctions.

... In the rapidly expanding world of online or virtual mediation, representational lawyers will be required to adapt to new technologies. Despite what platform the parties or the court chooses in the case of court-connected mediation ... it is critical to test the platform in advance of the mediation. Other preparations include (a) having backup technology available (*e.g.*, phone conference call number) (b) understanding the new ground rules (c) explaining the virtual mediation experience to your client — the possibility of being sent to breakout rooms — how you will communicate with the client during the mediation session (d) preparing in a practical way for the new environment — make sure you have a way to execute documents.

. . . Lawyers must not represent a client if the representation involves a conflict of interest . . . Courts have also held that absent consent, lawyers must refrain from taking on representation of a client if the representation would be adverse to the interests of a former client. . . .

In the United States, there is no national rule that requires lawyers to inform clients of ADR options for resolving their disputes. . . . In considering whether to discuss ADR options with a client, it is important to determine whether mediation is appropriate for your client's case. This involves a consideration of many questions. What are the costs and benefits of engaging in mediation? What other options are available? What are the BATNAs and WATNAs? . . . [A]fter lawyers have an understanding of their clients' needs, interests, and goals, they should make them aware of ADR options. . . .

Model Rule 3.2 requires that lawyers "make reasonable efforts to expedite litigation consistent with the interests of the client." Some of the traditional selling points for mediation are efficiency, speed, and party satisfaction. Acting in accordance with his client's interests, a lawyer might consider mediation as a process that could help to achieve the goals of Model Rule 3.2. . . .

[C]onsistent with Model Rule 1.1, the competent lawyer who represents a party in mediation should be prepared to give sound legal advice. . . . Lawyers should also be prepared for involvement in at least three other activities: the opening statement, enlisting the help of the mediator, and drafting the mediated settlement agreement.

. . . It has become common for some lawyers to suggest abandoning the opening statement in the interests of efficiency. The arguments are varied. . . . Despite the initial appeal of these arguments, abandoning the opportunity to give an opening statement deprives the lawyer and client of the opportunity to speak directly to the principal on the opposing side and to craft a narrative that could lead to settlement. . . .

The mediator can be a valuable asset to the attorney in furthering his client's goals. . . . Consistent with the duty under Model Rule 1.6 to keep clients' information confidential, lawyers should carefully plan what information they will share with the mediator and be clear on the extent to which the mediator should keep information confidential. Other suggestions for taking full advantage of the mediator's expertise include the following: (a) Consider how you might enlist the mediator in signaling your willingness to compromise to the other side. (b) Think about how the mediator can help overcome barriers to settlement. (c) Take advantage of the caucus and request assistance from the mediator in how to make an acceptable proposal or whether a particular proposal is likely to be acceptable or will result in alienating the parties. (d) Take advantage of the time that may exist between caucuses when you have informal opportunities to speak with the mediator as the process unfolds.

. . .

A lawyer is required to be a zealous advocate for his client in mediation. What does this mean when it comes to truthfulness? How honest should a lawyer be when communicating with a mediator? . . . There are some situations . . . when a higher degree of candor may be required in order to satisfy clients' interests and achieve their goals. The final footnote to [ABA Formal] Opinion 06-439 provides guidance in this regard:

> [C]omplete candor may be necessary to gain the mediator's trust or to provide the mediator with critical information regarding the client's goals or intentions so that the mediator can effectively assist the parties in forging an agreement. . . . Thus, in extreme cases, a failure to be forthcoming, even though not in contravention of Rule 4.1(a) could constitute a violation of the lawyer's duty to provide competent representation under Model Rule 1.1.

. . .

Lawyers should be familiar with two aspects of confidentiality protection in mediation. The first relates to the attorney-client relationship, and the second deals with the relationship between the attorney and the mediation process generally. . . .

It is important . . . for the representational lawyer in mediation to become familiar with the specific confidentiality requirements of the jurisdiction in which mediation occurs.

. . . [T]he attorney who represents his client in mediation in a jurisdiction where he is not admitted to practice faces exposure to sanctions under unauthorized-practice-of-law statutes. For example, in *In re Non-Member of State Bar of Arizona*, a lawyer who was licensed to practice in Virginia and Florida was found to have engaged in the unauthorized practice of law by representing parties in a mediation in Arizona. As a result, she was sanctioned with an "informal reprimand." [*In re Non-Member of St. Bar of Ariz.*, 152 P.3d 1183 (2007)] . . . .

Mediation Representation: Advocating as a Problem-Solver in Any Country or Culture

1, 2, 4, 5 (2010)
By Harold Abramson

The mediation process is indisputably different from other dispute resolution processes like arbitrations and judicial trial where the third party makes decisions. The adversarial strategies and techniques that have proven effective in these other forums do not work optimally in mediation. The familiar adversarial strategy of presenting the strongest partisan arguments and aggressively attacking the other side's case may be effective when each side is trying to convince a judge to make a favorable decision. But, in mediation, there is no neutral third-party decision-maker, only a third-party helper. The third party may not even be your primary audience. The primary audience is the other side, who is surely not neutral, can often be quite hostile, and ultimately must approve any settlement. In this different representational setting, the adversarial approach is less effective if not self-defeating.

You need a different representation approach, one tailored to realize the full benefits of this burgeoning and increasingly preferred forum for resolving disputes. Instead of advocating as a zealous adversary, you should advocate as a zealous problem-solver.

. . .

As a problem solver who is creative, you do more than just try to merely settle the dispute. You search for solutions that go beyond the traditional ones based on rights, obligations, and precedent. Rather than settling for win-lose outcomes, you search for solutions that can benefit both sides. You develop a collaborative relationship with the other side and the mediator, and participate throughout the process in a way that may produce solutions that are inventive as well as enduring . . .

Shifting between hard positional tactics and creative problem-solving ones during the course of mediation can undercut the problem-solving approach . . . you should pursue an intelligent adherence to problem-solving.

Lawyer's Representation of Clients in Mediation: Using Economics and Psychology to Structure Advocacy in a Nonadversarial Setting

14 Ohio St. J. on Disp. Resol. 269, 291–97 (1999)*
By Jean R. Sternlight

Attorney advocacy, properly defined, is entirely consistent with and supportive of mediation. While many commentators have attacked attorneys' use of advocacy in the mediation process . . . the problem is not advocacy per se, but rather certain kinds of advocacy or adversarial behavior employed under particular circumstances. However, some attorney behavior should be proscribed in mediation (as it is in litigation), and some attorneys have a lot to learn regarding how best to advocate for their clients in a mediation.

If advocacy is defined broadly as supporting or pleading the cause of another, there is no inconsistency between advocacy and mediation. Permitting an attorney to act as an advocate for her client simply allows that attorney to speak and make arguments on her client's behalf and to help her client achieve her goals. The purpose of mediation is to reach an agreement which is acceptable to and desired by all parties. To reach such an agreement, both parties may wish to share their views as to their likely success in court as well as to engage in problem-solving. While some

---

parties may be comfortable participating pro se, others may prefer to be aided by an attorney. If a party can advocate for her own interests, this Author sees no reason why her representative should not also be permitted to "advocate" on her behalf.

Nor is it clear why "adversarial" behavior, at least broadly defined, is necessarily inconsistent with mediation. To the extent that acting adversarially means advocating only on behalf of one's own client and not on behalf of any other party or on behalf of the process or system, the conduct is easy to reconcile with mediation. The problem-solving that works well in mediation does not require sacrifice of one's self-interest, but rather allows parties to search for solutions that are mutually beneficial.

Therefore, it is not at all clear to this Author why an attorney, hired by a party, should work toward achieving mediation results that, while helpful to others or supportive of a peaceful solution, do not serve the wishes of the client. Of course, if a client chooses to direct her attorney to work toward an agreement that benefits all parties equally, rather than one that benefits the client most, she should be able to do so, but it is not clear why a client should be obliged to have her attorney represent interests other than her own. Certainly a client should not be required to have the attorney she has retained act contrary to her interests. Were we to entirely forbid attorneys from advocating on behalf of their clients, to require them to be neutral between their own clients and others or to require them to disclose all that they know about their clients' interests and positions, many people would no doubt decide not to retain attorneys to help them in mediation.

Still, it is appropriate to place certain restraints on attorney and client advocacy and adversarial behavior in mediation, just as we have placed limits on such conduct in litigation. In litigation we require that attorneys and clients have an adequate basis for positions taken in pleadings, we require attorneys to disclose the existence of relevant binding precedent to a tribunal, and we limit attorneys' ability to lie on behalf of their clients. These and other constraints may be appropriate in the mediation context as well.

Nor does this endorsement of advocacy mean that attorneys are relegated to being mere "hired guns." A vast professional responsibility literature contains many works urging that attorneys do and should have their own sense of morality, and it is entirely appropriate for attorneys to attempt to convince their clients that a particular course of action is unwise or immoral. Acceptance of such a view does not require abandonment of the principle that attorneys should serve as advocates for their clients.

Yet, while attorneys may appropriately advocate for their clients in mediation, it is certainly true that those attorneys who attempt to employ traditional "zealous" litigation tools when representing their clients in mediation may frequently (but not always) fail either to fulfill their clients' wishes or to serve their clients' interests. Those who would hoard information, rely solely on legal rather than emotional arguments, or refuse to let their clients speak freely will often have little success in mediation. This is not because attorneys ought not to advocate for their clients, but rather because attorneys ought not to advocate *poorly* on behalf of their clients . . .

The distinction between whether attorneys may advocate on behalf of their clients in mediation and how they may do so is not merely semantic. Once it is recognized that advocacy is permitted the question becomes when and how attorneys should best represent their clients in mediation. Attorneys need much more specific guidance on how to behave in mediations than the simple edict "thou shalt not advocate" or the equally simple "thou shalt advocate."

Notes and Questions

(1) Is advocacy the same as adversarialness? If not, how do they differ? For an argument that lawyers should advocate for their clients by learning to work effectively with mediators, see James K.L. Lawrence, *Mediation Advocacy: Partnering with the Mediator*, 15 Ohio St. J. on Disp. Resol. 425 (2000).

(2) Is advocating as a zealous problem-solver (Abramson) the same as conflict resolution advocacy (Macfarlane)?

(3) Professor Abramson argues that shifting between adversarial and problem-solving approaches during mediation can undercut the problem-solving approach. Is his view consistent with Professor Sternlight's point that attorneys can be advocates for their clients without being adversarial?

(4) Do lawyers need a distinctive set of professional rules to cover the role of the attorney in mediation and other forms of ADR? Is it feasible to have one set of professional rules governing litigation and another governing mediation or other forms of ADR, given that these processes may take place simultaneously?

What's a Lawyer to Do in Mediation?

18 Alternatives to the High Cost of Litigation 1 (July/Aug. 2000)*
By Jean R. Sternlight

What are lawyers supposed to do when they represent their clients in mediation? Should they act the same way many do in a deposition or trial, where they instruct the client not to volunteer information, and to carefully follow the attorney's lead? At the other extreme, should an attorney who is representing a client in a mediation even bother attending? If he or she does attend, should he or she largely sit silently, and let the client do the talking and run the show? Lawyers around the country are answering these questions in very different ways. The differences appear to stem not only from variations in individual philosophy but also from the culture of the local litigation and ADR community.

. . .

---

* Copyright © 2000 CPR Institute for Dispute Resolution. Founded in 1979 as Center for Public Resources/CPR Legal Program. Reprinted with permission. For a more complete version of this discussion, see Jean R. Sternlight, *Lawyers' Representation of Clients in Mediation: Using Economics and Psychology to Structure Advocacy in a Nonadversarial Setting*, 14 Ohio St. J. on Disp. Resol. 269 (1999).

Drawing on the psychological phenomena and strategic issues that arise in the lawyer-client relationship, set forth below are a few well-grounded tips for counsel representing a client in mediation.

. . .

Counsel should always keep in mind some of the basic insights offered by economists and psychologists who have studied the question of why disputes often fail to settle (or take a long time to settle), even where an early settlement is seemingly desirable for all. One key factor is the psychological differences in the way attorneys and clients view the world. Empirical studies have demonstrated that most people are affected by a series of phenomena that cause them to act in a less than an objective, reasoned manner when they attempt to resolve disputes. To provide a few examples, people tend to be over optimistic as to their chances of success; they are more willing to gamble regarding perceived losses than perceived gains; and they prefer settlements that appear to be "just."

Also influential is the different way an attorney dissects a dispute as compared to a client. Parties are frequently interested not merely in monetary outcomes but also in "venting," receiving or giving an apology, or achieving vengeance or publicity. Studies have shown that lawyers, as compared to their clients, tend to be far more objective in their settlement approach. Lawyers often focus on a settlement's bottom-line dollar value rather than process issues or surrounding emotional concerns.

These differences between lawyers and their clients can impede desirable settlements. Attorneys, rooted in their hyper-rational world, may not realize the importance of non-monetary benefits or processes such as venting or apologizing. They may think they are aiding their clients by pushing them to be objective, but the client might have preferred terms that appealed to his or her nonobjective, emotional wishes.

. . .

When attorneys attempt to settle their clients' disputes without using mediation, the clients remain very much in the background. While the attorney is ethically required to obtain the client's approval for any settlement, the attorney typically negotiates the deal on her own, merely consulting the client occasionally. The client is not present for the negotiation and therefore doesn't hear firsthand what the other side's position is; to hear the other side's anger; to assess the arguments of the opposing attorney; to explain the importance of non-monetary relief; to voice his feelings; or to give or receive an apology.

By contrast, in a mediation the client potentially can do each of these things and more, thereby enabling a settlement that would not otherwise have been possible. Mediation can permit the client to communicate directly with the opposing party and its attorney, and eliminate the erroneous transmissions that inevitably occur when one person acts as the agent for another.

Usually mediation can serve this beneficial purpose only where clients are permitted to play an active role in the mediation. If a client, while attending the mediation, does not express his or her own views in his or her own voice, neither the client nor the opposing party will secure many of the mediation's potential benefits. Where the attorneys "take over" the mediation and silence their own clients, they remove one of the mediation's primary potential benefits and convert the mediation back into a negotiation among attorneys.

Thus, in many instances it will be wise for an attorney to permit the client to participate vigorously, both by giving an opening statement and by speaking freely in other parts of the mediation. This participation will help the clients on both sides to communicate more directly, and to avoid some of the problems caused by differences between clients and their attorneys. For similar reasons, it also often will be desirable to permit much of the mediation to occur as a joint session, rather than moving immediately to caucus.

. . .

In preparing for a mediation an attorney should try to think about why the case has not already settled. What might be some of the barriers? Perhaps the opposing party is blocking settlement because it has unrealistic expectations due to a lack of factual or legal information, or maybe the opposing party has unmet non-monetary goals. Maybe it is the opposing party's attorney who is blocking settlement, based on the attorney's lack of information or unmet monetary or non-monetary goals. Many times an attorney may realize that it is his or her own client's unrealistic expectations or unmet monetary or non-monetary needs that are preventing agreement. Occasionally an attorney may even have the insight that it is his or her own concerns that are the problem.

Once an attorney begins to understand why the dispute is not settling, the attorney often can see that clients' active participation in mediation might prove helpful. For example, if the opposing party or opposing attorney is blocking settlement because either has unrealistically high expectations regarding how the facts will play at trial, a client may be well qualified to teach the opposing party that the case is not as strong as the opposing party thought. Where the client tells his or her story compellingly and convincingly in the mediation, the opposing client and attorney may learn their case is not as strong as they believed.

Similarly, where the opposing client has unmet non-monetary needs, it may be critical for an attorney to have his or her client participate actively. The client is far better suited than the attorney to provide a meaningful apology. Where the opposing party needs to "vent" his anger or concerns, he or she may need to do so against a live opposing client, and not merely an attorney. A client also may be better than the attorney at helping to think up creative "win/win" solutions based on the disputants' mutual needs and interests.

Turning to blockages due to a client's misperceptions, active client participation on both sides can be critical in bringing a dose of reality to the client. Finally, allowing a client to participate actively can alleviate stresses due to the client's perception that an attorney may be acting out of self interest. These few examples illustrate that clients' active participation can be critical.

. . .

There are situations in which attorneys would do their clients a real disservice by failing to attend or failing to participate actively. For example, sometimes the parties' failure to settle a dispute may be attributable not to lack of emotional or informational exchange between the parties, but rather to one party's misguided view of the law. Here, the most useful mediation may be one in which the opposing attorney or mediator finds a way to educate the misguided client — or attorney — as to his likelihood of success. As well, some clients' basic personality or circumstances may be such that it is important for their attorney to play the role of protector. It would typically be unwise to design a family mediation to encourage active participation by both a perpetrator and a victim of domestic violence.

. . .

In sum, while there is no single recipe for mediation success, insights drawn from economics, psychology and agency theory reveal that active client participation is often critical to achieve the full benefits of mediation. Attorneys who consistently dominate the mediation, treating it like just another deposition or trial, or even allow their clients not to attend, often are doing their clients a disservice. Instead, drawing on the tools offered by social science, attorneys should attempt to assess what steps they and their clients should take to overcome whatever barriers may exist to a desirable settlement. Often this analysis will reveal that attorneys should foster rather than inhibit active client participation in mediation.

20 Common Errors in Mediation Advocacy
13 Alternatives to the High Cost of Litigation 69 (May 1995)*
By Tom Arnold

Trial lawyers who are unaccustomed to being mediation advocates often miss important arguments. Here are 20 common errors, and ways to correct them.

Problem 1: Wrong Client in the Room

CEOs settle more cases than vice presidents, house counsel or other agents. Why? For one thing, they don't need to worry about criticism back at the office. Any lesser agent, even with explicit "authority," typically must please a constituency which was not a participant in the give and take of the mediation. That makes it hard to settle cases.

A client's personality also can be a factor. A "Rambo," who is aggressive, critical, unforgiving, or self-righteous doesn't tend to be conciliatory. The best peace-makers show creativity, and tolerance for the mistakes of others. Of course, it also helps to know the subject.

Problem 2: Wrong lawyer in the Room

Many capable trial lawyers are so confident that they can persuade a jury of anything (after all, they've done it before), that they discount the importance of preserving relationships, as well as the exorbitant costs and emotional drain of litigation. They can smell a "win" in the court room, and so approach mediation with a measure of ambivalence.

Transaction lawyers, in contrast, tend to be better mediation counsel. At a minimum, parties should look for sensitive, flexible, understanding people who will do their homework, no matter their job experience. Good preparation makes for more and better settlements. A lawyer who won't prepare is the wrong lawyer.

Problem 3: Wrong Mediator in the Room

Some mediators are generous about lending their conference rooms but bring nothing to the table. Some of them determine their view of the case and urge the parties to accept that view without exploring likely win-win alternatives.

. . .

Masters of the process can render valuable services whether or not they have substantive expertise. When do the parties need an expert? When they want an evaluative mediator, or someone who can cast meaningful lights and shadows on the merits of the case and alternative settlements.

It may not always be possible to know and evaluate a mediator and fit the choice of mediator to your case. But the wrong mediator may fail to get a settlement another mediator might have finessed.

Problem 4: Wrong case

Almost every type of case, from antitrust or patent infringement to unfair competition and employment disputes, is a likely candidate for mediation. Occasionally, cases don't fit the mold, not because of the substance of the dispute, but because one or both parties want to set a precedent.

. . .

Problem 5: Omitting Client Preparation

Lawyers should educate their clients about the process. Clients need to know the answers to the types of questions the mediator is likely to ask. At the same time, they need to understand that the other party (rather than the mediator) should be the focus of each side's presentation.

In addition, lawyers should interview clients about the client's and the adversary's "best alternative to negotiated agreement," and "worst alternative to negotiated agreement," terms coined by William Ury and Roger Fisher in their book, *Getting to YES*. A party should accept any offer better than his perceived BATNA and reject any offer seen as worse than his perceived WATNA.... A weak or false understanding of either party's BATNA or WATNA obstructs settlements and begets bad settlements.

Other topics to cover with the client:

— the difference between their interests and their legal positions;

— the variety of options that might settle the case;

— the strengths and weaknesses of their case;

— objective independent standards of evaluation;

— the importance of apology and empathy.

Problem 6: Not Letting a Client Open for Herself

At least as often as not, letting the properly coached client do most, or even all, of the opening and tell the story in her own words works much better than lengthy openings by the lawyer.

To prepare for mediation, rehearse answers to the following questions, which the mediator is likely to ask:

— How do you feel about this dispute?

— Or about the other party?

— What do you really want in the resolution of this dispute?

— What are your expectations from a trial? Are they realistic?

— What are the weaknesses in your case?

— What law or fact in your case would you like to change?

— What scares you most?

— What would it feel like to be in your adversary's shoes?

— What specific evidence do you have to support each element of your case?

— What will the jury charge and interrogatories probably be?

— What is the probability of a verdict your way on liability?

— What is the range of damages you think a jury would return in this case if it found liability?

— What are the likely settlement structures, from among the following possibilities: Terms, dollars, injunction, services, performance, product, recision [sic], apology, costs, attorney fees, releases?

— What constituency pressures burden the other party? Which ones burden you?

Problem 7: Addressing the Mediator Instead of the Other Side

Most lawyers open the mediation with a statement directed at the mediator, comparable to opening statements to a judge or jury. Highly adversarial in tone, it overlooks the interests of the other side that gave rise to the dispute.

Why is this strategy a mistake? The "judge or jury" you should be trying to persuade in a mediation is not the mediator, but the adversary. If you want to make the other party sympathetic to your cause, don't hurt him.

For the same reason, plenary sessions should demonstrate your client's humanity, respect, warmth, apologies and sympathy. Stay away from inflammatory issues, which are better addressed by the mediator in private caucuses with the other side.

Problem 8: Making the Lawyer the Center of the Process

Unless the client is highly unappealing or inarticulate, the client should be the center of the process. The company representative for the other side may not have attended depositions, so is unaware of the impact your client could have on a judge or jury if the mediation fails. People pay more attention to appealing plaintiffs, so show them off.

Prepare the client to speak and be spoken to by the mediator and the adversary. He should be able to explain why he feels the way he does, why he is or is not responsible, and why any damages he *caused* are great or only peanuts. But he should also extend empathy to the other party.

Problem 9: Failure to Use Advocacy Tools Effectively

You'll want to prepare your materials for maximum persuasive impact. Exhibits, charts, and copies of relevant cases or contracts with key phrases highlighted can be valuable visual aids. A 90-second video showing key witnesses in depositions making important admissions, followed by a readable size copy of an important document with some relevant language underlined, can pack a punch.

Problem 10: Timing Mistakes

Get and give critical discovery, but don't spend exorbitant time or sums in discovery and trial prep before seeking mediation.

Mediation can identify what's truly necessary discovery and avoid unnecessary discovery. One of my own war stories: With a mediation under way and both parties relying on their perception of the views of a certain vice president, I leaned over, picked up the phone, called the vice president, introduced myself as the mediator, and asked whether he could give us a deposition the following morning. "No," said he, "I've got a Board meeting at 10:00."

"How about 7:30 a.m., with a one-hour limit?" I asked. "It really is pretty important that this decision not be delayed." The parties took the deposition and settled the case before the 10:00 board meeting.

Problem 11: Failure to Listen to the Other Side

Many lawyers and clients seem incapable of giving open-minded attention to what the other side is saying. That could cost a settlement.

Problem 12: Failure to Identify Perceptions and Motivations

Seek first to understand, only then to be understood. Messrs. Fisher and Ury suggest you brainstorm to determine the other party's motivations and perceptions. Prepare a chart summarizing how your adversary sees the issues. . . .

Problem 13: Hurting, Humiliating, Threatening, or Commanding

Don't poison the well from which you must drink to get a settlement. That means you don't hurt, humiliate or ridicule the other folks. Avoid pejoratives like "malingerer," "fraud," "cheat," "crook," or "liar." You can be strong on what your evidence will be and still be a decent human being.

All settlements are based upon trust to some degree. If you anger the other side, they won't trust you. This inhibits settlement.

The same can be said for threats, like a threat to get the other lawyer's license revoked for pursuing such a frivolous cause, or for his grossly inaccurate pleadings.

Ultimatums destroy the process, and destroy credibility. Yes, there is a time in mediation to walk out — whether or not you plan to return. But a series of ultimatums, or even one ultimatum, most often is very counterproductive.

Problem 14: The Backwards Step

A party who offered to pay $300,000 before the mediation, and comes to the mediation table willing to offer only $200,000, injures its own credibility and engenders bad feelings from the other side. Without some clear and dramatic reasons for the reduction in the offer, it can be hard to overcome the damage done.

Problem 15: Too many people

Advisors — people to whom the decision-maker must display respect and courtesy, people who feel that since they are there they must put in their two bits worth — all delay a mediation immeasurably. A caucus that with only one lawyer and vice president would take 20 minutes, with five people could take an hour and 20 minutes. What could have been a one-day mediation stretches to two or three.

This is one context in which I use the "one-martini lunch." Once I think that everyone present understands all the issues, I will send principals who have been respectful out to negotiate alone. Most come back with an expression of oral settlement within three hours. Of course, the next step is to brush up on details they overlooked, draw up a written agreement and get it signed. But usually those finishing touches don't ruin the deal.

Problem 16: Closing Too Fast

A party who opens at $1 million, and moves immediately to $500,000, gives the impression of having more to give. Rightly or wrongly, the other side probably will not accept the $500,000 offer because they expect more give.

The "dance" is part of communication. Skip the dance, lose the communication, and risk losing settlement at your own figure.

Problem 17: Failure to Truly Close

Unless parties have strong reasons to "sleep on" their agreement, to further evaluate the deal, or to check on possibly forgotten details, it is better to get some sort of enforceable contract written and signed before the parties separate. Too often, when left to think overnight and draft tomorrow, the parties think of new ideas that delay or prevent closing.

Problem 18: Breaching a Confidentiality

Sometimes parties to a mediation unthinkingly, or irresponsibly, disclose in open court information revealed confidentially in a mediation.

When information is highly sensitive, consider keeping it confidential with the mediator. Or if revealed to the adversary in a mediation where the case did not settle, consider moving before the trial begins for an order in *limine* to bind both sides to the confidentiality agreement.

Problem 19: Lack of Patience and Perseverance

The mediation "dance" takes time. Good mediation advocates have patience and perseverance.

Problem 20: Misunderstanding conflict

A dispute is a problem to be solved together, not a combat to be won.

Sharing a Mediator's Powers — Effective Advocacy in Settlement

American Bar Association (2013)*
Pages ix, x, 33, 37–38, 40–42, 44–48, 52, 72, 87–91
By Dwight Golann

This book is written for lawyers who represent parties in mediation. It explains how to use the mediation process, and the special abilities of mediators, to achieve optimal results in settling cases.

. . .

The point is not to approach mediation passively, and instead use the process to advance your clients' goals.

. . .

Focus Discussion and Exchange Information

1. Emphasize Key Issues

Good negotiators know that a mediator will usually act as the moderator of discussion . . . As a result, mediators have significant influence over what is discussed

---

* Reprinted with permission.

and how. Skilled lawyers tell their mediator what they would like her to stress and how they would like points articulated in the other room.

. . .

2. Exchange Data

. . .

[P]arties in litigation typically play "hide the ball," concealing information from each other as much as possible. In mediation, however, the calculus can be different: Disputants know that settlement is likely and that exchanging information may increase their chances of success. . . .

. . . Lawyers know . . . that they can disclose data in mediation without necessarily exposing it to use at trial . . . All this makes litigants more willing to exchange information in mediation than in direct bargaining.

The most straightforward way to convey data is by talking directly with the attorney and client on the other side. The opening session is an excellent opportunity to do this.

Inadequate information is a special problem when parties mediate early in a case, before conducting full discovery. . . . Data problems are also likely to arise when parties consider non-legal solutions to a dispute, because the evidence gathered in litigation is often irrelevant to their non-legal interests.

a. Gather Information

Lawyers can enlist mediator's help to obtain data from an adversary, or convince their own client why it makes sense to provide information to an opponent. Ask the mediator to suggest that it's in the other side's interest to provide the data you need to compromise. In some cases the problem may lie with your own client. A corporation, for instance, may drag its feet producing data because the person responsible is afraid of being blamed for a costly settlement or simply doesn't see the request as a priority. In such cases, prompt the mediator to ask for information from your client . . .

Co-defendants sometimes hide data from each other to minimize their share of a settlement . . . If your client is being pressed to pick up an unfair portion of a bill for a group of defendants, ask the mediator to help the defendants cooperate, first to get the group the best possible deal from the plaintiff and then to allocate the cost fairly among them.

b. Convey Data

It is also possible to use mediation to help convey data, either to the mediator or to your opponent.

. . . If you have hidden evidence that may influence a mediator's view of your case, when should you disclose it? In general, it's better to offer such evidence near the beginning of the process, when the mediator is focused on gathering information and understanding the issues. . . .

[M]ediation can increase an opponent's willingness to listen to information with a more open mind. This is due to . . . "reactive devaluation" — the tendency of people to react negatively to anything presented by someone they see as an adversary.

. . .

c. Take Advantage of Confidentiality

The fact that mediation is a confidential process can allow lawyers to use evidence for settlement purposes with less risk their opponents will be able to use it in litigation if the process is not successful. . . .

Regardless of applicable law, you can use several techniques to enhance the confidentiality of the information you provide in mediation.

. . . The simplest option is to present evidence to the mediator, but forbid her from disclosing it to your opponent.

. . . The fact that you forbid a mediator from disclosing information at one point in the process . . . does not prevent you from authorizing disclosure later when the risk/reward balance appears more favorable. . . .

. . . You can give the mediator discretion to make the disclosure, but under a restrictive condition ("You can show them the affidavit, but only if you think it will tie down a deal" . . .).

Still another option is to limit the form in which the documentary evidence is disclosed to the opponent, reducing the risk it will come back to bite you,

- Have the mediator write "Confidential Mediation Communication" or similar words on a document and initial and date it. . . .

- Have the mediator write "No copies to be made" on the document. . . .

- Provide data visually only. . . .

Still another option is to give a document to the mediator under the condition that the neutral can read it, take notes, and tell the other side what the document contains, but may not take the document physically into the other room. . . .

3. Gather or Provide Information about Intentions

. . . [T]he most important data in a negotiation often concerns the other side's intentions. Mediators may give an interpretation of one party's state of mind to the other. . . . The fact that mediators can convey intentions as well as facts offers another opportunity to use the process to advantage. . . .

. . . If you ask a mediator explicitly for her impressions of the other side's bargaining intentions, to the extent the mediator knows and can answer without violating a confidence or impeding the process, she may do so. . . .

Bear in mind that if you ask for information about your opponent's attitude, the mediator may take it as implied permission to give the other side similar information about you. Make it clear what you want withheld, and accept that data transmission is usually a two-way street. . . .

Build a cooperative strategy

. . . Given the strong tendency of litigants to use competitive tactics, if nothing is done ahead of time your opponent is likely to arrive at mediation prepared to bargain in a competitive framework. To avoid this, ask the mediator to lay groundwork for the approach you prefer. . . .

Respond to Competitive Tactics

One reason parties adopt a competitive stance is to respond to such tactics from an opponent. If you would prefer a cooperative or creative approach, but are dealing with an adversary using hardball tactics, how can mediation help you respond?

Educate the mediator. . . . If the mediator appears to be missing something that helps to explain the other side's tactic or exposes its unreasonableness, educate him.

Ask about motivation. Extreme offers are usually driven by factors other than the legal merits, such as strong emotions or a determination not to be the first to show weakness. If you're not sure what is motivating a tactic, ask the neutral about it. . . .

Ask about the reasoning. If you receive an extreme offer ask the mediator about the assumptions and reasoning that underlie it. . . . If there is no convincing justification on the merits, and for an extreme offer almost by definition there won't be, you can ask the mediator to press for a better explanation or for a better offer that reflects the realities of the case. By doing this, of course, you are also suggesting a better way to bargain.

Ask for advice. A disputant—usually the other side but sometimes your own client—may be acting competitively because he thinks that is "how the game is played," or in response to what he perceives as the other side's unreasonableness (a special problem because of each side's tendency to want the other to compromise first). If this occurs, ask the mediator for advice, perhaps including the neutral's prediction of the likely response to a proposed tactic. . . .

You can ask the mediator what she thinks the other side expects you to do. . . . You can also ask what would motivate them to compromise. . . .

Work on the merits. If a disparity in positions is based on disagreement about a legal or factual issue, suggest exchanging information about it, or propose a process to do so. . . .

Deal with emotions. If angry feelings are driving the disagreement, suggest a response. ("Should the two CEOs get together to talk about how we got to this point?") If the issue is with your own client, ask the mediator to talk with him privately, ideally before the mediation begins but if necessary in caucus. Having the chance to vent anger or other feelings in private, and being assured the mediator will communicate his anger to the other side, will sometimes persuade a client to modify an unhelpful offer before it is made.

Ask the mediator to take responsibility. If you opt to answer a competitive move with a relatively reasonable offer, you can ask the mediator to take responsibility for it. This allows your client to combine a productive step with a gesture of resolve.... A variant is to ask the mediator to deliver the message as your own ("Tell them we are making a large concession to cut to the chase, and we expect them to reciprocate.")

Ask for internal mediation. If the problem is that your client is a group of people with varying opinions, ask the mediator to mediate among them. Remember, though, that a mediator probably won't know about your internal dynamics; you will need to fill her in, either through an advance call or a hallway conversation.

. . .

Respond to the move. Eventually you will have to make a counteroffer or respond in some other way. You have several alternatives. The simplest is to respond in kind, with an extreme offer, committing at least temporarily to a competitive process. If you do, explain to the mediator your preference for a more realistic approach and have him communicate this to your opponent....

Another option is to make a relatively reasonable offer that ignores the opponent's hardball tactic. Ask the mediator to explain what you are doing and see if the opponent responds cooperatively. If not you can limit your next move, explaining that you are not willing to continue on a reasonable path unilaterally. A relatively good first offer followed by modest concessions arguably communicates as much firmness as making an extreme first offer, followed by larger later moves.

You can also seek to avoid positional bargaining entirely, by asking about the merits or exploring non-monetary concerns. Again you should ask the mediator to explain what you are doing and why. Whatever your response, a mediator can help you implement it.

. . .

... Good lawyers know a mediator can help them navigate effectively, and are not bashful about asking for help.

Notes and Questions

(1) Several books focus explicitly on how lawyers should represent their clients in mediation. *See* Harold I. Abramson, *Mediation Representation: Advocating as a Problem-Solver* (3d ed., 2013); Eric Galton, *Representing Clients in Mediation* (1994); John W. Cooley, *Mediation Advocacy* (1996). For useful articles, see Harold Abramson, *Problem-Solving Advocacy in Mediation: A Model of Client Representation*, 10 Harv. Neg. L. Rev. 103 (2005); James K. L. Lawrence, *Mediation Advocacy: Partnering with the Mediator*, 15 Ohio St. J. on Disp. Resol. 425 (2000). For a thoughtful article discussing mediation advocacy on behalf of parents in the context of dependency mediation, see Debra Ratterman Baker, *Dependency Mediation: Strategies for Parents' Attorneys*, 18 A.B.A. Child L. Prac. 124 (1999).

(2) How do you believe lawyers and their clients should divide responsibilities in a mediation? If you believe the determination should vary from case to case, what factors do you believe are important to consider?

(3) Do you believe that the degree of participation of lawyer or client in a mediation has any impact on whether the mediation ultimately results in a settlement? Why or why not? As between the attorney and the client, who should decide on their respective degrees of participation in a mediation? Are ethical rules relevant to the consideration of this question?

(4) Professor Golann states that, "When a mediator's proposal fails, it is not the end of the process. Experienced neutrals know that a party who has rejected a proposal will often feel an obligation to do something to make up for his refusal — typically, by offering a smaller concession. A good mediator will therefore react to a no by asking 'If you won't take that, what *would* you take . . . ?' and then 'Can I propose that to the other side?'" As an attorney, how would you feel about the mediation continuing after the mediator has made a proposal which is not favorable to your client? How does a mediator proposal comport with your understanding of mediator neutrality?

4. What Ethical Constraints Apply to Lawyers in Mediation?

Existing ethical rules restrain lawyers from lying in litigation, arbitration, or negotiation. In this section, ethical rules governing negotiation in the context of mediation are considered.

ABA Model Rule 3.3 prohibits a lawyer, *inter alia*, from knowingly "mak[ing] a false statement of material fact or law to a tribunal," "fail[ing] to disclose a material fact to a tribunal when disclosure is necessary to avoid assisting a criminal or fraudulent act by the client," or "fail[ing] to disclose to the tribunal legal authority in the controlling jurisdiction known to the lawyer to be directly adverse to the position of the client and not disclosed by opposing counsel." ABA Model Rule 1.0(m) defines the term "tribunal" to include arbitrators who issue binding awards, as well as courts. ABA Model Rule 4.1 prohibits a lawyer, in the course of representation, from "mak[ing] a false statement of material fact or law" or "fail[ing] to disclose a material fact to a third party when disclosure is necessary to avoid assisting a criminal or fraudulent act. . . ." However, the Official Comment to Rule 4.1 significantly notes: "Under generally accepted conventions in negotiation, certain types of statements ordinarily are not taken as statements of material fact. Estimates of price or value placed on the subject of a transaction and a party's intentions as to an acceptable settlement of a claim are in this category. . . ."

Two important excerpts on this topic appear below. In 2006, the American Bar Association issued a formal opinion stating that the dictates of Rule 4.1 apply to mediation (and not the stricter standard of truthfulness required by Rule 3.3).

Previously, Professor James Alfini had argued that there is a need to revise Rule 4.1 to create a more suitable ethics infrastructure to support mediation and other ADR proceedings. Do you think a revision to Rule 4.1 is necessary? If so, do you think the practicing bar would find Alfini's revision acceptable?

Formal Opinion 06-439, April 12, 2006

Lawyer's Obligation of Truthfulness When Representing a Client in Negotiation:
Application to Caucused Mediation

. . .

In this opinion, we discuss the obligation of a lawyer to be truthful when making statements on behalf of clients in negotiations, including the specialized form of negotiation known as caucused mediation.

. . . [T]he ethical principles governing lawyer truthfulness do not permit a distinction to be drawn between the caucused mediation context and other negotiation settings. The Model Rules do not require a higher standard of truthfulness in any particular negotiation contexts. Except for Rule 3.3, which is applicable only to statements before a "tribunal," the ethical prohibitions against lawyer misrepresentations apply equally in all environments. Nor is a lower standard of truthfulness warranted because of the consensual nature of mediation. Parties otherwise protected against lawyer misrepresentation by Rule 4.1 are not permitted to waive that protection, whether explicitly through informed consent, or implicitly by agreeing to engage in a process in which it is somehow "understood" that false statements will be made. Thus, the same standards that apply to lawyers engaged in negotiations must apply to them in the context of caucused mediation. . . . We emphasize that, whether in a direct negotiation or in a caucused mediation, care must be taken by the lawyer to ensure that communications regarding the client's position, which otherwise would not be considered statements "of fact," are not conveyed in language that converts them, even inadvertently, into false factual representations. For example, even though a client's Board of Directors has authorized a higher settlement figure, a lawyer may state in a negotiation that the client does not wish to settle for more than $50. However, it would not be permissible for the lawyer to state that the Board of Directors had formally disapproved any settlement in excess of $50, when authority had in fact been granted to settle for a higher sum.

Conclusion

Under Model Rule 4.1, in the context of a negotiation, including a caucused mediation, a lawyer representing a party may not make a false statement of material fact to a third person. However, statements regarding a party's negotiating goals or its willingness to compromise, as well as statements that can fairly be characterized as negotiation "puffing," are ordinarily not considered "false statements of material fact" within the meaning of the Model Rules.

Settlement Ethics and Lawyering in ADR Proceedings: A Proposal to Revise Rule 4.1

19 N. Ill. U. L. Rev. 255, 270–71 (1999)*
By James Alfini

RULE 4.1 TRUTHFULNESS IN STATEMENTS TO OTHERS [Alfini Proposal]

In the course of representing a client a lawyer shall not knowingly:

(a) make a false statement of material fact or law to a third person; or

<u>(b) assist the client in reaching a settlement agreement that is based on reliance upon a false statement of fact made by the lawyer's client; or</u>

~~(b)~~ <u>(c)</u> fail to disclose a material fact to a third person when disclosure is necessary to avoid assisting a criminal or fraudulent act by a client, unless disclosure is prohibited by Rule 1.6.

Comment

Misrepresentation

[1] A lawyer is required to be truthful when dealing with others on a client's behalf, but generally has no affirmative duty to inform an opposing party of relevant facts. A misrepresentation can occur if the lawyer incorporates or affirms a statement of another person that the lawyer knows is false. Misrepresentations can also occur by failure to act.

~~Statements of Fact~~

~~[2] This Rule refers to statements of fact. Whether a particular statement should be regarded as one of fact can depend on the circumstances. Under generally accepted conventions in negotiation, certain types of statements ordinarily are not taken as statements of material fact. Estimates of price or value placed on the subject of a transaction and a party's intentions as to an acceptable settlement of a claim are in this category, and so is the existence of an undisclosed principal except where nondisclosure of the principal would constitute fraud.~~

Alternative Dispute Resolution

<u>[2] A lawyer's duty of truthfulness applies beyond formal tribunals (see Rule 3.3) to less formal settings. The obligation to be truthful is particularly essential with the increased use by courts of dispute resolution alternatives such as mediation, arbitration, mini-trial, and summary jury trial to effect settlement. When representing a client in these less formal settings, the lawyer may often encounter situations where both the lawyer and his or her client participate freely in open and frank discussions unconstrained by rules of evidence or procedure. The lawyer should therefore inform the client of the lawyer's duty to be truthful and the lawyer's inability to</u>

assist the client in reaching a settlement agreement that is procured in whole or in part as a result of a false statement of material fact or law made by the client.

Fraud by Client

[3] Paragraph (b) recognizes that substantive law may require a lawyer to disclose certain information to avoid being deemed to have assisted the client's crime or fraud. The requirement of disclosure created by this paragraph is, however, subject to the obligations created by Rule 1.6.

Notes and Questions

(1) Do you think it is feasible to have one standard of truth-telling in mediation, another in negotiation, and still another in court?

(2) In *In re Fee*, 898 P.2d 975, 980 (Ariz. 1995), the Arizona Supreme Court held that attorneys violated their duty of candor to a tribunal by failing to disclose their complete fee agreement to a judge who was acting as settlement judge (mediator). If the "mediator" had not been a judge, should the case have been decided differently?

Chapter 11

Career Directions in Mediation

A. Introduction

Mediation is regularly used in multiple settings, including courts, business and service organizations, and educational institutions. Local political officials and community leaders often use it to address social conflicts that erupt in their communities over such matters as affordable housing, adequate health services or educational services, and in response to citizen groups protesting mass shootings or politically-divisive speakers.

For persons interested in pursuing career opportunities in mediation-related work, there are multiple paths. Recent societal developments have spurred an increased growth in ADR career opportunities: the Covid-19 global pandemic accelerated and expanded the use of technology to conduct mediation sessions in an on-line environment; polarizing community and political events stimulated the expanded use of government agencies to provide mediation and conciliation services; and the increased adoption of presumptive and mandatory ADR regimes within courts around the country created mediator and ADR administrative employment opportunities. Section B identifies current program and substantive law areas in which private sector professional mediator practitioner services are established; Section C examines organization-based opportunities to be employed as a mediator or work as an administrator in ADR-provider organizations. Section D identifies sample websites containing the biographies of individuals who have successfully developed mediation careers, and introduces a small number of individuals whose engagement with mediation careers and services is reflected in Sections B and C.

B. Independent Mediation Practices

All parties to a mediation want an experienced mediator to assist them. But the Catch-22 is: how does one gain that experience? Unlike a traditional legal practice in which law firm partners utilize associates to assist in the research and presentation of a case, mediating is primarily a solo activity. How can a mediator and potential client become linked?

There are several avenues: a person who participates in an established law practice or business activity can, over time, develop relationships with clients and other persons who might have a future need for a mediator. Alternatively, a mediator, like other professional and business personnel, may engage in networking activities by participating actively in social or community activities. Additionally, many courts, governmental agencies (both federal and state), and not-for-profit organizations develop "panels" of mediators. In some instances, that governing agency appoints a panel member to mediate a case, while in other situations, the agency provides the negotiating parties with a list of selected panel members and leaves it to the parties to choose their mediator; under either scenario, becoming a panel member is the critical avenue for gaining service as a mediator. Finally, a person can gain significant experience by providing pro bono mediation services for community-based mediation programs, school peer mediation projects, or court-sponsored "Settlement Week" activities.

Set out below are multiple substantive settings in which mediation service occurs. Not all command comparable compensation; not all provide daily work.

1. Small Claims Mediation and Neighborhood Justice Center Programs

This label references disputes that are typically filed or are about to be filed in a civil or criminal court system that involve limited financial demands and, often, multiple interpersonal dynamics. Some state court systems officially create a "small claims court" in which disputants can appear without counsel and present their cases to a judge for decision; some states or cities have developed other specialty courts, such as housing courts, for handling related conflicts. When the disputants arrive for the calendar call, they are encouraged (or often required) to attend a mediation conference offered through that court to attempt to settle their dispute. If they resolve it through mediation, the settlement is treated in the same manner as a court judgment. Neighborhood justice center disputes emerge along a different track: a complaining neighbor typically files their claim with a clerk in a prosecutor's office, and the prosecutor and court divert the case to mediation. Parties routinely appear and participate in each of these settings without lawyer representation.

Both types of these disputes involve multiple claims: alleged breach of contract for failure to make timely payments on a "rent-to-own" furniture contract; alleged theft of company property by a terminated employee; landlord claims for alleged rental arrears or tenant claims for a non-refunded security deposit; or one tenant alleging that the co-tenant failed to pay "agreed-upon shared" expenses, such as utility or internet service billings. In the neighborhood justice center setting, these financial claims are often intertwined with such interpersonal dynamics as a failed romantic relationship or harassing conduct.

A person who mediates these cases generally serves on a volunteer basis. For many practitioners, mediating these cases constitutes the most viable, initial source for gaining robust mediation experience.

2. Family and Dependency Mediation

Our family court system, though distinctive in each state, constitutes a forum that is pressed to serve an extensive range of family dynamics. Family court personnel have been pro-active in developing innovative programs — including the provision of mediation services — to serve parties in need.

These substantive conflicts are broad-based: married couples seeking a divorce; divorced couples seeking to revise parenting or financial arrangements; a divorced parent accusing the other of being unfit to parent due to drug, alcohol, or mental health problems; parents soliciting court assistance to secure their teen-age child's compliance with their parentally-imposed social curfew; child protective service agencies seeking to establish appropriate living arrangements for children feared to be victims of parental neglect or abuse. Mediators service all such matters.

Family mediation is a growing field and a practice arena in which building a private mediation practice after a few years of mediation and/or litigation experience is possible.

3. "Civil Law Cases"

This "catch-all" category references the broad range of lawsuits that could be or have been filed in a civil court at the state or federal level. Typically, pursuant to a relevant court rule, parties must first try to resolve that dispute through mediation. This practice domain is currently the largest source of compensated, sustained mediating case activity.

We highlight below six categories of legal claims in which mediation has been regularly used.

1. Personal Injury Disputes. These cases capture multiple tort actions: a "slip and fall" injury sustained by a grocery-store customer who slipped on a wet floor that the store owner's employee had recently mopped; a pedestrian injured by a car driver who had proceeded through an intersection against a red light; or an interested bystander at a construction site who is injured by flying debris that was accidentally dropped by project employees working on an elevated platform. Many lawyer advocates describe these legal claims as "routine," but everyone involved values a mediator's assistance in developing an increased understanding of the complexity of each person's perspective and feelings as a foundation for resolving the injury claims.

The PI dispute also captures the complex catastrophic tort action. These actions might involve the fatal loss of a loved one, cutting short a future full of hope. Consider the following: an 18-year-old high school senior who had compiled a perfect academic record, excelled in athletics, held leadership positions in student government, participated actively and without fanfare in various religious and community service activities, and gained admittance to attend a prestigious college to pursue their dream of becoming a scientist is fatally injured in an auto accident the night before his high school graduation. The deceased was driving his car at 2:00 a.m. on a country road; his car crossed the middle line only to be met by an oncoming car driven by a 19-year-old driver — unemployed and a high-school dropout — who was traveling at a speed far exceeding the speed limit. The deceased party was the parent's only child; there is some evidence that they were intoxicated while driving.

It is not difficult to imagine how complex and intense these discussions might be: the parents of the deceased student grieving over the loss of their only, and remarkably talented, child and their perception that the defendant driver had failed in every way that their son had excelled; a defendant who felt very badly about the accident but did not perceive the victim to be blameless, and his parent who loves him as much as the plaintiff's parents loved their son. Managing these conversations in a constructive, empathetic way is intellectually and emotionally exhausting for everyone, including the mediator. But many prefer it to reliving the tragedy in the context of a contested jury trial.

2. Medical Maltreatment Claims. From a legal perspective, medical matters often invite special attention, for one's health situation shapes their daily capacity and conduct. What "caused" a patient's compromised health condition following a medical procedure or treatment program can be complex: medical procedures addressing life-threatening situations may have low success probabilities; a hospital's technical resources and personnel capacity may be limited; post-operative recovery protocols might be difficult for a patient to implement. Using mediation to sort out these matters promotes prompt, private conversations that all participants welcome.

3. Construction. Roofs leak. Buildings collapse, through faulty material, unanticipated stresses, shoddy craftsmanship, or natural disasters. Air conditioning units or heating systems might fail to operate as promised. Delays in delivery of building supplies disrupts scheduled project work and can create project cost overruns. These disputes may involve multiple players: the building owner; architects; engineers; material suppliers; skilled tradespeople; bankers; insurance companies; and others. The construction process — and businesses — is team-dependent, whether the work involves building an apartment complex, a single-family home or an airport expansion. Organizing and facilitating multiple conversations simultaneously among numerous stakeholders and their representatives is the significant contribution that a mediator makes to resolving these predictable conflicts.

4. Labor and Employment. For most people, work is crucial: it importantly contributes to one's sense of self-dignity and the financial income from one's work often constitutes one's primary economic resource. If one's work life is made miserable by harassing or belittling remarks made by one's co-worker or supervisor, one wants to take action to stop it. If one is denied an employment opportunity or promotion because of one's age, race, sex or religion, one wants to correct that injustice. If a storeowner believes that an employee has stolen company property, they want to be able to terminate that individual quickly. Mediators are regularly used to assist both parties address such individual claims as well as service class action discrimination lawsuits.

Every workplace participant—owners, supervisors, and co-workers—has a stake in participating in an effective, stimulating employment environment. No one needs to wait until someone files a lawsuit before encouraging contesting parties to meet with a mediator to discuss their challenges. As noted previously, the U.S. Postal Service created its REDRESS (Resolve Employment Disputes Reach Equitable Solutions Swiftly) mediation program to encourage employees to promptly and effectively address workplace challenges with the assistance of a mediator; the Service recruits, appoints and compensates the individuals (none of whom work for the postal service) who have been trained to serve as mediators. Similarly, the U.S. Department of Justice oversees the enforcement of the American with Disabilities Act, in part, by encouraging affected parties to seek resolution involving such matters by using private sector mediators specially trained by the Department. In growing numbers, private sector employers, colleges and universities, and other organizations are designing dispute resolution systems that encourage or require that disputing employees use a mediator to promote settlement discussions before anyone can file formal court papers.

5. Intellectual Property. Copyrights, patents, and trademarks are valuable. These protections exist in order to stimulate intellectual imagination, scientific and engineering creativity, and business acumen. When a person believes that others have pirated their creation, they seek recompense and recognition. These disputants need to discuss their contentions thoroughly but in a manner that does not reveal competitive secrets. Some discussions involve complex technical matters; others involve a careful analysis of the creative process. Time is often of the essence, at least to one party. Using a mediator perfectly meets these needs.

6. Business and Contract Disputes. Business enterprises can thrive and prosper, or they can fail; in either setting, disputes emerge. If success envelops the business, owners can fight over allocating profits, development plans, or employment practices; if the business fails, agreements must be reached regarding creditor payoffs, asset sales, and terminating employment contracts. Whether the case comes as a court-referral of a litigated matter or because business partners and their advisors proactively seek assistance, experienced business lawyers or savvy business personnel serving as mediators provide valuable services to such disputants.

4. Elder Care

Advances in medical science and technology enable us to live longer. For many persons, though, the quality of that expanded biological existence distinctly varies. With aging, a person's physical mobility diminishes; one's memory deterioration, whether prompted by natural causes or accelerated by Alzheimer or other diseases, compromises independence. What were once routine trips and falls generate more complex orthopedic injuries. When these and other elder care challenges arise, family members often shape and implement a supporting service network for their parents or loved ones. But developing and implementing such a network can trigger conflict: who will pay for support expenses? How is caring time by loved ones, not professionals, divided between spouse and children? How is caring time by loved ones compensated, if at all? How are different opinions among family members about appropriate treatment options resolved? What procedures are there for making significant health-care and quality of life decisions? These challenges are emotionally excruciating, take time and patience to address, and require developing supportive, sustained relationships with multiple stakeholders. Mediators play a pivotal role in developing and managing these poignant discussions among multiple stakeholders.

5. Probate

Death invites disputes. In the family context, those controversies may be wrapped in years of emotional and intellectual engagement; if a family member's demise was preceded by a sustained period of illness that triggered its own treatment disputes, that complex history additionally shapes the discussion and resolution of disputes regarding estate matters.

But probate disputes are not confined to families. Persons or organizations that expected to be beneficiaries of someone's largesse but are then informed otherwise are properly suspicious. The distribution of art collections or valued musical instruments can generate intense controversy since, by definition, persons are dealing with one-of-a-kind objects. The components of a person's estate could be more sentimental than financial, but the discussion and debate over its distribution — whether it involves the decedent's extensive collection of auto repair tools, unpublished manuscripts, book collection, or entertainment dinnerware and crystal glasses — might be explosive. Persons involved in these situations often want prompt, private resolution of these controversies, and they seek mediator assistance to secure it.

6. Peer Mediation

In the K-12 school setting, students, as do adults, get mired in conflict. The conflict can erupt over personal property — taking someone's school supplies or iPod — or involve more intense, interpersonal dynamics such as bullying, teasing, or "messing with my friend." School systems regularly hire an independent mediator to design or administer the school's "dispute resolution program," which includes training students to become peer mediators, supervising student mediator conduct, and initiating educational programs about conflict resolution processes and skills for all members of the school community.

7. Bioethical Disputes

The adage that life is uncertain is accurate. It is made more painful when one is forced to choose among medical care options that lead to disability, suffering, or death — and, often, to be forced to make that decision within severely curtailed time constraints. The litigated fight between the husband and parents of Terri Schiavo over whether and how her medical care should be terminated was highly publicized. But disputes similar in kind occur regularly — without the fanfare — throughout the country.

These disputes often arise in the context of a medical care facility — a hospital or nursing home — in which a patient either enters the care facility with a life-altering medical condition or, while receiving medical treatment, acquires such a condition. Loved ones — spouses, children, parents — of the patient must, in consultation with treating physicians, other health-care professionals, social workers, medical students, and perhaps medical ethicists, develop an acceptable treatment plan. When there are disagreements, the challenge becomes to create a mutually-acceptable plan acceptable so that a final treatment decision can be effectively implemented. Some hospitals have established Bioethics Consultation Services (BCS) to handle such matters; law-trained and philosophically trained individuals, each of whom is also trained as a mediator, staff these services.

8. Environmental Disputes

Environmental controversies pierce geographic boundaries. Air quality; water purity; toxic waste sites; nuclear waste contamination; forest preservation or deterioration — all impact the quality of our life. But they collide with other practices that people enjoy: driving cars powered by fossil fuels; building highways that redefine previously established neighborhood boundaries; snow skiing on mountain paths made possible by razing trees; or tearing down old buildings that some view as historically precious but others view as impediments to contemporary construction technology and aesthetic possibilities. The world of urban and regional planning in an era of increased environmental consciousness is a world of controversy involving multiple players, both private and governmental. Persons who mediate such controversies are knowledgeable about political processes, community organizations, and business practices. They are creative in persuading private foundations or donors to provide economic resources to facilitate broad-based, sustained participation by multiple parties. They often work in teams, blending technical and professional backgrounds in service of the disputants.

9. Public Policy Disputes

We live in exciting times, confronting significant challenges — economic polarity, immigration policy, educational restructuring — that test the continued viability of democratic governance. For some of these public policy disputes — how to finance public educational systems — citizens can anticipate and deliberate about them; other disputes simply erupt, such as the reaction to the police murder of George Floyd in Minneapolis, the shooting massacre of students in Uvalde, Texas or Parkland, Florida, or the protests surrounding local citizen initiatives regarding reproductive rights and practices. Mediated discussions of public policy controversies can enhance, not undermine, democratic governance. Recent initiatives such as Rebuild Congress, the National Institute for Civil Discourse, and The Democracy Project aspire to trigger such public participation. More modest initiatives, such as helping a public high school develop a policy to govern cell phone use by its community members, also dot the landscape. Engagement in these settings develops in multiple ways: a community or political leader may encourage it; an established, respected business or social organization may suggest it; or a dispute resolution entity — be it a bar association committee, a community dispute resolution program, or a university institute — may explore possible service, using private mediators to deliver the service.

10. Special Education Disputes

Special education mediation is a mediation where the parents of a student with disabilities and the school district personnel meet to negotiate disputes surrounding the appropriate educational services required to sustain the student's learning. Federal law requires that school districts make mediation available to allow resolution of disputes regarding the identification, evaluation, educational placement or provision of free, appropriate public educational services to a student with a disability or a student suspected of having a disability. The school district and the parent must agree to participate in the process. Mediators are usually assigned to cases through their participation on a mediator panel developed by the district or by a community dispute resolution center. Mediators undergo specific training on both the administrative and legal aspects of special education.

C. Organization-Based Employment Opportunities

Persons interested in pursuing employment opportunities in mediation may not want to operate independent solo practices; for multiple reasons, both professional and personal, they may seek or prefer salaried job opportunities connected with institutions. Two such options exist: staff mediator positions with agencies or organizations, and staff positions with dispute resolution programs which include, but are not limited to, serving as a mediator. The method for gaining entry to each realm differs significantly, but this can be a successful entrée to a career in mediation and ADR.

1. Mediator Positions in Agencies and Organizations

There are some organizations, mostly governmentally based, that hire full-time staff mediators. Historically, most of these positions are in governmental units that provide mediation and technical assistance to participants in union-management relations. The Federal Mediation and Conciliation Service (FMCS), for example, employs staff mediators to assist private-sector labor-management representatives conduct their collective bargaining sessions. With the explosive growth of formal union-management relations involving public sector employees beginning in the late 1960s, state governments created agencies comparable to FMCS to serve collective bargaining needs involving public sector unions and management; these are variously referred to as Public Employment Relations Boards (PERBs) or Public Employment Relations Commissions (PERCs). A limited number of governmental agencies exist at both the federal and state level that provide mediators and conciliators to help resolve controversies involving civil rights or civil disturbances; the leading example is the Community Relations Service (CRS) of the U.S. Department of Justice, but examples at the state and local levels include New Jersey's Community Relations Unit in the Attorney General's Division on Civil Rights and California's Community Conflict Resolution Unit in its Civil Rights Department. Other federal government agencies, such as the Department of Defense, hire staff mediators, and various state government offices, such as Worker Compensation Offices, Human Rights Agencies, or Departments of Education, regularly recruit for staff mediators. Finally, many state and federal court systems have hired staff persons to serve as mediators both in subject-specific areas, such as family or juvenile court settings, and for cases involving general civil and appellate matters.

These agencies, in their recruiting process, seek individuals who have gained experience in the targeted service domain. Persons hired as staff mediators for agencies servicing union-management collective bargaining, for example, normally have employment experience related to that area either in union leadership positions, as management staff in labor-relations offices in either the private or public sector, or as professional advocates who represented unions or management in grievance arbitration cases. For agency-based opportunities that serve other constituencies — *e.g.*, family, workers compensation, civil rights, peer mediation — the relevant range of lived experiences are considerably more robust and so become viable employment opportunities for persons who are early in their professional careers. Similarly, persons appointed to court mediator positions often have professional law practice experience, although the educational and practice opportunities some persons acquire as law students participating in various mediation classes, clinics, internship programs and competitions can be sufficient.

2. Working for a Dispute Resolution Agency

There are multiple employment opportunities for persons who want to enter the mediation field immediately following their formal educational training. However, many involve working in settings in which one performs various organizational activities, not just mediating. These organizational-employment opportunities fall into two categories.

a. Dispute Resolution Agencies That Provide Direct Service

There are many not-for-profit organizations that provide mediation and other dispute resolution services to their communities. Some are free-standing, privately-financed programs, such as the Community Boards Program in San Francisco. Other agencies have contractual relationships with their local court systems, school systems, family service agencies, business federations, and other organizations pursuant to which that organization refers its conflicts to the dispute resolution agency, which then provides mediation services. Staff members at these dispute resolution centers, such as the multiple offices of the Community Dispute Resolution Centers Programs in New York and Michigan, not only mediate disputes but also recruit and train community residents to serve as mediators as well as engage in community education and outreach activity. These dispute resolution agencies typically recruit staff members whose qualifications are predicated more heavily on their formal educational training and lived experiences than on their dispute resolution experience.

There are also significant employment opportunities situated within more traditional business and educational organizations for persons with mediation/dispute resolution training and skills but whose job title does not reflect a dispute resolution designation. Persons who work in a company's human resource department routinely deploy "dispute resolution skills"; colleges and universities often recruit administrators to supervise student judicial councils that conduct hearings ranging from allegations of student harassment to charges of plagiarism or cheating on examinations. Some organizations, both for-profit and not-for-profit, hire individuals to work in their ombudsperson office.

Persons entering the dispute resolution field through these avenues rapidly develop or sharpen multiple employment skills, including supervisory and budgeting expertise, staff training, grant development experience, public presentation competency, and program development proficiency; with this robust employment profile, particularly when joined with formal legal training, a person enjoys a competitive advantage in pursuing mediation employment opportunities in organizational settings or in the development of an independent mediation practice.

b. Working for a DR Administrative or Provider Organization

Some organizations provide education, technical assistance, and administrative support to parties who use dispute resolution services. While these institutions want their professional staff to be persons who are knowledgeable about mediation theory and practice, staff personnel themselves do not perform an official mediating role. Working in these administrative positions, though, enables someone who is interested in mediation to immediately obtain employment in the dispute resolution field and to interact with multiple players, including parties to a controversy and mediators. For example, in the public sector, there are dispute resolution programs placed organizationally within the administrative offices of a state's supreme court.

Persons employed in these offices conduct research about experimental programs in mediation, assist in developing prototype mediation programs and institutionalizing their use, and provide technical assistance and training to courts, bar associations, judicial conferences, and community organizations that are interested in promoting mediation's use. While only some of these court employees are able to mediate cases while in their position, they will definitely acquire experience and expertise about process design, skill development and training, while positioning themselves, if they choose, for more direct service opportunities.

There are also entities referred to as "provider" organizations. The structure and operation of the American Arbitration Association (AAA), the oldest of such organizations, is characteristic: the AAA develops "panels" of mediators and arbitrators. When parties to a controversy want to hire a mediator, they contact the AAA and, with appropriate compensation for its administrative services, engage AAA to identify possible mediators (or select one for the parties), arrange for the conference meeting place and time, handle the transmission of all documents among the parties and mediator, and, at the case's end, close out the file by sending appropriate billings. The important contribution of the AAA staff member to the proceeding is primarily procedural. Much like the employment experience in the administrative office of a state's supreme court, discussed previously, securing an administrative position with a private provider organization enables someone with an interest in mediation to begin working immediately in the dispute resolution field and gain valuable insights into how parties, their representatives, and mediators perform their work. Provider-organizations such as the AAA, the International Institute for Conflict Prevention and Resolution, and JAMS (formerly Judicial Arbitration and Mediation Services) have offices and provide services throughout the United States.

D. Practitioner Profiles

People who mediate regularly or work for ADR provider organizations have multiple profiles. Many are law-trained; persons with professional training in the helping professions often mediate, particularly family cases. Some private practitioners serve clients in multiple parts of the country while others target a client base within their own geographical area. Since conducting mediation sessions via videoconferencing mediation through applications like Zoom or Webex has become widespread, many mediators are able to convene cases from the comfort of their own office or home. Doing so has enabled some practitioners to expand from a local practice to a national one. Many persons combine mediating with engaging in other professional or business practices, and some persons mediate only as volunteers for local programs.

Persons with an independent mediation practice market their business. While engaging in professional association activities and community service are significant ways in which a person meets others and develops a network, individual and practice groups use multiple electronic and social media formats — websites, Facebook, Linkedin, and the like — to share their background and experiences. Persons working as a mediator in agency-based organizations, either government or non-profit, often have their profiles appear on their respective organization websites.

Set out below are the biographies of three mediators. These biographies illustrate the professional and personal experiences — "pathways" — that led them into mediation work. They also reflect, both within and across practitioner categories, the continuing need and challenges signaled in Chapter 7 for the "mediator pool" to more richly reflect diversity along racial, ethnic, gender, and generational dimensions.

These profiles are illustrative. There are additional resources referenced below, specifically the blog *ADR as a 1st Career,* which highlights (and thereby celebrates) that one can begin a career in mediation and ADR shortly after completing one's formal education. These individuals who have joined the ADR profession over the past twenty-five years confirm that the old adage that "you have to have grey hair on your head to be a successful mediator" is passe.

ADR Personalities and Practice Tips

49–52 (James J. Alfini & Eric R. Galton, Eds., 1998)*
By Dana L. Curtis

[Dana L. Curtis mediates civil disputes in a wide range of substantive areas. . . . She began practice as a full-time mediator in 1991 with Mediation Law Offices in Mill Valley and served as Circuit Mediator with the U.S. Court of Appeals for the Ninth Circuit in San Francisco until 1997. . . . Her solo practice is based in Sausalito, California.]

I knew I wanted to be a mediator when I was introduced to mediation in a second-year law school course. My other courses, though interesting intellectually, minimized the role of the human being behind the legal claims. Mediation focused on the individuals involved and on the meaning they attached to the dispute. The parties' priorities could be the most important reference point for resolution. In addition to, or instead of, the rule of law, their concerns, needs, fears, hopes and desires all mattered. As well as seeing how mediation could better meet the needs of the parties than a litigated resolution, I realized that mediation better utilized my strengths. As a mediator, I could use relationship and communication skills I had developed in my first career as a teacher.

Full of enthusiasm for mediation, I asked my professor where to learn about mediating as a career. He referred me to Gary Friedman, a pioneer lawyer mediator and Director of the Center for Mediation in Law in Mill Valley, California. I sought Gary's advice about mediating employment and other commercial disputes. He encouraged me, but warned that such a career would be difficult to forge, as the application of mediation in civil disputes was uncommon at that time. He also noted that I seemed to have what it would take — the commitment to mediation and an entrepreneurial spirit, evidenced by the fact that I had entered law school as a single mother after moving to California from Idaho with my three children.

Gary advised me to remain committed, to be patient and to get litigation experience to enhance my credibility with lawyers and my understanding of the legal process. Following his advice, after law school I clerked for a California Supreme Court associate justice and thereafter joined a large San Francisco law firm, practicing commercial and employment litigation in San Jose and San Francisco. I began as an enthusiastic associate and during much of my first year of practice seriously considered a long-term litigation career. Before long, my enthusiasm abated. The enormity of financial and human resources spent on litigation astounded me. The inefficiency of the discovery process (where the object, it seemed to me, was to provide the other side with as little information as possible), the lack of predictability and fairness of jury trials, and the failure of litigation to address the clients' true needs all left me disaffected.

In addition, the demands of big firm practice, the often sixty-and sometimes eighty-hour work weeks, and the isolation I experienced among 200 other big firm lawyers convinced me that I was not willing to sacrifice more years of "being" for "becoming." The idea of partnership became unthinkable. As one of my law school friends put it, partnership is like a pie eating contest where the prize is more pie.

I dreamed of mediating. Although I had trained as a mediator and had been teaching mediation for several years, I was unable to see a way to make the transition. During this time of profound dissatisfaction with my career, I spent an evening with four dear women friends, as I had been doing on a bimonthly basis for several years. That night I spoke of my life consumed with work, of the months without a day off, of the weeks in a hotel room, of the frustrations of a difficult trial and of the day-to-day failure of my career to provide deep, personal meaning for me. What followed caused me finally to initiate change in my life. One of my friends looked me in the eye and said, "Dana, you will die if you don't leave your job." I knew she was right. If not physically, I was dying spiritually. The next day, without knowing what else I would do, I gave notice that I would be leaving the firm.

A few days later, I ran into Gary Friedman on the street in San Francisco. When he discovered I was leaving my law practice, he invited me to meet with him. Over a series of meetings, I learned that he was becoming increasingly interested in mediation of civil disputes and would like to work closely with lawyers who were pursuing commercial mediation. Within a few months, I hung out my mediation shingle (literally!) at Gary's office in Mill Valley. There, I practiced mediation for two years with Laura Farrow, another lawyer who left the firm at the same time I did. . . . .

The years I spent at Mediation Law Offices enabled me to develop a successful practice and to build a foundation that has been important in my practice and in my teaching. By working closely with Gary, I became more effective and more reflective. Following most mediations, I would write a critique of the process and meet with Gary to reflect on the dynamic between the parties and within myself....

After two years at Mediation Law Offices, I had the opportunity to become a Circuit Court Mediator for the U.S. Court of Appeals for the Ninth Circuit in San Francisco. I was persuaded to leave private practice by the promise of an endless array of federal cases to mediate and steady paychecks. In the Ninth Circuit Mediation Program, I worked with five other full-time mediators to resolve cases on appeal. It was a mediator's dream come true. We selected our caseload from hundreds of diverse civil appeals. On any day, we might conduct a telephone mediation in a securities case, an employment discrimination dispute, a products liability matter, an IRS appeal, a bankruptcy case or an insurance coverage dispute. Several times a month, I would mediate in person, often in complex multi-party disputes. It was a time of applying my experience and knowledge of a face-to-face mediation model, where the parties could reach understanding in order to craft a resolution that addressed their priorities, not just their assessment of their legal positions....

During the three years I worked at the Ninth Circuit, I mediated hundreds of appeals. I learned that it is never too late for mediation. It was not unusual for a case to have been in litigation for ten years or more — and still settle! ...

A year ago, I left the Ninth Circuit to return to private mediation practice and to join the Negotiation and Mediation Program at Stanford Law School, where I am a lecturer teaching two mediation courses a year.

Profiles in ADR: Grande Lum

20 Disp. Resol. Mag. 41 (2014)

On April 4, [2017] Grande Lum, Director of the US Department of Justice's Community Relations Service, accepted the ABA's Lawyer as Problem Solver Award on behalf of CRS. The editors of Dispute Resolution Magazine took this opportunity to interview Lum about CRS and the people who work in it.[1] ...

Q: What about your career path?

A: I took the Harvard Law School Negotiation Workshop from *Getting To Yes* co-author Roger Fisher in my first year of law school, which dramatically altered my career trajectory, as I went into law school thinking I would become a civil rights litigator. It was so unlike all my other law classes in its emphasis on joint problem solving and collaboration. I received an offer to join Conflict Management, Inc., CMI, which was basically a spinoff of the Harvard Negotiation Project. From there I have been blessed with 20 years in dispute resolution that have been fulfilling and

---

1. Since the publication of this article, Grande Lum has transitioned from CRS to other positions including the Director of the Divided Community Project at The Ohio State University Moritz College of Law, Provost and Vice President of Academic Affairs at Menlo College and most recently, the Director of the Martin Daniel Gould Center for Conflict Resolution at Stanford Law School.

adventurous. I became a partner at CMI, co-founded Thought Bridge, a mediation firm, then started Accordance, a training company, and wrote two books. I landed a dream job as clinical professor at the University of California Hastings School of the Law, where I directed its Center for Negotiation and Dispute Resolution. It was joyful working with students and great colleagues, and we grew the program to one of the top law school dispute resolution programs in the country. I would still be there but for the fact that I had the unexpected opportunity to join the Obama administration. I first worked at the Small Business Administration, running a program to increase government contracting and jobs in poor areas of the country. I was then nominated by the President and confirmed by the Senate as CRS Director, which for me was a once-in-a-lifetime opportunity to lead an organization I had long admired. . . .

Q: Is there a traditional career path for CRS conciliators?

A: The career path each staff member traveled before arriving at the agency is as diverse as the fabric of the communities they serve. CRS staff hail from all walks of life: civil rights, advocacy, community organizing, education, law enforcement, conflict resolution, law, social work, psychology, journalism and communications, labor, government, and even astrophysics. No matter what discipline CRS staff have come from, they joined the agency because of their heartfelt desire to help people resolve disputes.

Profiles in ADR: Doug Van Epps
23 Disp. Resol. Mag. 32 (2017)
By Zena Zumeta

Doug Van Epps is the Director of the Michigan Office of Dispute Resolution, based in the State Court Administrative Office. The first and only director of that office, he has shaped the position in the 28 years he has held it, moving from creating a system of volunteer mediation centers around the state to being a force for dispute resolution within state government and throughout the Michigan court system.[2]

Q: What did you do before you got to the Office of Dispute Resolution?

A: Out of law school, I went to the prosecutor's office in the state capitol and stayed three years. Back then, the natural progression after that was to move to a law firm, but listening to attorneys in the courthouse halls gave me the impression that practicing law would be increasingly acrimonious and contentious. Lawyers were settling cases on the courthouse steps but not solving problems, which is what I went to law school to do: help people solve problems. Treating every problem as if it's a war just isn't my nature.

So not seeing a place for myself in practicing law, and I suppose to take stock of things, I sold everything and went to Europe for a year. While there, I heard the first CDs on the market, and returned home to start a music store called the Compact

---

2. Doug Van Epps retired from his position with the Michigan Courts in May 2021.

Disc Emporium. It was the second CD-only store in the country and for its novelty was featured on the cover of *Billboard*. What I loved most there was talking to people about music and introducing them to new types of music. The business grew very quickly, and when it was time to consider opening more stores, it occurred to me that doing that would likely distance me from what I most liked: just talking with people and playing music. So instead of expanding, I sold it, and fortuitously just in time before the music business changed so radically. And traveled again (are you picking up a theme here?), this time to various points in the Pacific, Asia, and Australia. . . .

Q: How did you end up at the Office of Dispute Resolution?

A: I was in the process of starting another business when a friend sent me the job description for the Director of the Community Dispute Resolution Program with a note that said "You can't run from the law forever!" While I was at the prosecutor's office, I had taken a mediation training and helped start a local mediation center, the first I knew of in Michigan. Like people in most local mediation nonprofits, everyone involved was passionate about solving problems, and the experience seemed to directly respond to my concerns about the practice of law in the first place. So when I received the job application, I thought the position might afford me the opportunity to actually do something about the sad state of affairs in the profession. Somewhat ironically, for not having practiced law for a number of years, I was hired chiefly because of my entrepreneurial experience. They wanted someone who could build a statewide program from the ground up. So it was a zigzag way into the profession, similar to the way many of us got into ADR. I thought I might help launch the program and then leave, but I'm still here 28 years later.

Important Resources for Careers in Mediation

There are multiple online and print resources that display the biographies of women and men who have forged sustained work in the mediation field.

- Professor Alyson Carrell created the *ADR as 1st Career* blog which celebrates the stories of individuals who successfully launched a career in Alternative Dispute Resolution immediately, or soon after, graduating with an advanced degree. The blog has over 50 videos in which persons share their stories of perseverance to quickly reach a career in ADR.

- *The Mediators: Views from the Eye of the Storm* (Mediate.com) is a DVD recording containing extensive individual interviews with 64 persons who describe the development of their mediation career and their approach to mediation. In its promotional material, Mediate.com described these individuals as "the best known and most experienced mediators in the world."

- The American Bar Association published *ADR Personalities and Practice Tips* (J. Alfini & E. Galton, E. eds., 1998), in which invited mediators wrote entries describing their personal journeys into mediation work.

- More recently, short autobiographies of 23 prominent participants in the development of the field appeared in *Evolution of a Field: Personal Histories in Conflict Resolution* (H. Gadlin & N. Welsh eds., 2020).

Notes and Questions

When trying to develop one's practice, what types of ethical dilemmas might a mediator encounter advertising one's services? Would sending potential clients a complimentary ball-point pen or calendar bearing the mediator's name violate any ethical norms for mediators? If a mediator's website contains, among other things, her client list, would that be acceptable? See Chapter 8 *supra*, for additional challenges posed when mediators engage in business development activities.

E. Mediation's Promise

Barring dramatic social and political changes, most United States residents can be confident that our basic legal institutions and processes will continue to operate in predictable form well into the future.

Many signs also point to sustained mediation activity: expansion of mandatory court-connected mediation programs in state and local courts; state and federal legislation supporting mediation's use in various sectors; courses on mediation at universities and law schools throughout the country; and a social climate in which persons and businesses demand that their dispute resolution budgets support flexible, efficient, and varied dispute resolution processes.

But a contrary vision about mediation is also plausible. Despite expanding mediation activity, most persons still believe suing someone is the most desirable way to resolve controversies. As depicted in movies, streaming resources, and courtroom novels, our role model of the heroic problem solver is the strong, aggressive courtroom advocate. Few communication networks portray the power and skills of negotiators and mediators; and many lawyers continue to view mediation as only an incidental, required hurdle to jump in the litigation process.

Several dominant lessons emerge from the mediation story, though, that provide powerful reasons for believing that mediation's place in our democratic society is vital and secure. What are they?

First, wherever persons want to participate responsibly in resolving controversies in which they are a stakeholder, using mediation can help make that happen. There are important social practices within our own country that appear ripe for reconsideration and reconstruction: health care delivery, public school systems, and banking practices are just three examples of significant institutions that are undergoing significant transformations. Trained mediators can be a force for creating constructive dialogue among concerned stakeholders on such pivotal matters.

Second, we are becoming better educated about mediation. Many of today's law students, unlike their predecessors, attended a middle school or high school in which there was a peer mediation program; they might very well have served as mediators themselves. But the education initiative is much broader than a law school curriculum: workshops at professional and business organizations are replete with topics relating to negotiation and consensus-building; and academic and certificate programs in dispute resolution at both the undergraduate and graduate levels are expanding, with students in business, nursing, and natural resources being required to take mediation and facilitation courses. There is a slow, steady climate change occurring with respect to how persons choose to deal with differences, and the study and use of mediation is a part of that change.

Finally, persons drawn to this work, by and large, are remarkably strong, energetic, thoughtful, and resourceful individuals. Their energy in, and commitment to, this work has been shaped by personal experiences and perspectives that give them confidence in the integrity and value of mediation. They are persistent, imaginative, and committed to serving the parties at the highest standards of excellence. They experience an extraordinary sense of satisfaction in helping parties overcome what had previously been perceived as insuperable barriers. They know that each mediation session involves persons with distinctive aspirations, values, and priorities — and that fact mandates their treating each party with empathy and respect. Engaging talented, compassionate individuals who do the work of mediation plays a significant role in shaping its future. As long as fellow community members seek to be treated with dignity, as is their right, and as long as persons of character and conviction continue to assume the mediator's role, there will be a role for mediation.

Appendices

Appendix A

Model Standards of Conduct for Mediators

AMERICAN ARBITRATION ASSOCIATION
(ADOPTED SEPTEMBER 8, 2005)

AMERICAN BAR ASSOCIATION
(ADOPTED AUGUST 9, 2005)

ASSOCIATION FOR CONFLICT RESOLUTION
(ADOPTED AUGUST 22, 2005)

SEPTEMBER 2005

The Model Standards of Conduct for Mediators was prepared in 1994 by the American Arbitration Association, the American Bar Association's Section of Dispute Resolution, and the Association for Conflict Resolution.[1] A joint committee consisting of representatives from the same successor organizations revised the Model Standards in 2005.[2] Both the original 1994 version and the 2005 revision have been approved by each participating organization.[3]

Preamble

Mediation is used to resolve a broad range of conflicts within a variety of settings. These Standards are designed to serve as fundamental ethical guidelines for persons mediating in all practice contexts. They serve three primary goals: to guide the conduct of mediators; to inform the mediating parties; and to promote public confidence in mediation as a process for resolving disputes.

---

1. The Association for Conflict Resolution is a merged organization of the Academy of Family Mediators, the Conflict Resolution Education Network and the Society of Professionals in Dispute Resolution (SPIDR). SPIDR was the third participating organization in the development of the 1994 Standards.

2. Reporter's Notes, which are not part of these Standards and therefore have not been specifically approved by any of the organizations, provide commentary regarding these revisions.

3. The 2005 revisions to the Model Standards were approved by the American Bar Association's House of Delegates on August 9, 2005, the Board of the Association for Conflict Resolution on August 22, 2005 and the Executive Committee of the American Arbitration Association on September 8, 2005.

Mediation is a process in which an impartial third party facilitates communication and negotiation and promotes voluntary decision making by the parties to the dispute.

Mediation serves various purposes, including providing the opportunity for parties to define and clarify issues, understand different perspectives, identify interests, explore and assess possible solutions, and reach mutually satisfactory agreements, when desired.

Note on Construction

These Standards are to be read and construed in their entirety. There is no priority significance attached to the sequence in which the Standards appear.

The use of the term "shall" in a Standard indicates that the mediator must follow the practice described. The use of the term "should" indicates that the practice described in the standard is highly desirable, but not required, and is to be departed from only for very strong reasons and requires careful use of judgment and discretion.

The use of the term "mediator" is understood to be inclusive so that it applies to co-mediator models.

These Standards do not include specific temporal parameters when referencing a mediation, and therefore, do not define the exact beginning or ending of a mediation.

Various aspects of a mediation, including some matters covered by these Standards, may also be affected by applicable law, court rules, regulations, other applicable professional rules, mediation rules to which the parties have agreed and other agreements of the parties. These sources may create conflicts with, and may take precedence over, these Standards. However, a mediator should make every effort to comply with the spirit and intent of these Standards in resolving such conflicts. This effort should include honoring all remaining Standards not in conflict with these other sources.

These Standards, unless and until adopted by a court or other regulatory authority do not have the force of law. Nonetheless, the fact that these Standards have been adopted by the respective sponsoring entities, should alert mediators to the fact that the Standards might be viewed as establishing a standard of care for mediators.

STANDARD I. SELF-DETERMINATION

A. A mediator shall conduct a mediation based on the principle of party self-determination. Self-determination is the act of coming to a voluntary, uncoerced decision in which each party makes free and informed choices as to process and outcome. Parties may exercise self-determination at any stage of a mediation, including mediator selection, process design, participation in or withdrawal from the process, and outcomes.

1. Although party self-determination for process design is a fundamental principle of mediation practice, a mediator may need to balance such party self-determination with a mediator's duty to conduct a quality process in accordance with these Standards.

2. A mediator cannot personally ensure that each party has made free and informed choices to reach particular decisions, but, where appropriate, a mediator should make the parties aware of the importance of consulting other professionals to help them make informed choices.

B. A mediator shall not undermine party self-determination by any party for reasons such as higher settlement rates, egos, increased fees, or outside pressures from court personnel, program administrators, provider organizations, the media or others.

STANDARD II. IMPARTIALITY

A. A mediator shall decline a mediation if the mediator cannot conduct it in an impartial manner. Impartiality means freedom from favoritism, bias or prejudice.

B. A mediator shall conduct a mediation in an impartial manner and avoid conduct that gives the appearance of partiality.

1. A mediator should not act with partiality or prejudice based on any participant's personal characteristics, background, values and beliefs, or performance at a mediation, or any other reason.

2. A mediator should neither give nor accept a gift, favor, loan or other item of value that raises a question as to the mediator's actual or perceived impartiality.

3. A mediator may accept or give de minimis gifts or incidental items or services that are provided to facilitate a mediation or respect cultural norms so long as such practices do not raise questions as to a mediator's actual or perceived impartiality.

C. If at any time a mediator is unable to conduct a mediation in an impartial manner, the mediator shall withdraw.

STANDARD III. CONFLICTS OF INTEREST

A. A mediator shall avoid a conflict of interest or the appearance of a conflict of interest during and after a mediation. A conflict of interest can arise from involvement by a mediator with the subject matter of the dispute or from any relationship between a mediator and any mediation participant, whether past or present, personal or professional, that reasonably raises a question of a mediator's impartiality.

B. A mediator shall make a reasonable inquiry to determine whether there are any facts that a reasonable individual would consider likely to create a potential or actual conflict of interest for a mediator. A mediator's actions necessary to accomplish a reasonable inquiry into potential conflicts of interest may vary based on practice context.

C. A mediator shall disclose, as soon as practicable, all actual and potential conflicts of interest that are reasonably known to the mediator and could reasonably be seen as raising a question about the mediator's impartiality. After disclosure, if all parties agree, the mediator may proceed with the mediation.

D. If a mediator learns any fact after accepting a mediation that raises a question with respect to that mediator's service creating a potential or actual conflict of interest, the mediator shall disclose it as quickly as practicable. After disclosure, if all parties agree, the mediator may proceed with the mediation.

E. If a mediator's conflict of interest might reasonably be viewed as undermining the integrity of the mediation, a mediator shall withdraw from or decline to proceed with the mediation regardless of the expressed desire or agreement of the parties to the contrary.

F. Subsequent to a mediation, a mediator shall not establish another relationship with any of the participants in any matter that would raise questions about the integrity of the mediation. When a mediator develops personal or professional relationships with parties, other individuals or organizations following a mediation in which they were involved, the mediator should consider factors such as time elapsed following the mediation, the nature of the relationships established, and services offered when determining whether the relationships might create a perceived or actual conflict of interest.

STANDARD IV. COMPETENCE

A. A mediator shall mediate only when the mediator has the necessary competence to satisfy the reasonable expectations of the parties.

1. Any person may be selected as a mediator, provided that the parties are satisfied with the mediator's competence and qualifications. Training, experience in mediation, skills, cultural understandings and other qualities are often necessary for mediator competence. A person who offers to serve as a mediator creates the expectation that the person is competent to mediate effectively.

2. A mediator should attend educational programs and related activities to maintain and enhance the mediator's knowledge and skills related to mediation.

3. A mediator should have available for the parties' information relevant to the mediator's training, education, experience and approach to conducting a mediation.

B. If a mediator, during the course of a mediation determines that the mediator cannot conduct the mediation competently, the mediator shall discuss that determination with the parties as soon as is practicable and take appropriate steps to address the situation, including, but not limited to, withdrawing or requesting appropriate assistance.

C. If a mediator's ability to conduct a mediation is impaired by drugs, alcohol, medication or otherwise, the mediator shall not conduct the mediation.

STANDARD V. CONFIDENTIALITY

A. A mediator shall maintain the confidentiality of all information obtained by the mediator in mediation, unless otherwise agreed to by the parties or required by applicable law.

   1. If the parties to a mediation agree that the mediator may disclose information obtained during the mediation, the mediator may do so.

   2. A mediator should not communicate to any non-participant information about how the parties acted in the mediation. A mediator may report, if required, whether parties appeared at a scheduled mediation and whether or not the parties reached a resolution.

   3. If a mediator participates in teaching, research or evaluation of mediation, the mediator should protect the anonymity of the parties and abide by their reasonable expectations regarding confidentiality.

B. A mediator who meets with any persons in private session during a mediation shall not convey directly or indirectly to any other person, any information that was obtained during that private session without the consent of the disclosing person.

C. A mediator shall promote understanding among the parties of the extent to which the parties will maintain confidentiality of information they obtain in a mediation.

D. Depending on the circumstance of a mediation, the parties may have varying expectations regarding confidentiality that a mediator should address. The parties may make their own rules with respect to confidentiality, or the accepted practice of an individual mediator or institution may dictate a particular set of expectations.

STANDARD VI. QUALITY OF THE PROCESS

A. A mediator shall conduct a mediation in accordance with these Standards and in a manner that promotes diligence, timeliness, safety, presence of the appropriate participants, party participation, procedural fairness, party competency and mutual respect among all participants.

   1. A mediator should agree to mediate only when the mediator is prepared to commit the attention essential to an effective mediation.

   2. A mediator should only accept cases when the mediator can satisfy the reasonable expectation of the parties concerning the timing of a mediation.

3. The presence or absence of persons at a mediation depends on the agreement of the parties and the mediator. The parties and mediator may agree that others may be excluded from particular sessions or from all sessions.

4. A mediator should promote honesty and candor between and among all participants, and a mediator shall not knowingly misrepresent any material fact or circumstance in the course of a mediation.

5. The role of a mediator differs substantially from other professional roles. Mixing the role of a mediator and the role of another profession is problematic and thus, a mediator should distinguish between the roles. A mediator may provide information that the mediator is qualified by training or experience to provide, only if the mediator can do so consistent with these Standards.

6. A mediator shall not conduct a dispute resolution procedure other than mediation but label it mediation in an effort to gain the protection of rules, statutes, or other governing authorities pertaining to mediation.

7. A mediator may recommend, when appropriate, that parties consider resolving their dispute through arbitration, counseling, neutral evaluation or other processes.

8. A mediator shall not undertake an additional dispute resolution role in the same matter without the consent of the parties. Before providing such service, a mediator shall inform the parties of the implications of the change in process and obtain their consent to the change. A mediator who undertakes such role assumes different duties and responsibilities that may be governed by other standards.

9. If a mediation is being used to further criminal conduct, a mediator should take appropriate steps including, if necessary, postponing, withdrawing from or terminating the mediation.

10. If a party appears to have difficulty comprehending the process, issues, or settlement options, or difficulty participating in a mediation, the mediator should explore the circumstances and potential accommodations, modifications or adjustments that would make possible the party's capacity to comprehend, participate and exercise self-determination.

B. If a mediator is made aware of domestic abuse or violence among the parties, the mediator shall take appropriate steps including, if necessary, postponing, withdrawing from or terminating the mediation.

C. If a mediator believes that participant conduct, including that of the mediator, jeopardizes conducting a mediation consistent with these Standards, a mediator shall take appropriate steps including, if necessary, postponing, withdrawing from or terminating the mediation.

STANDARD VII. ADVERTISING AND SOLICITATION

A. A mediator shall be truthful and not misleading when advertising, soliciting or otherwise communicating the mediator's qualifications, experience, services and fees.

   1. A mediator should not include any promises as to outcome in communications, including business cards, stationery, or computer-based communications.

   2. A mediator should only claim to meet the mediator qualifications of a governmental entity or private organization if that entity or organization has a recognized procedure for qualifying mediators and it grants such status to the mediator.

B. A mediator shall not solicit in a manner that gives an appearance of partiality for or against a party or otherwise undermines the integrity of the process.

C. A mediator shall not communicate to others, in promotional materials or through other forms of communication, the names of persons served without their permission.

STANDARD VIII. FEES AND OTHER CHARGES

A. A mediator shall provide each party or each party's representative true and complete information about mediation fees, expenses and any other actual or potential charges that may be incurred in connection with a mediation.

   1. If a mediator charges fees, the mediator should develop them in light of all relevant factors, including the type and complexity of the matter, the qualifications of the mediator, the time required and the rates customary for such mediation services.

   2. A mediator's fee arrangement should be in writing unless the parties request otherwise.

B. A mediator shall not charge fees in a manner that impairs a mediator's impartiality.

   1. A mediator should not enter into a fee agreement which is contingent upon the result of the mediation or amount of the settlement.

   2. While a mediator may accept unequal fee payments from the parties, a mediator should not use fee arrangements that adversely impact the mediator's ability to conduct a mediation in an impartial manner.

STANDARD IX. ADVANCEMENT OF MEDIATION PRACTICE

A. A mediator should act in a manner that advances the practice of mediation. A mediator promotes this Standard by engaging in some or all of the following:

   1. Fostering diversity within the field of mediation.

   2. Striving to make mediation accessible to those who elect touse it, including providing services at a reduced rate or on a pro bono basis as appropriate.

3. Participating in research when given the opportunity, including obtaining participant feedback when appropriate.

4. Participating in outreach and education efforts to assist the public in developing an improved understanding of, and appreciation for, mediation.

5. Assisting newer mediators through training, mentoring and networking.

B. A mediator should demonstrate respect for differing points of view within the field, seek to learn from other mediators and work together with other mediators to improve the profession and better serve people in conflict.

Reporter's Notes to Model Standards of Conduct for Mediators (September 9, 2005)

I. Introduction

During the 1992–94 period, representatives from the American Arbitration Association, the American Bar Association's Section of Dispute Resolution, and the Association for Conflict Resolution[1] developed the Model Standards of Conduct for Mediators (hereinafter referred to as 1994 Version). These Standards had three stated functions: to serve as a guide for the conduct of mediators; to inform the mediating parties; and to promote public confidence in mediation as a process for resolving disputes.

The 1994 Version has performed these functions with remarkable success. Two salient signs of such success are that various state programs adopted it in total or with slight variations as their guide for mediator conduct,[2] and multiple educational texts reference it in their discussion of ethical norms for mediators.[3]

During the past decade, however, the use of mediation has grown exponentially. State jurisdictions authorize referrals to mediation across a broad range of cases; Florida, as a single state, reported more than 100,000 cases being mediated in a given year. At the federal level, both district and circuit courts have experimented with various mediation initiatives. Delivery systems vary: some jurisdictions support the development of private marketplace mediator service delivery while others hire staff mediators in order to provide mediation services to all parties without additional cost to them. As use has grown, so have guidelines and rules; partly in response to

---

1. The Association for Conflict Resolution is the merged organization of three entities: the Academy of Family Mediators, the Conflict Resolution Education Network, and the Society of Professionals in Dispute Resolution. The Society of Professionals in Dispute Resolution was the third participating organization in the development of the 1994 Standards.

2. Such states include Alabama, Arkansas, Arizona, California, Georgia, Kansas, Louisiana, and Virginia.

3. Examples include Alfini, *et al.*, *Mediation Theory and Practice*, Goldberg, Sander, *et al.*, *Dispute Resolution: Negotiation, Mediation, and Other Processes.*

the phenomenon that there are now more than 2200 statutory provisions or court rules shaping mediation's use, leaders in the field initiated efforts in the late 1990s that led to the development of the Uniform Mediation Act. And in contexts other than courts, such as peer mediation programs in middle schools and high schools, mediation systems in organizational contexts, and facilitated dialogue to resolve social policy conflicts, mediation's use has become prominent.

Given this expanded use, representatives from the original participating organizations believed it important to review the 1994 Version to assess whether changes were warranted. In September 2002, two designated representatives from each of the three original participating organizations convened (hereinafter referred to as Joint Committee) to initiate its review These persons included:

American Arbitration Association:

Eric P. Tuchmann

John H. Wilkinson

American Bar Association, Section of Dispute Resolution

R. Wayne Thorpe

Susan M. Yates

Association for Conflict Resolution

Sharon B. Press

Terrence T. Wheeler

II. Guiding Principles

The members of the Joint Committee adopted the following principles to govern their work:

A. The three-fold major functions of the 1994 Version — to serve as a guide for the conduct of mediators; to inform the mediating parties; and to promote public confidence in mediation as a process for resolving disputes — should remain unchanged.

B. The Standards should retain their original function of serving as fundamental, basic ethical guidelines for persons mediating in all practice contexts while simultaneously recognizing that mediation practice in selected contexts may require additional standards in order to insure process integrity.

C. The basic architecture of the 1994 Version should be retained. Where possible, the original concepts should be retained, but changes should be made to correct, clarify or respond to new developments in mediation practice.

D Each Standard should target fundamental, ethical guidelines for mediators and exclude references to desirable behaviors or "best practices" in the statement of a Standard.

E. The process for conducting the Joint Committee's review of the 1994 Version should be accessible by the various publics interested in and affected by the practice of mediation.

F. Any changes to the Standards should be supported by a consensus of all Joint Committee members.

III. Joint Committee Schedule of Operations

The Joint Committee convened in September 2002 to begin its work. Members discussed basic governing principles to guide both procedural and substantive issues. It agreed to recruit a Reporter to assist it in its work.

At its meeting in March 2003 at the ABA's Section of Dispute Resolution Annual Conference in San Antonio, Texas, the Joint Committee adopted the following procedural guidelines:

a) Convene a series of Joint Committee meetings during the 2003–04 period at which the Committee members, in executive session, would analyze the 1994 Version, consider input from outside the Joint Committee, raise questions or concerns about its current vitality, and, if appropriate, develop and adopt alternative format, language, and content;

b) Conduct regular public sessions at the various conferences or meetings of the sponsoring organizations with the goal of eliciting comments and insights from practitioner audiences regarding appropriate questions to raise about the project's goals or particular elements of individual Standards; and

c) Publish the Committee's work through a web site in order to elicit broad-based comments and reactions to the Joint Committee's activities.

In July 2003, the Joint Committee, through its Reporter, sent letters of invitation to more than 50 organizations in the dispute resolution field requesting them to designate a liaison to the Joint Committee. The Committee Reporter was charged with contacting these organizational liaisons in timely, regular ways to alert them to the development of the Joint Committee work. While participation and comments were desired from all persons affected by the Joint Committee's work, the Joint Committee believed that having organizations identify such liaison personnel would expedite communication.

The Joint Committee met in executive session in May 2003, October 2003, January 2004, April 2004, November 2004 and December 2004. These in-person sessions were accompanied by extensive conference call discussions. The Joint Committee conducted public forum about its work at the annual conferences of the ABA's Section of Dispute Resolution (March 2003 and April 2004) and the Association for Conflict Resolution (October 2003 and October 2004). It established its website,

listing the 1994 version and inviting practitioner comment, in July 2003 (www
.moritzlaw.osu.edu/dr).

The Joint Committee posted a proposed revised Model Standards (January 2004) in
January 2004. It received public comments to the posting, both via website responses
and the workshop discussion at the ABA's Section of Dispute Resolution Annual
Meeting in April 2004. Throughout Summer 2004, the Joint Committee engaged in
extensive conference call discussions to analyze and address the various issues raised
by public comment. It posted Model Standards (September 2004) at the beginning of
September; this version reflected substantial changes to the Model Standards (January 2004) document, including a significant proposed revision for the role and shape
of the Reporter's Notes. At the time of the posting, the Joint Committee invited public
comments for an approximate 60-day period, noting that it planned to meet in early
November to begin consideration of its final draft. Public comments were received
through early December 2004 and considered at the Joint Committee's final sessions
on December 6–7, 2004. Through subsequent conference calls during December 2004,
the Joint Committee developed its December 2004 draft, a draft designed as a final
document, subject to consultation by Joint Committee members with their respective internal constituencies. The December 2004 draft and accompanying Reporter's
Notes (January 17, 2005) were posted to the website for public information purposes.
During the January–July, 2005 period, the Joint Committee examined targeted suggestions from constituent sources and developed the July 29, 2005 document.

The Joint Committee agreed unanimously to recommend to its respective
organizations for appropriate adoption the Model Standards of Conduct (July 2005);
for reasons explained below in Footnote 4, the document is referred to throughout
these Reporter's Notes as Model Standards (September 2005)).[4]

IV. Format of Model Standards
(September 2005)

General changes. The Joint Committee has recommended several significant
organizational format changes to the 1994 Version. The Joint Committee, with the
aid of sustained, thoughtful public comments, concluded that the 1994 Version
could be improved by adopting the following principles:

---

4. The Joint Committee formatted the first page of the Model Standards (September 2005) so as
to reflect an effective date. It agreed that the effective date would be that date on which, chronologically, the last of the three original participating organizations adopts the Model Standards.
The Joint Committee instructed its Reporter that, once an effective date was established, he should
revise the Reporter's Notes to change all references to "Model Standards (July 2005)" to reflect that
adoption date. As noted on the cover page for the Standards, the adoption dates by the respective organizations were: American Arbitration Association (September 8, 2005), the American
Bar Association House of Delegates (August 9, 2005), and the Association for Conflict Resolution
(August 22, 2005).

(1) separate the statement of the Standard's title from a statement of the Standard itself; (2) divide the statement of the Standard into enumerated paragraphs and sub-paragraphs, thereby facilitating clarity of exposition and public discussion of distinct, albeit related concepts; (3) eliminate the ambiguous status of the "hanging paragraphs" that follow the statement of the Standard itself by drafting the document so that all entries provide meaningful guidance for mediator conduct; (4) distinguish the level of guidance provided to the mediator by the targeted use of the verbs, "shall" and "should," thereby eliminating the need for the categorical distinction between the statement of the Standard and "Comments"; (5) shape the document so that the language of the Standards guides the mediator's conduct rather than the conduct of other mediation participants; and (6) shape the document to provide guidance for mediator conduct in situations when the operation of two or more Standards might conflict with one another.

While believing that the 1994 Version could be improved in these ways, the Joint Committee wants to state publicly its collective admiration and respect for the efforts of those individuals who crafted the 1994 Version. The quality of their work is confirmed in multiple ways, including the numbers of states that have adopted the 1994 Version to govern its court-annexed mediation programs and the number of textbooks that cite it in discussions of mediator ethics. As the Joint Committee considered using alternative phrases and words in various Standards and Comments, it routinely returned to admiring the insight contained in the original Standards. And perhaps most significantly, the Joint Committee, after canvassing multiple codes and standards operating in courts and programs, enthusiastically confirmed that the drafters of the 1994 Version had served the public elegantly by providing a comprehensive, useable document organized around nine Standards. The Joint Committee has retained that basic architecture throughout its revisions.

Changes in format to the Model of Standards of Conduct for Mediators.

The Joint Committee attempted to incorporate and implement the above-noted principles throughout its multiple drafts. In the first posted revision, the Model Standards (January 2004) embraced the principles of having a title for each Standard, stating the Standard in declarative sentences targeted exclusively at guiding mediator conduct, enumerating them in appropriately separated sentences, and distinguishing the type of mediator guidance offered by a Standard or Comment by the use of "shall" and "should" respectively. Second, in terms of format, the Model Standards (January 2004) used footnotes to try to provide several types of information:

a) a definition of relevant terms; (b) examples of how a particular Standard or comment might operate at cross purposes with another Standard in a particular setting; (c) general comments regarding the significance of particular Standards, using verbatim the language of the 1994 Version; and (d) clarification, by way of example, of new elements being added to the 1994 Version. Third, the Model Standards (January 2004) suggested that the Reporter's Notes would be an official source to summarize or clarify matters relevant to the statement of the Model Standards.

Public comments to the Model Standards (January 2004) applauded the Joint Committee's effort to organize crisply the statement of the Standard and the Comment section. However, many noted that the use of footnotes was problematic: format-wise, it instantly prompted a reader to assess what status to accord them: were they binding? Were they of the same significance as a statement of a Standard or Comment? And, in the final analysis, what would be their relationship to an expanded version of the Reporter's Notes? Further, given that one of the Joint Committee's guiding principles was that substantive changes to the 1994 Version would be made only if there were evidence that current practice or policies warranted such changes, some charged that the footnotes, even in combination with enriched Reporter's Notes, did not systematically deliver on that promise. Finally, several persons suggested that the content or statement of particular footnotes needed clarification.

The Joint Committee, in its deliberations during the April–August 2004 period, found persuasive the public comments that argued that the use of footnotes created complexity and confusion rather than clarity. Accordingly, the Model Standards (September 2004), with two exceptions, contained no footnotes; those exceptions addressed two topics that the Joint Committee thought important to reflect in the document itself: first, that no participating organization had yet to consider and adopt the Model Standards (September 2004); and second, that the use of the term "mediator" in the Standards was to be understood to apply to persons operating in a co-mediator model as well as to those working in a solo capacity. In eliminating the footnotes, however, the Joint Committee proposed having the Reporter's Notes serve as the legislative history regarding the development and application of the Model Standards of Conduct for Mediators. Accordingly, it directed its Reporter to format and prepare the Reporter's Notes so that the Notes contained a discussion of the following elements: the concerns and rationale the Joint Committee found persuasive for offering substantive changes to the 1994 Version; examples of application questions that the footnotes in the Model Standards (January 2004) were designed to address; and a recounting, at least in a general way, of the types of concerns and comments raised by public participants and the manner in which the Joint Committee addressed those comments in its current draft.

In response to public and organizational comments to the Model Standards (September 2004), the Committee made three significant changes in developing the December 2004 draft. First, in response to public concerns about there being multiple documents (i.e., the Model Standards and the Reporter Notes), the Joint Committee chose to develop a format for the Standards such that the document itself constituted a complete statement. The Joint Committee concluded that it would not try to integrate or weave the Reporter's Notes or any other commentary into the final statement of the Model Standards nor have the Reporter's Notes viewed as an independent but necessary component of the publication of the Standards for which formal adoption by participating organizations would be sought. Each Joint Committee member agrees, though, that these Reporter Notes accurately reflect the commentary, history and deliberations of the Revision process and hopes that they serve their intended educational role.

Second, the Joint Committee chose to eliminate organizationally the distinction between Standards and Comments, opting to address through clear language in each entry the precise guidance provided to a mediator.

Finally, the Joint Committee included explicit provisions directed to considerations of interpretative construction.

V. Analysis of Model of Standards of Conduct for Mediators (September 2005).

Preamble

The Model Standards (September 2005) amends the organizational format of the 1994 Version. It identifies an effective date for the adoption of the Standards by participating organizations, begins with a paragraph describing the historical context of the document and its revision, and substitutes a Preamble and Note on Construction for the "Introductory Note" and "Preface."

The Joint Committee determined that the Model Standards, to be most effective, must operate as a single, self-contained, defining document. As a result, while it noted that that the Reporter's Notes could serve a valuable educational function for the public regarding the rationale for various changes, the Joint Committee concluded that its prior consideration to have the Reporter's Notes serve an integral role as an interpretative resource for the Standards was misdirected. Further, the Joint Committee determined that the distinction between a statement of a "Standard" and the "Comments" relevant to that Standard was ultimately not helpful; although this distinction occurs in the 1994 Version and had been retained by the Joint Committee in both the Model Standards (January 2004) and Model Standards (September 2004), the Joint Committee decided that the fundamental difference for guiding mediator conduct contained in this categorical distinction was more effectively communicated in clear language for each entry. To promote clarity, the Model Standards (September 2005) contains a new section entitled Note on Construction with material that explains the level of mediator guidance provided by each entry. With these significant format changes, the Joint Committee believes the Model Standards (September 2005) can operate effectively as a self-contained document.

In the Preamble, the Model Standards (September 2005) revises the definition of mediation in order to make it consistent with changes in Standard I that recognize that party self-determination operates over not just voluntary decision-making as to outcomes but to multiple process components as well. Since the publication of the 1994 Version, there has been significant academic and policy discussion focused on mediation style or theory. In particular, the terms, facilitative and evaluative, to describe mediator orientations have taken on particular meanings in the popular literature and approaches to mediation differently conceptualized in such frameworks as problem-solving or transformative have been trenchantly analyzed. The revised definition of mediation is not designed to exclude any mediation style or approach consistent with Standard I's commitment to support and respect the parties' decision-making roles in the process.

Note on Construction

This section is designed to provide clarity to the interpretation and application of the Standards, both individually and collectively.

The Model Standards (September 2005) retain the 9-Standard architecture of the 1994 Version. The Note indicates that the Standards are to be read and construed in their entirety. The interpretative principle that mandates that each Standard be read and interpreted in such a manner as to promote consistency with all other Standards is the presumed operative principle guiding the drafting of the Model Standards (September 2005).

By eliminating the structural framework that led to using "shall" and "should" in the statement of the Standard and Comment respectively, the Joint Committee believed it important to define these terms, given the purposes and goals of these Standards. The definition of "shall" prescribes mandatory mediator conduct. The definition of "should," more sharply than conventional understanding might otherwise suggest, stipulates that the recommended guidance to a mediator, though not mandated, can be discarded only for compelling reasons. The combined message is clear: the Standards, in their various statements, provide strong guidance for mediator conduct; while not presuming to be a "rule-book" that anticipates and answers every possibility, the Standards provide meaningful guidance for most situations and the burden transfers to an individual mediator to justify a departure from its prescriptions.

While some sections of the Model Standards (September 2005), such as Standards III (A–F) and IV (B), make reference to a time frame for a mediation (using language such as "during and after a mediation,") the Note on Construction notes clearly that the Model Standards (September 2005) do not try to provide precise definitions for the beginning and ending of a mediation. The Joint Committee recognizes that such definitional precision might be important in some contexts, such as where court rules, statutes or other regulations govern a mediation; however, in other settings, the exact beginning or end of a mediation is not always clear, yet the Model Standards (September 2005) are designed to guide mediator conduct even in such contexts of ambiguity.

The Note explicitly addresses the fact that a mediator's conduct may be affected by applicable law, court rules, regulations, other applicable professional rules, mediation rules to which the parties have agreed, and agreement of the parties, some of which may conflict with and take precedence over compliance with these Standards. This topic is noted here for both format and substantive reasons. Organizationally, it became clumsy to represent this conflict throughout the document with such phrases as "unless otherwise required by law;" while that phrase has been used once in the statement of a provision of Standard V dealing with Confidentiality (a significantly law-regulated area of mediator activity), the Joint Committee believed it best to state this basic proposition at the beginning of the document so that it would operate as a presumed understanding throughout.

Substantively, the Joint Committee, in response to comments, believed it important to clarify for a mediator what posture he or she should adopt when confronted with such a conflict. The basic principle, while straightforward, requires elaboration. The principle that guides mediator conduct in such contexts is: in the event of a conflict between a provision of a Standard and one or more external sources identified in the Note, a mediator ought to conduct oneself in a manner that retains and remains faithful to as much of the spirit and intent of the affected Standard, and all other Standards, as is possible. The following example is illustrative: Assume that a court orders a party to mediation; one party's counsel telephones the mediator and states that neither the lawyer nor client plans to attend, believing any such session to be worthless for this case. The mediator reminds the attorney of the court directive; indeed, in some jurisdictions, since the mediator may even have a duty to report participant non-attendance to the referring court, the mediator may remind the attorney of that matter, too. Here is a conflict between a court rule and Standard I: a mediator cannot consistently adhere to the court rule and simultaneously honor the prescription in Standard I that a mediator conduct the mediation based on party self-determination with regard to "... participation in [a mediation.]" When a mediator in this situation recognizes that the court rule takes precedence over this provision of Standard I, a mediator still has an ethical responsibility to conduct that mediation in a manner consistent with all other aspects of Standard I — e.g., respecting and promoting self-determination with respect to process design and outcomes — as well as consistent with all other Standards. The current language of the penultimate paragraph reflects the Joint Committee's decision that a mediator must act in various practice contexts in a manner that retains and advances as much of the spirit and intent of the Standards as is possible.

The Joint Committee has consistently noted that the Standards can be used in multiple ways by individuals, programs, or organizations, including requiring compliance with these Standards as a condition for continuing membership in a program or organization. The Joint Committee, however, has added a final paragraph under Note to clarify for mediators that courts or other entities may use these Standards to establish the expected level of care for mediator conduct.

Standard I: Self-Determination

There are two significant changes proposed to the 1994 Version. First, the 1994 Version focuses exclusively on exercising self-determination with respect to outcome; it is silent with regard to such matters as mediator selection, designing procedural aspects of the mediation process to suit individual needs, and choosing whether to participate in or withdraw from the process. The Model Standards (September 2005) extends the scope of self-determination to these other areas.

Second, the 1994 Version does not address the question of the interplay among the Standards. In some instances, the interplay is consistent but the mediator must be cognizant of it. For example, while parties can exercise self-determination in the selection of their mediator, a mediator must consider Standard III: Conflicts of Interests and Standard IV: Competence when deciding whether to accept the invitation to serve. Alternatively, the interplay among Standards may result in a conflict; a mediator, for example, may feel pulled in conflicting directions when the mediator, duty-bound to support party self-determination (Standard I), recognizes that parties are trying to design a process that is not mediation but want to call it mediation to gain confidentiality protections, thereby undermining the mediator's obligation to sustain a quality process (Standard VI). Standard I(A)(1) and I(B) explicitly recognize this potential for conflict and indicates to the mediator that sustaining a quality process places limits on the extent to which party autonomy, external influences, and mediator self-interest should shape participant conduct.

Standard I (B) directly addresses the concern that mediators may undermine party self-determination or themselves experience conflicts of interest as a result of pressure or incentives generated by court personnel, program administrators, provider organizations, the media, or other outside influences. Many factors can operate this way, intended or not: for instance, a program administrator might suggest to one mediator that more cases shall be assigned to another mediator because that person "always gets a settlement," or a news media writer might report settlement talks as having stalled in a way that might possibly harm the reputation of the identified mediator. The result is that such pressures or influences prompt the mediator to engage in conduct to override party self-determination in an effort to gain resolution. The Joint Committee reaffirms the Comment in the 1994 Version on this point that the mediator's commitment to the parties and process must remain steadfast and a mediator must not coerce parties to settle; the language of the Model Standards (September 2005) has been sharpened to eliminate any ambiguity regarding that duty.

Several public comments raised concerns that the language of the 1994 Version stating, "Self-determination is the fundamental principle of mediation" had not been retained. The Joint Committee believes that the expanded statement of Standard I, together with the definition of mediation appearing in the Preamble, appropriately reaffirms the central responsibility that a mediator has to actively support party self-determination, prohibits conflict of interest issues from undermining a mediator's commitment to promoting party self-determination (I(B)), yet recognizes, as noted above, that Standards may conflict.

Other public comments suggested that the Standard should contain language that requires the mediator to make certain that the parties made informed decisions; given the significant controversy about whether and how a mediator might insure that a party's decisions are suitably informed, the Joint Committee reaffirmed retaining the language of the 1994 Version as I (B). Additionally, several public comments noted that parties can be effectively ordered to mediation by a judge, thereby rendering self-determination as to process irrelevant. The Joint Committee addresses this dynamic in the Preamble in its discussion of the potential conflict between the operation of the Model Standards (September 2005) and other sources that might govern an individual mediator's conduct. Finally, some public comments suggested that Standard I should contain guidance to a mediator regarding his or her duty to report "good faith" participation by various mediation participants. To the degree that might be required by other rules governing mediator behavior in a particular setting, the Joint Committee addresses this topic in the Note on Construction's statement regarding potential conflicts. However, in Standard V (A) (2) on confidentiality, the Joint Committee explicitly supports the position widely adopted in practice and program rules that a mediator can override confidentiality, if required, for only two purposes: to report whether parties appeared at a scheduled mediation or to report whether the parties reached a resolution; the Joint Committee rejected overriding the confidentiality requirement for any other purpose.

Standard II: Impartiality

The Joint Committee believes that several developments of the past decade's growth in mediation practice warrant changes to the 1994 Version of Standard II. First, with the expanded growth of private sector mediation practices, the range of business practices and practices regarding fees raises concerns about the mediator being perceived as partial. Second, with the remarkable diversity of participants in mediation, challenges have arisen with regard to sustaining a mediator's impartiality while simultaneously respecting practices grounded in different cultures.

The Model Standards (September 2005) addresses these concerns in the following way. In Standard II (A), the Joint Committee reaffirms the central role of the need for a mediator to be impartial; disclosure of potential conflicts of interests, and parties choosing to proceed following such disclosure, is a separate consideration addressed in Standard III.

Second, the propriety and impact of fee arrangements, including success fees or practices involving unequal payment of the mediator's fee by the parties, affects several Standards; the Joint Committee chose to address these matters in Standard VIII: Fees and Other Charges.

In response to insightful public comment, the Joint Committee revised the language of what is now Standard II (B)(1) to reflect that the mediator must not act in a manner that favors or prejudices any mediation participant based on the personal characteristics, background, values and beliefs, or performance at a mediation of that individual; the proscription governs the mediator's conduct towards any participant, not just the parties. While the Standard delineates recognizable elements that operate to undermine mediator impartiality, the list is not exhaustive. Additionally, the Joint Committee decided to strengthen the 1994 Version by shaping the Standards both to guide the conduct of mediators rather than other mediation participants and to provide guidance for mediator conduct through the defined use of "shall" and "should"; by so doing, the Joint Committee agreed that the phrase, "should guard against," that is used in the 1994 Version in this section was not consistent with such changes.

Some public comments urged the Joint Committee to adopt language that required the mediator, when his or her ability to remain impartial was undermined, to withdraw from the mediation "without harming any party's interests." Individual members of the Joint Committee questioned whether withdrawal without harm to at least some interests of one or more parties is always possible, even though all agreed that the duty to withdraw in these circumstances is clear. The Joint Committee believes that the manner of withdrawal is a matter of "best practices"; further, throughout the Standards, the Joint Committee has declined to insert language that requires a mediator to insure a particular outcome.

Finally, potential challenges to a mediator's impartiality in private sector practice arise with remarkable frequency. For example, if all parties, their representatives and the mediator are immersed in discussions in an all-day mediation and they decide to order food for lunch, does the mediator violate Standard II if the lawyer for one of the parties offers to pay for everyone's lunch? If a mediator accepts a small gift from a grateful party following a successful mediation, must the mediator return it on pain of violating the impartiality requirement? And these matters become more complex when practices grounded in cultural traditions surface: if the cultural tradition of one party prompts that individual to bring a ceremonial gift to the mediator in order to reaffirm the seriousness of the talks and the well-wishes that the talks proceed constructively, can the mediator accept it? The Joint Committee supports the individual mediator, whether in a private practice setting or government or organizational program setting, responding sensitively and comfortably to such contemporary practices, but with the caveat that all such conduct be grounded in a sincere assessment as to whether accepting such benefits or giving such gifts will raise questions as to that mediator's actual or perceived impartiality; by using the term "de minimis gifts or incidental items," the Standard signals to the practicing mediator that the threshold for questioning whether a mediator is no longer impartial for these types of matters is low.

There were several public comments expressing concern that the following language from the 1994 Version's Comment Section of Standard II had not been retained in the posted Model Standards (January 2004):

> "When mediators are appointed by a court or institution, the appointing agency shall make reasonable efforts to ensure that mediators serve impartially."

Comparable comments were received regarding the role of program administrators in government or organizational mediation programs. The Joint Committee appreciates the conviction expressed by program administrators operating in court or other institutional settings that the cited language serves a critically important role in assisting program administrators to advance quality mediation practice. However, one goal of the Model Standards (September 2005) is to have all language focus sharply and exclusively on guiding mediator conduct; for that reason, the Joint Committee has consistently resisted suggestions that it develop language that recognized and extended coverage of the Standards to administrators of mediation programs in court, administrative and organizational contexts. That is not to suggest, however, that the Standards will not influence the conduct of these other participants, indirectly or directly; for instance, the Joint Committee explicitly addresses the concerns raised by these comments in Standard I (B): Self-Determination where the language of the Standard reinforces the mediator's duty to the parties and process when responding to pressure being exerted by such outside influences as court personnel or provider organizations.

Standard III: Conflicts of Interest

Standard III (A) defines a conflict of interest as a dealing or relationship that undermines a mediator's impartiality; while Standard II and III are explicitly connected in a fundamental manner, the Joint Committee felt it important to retain the distinction in order to emphasize that a mediator's impartiality is central to the mediation process and that mediator conduct that raises questions of conflicts of interest serves to undermine public or party confidence in the central integrity of the process.

Standard III (A) notes that a conflict of interest can arise from multiple sources in multiple time dimensions. A mediator must canvass this extensive range of possible disqualifying activities, attuned to the notion that his or her immediate duty is to disclose information that might create a possible conflict of interest; if parties, with knowledge of the relationship, consent to that mediator's service, then the mediator, pursuant to Standard I, could proceed. However, the Model Standards (September 2005) retains content and language of the 1994 Version that notes that if the conflict of interest casts serious doubts on process integrity, then the mediator shall decline to proceed despite the preferences of the parties.

Public comment requested clarification of the interplay between such sections as Standard III (C) or III (D) with Standard II (C): Impartiality. As is referenced in the Reporter's Notes in Note on Construction, the interpretative principle mandates that each Standard be read in a manner that promotes consistency. Applying that principle, in Standard II (C), the Joint Committee supports the posture that a mediator shall not conduct a mediation if he or she is unable to conduct it in an impartial manner; even if participants, under Standard III (C) or III (D) gave consent to the mediator to proceed after a mediator disclosed an actual or potential conflict of interest, Standard II (C) prohibits the mediator from proceeding.

Some Committee members were disturbed to hear reported that a common practice among some mediators is for the mediator not to disclose with all mediation

parties and their representatives that the mediator has served previously as a mediator in situations involving some of the mediation parties or their representatives; the
language of III (A) seriously questions the integrity of such a practice.

Standard III (B) explicitly acknowledges that how one conducts a conflicts check
varies by practice context. For a complex case that comes to a mediator through
his or her law firm, best practice consists of making a firm-wide conflicts check at
the pre-mediation phase. By contrast, for a mediator of an interpersonal dispute
administered by a community mediation agency who is charged with mediating
the case immediately upon referral, making an inquiry of the parties and participants at the time of the mediation regarding potential conflicts of interest may be
sufficient.

In drafting Standard III (C), public comments highlighted one particular
source of potential conflict as being that situation in which a significant portion
of a mediator's work, particularly when compensated, comes from a single source;
these commentators suggested that that situation be explicitly addressed. The Joint
Committee, as individuals, agreed that such a situation creates a serious potential conflict and that there would be a duty minimally to disclose that situation.
However, as other public comments noted, there are multiple examples of relationships between one party and a mediator that give rise to the same concern about
conflicts of interest; if one attempted to catalogue a comprehensive list, then failure (through oversight) to include some relationship might be seen, incorrectly,
to license that conduct. Therefore, the Joint Committee developed language of a
general nature.

In performing the mediator's role, an individual displays multiple analytical and
interpersonal skills; therefore, it is not surprising that a mediation participant who
witnesses such talent might consider employing that mediator again. If a mediation
participant, be it a party, party representative, witness or some other participant
wants to employ the individual mediator in a subsequent mediation, or in another
role (such as a personal lawyer, therapist, or a consultant to their business), then the
individual serving as mediator must make certain that entering into such a new
relationship does not cast doubt about the integrity of the mediation process. The
Model Standards (January 2004) contained an explicit enumeration (Paragraph C)
that prohibited a mediator from soliciting any type of future professional services;
in response to public comments critical of the broad, absolutist language of that
paragraph, the Joint Committee deleted that provision in the Model Standards (September 2004) and revised the language of what was then Comment 3 to address this
matter. The final language appears in Model Standards (September 2005) as Standard III (F). Unlike some other Codes, Standard III (F) does not impose rigid time
lines to regulate the development of such relationships but does suggest that the
amount of time that has elapsed is a factor to consider.

Standard IV: Competence

Mediators operate in many contexts and reflect a broad range of backgrounds, trainings, and competencies. The Model Standards (September 2005) retains the commitment expressed in the 1994 Version that the Standards not create artificial or arbitrary barriers to serve the public as a mediator. But to promote public confidence in the integrity and usefulness of the process and to protect the members of the public, an individual representing himself or herself as a mediator must be committed to serving only in those situations for which he or she possesses the basic competency to assist.

The Joint Committee, Standard IV (A), changes the language of the 1994 Version to use the term, "competence" in place of "qualification." In elaborating on IV (A), Standard IV (A) (1) indicates that such elements as training, experience in mediation, and cultural understandings are often necessary in order to provide effective service. But the Joint Committee understands its language to explicitly reject two notions with regard to the operations of this Standard: first, that possessing particular educational degrees is an absolute requirement to establish mediator competency, and second, that the list of desirable competencies means that each competency is required for effective service in every mediation.

Standard IV (B) recognizes the situation in which a mediator, upon agreeing to serve, learns during the course of the discussions that the matters are more complex than originally anticipated and beyond his or her competency. In such a situation, Standard IV (B) imposes a duty on that mediator to take affirmative steps with the parties to address the situation and make appropriate arrangements for serving them (perhaps through hiring co-mediators with relevant competencies or the selection of an alternative mediator).

Public comments on the Model Standards (January 2004) strongly supported language that reaffirmed, as a central feature of Standard IV, that training and experience are the necessary and sufficient conditions for service as a mediator. The Joint Committee believes that its current language reflects that commitment and that it appropriately appears in Standard IV (A) (1). The Joint Committee also wanted to emphasize that mediator competency also includes cultural understandings, a dimension that the 1994 Version does not address. Additional public comments suggested that the language of the Standards include reference to an individual's meeting the qualification requirements set forth by relevant state statutes; the Joint Committee believed that its statements in the Note on Construction regarding the relationship between the Standards and state law addressed this matter, together with its Preamble statement that the Standards are considered as fundamental ethical guidelines; particular programs or practice areas might require additional elements for service.

Standard IV (C) mandates that a mediator not conduct the mediation if she or he is impaired by drugs, alcohol, medication or otherwise. If a mediator has the ability to correct this impairment, then she or he can initiate or continue service.

Standard V: Confidentiality

One of the most significant developments surrounding the practice of mediation that has occurred since the adoption of the 1994 Version has been the development of the Uniform Mediation Act (2003). That undertaking significantly enhanced professional conversation and awareness of the policy goals advanced by the presumption that parties should determine their own rules regarding confidentiality and that communications made for purposes of advancing a mediation conversation should not be available for use in subsequent proceedings. Discussion and debate surrounding that uniform law focused significantly on whether the parties and the mediator or just the parties should hold the privilege independently, and what exceptions to the privilege should be made a part of law. While this Standard is consistent with the confidentiality policy goals of the Uniform Mediation Act, it is not designed to match its substantive provisions and nuances in every dimension.

Standard V directs mediator conduct in two ways. First, it imposes a duty on the mediator not to share with others information obtained as a result of serving as a mediator. Even if the parties agree that the mediator shall disclose it (pursuant to Standard I (A)), Standard V (A) (1) states that the mediator may do so but is not required to do so. Second, Standard V imposes a duty on the mediator to promote participant understanding of the extent to which information shared and comments made for purposes of mediation are confidential. What is crucial to the effective operation of the Standard — and hence to the integrity of the process — is that all participants to the mediation, including the mediator, actively seek to understand the nature and extent of the confidential status of communications made during the mediation. The current language promotes that goal.

Some public comments to prior versions urged the Joint Committee to adopt language that explicitly linked or tracked the Standard to the requirements of state or Federal law; as noted above in a related matter, the Joint Committee placed references in the Note on Construction to the interplay between the Standards and relevant legal guidelines, in part to enhance the fluidity of the language of the Standards and in some measure to resist a perceived tendency to over regulate mediation practice. The Model Standards (September 2005) retains, in both V (A) and V (A) (2), references to recognized exceptions to the confidentiality reach.

Standard V(A)(3) tracks the concept of the 1994 Version in which its drafters sought to insure that the Confidentiality Standard did not prohibit monitoring, research, evaluation or education of mediation by responsible persons. However, since the language of the Standards is targeted to guide mediator conduct, the language of the 1994 Version required modification. Further, when reflecting on the nature of how the teaching, research and evaluation of mediation could appropriately go forward, the Joint Committee thought it appropriate to adopt a two-fold goal: first, protect the identity of individual participants, so that a mediator participating in teaching, research and evaluation could discuss aspects of the case but doing so in a way that does not readily enable people to discern the identities of the parties; second, to permit teaching, research and evaluation to proceed without imposing undue requirements for gaining party consent to every initiative — for example, if a court system sought to evaluate its mediation program, it would be an undue requirement to insist that the evaluator affirmatively obtain from every party or party representative to a mediation his or her consent to have reported such elements as the length of a mediation session.

Some public comments suggested that a mediator, when conducting a caucus, can appropriately place the responsibility on the party with whom she or he is caucusing to flag each element of information that the party wishes the mediator to keep confidential. In Standard V (B), the Joint Committee rejects that approach to the degree that it is not consistent with securing meaningful and timely party consent. At a practice level, the Joint Committee notes that some mediators advise the participants that the mediator will keep confidential those matters disclosed by a participant if the participant so requests; otherwise, the mediator shall treat comments made in the caucus as being ones that he or she could use in subsequent caucuses if doing so, in the mediator's judgment, would help advance discussion. By contrast, the practice of other mediators when conducting a caucus is to advise the participants that a mediator will treat all matters shared with him or her as confidential but shall ask at the end of a particular caucus whether the mediator has the participant's consent to use any or all of that developed information in subsequent caucuses. Whichever practice is adopted by a mediator, Standard V (B) affirms that it is a mediator's duty to insure that party consent to the approach is known, meaningful and timely.

Standard V (C) targets a mediator's responsibility to make certain that the parties understand the extent to which they, not the mediator, will maintain confidentiality of information that surface in mediation. Section V (D) is a provision that applies equally to V (A–C); while some might believe it implicit in each of the preceding paragraphs of the Standards, the Joint Committee thought it important to emphasize, even if somewhat redundant, the need for participant understanding of the confidentiality guidelines governing the conversation.

Standard VI: Quality of the Process

The 1994 Version sets forth in the statement of the Standard and in its "hanging paragraph" a series of distinct, concrete ways in which a mediator could act to advance a quality process. The Model Standards (September 2005) captures those elements in its statement of VI(A), incorporating from public comment a revision that requires a mediator to conduct a process that advances procedural fairness, not, as in the Model Standards (January 2004), "process fairness."

Public comments to both the Model Standards (January 2004) and the Model Standards (September 2004), combined with further Joint Committee discussion, resulted in several changes reflected in the Model Standards (September 2005). In summary form, those changes include:

1. Comment 1 from the Model Standards (January 2004) read as follows: "A mediator should conduct mediation in a way that prevents one or more parties from manipulating the process to advance personal goals that are inconsistent with mediation principles and values." That comment has been deleted for two reasons: first, the Model Standards (September 2005) focus on guiding mediator behavior and not that of other participants in the mediation process; second, the Model Standards (September 2005) capture the goal of preventing such participant behavior in provisions such as VI (A) (6).

2. Standard VI (A) (1–9) is sequenced to reflect the presumptive order in which a mediator might confront these considerations in practice.

3. Standard VI (A) (4) reflects the nuanced environment in which mediation occurs. The language of Standard VI(A)(4) prohibits a mediator from knowingly misrepresenting a material fact or circumstance to a mediation participant while it acknowledges that resolving matters in mediation is not always predicated on there having been complete honesty and candor among those present. To state the matter differently, while mediation participants might engage in negotiating tactics such as bluffing or exaggerating that are designed to deceive other parties as to their acceptable positions, a mediator must not knowingly misrepresent a material fact or circumstance in order to advance settlement discussions.

4. Standard VI (A) (5–8) reflects an effort to reorganize and distinguish more sharply among related but importantly different directions to the mediator. VI (A)(5) announces that the mediator's role differs substantially from that of other professional roles; the goal is to distinguish between a mediator's role and such other roles as being a lawyer, mental health counselor, and the like. Yet, (A)(5) also recognizes that the insights and training the mediator draws upon to assist parties in mediation might simultaneously constitute an important element of enabling a mediator to be competent and effective to serve the parties in that setting and be drawn from the mediator's training and experience in those other professional roles. So, the language of VI (A) (5) recognizes the differing roles that a mediator as an individual assumes in his or her life and then supports the mediator sharing information that he or she is qualified by training or experience to provide only if it is done in a manner consistent with other Standards, most notably promoting party self-determination and sustaining mediator impartiality.

Standard VI (A) (6) makes it explicit that a mediator cannot engage in a ruse of labeling a dispute resolution process as "mediation" in order to gain its benefits (such as confidentiality protections) when it is apparent that the participants have designed and participated in some other form of dispute resolution. (A)(7), as a stand-alone entry, notes that it certainly is plausible for a mediator to recommend, when appropriate, that the parties consider resolving their dispute through some other third-party process. This guideline makes at least two presumptions: first, that a mediator might identify such an option when it seems an appropriate track to pursue as a matter of process choice (i.e. "fitting the forum to the fuss") or after mediation efforts to resolve the issue(s) have not been successful in resolving all issues to each party's satisfaction; and second, that the mediator is qualified by training or experience to explain to the parties, if requested, how these various processes operate. Finally, (A) (8) clarifies that a mediator shall not undertake in the same matter that he or she is mediating a different intervener role (such as those described in (A)(7)) without party consent, without explaining to the parties and their representatives the implications of changing processes (e.g. a third-party decision-maker might have to make decisions regarding participant credibility that was not necessary in a mediation process), and without being cognizant that undertaking a new role might be governed by standards governing other third-party professions, such as a Code of Ethics for Arbitrators.

5. Standard VI (A)(9) reflects revised language to the 1994 Version by targeting guidance to the mediator more sharply: it guides a mediator who confronts mediation participants using mediation to further criminal conduct, not simply illegal conduct, to take appropriate steps to deter them from accomplishing that goal. Several public comments suggested that the mediator's duty in such a situation was to affirmatively report such conduct to appropriate legal authorities. The Joint Committee rejected that suggestion for two reasons. First,, the subtly of such matters—including there being multi-issue cases in which only one issue raised a specter of criminal conduct—requires that a mediator be firm but flexible in addressing such a situation; second, confidentiality laws or agreements may prevent it, such that unless there were an exception in the confidentiality agreement for this situation or a mediator had a duty to report such conduct, a mediator might expose himself or herself to liability by reporting such conduct.

6. Standard VI (A) (10) reflects new language that addresses the situation involving a mediator's obligation when conducting a mediation with persons with recognized disabilities. The Joint Committee recognizes that the language of Comment 8 in its Model Standards (January 2004), while included by oversight but actually reflecting the language contained in the 1994 Version, was completely unacceptable. Public comments thoughtfully suggested a variety of possible clauses to address this situation; Comment 8 in the Model Standards (September 2004) reflected the Joint Committee's judgment as to the best expression of the multiple commitments involved in such a situation and it received positive endorsement from several public stakeholders. That September language remains unchanged and appears as (A) (10).

7. The Joint Committee believes that developments in practice regarding the mediation of cases in which allegations of domestic abuse arise must be addressed in any revision to the 1994 Version. Public comments strongly endorsed amending the 1994 Version to address this topic and

Standard VI (B) reflects that effort. The Joint Committee understands the term, "domestic abuse," to apply to acts of both physical violence and psychological coercion among persons in a domestic relationship. Standard VI (B) also provides guidance to mediators for situations in which mediation participants in non-domestic relationships have engaged in acts of violence towards one another. Mediator guidance for addressing challenges posed by the threat of violent conduct among participants is reinforced through such other provisions as Standards I and VI (A).

Some public comments suggested that any provision targeted at mediations involving domestic abuse should contain a detailed prescription regarding the manner in which the mediator should screen participants, the requisite training to serve as a mediator in such situations, the requirement to report such matters to appropriate agencies if one is a mandatory reporter, and the like; the Joint Committee chose to retain the targeted, albeit general language of VI (B), with the notion that Standards for particular programs might choose to build in more elaborate requirements.

Standard VII: Advertising and Solicitation

With increased private sector activity in the provision of mediation services, the Joint Committee believed that the 1994 Version required modest amendment to provide guidance to mediators in a more complex, technological world. The language of Standard VII (A) addresses the complexity that confronts a mediator who seeks to communicate effectively the nature of his or her services as a mediator and his or her expertise without making representations that are inconsistent with such principles as party self-determination and mediator impartiality. Standard VII (A) (1) reaffirms the 1994 Version's commitment that a mediator must not include any promise as to outcome.

Standard VII (A) (2) addresses the concern that a mediator representing to the public that he or she is a "certified" mediator might be misunderstood by the public as suggesting that the mediator has met a more stringent level of selectivity than is otherwise the case. The 1994 Version addresses this challenge as well. Some governmental entities, including courts or administrative agencies, and private sector organizations have developed, publicized procedures through which an individual mediator can obtain status as having been "certified" to be on that entity's mediator roster. If a person has been granted that status by a governmental entity or private organization, then he or she is free to so advertise it. The Joint Committee notes, however, that it would mislead the public — and be prohibited by VII (A)(2) — were an individual to complete a privately-offered mediator training program, receive a

"Certificate" that states that he or she has successfully completed that course, and then advertise that he or she is a "Certified" mediator.

Standard VII (B) addresses the increasing challenge of blending appropriate communication and marketing of a mediator's services without soliciting business in a manner that results in compromising that individual's actual or perceived impartiality, and VII(C) prohibits a mediator from listing the names of clients or persons served in mediation without their permission.

Standard VIII: Fees and Other Charges

The Model Standards (September 2005) amends the title of this Standard from the 1994 Version by adding the words, "and other Charges."

Several developments have prompted amendments to the 1994 Version. The language of VIII (A) and VIII (A) (1) provide guidance to a mediator regarding basic principles on which to construct a fee; the language of VIII (B), while not prohibiting the amount a person might charge for his or her mediation services, does mandate that the method or structure for fee payments cannot operate at cross purposes with such fundamental values of the mediation process as party self-determination or mediator impartiality.

Some scholars and practitioners have urged members of the "mediation field" to carefully examine the relationship between mediator fees and mediated outcomes. Recognizing that there remains significant controversy about whether or how success or contingent fees might operate consistently with other Standards, the Joint Committee, in Standard VIII (B)(1), retained the language of the 1994 Version regarding these matters.

A significant, controversial practice that has developed in private sector mediation practice during the past decade is the situation in which the mediator's fee is paid in unequal amounts by the parties. The presumptive norm had been that parties pay the mediator's fees in equal amounts, thereby insuring that the mediator's impartiality, both in perception and reality, was secured. The reality of contemporary practice in some sectors is that one party pays the entire fee and that all parties are comfortable with that arrangement. This practice occurs routinely in such areas as the mediation of employment discrimination lawsuits, where the defendant employer pays the mediator's fee, personal injury litigation, and the like. Some argue that parties would not have access to the benefits of mediation if such fee payment arrangements were not available.

The Joint Committee believed that, at the practical level, this practice of parties' paying unequal amounts of the mediator's fee creates the danger of undermining process integrity in two important ways: first, if the parties were not aware of this arrangement, one party, upon learning of it at a later date, might believe the outcomes had been skewed in favor of the party who had paid the higher percentage of the mediator's fee; second, if the payer of the higher fee percentage is that mediator's

primary or exclusive client, the practice might create the impression that the mediator's financial interest in servicing that client outweighed his or her commitment
to conducting a quality process in an impartial manner. For both situations, the
Joint Committee believed that the appropriate stance of the Standard should, in
the first instance, support disclosure of the arrangement to all participants, since
unequal payments of fees almost always creates a perception of partiality; further,
the Standard should require the mediator to be attentive to how that practice, even
when acceptable to all parties, impacts the integrity of the process. Standard VIII
(B) addresses these concerns.

The Model Standards (September 2005) eliminates the proposed language of
the Model Standards (January 2004) regarding excepting administrative fees from
the concept of referral fees; public comment raised important questions about the
meaning of "administrative expense" and the Joint Committee refocused its comments to address the mediator, not provider agencies or other program sponsors.

Standard IX: Advancement of Mediation Practice

The Model Standards (September 2005) changes the title of this Standard from
the 1994 Version, replacing "Obligations to the Process" with "Advancement of
Mediation Practice." The Joint Committee believes the proposed title more accurately reflects the Standard's intended focus.

Standard IX (A) (1–5) delineates some of the ways in which an individual can participate in advancing mediation practice. Given the targeted definitions provided
to the terms "shall" and "should" in the Model Standards (September 2005), and
consistent with public suggestions, the Joint Committee uses the term, "should,"
in the statement of Standard IX. The Joint Committee does not believe the delineated list of activities for advancing the practice of mediation is exhaustive nor that
a mediator need engage in all of these initiatives all the time; the second sentence of
Standard IX (A) reflects that judgment. Finally, the Joint Committee embraced as
persuasive the thoughtful public comments that recommended that the language of
Standard IX (B) substitute the word "respect" for "tolerate."

Joseph B. Stulberg, JD, Ph.D.
Reporter
Professor of Law
Moritz College of Law, The Ohio State University Columbus, Ohio

Membership of Joint Committee for the Model Standards of Conduct for Mediators
(July 29, 2005)

Sharon B. Press, Attorney/Mediator
Director, Florida Dispute Resolution Center
Adjunct Professor, Florida State University College of Law Tallahassee, Florida

R. Wayne Thorpe Mediator/Arbitrator
JAMS Atlanta Office Director Atlanta, Georgia

Eric P. Tuchmann
General Counsel
American Arbitration Association New York, New York

Terrence T. Wheeler
Attorney/Mediator
Artz & Dewhirst, LLP
Adjunct Professor, Capital University Law School
Co-Director, Center for Dispute Resolution at CULS
Columbus, Ohio

John H. Wilkinson
Attorney/Mediator
Fulton, Rowe & Hart
New York, New York

Susan M. Yates
Mediator
Executive Director
Center for Analysis of Alternative Dispute Resolution Systems
Chicago, Illinois

Appendix C

Florida Rules for Certified and Court-Appointed Mediators

Part III Mediation Certification and Applications Discipline

Rule 10.700 Scope and Purpose

These rules apply to all proceedings before investigatory committees and adjudicatory panels of the Mediator Qualifications and Discipline Review Board (MQDRB) involving applications for certification or discipline of certified and court-appointed mediators. The purpose of these rules is to provide a means for enforcing the Florida Rules for Certified and Court-Appointed Mediators (Rules).

Rule 10.710 Privilege to Mediate

The privilege to mediate as a certified or court-appointed mediator is conditional, confers no vested right, and is revocable for cause.

Rule 10.720 Definitions

(a) Applicant. A new applicant with no previous certifications, an applicant for renewal of a current certification, an applicant for additional certifications, and an applicant for reinstatement of certification.

(b) Court-Appointed. Being appointed by the court or selected by the parties as the mediator in a court-ordered mediation.

(c) Division. One of the standing divisions of the MQDRB established on a regional basis.

(d) DRC or Center. The Florida Dispute Resolution Center of the Office of the State Courts Administrator.

(e) File. To deliver to the office of the Florida Dispute Resolution Center of the Office of the State Courts Administrator pleadings, motions, instruments, and other papers for preservation and reference.

(f) Good Moral Character Inquiry. A process which is initiated based on information which comes to the attention of the DRC relating to the good moral character of a certified or court-appointed mediator or applicant for certification.

(g) Investigator. A certified mediator, lawyer, or other qualified individual retained by the DRC at the direction of a RVCC or a QIC to conduct an investigation.

(h) MQDRB or Board. The Mediator Qualifications and Discipline Review Board.

(i) Panel. Five members of the MQDRB selected by the DRC by rotation to adjudicate the formal charges associated with a rule violation or a good moral character complaint, selected from the division in which the complaint arose unless, in the discretion of the DRC Director, there is good reason to choose members from 1 of the other divisions.

(j) Panel Adviser. A member of The Florida Bar retained by the DRC to assist a panel in performing its functions during a hearing. A panel adviser provides procedural advice only, is in attendance at the hearing, is not part of the panel's private deliberations, but may sit in on deliberations in order to answer procedural questions and is authorized to draft the decision and opinion of the panel for approval by the full panel and execution by the Chair.

(k) Prosecutor. A member of The Florida Bar in good standing retained by the DRC to prosecute a complaint before a hearing panel. The Prosecutor is authorized to perform additional investigation in order to prepare the case, negotiate a consent to charges and an agreement to the imposition of sanctions to be presented to the panel prior to the hearing, and to fully prosecute the case, including any post hearing proceedings.

(l) Qualifications Inquiry Committee or QIC. Four members of the MQDRB, no more than 1 from each division, selected by the DRC by rotation to serve for a 1-year period to conduct investigations and disposition of any good moral character inquiry for any applicant.

(m) Rule Violation Complaint. Formal submission of alleged violation(s) of the Florida Rules for Certified and Court-Appointed Mediators. A complaint may originate from any person or from the DRC.

(n) Rule Violation Complaint Committee or RVCC. Three members of the MQDRB selected by the DRC by rotation to conduct the investigation and disposition of any rule violation complaint.

Rule 10.730 Mediator Qualifications and Discipline Review Board

(a) Generally. The Mediator Qualifications and Discipline Review Board (MQDRB) shall be composed of 4 standing divisions that shall be located in the following regions:

> (1) Northern: encompassing the First, Second, Third, Fourth, Eighth, and Fourteenth judicial circuits;
>
> (2) Central: encompassing the Fifth, Seventh, Ninth, Tenth, Eighteenth and Nineteenth judicial circuits;

(3) Southeast: encompassing the Eleventh, Fifteenth, Sixteenth, and Seventeenth judicial circuits; and

(4) Southwest: encompassing the Sixth, Twelfth, Thirteenth, and Twentieth judicial circuits.

Other divisions may be formed by the Supreme Court of Florida based on need.

(b) Composition of Divisions. Each division of the MQDRB shall be composed of:

(1) Judges: three circuit, county, or appellate judges;

(2) County Mediators: three certified county mediators;

(3) Circuit Mediators: three certified circuit court mediators;

(4) Family Mediators: three certified family mediators, at least 2 of whom shall be non-lawyers;

(5) Dependency Mediators: not less than 1 nor more than 3 certified dependency mediators, at least 1 of whom shall be a non-lawyer;

(6) Appellate Mediators: not less than 1 nor more than 3 certified appellate mediators; and

(7) Attorneys: three attorneys who are currently or were previously licensed to practice law in Florida for at least 3 years who have or had a substantial trial or appellate practice and are neither certified as mediators nor judicial officers during their terms of service on the MQDRB but who have a knowledge of and experience with mediation practice, statutes, and rules, at least 1 of whom shall have a substantial family law practice.

(c) Appointment and Term. Eligible persons shall be appointed to the MQDRB by the chief justice of the Supreme Court of Florida for a period of 4 years. The terms of the MQDRB members shall be staggered. No member of the MQDRB shall serve more than 3 consecutive terms. The term of any member serving on a committee or panel may continue until the final disposition of their service on a case.

(d) Rule Violation Complaint Committee (RVCC). Each RVCC shall be composed of 3 members of the MQDRB selected by the DRC on a rotation basis. To the extent possible, members of a RVCC shall be selected from the division in which the alleged violation occurred. RVCCs are assigned to a single case; however they may be assigned to related cases to be disposed of collectively as is deemed appropriate by the DRC Director. A RVCC shall cease to exist after the disposition of the case(s) to which they are assigned. Each RVCC shall be composed of:

(1) one judge or attorney, who shall act as the chair of the committee;

(2) one mediator, who is certified in the area to which the complaint refers; and

(3) one other certified mediator.

(e) Qualifications Inquiry Committee (QIC). Each QIC shall be composed of 4 members, 1 from each of the 4 divisions of the MQDRB, selected by the DRC on a rotation basis to serve for a period of 1 year or until completion of all assigned cases, whichever occurs later. The QIC shall be composed of:

   (1) one judge or attorney, who shall act as the chair of the committee; and

   (2) three certified mediators.

   (f) Panels. Each panel shall be composed of 5 members of the MQDRB selected by the DRC on a rotation basis. To the extent possible, members shall be selected from the division in which the alleged violation occurred or, in the case of a good moral character inquiry, from the division based on the Florida address of the subject of the inquiry. Panels are assigned to a single case; however, they may be assigned to related cases to be disposed of collectively as is deemed appropriate by the DRC Director. A panel shall cease to exist after disposing of all cases to which it is assigned. Each panel shall be composed of:

   (1) one judge, who shall serve as the chair;

   (2) three certified mediators, at least 1 of whom shall be certified in the area to which the complaint or inquiry refers; and

   (3) one attorney who shall serve as vice-chair. The vice-chair shall act as the chair of the panel in the event of the unavailability of the chair.

   (g) Decision making. For all RVCCs, QICs, and panels, while unanimity is the preferred method of decision making, a majority vote shall rule.

Committee Notes

2000 Revision. In relation to (b)(5), the Committee believes that the chief justice should have discretion in the number of dependency mediators appointed to the board depending on the number of certified dependency mediators available for appointment. It is the intention of the Committee that when dependency mediation reaches a comparable level of activity to the other 3 areas of certification, the full complement of 3 representatives per division should be realized.

Rule 10.740 Jurisdiction and Powers

   (a) RVCC. Each RVCC shall have such jurisdiction and powers as are necessary to conduct the proper and speedy investigation and disposition of any complaint. The judge or attorney chairing the RVCC shall have the power to compel:

   (1) attendance of any person at a RVCC proceeding;

   (2) statements, testimony, and depositions of any person; and

   (3) production of documents, records, and other evidence.

The RVCC shall perform its investigatory function and have concomitant power to resolve cases prior to panel referral.

   (b) QIC. The QIC shall have such jurisdiction and powers as are necessary to conduct the proper and speedy investigation and disposition of: any good moral character inquiry pursuant to rule 10.800; petitions for reinstatement; or other matters referred by the DRC. The judge or attorney chairing the QIC shall have the power to compel:

(1) attendance of any person at a QIC proceeding;

(2) statements, testimony, and depositions of any person; and

(3) production of documents, records, and other evidence.

The QIC shall perform its investigatory function and have concomitant power to resolve cases prior to panel referral.

(c) Panel. Each panel shall have such jurisdiction and powers as are necessary to conduct the proper and speedy adjudication and disposition of any proceeding before it. The panel shall perform the adjudicatory function, but shall not have any investigatory functions.

(d) Panel Chair. The chair of a panel shall have the power to:

(1) compel the attendance of witnesses;

(2) issue subpoenas to compel the depositions of witnesses;

(3) order the production of records or other documentary evidence;

(4) hold anyone in contempt prior to and during the hearing;

(5) implement procedures during the hearing;

(6) determine admissibility of evidence; and

(7) decide motions prior to or during the hearing.

The vice-chair of a panel, upon the unavailability of the chair, is authorized only to issue subpoenas or order the production of records or other documentary evidence.

(e) Contempt/Disqualification Judge. One MQDRB judge member from each division shall be designated by the DRC, to serve for a term of 1 year, to hear all motions for contempt at the complaint committee level (RVCC or QIC) and hear motions for disqualification of any member of a RVCC, QIC or panel.

Rule 10.750 Contempt Process

(a) General. Should any person fail, without justification, to respond to the lawful subpoena of a RVCC, QIC, or panel, or, having responded, fail or refuse to answer all inquiries or to turn over evidence that has been lawfully subpoenaed, or should any person be guilty of disorderly conduct, that person may be found to be in contempt.

(b) RVCC or QIC Contempt. A motion for contempt based on the grounds delineated in subdivision (a) above along with a proposed order to show cause may be filed before the contempt/disqualification judge in the division in which the matter is pending. The motion shall allege the specific failure on the part of the person or the specific disorderly or contemptuous act of the person which forms the basis of the alleged contempt.

(c) Panel Contempt. The chair of a panel may hear any motions filed either before or during a hearing or hold any person in contempt for conduct occurring during the hearing.

Rule 10.760 Duty to Inform

A certified mediator shall inform the DRC in writing within 30 days of having been reprimanded, sanctioned, or otherwise disciplined by any court, administrative agency, bar association, or other professional group.

Rule 10.770 Staff

The DRC shall provide all staff support to the MQDRB necessary to fulfill its duties and responsibilities under these rules and perform all other functions specified in these rules.

Rule 10.800 Good Moral Character Inquiry Process

(a) Generally. Good moral character issues of applicants shall be heard by the QIC to determine if an applicant has the good moral character necessary to be certified pursuant to rule 10.110. If, during the term of certification of a mediator, the DRC becomes aware of any information concerning a certified mediator which could constitute credible evidence of a lack of good moral character under rule 10.110, the DRC shall refer such information to a RVCC as a rule violation complaint pursuant to 10.810. The QIC and RVCC shall be informed of the applicant's or mediator's prior disciplinary history.

(b) Meetings. The QIC shall convene as necessary by conference call or other electronic means to consider all cases currently pending before it.

(c) Initial Review. Prior to approving a new or renewal application for certification, the DRC shall review the application and any other information to determine whether the applicant appears to meet the standards for good moral character under rule 10.110. If the DRC's review of an application for certification or renewal raises any questions regarding the applicant's good moral character, the DRC shall request the applicant to supply additional information as necessary. Upon completing this extended review, if the information continues to raise questions regarding the applicant's good moral character, the DRC shall forward the application and supporting material as an inquiry to the QIC.

(d) Process. In reviewing all documentation relating to the good moral character of any applicant, the QIC shall follow the process below.

(1) In relation to a new application, the QIC shall either recommend approval or, if it finds there is reason to believe that the applicant lacks good moral character, the QIC may do 1 or more of the following:

(A) offer the applicant the opportunity to withdraw his/her application prior to the finding of probable cause;

(B) offer the applicant the opportunity to satisfy additional conditions prior to approval of application; or

(C) prepare a complaint and submit the complaint to the DRC for forwarding to the applicant. The complaint shall state with particularity the specific facts and details that form the basis of the complaint. The applicant shall respond within 20 days of receipt of the complaint unless the time is otherwise extended by the DRC in writing.

  (i) After the response is received, the QIC may:

   1. dismiss the complaint and approve the application; or

   2. make a finding of probable cause, prepare formal charges, and refer the matter to the DRC for assignment to a panel.

(2) In relation to a renewal application, the QIC shall either recommend approval or, if it finds there is reason to believe that the renewal applicant lacks good moral character, the QIC may do 1 or more of the following:

(A) offer the renewal applicant the opportunity to withdraw his/her application and may include the necessity to resign any other certifications prior to the finding of probable cause; or

(B) offer the applicant the opportunity to satisfy additional conditions prior to approval of application; or

(C) prepare a complaint and submit same to the DRC for forwarding to the applicant. The complaint shall state with particularity the specific facts and details that form the basis of the complaint. The applicant shall respond to the complaint within 20 days of receipt unless otherwise extended by the DRC in writing.

  (i) After the response is received, the QIC may:

   1. dismiss the complaint and approve the renewal application; or

   2. make a finding of probable cause, prepare formal charges and refer the matter to the DRC for assignment to a panel.

(e) Notification. Within 10 days of a matter being referred to the QIC, the DRC shall send notification to the applicant of the existence of a good moral character inquiry. Notification to the applicant shall be made by certified mail addressed to the applicant's physical address on file with the DRC until such time as the mediator expressly agrees in writing to accept service electronically and then notification shall be made to the applicant's e-mail address on file with the DRC.

(f) Investigation. The QIC, after review of the information presented, may direct the DRC to retain the services of an investigator to assist the QIC in any of its functions. The QIC, or any member or members thereof, may also conduct an investigation if authorized by the QIC chair. Any investigation may include meeting with the applicant or any other person.

(g) QIC Meeting with the Applicant. Notwithstanding any other provision in this rule, at any time while the QIC has jurisdiction, it may meet with the applicant in an effort to resolve the matter. This resolution may include additional conditions to certification if agreed to by the applicant. If additional conditions are accepted, all relevant documentation shall be forwarded to the DRC. These meetings may be in person, by teleconference, or other communication method at the discretion of the QIC.

(h) Notice and Publication. Any consensual resolution agreement with an applicant which includes sanctions shall be distributed by the DRC to all circuits and districts through the chief judges, all trial and appellate court administrators, the ADR directors, and mediation coordinators and published on the DRC page of the Florida Courts website with a summary of the case and a copy of the agreement.

(i) Review. If no other disposition has occurred, the QIC shall review all available information including the applicant's response to a complaint, any investigative report, and any underlying documentation to determine whether there is probable cause to believe that the alleged conduct would constitute evidence of the applicant's lack of good moral character.

(j) No Probable Cause. If the QIC finds no probable cause, it shall close the inquiry by dismissal and so advise the applicant in writing.

(k) Probable Cause and Formal Charges. If the QIC finds probable cause to believe the applicant lacks the good moral character necessary to be certified as a mediator, the QIC shall draft formal charges and forward such charges to the DRC for assignment to a panel. The charges shall include a statement of the matters regarding the applicant's lack of good moral character and references to the rules relating to those matters. At the request of the QIC, the DRC may retain a member in good standing of The Florida Bar to conduct such additional investigation as necessary and to draft the formal charges for the QIC. The formal charges shall be signed by the chair, or, in the alternative, by the remaining 3 members of the QIC.

(l) Withdrawal of Application. A withdrawal of an application does not result in the loss of jurisdiction by the QIC.

(m) Panel. If a matter is referred to a panel under this section, the process shall proceed pursuant to rule 10.820.

Committee Notes

2015 Revision. A lack of good moral character may be determined not only by 1 incident but also by the cumulative effect of many instances. In reviewing an application for matters concerning the good moral character of any applicant, prior disciplinary actions against the applicant, from whatever source, should be provided to the QIC for their review and consideration.

Rule 10.810 Rule Violations Complaint Process

(a) Initiation of Complaint. Any individual or the DRC may make a complaint alleging that a mediator has violated 1 or more provisions of these rules. The complaint from an individual shall be written, sworn to under oath and notarized using a form supplied by the DRC. A complaint initiated by the DRC need not be sworn nor notarized but shall be signed by the director or the DRC staff attorney, if any. The complaint shall state with particularity the specific facts and details that form the basis of the complaint.

(b) Filing. The complaint shall be filed with the DRC. Once received by the DRC, the complaint shall be stamped with the date of receipt.

(c) Assignment to a Rules Violation Complaint Committee (RVCC). Upon receipt of a complaint, the DRC shall assign the complaint to a RVCC within a reasonable period of time. The RVCC shall be informed by the DRC of the mediator's prior disciplinary history. As soon as practical after the receipt of a complaint from an individual, the DRC shall send a notification of the receipt of the complaint to the complainant.

(d) Facial Sufficiency Determination. The RVCC shall convene by conference call to determine whether the allegation(s), if true, would constitute a violation of these rules.

(1) If the RVCC finds a complaint against a mediator to be facially insufficient, the complaint shall be dismissed without prejudice and the complainant shall be so notified and given an opportunity to re-file within a 20-day time period. No complainant whose complaint is dismissed without prejudice pursuant to this section shall be permitted more than 1 additional filing to establish facial sufficiency.

(2) If the complaint is found to be facially sufficient, the RVCC shall prepare a list of any rule or rules which may have been violated and shall submit same to the DRC.

(e) Service. Upon the finding of facial sufficiency of a complaint, the DRC shall serve on the mediator a copy of the list of alleged rule violations, a copy of the complaint, and a link to an electronic copy of these rules or the rules which were in effect at the time of the alleged violation. Service on the mediator shall be made either electronically or by certified mail addressed to the mediator's physical or e-mail address on file with the DRC.

(f) Response. Within 20 days of the receipt of the list of alleged rule violations and the complaint, the mediator shall send a written, sworn under oath, and notarized response to the DRC by registered or certified mail. Unless extended in writing by the DRC, if the mediator does not respond within the 20-day time frame, the allegations shall be deemed admitted and the matter may be referred to a panel.

(g) Resignation of Certification. A resignation of certification by a mediator after the filing of a complaint does not result in the loss of jurisdiction by the MQDRB.

(h) Investigation. The RVCC, after review of the complaint and response, may direct the DRC to appoint an investigator to assist the RVCC in any of its functions. The RVCC, or any member or members thereof, may also conduct an investigation if authorized by the RVCC chair. Any investigation may include meeting with the mediator, the complainant or any other person.

(i) RVCC Meeting with the Complainant and Mediator. Notwithstanding any other provision in this rule, at any time while the RVCC has jurisdiction, it may meet with the complainant and the mediator, jointly or separately, in an effort to resolve the matter. This resolution may include sanctions as set forth in rule 10.840(a) if agreed to by the mediator. If sanctions are accepted, all relevant documentation shall be forwarded to the DRC. Such meetings may be in person, by teleconference, or other communication method, at the discretion of the RVCC.

(j) Notice and Publication. Any consensual resolution agreement which includes sanctions shall be distributed by the DRC to all circuits and districts through the chief judges, all trial and appellate court administrators, the ADR directors, and mediation coordinators and published on the DRC page of the Florida Courts website with a summary of the case, the rule or rules listed as violated, the circumstances surrounding the violation of the rules, and a copy of the agreement.

(k) Review. If no other disposition has occurred, the RVCC shall review the complaint, the response, and any investigative report, including any underlying documentation, to determine whether there is probable cause to believe that the alleged misconduct occurred and would constitute a violation of the rules.

(l) No Probable Cause. If the RVCC finds no probable cause, it shall dismiss the complaint with prejudice and so advise the complainant and the mediator in writing. Such decision shall be final.

(m) Probable Cause Found. If the RVCC finds that probable cause exists, it may:

(1) draft formal charges and forward such charges to the DRC for assignment to a panel;

or

(2) decide not to proceed with the case by filing an Order of Non-Referral containing a short and plain statement of the rules for which probable cause was found and the reason or reasons for non-referral, and so advise the complainant and the mediator in writing.

(n) Formal Charges and Counsel. If the RVCC finds probable cause that the mediator has violated 1 or more of these rules, the RVCC shall draft formal charges and forward such charges to the DRC for assignment to a panel. The charges shall include a statement of the matters asserted in the complaint relevant to the finding of rules violations, any additional information relevant to the finding of rules violations, and references to the particular sections of the rules violated. The formal charges shall be signed by the chair, or, in the alternative, by the other 2 members of the RVCC. At the request of the RVCC, the DRC may retain a member in good standing of The Florida Bar to conduct such additional investigation as necessary and draft the formal charges.

(o) Dismissal. Upon the filing of a stipulation of dismissal signed by the complainant and the mediator, and with the concurrence of the RVCC, which may withhold concurrence, the complaint shall be dismissed with prejudice.

Rule 10.820 Hearing Panel Procedures

(a) Notification of Formal Charges. Upon the referral of formal charges to the DRC from a RVCC or QIC, the DRC shall promptly send a copy of the formal charges to the mediator or applicant and complainant, if any, by certified mail, return receipt requested.

(b) Prosecutor. Upon the referral of formal charges, the DRC shall retain the services of a member in good standing of The Florida Bar to prosecute the case.

(c) Panel Adviser. After the referral of formal charges, the DRC may retain the services of a member in good standing of The Florida Bar to attend the hearing and advise and assist the panel on procedural and administrative matters.

(d) Assignment to Panel. After the referral of formal charges to the DRC, the DRC shall send to the complainant, if any, and the mediator or applicant a Notice of Assignment of the case to a panel. No member of the RVCC or QIC that referred the formal charges shall serve as a member of the panel.

(e) Assignment of Related Cases. If the DRC assigns related cases to a panel for a single hearing, any party to those cases may make a motion for severance which shall be heard by the chair of the panel.

(f) Time of the Hearing. Absent stipulation of the parties or good cause, the DRC shall set the hearing for a date not more than 120 days nor less than 30 days from the date of the notice of assignment of the case to the panel. Within 10 days of the scheduling of the hearing, a notice of hearing shall be sent by certified mail to the mediator or applicant and his or her attorney, if any.

(g) Admission to Charges. At any time prior to the hearing, the panel may accept an admission to any or all charges and impose sanctions upon the mediator or applicant. The panel shall not be required to meet in person to accept any such admission and imposition of sanctions.

(h) Dismissal by Stipulation. Upon the filing of a stipulation of dismissal signed by the complainant, if any, the mediator or applicant, and the prosecutor and with the review and concurrence of the panel, which concurrence may be withheld, the case shall be dismissed with prejudice. Upon dismissal, the panel shall promptly forward a copy of the dismissal order to the DRC.

(i) Procedures for Hearing. The procedures for a hearing shall be as follows:

    (1) Panel Presence. No hearing shall be conducted without the chair being physically present. All other panel members must be physically present unless the chair determines that exceptional circumstances are shown to exist which include, but are not limited to, unexpected illness, unexpected incapacity, or unforeseeable and unavoidable absence of a panel member. Upon such determination, the hearing may proceed with no fewer than 4 panel members, of which 1 is the chair. In the event only 4 of the panel members are present, at least 3 members of the panel must agree on the decisions of the panel. If

3 members of the panel cannot agree on the decision, the hearing shall be rescheduled.

(2) Decorum. The hearing may be conducted informally but with decorum.

(3) Oath. Anyone testifying in the hearing shall swear or affirm to tell the truth.

(4) Florida Evidence Code. The rules of evidence applicable to trials of civil actions shall apply but are to be liberally construed.

(5) Testimony. Testimony at the hearing may be given through the use of telephonic or other communication equipment upon a showing of good cause to the chair of the panel within a reasonable time prior to the hearing.

(6) Right to Defend. A mediator or applicant shall have the right: to defend against all charges; to be represented by an attorney; to examine and cross-examine witnesses; to compel the attendance of witnesses to testify; and to compel the production of documents and other evidentiary matter through the subpoena power of the panel.

(7) Mediator or Applicant Discovery. The prosecutor shall, upon written demand of a mediator, applicant, or counsel of record, promptly furnish the following: the names and addresses of all witnesses whose testimony is expected to be offered at the hearing; copies of all written statements and transcripts of the testimony of such witnesses in the possession of the prosecutor or the DRC which are relevant to the subject matter of the hearing and which have not previously been furnished; and copies of any exhibits which are expected to be offered at the hearing.

(8) Prosecutor Discovery. The mediator, applicant, or their counsel of record shall, upon written demand of the prosecutor, promptly furnish the following: the names and addresses of all witnesses whose testimony is expected to be offered at the hearing; copies of all written statements and transcripts of the testimony of such witnesses in the possession of the mediator, applicant or their counsel of record which are relevant to the subject matter of the hearing and which have not previously been furnished; and copies of any exhibits which are expected to be offered at the hearing.

(9) Complainant's Failure to Appear. Absent a showing of good cause, if the complainant fails to appear at the hearing, the panel may dismiss the case.

(10) Mediator's or Applicant's Failure to Appear. If the mediator or applicant has failed to answer the underlying complaint or fails to appear, the panel may proceed with the hearing.

(A) If the hearing is conducted in the absence of a mediator or applicant who failed to respond to the underlying complaint and the allegations were therefore admitted, no further notice to the mediator or applicant is necessary and the decision of the panel shall be final.

(B) If the hearing is conducted in the absence of a mediator or applicant who submitted a response to the underlying complaint, the DRC shall notify the mediator or applicant that the hearing occurred and whether the matter was dismissed or if sanctions were imposed. The mediator or applicant may petition for rehearing by showing good cause for such absence. A petition for rehearing must be received by the DRC and the prosecutor no later than 10 days from receipt of the DRC notification. The prosecutor shall file a response, if any, within 5 days from receipt of the petition for rehearing. The disposition of the petition shall be decided solely by the chair of the panel and any hearing required by the chair of the panel may be conducted telephonically or by other communication equipment.

(11) Reporting of Proceedings. Any party shall have the right, without any order or approval, to have all or any portion of the testimony in the proceedings reported and transcribed by a court reporter at the party's expense.

(j) Decision of Panel. Upon making a determination that the case shall be dismissed or that the imposition of sanctions or denial of application is appropriate, the panel shall promptly notify the DRC of the decision including factual findings and conclusions signed by the chair of the panel. The DRC shall thereafter promptly mail a copy of the decision to all parties.

(k) Notice to Circuits and Districts. In every case in which a mediator or applicant has had sanctions imposed by agreement or decision, such agreement or decision shall be sent by the DRC to all circuits and districts through the chief judges, all trial and appellate court administrators, the ADR directors, and mediation coordinators.

(l) Publication. Upon the imposition of sanctions, whether by consent of the mediator or applicant and approval by the panel or by decision of the panel after a hearing, the DRC shall publish the name of the mediator or applicant, a summary of the case, a list of the rule or rules which were violated, the circumstances surrounding the violation, and a copy of the decision of the panel. Such publication shall be on the DRC page of the Florida Courts website and in any outside publication at the discretion of the DRC Director.

Rule 10.830 Burden of Proof

(a) Rule Violation. The burden of proof for rule violations other than good moral character is clear and convincing evidence.

(b) Good Moral Character. The burden of proof for any good moral character issue is the preponderance of the evidence.

Rule 10.840 Sanctions

(a) Generally. The mediator or applicant may be sanctioned pursuant to the following:

(1) by agreement with a RVCC or QIC;

(2) by agreement with a panel to the imposition of sanctions; or

(3) by imposition of sanctions by a panel as a result of their deliberations.

(b) Types of Sanctions. Sanctions may include 1 or more of the following:

(1) denial of an application;

(2) oral admonishment;

(3) written reprimand;

(4) additional training, which may include the observation of mediations;

(5) restriction on types of cases which can be mediated in the future;

(6) supervised mediation;

(7) suspension for a period of up to 1 year;

(8) decertification or, if the mediator is not certified, bar from service as a mediator under any rule of court or statute pertaining to certified or court-appointed mediators;

(9) costs incurred prior to, during, and subsequent to the hearing. The specific categories and amounts of such costs are to be decided by the chair of the panel upon submission of costs by the DRC or the prosecutor, and shall include only:

(A) all travel expenses for members of the panel;

(B) all travel expenses for witnesses, prosecutor, panel adviser, and DRC Director or designee;

(C) court reporter fees and transcription;

(D) fees and costs for all investigation services;

(E) telephone/conference call charges;

(F) postage and delivery;

(G) notary charges;

(H) interpretation and translation services; and

(I) copy costs.

(10) any other sanctions as deemed appropriate by the panel.

(c) Failure to Comply With Sanctions.

(1) If there is a reasonable belief that a mediator or applicant failed to comply with any sanction, unless otherwise provided for in the agreement with a RVCC or QIC or the decision of the panel, the DRC may file a motion for contempt with the Contempt/Disqualification Judge of the division in which the sanctions were agreed to or imposed and serve the mediator or applicant with a copy of the motion.

(2) The mediator or applicant shall file a response within 20 days of receipt of the motion for contempt.

(3) If no response is filed, the allegations of the motion are admitted.

(4) The DRC shall thereafter set a hearing with the Contempt/Disqualification Judge and provide notice to the mediator or applicant. The holding of a hearing shall not preclude subsequent hearings on any other alleged failure.

(5) Any sanction in effect at the time that the DRC has a reasonable belief that a violation of the sanctions has occurred shall continue in effect until a decision is reached by the Contempt/Disqualification Judge.

(6) A finding by the Contempt/Disqualification Judge that there was a willful failure to substantially comply with any imposed or agreed-to sanction shall result in the automatic decertification of the mediator for no less than 2 years after which the mediator shall be required to apply as a new applicant.

Rule 10.850 Suspension, Decertification, Denial of Application, and Removal

(a) Suspension. During the period of suspension, compliance with all requirements for certification must be met including, but not limited to, submittal of renewal application, fees and continuing education requirements.

(b) Reinstatement after Suspension. A mediator who has been suspended shall be reinstated as a certified mediator, unless otherwise ineligible, upon the expiration of the suspension period and satisfaction of any additional obligations contained in the sanction document.

(c) Automatic Decertification or Automatic Denial of Application. A mediator or applicant shall automatically be decertified or denied application approval without the need for a hearing upon the following:

(1) Conviction of Felony of Certified Mediator. If the DRC finds that a certified mediator has a felony conviction, the mediator shall automatically be decertified from all certifications and notification and publication of such decertification shall proceed pursuant to rule 10.820(j) and (k). The decertified mediator may not apply for any certification for a period of 2 years or until restoration of civil rights, whichever comes later.

(2) Conviction of Felony of Applicant. If the DRC finds that an applicant for certification has a felony conviction and has not had civil rights restored, the application shall be automatically denied and may not be resubmitted for consideration until restoration of civil rights.

(3) Revocation of Professional License of Certified Mediator. If the DRC finds that a certified mediator has been disbarred from any state or federal bar or has had any professional license revoked, the mediator shall be automatically decertified and cannot reapply for certification for a period of 2 years.

(4) Revocation of Professional License of Applicant. If the DRC finds that an applicant for certification has been disbarred from any state or federal bar or has had any professional license revoked, the applicant shall be

automatically denied approval and cannot reapply for certification for a period of 2 years.

(5) Notification and Publication. In the event of an automatic denial of an application or decertification, the DRC shall follow all procedures for notification and publication as stated in rule 10.820(k) and (l).

(d) Decertified Mediators. If a mediator or applicant has been decertified or barred from service pursuant to these rules, the mediator or applicant shall not thereafter be assigned or appointed to mediate a case pursuant to court rule or order or be designated as a mediator by the parties in any court proceeding.

(e) Removal from Supreme Court Committees. If a member of the MQDRB, the ADR Rules and Policy Committee, the Mediator Ethics Advisory Committee, the Mediation Training Review Board, or any supreme court committee related to alternative dispute resolution processes established in the future, is disciplined, suspended, or decertified, the DRC shall immediately remove that member from the committee or board on which the member serves.

(f) Reinstatement after Decertification.

(1) Except if inconsistent with rule 10.110, or subdivision (b) of this rule, a mediator who has been decertified may be reinstated as a certified mediator after application unless the document decertifying the mediator states otherwise.

(2) Unless a greater time period has been imposed by a panel or rule, no application for reinstatement may be submitted prior to 1 year after the date of decertification.

(3) The reinstatement procedures shall be as follows:

(A) A petition for reinstatement shall be made in writing, sworn to by the petitioner, notarized under oath, and filed with the DRC.

(B) The petition shall contain:

(i) a new and current application for mediator certification along with required fees;

(ii) a description of the offense or misconduct upon which the decertification was based, together with the date of such decertification and the case number;

(iii) a copy of the sanction document decertifying the mediator;

(iv) a statement of facts claimed to justify reinstatement as a certified mediator; and

(v) if the period of decertification is 2 years or more, the petitioner shall complete a certified mediation training program of the type for which the petitioner seeks to be reinstated and complete all mentorship and other requirements in effect at the time.

(C) The DRC shall refer the petition for reinstatement to the current QIC.

(D) The QIC shall review the petition for reinstatement. If there are no matters which make the mediator otherwise ineligible and if the petitioner is found to have met the requirements for certification, the QIC shall notify the DRC and the DRC shall reinstate the petitioner as a certified mediator. However, if the decertification was for 2 or more years, reinstatement shall be contingent on the petitioner's completion of a certified mediation training program of the type for which the petitioner seeks to be reinstated.

Rule 10.860 Subpoenas

(a) RVCC or QIC. Subpoenas for the production of documents or other evidence and for the appearance of any person before a RVCC or QIC, or any member thereof, may be issued by the chair of the RVCC or QIC. If the chair is unavailable, the subpoena may be issued by the remaining members of the RVCC or QIC.

(b) Panel. Subpoenas for the attendance of witnesses and the production of documents or other evidence before a panel may be issued by the chair of the panel. If the chair of a panel is unavailable, the subpoena may be issued by the vice-chair.

(c) Service. Subpoenas may be served in any manner provided by law for the service of witness subpoenas in a civil action.

(d) Failure to Obey. Any person who, without good cause shown, fails to obey a duly served subpoena may be cited for contempt in accordance with rule 10.750.

Rule 10.870 Confidentiality

(a) Generally. Until the finding of probable cause, all communications and proceedings shall be confidential. Upon the filing of formal charges, the formal charges and all documents created subsequent to the filing of formal charges shall be public with the exception of those matters which are otherwise confidential under law or rule of the supreme court, regardless of the outcome of any appeal. If a consensual agreement is reached between a mediator or applicant and a RVCC or QIC, only a summary of the allegations and a link or copy of the agreement may be released to the public and placed on the DRC page of the Florida Courts website.

(b) Breach of Confidentiality. Violation of confidentiality by a member of the MQDRB shall subject the member to discipline under these rules and removal from the MQDRB by the chief justice of the Supreme Court of Florida.

Committee Notes

2008 Revision. The recent adoption of the Florida Mediation Confidentiality and Privilege Act, sections 44.401–44.406, Florida Statutes, renders the first paragraph of the 1995 Revision Committee Notes inoperative. The second paragraph explains the initial rationale for the rule, which is useful now from a historical standpoint.

1995 Revision. The Committee believed the rule regarding confidentiality should be amended in deference to the 1993 amendment to section 44.102, Florida Statutes, that engrafted an exception to the general confidentiality requirement for all media-tion sessions for the purpose of investigating complaints filed against mediators. Section 44.102(4) specifically provides that "the disclosure of an otherwise privi-leged communication shall be used only for the internal use of the body conduct-ing the investigation" and that "[Prior] to the release of any disciplinary files to the public, all references to otherwise privileged communications shall be deleted from the record."

These provisions created a substantial potential problem when read in conjunction with the previous rule on confidentiality, which made public all proceedings after formal charges were filed. In addition to the possibly substantial burden of redact-ing the files for public release, there was the potentially greater problem of conduct-ing panel hearings in such a manner as to preclude the possibility that confidential communications would be revealed during testimony, specifically the possibility that any public observers would have to be removed prior to the elicitation of any such communication only to be allowed to return until the next potentially confi-dential revelation. The Committee believes that under the amended rule the integ-rity of the disciplinary system can be maintained by releasing the results of any disciplinary action together with a redacted transcript of panel proceedings, while still maintaining the integrity of the mediation process.

Rule 10.880 Disqualification and Removal of Members of a Committee, Panel or Board

(a) Disqualification of Member. A member of the MQDRB is disqualified from serving on a RVCC, QIC or panel involving that member's own discipline or decertification.

(b) Party Request for Disqualification of a MQDRB Member. Any party may move to disqualify a member of the committee or panel before which the case is pending. Factors to be considered include, but are not limited to:

(1) the member or some person related to that member is interested in the result of the case;

(2) the member is related to an attorney or counselor of record in the case; or

(3) the member is a material witness for or against 1 of the parties to the case.

(c) Facts to Be Alleged. Any motion to disqualify shall be in writing, allege the facts relied on to show the grounds for disqualification and shall be made under oath by the moving party.

(d) Time for Motion. A party shall file a motion to disqualify with the DRC not later than 10 days after the movant discovered or reasonably should have discovered the facts which would constitute grounds for disqualification.

(e) Action by Contempt/Disqualification Judge. One of the Contempt/Disqualification Judges shall rule on any motions for disqualification.

(f) Board Member Initiative. A member of any committee or panel may disqualify him/herself on the member's own initiative at any time.

(g) Replacement. Depending on the circumstances, the DRC may replace any disqualified member.

(h) Qualifications for New Member. Each new member serving as a replacement shall have the same qualifications as the disqualified member, but, if needed, may be chosen from a different division of the MQDRB.

Rule 10.890 Limitation on Time to Initiate a Complaint

(a) Rule Violations. Except as otherwise provided in this rule, complaints alleging violations of the Florida Rules for Certified and Court-Appointed Mediators shall not be filed later than 2 years after the date on which the party had a reasonable opportunity to discover the violation, but in no case more than 4 years after the date of the violation.

(b) Felonies. There shall be no limit on the time in which to file a complaint alleging a conviction of a felony by an applicant or mediator.

(c) Good Moral Character. A complaint alleging lack of good moral character in connection with an application under these rules shall not be filed later than 4 years after the date of the discovery by the DRC of the matter(s) evidencing a lack of good moral character.

Rule 10.900 Supreme Court Chief Justice Review

(a) Right of Review. Any mediator or applicant found to have committed a violation of these rules or otherwise sanctioned by a hearing panel shall have a right of review of that action. Review of this type shall be by the chief justice of the Supreme Court of Florida or by the chief justice's designee. A mediator shall have no right of review of any resolution reached under rule 10.800(g) and 10.810(i).

(b) Rules of Procedure. The Florida Rules of Appellate Procedure, to the extent applicable and except as otherwise provided in this rule, shall control all appeals of mediator disciplinary matters.

  (1) The jurisdiction to seek review of disciplinary action shall be invoked by filing a Notice of Review of Mediator Disciplinary Action with the clerk of the supreme court within 30 days of the panel's decision. A copy shall be provided to the DRC.

  (2) The notice of review shall be substantially in the form prescribed by rule 9.900(a), Florida Rules of Appellate Procedure. A copy of the panel decision shall be attached to the notice.

  (3) Appellant's initial brief, accompanied by an appendix as prescribed by rule 9.210, Florida Rules of Appellate Procedure, shall be served within 30 days

of submitting the notice of review. Additional briefs shall be served as prescribed by rule 9.210, Florida Rules of Appellate Procedure.

(c) Standard of Review. The review shall be conducted in accordance with the following standard of review:

(1) The chief justice or designee shall review the findings and conclusions of the panel using a competent substantial evidence standard, neither reweighing the evidence in the record nor substituting the reviewer's judgment for that of the panel.

(2) Decisions of the chief justice or designee shall be final upon issuance of a mandate under rule 9.340, Florida Rules of Appellate Procedure.

Rule 10.910 Mediator Ethics Advisory Committee

(a) Scope and Purpose. The Mediator Ethics Advisory Committee shall provide written advisory opinions to mediators subject to these rules in response to ethical questions arising from the Standards of Professional Conduct. Such opinions shall be consistent with supreme court decisions on mediator discipline.

(b) Appointment. The Mediator Ethics Advisory Committee shall be composed of 9 members, 2 from each of the 4 divisions of the Mediator Qualifications and Discipline Review Board and the ninth member from any of the 4 divisions. No member of the Mediator Qualifications and Discipline Review Board shall serve on the committee.

(c) Membership and Terms. The membership of the committee, appointed by the chief justice, shall be composed of 1 county mediator, 1 family mediator, 1 circuit mediator, 1 dependency mediator, 1 appellate mediator and 4 additional members who hold any type of Florida Supreme Court mediator certification. All appointments shall be for 4 years. No member shall serve more than 2 consecutive terms. The committee shall select 1 member as chair and 1 member as vice-chair.

(d) Meetings. The committee shall meet in person or by telephone conference as necessary at the direction of the chair to consider requests for advisory opinions. A quorum shall consist of a majority of the members appointed to the committee. All requests for advisory opinions shall be in writing. The committee may vote by any means as directed by the chair.

(e) Opinions. Upon due deliberation, and upon the concurrence of a majority of the committee, the committee shall render opinions. A majority of all members shall be required to concur in any advisory opinion issued by the committee. The opinions shall be signed by the chair, or vice-chair in the absence of the chair, filed with the Dispute Resolution Center, published by the Dispute Resolution Center, in its newsletter, or by posting on the DRC website, and be made available upon request.

(f) Effect of Opinions. While reliance by a mediator on an opinion of the committee shall not constitute a defense in any disciplinary proceeding, it shall be evidence of good faith and may be considered by the board in relation to any determination of guilt or in mitigation of punishment.

(g) Confidentiality. Prior to publication, all references to the requesting mediator or any other real person, firm, organization, or corporation shall be deleted from any request for an opinion, any document associated with the preparation of an opinion, and any opinion issued by the committee. This rule shall apply to all opinions, past and future.

(h) Support. The Dispute Resolution Center shall provide all support necessary for the committee to fulfill its duties under these rules.

Committee Notes

2000 Revision. The Mediator Ethics Advisory Committee was formerly the Mediator Qualifications Advisory Panel.

Appendix D

Uniform Mediation Act

UNIFORM MEDIATION ACT
(Last Revised or Amended in 2003)

Drafted by the
NATIONAL CONFERENCE OF COMMISSIONERS
ON UNIFORM STATE LAWS
and by it
APPROVED AND RECOMMENDED FOR ENACTMENT
IN ALL THE STATES
at its
ANNUAL CONFERENCE
MEETING IN ITS ONE-HUNDRED-AND-TENTH YEAR
WHITE SULPHUR SPRINGS, WEST VIRGINIA
AUGUST 10–17, 2001 AMENDMENTS APPROVED
at its
ANNUAL CONFERENCE
MEETING IN ITS ONE-HUNDRED-AND-TWELFTH YEAR
IN WASHINGTON, DC
AUGUST 1–7, 2003

SECTION 1. TITLE. This [Act] may be cited as the Uniform Mediation Act.

SECTION 2. DEFINITIONS. In this [Act]:

(1) "Mediation" means a process in which a mediator facilitates communication and negotiation between parties to assist them in reaching a voluntary agreement regarding their dispute.

(2) "Mediation communication" means a statement, whether oral or in a record or verbal or nonverbal, that occurs during a mediation or is made for purposes of considering, conducting, participating in, initiating, continuing, or reconvening a mediation or retaining a mediator.

(3) "Mediator" means an individual who conducts a mediation.

(4) "Nonparty participant" means a person, other than a party or mediator, that participates in a mediation.

(5) "Mediation party" means a person that participates in a mediation and whose agreement is necessary to resolve the dispute.

561

(6) "Person" means an individual, corporation, business trust, estate, trust, partnership, limited liability company, association, joint venture, government; governmental subdivision, agency, or instrumentality; public corporation, or any other legal or commercial entity.

(7) "Proceeding" means:

(A) a judicial, administrative, arbitral, or other adjudicative process, including related pre-hearing and post-hearing motions, conferences, and discovery; or

(B) a legislative hearing or similar process.

(8) "Record" means information that is inscribed on a tangible medium or that is stored in an electronic or other medium and is retrievable in perceivable form.

(9) "Sign" means:

(A) to execute or adopt a tangible symbol with the present intent to authenticate a record; or

(B) to attach or logically associate an electronic symbol, sound, or process to or with a record with the present intent to authenticate a record.

SECTION 3. SCOPE.

(a) Except as otherwise provided in subsection (b) or (c), this [Act] applies to a mediation in which:

(1) the mediation parties are required to mediate by statute or court or administrative agency rule or referred to mediation by a court, administrative agency, or arbitrator;

(2) the mediation parties and the mediator agree to mediate in a record that demonstrates an expectation that mediation communications will be privileged against disclosure; or

(3) the mediation parties use as a mediator an individual who holds himself or herself out as a mediator or the mediation is provided by a person that holds itself out as providing mediation.

(b) The [Act] does not apply to a mediation:

(1) relating to the establishment, negotiation, administration, or termination of a collective bargaining relationship;

(2) relating to a dispute that is pending under or is part of the processes established by a collective bargaining agreement, except that the [Act] applies to a mediation arising out of a dispute that has been filed with an administrative agency or court;

(3) conducted by a judge who might make a ruling on the case; or

(4) conducted under the auspices of:

(A) a primary or secondary school if all the parties are students or

(B) a correctional institution for youths if all the parties are residents of that institution.

(c) If the parties agree in advance in a signed record, or a record of proceeding reflects agreement by the parties, that all or part of a mediation is not privileged, the privileges under Sections 4 through 6 do not apply to the mediation or part agreed upon. However, Sections 4 through 6 apply to a mediation communication made by a person that has not received actual notice of the agreement before the communication is made.

Legislative Note: To the extent that the Act applies to mediations conducted under the authority of a State's courts, State judiciaries should consider enacting conforming court rules.

SECTION 4. PRIVILEGE AGAINST DISCLOSURE; ADMISSIBILITY; DISCOVERY.

(a) Except as otherwise provided in Section 6, a mediation communication is privileged as provided in subsection (b) and is not subject to discovery or admissible in evidence in a proceeding unless waived or precluded as provided by Section 5.

(b) In a proceeding, the following privileges apply:

(1) A mediation party may refuse to disclose, and may prevent any other person from disclosing, a mediation communication.

(2) A mediator may refuse to disclose a mediation communication, and may prevent any other person from disclosing a mediation communication of the mediator.

(3) A nonparty participant may refuse to disclose, and may prevent any other person from disclosing, a mediation communication of the nonparty participant.

(c) Evidence or information that is otherwise admissible or subject to discovery does not become inadmissible or protected from discovery solely by reason of its disclosure or use in a mediation.

Legislative Note: The Act does not supersede existing state statutes that make mediators incompetent to testify, or that provide for costs and attorney fees to mediators who are wrongfully subpoenaed. See, e.g., Cal. Evid. Code Section 703.5 (West 1994).

SECTION 5. WAIVER AND PRECLUSION OF PRIVILEGE.

(a) A privilege under Section 4 may be waived in a record or orally during a proceeding if it is expressly waived by all parties to the mediation and:

(1) in the case of the privilege of a mediator, it is expressly waived by the mediator; and

(2) in the case of the privilege of a nonparty participant, it is expressly waived by the nonparty participant.

(b) A person that discloses or makes a representation about a mediation communication which prejudices another person in a proceeding is precluded from asserting a privilege under Section 4, but only to the extent necessary for the person prejudiced to respond to the representation or disclosure.

(c) A person that intentionally uses a mediation to plan, attempt to commit or commit a crime, or to conceal an ongoing crime or ongoing criminal activity is precluded from asserting a privilege under Section 4.

SECTION 6. EXCEPTIONS TO PRIVILEGE.

(a) There is no privilege under Section 4 for a mediation communication that is:

(1) in an agreement evidenced by a record signed by all parties to the agreement;

(2) available to the public under [insert statutory reference to open records act] or made during a session of a mediation which is open, or is required by law to be open, to the public;

(3) a threat or statement of a plan to inflict bodily injury or commit a crime of violence;

(4) intentionally used to plan a crime, attempt to commit or commit a crime, or to conceal an ongoing crime or ongoing criminal activity;

(5) sought or offered to prove or disprove a claim or complaint of professional misconduct or malpractice filed against a mediator;

(6) except as otherwise provided in subsection (c), sought or offered to prove or disprove a claim or complaint of professional misconduct or malpractice filed against a mediation party, nonparty participant, or representative of a party based on conduct occurring during a mediation; or

(7) sought or offered to prove or disprove abuse, neglect, abandonment, or exploitation in a proceeding in which a child or adult protective services agency is a party, unless the

[Alternative A: [State to insert, for example, child or adult protection] case is referred by a court to mediation and a public agency participates.]

[Alternative B: public agency participates in the [State to insert, for example, child or adult protection] mediation].

(b) There is no privilege under Section 4 if a court, administrative agency, or arbitrator finds, after a hearing in camera, that the party seeking discovery or the proponent of the evidence has shown that the evidence is not otherwise available, that there is a need for the evidence that substantially outweighs the interest in protecting confidentiality, and that the mediation communication is sought or offered in:

(1) a court proceeding involving a felony [or misdemeanor]; or

(2) except as otherwise provided in subsection (c), a proceeding to prove a claim to rescind or reform or a defense to avoid liability on a contract arising out of the mediation.

(c) A mediator may not be compelled to provide evidence of a mediation communication referred to in subsection (a)(6) or (b)(2).

(d) If a mediation communication is not privileged under subsection (a) or (b), only the portion of the communication necessary for the application of the exception from nondisclosure may be admitted. Admission of evidence under subsection (a) or (b) does not render the evidence, or any other mediation communication, discoverable or admissible for any other purpose.

Legislative Note: If the enacting state does not have an open records act, the following language in paragraph (2) of subsection (a) needs to be deleted: "available to the public under [insert statutory reference to open records act] or".

SECTION 7. PROHIBITED MEDIATOR REPORTS.

(a) Except as required in subsection (b), a mediator may not make a report, assessment, evaluation, recommendation, finding, or other communication regarding a mediation to a court, administrative agency, or other authority that may make a ruling on the dispute that is the subject of the mediation.

(b) A mediator may disclose:

(1) whether the mediation occurred or has terminated, whether a settlement was reached, and attendance;

(2) a mediation communication as permitted under Section 6; or

(3) a mediation communication evidencing abuse, neglect, abandonment, or exploitation of an individual to a public agency responsible for protecting individuals against such mistreatment.

(c) A communication made in violation of subsection (a) may not be considered by a court, administrative agency, or arbitrator.

SECTION 8. CONFIDENTIALITY.
Unless subject to the [insert statutory references to open meetings act and open records act], mediation communications are confidential to the extent agreed by the parties or provided by other law or rule of this State.

SECTION 9. MEDIATOR'S DISCLOSURE OF CONFLICTS OF INTEREST; BACKGROUND.

(a) Before accepting a mediation, an individual who is requested to serve as a mediator shall:

(1) make an inquiry that is reasonable under the circumstances to determine whether there are any known facts that a reasonable individual would consider likely to affect the impartiality of the mediator, including a financial or personal interest in the outcome of the mediation and an existing or past relationship with a mediation party or foreseeable participant in the mediation; and

(2) disclose any such known fact to the mediation parties as soon as is practical before accepting a mediation.

(b) If a mediator learns any fact described in subsection (a)(1) after accepting a mediation, the mediator shall disclose it as soon as is practicable.

(c) At the request of a mediation party, an individual who is requested to serve as a mediator shall disclose the mediator's qualifications to mediate a dispute.

(d) A person that violates subsection [(a) or (b)][(a), (b), or (g)] is precluded by the violation from asserting a privilege under Section 4.

(e) Subsections (a), (b), [and] (c), [and] [(g)] do not apply to an individual acting as a judge.

(f) This [Act] does not require that a mediator have a special qualification by background or profession.

(g) A mediator must be impartial, unless after disclosure of the facts required in subsections (a) and (b) to be disclosed, the parties agree otherwise.]

SECTION 10. PARTICIPATION IN MEDIATION. An attorney or other individual designated by a party may accompany the party to and participate in a mediation. A waiver of participation given before the mediation may be rescinded.

SECTION 11. INTERNATIONAL COMMERCIAL MEDIATION.

(a) In this section, "Model Law" means the Model Law on International Commercial Conciliation adopted by the United Nations Commission on International Trade Law on 28 June 2002 and recommended by the United Nations General Assembly in a resolution (A/RES/57/18) dated 19 November 2002, and "international commercial mediation" means an international commercial conciliation as defined in Article 1 of the Model Law.

(b) Except as otherwise provided in subsections (c) and (d), if a mediation is an international commercial mediation, the mediation is governed by the Model Law.

(c) Unless the parties agree in accordance with Section 3(c) of this [Act] that all or part of an international commercial mediation is not privileged, Sections 4, 5, and 6 and any applicable definitions in Section 2 of this [Act] also apply to the mediation and nothing in Article 10 of the Model Law derogates from Sections 4, 5, and 6.

(d) If the parties to an international commercial mediation agree under Article 1, subsection (7), of the Model Law that the Model Law does not apply, this [Act] applies.

Legislative Note. The UNCITRAL Model Law on International Commercial Conciliation may be found at www.uncitral.org/en-index.htm. Important comments on interpretation are included in the Draft Guide to Enactment and Use of UNCITRAL Model Law on International Commercial Conciliation. The States should note the Draft Guide in a Legislative Note to the Act. This is especially important with respect to interpretation of Article 9 of the Model Law.

SECTION 12. RELATION TO ELECTRONIC SIGNATURES IN GLOBAL AND NATIONAL COMMERCE ACT. This [Act] modifies, limits, or supersedes the federal Electronic Signatures in Global and National Commerce Act, 15 U.S.C. Section 7001 *et seq.*, but this [Act] does not modify, limit, or supersede Section 101(c) of that Act or authorize electronic delivery of any of the notices described in Section 103(b) of that Act.

SECTION 13. UNIFORMITY OF APPLICATION AND CONSTRUCTION. In applying and construing this [Act], consideration should be given to the need to promote uniformity of the law with respect to its subject matter among States that enact it.

SECTION 14. SEVERABILITY CLAUSE. If any provision of this [Act] or its application to any person or circumstance is held invalid, the invalidity does not affect other provisions or applications of this [Act] which can be given effect without the invalid provision or application, and to this end the provisions of this [Act] are severable.

SECTION 15. EFFECTIVE DATE. This [Act] takes effect. . . . .

SECTION 16. REPEALS. The following acts and parts of acts are hereby repealed:

(1)

(2)

(3)

SECTION 17. APPLICATION TO EXISTING AGREEMENTS OR REFERRALS.

(a) This [Act] governs a mediation pursuant to a referral or an agreement to mediate made on or after [the effective date of this [Act]].

(b) On or after [a delayed date], this [Act] governs an agreement to mediate whenever made.

References

Chapter 1

ABRAMSON, Harold I. (2004) *Mediation Representation: Advocating in a Problem-Solving Process*. South Bend: The Nat'l Inst. for Trial Advocacy.

AUERBACH, Jerold S. (1983) *Justice Without Law?* New York: Oxford Univ. Press.

BUSH, Robert A. Baruch, and FOLGER, Joseph. (1994) *The Promise of Mediation*. San Francisco: Jossey-Bass.

CARPENTER, Susan C., and KENNEDY, W.J.D. (1988) *Managing Public Disputes*. San Francisco: Jossey-Bass.

COLE, Sara et al., eds. (2011) Mediation: Law, Policy and Practice (2012 ed.) St. Paul: Thompson-West.

DANZIG, Richard. (1973) *Toward the Creation of a Complementary, Decentralized System of Criminal Justice*, 26 Stan. L. Rev. 1

DEUTSCH, Martin. (1973) *The Resolution of Conflict*. New Haven: Yale Univ. Press.

FELSTINER, William, ABEL, Richard L., and SARAT, Austin. (1980-81) *The Emergence and Transformation of Disputes: Naming, Blaming, Claiming*, 15 L. & Soc'y Rev. 631.

FISHER, Roger, and URY, William. (1981) *Getting to Yes*. Boston: Houghton Mifflin.

FOLBERG, Jay, and TAYLOR, Alison. (1984) *Mediation*. San Francisco: Jossey-Bass.

FULLER, Lon. (1971) *Mediation: Its Forms and Functions*, 44 S. Cal. L. Rev. 305.

GALTON, Eric R., and LOVE, Lela P., eds. (2012) Stories Mediators Tell. Washington, D.C.: Am. Bar Ass'n Sec. on Disp. Resol.

GOLANN, Dwight. (1997) *Mediating Legal Disputes: Effective Strategies for Lawyers and Mediators*. New York: Aspen Publishers.

GOLDMANN, Robert. (1980) *Roundtable Justice*. Boulder: Westview Press.

HAYNES, John. (1994) *The Fundamentals of Family Mediation*. Albany: State Univ. of New York Press.

KATSH, Ethan, RIFKIN, Janet, and GAITENBY, Alan. (2000) *E-Commerce, E-Disputes, and E-Dispute Resolution: In the Shadow of "eBay Law,"* 15 Ohio St. J. on Disp. Resol. 705.

KOLB, Deborah. (1994) *When Talk Works: Profiles of Mediators*. San Francisco: Jossey-Bass.

LAX, David, and SEBENIUS, James. (1986) *The Manager as Negotiator*. New York: The Free Press.

LEVINE, Bertram, and LUM, Grande. (2020) *America's Peacemakers: The Community Relations Service and Civil Rights*. University of Missouri Press.

MAGGIOLO, Walter. (1985) *Techniques of Labor Mediation*. New York: Oceana Publications.

McGILLIS, Daniel, and MULLEN, Joan. (1977) *Neighborhood Justice Centers: An Analysis of Potential Models*. Washington, D.C.: U.S. Department of Justice.

MNOOKIN, Robert H. (2000) *Beyond Winning: Negotiating to Create Value in Deals and Disputes*. Cambridge: Harvard Univ. Press.

MOORE, Christopher. (2003) The Mediation Process: Practical Strategies for Resolving Conflict (3d ed.). San Francisco: Jossey-Bass.

PODZIBA, Susan L. (2012) Civic Fusion: Mediating Polarized Public Disputes. Washington, D.C.: Am. Bar Ass'n Sec. on Disp. Resol.

RAIFFA, Howard. (1982) *The Art and Science of Negotiation*. Cambridge: Harvard Univ. Press.

RISKIN, Leonard L. (1996) *Understanding Mediators' Orientations, Strategies, and Techniques: A Grid for the Perplexed*, 1 Harv. Negot. L. Rev. 7.

ROGERS, Nancy, and McEWEN, Craig. (1994) Mediation: Law, Policy, Practice (2d ed.). St. Paul: West Publishing Co.

SCHELLING, Thomas. (1960) *The Strategy of Conflict*. Cambridge: MA: Harvard Univ. Press.

SIMKIN, William, and FIDANDIS, Nicolas. (1986) Mediation and the Dynamics of Collective Bargaining (2d ed.). Washington, D.C.: Bureau of Nat'l Affairs.

STULBERG, Joseph B. (1987) *Taking Charge/Managing Conflict*. Lexington, MA: Lexington Press.

STULBERG, Joseph B. (1981) *The Theory and Practice of Mediation: A Reply to Professor Susskind*, 6 Vt. L. Rev. 85.

STULBERG, Joseph B. and LOVE, Lela P. (2013) The Middle Voice: Mediating Conflict Successfully (2d ed.). Durham: Carolina Acad. Press.

SUSSKIND, Lawrence, and CRUIKSHANK, Jeffrey. (1985) *Breaking the Impasse*. New York: Basic Books.

SUSSKIND, Lawrence. (1981) *Environmental Mediation and the Accountability Problem*, 6 Vt. L. Rev. 1.

WALTON, Richard, and MCKERSIE, Robert. (1991) A Behavioral Theory of Labor Negotiations (2d ed.). Ithaca, N.Y.: ILR Press.

WAHRHAFTIG, Paul, and ASSEFA, Hizkias. (1988) *Extremist Groups and Conflict Resolution: the MOVE crisis in Philadelphia*. New York: Praeger.

Chapter 2

ALFINI, James J. (1999) *Settlement Ethics and Lawyering in ADR Proceedings: A Proposal to Revise Rule 4.1*, 19 N. Ill. U. L. Rev. 255.

AMERICAN BAR ASSOCIATION, *Model Rules of Professional Conduct, Rule 4.1.*, Chicago: American Bar Association.

ARROW, Kenneth, ed. (1995) *Barriers to Conflict Resolution*. New York: W. W. Norton.

BIRKE, Richard, and FOX, Craig R. (1999) *Psychological Principles in Negotiating Civil Settlements*, 4 Harv. Negot. L. Rev. 1.

BRESLIN, J. William, and RUBIN, Jeffrey Z., eds. (1991) *Negotiation Theory and Practice*. Cambridge, MA.: Program on Negotiation.

BROWN, Jennifer Gerarda. (1997) *The Role of Hope in Negotiation*, 44 UCLA L. Rev. 1661.

BUSH, Robert A. Baruch. (1997) *"What Do We Need a Mediator For?": Mediation's "Value-Added" for Negotiators*, 12 Ohio St. J. Disp. Resol. 1.

CHAMBERS, John R., and De DREU, K.W. (2014) *Egocentrism Drives Misunderstanding in Conflict and Negotiation*, 51 J. Experimental Soc. Psych. 15.

CIALDINI, Robert B. (1993) Influence: The Psychology of Persuasion (rev. ed.). New York: Morrow.

CRAVER, Charles B. (2002) *The Intelligent Negotiator: What to Say, What to Do, and How to Get What You Want—Every Time*. Roseville, Calif.: Prima Publishing.

CRAVER, Charles B. (1997) Symposium: *The Lawyer's Duties and Responsibilities in Dispute Resolution: Article: Post-Conference Reflection: Negotiation Ethics: How to be Deceptive Without Being Dishonest/How to Be Assertive Without Being Offensive*, 38 S. Tex. L. Rev. 713.

CRAVER, Charles B. (1997) Effective Legal Negotiation and Settlement (3d ed.). Charlottesville: Michie.

EBNER, Noam, and KAMP, Adam. (2010) Relationship 2.0, in Rethinking Negotiation Teaching: Venturing Beyond the Classroom (Christopher Honeyman et al., eds.). St. Paul: DRI Press.

EBNER, Noam et al., eds. (2012) *Rethinking Negotiation Teaching: Assessing Our Students, Assessing Ourselves*. St. Paul: DRI Press.

EBNER, Noam, et al. (2009) *You've Got Agreement: Negotiating via Email*, in Rethinking Negotiation Teaching: Innovations for Context and Culture (Christopher Honeyman et al., eds.). St. Paul: DRI Press.

EBNER, Noam. (2010) Relationship 2.0 *in* Rethinking Negotiation Teaching: Venturing Beyond the Classroom (Honeyman et al., eds), DRI Press.

ECKBLAD, Ariel. (2020) *In Pursuit of Fairness: Re-Negotiating Embedded Norms & Re-Imagining Interest-Based Negotiation*, 26 Harv. Negot. L. Rev. 1.

FISHER, Roger, URY, William, and PATTON, Bruce. (1981, 1991) *Getting to Yes: Negotiating Agreement Without Giving In* (2d. ed.). New York: Penguin Books.

FISHER, Roger. (1984) *Comment*, 34 J. Legal. Educ. 120.

FOX, Lawrence J. (2001) Those Who Worry About the Ethics of Negotiation Should Never be Viewed as Just Another Set of Service Providers, 52 Mercer L. Rev. 977.

FRASE, Laura A. (2020-21), *Refining our Thinking About Thinking: Battling the Sway of Cognitive Biases in Negotiation*, 51 Cumb. L. Rev. 347

FRESHMAN, Clark et al. (2002) *The Lawyer-Negotiator as Mood Scientist: What We Know and Don't Know About How Mood Relates to Successful Negotiation*, 2002 J. Disp. Resol. 1.

GIFFORD, Donald G. (1989) *Legal Negotiation*. St. Paul: West Publishing Co.

GOODPASTER, Gary. (1996) *A Primer on Competitive Bargaining*, 1996 J. Disp. Resol. 325.

GUERNSEY, Thomas F., and ZWIER, Paul J. (2005) *Advanced Negotiation and Mediation Theory and Practice: A Realistic Integrated Approach. National Institute for Trial Advocacy.*

HINSHAW, Art, and ALBERTS, Jess K. (2011) *Doing the Right Thing: An Empirical Study of Attorney Negotiation Ethics*, 16 Harv. Negot. L. Rev. 95.

HOFLING, Charles, et al. (1966) *An Experimental Study of Nurse-Physician Relationships*, 143 J. Nervous & Mental Disease 171.

HONEYMAN, Christopher et al., eds. (2009) *Rethinking Negotiation Teaching: Innovations for Context and Culture.* St. Paul: DRI Press.

HONEYMAN, Christopher et al., eds. (2010) *Rethinking Negotiation Teaching: Venturing Beyond the Classroom.* St. Paul: DRI Press.

HONEYMAN, Christopher et al., eds. (2013) *Rethinking Negotiation Teaching: Educating Negotiators for a Connected World*. St. Paul: DRI Press.

HONEYMAN, C. and SCHNEIDER, A. (eds.) *The Negotiator's Desk Reference*, Vols. 1 & 2. DRI Press: 2017

HSU, Shi-Ling. (2002) *A Game-Theoretic Approach to Regulatory Negotiation and a Framework for Empirical Analysis*, 26 Harv. Envtl. L. Rev. 33.

JOLLS, Christine et al. (1998) *A Behavioral Approach to Law and Economics*, 50 Stan. L. Rev. 1471.

KAHNEMAN, Daniel et al., eds. (1982) *Judgment Under Uncertainty: Heuristics and Biases*. Cambridge: Cambridge University Press.

KAHNEMAN, Daniel, and TVERSKY, Amos. (1995) *Conflict Resolution: Cognitive Perspective, in Barriers to Conflict Resolution* (K. Arrow, ed.). New York: W. W. Norton.

KOLB, Deborah M., and WILLIAMS, Judith. (2003) Everyday Negotiation: Navigating the Hidden Agendas in Bargaining (Rev. ed.). San Francisco: Jossey-Bass.

KOROBKIN, Russell. (2008) *Against Integrative Bargaining*, 58 Case W. Res. L. Rev. 1323.

KOROBKIN, Russell. (2002) *A Positive Theory of Legal Negotiation*, 88 Geo. L.J. 1789.

KOROBKIN, Russell et al. (1997) *Psychology, Economics, and Settlement: A New Look at the Role of the Lawyer*, 76 Tex. L. Rev. 77.

KOROBKIN, Russell, and GUTHRIE, Chris. (1994) *Psychological Barriers to Litigation Settlement: An Experimental View*, 93 Mich. L. Rev. 107.

KRAMER, Henry S. (2001) *Game Set, Match: Winning the Negotiations Game*. New York: ALM Publishing.

KRITEK, Phyllis Beck. (2002) Negotiating at an Uneven Table: Developing Moral Courage in Resolving Our Conflicts (2d ed.). San Francisco: Jossey-Bass.

LAX, David A., and SEBENIUS, James K. (1986) The Manager as Negotiator: Bargaining for Cooperation & Competitive Gain. New York: Free Press.

LEWICKI, Roy J. et al. (2004) Essentials of Negotiation (3d ed.). New York: McGraw-Hill/Irwin.

LEWICKI, Roy J. et al. (2009) Negotiation: Readings, Exercises, and Cases (6th ed.). New York: McGraw-Hill/Irwin.

LUBAN, David. (1988) *The Quality of Justice, Institute for Legal Studies*, Working Papers Series 8.

LUM, Grande et al. (2002) *Expand the Pie: How to Create More Value in Any Negotiation*. Seattle: Castle Pac. Publ'g.

MENKEL-MEADOW, Carrie. (1984) *Toward Another View of Legal Negotiation: The Structure of Problem Solving*, 31 UCLA L. Rev. 754.

MEYERSON, Bruce. (1997) *Telling the Truth in Mediation: Mediator Owed Duty of Candor*, Disp. Resol. Magazine, Vol. 4, No. 17 (Winter 1997).

MILGRAM, Stanley. (1974) *Obedience to Authority: An Experimental View*. New York: Harper & Row.

MNOOKIN, Robert H. (2003) Strategic Barriers to Dispute Resolution: A Comparison of Bilateral and Multilateral Negotiations, 8 Harv. Negot. L. Rev. 1.

MNOOKIN, Robert H., PEPPET, Scott, and TULUMELLO, Andrew. (2000) *Beyond Winning: Negotiating to Create Value in Deals and Disputes*. Cambridge: Belknap Press of Harvard Univ. Press.

MNOOKIN, Robert H., and ROSS, Lee. (1995) Introduction to Barriers to Conflict Resolution 3 (Kenneth J. Arrow, ed.). New York: W. W. Norton.

MNOOKIN, Robert H. (1993) *Why Negotiations Fail: An Exploration of Barriers to the Resolution of Conflict*, 8 Ohio St. J. on Disp. Resol. 235.

MNOOKIN, Robert H., and WILSON, Robert R. (1989) *Rational Bargaining and Market Efficiency: Understanding* Pennzoil v. Texaco, 75 Va. L. Rev. 295.

NELKEN, Melissa L. (2001) *Understanding Negotiation*. Cincinnati: Anderson Publishing Co.

PALMER, Michael Palmer. (2010) *Which Is Better? The Deal or the Ordeal? An Examination of Some Challenges of Case Valuation*, 36 Vt. B.J. 34 (fall).

PRUITT, Dean G., and LEWIS, Steven A. (1977) The Psychology of Integrative Bargaining (in) Negotiations: Social-Psychological Perspectives (D. Druckman, ed.). Beverly Hills: Sage.

RACHLINSKI, Jeffrey J. (1996) *Gains, Losses, and the Psychology of Litigation*, 70 S. Cal. L. Rev. 113.

RAIFFA, Howard et al. (2007) *Negotiation Analysis: The Science and Art of Collaborative Decision Making*. Cambridge: Belknap Press of Harvard Univ. Press.

RAIFFA, Howard. (1982) *The Art & Science of Negotiation*. Cambridge: Harvard Univ. Press.

RAINEY, Daniel, et al, eds. (2021) *Online Dispute Resolution: Theory and Practice*, Eleven International Publishing.

RAMBO, Lynne H. (2000) *Impeaching Lying Parties With Their Statements During Negotiation: Demysticizing the Public Policy Rationale Behind Evidence Rule 408 and the Mediation-Privilege Statutes*, 75 Wash. L. Rev. 1037.

ROBINSON, Rob J. et al. (June 1990) *Misconstruing the Views of the "Other Side": Real and Perceived Differences in Three Ideological Conflicts*, Stanford Center on Conflict and Negotiation Working Paper No. 18.

ROSS, Lee, and STILLINGER, Constance. (1991) *Barriers to Conflict Resolution*, 7 Negot. J. 389.

SCHNEIDER, Andrea Kupfer. (2002) *Shattering Negotiation Myths: Empirical Evidence on the Effectiveness of Negotiation Style*, 7 Harv. Negot. L. Rev. 143.

SCHNEIDER, Andrea Kupfer. (1994) *Effective Responses to Offensive Comments*, 1994 Negot. J. 107.

SCHNEIDER, Andrea Kupfer. (2012) *Teaching a New Negotiation Skills Paradigm*, 39 Wash. U. J.L. & Pol'y 13.

SCHNEIDER, Andrea Kupfer, and HONEYMAN, Christopher, eds. (2006) The Negotiator's Fieldbook: The Desk Reference for the Experienced Negotiator. Washington, D.C.: Am. Bar Ass'n Sec. on Disp. Resol.

SGOUREY, Stoyan V. (Sgourev, *Lake Wobegon Upside Down: The Paradox of Status-Devaluation*, 84 Soc. Forces 1497

SIMONS, Herbert W. (1986) *Persuasion: Understanding, Practice and Analysis*. New York: McGraw-Hill College.

STERNLIGHT, Jean R. (1999) *Lawyers' Representation of Clients in Mediation: Using Economics and Psychology to Structure Advocacy in an Nonadversarial Setting*, 14 Ohio St. J. on Disp. Resol. 259.

STERNLIGHT, Jean R. and ROBBENNOLT, Jennifer K. (2022) *In-Person or Via Technology?: Drawing on Psychology to Choose and Design Dispute Resolution Processes*, 71 DePaul L. Rev 537

STILLINGER, Constance A. et al. (1988) *The Reactive Devaluation Barrier to Conflict Resolution*, Stanford Center on Conflict and Negotiation, Working Paper No. 3. *Symposium: The Emerging Interdisciplinary Canon of Negotiation*, 87 Marq. L. Rev. 637 (2004).

THURMAN, Ruth Fleet. (1990) *Chipping Away at Lawyer Veracity: The ABA's Turn Toward Situation Ethics in Negotiations*, 1990 J. Disp. Resol. 103.

TVERSKY, Amos et al. (1990) *The Causes of Preference Reversals*, 80 Am. Econ. Rev. 204.

TVERSKY, Amos, and KAHNEMAN, Daniel. (1991) *Loss Aversion in Riskless Choice: A Reference-Dependent Model*, 106 Q.J. Econ. 1038.

TVERSKY, Amos, and THALER, Richard. (1990) *Anomalies: Preference Reversals*, 4 J. Econ. Persp. 201.

WHITE, James. (1980) *Machiavelli and the Bar: Ethical Limitations on Lying in Negotiation*, 1980 Am. B. Found. Res. J. 926.

WHITE, James J. (1984) *The Pros and Cons of Getting to Yes*, 34 J. Legal Educ. 115.

WILLIAMS, Gerald R. (1983) *Legal Negotiation and Settlement*. St. Paul: West Publishing Co.

ZOGHBY, Marguerite. (2001) *The Prohibition of Communication with Adverse Parties in Civil Negotiations: Protecting Clients or Preventing Solutions?* 14 Geo. J. Legal Ethics 1165.

Chapter 3

AARON, Marjorie Corman. (2005) *Do's and Don'ts for Mediation Practice*, Disp. Resol. Magazine, Vol. XI, No. II (Winter 2005).

BUSH, Robert A. Baruch, and FOLGER, Joseph P. (1996) *Transformative Mediation and Third-Party Intervention: Ten Hallmarks of a Transformative Approach to Practice*, 13 Mediation Q. 263.

FOLBERG, Jay, and TAYLOR, Alison. (1988) *Mediation: A Comprehensive Guide to Resolving Conflicts without Litigation*. San Francisco: Jossey-Bass.

HAYNES, John M., and HAYNES, Gretchen L. (1989) *Mediating Divorce*. San Francisco: Jossey-Bass.

MOORE, Christopher W. (1991) *The Mediation Process: Practical Strategies for Resolving Conflict*. San Francisco: Jossey-Bass.

PRESS, Sharon, and KOSCH, Kimberly. (2013) *County Mediator's Manual*. Tallahassee, FL: Florida Disp. Resol. Center.

RISKIN, L. (2023) *Managing Conflict Mindfully*. West Academic Publishing.

STULBERG, Joseph B. and LOVE, Lela P. (2019) The Middle Voice: Mediating Conflict Successfully (3d ed.). Durham: Carolina Acad. Press.

THE TEST DESIGN PROJECT. (1995) *Performance-Based Assessment: A Methodology, for Use in Selecting, Training and Evaluating Mediators*. Washington, DC: Nat'l Inst. for Disp. Resol.

WISSLER, Roselle L. and HINSHAW, Art. (2022) *What Happens Before the First Mediation Session? An Empirical Study of Pre-Session Communications*, 23 Cardozo J. Conflict Resol. 143.

Chapter 4

ABA Section of Dispute Resolution (2017) *Report on the Task Force on Research on Mediator Techniques*.

AARON, Marjorie Corman. (1996) Evaluation in Mediation (in) Mediating Legal Disputes (Dwight Golann, ed.). New York: Aspen Law and Business.

ALFINI, James J. (1991) *Trashing, Bashing, and Hashing It out: Is This the End of "Good Mediation"?*, 19 Fla. St. U. L. Rev. 47.

AMSLER, Lisa Blomgren, MARTINEZ, Janet K., and SMITH, Stephanie E. (2020) *Dispute Systems Design: Preventing, Managing, and Resolving Conflict.* Stanford University Press.

ANDERSON, Jonathan F., and BINGHAM, Linda. (1997) *Upstream Effects from Mediation of Workplace Disputes: Some Preliminary Evidence from the USPS*, 48 Lab. L.J. 601.

ANTES, James R., FOLGER, Joseph P., and DELLA NOCE, Dorothy J. (2001) *Transforming Conflict Interactions in the Workplace: Documented Effects of the USPS REDRESS Program*, 18 Hofstra Lab. & Emp. L.J. 429.

BERNARD, Sydney E. et al. (1984) *The Neutral Mediator: Value Dilemmas in Divorce Mediation*, 4 Mediation Q. 61.

BICKERMAN, John. (2012) *Adapting Mediation to What Users Want*, 45 Md. Bar J. 55.

BICKERMAN, John. (1996) *Evaluative Mediator Responds*, 14 Alternatives to the High Cost of Litigation 70.

BINGHAM, Linda, KIM, Kiwhan, and RAINES, Susan Summers. (2002) *Exploring the Role of Representation in Employment Mediation at the USPS*, 17 Ohio St. J. on Disp. Resol. 341.

BRETT, Jeanne M. et al. (1986) *Mediator Style and Mediation Effectiveness*, 1986 Negot. J. 277.

BUSH, Robert A. Baruch. (1989) *Efficiency and Protection, or Empowerment and Recognition?: The Mediator's Role and Ethical Standards in Mediation*, 41 Fla. L. Rev. 253.

BUSH, Robert A. Baruch, and FOLGER, Joseph. (1994) *The Promise of Mediation: Responding to Conflict Through Empowerment and Recognition.* San Francisco: Jossey-Bass.

BUSH, Robert A. Baruch, and FOLGER, Joseph P. (2005) *The Promise of Mediation: The Transformative Approach to Mediation* (2d ed.). San Francisco: Jossey-Bass.

BUSH, Robert A. Baruch, and FOLGER, Joseph P. (1996) *Transformative Mediation and Third-Party Intervention: Ten Hallmarks of a Trans-formative Approach to Practice*, 13 Mediation Q. 263.

CHARKOUDIAN, Lorig, and WAYNE, E.K. (2010) *Fairness, understanding, and satisfaction: Impact of mediator and participant race and gender on participants' perception of mediation*, Conflict Resol. Q. 23 (Fall, Vol. 28, Issue 1).

CHARKOUDIAN, Lorig. (2012) *Just My Style: The Practical, Ethical, and Empirical Dangers of the Lack of Consensus about Definitions of Mediation Styles*, Negotiation and Conflict Management Research 325 (Vol. 5, Issue 4).

CHARKOUDIAN, Lorig et al. (2019) *What Works in Alternative Dispute Resolution? The Impact of Third-Party Neutral Strategies in Small Claims Cases*, Conflict Resol. Q. 101 (Winter, Vol. 37, Issue 2).

COBB, Sara, and RIFKIN, Janet. (1991) *Practice and Paradox: Deconstructing Neutrality in Mediation*, 16 Law & Soc'y Inquiry 35.

EISENBERG, Deborah Thompson. (2016) *What we Know and Need to Know about Court-Annexed Dispute Resolution*, 67 S.C. L. Rev. 245.

FEERICK, John et al. (1995) *Standards of Professional Conduct in Alternative Dispute Resolution*, 1995 J. Disp. Resol. 95.

FOLBERG, Jay, and TAYLOR, Alison. (1984) *Mediation: A Comprehensive Guide to Resolving Conflicts Without Litigation*. San Francisco: Jossey-Bass.

FOLGER, Joseph P., and BUSH, Robert A. Baruch. (1996) *Transformative Mediation and Third-Party Intervention: Ten Hallmarks of a Transformative Approach to Practice*, 13 Mediation Q. 263.

FOLGER, Joseph P., BUSH, Robert A. Baruch, and DELLA NOCE, Dorothy J., eds. (2010) *Transformative Mediation: A Sourcebook*. Reston, VA: Ass'n for Conflict Resol. & Inst. for the Study of Conflict Transformation.

FRIEDMAN, Gary J. (1993) *A Guide to Divorce Mediation*. New York: Workman Publications.

FRIEDMAN, Gary J. and HIMMELSTEIN, Jack. (2008) Challenging Conflict Mediation Through Understanding. Washington, D.C.: Am. Bar Ass'n Sec. on Disp. Resol.

FRIEDMAN, Gary J. and HIMMELSTEIN, Jack (2006) *Resolving Conflict Together: The Understanding-Based Model of Mediation*, 2006 J. Disp. Resol. 523.

FULLER, Lon L. (1971) *Mediation: Its Forms and Functions*, 44 S. Cal. L. Rev. 305.

GAYNIER, Lisa P. (2005) *Transformative Mediation: In Search of a Theory of Practice*, 22 Conflict Resol. Q. 397.

GOLANN, Dwight, and AARON, Marjorie Corman. (2019) *Beyond Abstinence: The Need for Safe, Impartial Evaluation in Mediation*, Disp. Resol. Mag. 22 (No. 4).

GOLANN, Dwight, ed. (1996) *Mediating Legal Disputes*. New York: Aspen Law and Business.

HARMON-DARROW, Caroline, et al. (2020) *Defining Inclusive Mediation: Theory, Practice, and Research*. Conflict Resolution Q. 305.

HAYNES, John M. (1992) *Mediation and Therapy: An Alternative View*, 10 Mediation Q. 21.

HANSEN, Toran. (2004) *The Narrative Approach to Mediation*, 4 Pepp. Disp. Resol. L.J. 297.

HINSHAW, Art, SCHNEIDER, Andrea Kupfer, and COLE, Sarah Rudolph. (2021) *Discussions in Dispute Resolution: The Foundational Articles*. Oxford University Press.

KOLB, Deborah. (1994) *When Talk Works: Profiles of Mediators*. San Francisco: Jossey-Bass.

KOLB, Deborah. (1983) The Mediator *s*. Cambridge: MIT Press.

KOVACH, Kimberlee, and LOVE, Lela. (1996) *Evaluative Mediation Is an Oxymoron*, 14 Alternatives to the High Cost of Litigation 31.

KRESSEL, Kenneth et al. (1994) *The Settlement-Orientation vs. the Problem-Solving Style in Custody Mediation*, 50 J. Soc. Issues 67.

KRESSEL, Kenneth. (1994) Frances Butler: Questions That Lead to Answers in Child Custody Mediation (in) When Talk Works: Profiles of Mediators (Deborah M. Kolb ed.). San Francisco: Jossey-Bass.

LANDE, John. (2023) *Real Mediation Systems to Help Parties and Mediators Achieve Their Goals*, 24 Cardozo J. Conflict Resol. 347.

LANG, Michael, guest ed. (1996) *Transformative Approaches to Mediation: Special Issue*, 13 Mediation Q. 4.

LOVE, Lela P. (1997) *The Top Ten Reasons Why Mediators Should Not Evaluate*, 24 Fla. St. U. L. Rev. 937.

MAUTE, Judith. (1991) *Public Values and Private Justice: A Case for Mediator Accountability*, 4 Geo. J. Legal Ethics 503.

MAYER, Bernard S., STULBERG, Joseph B., and SUSSKIND, Lawrence. (2012) *Core Values of Dispute Resolution: Is Neutrality Necessary?* , 95 Marq. L. Rev. 805.

MAYER, Bernard S., and FONT-GUZMAN, Jacqueline (2022) *The Neutrality Trap: Disrupting and Connecting for Social Change*. Wiley.

McDERMOTT, E. Patrick. (2012) *Discovering the Importance of Mediator Style — An Interdisciplinary Challenge, Negotiation and Conflict Management Research* 340 (November; Issue 4).

MENKEL-MEADOW, Carrie. (1995) *The Many Ways of Mediation: The Transformation of Traditions, Ideologies, Paradigms, and Practices*, 11 Negot. J. 217.

NAUSS EXON, Susan. (2008) *The Effects That Mediator Styles Impose on Neutrality and Impartiality Requirements of Mediation*, 42 U.S.F. L. Rev. 577.

NOLAN-HALEY, Jacqueline. (1999) *Informed Consent in Mediation: A Guiding Principle for Truly Educated Decisionmaking*, 74 Notre Dame L. Rev. 775.

PRESS, Sharon, and DEASON, Ellen E. (2021) *Mediation: Embedded Assumptions of Whiteness*, 22 Cardozo J. Conflict Resol. 453.

RISKIN, Leonard L. (2003) *Decisionmaking in Mediation: The New Old Grid and the New New Grid System*, 79 Notre Dame L. Rev. 1.

RISKIN, Leonard L. (1996) *Understanding Mediators' Orientations, Strategies, and Techniques: A Grid for the Perplexed*, 1 Harv. Negot. L. Rev. 7.

RISKIN, Leonard L. (1994) *Mediator Orientations, Strategies and Techniques*, 12 Alternatives to the High Cost of Litigation 111.

RISKIN, Leonard L. (1982) *Mediation and Lawyers*, 43 Ohio St. L.J. 29.

RISKIN, Leonard L. (1984) *Toward New Standards for the Neutral Lawyer in Mediation*, 26 Ariz. L. Rev. 329.

ROGERS, Nancy H. (2nd ed. 2019) *Designing Systems and Processes for Managing Disputes.* Wolters Kluwer.

SHETOWSKY, Donna. (2017) *When Ignorance is Not Bliss: An Empirical Study of Litigants' Awareness of Court-Sponsored Alternative Dispute Resolution Programs*, 22 Harv. Negot. L. Rev. 189.

SIBLEY, Susan S., and MERRY, Sally E. (1986) *Mediator Settlement Strategies*, 8 Law & Pol'y 7.

STARK, James. (1997) *The Ethics of Mediation Evaluation: Some Troublesome Questions and Tentative Proposals, from an Evaluative Lawyer Mediator*, 38 S. Tex. L. Rev. 769.

STIPANOWICH, Thomas J. (1998) *The Multi-Door Contract and Other Possibilities*, 13 Ohio St. J. on Disp. Resol. 303.

STULBERG, Joseph B. (1987) *Taking Charge/Managing Conflict.* Lexington, MA: Lexington Press.

STULBERG, Joseph B. (1981) *The Theory and Practice of Mediation: A Reply to Professor Susskind*, 6 Vt. L. Rev. 85.

STULBERG, Joseph B. and LOVE, Lela P. (2019) The Middle Voice: Mediating Conflict Successfully (3d ed.). Durham: Carolina Acad. Press.

STULBERG, Joseph B. and SUSSKIND, Lawrence. (2012) *Core Values of Dispute Resolution: Is Neutrality Necessary?*, 95 Marq. L. Rev. 805.

SUSSKIND, Lawrence. (1981) *Environmental Mediation and the Accountability Problem*, 6 Vt. L. Rev. 1.

SUSSKIND, Lawrence, et al. Judicial Dispute Resolution (JDR): New Roles for Judges in Ensuring Justice. Anthem Press: 2023

WECKSTEIN, Donald T. (1997) *In Praise of Party Empowerment — And of Mediator Activism*, 33 Willamette L. Rev. 501.

WILLIAMS, Michael. (1997) *Can't I Get No Satisfaction?: Thoughts on The Promise of Mediation*, 15 Mediation Q. 143.

WINSLADE, John, and MONK, Gerald. (2000) *Narrative Mediation: A New Approach to Conflict Resolution*. San Francisco: Jossey-Bass.

Chapter 5

BROWN, Jennifer Gerarda, and AYRES, Ian. (1994) *Economic Rationales for Mediation*, 80 Va. L. Rev. 323.

BRUNET, Edward. (1987) *Questioning the Quality of Alternative Dispute Resolution*, 62 Tul. L. Rev. 1.

COLE, Sara et al., eds. (2011) Mediation: Law, Policy and Practice (2012 ed.). St. Paul: Thompson-West.

DEASON, Ellen F. (2006) *The Need for Trust as a Justification for Confidentiality in Mediation: A Cross-Disciplinary Approach*, 54 U. Kan. L. Rev. 1387

DEASON, Ellen E. (2002) *Predictable Mediation Confidentiality in the U.S. Federal System*, 17 Ohio St. J. on Disp. Resol. 239.

DEASON, Ellen E. (2002) Uniform Mediation Act — Law Ensures Confidentiality, Neutrality of Process, Disp. Resol. Magazine (Summer 2002), at 7, 9.

EHRHARDT, Charles W. (1999) *Confidentiality, Privilege and Rule 408: the Protection of Mediation Proceedings in Federal Court*, 60 La. L. Rev. 91.

FEINBERG, Kenneth R. (1989) *A Preferred Method of Dispute Resolution*, 16 Pepp. L. Rev. 55.

FREEDMAN, Lawrence R., and PRIGOFF, Michael. (1986) *Confidentiality in Mediation: The Need for Protection*, 2 Ohio St. J. on Disp. Resol. 37.

HARTER, Phillip J. (1989) *Neither Cop Nor Collection Agent: Encouraging Administrative Settlements by Ensuring Mediator Confidentiality*, 41 Admin. L.J. 315.

HUGHES, Scott H. (1998) *A Closer Look: The Case for a Mediation Confi dentiality Privilege Still Has Not Been Made*, Disp. Resol. Magazine, Vol. 5, No. 14 (Winter 1998).

IZUMI, Carol. (1995) Remarks in *Symposium on Standards of Professional Conduct in Alternative Dispute Resolution*, 1995 J. Disp. Resol. 95.

KATZ, Lucy V. (1988) *Enforcing an ADR Clause — Are Good Intentions All You Have?* 26 Am. Bus. L.J. 575.

KIRTLEY, Alan. (1995) *The Mediation Privilege's Transition from Theory to Implementation: Designing a Mediation Privilege Standard to Protect Mediation Participants, the Process and the Public Interest*, 1995 J. Disp. Resol. 1.

PERINO, Michael A. (1995) *Drafting Mediation Privileges: Lessons from the Civil Justice Reform Act*, 26 Seton Hall L. Rev. 1.

PRESS, Sharon and FIRESTONE, Gregory (2022) *Privadentiality: What is It and Why do we need it?* 26 Dispute Resolution Magazine 24–26.

PRIGOFF, Michael L. (1988) *Toward Candor or Chaos: The Case of Confidentiality in Mediation*, 12 Seton Hall Legis. J. 1.

REUBEN, Richard C. (2003) *The Sound of Dust Settling: A Response to Criticisms of the UMA*, 2003 J. Disp. Resol. 99.

SHANNON, Brian D. (2003) *Dancing with the One That "Brung Us" — Why the Texas ADR Community Has Declined to Embrace the UMA*, 2003 J. Disp. Resol. 197.

SHERMAN, Edward F. (1997) *Confidentiality in ADR Proceedings: Policy Issues Arising From the Texas Experience*, 38 S. Tex. L. Rev. 541.

WELSH, Nancy A. (2011) *Musings on Mediation, Kleenex, and (Smudged) White Hats*, 33 U. La Verne L. Rev. 5.

Chapter 6

AMERICAN BAR ASSOCIATION. (2004) *Resolution on Good Faith Requirements for Mediators and Mediation Advocates in Court-Mandated Mediation Programs*, ABA Section of Dispute Resolution, Approved by Section Council, August 7, 2004.

BOULLE, Laurence (2014) *International Enforceability of Mediated Settlement Agreements* 7 Contemp. Asia Arb. J. 35.

CARTER, Roger L. (2002) *Oh Ye of Little [Good] Faith: Questions, Concerns and Commentary on Efforts to Regulate Participant Conduct in Mediations*, 2002 J. Dis. Res. 367.

COBEN, James R., and THOMPSON, Peter N. (1999) *The Haghighi Trilogy and the Minnesota Civil Mediation Act: Exposing a Phantom Menace Casting a Pall Over the Development of ADR in Minnesota*, 20 Hamline J. Pub. L. & Pol'y 299.

COLE, Sara et al., eds. (2011) Mediation: Law, Policy and Practice (2012 ed.). St. Paul: Thompson-West.

DEASON, Ellen E. (2001) *Enforcing Mediated Settlement Agreements: Contract Law Collides with Confidentiality*, 35 U.C. Davis L. Rev. 33.

GLEASON ALVAREZ, Erin E. (2022). *What is Bad Faith in Mediation?* (2022) ALM LAW.

IZUMI, Carol L., and LA RUE, Homer C. (2003) *Prohibiting "Good Faith" Reports Under the Uniform Mediation Act: Keeping the Adjudication Camel out of the Mediation Tent*, 2003 J. Disp. Resol. 67.

KOVACH, Kimberlee K. (1997) *Good Faith Mediation — Requested, Recommended, or Required? A New Ethic*, 38 S. Tex. L. Rev. 575.

KOVACH, Kimberlee K. (1997) *Lawyer Ethics in Mediation: Time for A Requirement of Good Faith in Mediation*, Disp. Resol. Magazine (Winter 1997), at 9.

LANDE, John. (2002) *Using Dispute System Design Methods to Promote Good-Faith Participation in Court-Connected Mediation Programs*, 50 UCLA L. Rev. 69.

SHERMAN, Edward F. (1993) *Court-Mandated Alternative Dispute Resolution: What Form of Participation Should Be Required?*, 46 SMU L. Rev. 2079.

SHERMAN, Edward F. (1997) *"Good Faith" Participation in Mediation: Aspirational, Not Mandatory*, Disp. Resol. Magazine (Winter 1997), at 14.

THOMPSON, Peter N. (2011) *Good Faith Mediation in the Federal Courts*, 26 Ohio St. J. on Disp. Resol. 363.

YEO, Walter (2021) *Understanding and Encouraging Good Faith in Mediation* in Joel Lee & Marcus Lim (ed.) Contemporary Issues in Mediation.

Chapter 7

ADLER, Robert. (1988) Sharing the Children: How to Resolve Custody Problems and Get on with Your Life.

ALFINI, James J. (1991) *Trashing, Bashing, and Hashing It Out: Is This The End of "Good Mediation"?*, 19 Fla. St. U. L. Rev. 47.

ASSOCIATION FOR CONFLICT RESOLUTION ANNUAL CONFERENCE 2003. (2004) *The World of Conflict Resolution: A Mosaic of Possibilities*, 5 Cardozo J. Conflict Resol. 190.

AUGSBURGER, D.W. (1992). *Conflict Mediation Across Cultures*. Louisville, KY: Westminister/John Knox Press.

BABCOCK, Linda, and LASCHEVER, Sara. (2003) *Women Don't Ask: Negotiation and the Gender Divide*. Princeton, NJ: Princeton Univ. Press.

BARNES, Bruce. (1994) *Conflict Resolution Across Cultures: A Hawaii Perspective and a Pacific Mediation Model*, 12 Mediation Q. 117.

BOWLAND, S.Y., et al., eds. (2022). *Beyond Equity and Inclusion in Conflict Resolution: Recentering the Profession*. Rowman & Littlefield.

BRYAN, Penelope E. (1992) *Killing Us Softly: Divorce Mediation and the Politics of Power*, 40 Buff. L. Rev. 441.

BUSCH, Dominic, ed. (2023) *The Routledge Handbook of Intercultural Mediation*. Routledge.

COBB, Sara, and RIFKIN, Janet. (1991) *Practice and Paradox: Deconstructing Neutrality in Mediation*, 16 Law & Soc. Inquiry 35.

CHALMERS, W. Ellison. (1974) *Racial Negotiations: Potentials & Limitations*. Ann Arbor: Inst. of Lab. and Indus. Rel.

CIVIL RIGHTS MEDIATION ORAL HISTORY PROJECT, https://civilrightsmediation.org/ and https://youtube.com/@crmediation.

COLE, Sarah Rudolph et al. (2023), *"Framing" in Public Initiatives to Advance Racial Equity*, 38, Ohio St. J. Disp. Resol. 255.

COKER, Donna. (1999) *Enhancing Autonomy for Battered Women: Lessons from Navajo Peacemaking*, 47 UCLA L. Rev. 1.

DAHL, Robert A. (1989) *Democracy and Its Critics*. New Haven: Yale Univ. Press.

DELGADO, Richard et al. (1985) *Fairness and Formality: Minimizing the Risk of Prejudice in Alternative Dispute Resolution*, 1985 Wis. L. Rev. 1359.

DIVIDED COMMUNITY PROJECT, *Virtual Toolkit*, https://go.osu.edu/dcptoolkit.

DODD, Carley H. (1987) *Dynamics of Intercultural Communication*. Dubuque: W.C. Brown.

DUKES, Frank, and COZART, Selena. (2023), *Rethinking Systems Design for Racial Justice & Equity: "We Don't Want Any of That Neutrality" and Other Lessons from Mediating Race and Equity*, 38 Ohio St. J. Disp. Resol. 341

DURYEA, Michelle LeBaron, and GRUNDISON, J. Bruce. (1993) *Conflict and Culture: Research in Five Communities in Vancouver, British Colombia*. Victoria, BC: UVic. Inst. for Disp. Resol.

FELSTINER, William, ABEL, Richard L., and SARAT, Austin. (1980–81) *The Emergence and Transformation of Disputes: Naming, Blaming, Claiming*, 15 Law & Soc'y Rev. 631.

FISS, Owen. (1984). *Against Settlement*, 93 Yale L.J. 1073.

FOLBERG, Jay, and TAYLOR, Alison. (1984) *Mediation*. San Francisco: Jossey-Bass.

FROEHLICH, William, ROGERS, Nancy H., and STULBERG, Joseph B. (2020) *Sharing Dispute Resolution Practices with Leaders of a Divided Community or Campus: Strategies for Two Crucial Conversations*, 35 Ohio St. J. on Disp. Resol. 781.

FULLER, Lon. (1958) *Positivism and Fidelity to Law — A Reply to Professor Hart*, 71 Harv. L. Rev. 630.

GAGNON, Andree G. (1992) *Ending Mandatory Divorce Mediation for Battered Women*, 15 Harv. Women's L.J. 272.

GILLIGAN, Carol. (1982) *In a Different Voice*. Cambridge: Harvard Univ. Press.

GOLDBERG, Stephen B., SANDER, Frank E.A., ROGERS, Nancy H., and COLE, Sarah Rudolph. (2007) Dispute Resolution: Negotiation, Mediation, and Other Processes (5th ed.). New York: Wolters Kluwer.

GRILLO, Trina. (1990) *Process Dangers for Women*, 100 Yale L.J. 1545.

GULLIVER, P.H. (1979) *Disputes and Negotiations: A Cross-Cultural Perspective*. San Diego: Academic Press.

GUNNING, Isabelle. (2022) *Justice for All in Mediation: What the Pandemic, Racial Justice Movement, and the Recognition of Structural Racism Calls us to do as Mediators*, 68 Wash. U. J.L. & Pol'y 36.

GUTMANN, Amy, and THOMPSON, Dennis. (1996) *Democracy and Disagreement*. Cambridge: Belknap Press of Harvard Univ.

HALL, Edward T., and HALL, Mildred R. (1987) *Hidden Differences*. Garden City, N.Y.: Anchor Press.

HART, H.L.A. (1994) *The Concept of Law* (2d ed.). Oxford: Clarendon Press.

HART, H.L.A. (1958) *Positivism and the Separation of Law and Morals*, 71 Harv. L. Rev. 593.

HENSLER, Deborah R. (2002) *Suppose It's Not True: Challenging Mediation Ideology*, 2002 J. Disp. Resol. 81.

HERMANN, Michelle, et al. (1993) *An Empirical Study of the Effects of Race and Gender on Small Claims Adjudication and Mediation*. Albuquerque: Inst. of Pub. L., Univ. of New Mexico.

HOFFMAN, David, and WINTER, Helen (2022) *Follow the Science: Proven Strategies for Reducing Unconscious Bias*, 28 Harv. Neg. L. Rev. 1.

HUGHES, Scott. (1995) *Elizabeth's Story*, 8 Geo. J. Legal Ethics 553.

HYMAN, Jonathan M. (2004) *Swimming in the Deep End: Dealing with Justice in Mediation*, 6 Cardozo J. Conflict Resol. 19.

HYMAN, Jonathan M., and LOVE, Lela P. (2002) *If Portia Were a Mediator: An Inquiry Into Justice in Mediation*, 9 Clinical L. Rev. 159.

IZUMI, Carol. (2010) *Implicit Bias and the Illusion of Mediator Neutrality*, 34 Wash. U. J.L. & Pol'y 71.

IZUMI, Carol L. (2017) *Implicit Bias and Prejudice in Mediation*, 70 SMU L. Rev. 681.

KANG, Sooyeon. (2023) *Constructing Community Cohesion Organically and Strategically*, 38, Ohio St. J. Disp. Resol. 139.

KELLY, Joan B. (1989) *Mediated and Adversarial Divorce: Respondents' Perception of Their Processes and Outcomes*, 24 Mediation Q. 71.

KOLB, Deborah M. (2009) *Too Bad for the Women or Does It Have to Be? Gender and Negotiation Research over the Past Twenty-Five Years*, 2009 Negot. J. 515.

KOLB, Deborah M., and COOLIDGE, Gloria C. (1991) Her Place at the Table: A Consideration of Gender Issues in Negotiation, in Negotiation Theory and Practice (William Breslin & Jeffrey Z. Rubin, eds.). Cambridge: The Harvard Program on Negot. Books.

KOLB, Deborah M., and WILLIAMS, Judith. (2000) *The Shadow Negotiation: How Women Can Master the Hidden Agendas That Determine Bargaining Success.* New York: Simon & Shuster.

LANDRUM, Susan. (2011) *The On-Going Debate About Mediation in the Context of Domestic Violence: A Call for Empirical Studies of Mediation's Effectiveness*, 12 Cardozo J. Conflict Resol. 425.

LEVINE, Bertram, and LUM, Grande. (2020) *America's Peacemakers: The Community Relations Service and Civil Rights.* University of Missouri Press.

LOVE, Lela, and MCDONALD, Cheryl B. (1997) *A Tale of Two Cities: Day Labor and Conflict Resolution for Communities in Crisis.* Disp. Resol. Magazine (Fall 1997), at 8.

LUBAN, David. (1995) *Settlement and the Erosion of the Public Realm*, 83 Geo. L.J. 2619.

MACKINNON, Catherine A. (1993) *Only Words.* Cambridge: Harvard Univ. Press.

MATSUDA, Mari J. (1989) *Public Response to Racist Speech: Considering the Victim's Story*, 87 Mich. L. Rev. 2320.

MAYER, Bernard S., and FONT-GUZMAN, Jacqueline (2022) *The Neutrality Trap: Disrupting and Connecting for Social Change.* Wiley.

MCEWEN, Craig A., and MAIMAN, Richard M. (1984) Mediation in Small Claims Court: Achieving Compliance Through Consent, 19 Law & Soc'y Rev. 11.

MCEWEN, Craig A., and MAIMAN, Richard M. (1986) *The Relative Significance of Disputing Forum and Dispute Characteristics for Outcome and Compliance*, 20 Law & Soc'y Rev. 439.

MCEWEN, Craig A., and WILLIAMS, Laura. (1998) *Legal Policy and Access to Justice Through Courts and Mediation*, 13 Ohio St. J. on Disp. Resol. 865.

MENKEL-MEADOW, Carrie. (1995) *Whose Dispute is it Anyway? A Philosophical and Democratic Defense of Settlement (In Some Cases)*, 83 Geo. L.J. 2663.

NOLAN-HALEY, Jacqueline. (1999) *Informed Consent in Mediation: A Guiding Principle for Truly Educated Decisionmaking*, 74 Notre Dame L. Rev. 775.

O'CONNELL CORCORAN, Kathleen, and MELAMED, James C. (1990) *From Coercion to Empowerment: Spousal Abuse and Mediation*, 7 Mediation Q. 303.

PEARSON, Jessica. (1991) *The Equity of Mediated Agreements*, 9 Mediation Q. 179.

PEARSON, Jessica. (1997) *Mediating When Domestic Violence Is a Factor: Policies and Practices in Court-Based Divorce Mediation Programs*, 14 Mediation Q. 319.

PENA-GRATEREAUX, Mary E., and JESSOP, Maria I. (2000) *Mediation and Culture: Conversations with New York Mediators from Around the World*. New York: Washington Heights Inwood Coalition Mediation Program.

PFUND, Alicia, ed. (2013) *From Conflict Resolution to Social Justice: The Work and Legacy of Wallace Warfield*. Bloomsbury Academic.

POWELL, john, and Conner, Ned (2023), *Form and Substance: Understanding Conceptual and Design Differences Among Racial Equity Proposals and a Bold Application*, 38 Ohio St. J. Disp. Resol. 13.

PRESS, Sharon, and DEASON, Ellen E. (2021) *Mediation: Embedded Assumptions of Whiteness*, 22 Cardozo J. Conflict Resol. 453.

PRESS, Sharon. (2020) *Using Dispute Resolution Skills to Heal a Community*, 35 Ohio St. J. Disp. Resol. 645.

REISMAN, W. Michael. (1983*) Looking, Staring, and Glaring: Microlegal Systems and Public Order*, 12 Denv. J. Int'l L. & Pol'y 165.

RIMELSPACH, Rene. (2001) *Mediating Family Disputes in a World With Domestic Violence: How to Devise a Safe and Effective Court-Connected Mediation Program*, 17 Ohio St. J. on Disp. Resol. 95.

ROGERS, Nancy H. (2015) *When Conflicts Polarize Communities: Designing Localized Offices that Intervene Collaboratively*, 30 Ohio St. J. Disp. Resol. 173.

ROTHMAN, Jay (2006). *Identity and Conflict: Collaboratively Addressing Police-Community Conflict in Cincinnati, Ohio*, 22 Ohio St. J. Disp. Resol. 105.

ROSENBERG, Joshua D. (1991) *In Defense of Mediation*, 33 Ariz. L. Rev. 467.

ROTHMAN, Jay. (2003) *Improving Police-Community Relations in Cincinnati: A Collaborative Approach*. Cincinnati Enquirer (Fall 2003).

RUBIN, Jeffrey Z., and SANDER, Frank E.A. (1991) *Culture, Negotiation, and the Eye of the Beholder*, 7 Negot. J. 249.

SAPOSNEK, Donald T. (1983) *Mediating Child Custody Disputes.* San Francisco: Jossey-Bass.

STULBERG, Joseph B. (1998) *Mediation and Fairness*, 13 Ohio St. J. on Disp. Resol. 909.

STULBERG, Joseph B., and LOVE, Lela P. (1996) Community Dispute Resolution Training Manual (rev. ed.). Lansing: Mich. Sup. Ct.

TANNEN, Deborah. (1990) *You Just Don't Understand.* New York: HarperCollins.

TANNEN, Deborah. (1995) *Talking 9 to 5: Women and Men at Work.* New York: HarperCollins.

TERVALON, Melanie, and MURRAY-GARCIA, Jann. (1998) *Cultural Humility Versus Cultural Competence: A Critical Distinction in Defining Physician Training Outcomes in Multicultural Education*, Journal of Health Care for the Poor and Underserved 117 (Vol. 9, No.2).

TRUJILLO, Mary Adams et al., eds. (2008) *Re-Centering Culture and Knowledge in Conflict Resolution Practice.* Syracuse University Press.

WELSH, Nancy A. (2002) *Disputant's Decision Control in Court-Annexed Mediation: A Hollow Promise Without Procedural Justice*, 2002 J. Disp. Resol. 179.

WISSLER, Roselle. (1995) *Mediation and Adjudication in the Small Claims Court: The Effects of Process and Case Characteristics*, 29 Law & Soc'y Rev. 323.

Chapter 8

AMERICAN ARBITRATION ASSOCIATION, AMERICAN BAR ASSOCIATION, Society of Professionals in Dispute Resolution. *Standards of Conduct For Mediators.* (1994)

AMERICAN ARBITRATION ASSOCIATION, AMERICAN BAR ASSOCIATION, Society of Professionals in Dispute Resolution. *Standards of Conduct For Mediators: Reporter's Notes.* (1994)

AMERICAN BAR ASSOCIATION. *Model Rules of Professional Conduct, Rule 2.4,* Chicago: American Bar Association.

ASSOCIATION OF FAMILY AND CONCILIATION COURTS, Model Standards of Practice for Family and Divorce Mediation, Association (2000)

BARRETT, Robert. (1996) *Mediator Certification: Should California Enact Legislation?* 30 U.S.F. L. Rev 619.

BENNS, Whitney, *A Conversation with Whitney Benns, Educator, Facilitator, and Emotional Labor Organizer On 'experts,' neutrality, and protest as a powerful tool*, Disp. Resol. Magazine, Vol. 27, No. 1 (January 2021).

BERSTEIN, Dan, *Preventing Unintentional Discrimination in Dispute Resolution*, Disp. Resol. Magazine, Vol. 29, No. 1 (January 2023).

BUSH, Robert A. Baruch. (1992) *The Dilemmas of Mediation Practice: A Study of Ethical Dilemmas and Policy Implications*, National Institute for Dispute Resolution.

COBEN, James R., and LOVE, Lela P. (2010) *Trick or Treat: The Ethics of Mediator Manipulation*. Disp. Resol. Magazine, Vol. 17, No. 18 (Fall 2010).

Florida Rules for Certified and Court-Appointed Mediators, 10.100 *et. seq.*, effective August 2021.

KNISLEY, Nikki and PRESS, Sharon, *Mental Health and Mediation*. Disp. Resol. Magazine, Vol. 28, No. 2 (April 2022).

LAFLIN, Maureen E. (2000) *Preserving the Integrity of Mediation Through the Adoption of Ethical Rules for Lawyer Mediators*, 14 Notre Dame J.L. Ethics & Pub. Pol'y 479.

MAUTE, Judith. (1991) *Public Values and Private Justice: A Case for Mediator Accountability*, 4 Geo. J. Legal Ethics 503.

MENKEL-MEADOW, Carrie. (1996) *Mediation and the Legal System: Is Mediation the Practice of Law?*, 14 Alternatives 57.

MEYERSON, Bruce. (1996) *Lawyers Who Mediate Are Not Practicing Law*, 14 Alternatives 74.

MOFFITT, Michael. (2003) *Ten Ways to Get Sued: A Guide for Mediators*, 8 Harv. Negot. L. Rev. 81.

PEPPET, Scott. (2003) *Contractarian Economics and Mediation Ethics: The Case for Customizing Neutrality Through Contingency Fee Mediation*, 82 Tex. L. Rev. 227.

PLIMPTON, David. (2000) *Liability Pitfalls May Be Waiting for Lawyer-Neutrals*, 18 Alternatives to the High Cost of Litigation 65.

RAVINDRA, Geetha. (2000) *The Response: The Goal is to Inform, Not Impede, ADR*, 18 Alternatives 124.

RUBIN, Melvin. (2010) *Mediatory Malpractice: A Proposed Defensive Path Through the Minefield*, Disp. Resol. Magazine Vol. 17, No. 1 (Fall 2010).

SHAPIRA, Omer (2021) *Mediation Ethics: A Practitioner's Guide* (American Bar Association).

STEMPEL, Jeffrey W. (1997) *Beyond Formalism and False Dichotomies: The Need for Institutionalizing a Flexible Concept of the Mediator's Role*, 24 Fla. St. U. L. Rev. 949.

WELSH, Nancy. (2001) *The Thinning Vision of Self-Determination in Court-Connected Mediation: the Inevitable Price of Institutionalization?*, 6 Harv. Negot. L. Rev. 1.

WING, Leah, and RIFKIN, Janet. (2001) Racial Identity Development and the Mediation of Conflicts, in New Perspectives on Racial Identity Development (Charmaine L. Wijevesinghe and Bailey W. Jackson III, eds.). New York: New York Univ. Press.

With Conflicts at Issue, Florida Firm and Its Former Partners Restructure ADR— Again (1997), 15 Alternatives to the High Cost of Litigation 131.

YOUNG, Paula M. (2021) *The Crisis in Insurance Coverage for Mediators, Part 3: Underwriters at Lloyds, London Offers a Meaningful Option for Mediators* 20 Appalachian J.L. 191.

YOUNG, Paula M. (2019-2020) *The Crisis in Insurance Coverage for Mediators, Part 2: Coverage for Mediators Entering the Field from the Mental Health Professions—You May as Well be "Going Bare" Because "There's No There, There"* 19 Appalachian J.L. 79.

YOUNG, Paula M. (2016) *The Crisis in Insurance Coverage for Mediators—Part 1: Even Lawyer-Mediators are "Going Bare* 15 Appalachian J.L. 1.

YOUNG, Paula M. (2008) *A Connecticut Mediator in a Kangaroo Court?: Successfully Communicating the "Authorized Practice of Mediation" Paradigm to "Unauthorized Practice of Law" Disciplinary Bodies*, 2008 S. Tex. L. Rev. 1047.

YOUNG, Paula M. (2006) *Take It or Leave It. Lump It or Grieve It: Designing Mediator Complaint Systems That Protect Mediators, Unhappy Parties, Attorneys, Courts, the Process, and the Field*, 21 Ohio St. J. on Disp. Resol. 721.

Chapter 9

ALFINI, James J. et al. (1994) *What Happens When Mediation Is Institutionalized?: To the Parties, Practitioners, and Host Institutions*, 9 Ohio St. J. on Disp. Resol. 307.

ALFINI, James J., and McCABE, Catherine G. (2001) *Mediating in the Shadow of the Courts: A Survey of the Emerging Case Law*, 54 Ark. L. Rev. 171.

BINGHAM, Lisa A. (1997) *Mediating Employment Disputes: Perceptions of REDRESS at the United States Postal Service*, 20 Rev. of Pub. Personnel Admin. 20 (Spring 1997).

BRAZIL, Wayne D. (2002) *Court ADR 25 Years After Pound: Have We Found a Better Way?*, 18 Ohio St. J. on Disp. Resol. 93.

BUSH, Robert. A. Baruch. (1989) *Mediation and Adjudication, Dispute Resolution and Ideology: An Imaginary Conversation*, 3 J. Contemp. Legal Issues 1.

CHARKOUDIAN, Lorig, EISENBERG, Deborah T. & WALTER, Jamie L. (2017) *What Difference Does ADR Make? Comparison of ADR and Trial Outcomes in Small Claims Court*, 35 Conflict Resol. Q. 1.

COLE, Sara et al., eds. (2011) Mediation: Law, Policy and Practice (2012 ed.). St. Paul: Thompson-West.

CRATSLEY, John C. (2006) *Judicial Ethics and Judicial Settlement Practices: Time for Two Strangers to Meet*, 21 Ohio St. J. on Disp. Resol. 569.

HARE, Rebecca. (2020) *Mitigating Power Imbalance in Eviction Mediation: A Model for Minnesota*, 38(1) Law & Ineq.

HINSHAW, Art. (2016) *Regulating Mediators,* 21 Harv. Negot. L. Rev. 163.

JOHNSON, Earl. (2012) The Pound Conference Remembered. Disp. Resol. Magazine (Fall 2012).

KELLY, Joan B. (2004) *Family Mediation Research: Is There Empirical Support for the Field?*, 22 Conflict Resol. Q. 3.

LANDE, John. (2000) *Getting the Faith: Why Business Lawyers and Executives Believe in Mediation*, 5 Harv. Negot. L. Rev. 137.

MACFARLANE, Julie, and KEET, Michaela. (2005) *Civil Justice Reform and Mandatory Civil Mediation in Saskatchewan: Lessons from a Maturing Program*, 42 Alberta L. Rev. 677.

McADOO, Bobbi, and HINSHAW, Art. (2002) *The Challenge of Institutionalizing Alternative Dispute Resolution: Attorney Perspectives on the Effect of Rule 17 on Civil Litigation in Missouri*, 67 Mo. L. Rev. 473.

McADOO, Bobbi et al. (2004) *Institutionalization: What Do Empirical Studies Tell Us About Court Mediation?*, Disp. Resol. Magazine (Winter 2003).

McADOO, Bobbi. (2002) *A Report to the Minnesota Supreme Court: The Impact of Rule 114 on Civil Litigation Practice in Minnesota*, 25 Hamline L. Rev. 401.

McCRORY, John P. (1999) *Mandated Mediation of Civil Cases in State Courts: A Litigant's Perspective on Program Model Choices*, 14 Ohio St. J. on Disp. Resol. 813.

McDERMOTT, E. Patrick & OBAR, Ruth (2022), *The Equal Employment Opportunity Commission Mediation Participants Experience in Online Mediation and Comparison to In-Person Mediation,* https://www.eeoc.gov/sites/default/files/2022-06/508%20Final_PARTICIPANT%20FINAL_3_4_2022.pdf.

McDERMOTT, E. Patrick & OBAR, Ruth (2022), *Equal Employment Opportunity Commission Mediators' Perception of Remote Mediation and Comparisons to In-Person Mediation,* https://www.eeoc.gov/sites/default/files/2022-06/508%20Final_Mediator_FINAL%20EEOC%20REPORT_3_4.pdf.

MENKEL-MEADOW, Carrie. (1991) *Pursuing Settlement in an Adversary Culture: a Tale of Innovation Co-Opted or "The Law of ADR,"* 19 Fla. St. L. Rev. 1.

PRESS, Sharon. (1992–93) *Building and Maintaining a Statewide Mediation Program: A View from the Field*, 81 Ky. L.J. 1029.

PRESS, Sharon. (1997) *Institutionalization: Savior or Saboteur of Mediation?*, 24 Fla. St. U. L. Rev. 903.

PRESS, Sharon. (2003) *Institutionalization of Mediation in Florida: At the Crossroads*, 108 Penn St. L. Rev. 43.

ROBINSON, Peter. (2012) *Opening Pandora's Box: An Empirical Exploration of Judicial Settlement Ethics and Techniques*, 27 Ohio St. J. on Disp. Resol. 53.

RUBINSON, Robert. (2016) *Of Grids and Gatekeepers: The Socioeconomics of Mediation*, 17 Cardozo J. Conflict Resol., 873.

SANDER, Frank E.A. (2000) *The Future of ADR*, 2000 J. Disp. Resol. 3.

SHACK, Jennifer. (2003) *Efficiency: Mediation in Courts Can Bring Gains, But Under What Conditions?* Disp. Resol. Magazine , at 11 (Winter 2003).

SHESTOWSKY, Donna. (2017) *When Ignorance is Not Bliss: An Empirical Study of Litigants' Awareness of Court-Sponsored Alternative Dispute Resolution Programs,* 22 Harv. Negot. L. Rev. 189.

WALDMAN, Ellen. (1996) *The Challenge of Certification: How to Ensure Mediator Competence While Preserving Diversity*, 30 U.S.F. L. Rev. 723.

WECKSTEIN, Donald T. (1996) *Mediator Certification: Why and How*, 30 U.S.F. L. Rev. 757.

WELSH, Nancy A. (2004) *The Place of Court-Connected Mediation in a Democratic Justice System*, 5 Cardozo J. Conflict Resol. 117.

WELSH, Nancy A. (2017) *Do You Believe in Magic?: Self Determination and Procedural Justice Meet Inequality in Court-Connected Mediation,* 70 SMU L. Rev. 721

WISSLER, Roselle L. (2004) *The Effectiveness of Court-Connected Dispute Resolution in Civil Cases*, 22 Conflict Resol. Q. 3.

WISSLER, Roselle L. (2010) *Representation in Mediation: What We Know from Empirical Research*, 37 Fordham Urb. L.J. 419.

WISSLER, Roselle L. (2011) *Party Participation and Voice in Mediation*, Disp. Resol. Magazine, at 20 (Fall 2011).

Chapter 10

ABRAMSON, Harold I. (2013) Mediation Representation: Advocating as a Problem-Solver (3d rev. ed.) New York: Oxford Univ. Press.

ABRAMSON, Harold I. (2010) *Mediation Representation: Advocating as a Problem-Solver in any Country or Culture.* South Bend: The Nat'l Inst. for Trial Advocacy.

ABRAMSON, Harold I. (2005) *Problem-Solving Advocacy in Mediation: A Model of Client Representation*, 10 Harv. Negot. L. Rev. 103.

ALFINI, James J. (1999) *Settlement Ethics and Lawyering in ADR Proceedings: A Proposal to Revise Rule 4.1*, 19 N. Ill. U. L. Rev. 255.

ARNOLD, Tom. (1995) *20 Common Errors in Mediation Advocacy*, 13 Alternatives to the High Cost of Litigation 69.

BAKER, Debra Ratterman. (1999) *Dependency Mediation: Strategies for Parents' Attorneys*, 18 ABA Child L. Prac. 124.

BECKWITH, Sandra S., and SLOVIN, Sherri. (2003) *The Collaborative Lawyer as Advocate: A Response*, 18 Ohio St. J. on Disp. Resol. 497.

BREGER, Marshall J. (2000) *Should an Attorney be Required to Advise a Client of ADR Options?*, 13 Geo. J. Legal Ethics 427.

COCHRAN, Robert F. Jr. (1999) *ADR, the ABA, and Client Control: A Proposal that the Model Rules Require Lawyers to Present ADR Options to Clients*, 41 S. Tex. L. Rev. 183.

COCHRAN, Robert F. Jr. (1990) *Legal Representation and the Next Steps Toward Client Control: Attorney Malpractice for the Failure to Allow the Client to Control Negotiation and Pursue Alternatives to Litigation*, 47 Wash. & Lee L. Rev. 819.

COOLEY, John W. (1996) *Mediation Advocacy*. South Bend: Nat'l Inst. for Trial Advocacy.

FAIRMAN, Christopher M. (2003) *Ethics and Collaborative Lawyering: Why Put Old Hats on New Heads?*, 18 Ohio St. J. on Disp. Resol. 505.

FISHER, Roger, URY, William, and PATTON, Bruce. (1981, 1991) Getting to Yes: Negotiating Agreement Without Giving in (2d ed.). New York: Penguin Books.

GALTON, Eric. (1994) *Representing Clients in Mediation*. Dallas: American Lawyer Media.

GERONEMUS, David. (1999) *Mediation of Legal Malpractice Cases: Prevention and Resolution*, Practicing Law Institute Litigation and Administrative Practice Course Handbook Series Litigation PLI Order No. H0-003Q, 609 PLI/Lit 847 (June 1999).

GOLANN, Dwight. (2013) *Shatrin a Mediator's Powers — Effective Advocacy in Settlement*. Am. Bar Ass'n Sec. on Disp. Resol.

GUTHRIE, Chris. (2001) *The Lawyer's Philosophical Map and the Disputant's Perceptual Map: Impediments to Facilitative Mediation and Lawyering*, 6 Harv. Negot. L. Rev. 145.

LANDE, John. (1997) *How Will Lawyering and Mediation Transform Each Other?*, 24 Fla. St. U. L. Rev. 839.

LAWRENCE, James K.L. (2002) *Collaborative Lawyering: A New Development in Conflict Resolution*, 17 Ohio St. J. on Disp. Resol. 431.

LAWRENCE, James K.L. (2000) *Mediation Advocacy: Partnering with the Mediators*, 15 Ohio St. J. on Disp. Resol. 425.

LUBAN, David. (1981) *Paternalism and the Legal Profession*, 1981 Wis. L. Rev. 454.

MACFARLANE, Julie. (2008) *The Evolution of the New Lawyer: How Lawyers are Reshaping the Practice of Law*, 2008 J. Disp. Resol. 61.

MACFARLANE, Julie, and KEET, Michaela. (2005) *Civil Justice Reform and Mandatory Civil Mediation in Saskatchewan: Lessons from a Maturing Program*, 42 Alberta L. Rev. 677.

McADOO, Bobbi. (2002) *A Report to the Minnesota Supreme Court: The Impact of Rule 114 on Civil Litigation Practice in Minnesota*, 25 Hamline L. Rev. 401.

McADOO, Bobbi, PRESS, Sharon, and GRIFFIN, Chelsea. (2012) *It's Time to Get it Right: Problem-Solving in the First-Year Curriculum*, 39 Wash. U. J.L. Pol'y 39.

McADOO, Bobbi, and HINSHAW, Art. (2002) *The Challenge of Institutionalizing Alternative Dispute Resolution: Attorney Perspectives on the Effect of Rule 17 on Civil Litigation in Missouri*, 67 Mo. L. Rev. 473.

McEWEN, Craig A. et al. (1995) *Bring in the Lawyers: Challenging the Dominant Approaches to Ensuring Fairness in Divorce Mediation*, 79 Minn. L. Rev. 1317.

MENKEL-MEADOW, Carrie. (1997) *Ethics in Alternative Dispute Resolution: New Issues, No Answers from the Adversary Conception of Lawyers' Responsibilities*, 38 S. Tex. L. Rev. 407.

MEYERSON, Bruce. (1997) *Telling the Truth in Mediation: Mediator Owed Duty of Candor*, 4 Disp. Resol. Magazine 17.

MNOOKIN, Robert H., and KORNHAUSER, Lewis. (1979) *Bargaining in the Shadow of the Law: The Case of Divorce*, 88 Yale L.J. 950.

MNOOKIN, Robert H. (2000) *Beyond Winning: Negotiating to Create Value in Deals and Disputes.* Cambridge: Harvard Univ. Press.

NOLAN-HALEY, Jacqueline M. (2021) *Lawyers Representation in Mediation, Mediation Ethics: A Practitioner's Guide* (ed. Omer Shapira).

NOLAN-HALEY, Jacqueline M. (1998) *Lawyers, Clients and Mediation*, 73 Notre Dame L. Rev. 1369.

PEDONE, Nicole. (1998) *Lawyer's Duty to Discuss Alternative Dispute Resolution: In the Best Interest of Children*, 36 Fam. & Conciliation Cts. Rev. 65.

PRIGOFF, Michael L. (1990) At Issue: *Professional Responsibility: Should There Be a Duty to Advise of ADR Options? NO: An Unreasonable Burden*, 76 A.B.A. J. 51 (Nov. 1990).

REUBEN, Richard C. (2000) *Constitutional Gravity: A Unitary Theory of Alternative Dispute Resolution and Public Civil Justice*, 47 UCLA L. Rev. 949.

RISKIN, Leonard. (1982) *Mediation and Lawyers*, 43 Ohio St. L.J. 29.

RISKIN, Leonard L. (1994) Mediator Orientations, Strategies and Techniques, 12 Alternatives to the High Cost of Litigation 111.

RISKIN, Leonard L. (1996) *Understanding Mediators' Orientations, Strategies, and Techniques: A Grid for the Perplexed*, 1 Harv. Negot. L. Rev. 7.

ROGERS, Nancy H., and McEWEN, Craig A. (1998) *Employing the Law to Increase the Use of Mediation and to Encourage Direct and Early Negotiations*, 13 Ohio St. J. on Disp. Resol. 831.

RUBINSON, Robert. (2004) *Client Counseling, Mediation, and Alternative Narratives of Dispute Resolution*, 10 Clinical L. Rev. 833.

RUTHERFORD, Mark C. (1986) *Lawyers and Divorce Mediation: Designing the Role of "Outside Counsel,"* Mediation Q. (June 1986), at 17.

SANDER, Frank E.A. (1990) *At Issue: Professional Responsibility Should There be a Duty to Advise of ADR Options? Yes: An Aid to Clients*, 76 A.B.A. J. 50 (Nov. 1990).

SCHMITZ, Suzanne J. (1999) *Giving Meaning to the Second Generation of ADR Education: Attorney's Duty to Learn about ADR and What They Must Learn*, 1999 J. Disp. Resol. 29.

SPIEGEL, Mark. (1979) *Lawyering and Client Decisionmaking: Informed Consent and the Legal Profession*, 128 U. Pa. L. Rev. 41.

STERNLIGHT, Jean R. (1999) *Lawyers' Representation of Clients in Mediation: Using Economics and Psychology to Structure Advocacy in an Nonadversarial Setting*, 14 Ohio St. J. on Disp. Resol. 259.

STERNLIGHT, Jean R. (2005) *Separate and Not Equal: Integrating Civil Procedure and ADR in Legal Academia*, 80 Notre Dame L. Rev. 681.

STERNLIGHT, Jean R. (2000) *What's a Lawyer to Do in Mediation?* 18 Alternatives to the High Cost of Litigation 1.

WARMBROD, Monica L. (1996–7) *Could an Attorney Face Disciplinary Actions or Even Legal Liability for Failure to Inform Clients of Alternative Dispute Resolution?* 27 Cumb. L. Rev. 791.

WIDMAN, Stuart M. (1993 symposium issue) *Attorneys' Ethical Duties to Know and Advise Clients About Alternative Dispute Resolution*, Prof. Law. 18.

WISSLER, Roselle L. (2004) *Barriers to Attorneys' Discussion and Use of ADR*, 19 Ohio St. J. on Disp. Resol. 460.

WISSLER, Roselle L. (2002) *When Does Familiarity Breed Content? A Study of the Role of Different Forms of ADR Education and Experience in Attorneys' ADR Recommendations*, 2 Pepp. Disp. Resol. L.J. 199.

Chapter 11:

Profiles in ADR: Grande Lum, Disp. Resol. Magazine at 41 (Spring 2014)

ALFINI, James J., and GALTON, Eric R. (1998) *ADR Personalities and Practice Tips.* Washington, D.C.: Am. Bar Ass'n Sec. on Disp. Resol. The Mediators: Views from the Eye of the Storm (Mediate.com 2006).

GADLIN, Howard and WELSH, Nancy. (2020) *Evolution of a Field: Personal Histories in Conflict Resolution.*

ZENA, Zumeta., (2017) *Profiles in ADR: Doug Van Epps,* Disp. Resol. Magazine at 32 (Spring 2017)

Table of Cases

Index